CRISIS AND HOPE

IN LATIN AMERICA

an Evangelical Perspective

Revised Edition

Emilio Antonio Núñez C.
William David Taylor

Foreword by Samuel Escobar

WCL

WEF

First Edition published by Moody Press, Chicago, Illinois
Revised Edition published jointly by
William Carey Library
P.O. Box 40129
Pasadena, CA 91114
(818) 798-0819
        and
WEF, an imprint of Paternoster Publishing,
P.O. Box 300
Carlisle, Cumbria, CA3 0QS
United Kingdom

Library of Congress Cataloging-in-Publication Data

Núñez C., Emilio Antonio.
     Crisis and Hope in Latin America: an evangelical perspectives /Emilio Antonio Núñez C., William David Taylor. -- Rev. ed.
          p.   cm.
     Rev. ed. of: Crisis in Latin America. c1989.
     Includes bibliographica l references and indexes.
     ISBN 0-87808-766-4 (alk. paper)
          1. Christianity--Latin America.   2. Latin America--History--1948- 3. Latin America--Church history--20th century.   4. Catholic Church-- Latin America--History--20th century.   5. Evangelicalism--Latin America--History--20th century.   6. Missions--Latin America.
     7. Evangelicalism--Relations--Catholic Church.   8. Catholic Church-- Relations--
     Evangelicalism.   I. Núñez C., Emilio Antonio.   Crisis
in Latin America.   II. Title.
BR600.N86   1996
278--dc20
                                                                                    96-21251
                                                                                    CIP

British Library Cataloging-in-Publication Data
A catalogue record for this book is available from the British Library
ISBN 1-900890-01-1

Photo Credits: Page 24, bottom; page 25, bottom; page 119; page 140; page 147 used courtesy of Latin America Mission.

1 2 3 4 Printing / Year 00 99 98 97 96

Printed in the United States of America

Dedication to the Revised Edition

We affectionately dedicate our book to those who have encouraged us to write.

With deep gratitude to our colleagues
    M. Daniel Carroll-Rodas
    Samuel Escobar
    William Harris Taylor

    and our wives ...
    Sara Monterrosa Echegoyén de Núñez
    Yvonne Christine DeAcutis de Taylor

... Faithful companions in ministry
... Cross-cultural servants of Christ

Contents

Evangelical Self-Theologizing in Latin America

PART THREE
Update and Concluding Perspectives for Latin America
William David Taylor and Emilio Antonio Núñez

Foreword to the Revised Edition

During fifteen years of living and working in Latin America I tried to read widely on that continent: its history, its politics, its religious background and contemporary religious scene, its society, its problems and challenges for the future. I wish that a book such as this one had been available when I ministered in Latin America. I probably read several dozen books before approaching the scope covered in this one volume. I know of no equivalent work today that covers the same depth and the breadth of study from an evangelical perspective.

If one wishes to get an overview of the history of Latin America, this book has it in readable and fast-flowing language. If one wishes to understand the people and races of Latin America, here is a superb introduction. If one wishes a succinct summary of liberation theology, here is a peerless source directly from the heart of the continent that gave birth to that theology. If one wishes insights into Roman Catholicism as it is manifest in Latin America today, here is a sympathetic yet analytical and critical study. And on any of the topics covered, the footnotes and bibliography provide an enormous source for further study. The personal experiences and insights that are woven into the fabric of the book make for easy reading and clarity of illustration.

Few people in Latin America today are more qualified to collaborate on a book of this scope than authors Emilio Antonio Núñex and William D. Taylor. These godly men have known each other since Dr. Taylor (the younger of the two) was a boy. They have worked together for more than seventeen years as colleagues in theological education and church ministry. They have challenged each other as iron sharpening iron; they have learned from each other; they have cooperated together in ministry. Because of his ethnic roots, his professional and theological preparation, his long years of fruitful ministry in teaching and preaching, his breadth of reading and travel, plus his warm-hearted commitment to the Lord, Dr. Núñez stands tall among evangelical thoelogians of Latin America today. He commands a respect that few can equal among all segments of the Christian community. His unquestioned scholarship, his careful and fair evaluation of trends and movements, combined with his irenic and loving spirit, command a hearing among evangelicals, mainline Protestant denominations, and Roman Catholics as few other evangelicals can. When he writes, we listen because he writes from his head and his heart combined.

Dr. Taylor is one of those rare and fortunate persons who can live in two very different cultures, understanding and ministering to both worlds with equal freedom. Most of his formative years were spent in Latin America, where he was born and reared, while his formal higher education was completed in the United States. Then most of his adult ministry has been on the grass roots level of church planting, teaching, and discipling in Central America. He combines the disciplines of rigorous academic study on the highest level with a theological depth that comes from his personal study of the Scriptures and his daily walk with the Lord. Therefore, he speaks and writes with an authenticity that invites respect and response.

On the personal level I wish to add one further comment. As a member of the Executive Council of the World Evangelical Fellowship, Dr. Núñez is a member of my board of directors to whom I report. As executive secretary of the Missions Commission of the World Evangelical Fellowship, Dr. Taylor is one of my colleagues who reports to me. Thus I am honored to be asked to participate in this highly significant book written by two of my very dear friends, both of whom have ministered to me by their lives and friendship.

My prayers go with this book—a book that will give new understanding about the people and challenges of the great and crucial continent of Latin America.

David M. Howard

Foreword to the Revised Edition

LATIN AMERICA: LAND OF CRISIS AND HOPE

Samuel Escobar

Three decades ago, few people would have expected the kind of painful transitions that Latin America has experienced in recent years. By the mid-sixties the dreams of social utopias that were to follow popular revolutions filled the air with combative songs and the walls with communist slogans. In 1995 poetry has given way to figures and now the average citizen has to become conversant with the economic lingo of the market: investments, interest rates, privatization and stabilization. The cities look more crowded, there are more children begging in the streets, and in some countries the ideological terror of the guerrillas and the armed forces has been replaced by the armed violence of drug traffickers and common criminals. Against the background of such social and political turmoil there is an explosion of religious activity that has taken social scientists as well as Christian leaders by surprise. In almost every city you come across theaters converted into worship places, in Santiago de Chile you find a Maryknoll priest preaching in the open air just like Pentecostal pastors, and in radio stations of Brazil and Peru, Catholic and Protestant broadcasts are so much alike that it is difficult to distinguish one from the other.

In order to understand what is going on in Latin America, an acquaintance with religious history as well as a theological frame of reference are indispensable. That is what William Taylor and Emilio Antonio Núñez offer in this book. Their intention is to provide a panorama of the Latin American world, ordering an enormous amount of data around an outline that stands on the firm ground of Christian missiological convictions. The book does not claim neutrality or objectivity. The authors have convictions about the mission of the Christian church, and they look at social, cultural and religious transitions from the perspective of the evangelical communities that are now growing in the Latin world. Their awareness of crisis as well as their proposal of hope are closely linked to their faith in Jesus Christ and their enthusiasm to proclaim his gospel. They have traveled extensively throughout the continent and they have taught in several theological institutions. They write from the vantage point of two Latin American insiders, but they are also conversant with the culture of the English-speaking readers to whom the book is addressed. I consider that the demand for a new edition of their book is enough evidence that it is a significant and useful contribution to the literature about Latin America. I would like to outline here some developments that can only be understood within the frame provided by this work.

Christendom's Crisis

It may sound as a typical Latin American exaggeration to say that the future of Christianity is at stake in what happens in Latin America today. However, when we pay attention to figures we may have to conclude that there is no exaggeration in that statement. Almost half of the Catholics of all the world live in Latin America. Consequently the Catholic hierarchies consider the region as a reservoir of human and material resources for their missionary work in the future. On the other hand, Latin America happens to be the continent where popular forms of Protestantism grow faster than anywhere else, and they grow at the expense of the Catholic Church. During the most recent decades more people have left Catholicism in order to become Protestant than at the time of the Reformation in the sixteenth century. Brazil, with its population of over 140 million, is considered the largest Catholic nation in the world, but the Catholic percentage of the population went down from 92.8% in 1970 to 88.4% in 1980, and decline has continued. In fact, the 22 million Protestants of Brazil might well be now a religious majority in comparison with the number of Catholics who actually practice their religion.

The more conservative sectors of Catholicism tend to interpret these facts attributing them to a foreign conspiracy. In his opening address to the Latin American Bishops Conference at Santo Domingo (October 1992), Pope John Paul II challenged them to "defend" their flock from "rapacious wolves." It was a clear allusion to the growth of evangelical churches, usually described as "sects" in Catholic documents. The Pope added: "[W]e should not underestimate a particular strategy aimed at weakening the bonds that unite Latin American countries and so to undermine the kinds of strength provided by unity. To that end, significant amounts of money are offered to subsidize proselytizing campaigns that try to shatter such Catholic unity."[1] Other Catholic leaders and scholars, especially those with pastoral experience in Latin America, are openly critical of this "conspiracy theory" approach. Dominican Edward Cleary commenting on the Pope's speech wrote: "Ten years of study has convinced me that there is not a strong relation between money spent and results. The great advances seen in Protestant growth in Latin America are not the results of dollars from the United States."

Research and observation have led other Catholic specialists to agree with Cleary, because the churches that are growing faster are the ones that do not depend on connections outside their countries. They acknowledge that Latin America lives in a crucial moment in the history of Christianity. This demands an effort to know objectively the reality of the Protestant advance and the challenge it represents.[3] Latin America is an example of a Christendom situation that shows signs of decline and fatigue, and Latin America faces the presence of vigorous minorities committed to evangelize. It is important to remember that there are also other regions where established or "mainline" churches are facing the same situation. It is the case of some state churches in Europe and of so-called historic or mainline denominations in places like North America and Australia. But the growth of Catholicism or new denominations in the United States and Australia has not evoked the kind of passionate reaction that the growth of Protestantism in Latin America has produced among some Roman Catholics there.

At a time of great spiritual vacuum and deep social disturbances caused by colossal transitions, Protestants and Catholics in Latin America could learn from one another. After all, they have to respond to the cries of the urban masses in exploding cities and to the selfishness of powerful elites that use every available means to maintain their privileges. This part of the world is like a laboratory where some of the most acute questions about cooperation of Christians for mission are being tested but with negative results. As this book demonstrates, the present difficulties for ecumenism and cooperation are rooted in a long religious and social history with which it is not easy to come to terms. A first step in that direction is to become familiar with the historical and cultural traits that are uniquely Latin American, and that is not possible without processing a mass of data like these authors have done.

Perestroika and the Emergence of the Poor

Acquaintance with the past will help to understand the significant transitions of the present. The sudden and profound changes in Eastern Europe symbolized by the fall of the Berlin Wall in 1989 have had a strong repercussion in Latin America. Leftist intellectuals and political parties were unable to understand the social dynamism boiling at the grassroots level during the decade of the '80s. During this period four phenomena that were always considered characteristic of Latin American politics have disappeared or are in the process of waning away. Populism, academic Marxism, militarism, four-digit inflation and protected economies have given way to a modernization process characterized by administrative reforms of the state, elected governments, ideological uncertainty and openness to market economies. Society has changed and the churches have also changed. Just as in North America and Europe there are signs of a post-denominational situation in which all kinds of ecclesiastical barriers are crossed not so much as an intentional ecumenical effort but rather as a flux created by lack of permanent loyalties.

Part of the unique social dynamics m Latin America has been the relentless process of urban accumulation that has turned cities into urban labyrinths. This has brought to light the emergence of new segments of the population that in the past could be hidden in the distant rural areas but have now massively invaded the streets of capitals like Lima, Mexico, Guatemala, Sao Paulo, Caracas and Bogota. These emerging popular sectors have demonstrated their ability to become social and economic actors without the tutorial paternalism of Marxist parties and their outdated theories. They constitute the appearance of *The Other Path* as economist Hernando de Soto has called it, in a clear contrasting allusion to the classic revolutionary way symbolized by the Maoism of Shining Path in Perú.[4] De Soto has demonstrated that the vastness of informal economies prove that the poor have entrepreneurial abilities to survive and emerge in spite of oppressive bureaucratic control and inefficient socializing measures. There is also a religious dimension of this emergence. The expansion of popular Protestantism in the form of popular churches among these emerging masses has become a surprising phenomenon.

The factor that is changing the religious map of Latin America is the growth of a variety of churches that could be described as "popular Protestantism" and has become a new force to be reckoned with on the social and political scene. The bulk of this growth corresponds to Pentecostal churches and some observers predict that this will become the predominant religious force in Latin America on the eve of the Third Millennium. They are indigenous in nature and inspired by a contagious proselytistic spirit. They show some of the marks of the early Pentecostal movement in North America that Hollenweger also associates with indigenous non-white churches in other parts of the world, namely, glossolalia, oral liturgy, a narrative style in the communication of their message, maximum participation of all the faithful in the prayers and decision-making, inclusion of dreams and visions in public meetings, and a unique understanding of the body/mind relationship applied in healing by prayer.[5] These Pentecostal churches grew especially among the most marginalized social groups in the urban areas, usually unnoticed during their first decades. However, in some cases political circumstances brought them to public attention, especially when governments had tensions with the Roman Catholic Church and looked for other sources of religious legitimization.

Sociology and Theology

It could be said that these popular Protestant churches have become alternative societies that create a closed world where people are accepted and become actors, not on the basis of what gives them status in the world around but of values that come from their vision of the Kingdom of God. This fact has especially caught the attention of social scientists. After long years of academic and journalistic hostility and misrepresentation of Latin American evangelicals, a new generation of social scientists working at the micro-level have brought to light the transforming nature of the spiritual experience offered by these churches.[6] British sociologist David Martin has summarized and interpreted a vast amount of data from the accumulated research of the last two decades. He finds that the massive migration from countryside to megacity is the background for the religious transformation: "The new society now emerging in Latin America has to do with movement, and evangelicals constitute a movement. Evangelical Christianity is a dramatic migration of the spirit matching and accompanying a dramatic migration of bodies."[7]

Observers and scholars have had to come to terms with the fact that in spite of all good theory and good intentions many actions in favor of the poor were tainted by a paternalistic approach. Social and political conscientization took the form of a struggle for the poor, trying to create a more just society for them rather than with them. Historical churches connected to world communities and denominational families had access to funds, foreign press and even diplomatic ties that were used in an effort to help the victims of poverty or state terrorism. Incarnation among the poor has been many times the source of these movements, but they have failed in mobilizing the poor themselves. By contrast, the popular Protestant churches are popular movements in themselves. Their pastors and leaders do not have to identify with the poor, *they are the poor*. They do not have a social agenda but an intense spiritual agenda and it is through that agenda that they have been able to have a social impact. As Martin observes about the impact of the Pentecostal experience, "Above all it renews the innermost cell of the family and protects the woman from the ravages of male desertion and violence. A new faith is able to implant new disciplines, reorder priorities counter corruption and destructive machismo, and reverse the indifferent and injurious hierarchies of the outside world."[8]

All Christians in Latin America have to ask themselves what significance these realities which sociology has now described and interpreted has for their faith. What light do these events shed for our understanding of what is the gospel and the mission of the church? The questions have become important now that thousands of Latin American evangelicals migrating to Japan, United States and Europe are becoming lay missionaries like those that went from Jerusalem to Antioch in New Testament times.[9] They are important questions also for the many missionary-training schools and missionary-sending organizations that are spreading all over Latin America. Catholics would like to see the same missionary vision in their ranks, but they acknowledge that though Latin Americans constitute 42% of the Catholics of the world, only 2% of the Catholic missionary force comes from Latin America.[10]

For evangelical leaders and Catholic pastors or for anyone who would like to accompany evangelical churches in new forms of missionary partnership, the theological questions will have to be considered sooner or later. Missiology must take very seriously the material and the questions that come from the historical record and sociological interpretation. But missiological discernment requires also theological clarity. This book helps in providing a critical record and evaluation of theological developments in Latin America during the more recent decades. Liberation theologies, fundamentalist or economic mission patterns, as well as evangelical missiology are here described and evaluated. Readers may not always agree with Taylor and Núñez, but because these authors strive to present a fair description and a logical argument, readers will be helped to clarify their own ideas and sort out their options. The book does not end with academic conclusions but with a plea for a renewed sense of mission, for the adoption of new missionary patterns. I am challenged by their call for a new attitude, one that is realistic about the crisis and courageous on the basis of the hope that comes from Jesus Christ.

Samuel Escobar, Eastern Baptist Theological Seminary
Philadelphia, December 1994

Dr. Escobar, a Peruvian by birth, divides his time between duties in the USA as Professor of Missions at Eastern Baptist Theological Seminary in Philadelphia, Pennsylvia, and those in Peru. He served before as regional secretary for Latin America of the International Fellowship of Evangelical Students. A theologian, writer and mentor, he is honorary president of the Latin American Theological Fraternity.

Notes

1. Alfred T. Hennelly, S.J., ed., *Santo Domingo and Beyond* (Maryknoll: Orbis, 1993), p.48.

2. "John Paul Cries 'Wolf'," *Commonweal,* 20 Nov. 1992, p. 7.

3. I have summarized pastoral observations from Catholic authors that follow this approach in "Mission in Latin America: an Evangelical Perspective," *Missiology* 20 (2), pp.241-253.

4. Hernando de Soto, *The Other Path* (London: I.B.Tauris, 1989).

5. Walter J. Hollenweger, "After Twenty Years' Research on Pentecostalism," *International Review of Mission* 75(297), pp. 3-12.

6. I have studied the conflicting approaches to popular Protestantism in "The Promise and Precariousness of Latin American Protestantism," in *Coming of Age. Protestantism in Contemporary Latin America,* Daniel R. Miller, ed. (Lanham: University Press of America, 1994), pp. 3-35.

7. David Martin, *Tongues of Fire* (Oxford: Basil Blackwell, 1990), p. 284.

8. *Idem.*

9. Acts 11:19-21.

10. This was the concern expressed during the Catholic Latin America Missionary Congress COMLA-4 in Lima, February 1991, *Memorias del COMLA-4* (Lima: C0MLA4, 1991).

Introduction:

Approaching Latin America in Crisis and Hope

William David Taylor

AS WE BEGIN THIS BOOK

It was a kind of epiphany, a transforming moment that recent evening in 1994 that transported me beyond the concrete world I observed from the balcony of my window in the capital city of El Salvador. Dusk gently fell over the entire capital city valley. On the far eastern side an evening thunderstorm marched across the city, the sheets of rain marked in slanted lines, the dark clouds heavy. As far as my eye could see the lights gradually blinked on, covering the valley like bright jewels on black velvet. But beyond the physical I saw something else . . . a vision of crisis and hope.

That evening was unavoidably juxtaposed with a previous visit to that same city only a few years ago. Back then as dusk fell people rushed home from work to safety, the streets dangerous; at any time you could expect the unmistakable sounds of rifles and machine guns, the terrible thud of bombs. Who was shooting? It depended; it could have been angry and nervous government troops, or lawless right-wing death squads, or the committed guerrilla movements. God's people still met in their homes and church buildings; but well aware of danger, they were prepared with portable electric generators and offered rides home for believers without transportation. Back then the war economy was kept alive by brave Salvadorans and massive injections of foreign funds, primarily from the USA. El Salvador was not a safe place. Its citizens lived in tension. There was no hope. Countless thousands had emigrated and tens of thousands had died in that nasty war. The nation was in crisis; it was a microcosm of Latin Americafor in a context of violence and injustice, the church of Christ grew in ways that astonished everybody.

But as that evening storm moved across the valley and the lights came on, something profound moved inside my heart. It was as if this small nation was moving from death to life, from war to peace, from fear to hope. The long-desired peace accord between government/military and the Marxist movements was transforming the national psyche. The construction industry, paralyzed for twelve years, now boomed. Creative and hard-working citizens were now free to dream up new business and to edge their economy into modern times—with all of its benefits and perils. People walked and drove in relative peace, even at night. Churches sensed the change and had to challenge their people not from a context of fear but of hope and potential prosperity. As I saw the city come alive that night with light, it seemed to picture the growth of the church of Jesus Christ, light advancing in the darkness. Hope in the midst of crisis.

Yet those storm clouds bode another impression, for not all was positive. The transformation from a war economy to a peace economy had left thousands of former warriors with no skills for the new society. Many of them had turned to highway banditry, to common violence or to gang warfare. At night the highways and streets were only partially safe, and people still experienced fear. The wealthy minority drove with nervous peace in their Mercedes Benz and their high-tech Mitsubishi Monteros. The less fortunate majority still struggled to make ends meet. Questions remained: would the right-to-center governement serve the interests of the entire nation? Encouraging signs emerged, such as genuine empowerment of former shanty-town citizens who now experienced the privilege and responsibility of new home ownership. The government had delivered some promises. Was this a sign of hope?

Similar stories come from other Latin nations in clear transition, but too many questions remain. What about the masses? The urban and rural poor? The younger generations, restless, with no clear cause? What about the military, back in the barracks for the most part but nervous, involved in drug dealing in some nations? Would the structures of the new society truly change? Would endemic corruption—creating its own pathological peace—woven into the fabric of these nations be rooted out by leaders of integrity? Would Latin nations recognize their genuine need for each other and develop regional and continental trade covenants? Could countries alone make it in the global economy? And where was God in all of this?

As I pondered these issues that night, I was swept by conflicting waves of emotion. Was Latin America finally moving from ongoing crises and structural weaknesses into a context of expectation and promise? The questions gave me hope, nagged at me as well. I was drawn to remember again the sovereignty, mystery and message of God in Christ. A God of hope. A God of transformation. A God of the poor (the Latin majority) and a God of the wealthy (such small but powerful minorities). A God whose Word was being unleashed in power, yet shackled in religious traditions—whether Catholic or even evangelical. What did God require of his people in the context of a changing, crises-ridden but hopeful Latin America?

These thoughts surged through me that night. And they seemed fitting as we move into this second edition of our re-titled book on this beloved continent, *Crisis and Hope in Latin America*. It was not coincidental that my epiphany took place in El Salvador, the birth country of my colleague and mentor, Emilio Antonio Núñez, for in a special way it brought us back together again in "nuestra América Latina."

Latin America . . . that rich, multi-colored tapestry of race, language, religion, geography, history and politics! A collage of the contemporary juxtaposing itself alongside the ancient. Where traditional value systems and family structures pressured by modern secularization are experiencing major disintegration. Where the search continues for a political and economic system that will reverse the development of underdevelopment. Where a sense of gloom can sweep in when one contemplates the structural inequities that generate endemic poverty and human tragedy.

Latin America . . . with its multi-billion-dollar, sophisticated drug industry (supplying local and international demands), its history of traditional dictatorships and the facile image of the "banana republics" with revolving-door governments. Latin America with its Central American scenario that had so upset USA policies, generating the temporary fear of a mainland Marxist government. Latin America . . . hopelessly mired in its unprecedented external debt while threatening to default on her international debts. Latin America . . . with the traditional image of a man asleep under his sombrero, with that man's guerrilla son, having tensely grasped a machine gun in recent years, but perhaps the grandson holds a cellular phone to keep in contact with his own business. Latin America... spawning ground of Liberation Theology, that blend of Marxist ideology and Christian theology that both fascinates and repels, and now in its own crisis due to the collapse of philosophical, European Marxism.

Latin America . . . continent in crisis, but also hope. Political, economic, cultural, social, and spiritual factors still conspire to generate instability, uncontrolled change, violence and chaos. Sadly approaching the end of his life, Simon Bolivar, *El Libertador,* champion of Spanish American independence, sorrowfully observed, "America is ungovernable." Were he to return today he would discover his lament tragically compounded. Or might he be encouraged, even hopeful?

Finally, Latin America, scenario of God's providence with perhaps fifty-three million evangelicals (some estimates surge to sixty-five million) out of a population over 452.5 million; with God's people on the move, evangelizing, establishing new churches, developing new sensitivities to the social implications of the gospel, and increasingly involved in the political arenas (with mixed results). Evangelicals committed to self-theologizing and also obedient to their appropriation of globalized missions vision. The Word of God has never assured the church that peace, prosperity, power and privilege are necessary to her growth. To the contrary, Christ promised that his church would be built in spite of the conflictive forces of Hades. Latin American Christians have lived this reality, and from a context of poverty and powerlessness God has blessed. Now they will face growing secularization and materialism. Would nominalism eat up and neutralize their vibrant core values? Are we seeing a new and dangerous "cultural evangelicalism"?

Latin America is all of the above and so much more. With all of the available resources on Latin America—in a recent index of books in print over 3,296 new titles for sale dealt with our area—why one more?

THIS STILL COMES AS AN URGENTLY NEEDED BOOK

Why one more? Simply because there is no major contemporary work on this magnificent continent which will *inform* evangelical Christians on a broad scale about Latin America's history, culture, social reality and spiritual dynamics. We urgently need an updated book that, from an evangelical perspective, will also *shape* opinions and missiological reflection which will lead to restructured missions attitudes and action in Latin America.

This book therefore should fill a significant gap in evangelical literature. We will attempt to explain *what* is happening today. But even more important, we want to develop *why* Latin America is the way it is today. Because of this, our work is openly interpretative; it is *our* perspective, as Samuel Escobar notes in his provocative essay. The reader may discover differences of emphasis even between the two major authors, but hopefully the reader will be challenged to develop an inquiring mindset. The present-day conflicts which have ripped the very fabric of Latin America do have a particular background history that will lead us all toward greater understanding.

For example, what makes each Latin country unique? Take a "small example." Why is Nicaragua what and where it is today? The answer forces us to return 500 years to Hernán Cortéz and the other Spanish *conquistadores* to examine the system which they imposed on this "New World." Only then we can place into context the sad litany of misdirected North American foreign policy. Add to this the explosive idealism of Marxist socialism which appealed at a certain moment in history to the Sandinista leaders of a poverty-wracked nation. Then came the shocking elections which replaced that political regime. Finally, reflect upon the greedy, corrupt and sinful nature of humanity, coupled with demonic elements at work in all of our societies—left, center or right wing. But even these simplifications cannot explain Nicaragua adequately. Every country has its own particular story.

THIS IS A PANORAMIC BOOK

It would be impossible to treat this continent exhaustively; and the reader who wishes to do so can utilize the many sources cited in the various chapters to delve deeper into subtopics. We want to provide a sweeping perspective with a primary focus on the nineteen nations which have an Iberian heritage: Mexico, Guatemala, El Salvador, Honduras, Nicaragua, Costa Rica, Panama, Dominican Republic, Cuba, Colombia, Ecuador, Peru, Bolivia, Chile, Argentina, Uruguay, Paraguay, Venezuela and Brazil.[1] We will not deal specifically with Puerto Rico, nor the unique Hispanic world of the United States which explodes with growth due to high birth rates, as well as legal and illegal immigration—seeking the myth of the American Dream. These require an independent analysis, although they are part of the broader Latin American reality. The treatment will probably be uneven, simply because we the authors do not possess all of the knowledge necessary. We will have to generalize.[2]

PART I: William Taylor

Chapter 1 offers a sweeping panorama of Latin America, its rich geography, races, population dynamics, political, religious and cultural fabrics. Chapter 2 develops a brief history of the area from pre-Columbian days up to the contemporary scenario. The book by nature of ongoing current events will be dated; but this should not weaken its overall goals. Following our historical survey, Chapter 3 examines some of the political and socio-economic realities which operate today in Latin America. This will become significant for anyone who wishes to serve with understanding in Latin America. Too many Christians, including a significant percentage of the evangelical missionary force, have formed their attitudes about Latin America without even a simple knowledge of its historical formation. Chapter 4 looks at some of the religious dynamics at work today in Latin America. This includes Roman Catholicism as well as the rise of Protestantism within that religious context. One of the significant realities about the Protestant movement in Latin America is that the overwhelming majority of its members are thorough-going evangelicals. However, the spirit of error is at work today in Latin America. This can be best observed in the exploding growth of spiritism, particularly visible in Brazil where some 35% of the population practice some kind of spiritism. Part I concludes with a chapter exploring certain facets of the Latin American worldview, mentality and value systems. This last section will be a personal perspective by one born in Costa Rica and who has lived thirty years in Latin America.

PART II: Emilio A. Núñez C.

This section, beginning with Chapter 6, will examine the various Christs who have been brought to Latin America. Of special interest to students of Latin America is the Post-Vatican Council II Roman Catholicism of Latin America; four chapters will deal with this topic. Chapter 7, written at a particular moment of history, discusses the most recent reawakenings and search for renewal which the Roman church has been experiencing in a singular way in Latin America. Many significant developments have permanently changed Latin American Catholicism since the mid-sixties, with another cluster of changes coming in the last decade. And even as we write there are continuing modifications that aggravate an already complex scenario. For example, in some sectors of the Roman church there is a disturbing return to pre-Vatican II values, with evangelicals becoming once again members of the "sects," and no longer enjoying what they had been for a season, "separated brethren."

Chapter 8 investigates the revolutionary ferment expressed in Liberation Theology. The strength of this particular essay stems from the fact that the author is a son of the proletariat, one who has personally lived poverty and hence can understand the legitimate causes behind this distinctive theological-ideological system with its particular analysis and purported solutions. He also writes about the pastoral revolution as expressed in the Basic Ecclesial Communities. These two revolutionary changes offer particular challenges to the evangelicals of Latin America.

Núñez then reviews in Chapter 9 the challenge of the charismatic movement, particularly within the Catholic Church. The reality that perhaps 70% of all Latin American evangelicals are involved in various charismatic-Pentecostal groups cannot be underestimated. This religious phenomenon can be observed sweeping through Catholicism, Protestantism, and even outside of these two major bodies. It presents new spiritual equations unheard of before in the area. Chapter 10 concludes the section on Roman Catholicism by focusing on the viability of structural changes within this church. Some writers suggest that Latin Catholicism faces today a crossroads similar to Luther's, with the option of true biblical change. Others doubt this scenario. Núñez speaks to this issue, both from a historical and contemporary basis in his update in the new chapter of this book.

How can we do *theology* in Latin America? What does it mean to contextualize the Word of God within the Latin American context? With the highest view of the Scriptures and their authority, Chapter 11 argues that too much Christianity has been transported to Latin America in foreign pots and soil. It is time that non-Latin Christians learn to trust the leadership of the Holy Spirit in the lives of his Latin servants, and to respect their ability to discern and apply the Scriptures with redeeming power and effectiveness within the context of their own reality. The Latin American churches have been largely self-supporting, self-governing and self-propagating. Now they must become self-theologizing. Particular emphasis is given to evangelical contextualization of theological education in Latin America.

Chapter 12 looks at the challenge of Christian social responsibility in Latin America. From within Latin American soil, based on Scripture and stirred by the speaking and writing of key leaders, evangelicals in Latin America have recently reawakened to a new and high calling as they apply the social implications of the gospel to their context. This has called for a re-examination of the global mission of the church. Without diminishing the call to personal salvation by faith through the work of Christ, this new awakening has led not only to a sensitive social involvement but also to a commitment to social development and full participation in the political arena that could lead to national transformation.

PART III: William Taylor and Emilio A. Núñez C.

In Chapter 14 Taylor attempts to summarize Latin events and realities shaping this continent since the first edition was published. Space allows only the briefest updating. Taylor writes of the general socio-politico-economic and religious pictures. In Chapter 15 Núñez focuses on recent changes taking place in both the Roman Catholic Church and Liberation Theology. In Chapter 16 Taylor renews his call for the awakening of careful, loving attitudes and behavior with regards to Latin America. This part of the world has its own particular ethos. While the needs of Latin America may perhaps seem similar to those of the Western nations, they are in reality profoundly different.

Every Christian servant committed to Latin America must understand and appreciate the complex cluster of historical, cultural and socioeconomic factors that make Latin America what it is today. The future for the evangelical church in Latin America could be unusually bright. However, this is contingent upon taking the implications of the Word seriously within the context of Latin America. Clearly national leaders must lead the way. Major lessons must be learned by expatriate evangelical mission agencies working in Latin America. Some of these lessons must be learned by Latin leaders also. But no longer can non-Latin agencies be run as transnational corporations where decisions are made far from the local context and with little regard for those at the grassroots who are primarily impacted by the decisions that seriously affect the Latin American churches and leadership. This must change. No longer can foreign missionaries operate without a sensitive commitment to partnership in mission or without a loving understanding of history and culture. These lessons will apply as well to those non-Latin intercessory friends of Latin America, who can then pray with greater insight and wisdom.

THIS IS AN EVANGELICAL BOOK

Both authors are committed evangelicals whose shared ecclesiastical roots are grounded in Latin soil. We are Protestants by heritage, and we wish to identify ourselves with other writers whose perspective on Latin America has been guided by that tradition.[3] A few works stand out as significant in their treatment of Latin America. That magnificent work, *The Other Spanish Christ,* by John A. Mackay (1932) remains an unparalleled classic. Mackay called it "[a] study in the spiritual history of Spain and South America." We acknowledge our debt to this astute observer of human nature and spiritual truth who served as a Presbyterian missionary to Peru.

Then in 1958 W. Stanley Rycroft wrote *Religion and Faith in Latin America,* a penetrating study of what at that time was the start of the evangelical growth in Latin America. Wilfred Scopes edited (1962) *The Christian Ministry in Latin America and the Caribbean,* commissioned by and guided by the perspective of the World Council of Churches and with significant information. It was *Latin American Church Growth* (1969), authored by William R. Read, Victor M. Monterroso and Harmon A. Johnson, that first documented with greater care the growth of this work of God. While some of the statistics were disputed, this was the first volume that compiled so many facts on Latin America. Since then, others have written, such as North American J. Edwin Orr in 1978 with *Evangelical Awakenings in Latin America*, and Bolivian Methodists Esther and Mortimer Arias with their passionate and provocative *The Cry of My People*.

More recent publications can be mentioned. Written from the perspective of the sociology of religion, British scholar David Martin in *Tongues of Fire: The Explosion of Protestantism in Latin America* sympathetically documents spiritual phenomena which secular and Catholic scholars had not taken into account. Guillermo Cook, *New Face of the Church in Latin America, Between Tradition and Change*, has edited a very profitable work addressing the church from an interconfessional perspective. And Mike Berg and Paul Pretiz give us a popular presentation of Latin evangelical growth in *The Gospel People*. We would like this work of ours to stand as an evangelical expression from within Latin America.

THIS IS A RISKY BOOK

Others more qualified will be quick to underscore the shortcomings and limited perspectives of *Crisis and Hope in Latin America*. We have traveled throughout all the Latin American countries, yet our knowledge is incomplete. Some will feel overwhelmed with the plethora of information, with the details and statistics, or complain of dated material. It's "too academic and dry," some will say, and others, "too superficial." Yet others will criticize our theological presuppositions, or perhaps our apparent socio-political-economic naiveté and lack of major condemnation of North American foreign policy.

An inherent shortcoming in this type of a book is the documentation time-limitation. We are writing about dynamic realities, not merely fixed historical events. Therefore the day after the manuscript is sent in, current events change history. This happened to us in the process of writing drafts of the first edition, as well as this revised one. So forgive us. We write with the panorama of data before us, but we also write from the heart and from experience.

Some may feel that our weakness is in what we did not say, or what we avoided writing to evade problems. They may say that we should have spent more time on political and economic issues and less on "triumphalist Latin American evangelical progress." To all of our readers and evaluators we will be grateful if you let us know what we might have done to strengthen the book. For now this again is *our* attempt, *our* reading, and *our* set of priorities as we study Latin America from a Christian point of view.

THIS IS A LOVING PERSPECTIVE

It is written by a Salvadoran theologian/writer/pastor/teacher/mentor with his Christian ministry based in neighboring Guatemala for over fifty years, primarily at the Central American Theological Seminary. He has been privileged by God's grace to travel and to speak widely, as well as to participate in major Latin American as well as global evangelical developments in recent decades. It is co-authored by a hybrid semi-norteamericano who has based his ministry for seventeen years also in Guatemala and who has lived for thirty years in Central America. He is currently director of the Missions Commission, World Evangelical Fellowship, serving the international body of evangelicals.

We write with both passion and a clear mind, fully responsible for what we affirm and defend. Our love is focused on Latin America, her ethos, her nations and her people, on what they are as a product of culture, geography, human history and God's grace. Undoubtedly Latin America is a continent in crisis. The meaning of this term "crisis" is well expressed in the Quiché Maya language synonym. Actually it is a phrase, *xak quieb cubij pakawi*—literally, "just two it says on us." The dynamic equivalent is "something I'm in and either way I go it's trouble." And that is the case with Latin America, where semmingly whatever road it takes is trouble. Yet we also see rays of hope in two dimensions, the secular and the spiritual. However, our ultimate hope is placed in a sovereign God who has a future for these nations, her peoples, and his church.

William David Taylor
December 1995

NOTES

1   We are limiting our work to the nations which are a result of Spanish or Portuguese colonization and which speak either of those two languages. We are excluding territories which are products of French, Dutch or English colonization. Puerto Rico continues as a commonwealth of the United States, with its particular history and

ethos, but much of this book will still apply to Puerto Rico, and statistical information will be included at different times.

2   This revision has left the fourteen chapters of the first edition almost intact. A few changes were made, primarily in the statistical data, and some obviously changed political sections (such as Nicaragua).

3   John MacKay, *The Other Spanish Christ* (The MacMillan Company, 1932). W. Stanley Rycroft, *Religion and Faith in Latin America* (The Westminster Press, 1958). Wilfred Scopes, ed., *The Christian Ministry in Latin America and the Caribbean* (Commission on World Mission and Evangelism, World Council of Churches, 1962). William R. Read, Victor M. Monterroso, and Harmon A Johnson, *Latin American Church Growth* (William B. Eerdmans Publishing Company, 1969). J. Edwin Orr, *Evangelical Awakenings in Latin America* (Bethany Fellowship, Inc., 1978). Esther and Mortimer Arias, *The Cry of My People* (Friendship Press, 1980). The Arias book must be read taking into account their deep commitment to many themes of Liberation Theology. David Martin, *Tongues of Fire: The Explosion of Protestantism in Latin America* (Blackwell, 1991). Guillermo Cook, *New Face of the Church in Latin America, Between Tradition and Change* (Orbis, 1994). Mike Berg and Paul Pretiz, *The Gospel People* (MARC/LAM, 1992).

Part One

Critical Background Issues in Latin America

William David Taylor

1

A Contemporary Panorama
of Latin America

Latin America is a dynamic tapestry, a living mosaic, a collage, a kaleidoscope. No one analogy does justice to this continent in crisis. Clearly, a personal perspective depends on presuppositions and desires. The tourist views the very narrow slice, only what is on the tour, seldom if ever observing the broader Latin American reality. The journalist has a story to research as briefly as possible, and then to write. Some, in search of "more bang and blood for their buck," will report what may not be the truth. Very seldom, if ever, will either the tourist or the journalist understand the complex historical and spiritual textures of this tapestry.

The Marxist, the secular or religious historian, the involved participant in Latin American life and history: they each have their perspective. So does the Christian student of Latin America. But, one hopes, the believer in Jesus Christ will utilize all the resources at hand to study and to appreciate this region and its people. Christians are not neutral; we operate with a set of presuppositions that guide our perception of reality and establish ultimate truth. We are controlled by our pre-understandings—those subconscious sets of values that shape us. An evangelical product of a middle-class background, even a foreign missionary, will perceive reality through his particular socioeconomic lens. But as we approach Latin America, let us ask the Spirit of God to guide us into all truth, including an historical understanding which can translate into sensitive action today.

15

THERE IS NO ONE LATIN AMERICA: YET—

The Varieties

Anyone who travels throughout the area, even within a single country, might conclude that there are many Latin Americas. We could, for example, focus on the multiple races—Spanish, Portuguese and other Europeans, the Indians, the Africans, the Orientals, and the genetic mixtures that make up Latin America. We could look at the variegated geography, from sere deserts to impenetrable jungles, from the wide pampas to the rugged Andes and their ski slopes. We could examine the various political systems operating in the area, each one vying for the people's allegiance, or the conflicting but perhaps appealing religious alternatives that woo and call for spiritual commitment. Or we could think regionally: Mexico in the north, the Caribbean nations (tending to include Venezuela), Central America, and Panama—connecting continents, the Andean nations, mammoth Brazil, and the Southern Cone of Argentina, Chile, Paraguay, and Uruguay.

There is no single language spoken by all, and many nations are polyglot. Spanish is the national language for some 285 million inhabitants, while Portuguese is spoken by more than 158 million. But about 670 other languages are spoken, for multiplied millions claim a mother tongue spoken even before Columbus touched *tierra firme* in this "New World." For example, in Guatemala there are more than twenty-three different languages. If you factor in socio-economic elements you have even more Americas to confuse the observer: the minuscule plutocracy (two percent?) governs from the top while the "popular classes" (up to eighty percent) subsist and serve on the bottom. With relatively small middle classes (eighteen percent?), the present social dichotomy offers a smoldering fuse that could potentially convulse the entire continent.

The Controvery Over the Name

So, if there is no single, easily-defined Latin America, what are we to make of "Latin America"? The magnificent Columbian writer Germán Arcineigas argues for a novel approach—to call the entire continent "America" subdividing it into four ethnic regions entitled: Hispano America, Portuguese America, English America of the USA, and Anglo-French America of Canada. With warm eloquence he affirms:

When the four historical processes of the four Americas are explained in this summary manner, a better understanding of their differences and likenesses is possible. Because of a long series of experiences, the inhabitants of Hispano-America express themselves in Spanish, and along with their language they have retained the Catholic religion, Roman law, and a tendency toward quixotic flights of fancy. The free fusion of bloods has created in them a certain instability, which was augmented by the profoundly revolutionary rupture of 1810, when the spirit of republicanism rebelled against the centuries-old tradition of powerful hierarchies that had kept the colonies under the rule of a remote power. Since then, the Spanish language in America has taken on the ring of an aggressive idiom.

The Portuguese America of Brazil have come to speak Portuguese with a caressing, delightful, almost danceable accent, warm and bright with sun and carnival. While others were spending their time thinking of armaments, the Brazilians were devoting their time to study. Once having spanned their Amazon of politics with bridges of intelligent and peaceful agreement, these people are replete with good sense and serenity that have given their language a tinge of philosophical humor.

The people of the English America of the United States have expanded their language into a lively, constructive idiom as rich as their country, precise, unambiguous, spread over an America that has broadened as the contours of a prosperous democratic empire have expanded, one in which complications and difficulties arise only when races and traditions other than those of the white men of the thirteen original colonies come into play. This is a country in which religious freedom is practiced in many accents and with a tradition of work that has made its factories and its New York of steel-and-glass skyscrapers outstanding in the world.

The people of the Anglo-French America of Canada now speak both English and French. The two languages are not separated by an English Channel. The images of the saints in the Catholic churches are not decapitated. Canada, almost as large as all of Spanish America, contains fewer inhabitants than Colombia and Ecuador combined. It developed in peace; while others were spending their time winning independence through warfare, the Canadians were busy establishing industries, fell-ing pine forests to make paper, trapping beavers for fur coats, and converting waterfalls into electric energy. History has frozen there in the winter since the days of the Vikings. But when the snow melts, the eighteen million Canadians come forth and start back to work. A third of them speak a somewhat archaic French. To us, these four Americas are four great provinces on a continental mass, moving along their separate paths in search of the same thing: freedom. [1]

How did this vast area even become baptized with the name *America?* Certainly Christopher Columbus did not dream it up. He was convinced—even until his death—that he had discovered the shorter route to "Zipango,'" his term for Japan. One distinguished Argentine historian has argued that the area should have carried the name "Cristoforoso Colombo" in honor of the first discoverer.[2] Because Columbus was certain that he had arrived in the "Indies," he called the inhabitants *Indians.* Hence Spain called the area "The *West* Indies" on its map, and held to this title for almost four centuries. "By the time it had become clear that the discovered land was actually a new continent, or a New World, it was too late to rectify the error, or else there was no particular reason for doing so."[3]

The title *America* actually came from an Italian who followed Columbus.

Between 1499 and 1502 a Florentine businessman trading in Sevilla, Amerigo Vespucci, made three voyages in the course of which he discovered the mouth of the Amazon River and explored the coast of South America from Venezuela southward beyond the Rio de la Plata. His discoveries were so well publicized in Europe as opening up a New World, that his first name was affixed to the new continent and eventually to the entire hemisphere of Columbus. Seldom has fame so abundantly rewarded a man for so little, though in fact it was he, rather than Columbus, who first claimed to have discovered a new world.[4]

When the "United States of America" was chosen as the name for the new North American republic (and various names heatedly competed for the honor), the French began to call the Spanish- and Portuguese-speaking peoples "Latin Americans" because of the languages with Latin roots. That name has persevered. Still others have argued for "Hispanic

America," or "Iberoamerica." The reality is that no name alone will adequately describe the rich complexity of history and culture. And all of these names leave out the Indian and black heritage. What shall we make of this struggle regarding Latin America's name? Nothing much can be done at this point. Let us speak simply of *Latin America*.

Arciniegas has underscored some of the elements which bind these Latin American lands. Let us name as many as possible: a common pre-Columbian heritage; a conquest; a colonial period and an independence movement; languages; religion; a sense of supranational culture better experienced outside of the continent; and a cultural heritage largely from the Roman Mediterranean world. He concludes warmly:

> Furthermore, there is a unity in the Latin American republics. They constitute a bloc with a spirit all its own. José Martí, who was never inclined to use the expression "Latin America," spoke of "our America," a cordially definitive term that often is chosen to convey a more intimate vision of this geographical zone.[5]

THE GEOGRAPHICAL PANORAMA

On Thursday night, October 11, 1492, Columbus was the first known European to set eyes on the New World, and his first impressions of those historic days underscore the natural beauty he saw. His *diario,* possibly edited by the priest-historian Bartolomé de las Casas, has the notations: "Set upon shore, they saw very green trees and many waters and fruits of various kinds...." Later, "The island is quite large and very flat and with very green trees and many waters and a very large lake in the center, without any mountain."[6]

It Defies Description

To take it all in, you would have to travel 7,000 miles from the Rio Grande (Rio Bravo to the Mexicans) down to Cape Horn, and at its widest point you would trek 3,200 miles from Peru's Pacific shores through Brazil to the Atlantic Ocean. Latin America takes up fifteen percent of the world's land mass, close to 7.7 million square miles, and about eight percent of the world's population, 442 million people. This makes Latin America larger than the combined size of the United States and Canada, with their total of some 7.5 million square miles. Western Europe has

much less, just 1.4 million square miles.[7] Brazil alone takes up fifty percent of the Latin American land mass, is larger than the forty-eight con-
tiguous of the United States, and is twice as large as Western Europe.

From jungles to mountains, from lush tropical forests laden with exquisite orchids to barren plains, Latin America has it all. You will find
deserts in the high plateaus of northern Mexico and the mineral-rich
Atacama region of Chile, in the *llanos* of Colombia and Venezuela, in
the *caatinga* of northeastern Brazil, and in northwestern Argentina and
the Bolivian Andes. Latin America encompasses various mountain ranges, with a major rugged spine running from Mexico all the way down to
Cape Horn at the tip of Chile. Just the Andes alone extend 4,000 miles
and range between 100 and 400 miles wide. Mount Aconcagua, the highest peak of the hemisphere at 23,000 feet, rises majestically on the Ar-
gentine-Chilean border. Volcanoes, many active and others dormant for
now, puncture the skies with their green-blue-grey shapes and smoldering power.

The jungles evoke sweeping emotions—dark, dense, human-swal-
lowing, haunting. Dozer expresses it well:

> Almost completely unconquerable by white men has been
> the luxuriant, savage jungle or *selva*, where the few trails lead
> like dark caverns into the mysterious unknown and every step
> makes a pool in the boggy ground. This "Green Hell" has ex-
> erted a decisive influence upon the course of settlement. In the
> ancient Mayan country of Yucatan and Guatemala, in the
> southern part of the Central American isthmus, in large parts of
> the Amazon River basin, and in the swamplands of the Chaco
> in Paraguay, the tropical forests with their endless maze of
> trunks, lianas, creepers, ferns, roots, and plants that . . . twist
> about one another, climbing upward, have raised a menacing,
> impenetrable front to civilization. They inexorably smother out
> all would-be conquerors and all evidences of their handiwork
> in their tentaclelike embrace. In no other setting perhaps do
> man's efforts seem so puny and futile. Latin America has a
> larger expanse of rainy tropical area than any other continent.
> In the Amazon Basin the heavy rainfall, which exceeds 80
> inches a years, leaches away almost all surface fertility, and
> even the jungle trees maintain a precarious existence only by
> clutching a roothold in the dissolving terrain. A civilized ag-
> ricultural existence here is difficult if not impossible for white
> men.[8]

Yet many areas of these same jungles are in danger of being destroyed by humans. Larger than France and West Germany combined, the vast northeast area of Brazil, the *Sertao,* endures a perpetual drought crisis. The area is roughly 730 miles wide and 1,000 miles long, and millions of people remain there working the land and living in its large cities.[9] These conditions also spawn rebellion against Brazil's central government when officials ignore the area's social problems. Meanwhile the Panama Canal faces an uncertain future due to the destruction of the rain forest in the 1,300 square-mile watershed area along the route of the canal. "By 1950 some 20% of the forest had been cut. Now more than 70% has vanished, and about 800 acres of the remainder is being cleared every year."[10] Not only is the topsoil being washed away, but annual rainfall has decreased by as much as ten percent since 1900.

The Rivers

There are four major river systems in Latin America: the Magdalena in Colombia; the Rio de la Plata emerging in Buenos Aires and including the Uruguay, Paraguay, and Paraná rivers; the Orinoco of Venezuela, and the vast Amazon. While the Orinoco is not the best known, it boasts substantial statistics: 1,284 miles long; two known sources in Venezuela near the Brazilian border; many channels going into the ocean; small ocean-going vessels able to travel 260 miles up river and smaller ships able to sail for 500 miles above the Maipures and Atures rapids. Its total navigable length is 4,300 miles.[11] North American evangelicals might remember it for the mission that for years carried its name, the Orinoco River Mission—now merged with The Evangelical Alliance Mission.

It is the Amazon system that overpowers our imagination: containing more water than the combined Nile, Yangtze, and Mississippi rivers; more than 4,000 miles long; joined by more than 200 tributaries; deep, navigable water that allows large ships to sail 1,800 miles (equal to the distance from New York to Houston) up to Equitos, Peru, and smaller ships 1,000 miles farther upstream; 150 miles wide at its mouth; draining a basin close to the size of the United States, yet only some four million people live in that basin. The Peruvian novelist Ciro Alegria has

depicted life in the tropical rain forest dominated by the presence of a great river, the upper reaches of the Amazon. One of the characters of his novel *The Golden Serpent (La Serpiente de Oro,* 1935) gazes at the Amazon's tributary and exclaims,

"The river, yes, the river. I never thought of it. It is so large, so masterful, and it has made all this, hasn't it?"[12]

The river received its name as a result of an Indian attack in 1542 against Francisco Orellana, the first *conquistador* to explore the river. The Indians were led by a warrior who appeared to be female, and so the Spaniards called their attackers "Amazons" in memory of the female warriors of Greek mythology.

Chile: The Prime Example of Geographical Variety

Perhaps you have heard of the child's joke, "Dad, give me a country that can fit on a dinner plate!" Well, the answer obviously is Chile, the country whose name comes from an Indian term that means "where the land ends." It is a wrinkled ribbon of land stretching more than 2,600 miles from the Bolivian and Peruvian borders down to Cape Horn. Nevertheless that thin ribbon, never wider than 210 miles and as narrow as seventy-five miles, squeezes in an area larger than Texas. Chile also owns the Juan Fernández Islands of Robinson Crusoe fame, and Easter Island, 2,300 miles to the west in the Pacific Ocean. E. Bradford Burns, UCLA professor of Latin American studies, writes:

> No single country better illustrates the kaleidoscopic variety of Latin American geography than Chile, that long, lean land clinging to the Pacific shore for 2,600 miles. One of the world's bleakest and most forbidding deserts in the north gives way to rugged mountains with forests and alpine pastures. The Central Valley combines a Mediterranean climate with fertile plains, the heartland of Chile's agriculture and population. Moving southward, the traveler encounters dense mixed forests, heavy rainfall, and a cold climate, a warning of the glaciers and rugged coasts which lie beyond. Snow remains permanently in most of Terra del Fuego. [13]

Geography: The Mother of People

There is yet another dimension to geography, well expressed in an old Spanish proverb: "Tell me where you live and I'll tell you what kind of people you are" *(Dime dónde vives y te diré qué pueblo eres),* which underscores the fact that geography determines a people's destiny. The vast natural resources of Latin America have been only partially tapped, for many of them lie in hostile natural surroundings. Additionally, a historic-cultural mindset toward development has stymied healthy development of these resources.[14] The Andes Mountains, for all their beauty, have hindered internal and international communications since the colonial era up to the present. The colonial cities had more contact with the mother country even than with each other, and this has contributed to the fragmentation within Latin America today. Arocena said to me once, "Geography is not our mother, she is our stepmother."

THE RACES OF LATIN AMERICA

The Spectrum

Walk through the streets of any major city of Latin America and you cannot help but see the polychromatic spectrum of the races. From pure Indian—with hints of oriental features—to white European, from ebony black to shades of mulatto, brown, and yellow, Latin America presents a racial mosaic. Originally, three major racial stocks came together to define Latin America's people: Indians, Europeans of the Iberian peninsula, and blacks. The other races came much later. Dozer goes into detail:

> Latin America is inhabited by . . . almost all possible combinations of racial and national strains. The population of Argentina, for example, is 90 percent European in origin, whereas that of Paraguay, adjoining it to the north, is Guaraní Indian in about the same proportion.... Not only Spain, Portugal, France, England, and Holland, but also Germany, Italy, Africa, and even Asia are actively present in Latin America today. Here are white Argentines and black Venezuelans who speak the language of Castile; copper-colored Paraguayans who know only their native Guaraní; black Haitians who speak French patois; black Barbadians, Trinidadians, and Panamanians who speak Oxford English; Uruguayans of Italian origin who speak Spanish; Colombian *cholos,* completely Indian in face and figure, who haggle with customers in the market in Spanish; Curacaoans who live in Dutch colonial houses and speak a conglomerate idiom of French, Spanish, Dutch, and English called *papiamento;* German Chileans and Brazilians who have spoken the language of their German fatherland for four generations; Englishmen by whom Buenos Aires is always pro-

Portraits from the Latin
American Racial Mosaic

nounced "Bonuz Arez" and Managua always "Menaigu-wa'";
and a host of other linguistic groups. Spanish America is far
from being entirely Spanish in language. Brazil is far from being entirely Portuguese in either tongue or culture.... Latin
America is a crossroads of nationalities and races.[15]

The Indians

How many Indians were there when the Spanish *conquistadores* arrived? Estimates range widely from an unrealistic low of fifteen million
up to an extreme high of one hundred million. Probably a middle figure
would be closer to the truth, but nobody really knows. What is clearly
documented, however, is the tragic extermination of millions of Indians
because of the new diseases, war, and violent treatment introduced by the
conquistadores. Just in Mexico a 1532 study registered 16,871,408 Indians, but by 1608 this number had been reduced to 1,069,255.[16]

Throughout the centuries the Indians have attempted to hold to their
own social structure that focuses on the family, the clan, the tribe. Their
prime loyalties have been, and continue to be to this day, the local unit of
village or town. Their worldview is bound to the perception of the supernatural invading the totality of life. This view guides and shapes their
personal and communal history. They are basically animistic, worshiping
the spirits. Most have historically been tillers, herders, hunters. The three
major civilizations at the time of the conquest were the Aztecs of Mexico, the Mayans of the Yucatan and Guatemala, and the Incas of the Andean areas. More will be said about these major cultures later.

Today we have only estimates of the Indian populations. The countries classified as "Indian nations" are Mexico, Guatemala, Peru, Ecuador, Bolivia, and parts of Colombia. Hundreds of smaller Indian groups
live scattered throughout the other countries, primarily in Panama, Venezuela, and Brazil. Generally they are a people who have had to live under oppression since the conquest, although it must be said that some
were oppressors in their own right *before* the arrival of the Spanish. This
is documented by their own customs of slavery and in other cases even
human sacrifice. In some countries the Indian fighting blood has boiled
over. Indian guerillas have taken up arms in Guatemala, but the most vivid example of this violence is witnessed today in Peru with the *Sendero
Luminoso* (Shining Path). This guerilla movement originally attempted to
combine elements of Inca renaissance and Maoist thinking, but rapidly
degenerated into a desperate example of cruel violence in conflict with a
repressive military reaction.

Few countries have expressed a greater appreciation for their Indian heritage than Paraguay. Although Spanish is the official language, Guaraní remains the language of the heart; it is spoken in humble and wealthy homes as well as the highest government offices. The language is a gift of the Guaraní people, who were present at the conquest and whose language has "conquered" a modern nation. Today it is not so easy to establish just who is Indian and who is *mestizo*. The more recent census-takers establish the cultural identity of people not so much by race as by dress and language. If they are Indian by race but are dressed "Western" or speak Spanish, then they are no longer considered Indian in the official sense.

Significantly, the Indians are awakening to the fact that their large population serves also as a potential political block. Many towns of Guatemala formerly controlled by the *ladinos* (Spanish-Indian mixture) now rest in the hands of elected Indians. There is a new sense of self-worth, of *Indianismo*, surging in Latin America, a movement of perhaps up to four hundred local and regional groups. Their growing power is felt now in Brazil, Bolivia, Peru, Colombia, Guatemala, and Ecuador.[17] Evangelical ministries among the Indian peoples, such as Summer Institute of Linguistics-Wycliffe Bible Translators, are also feeling the negative side of radical *Indianismo*. In some of these cases SIL-WBT is under attack as a destroyer of culture and an imposer of foreign culture-religion.

Indianismo is also a phenomenon currently experienced among evangelicals, and particularly witnessed in the Quechua descendants of the Incas. In the highlands of Peru and Bolivia a people's movement is bringing thousands to a personal relationship with Christ. As Christians we clearly must respect the Indian as one created in God's image, precious, the object of Christ's love. We also must thank God for the dedicated ministries of Wycliffe Bible Translators and New Tribes Missions, whose study of both language and people has been made so that the Word of God might speak to Indian hearts in the mother tongue.

The Iberians—Spanish and Portuguese

The chapter dealing with the history of Latin America will analyze in greater detail the Iberians and their role in the New World. The Portuguese originally did not have a major interest westward. Their drive was toward Africa and Asia, and their royal navigators expertly plied the oceans. They became for a time Europe's major sea power and later monopolized for years the sea route finally discovered to India. Their initial goals, though, were commercial, not colonial.

However, these goals eventually and inevitably brought them into conflict with Spain's own colonial interests. "At Tordesillas in 1494, representatives of the two monarchs agreed to divide the world. An imaginary line running pole to pole 370 leagues west of the Cape Verde Islands gave Portugal everything discovered for 180 degrees east and Spain everything for 180 degrees west."[18] Later the line was pushed west in order to give Portugal what later became Brazil.

The Spanish aggressively settled the New World, their "West Indies." They brought the sword and the scepter, the cross and gunpowder to enforce "conversions" and establish their rule. Their *requerimento* was "a sort of outdoor theological treatise that every conquistador was obliged to read to possibly hostile natives before sounding his war trumpets, touching off his culverins, or charging his horses against the startled, bronze-hued tribes."[19]

They brought with them a complete culture, a language, a religion, a socio-political power structure that permanently marked Latin American history. They came in God's name, as well as in the king's name. They came, they stayed, they conquered. Not all was negative; for many of the motivations, attitudes, and practices had an authentic humanitarian motivation.

They also intermarried, though at first it was more a free union with Indian women. It is virtually impossible to find a Latin American painting that depicts the inevitable intermarriage in which the man is an Indian and the woman a Spaniard. It is always the opposite. These were men of fortune. If such a man had a wife, she was back in Spain waiting for his infrequent return. The Venezuelan Mariano Picón-Salas writes of this mixture of the races: "Miscegenation in Latin America is far more than a mere mingling of blood and race; indeed, it is a bringing together in the temple of history of the dissident temperaments, dispositions, forms, and ways of life in which our antagonistic tendencies have developed."[20]

The result of these unions was the *mestizo,* also called the *ladino* in other countries. This mixture of the bloods and races has caused a profound sense of malaise in many Latin American leaders, including Christians. One Nicaraguan author, a former Marxist now a charismatic Catholic, said to me recently: "The problem with us Nicaraguans is that we don't really know who we are. Our problem is *mestizaje.* Our blood is impure and this makes us insecure." A prominent Peruvian evangelical speaking in Central America expressed the problem this way:

When the Spanish male stepped on the shores of the New

World he sought for a woman to meet his needs. The only ones were Indians, and most of us are products of that union. But what are we, Spanish or Indian? We are neither, and since that first union we have been searching for our identity, for we are neither Indian nor Spanish. This is our inherent weakness.[21]

The Africans Arrive

When the Spaniards first arrived they utilized Indian labor—poorly paid, forced, or slave—to cultivate the land. That oppression erupted into a socio-theological debate: Does an Indian have a soul? Are Indians human? If they were human, possessing souls, then their treatment would have to change. Few argued as powerfully for the rights of the Indians as the two friars based in Santo Domingo, Antonio de Montesinos and Bartolomé de las Casas. Las Casas had traveled with Columbus on the original journey. In Cuba the Spanish crown had bequeathed to him an *encomienda,* the grant of a large section of land meant to be developed. If Indians already lived on the land, the *encomendero* assumed full responsibility for their temporal and spiritual welfare. In most cases this masqueraded as a smokescreen for slavery. But Bartolomé de las Casas renounced his *encomienda* and instead devoted himself to the defense of the Indians. In 1537 this "Apostle to the Indians" won from the pope a declaration that the Indians were indeed humans with souls. But the result was turned to tragedy when las Casas defended the Indians and asked for African slaves better suited for forced labor. There is some debate as to whether las Casas persisted in this attitude; apparently he later changed his mind regarding the black slave trade. But by then the flow of slaves had become a torrent.

It is believed that the first African slaves reached the New World as early as 1502. Later, the slave trade, carried on with the sanction of the Iberian monarchs, transported large number [sic] of blacks directly from Africa to the New World. Probably the first shipments of slaves arrived in Cuba in 1512 and in Brazil in 1538, and they continued until Brazil abolished its slave trade in 1850 and Spain finally terminated the slave trade to Cuba in 1866. As the American colonies grew, accommodated themselves to European demands, and developed plantation economies, the rhythm of slave importation accelerated. A majority of the 3 million slaves sold into Spanish America and the 5 million sold into Brazil over a period of approximately three centuries came from the west coast of Africa.[22]

And the blacks came, first as slaves and later as freed people. They have left their indelible mark on Latin America's history. In a sense one can imagine a black "people-ribbon" rimming the east coast of Latin America, where the major concentration of blacks is found. They form the dominant population in the Caribbean and have singularly affected Brazil. They applied their creativity to all the arts, trades, and crafts and became an indispensable human element in the New World of Latin America. They also introduced African spiritism to the New World. Geyer writes that "the talents, the temperaments, the beliefs, the physical traits of the Negro are ingredients in that new race of man—the American."[23] José Vasconcelos, Mexican writer and former Minister of Education, after a visit to Brazil wrote his lyrical work on the "Cosmic Race," that unique American Man who was the harbinger of a new world.[24]

The Later Europeans

Walk the streets of any major Latin American city, or enjoy your midmorning break by leisurely sipping an aromatic cup of coffee. Read the names on the downtown shops, scan the list of politicians campaigning, or observe the names of the Brazilian or Argentine World Cup soccer players. Once you become sensitive to the presence of non-Latin names, of fair-faced peoples of European extract, you will observe the results of some 150 years of active immigration.

In their desire to stimulate national development, many Latin American countries opened the doors wide to welcome immigrants from Europe. Many of the earliest arrivals came from Europe's lower classes. But with hard work and determination, they soon became an integral part of the newly emerging middle classes. This phenomenon particularly can be seen in the Southern Cone nations of South America. Sao Paulo, Brazil, gives us a good example.

While only about 4,200 Italians settled in Sao Paulo State between 1827 and 1873, more than 500,000 did so in the ten or so years between 1887 and 1898.... By the end of the 1930s, the state had 1 million Italian immigrants, and roughly half a million from both Portugal and other parts of Brazil. By then, an estimated 400,000 Spaniards and 200,000 Japanese also had arrived.[25]

Brazil invited waves of Italians, Portuguese, Spaniards, Germans, even Russians. Between 1891 and 1900 over 112,500 arrived annually, and just in the period of 1911–1913 alone, 500,000 immigrants came to start up a new life. In southern Brazil, for example, the German community is so strong that at times the visitor concludes he must be in the wrong country—he sees overwhelmingly fair-skinned, blue-eyed, German-speaking people and Lutheran churches. That is Brazil.

The perceptive visitor to Sao Paulo will observe a significant percentage of Japanese Brazilians. How did they get there? They came by invitation of the national government in two waves. In the late nineteenth century slavery had finally been abolished in Brazil. This provoked a crisis in labor, with a great need for specialized agricultural workers. Therefore the government of the state of Sao Paulo offered to pay passage across the Pacific for any Japanese immigrants. The second wave arrived during the 1960s to help develop more farming production centers. Today Brazil counts among its inhabitants about one million Japanese, assimilated into the Brazilian ethos. In 1984 the Minister of Petroleum was a Japanese-Brazilian. Japanese make up some seventeen percent of the students of the 45,000-strong University of Sao Paulo.[26] Significantly, some four percent of the Japanese of Sao Paulo identify themselves as members of evangelical churches. That is Brazil . . . a racial potpourri.

Between 1821 and 1914 Argentina welcomed some three million immigrants, mostly Italians and Spaniards. In 1914 thirty percent of the nation and fifty percent of Buenos Aires was foreign-born. Chile saw a similar influx before World War I. "They constituted at that time only 4 percent of the population. Yet, the foreign-born owned 32 percent of Chile's commercial establishments and 49 percent of the industries."[27] These immigrants contributed to rapid urban development, to the rise of a solid middle class, to industry and commerce, to the general modernization of the economies, to sports—particularly soccer—and even to the various Christian communities.

Dozer summarizes the Latin American racial melange and underscores the amazing new categories that have emerged:

> As a melting pot of races and nationalities Latin America has been active over a longer period of time and has accomplished a greater degree of amalgamation than has the United States. The general strains in that area are pure whites, pure Indians, pure Negroes; *mestizos*, called variously *ladinos, cholos,* and in Brazil *mamelucos, curibocas,* and c*aboclos,* who are descendants of mixed unions of whites and Indians; *zambos*

or *zambahigos* in the Caribbean area and *cafusos* in Brazil, who are of combined Indian and Negro parentage; *mulattoes,* who are of combined Negro and white parentage; and *pardos* in Brazil who are a mixture of all three colors. But these are the simple categories. The child of a mixed union of a *mestizo* and a white in the colonial period was called a *castizo;* of a mulatto and a white, a *morisco;* of a *morisco* and a white, a *chino;* of a *chino* and an Indian, a *salto atrás;* of a *salto atrás* and a mulatto, a *lobo;* of a *lobo* and a *chino*, a *jíbaro;* of a *jíbaro* and a mulatto, an *albarazado;* of an *albarazado* and a Negress, a *canbujo;* of a *canbujo* and an Indian, a *sanbaigo;* of a *sanbaigo* and a *lobo*, a *calpamulato;* and so on into almost infinite variety. Latin America contains almost every possible combination of colors, every mixture of mixtures. Mulattoes, for example, are characterized as *tercerones, quarterones, quinterones* and even *octorones*, depending upon the degree of color. During the colonial period Spanish law recognized approximately eighty possible racial combinations, and these have been increased since independence by mixtures with new immigrant strains.[28]

Mortimer Arias gives figures of the changing racial picture of Latin America from 1650 up to 1980:[29]

	White	Black	Indian	Mestizo
1650	138,000	67,000	12,000,000	670,000
1825	4,350,000	4,100,000	8,000,000	6,200,000
1950	72,000,000	13,729,000	14,000,000	61,000,000
1980	150,000,000	27,000,000	30,000,000	140,000,000

POPULATION EXPLOSION IN LATIN AMERICA

People, people, people is probably the overwhelming impression one gets from any significant visit to Latin America. Whether you go to a major city or travel to the interior the reality is always there: children, children, children, children, youth, youth, youth, adults, adults. Latin America is a population-young continent, with fifty-eight percent under the age of twenty-five. We shall deal in greater detail with population issues in chapter 3, but some items must be mentioned here. Note the growth of the population of Latin America compared to North America (United States and Canada).

Population Growth in Latin and North America: 1900-2025[30]

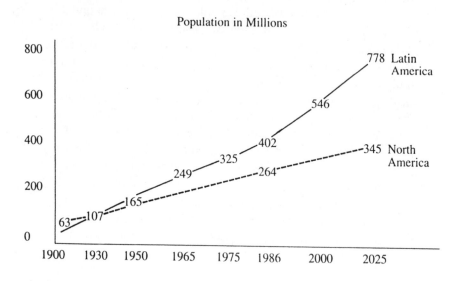

Population in Millions

Clearly Latin America contributes to the growing global weight-shift to the "South." By mid-1995 the world population was registered at 5.7 five billion, the more developed nations showing 1.17 billion (twenty-three percent), and the less developed nations registering 4.5 billion (seventy-seven percent). Today the United States has only 263 million, with a doubling time of 105 years. Greater Europe now has 729 million, but strikingly, a supposed doubling time of 500 years. Yet Latin America will double its population in thirty-six years. Some nations like Nicaragua can ill afford such growth, for they will double (if current rates of population growth continue) in a mere twenty-six years.[31]

What can be said of Latin America's population today? First, it is characterized by explosive growth. Marxist historian Edwardo Galeano says of his people: "They make love with enthusiasm, and without precaution."[32] Secondly, it has become an urban population, with sixty-seven percent now living in cities. Europe claims seventy-three percent urban, North America seventy-four percent, Africa only thirty percent, and Asia thirty-one percent. The challenge of the cities faces evangelicals in Latin America today as never before. John Maust underscores this need in his book *Cities of Change: Urban Growth and God's People in Ten Latin American Cities.*[33] The statistics on Mexico City are almost overwhelming: some twenty-one million people in 1989, surging to 31.6 by the year 2000; an additional one million new people annually; two million children unable to go to school simply because there is no school available; consumption of thirty percent of the nation's food; 2.4 million vehicles joined with thousands of factories polluting the air; one day's normal breathing equivalent to smoking close to two packs of cigarettes; the striking Chapultepec Park—an oxygen oasis in the heart of the city; an unbelievable and almost silent subway snaking its way underground, which packs in 3.5 million people per day; only 1,630 churches for an evangelical population numbering only one percent of the city.

Latin America's population is also young. There are some ninety-seven million youth ages fifteen to twenty-four out of a total of 442 million. The irony of modern medicine means that today there is a much higher survival rate for the young (eighty-nine percent of children will reach at least age twenty). Yet, tragically, millions of these children have been abandoned. Heart-wrenching scenes are common, particularly where they are most visible—in the large cities. Only God knows how many children wander the streets of Mexico City, Bogota, Lima, or Rio de Janeiro. There are millions just in Brazil alone. While it is impossible to get exact figures, we must see them as more than mere statistics. Rather, they are real children and real youths who wander about, living by their wits on garbage and petty crime.

Latin America's population is poor. Just one slum in Mexico City, Nezahualcoyotl, encompasses approximately three million people. Officials speak of some five hundred "lost cities," slums, in the city. Mexico City's garbage dump is a thriving "work" center. "Anywhere between 8,000 and 30,000 people make their living by collecting bones, cardboard, aluminum and virtually anything of value, and then selling it to a ringleader."[34] This stark picture can be easily duplicated in every major city.

Finally, it is a restless population keenly aware that no socio-political-economic system has managed to bring general prosperity or to distribute equitably the natural resources and wealth. It is a spiritually hungry population, willing to consider just about every spiritual claim. They need desperately to hear the message of a living, virile, victorious, powerful Christ who is able to transform their lives and even their society.

THE POLITICAL SCENARIO

The Picture Today

I will dedicate an entire chapter to some of the human crises of Latin America, but a few comments are in order here. Each country has its own unique political history, a record that has varied from decade to decade. Just twenty years ago the overall picture of Latin America would have been framed with the dark shadows of totalitarianism, mostly of the hard-line military right wing. But since then there has been a return to a semblance of democracy, or rather, a democracy that takes into account the political idiosyncracies of the Latin American social culture. Today the far right and far left of the spectrum coexist uneasily in Latin America. On the extreme right would be the Chilean strongman Augusto Pinochet, who had wanted to stay in power until 1997 but lost the October 1988 plebiscite and had to advance the return of democratic presidential elections in late 1989. Then there is Alfredo Stroessner of Paraguay, who after thirty-five years in power, was deposed in a bloody coup on February 3, 1989, and exiled to Brazil.

One country lines up on the far left. Cuba, openly and avowedly Marxist (though currently unhappy with some of the international implications of Mikhail Gorbachev's policies), is deeply indebted to the Russians, who yearly pumped in some six billion dollars to keep the island alive. Cuba paid off part of her debt by providing soldiers who serve as Marxist foreign-legion troops for Moscow. A recommended book to read about Cuba is Armando Valladares' prison memoir, a testimony to faith in God amidst human hell.[35] Nicaragua was ideologically close to Cuba and Marxist in orientation but unable to implement a doctrinaire approach. The Sandinista leadership claimed Nicaragua pluralistic in its economic policies and political freedoms. The Arias plan demonstrates the potential for true change and healing for Latin America, but only if the major players were willing to pay the price—including the United States. Nobody had forecast the electoral defeat for the Sandinistas.

Positioned between these two sets of extremes lies a broad-based middle with its own respective "left" and "right." Mexico, with its left-of-center one-party system, counters the Brazilian conservative forces emerging from years of rule by a military dictatorship. Argentina, as well as Peru, Ecuador, Uruguay, El Salvador, and Guatemala, is recovering from long periods of military bungling. Argentina has swung from a violent rightist military dictatorship all the way over to a progressive government which has tried, convicted, and jailed former military heads of state. Bolivia, with its revolving-door governments, has had so much political instability that no true change seems possible. High military and political officials have been accused of drug-industry involvement in a number of countries, with Bolivia, Colombia and Panama making current headlines. The remaining countries are developing their political experiments somewhere along the middle of the spectrum.

Latin America has also contributed to the international political leadership, primarily in the Organization of American States and the United Nations. Latins are justly proud of the gifted Peruvian, Javier Pérez de Cuellar, former Secretary-General of the United Nations, whose quiet diplomatic skills have been instrumental in resolving numerous international conflicts.

Threats to Stable Governments

It is important to underscore a few of the elements that undermine stable Latin American governments today. First comes the legacy of a colonial, centralized mindset that never had authentic desires for democracy. We see here a tragic history of mismanagement, a generations-long litany of the abuse of magnificent peoples. The legacy originated in Spain and was perpetuated by both civil as well as spiritual powers. The Roman Catholic Church must bear significant blame for her role in Latin American history. The church officially aligned herself with temporary power structures, condoning and blessing corrupt rulers; she imported a weak Christ incapable of authentic transformation of individual lives; she permitted a religious syncretism that never dealt with the non-Christian elements of Indian belief systems; and until recent years she limited the people's contact with the Word of God. And even to this day any perceived threat to her temporal power produces a strong reaction. In Guatemala, after evangelical General Efrain Ríos Montt was removed from power August 8, 1983, by a military coup, the Catholic leadership rejoiced openly. They held a huge open-air mass in Guatemala City on August 15 honoring the patron saint of the city, the Virgin of the Assumption. They thanked her for saving Guatemala from evil—meaning Ríos Montt. The new head of state, General Mejía Víctores, took over with the blessing of the church. He openly professed to be a faithful Catholic. And then he set a record for corruption in Guatemala's recent history. An outstanding evangelical lawyer echoed the thoughts of many when he stated sardonically: "Despite five hundred years of history the Catholics have yet to provide our country with an honest leader."

A second threat to stability stems from the inhuman social conditions prevalent in so many of these nations. This internal crisis of poverty, of personal and structural sin, of national and international economic debts soaring into the hundreds of billions of dollars, of the relationship of dependence upon foreign markets and prices for Latin raw materials and products, of the millions of families who are living and dying in the *favelas* and *villas de miseria* of Latin America, threatens to transform these nations into slowly ticking time bombs. Mexico is but one good example of this crisis, and there are many more.

A third threat is found in the active presence of subversive guerilla movements in many countries. We can cite but a few: Guatemala, Nicaragua, Colombia, and Peru. All but one of the movements are Marxist in orientation, and all are committed to a violent option for "solving" national problems. But, it must be said that if the cultures of poverty were not present neither would there be Marxist fighting. These Marxist radicals are not there merely because of Russia and its surrogate, Cuba. They are there and active primarily because of the long-standing social structures that generate poverty and underdevelopment. Never-theless, international Marxism thrives in such an environment, thereby encouraging Russia's former role in the area.

The drug industry threatens national stability, particularly in Bolivia, Peru, Colombia, and Panama. "Cocaine production rose in 1987. Some officials put drug export earning in Bolivia at US $2-billion, about three times the level of legal exports. In Peru the figure is about US $850-million and in Columbia US $4-billion."[36] Government officials on all levels, compromised and bought off, have become pawns of the vast drug cartels, the most famous being the Medellín Cartel. Even as I write, headlines and serious articles expose the radical corruption of Panama's military strongman Manuel Noriega, indicted by United States courts for direct leadership in the drug industry.

The most lucrative market for Latin American drug production is the United States, and for that reason the North American leadership pressures Latin governments and subsidizes economic and military programs to irradicate production. Some Latin observers also feel that Uncle Sam needs to work more on eliminating the drug demand, placing blame where it should be placed, and not primarily on the producers. Tragically, in Peru and Bolivia some believers are caught up in raising the coca leaf, simply because of the greater income it generates for their poor families.

The unchecked history of corruption and venality of so many Latin American leaders provides yet another threat. Seldom can one find a politician who has finished his term with a record of honesty. The Christian

Democrat movement, indebted to West German Catholic political theory, attempts to produce honest and clean politicians. But it is an uphill battle. The political arena has generally been considered a large personal pie of benefits to be distributed among family and friends, as well as a means of paying off political debts.

Finally, Latin American governments are unstable simply because no single political-economic-social system has yet been fashioned to fit the continent's unique history and reality.

The Political Future?

The above-mentioned factors have produced a spirit of pessimism in the minds of many secular and religious leaders of the area. They simply do not know what to do. Some try to sound optimistic in spite of the odds, others are extremely pessimistic, and yet others speak of the future in cautious terms couched in generalities. I personally foresee a continued pendulum-like movement over the next decades similar to the extremes of this century: a seesaw of totalitarianism versus "democracies." There will be an ongoing struggle provoked by the entrenched military, aristocracies and business elites, the subversive forces, the endemic human crises, the corrupt nature of humanity, and the demonic supernatural powers that provoke chaos and hell on earth. It will take some kind of godly, supernatural intervention in Latin America to produce healthy change.

THE RELIGIOUS PANORAMA

The religious panorama will be dealt with in detail later on, so what can be said here comes simply as an appetizer. My treatment of the subject obviously is made through an evangelical grid, and these presuppositions affect my analysis and conclusions. The secular, Liberationist, or Catholic observer-historian will obviously emphasize different themes.

A Religious Continent

The reality that Latin America is a religious continent is crucial to understanding this part of the world. The spiritual dimension weaves itself into the very fabric of the Latin American worldviews. Ultimately this comes from the way God has made humanity, but it is doubly true in

Latin America because the history of organized Christianity has been such an integral part of the history of these nations. The Indians continue with a well-developed cosmology in their fundamental animism. The Africans brought their spiritist worldviews with them. And while each variant will practice its own religion with its particular distinctives, Catholicism has proved remarkably open to syncretism by permitting the invasion of non-biblical belief systems into "Christianity." This produces a cultural "popular Catholicism."

The Catholic Church

Latin America has historically considered herself Catholic, but no longer do perceptive Catholic analysts feel at ease. Latins may be Catholic by tradition and culture, but they are not necessarily Christian. The percentage of practicing Catholics has diminished over the years. For example, today only fifteen percent of Sao Paulo would be considered faithful to their church. Too many Latins, says one Catholic leader, hold to a cultural Christianity more identified "with the environment culture.... One is obligated to adopt this religion to define oneself, or to be faithful to the group to which he belongs."[37]

Catholicism is no longer the monolithic structure it once was. The fragmentation that has come as a result of Vatican Council II, as well as the socio-cultural tensions particular to Latin American Catholicism, has revealed structural divisions in the church. While the old-line conservatives continue to seek solace in the Council of Trent, the liberation theologians on the left pressure for a radical departure from their church's traditional stance. The charismatic Catholics are finding unusual release in their new religious-emotional experience, which is opening them to further search for truth. The hierarchy is not finding it easy to reel these charismatics back into the historic fold.

Contemporary Latin American Catholics face challenges they previously never had to contemplate, challenges which have the potential to make permanent changes in the church.

The Evangelicals of Latin America

Perhaps forty million strong, evangelicals of Latin America grow much more rapidly than the national population rate, and one Roman Catholic source suggests there are fifty million.[33] Although they already constitute a political bloc in Guatemala, El Salvador, Chile, and Brazil, they are not united behind a particular ideology, political party, or specific candidates. Latin American evangelicals are overwhelmingly conservative in doctrine; many leaders call themselves *fundamentalistas* without the perjorative connotation which that term has in the United States. While many non-charismatic churches have a very high growth rate,[39] about seventy-five percent of all Latin American evangelicals belong to some Pentecostal or charismatic church. Their key to growth is "Lay, Say, Pray"; that is, they focus on lay activity, on personal witness, and intensive prayer.

Latin American evangelical leaders today face major issues that call them to serious reflection. First, how can they sustain the high numerical growth yet guarantee a quality conservation of those making decisions? As one pastor said, "Our churches may be large, but perhaps they are fat and not healthy!" It is imperative that more thought be given to biblical commitment and discipleship. Secondly, how can more leaders be trained for the growing churches? The present theological institutions are not producing sufficient leaders for the church today. Many of these schools are wrapped up with maintaining specific distinctives—both in program and theology—and have become unflexible. Other educators are polarized between residence and extension programs. Both thrusts are needed and must be combined for greater effectiveness.

A third challenge deals with contextualization within the Latin American reality. A fourth one deals with the social implications of the gospel in Latin America. And, finally, the challenge of world missions from Latin America to the cultures and peoples of the world has emerged. The November 1987 Congress of Missions of Ibero-America (COMIBAM), celebrated in Sao Paulo, was both an event and proof of a missionary ethos rippling through the churches of Latin America. The emphasis of COMIBAM has not been so much evangelism within one's culture—a perennial spirit of these churches—but rather cross-cultural evangelism and church planting both across Latin America's thousands of cultural lines as well as to the entire world.

The Explosion of Spiritism and Other Cults

The roots of Latin American spiritism find their origins in black African religious experience as well as in the Indian animistic worldview. The striking reality today is how respectable spiritism has become. In 1986, when a leading Brazilian spiritist died, the entire nation felt the impact. One government minister openly expressed his sorrow that one of his trusted advisors had died. The funeral appeared to be almost a state event. Evangelicals in Latin America, both nationals and expatriate missionaries, must be equipped to minister in light of the demonic forces openly at work. This will mean an understanding of the demonic worldview, of the ministry of deliverance, of counseling in light of these forces, and of greater sensitivity to these dimensions in the Scriptures. Such changes will require radical adjustments for many evangelical leaders.

In Conclusion

Spiritually, Latin America is wide open; and that means open for any message. All will be given a hearing, whether biblical, demonic or cultic, traditional or revolutionary. The challenges for evangelicals are vast. If they are to take advantage of the spiritual openness there will have to be serious study of the biblical nature of the church and its responsibility in the contemporary world.

CULTURE IN LATIN AMERICA

My focus here is not *culture* in the socio-anthropological sense of the term, but rather in terms of art, literature, theatre, music—in the use of skill and creative imagination to produce things of beauty and inner significance. And here Latin America has created a wealth widely ignored. While Latin American artists are indebted to the West—Europe primarily—the autochthonous dimensions, incredibly complex and beautiful, come into play as well. Other writers have dedicated themselves to a profound study of this cultural wealth,[40] so our purpose here is limited and merely illustrative.

The Various Art Forms of Latin America

Let me begin with painting. Whether the artist be a primitivist of Indian extract or a contemporary landscape painter, the gifts are undeniable. Perhaps what strikes many visitors to Latin America is the revolutionary emphasis of so many artists. Latins speak of *arte comprometido*, that is, art that is committed to a particular cause, generally nationalistic or revolutionary. The Mexican muralists Diego Rivera, Jose Clemente Orozco, and David Alfaro Siqueiros are outstanding examples of "art with message." They are not contemplative studies or delightful still lifes; by design they intend to disturb and shock emotionally. Nicaraguan *música de protesta* combines powerful political lyrics with stirring musical rhythms.

Latin American authors have been prolific and significant, while mastering the various literary forms. They include at least four Nobel literature prize winners: Gabriela Mistral (1945) and Pablo Neruda (1971), both of Chile; Miguel Angel Asturias (1967) of Guatemala; and Gabriel García Marquez (1982) of Colombia. Pick up any anthology of Latin writers and prepare to be stimulated. El Inca Garcilaso de la Vega (1539-1615), son of a Spanish conqueror and a Princess of the Sun, wrote some of the most important native chronicles of the Incas and the conquest. The Nicaraguan poet Ruben Darío led the late 1800s modernist movement. Partly borrowing from European influences, it had a nationalistic core in its inner heart. But the most powerful writers come from the twentieth century. Besides the prize winners already mentioned, they include Jorge Luis Borges of Argentina, Mario Vargas Llosa of Peru, Cabral de Melo Neto of Brazil, Carlos Fuentes and Octavio Paz of Mexico, Germán Arciniegas of Colombia, and many others. And then there is the whimsical and pungent Argentine comic strip *Mafalda,* the young girl with the piquant critique of society.

Music resonated in this New World long before Columbus. Even today in Indian communities one can hear melodies and ancient instruments. Autochthonous instruments include the marimba, the Venezuelan *Cuatro,* harps, flutes, drums, and the exquisite panpipes. Popular music brings rhythms of calypso, samba, and bossa nova. Contemporary, well-known classical musicians include Heitor Vila Lobos of Brazil, Carlos Chávez of Mexico, Jorge Sarmiento of Guatemala, and the bossanova master, Antonio Carlos Jobím of Brazil, who wrote the score for the classic Brazilian film *Black Orpheus.* Cuban Ernesto Lecuona goes down in musical history for the lush romantic melodies and rhythms of his Caribbean world. Even though most composers have studied in Europe, many of them have returned to Latin American themes in their music.

In dance who can surpass the visual beauty and rhythmic excitement of the Ballet Folklórico of Mexico, performing twice weekly in the Palace of Fine Arts? Latin America has its own traditional popular dances, some well-known: the *cha-cha, samba, conga, tango, rumba, joropa,* and *zapateado.* For blending art and architecture into a functional and pleasing whole, who can match the pre-Colombian creations of Aztecs, Mayans, and Incas? In a sense modern Brazilia fuses art and architecture on a massive scale. The elaborate mosaics of the library of the National Autonomous University of Mexico combine Indian, colonial, and modern themes.

Latin American art is committed art; it is art with a social conscience; it is art for political struggle; it is art that expresses national and Latin American identity; it is art that endlessly works the basic themes of the land, the Indian, the black, always in tension; many times it is surrealistic; it is art with a message that goes beyond the art form itself.

FINALLY

We return to affirm Latin America as a dynamic tapestry, a living mosaic, a collage, a kaleidoscope. Obviously it is so much more than that. I have attempted to portray in broad brush strokes something of the complexity of her geography, races, population, political and religious issues, and even art. But millions of written words cannot equal years of quality living in Latin America. Only the opportunity to meet her face to face, to develop sensitivity to her peoples, history, culture, issues, and currents, results in true understanding and compassion. And always one must come to terms with the underside of Latin America, that of the open veins, of the "120 million children in the eye of the hurricane."[41] Multiple pressures provoke social desintegration, and satisfying solutions seem elusive and ephemeral. Again, *xak quieb cubij päkawí* comes into play. Our confidence again and again has to be placed in the Lord and our commitment made to his church, in Latin America.

NOTES

1. Germán Arciniegas, *Latin America: A Cultural History* (New York: Alfred A. Knopf, 1972), pp. xxvi-xxvil.

2. Luis Arocena was my professor of Latin American civilization during my doctoral studies at the University of Texas, Austin, 1972–1974.

3 . Arciniegas, *Latin America,* p. xvi.

4. Donald Marquand Dozer, *Latin America: An Interpretive History*, rev. ed. (Tempe, AZ: Center for Latin American Studies, Arizona State University, 1979), p. 40.

5. Arciniegas, *Latin America,* p. xxvii.

6. Joseph Judge and James L. Stanfield, "The Island of Landfall," *National Geo-*

graphic, November 1986, pp. 583, 586.

7. Population Reference Bureau, Inc. *1987 World Population Data Sheet.* This annual publication is the best source of population information.

8. Dozer, *Latin America,* p. 5.

9. John Wilson and Gordon W. Gahan, "Drought Bedevils Brazil's Sertao," *National Geographic,* November 1972, pp. 704–22.

10. John Borrell, "Trouble Ahead for the Canal?" *Time,* 2 March 1987, p. 63.

11. *World Book,*s.v. "Amazon River."

12. E. Bradford Burns, *Latin America: A Concise Interpretive History,* 4th ed. (Englewood Cliffs, NJ: Prentice-Hall, 1986), pp. 6-7.

13. Ibid., p. 6.

14. Michael Novak, *The Spirit of Democratic Capitalism* (New York: A Touchstone Book; American Enterprise Institute/Simon & Schuster, 1982), p. 274.

15. Dozer, *Latin America,* pp. 8-9.

16. Enrique Dussel, *A History of the Church in Latin America: Colonialism to Liberation* (Grand Rapids: Eerdmans, 1981), p. 42.

17. Maria Elena Hurtado, "Exiles in their own countries," *South,* June 1987, pp. 149-51. This periodical is written from the perspective of the Two-Thirds World and hence offers a different slant on news that directly affects Asia, Africa, Latin America, and the Middle East.

18. Burns, *Latin America,* p. 14.

19. Mariano Picón-Salas, "The Initial Encounter," in *Man, State, and Society in Latin American History,* ed. Sheldon B. Liss and Peggy Liss (New York: Praeger, 1972), pp. 42-43.

20. Ibid., p. 46.

21. This is a free paraphrase from memory of an address given by Samuel Escobar at the Central American Theological Seminary in the early seventies.

22. Burns, *Latin America,* p. 23.

23. Georgie Anne Geyer, *The New Latins: Fateful Chane in South and Central America* (Garden City, NY: Doubleday, 1970), p. 15.

24. José Vasconcelos, *La Raza Cósmica,* Septima ed. (Colección Austral, Mexico: Espasa Calpe Mexicana, SA, 1982).

25. John Maust, *Cities of Change: Urban Crowth and God's People in Ten Latin American Cities* (Coral Gables, Fla.: Latin America Mission, 1984), p. 108.

26. Ibid.

27. Burns, *Latin America,* p. 164.

28. Dozer, *Latin America,* p. 9.

29. Esther and Mortimer Arias, *The Cry of My People: Out of Captivity in Latin America* (New York: Friendship Press, 1980), pp. 17-18.

30. Thomas W. Merrick, "Population Pressures in Latin Amenca," *Population Bulletin,* vol. 41, no. 3, July 1986.

31. *World Population Data Sheet, 1995.*

32. Eduardo Galeano, *Open Veins of Latin America: Five Centuries of the Pillage of a Continent* (New York: Monthly Review Press, 1973), p. 14.

33. Maust, *Cities of Change,* pp. 117-31.

34. Ibid., p. 125.

35 . Armando Valladares, *Against All Hope: The Prison Memoirs of Armando Valladares,* trans. Andrew Hurley (New York: Alfred A. Knopf, 1986).

36. Madlen Yopy, "Prospect 88. Latin America, an uphill battle," *South,* January 1988, p. 17.

37. Emilio Pin, S.J., *Elementos para una Sociología del Catolicismo Latinoamericano* (Madrid: FERES, 1963), p. 44.

38. Samuel Escobar, *La Fe Evangélica y las Teologías de la Liberación* (El Paso, TX: Casa Bautista de Publicaciones, 1987), p. 44.

39. In Guatemala, the Iglesias Evangélicas Centroamericanas, historically related to CAM Int., have demonstrated high rates of growth and may even today be the single largest denomination.

40. Jean Franco, *The Modern Culture of Latin America: Society and the Artist,* rev. ed. (Middlesex, England: Penguin Books 1970). See also Arturo Torres-Rioseco, *The Epic of Latin American Literature* (Berkeley, CA: University of California, 1967).

41. Galeano, *Open Veins,* p. 11.

2

A Synopsis of Latin American History

This relatively brief chapter attempts to integrate the vast information that forms such an integral part of the life of the Latin American peoples. On the desks around me lie seventeen major works dealing with this topic. Some of the perspectives are European, others are North American, yet others are Latin American, and one is Marxist.[1] Each has its own thrust, each claiming to have some kind of objectivity, each requiring evaluation by the careful student to unveil the prejudgments and value systems that control the recording of historical data. Total objectivity is impossible, and perhaps not truly needed, as long as the writer makes his presuppositions clear. The outline generally followed in this chapter comes from the late Dr. Luis Arocena, my Argentine professor of Latin American civilization at the University of Texas, Austin.

I write as an evangelical student, not a historian, of Latin American affairs. For that reason, I have tried to consult a great variety of sources, with ongoing attempts to sift the information received and then communicated on these pages. As a Christian, I see history moving toward a great denouement under the control of the Lord God himself. I also see the Kingdom of God at work today: not so much in the constructs of human government, but through the Word and Spirit of God, particularly as they transform the life of his people and his church. I see an integrated history. The sovereign eternal dimension penetrates human time, and God ultimately will be glorified. While humanity has struggled to produce on earth a society in which peace, freedom, and justice reign, their record is not very encouraging. The Christian can be grateful for the eternal option which is certain.

Let me clarify an important fact. The history of the Spanish-speaking countries is surprisingly different from that of Brazil. The reader therefore must be alerted to this variation and seek more complete sources for Brazil. Much of what will be said about the conquest and colonization applies primarily to Spanish America.

THE DISCOVERY: 1492

Time Line of Demarcation: 1492

The *Latin* aspect of this segment of history began in 1492, and that fact underscores a crucial element: there was a pre-Columbian history of supreme importance to us all. Life did not begin when Westerners, adventurers and explorers dedicated to despoiling, exploiting, enslaving, and converting, arrived on the shores of the New World. Since perhaps 20,000 B.C. humans had been in Mexico and had migrated as far south as Peru by no later than 12,000 B.C. Vast civilizations had come and gone; yet others in Mexico and Peru lingered in their glory to dazzle the Spanish *conquistadores*.

The year 1492 becomes then a double timeline of demarcation, a twin initiation of a new era. The first event was the Spaniard's discovery of the New World, the so-called Indies (which did not lead to the long-desired shorter route to the East—to China or to Japan). The second event lay in the New World's discovery of the Old. But in the final analysis the Old conquered the New and permanently changed its entire identity.

The Iberian Roots of the *Conquistadores*

These *conquistadores*, these men of fortune, cannot be understood without reflecting upon the historical and cultural backdrop that shaped them. H. B. Johnson has done an excellent job of evaluating the Iberian heritage:

> The men who conquered America were the cultural
> heirs of the *reconquistadores* of Iberia, warriors like the
> Cid who reestablished Christian culture and society be-

hind a moving frontier, which they pushed from the mountains of northern Spain to the Straits of Gibraltar during some four centuries of intermittent struggle against the Moors. Driven principally by a hunger for land and booty, these *reconquistadores* left in their wake, not only a belief in personal valor as the surest road to wealth and honor, but a frontier ethic as well, which was kept alive in the late medieval ballad tradition and the romances of chivalry.[2]

Many of the social structures carried to the New World were developed during the Iberian conquest. They include the *cabildo* (the municipal council) and the *latifundio* (large tracts of territory given to reward major pioneers). Other elements derived from medieval Europe, particularly the feudal lord-serf relationship. Black slavery, the quest for gold, and even the emerging sugar industry formed part of the social milieu of those years. The southern European trade competition pitted Italians, Spanish, and Portuguese against each other and then later against the northern European powers, Holland and England. The prime goal of all was to find a shorter route to India.

The Genoese sailor Cristobal Columbus committed himself to finding that elusive shorter route by sailing west. His entire life was dedicated to the proposition that the western seas led to the fabulous East, and he died persisting in the thought that he had realized his dream of reaching India. He was wrong; but once the seaways of empire had been traced out and a maritime bridge established, a culture and an ethos could be carried to the New World where they soon blended with indigenous elements to produce the variegated civilization of colonial Latin America....

In medieval Iberia, title to the lands taken from the Moors was derived from the fact of conquest, nicely legitimized and morally seconded by various papal declarations of crusade against the infidel.[3]

The Spaniards carried other values with them: religious zeal and intolerance, suspicion of non-Spaniards, more prestige for the soldier than the farmer or the family man, and a mentality of exploitation rather than development.

The Voyages to the Unknown West

J. Edwin Orr introduces his book on Latin America with the following panoramic perspective:

What an opportunity it was for Christendom when, in 1492, Columbus landed on an island in the Bahamas, and opened a door to the civilization, colonization and settlement of the Americas! A vast New World was brought into the circle of a nominally Christian society.

That same year, Alexander Borgia—whose personal life it is a kindness to ignore—ascended the papal throne. That same year, the last Muslim kingdom in Spain was reduced, releasing a burst of energy in the Iberian peninsula which helped create an empire in the West.

The same Alexander Borgia arbitrarily drew a line from the north pole to the south, designating the lands to the east of the Azores the proper domain of the King of Portugal, to the west, that of the King of Spain. By agreement, the line was shifted more than a thousand miles farther west, thus permitting the Portuguese to retain the land discovered by Cabral, the sub-continent of Brazil.[4]

The marriage of Ferdinand of Aragón and Isabella of Castilla in 1469 had united the two most powerful kingdoms of the Iberian Peninsula. Columbus and las Casas both speak highly of the queen in particular, emphasizing her high motives and Christian values as a leader and a benefactor of the Christian conquest.[5]

When Columbus finally received royal authority to travel, he outfitted three small caravals. Humanly speaking, it is very doubtful that the admiral really knew what he was doing. Although Columbus did not subscribe to the flat-earth theory, it was a risky sail into the uncharted oceans. What island did he reach first in the western Atlantic? Many have been named, and for years the prime honor went to what is today called Watling Island. However, Marden and Judge in *National Geographic*[6] have argued for Samana Cay, a relatively insignificant island, but sufficiently exciting for Columbus to have named it San Salvador "in commemoration of His Heavenly Majesty, who marvellously has given all this."[7] When the admiral navigator first viewed the island gleaming in the light of the moon, what could have surged through his mind? He truly found much more than the Orient or India in this history-changing voyage. The new lands were christened the Indies, and the conquest was on.

Columbus sailed four times to the New World. Soon other Spanish-sponsored sailors joined in the western discoveries. Among the first were Alonzo de Ojeda, Juan de la Cosa, Amerigo Vespucci (Columbus's fellow Italian, but bitter antagonist), Vicente Yáñez Pinzón, and Vasco Núñez de Balboa—who in crossing the isthmus of Panama discovered the Pacific Ocean as he searched for a shorter route to Peru. The Portuguese worked "their half" of the world by sailing east, and Vasco da Gama finally discovered during his long 1497–1499 voyage the shorter route around Africa to India. That trip produced fabulous wealth, and the Portuguese covered the seas in force. The 1494 Treaty of Tordesillas had now freed them to sail west; and in 1500 Cabral discovered Brazil and claimed it for the Portuguese crown.

In 1519 Fernao de Magalhaes (Magellan, who had switched his loyalty from Portugal to Spain) became the discoverer of the link between the Atlantic and the Pacific through what we now know as the Strait of Magellan. Dozer writes:

> The venturesome undertakings of the first wave of Spanish pioneers were surpassed by the exploits of their successors who pushed farther and farther into unknown wildernesses, where prospects never before seen by white men burst upon their astonished eyes and hardships almost beyond endurance had to be met. And yet, compensating for the hardships suffered by the *conquistadores* in this morning of America was the excitement that came from the ploughing of strange waters, the sighting of new headlands, the discovery of broad estuaries, the encounters with exotic animals and unintelligible natives, and the naming of new places. They moved about in a strange world, and in the embraces of the sensuous Indian women they forgot their homesickness and their toilsome labors.[8]

The explorers traveled in the name of Christ and their vicars as well as in the name of the crowns, bestowing Christian and Catholic names upon every possible location. "They were actuated by a supreme confidence in God and in themselves."[9]

The Peoples They Discovered

With his characteristic eloquence, Arciniegas writes:

The year that Columbus set foot on American soil drew a line through America's chronology not unlike the one drawn through Europe's reckoning of time by the birth of Christ. Christ was revealed to man in America in 1492, and for him the Christian era began with that year. Yet great civilizations, which we would term pagan, had flourished earlier under other gods, and an acquaintance with them is essential to the interpretation of the rest of history. A study of pre-Columbian life is as necessary to America as a knowledge of the pre-Christian civilizations of Assyria, Egypt, Greece, and ancient Rome is to the other hemisphere.[10]

These pre-Columbian ethnic groups, who in all probability had come over the Bering Straits, populated in varied degrees of concentration the lands from what is now the southwest United States to the southernmost tip of South America, as well as the islands. Most Latin Americanists emphasize the three major civilizations extant during the conquest: the Aztecs of central Mexico, the Mayans of southern Mexico and Guatemala, and the Incas of the Andes. But there were hundreds of other different groups; and as previously stated, a safe estimate of the total number of indigenous peoples would be over fifty million. These other groups include the Carib of the Caribbean islands and Central America, the Chibcha of Columbia, the Araucanian of Chile, the Guaraní of Paraguay, and the Tupi of Brazil. And now we have been introduced to some astonishing recent discoveries, which *National Geographic* calls "the New World's Richest Unlooted Tomb," which uncover the phenomenal wealth of the pre-Columbian Moche People of northwest Peru.[11]

Indigenous Scriptures might just as well have stated: "In the beginning was corn." Corn was to these peoples—from Mexico to South America—what wheat is to Europeans and rice to Asians. But not only their reverence for corn knitted these peoples together. Other characteristics included the focus on the family; clan or village; the profound faith in the supernatural forces that shaped and guided lives; the oral stories of the cultural hero-ancestor; the social sense of land ownership and land belonging to all; land tilling and the hunt; the sad record of internecine war, slavery, and oppression. At the same time, the differences among these peoples are vast. For that reason it is helpful to look briefly at the three major groups mentioned above.

The Maya people. In the classic period (fourth to tenth centuries)

Cultural Invasions from the North.

these people lived mainly in Guatemala. The late period, initiated by their sudden move to the Yucatan, lasted until the conquest. Their world revolved, and to a remarkable degree still does today, around corn. Their creation accounts speak of corn. Their sacred book, the *Popul Voh,* affirms that the gods "began to talk about the creation and the making of our first mother and father; of yellow corn and of white corn they made their flesh; of cornmeal dough they made the arms and the legs of man."[12] These Maya were agricultural experts and developed vast, sophisticated irrigation systems. Their major cities included the early complex, "El Mirador," in Guatemala; the religious center, Tikal, in Guatemala; their intellectual center, Copán, in Honduras; and Chichen Itzá and Mayapán, in the Yucatán peninsula. Their exquisite artistic ability is today seen in small figurines, animal sculptures, polychromed ceramics, weaving, featherwork, jewelry in gold and precious stones—all the way to soaring pyramids. They developed colors for painting that to this day preserve striking beauty. Burns refers to other achievements:

> Efficient agricultural methods produced corn surpluses and hence the leisure for a large priestly class to dedicate its talents to religion and to scientific study. Extraordinary intellectual achievements resulted. The Mayas progressed from the pictograph to the ideograph and thus invented a type of writing, the only Indians in the hemisphere to do so. Sophisticated in Mathematics, they discovered the zero and devised numeration by position. Astute observers of the heavens, they applied their mathematical skills to astronomy. Their careful studies of the heavens enabled them to predict eclipses, follow the path of the planet Venus, and prepare a calendar more accurate than the one used in Europe.[13]

Significantly, the Spanish *conquistadores* did not have a cataclysmic encounter with the Maya peoples, whose major centers of high civilization had slipped into strange eclipse during the tenth century. But the Spaniards did finish off what was left with a major battle fought in Guatemala by a Cortés associate. Don Pedro de Alvarado fought and conquered the Guatemala Mayans who were led by the legendary Tecun Umán. The invaders also virtually destroyed the Maya writings, leaving only about three codices intact. The most famous one is the sacred *Popol Vuh* of the Quiché of Guatemala—probably an oral tradition preserved with the help of R. P. Ximenez in the sixteenth century.

The Maya were a profoundly religious people with a pantheon of gods who cared for both cosmic and terrestrial affairs. The universe was one, and the supernatural invaded all of reality, merging the sacred and the secular. The cosmology was complex. These gods had to be appeased, and they were almost as bloodthirsty as the Aztec gods, with a demand for constant animal sacrifice. Yet there is controversy as to the amount of human sacrifice in Mayan religion. Once during a trip to Tikal, I listened to our guide explain Maya religion in English, and at the same time I could compare him to the Spanish-speaking guide in the next group. Our guide solemnly affirmed that there had been human sacrifice, and he explained how it was done. But the other guide strongly denied any such human bloodshed.

The Aztec people. By the fifteenth century the Aztecs had expanded and strengthened their hold on what is today the central valley of Mexico. Tenochtitlán was founded in 1325, and under the leadership of Moctezuma became an amazing city that later dazzled the eyes of Cortés and his 508 soldiers. The Aztecs also developed a complex and precise calendar, pictographs, impressive architecture, and a very efficient system of government. Their artistic and architectural accomplishments almost defy comparisons. The best place to observe the high accomplishments of the Aztecs is in the Mexico City Museum of Anthropology, where art and architecture combine so magnificently.

The Aztecs also were a religious people, and their universe had "unpronounceable gods and goddesses who presided over it and ruled man's fate."[14] There were great gods, creative deities, fertility gods, gods of rain and water, fire gods, pulque gods, planetary and stellar gods, gods of death and earth, and many variants of these gods. But their gods lusted for blood, and an astonishing number of human sacrifices were needed to appease them in their many ceremonies. The details of the callous brutality of the fire sacrifice or the sophisticated sacrifice of the Tezcatlipoca god are chilling. It is estimated that some twenty thousand people were sacrificed during the dedication of the enlarged great temple. Vaillant writes: "The application of human sacrifice to the most simple ceremonial act of thanksgiving offers a grisly contrast to the spirit in which these rituals were carried out."[15]

The Inca people. The Inca civilization was the "largest, oldest and best organized of the Indian civilizations . . . which flowered in the harsh environment of the Andes. By conquest, the empire extended in all directions from Cuzco, regarded as the center of the universe."[16] Within an area three thousand miles long (from Chile to Ecuador) and four hundred miles wide, these Inca regimented their centralized society with unique administrative ability. Theirs was a society led by a benevolent despot who appeared to desire the best for his subjects. Their counting system was based on the knotted strings, *quipu*, which probably had coded significance in the threads. The imperial language was Quechua. Their agricultural accomplishments were great in these dry highlands. Women played a significant role in society, the home, commerce, agriculture, arts, and textiles. Lake Titicaca, and the major city Tiahuanacu on its shore, share their glory with Cuzco and the fortress so well hidden in the high mountains, Machu Picchu.

The Inca also developed magnificent art, seen in textiles, multicolored ceramics, and gold. It was the Inca legend of El Dorado, based in Colombia, that ignited the imaginations of the *conquistadores* and made them willing to kill freely just so long as they could get their hands on the mythical golden man. Today the Gold Museum in the Bank of the Republic in Bogota has the world's outstanding collection of this historic gold art.

THE CONQUEST AND COLONIZATION: 1492-1810

The Conquest

The conquest was initiated by Columbus, who participated in the "pacification" of the West Indies peoples. It was a matter of "powerful persuasion," the cross and the sword, gunpowder and destruction. Within just fifty years the Spanish decapitated the indigenous societies and thus dominated a land mass that stretched from San Francisco, California, all the way to Tierra del Fuego, north of Antarctica. Armed with royal decrees and blessed by the church, the *conquistadores* marched and subdued.

John A. MacKay is passionate as he judges these men of fortune:

> Let us watch the crusaders in action. What magnificent *quijotadas* marked the course of the Conquest! North of the equator Hernán Cortéz burned his ten ships behind him, and, with a handful of daredevil Castilians, conquered the Aztec kingdom of Moctezuma. Francisco Pizarro, the ex-swineherd of Extremadura, marooned on a barren isle of the Pacific, drew a line on the sand with his sword, and invited every true Castilian to signify by crossing it that he would follow him thereafter to the

conquest of Peru. With the two hundred odd warriors who crossed the line, Pizarro scaled the Andean Cordillera and conquered the great Inca empire with its millions of subjects, taking captive the august Inca himself.[17]

One of the striking blends of politics and religion is seen in the *requerimento,* a kind of outdoor theological argument to be read by the Spanish to the "pagans" before charging in attack. It was read in Spanish, combined biblical passages with royal decrees, and affirmed that all the lands and the people conquered now belonged to the emperors of Spain or Brazil. In essence it summarized the Christian faith and demanded submission to the king and the Catholic faith. MacKay relates the encounter with Atahualpa, an Inca, after the formula was read to him.

> The Inca proudly replied that he would be vassal to no king. He denied the Pope's right to distribute lands that were not his. He refused to change his own sun-god for a God who had been put to death by the creatures he had made, and wanted to know where Valverde had learned such doctrines. When the Dominican handed him the Bible the Inca took it and threw it wrathfully to the ground. He swore he would have satisfaction for all the outrages committed by the Spaniards on their route from the coast. "The Gospel on the ground!" shouted the monk, "Christians, vengeance! Don't you see what is happening? Why dispute further with this arrogant dog? The fields are filling with Indians. At him, and I absolve you."[18]

After nine and a half months in captivity, Atahualpa was condemned to death by burning. In another case Caupolican, the Araucanian *Cacique,* desired to be baptised; but after his conversion he was forced to sit on a stake and was shot with arrows. The proud Cuban *Cacique,* Hatuay, was condemned to be burned alive but was also exhorted to convert and go to heaven. "Are there Christians in heaven?" he asked, and the reply was "Why, of course." Hatuay's rejoinder came: "Well, I don't want to go to any place where I shall have any chance of meeting them."[19] Many other examples can be given of similar responses by Indian leaders.

Ironically some of the Indian peoples welcomed the armored men, mistakenly concluding that horse and rider were one incredible creature of destruction. Miguel León-Portilla underscores the difference of perspective in the confrontation:

> When the Old World and the Aztecs in the New World met face to face on that November day in 1519, their attitudes toward each other were very different. The Aztecs . . . thought the strangers were Quetzalcoatl and other gods returning from over the sea, while the Spaniards—despite their amazement at the splendors of Tenochtitlan—considered the Aztecs barbarians and thought only of seizing their riches and of forcing them to become Christians and Spanish subjects.[20]

The war was won by the Spaniards but at a great price. Pedro de Valdivia founded the city of Santiago, Chile; but the Indians were not willing to give him their lands or provide him with the gold he demanded. And what was the end of this *conquistador?* "He was captured by the Araucanians in 1553 and killed—according to one legend, they poured molten gold down his throat."[21] Galeano mentions another high price of the conquest: the Caribbean island populations finally stopped paying tribute to Spain simply because they were exterminated.[22] The Indian populations were greatly reduced by forced work, disease, and war.

Many times the modern tourist, walking through the restored ruins of these indigenous peoples, will ask the naive question: "Where did all the Mayan peoples (or Aztec or Inca) disappear to?" The guide, controlling his impatience, has to say, "Sir, just look around you. There are multiplied millions living today." Other tourists see the religious practices of the contemporary Indian and comment on the "sincerity on the people's faces." What the non-Christian tourist does not know is how enslaved today's Indians are to their ancestral gods, to the demons that rule and destroy, to the hopelessness of life, to structural injustice, and to an eternity without the living Jesus Christ.

Thank God for the thousands of missionaries, expatriate and increasingly Latin American, who are dedicated to a full-orbed ministry to these magnificent peoples and tribes. This includes the missionary linguists as well as those who minister to established churches. Thank God for the growth of his church among the Indians—sometimes slow and discouraging, but other times pulsating with power as in the revivals sweeping today through the descendants of the Inca in the Andes (a movement that has come in part as a result of the freedom to use autochthonous instruments).

The Consolidation of Power and
Establishment of Colonial Structures

Understanding contemporary Latin America comes with the realization that the colonial social structures indelibly marked and shaped these peoples. To this very day many of the central problems can be traced back to colonial institutions. Here are some of the most significant ones.[23]

The institutions. The *Consejo de las Indias,* the Council of the Indies, was established in Spain in 1524 to advise the king on colonial affairs. Many of these decrees came in the form of *cédulas.* From distant Spain, multiplied thousands of laws and edicts were written to guide the new territories; by 1635 there were more than four hundred thousand of them in force at the same time. The viceroy was the Spanish captain general of the colonial areas and served as the king's personal representative. The *Alcaldes Mayores* were Spanish colonial officials appointed for judicial and administrative positions. The *audiencia* was a kind of court that dispensed justice and whose *oidores,* judges, shared functions of government with administrators and reviewed their work.

The *Real Patronato* reserved for the crown effective authority over the church in the Indies—an important contribution to the blending of church and state in the New World. The *repartimiento* was a system whereby the Indians were divided and forced to work in fields and mines as if they were slaves. The *donatorio* was an early and short-lived Portuguese system of colonial government. The *Capitao-mor* was the Portuguese head of militia responsible for distributing government orders.

Local authority was distributed according to the *cabildo* (the *senado da câmara* in Brazil). This was the town council (called an *ayuntamiento*), offering government at the first level by means of the *Regidores,* or councilors. From the start, the Crown authorized the *encomiendas,* grants based on the feudal model that gave both land and its people to *encomenderos,* who were charged with the development of that territory. They were also in charge of the spiritual and temporal welfare of the people on that land. These divisions later gave rise to the *latifundio,* massive ranches or plantations in the hands of a small number of people, in contrast to the *minifundio,* or smaller parcels of land to many people.

Those first favored with these grants were the *Peninsulares (Reinoes* in Brazil), people born in Iberia but living in the New World. The term *Indiano* was used then by the Spanish themselves for one born in

Spain and living in the New World but who identified with the mother country. These Spaniards came into conflict with the *Criollos* (*Criulos* in Brazil), American-born children of the *Peninsulares*. The *Mestizo* or *Ladino* was the child born of European and Indian parents.

The settlement of the land. The first Spaniards were men of fortune who came for gold, a commodity that offered easy shipment, imperishability, and precious value. They searched for it among the Indians, took it from them if found. Later they mined it, particularly in Colombia. The same was true for silver, with major strikes discovered in Mexico and Peru. In the sixteenth century Mexico shipped more than thirty-five million pesos of precious metals to Spain, and Colombia supplied some thirty million ounces of gold.[24] Brazilian gold came later on, in 1695, and then the rush to find fortune exploded. The *bandeirantes,* hardy explorers who often were of a multiracial blend, emerged as a special class of people—from folk hero to rascal.

From the beginning the land was to be tilled—obviously not by the Spaniards, but by the Indians. It was here that the *encomienda* came to play a central role. The previous chapter dealt with the issue of the human identity of the Indians and the major socio-theological controversy that ensued. We cannot overemphasize the crucial role played by men such as las Casas who dedicated themselves to the protection of the Indians. His image is found on Guatemala's most used coin, the *centavo*. Tragically, blacks were brought as slaves later on to work the sugar plantations of the Caribbean and Brazil.

Brazil's first formal settlement arose in 1532 at Sao Vicente, near present-day Santos. The initial goal of the Portuguese was to occupy rather than to settle or to populate the territory. Later, however, the development of an export economy ruled by an oligarchy of plantation owners began. For that reason they focused their attention primarily on the sugar plantations and the cattle ranches—and for both they needed slaves. Because the Portuguese were still more oriented to the development of Africa and the East Indies, it was not until they faced threats from France, England, and Holland that they populated the coast of Brazil in order to defend it. "By 1580, there were eight well-established captaincies, sixty sugar mills, a population of 17,000 to 25,000 Portuguese, 18,000 'civilized' Indians, and 14,000 black slaves."[25] There are significant parallels between plantation-oriented Brazil and the southern United States culture built around the values and behavior of the plantation world.

The predominance of the cities. The Spanish by 1600 had scores of towns and vast territories under their administration. Spain was eager to control its territorial possessions; and to consolidate them they introduced the full panoply of social structures already mentioned. This also stimulated the development of towns and cities with the more formal society.

> Of the 20 largest cities of Latin America, 16 were founded by 1580. All were physically planned in accord with the ideas of Emperor Charles V and King Philip II of Spain. As originally laid out, most cities had a central plaza, around which were situated the primary governmental and religious structures. Lots surrounding the plaza were allocated to the city's important families. Outward from the central plaza, streets were laid out in a gridiron pattern, with an eye to anticipating and facilitating future growth. Areas were set aside for the Indian population at some distance from the central plaza. These became *barrios,* each usually with its own plaza, church, and trading facilities.[26]

Some of the best examples of the Colonial cities today are Lima, Peru, and Antigua, Guatemala. Yet not all the cities were planned so well, as Mexico City, La Paz, and others clearly attest. These baroque cities brought together the major institutions of the colony: the imperial representatives, the regional and local civil government, the church, commerce—both internal and international—and the social and cultural life of the time. The focus on the few cities has also been a dominant factor in Latin American development. This has so favored the city that the interior is disregarded as inferior and is seen as necessary only in the way that it might supply and strengthen the urban world.

The church. The One, Holy, Roman Catholic church controlled most of New World life, not only in the cities but also in the interior and even into the remotest areas explored. Columbus had brought twelve friars with him on his second journey, while six Jesuits came with the first Brazilian governor-general. Their first task was to convert the pagan Indians; also they were to minister to the "Christians," the Iberians. The zeal of these missionaries is to be admired. They established missions for the Indians, many of which served to protect them from the rapacious exploitation of the Spaniards and Portuguese. Although the movie producers of *The Mission* took liberty in rewriting details, the crisis of the Indians is graphically portrayed in the film. It is based on the historical account of the Jesuit-Indian communities near the Iguazú Falls. The royal patronage system gave authority over the church in the New World to the royalty in all but purely spiritual matters. This obviously resulted in a double perversion: the church in the state and the state in the church. The church became very powerful as well as a major landowner, with her wealth concentrated in the cities. Sadly,

> The wealth reinforced the conservative inclinations of the Iberian Church. After the initial phase of evangelizing, it too exploited the Indians, as well as the African slaves, to till Church lands or to erect larger and more opulent edifices. To the masses it preached resignation. If God had made them poor, it would be a sin to question why. Poverty was to have its reward in the next life. It was not from the masses that the Church drew its leadership.... Thus, the highest ranks of the clergy, like those in the military and civil service, were associated with and filled by the aristocracy.[27]

Education. Education was provided by the church, and it preferred at first those of Spanish blood; only limited interest was shown in the schooling of Indians. Spanish education for the New World was crucial and schools on all levels were founded. The various Catholic orders took the initiative. There was hostile competition at times as they jostled for position and prestige, particularly between Dominicans and Jesuits. The first universities were founded in Mexico (1553) and Lima (1571) under the joint patronage of the king and pope—royal and pontificial universities. The classic "Seven Pillars" of medieval education were offered: theology (Aquinas and Scotus), Scripture, canons, arts (logic, physics, and metaphysics), laws, decretals, and rhetoric. Medicine followed shortly, joining with theology and law as the major courses of study. Tensions emerged when in those early years students of mixed blood found educational doors closed. At one time *mestizos* were rejected *in defecto natalium,* carrying a birth defect of mixed races, which made them inferior humans. Nevertheless, those early universities made educational history in the New World. Burns writes that

> before Harvard opened its doors in 1636, a dozen Spanish-American universities, drawing on medieval models, were offering a wide variety of courses in law, medicine, theology, and the arts, most of them taught in Latin. The universities made one major concession to the New

World: they taught theological students Indian languages
for their future benefit and effectiveness.[28]

However, education was dominated by a scholastic mindset which
condemned students to rote memory and limited educational content,
from primary through the university levels.[29]

Commerce. A mercantilist philosophy of commerce controlled both
business and trade. This meant that all major decisions were made in
Spain. They were designed to profit the mother country, not the colonies.
It was an exploitative dominance that prohibited internal development
and forced all trade routes to lead directly from the various colonial centers to Spain. No colonial infrastructure was allowed to develop. Actually, such ideas would have been considered heresy. The mercantilism centralized power in the hands of a few bureaucrats, thus allowing few
major decisions for local levels. Novak argues that "the Counter-
Reformation state impugned the religious value of commerce. It banned
or restricted enterprise in the private sector. It licensed certain entrepreneurs to develop state monopolies; it favored state mercantilism
over private mercantilism."[30] These attitudes prevail today in many sectors of Latin America, hindering socio-economic development.

Family structures. Much has been written about the differences in
family structure between the English and Spanish colonies. The Puritans
did not arrive to discover the land. That had already been done. They
came mostly with their entire families—men, women, and children—and
even communities, to till the soil of the New World. Their social structures revolved around this reality. They left Europe because of religious
and social persecution, and they arrived after tremendous sacrifice. They
came to stay and to build a Christian society. They were children of the
Reformation, Bible students committed to the priesthood of the believer,
to the high calling of physical labor, and to the sanctity of marriage and
children. They longed to worship God in liberty and were willing to pay
the price to settle where this freedom was theirs. They also came as British subjects with certain liberty to develop and elect their own local government.

Arciniegas significantly underscores these elements as he compares
the two colonial experiments. He includes in his book a segment of the
Mayflower Compact to illustrate the essence of the Puritan move.

> We, whose names are underwritten . . . Do by these
> Present, solemnly and mutually in the Presence of God
> and one another, covenant and combine ourselves to-

gether into a civil Body Politick, for our better Ordering
and Preservation and Furtherance of the Ends aforesaid;
And by Virtue hereof do enact, constitute, and frame,
such just and equal Laws, Ordinances, Acts, Constitutions, and Offices, from time to time, as shall be thought
meet and convenient for the General Good of the Colony.[31]

The contrast with the Iberian colonies is clear. They were conquered
and settled originally by men of fortune who had traveled without families and with no known desire to bring their families to the New World.
Their attitude to work was expressed by the words of Cortez: "I came for
gold, not to till the soil like a peasant." Their sexual needs were met by
Indian women, and a poor soldier could unite with—and perhaps later
marry—an Indian princess, a union that would bring prestige to both.
The great writer Inca Garcilazo de la Vega was the most famous child of
those unions. But that intermarriage, that mixture of the bloods, would
mark the self-image of the Latin American *mestizo* to the point that he
would to this day find himself searching for a clear identity.

The colonies were to be exploited, and state mercantilism assured
that the loaded galleons sailed the trade routes solely to Spain. The Iberians were children of the Counter-Reformation, faithful to their Holy
Church and suspicious of all potential heresy. The Bible was a closed
book; the priests were the intercessors. It was a matter of medieval miracle, mystery and authority, of mass conversion and nominal Christianity. These factors forged the Spanish colonies.

The reciprocal natural gifts of the Iberian colonies. Again it is Arciniegas who lists the fascinating exchange. The Spaniards brought a total society to the New World—state, church, language, education, legal
system, music. They brought ships and the wheel as functional instruments of mobility. They also brought the horse (with the cowboy or
soldier) and the donkey, the cow and ox, chickens and mice, pigs and
cats, the silkworm and sugar cane, bananas and rice, mangos, peaches,
apples, pears, plums, quince, figs, pomegranate, oranges, garlic, onions,
olives, roses, wheat, grapes and wine, syphilis and measles, black slaves,
guns and explosives.

The New World in exchange gave tobacco, pineapples, corn, to-
matoes, potatoes, chocolate, guine, sarsaparilla, vanilla, sweet potatoes,
red beans, bouganvillea, avocados, papaya, chili, rubber, and peanuts.
They also gave their land, their peoples to work the land, their beauty,
art, and music.[32]

Some Final Observations on This Period

As the colonial era came to a conclusion, internal and international currents began moving inexorably, which would produce cataclysmic change in the New World. The initial moves toward some kind of independence were under way both in Europe and in the colonies.

THE REVOLUTION AND INDEPENDENCE
OF LATIN AMERIA: 1810-1824

First Signs of Unrest

The Spanish and Portuguese colonial governments had served to exploit the New World for the mother countries. Inevitably some changes took place, and the eighteenth century in Latin America brought about limited liberalization in both trade and government. At the same time there had been a series of low-level danger signals that augured major structural changes.

Unrest in the Indian population. The Indians began to rebel in sporadic revolts, some of them significant, as in the case of the Chilean Araucanians. One of the most important rebellions took place in the Andean highlands, and has had long-term international implications, including the contemporary Argentine guerilla movement Tupamaros.

> In 1780 José Gabriel Condorcanqui (1742-81), a direct descendant of the Incas, who had assumed the name Tupac Amarú in 1771, led an abortive Indian rebellion in Peru after proclaiming himself emperor of his part of America. After a brief success, he was captured and put to death with great brutality. But on the plains of Venezuela people still speak of him as king, and people on the pampas remember that he died to bring about some of the reforms that actually came later.[33]

Unrest in Europe. The Spanish crown faced a series of changes and crises. While Brazil was able to sustain just about all of its territorial integrity, Spain began to lose land as the Spanish political alliances shifted. Santo Domingo went to France in 1797; then followed the massive loss of Louisiana in 1801 to France, who in turn sold it two years later to the United States. This territory of 827,987 square miles stretched from New

Orleans up into Canada. In 1819 a weakened Spain sold Florida to the United States.

Spain's and Portugal's own problems came as a result of the struggle with Napoleon's expansionist dreams. When Portugal refused to obey the French emperor, he invaded Portugal; and the entire Lisbon court by a matter of hours barely escaped the invading army and sailed off to Brazil. Napoleonic forces converted Spain into a battleground in 1808, which obligated the distant colonial vice-royalties to make many decisions on their own.

Yet another cause of the European unrest came with the expansionist designs of the English, French, and Dutch. Their original interests lay more in the islands of the West Indies, which today conserve the name originally given to the New World. The British based their sugar economy in the islands. Spain gradually lost control of Jamaica; and eventually that island was ceded to the British in a 1670 treaty. The British had great trade interests in the area and constantly pressured Spain on the open seas. For about three hundred years they effectively used privateers and buccaneers who plied the Caribbean seas, attacking and capturing Spanish ships. North American children will remember Sir Francis Drake, but every Ibero-American child grew up calling him "Drake the pirate"—a matter of perspective.

Curacao and the three Guianas—British, French, and Dutch—on the northern rim of South America are vestiges of that non-Iberian influence. However, it was the Dutch who tried to take advantage of Portuguese weaknesses in Brazil. Their interests were sugar, salt, and contraband trade. They actually invaded the northeastern corner and kept it from 1630 until 1654. To this day Dutch architecture can be observed in the city of Olinda.[34]

• *Unrest in the Criollos.* Back in the New World the rigid colonial class system faced structural stresses. The *criollos* were growing increasingly restive and resentful of the *peninsulares* dominating them. The Iberians monopolized the major posts in the government, the military, the church, and social and economic life. The *criollos* were left out, even though they were direct, pure-blood descendants of the Spaniards. Wealth continued to be siphoned off to Spain, and the trade routes still were forcibly limited to Spain. One notch down, the *mestizo* continued to battle the problem of identity, receiving limited acceptance from either those above or the Indians and blacks below. Those on the underside of society, Indians and blacks, were cut out of power completely. The first stages of nationalism were being felt, the class struggle had started, and these signs both augured ill for imperial Spain.

Radically new concepts began to emerge in Europe—revolution and independence. The basic ideas had been sown in the English and French Enlightenment by the *philosophes* and *encyclopaedists*. The unprecedented dreams of liberty, equality, and fraternity inspired some of the *criollos,* particularly those of the high class who were studying in Europe. They began reading the Enlightenment writings, the same literature that fueled the North American colonies. By the second half of the eighteenth century, the writings of Voltaire, Rousseau, Montesquieu, Locke, and others were being digested in light of their application to the Spanish colonies.

The American Revolution of 1776 seemed to provide an excellent model, at least on paper and in theory, for the Spanish colonies. The French Revolution of 1789 at first had encouraged the emancipation-minded *criollos.* "On the other hand, the Reign of Terror in France proved to be a sobering influence, for the majority of Creoles scarcely sought a completely egalitarian society in which their own advantages might disappear. They were determined upon changes, but hoped to achieve them within the framework of monarchy."[35]

Yet another revolutionary model emerged in Haiti, where an authentic slave rebellion expelled the French masters in 1791. A black Haitian military officer, Pierre Francois Dominique Toussaint l'Ouverture, led the revolt, but he was later tricked into captivity, chained, and sent to France to die in prison there. But in 1804 another black, Jean Jacques Dessalines, proclaimed Haiti's freedom and pronounced himself emperor.

Explosions: Battles and the Triumph of Independence

Simon Bolivar, the great Liberator—the Latin American's George Washington—declared that the wars were justified because of "the Laws of the Indies, the rule of the old executives, the influence of religion and of foreign domination, . . . the ferocity of our enemies and our national temperament."[36]

The first revolts. Initial uprisings in Spanish America were spontaneous and localized, fundamentally unrelated among the three major fronts of Mexico, Venezuela-Columbia, and Argentina-Chile. There was no unified command to bind the leaders—the "Patriots"—in strategy and goals. The colonial era had neutralized an infrastructure of continental interaction and communication. But the first battles exploded on all three major fronts: Mexico, Venezuela, and Argentina. In some cases the struggle began when the *criollos* took control of local *cabildos.* Buenos

Aires caught the independence virus after the English tried to take the city and fared only calamitous defeat at the hands of the local citizens.

Mexico. Mexico's case is unique because the battles ripped through the rural sector in 1810. The war started in the little Indian town of Dolores under the leadership of the parish priest, Miguel Hidalgo y Costilla. This case is also singular because of the Indian role in the struggle—a factor that led the city *criollos* to deny their support. The famous battle cry, the *Grito de Dolores,* unfortunately led to mob plunder and killing. Hidalgo was captured and executed by royalist forces; but in 1815 the *mestizo* priest José María Morelos led another revolt. He also was executed; and it was not until September 1821 that *criollo* Agustín de Iturbide emerged as the military leader destined to protest the repressive policies of a revitalized Spain. He so alarmed the *criollos,* even the most conservative, that they aligned behind the rebel leader. "In September 1821 Iturbide entered Mexico City in triumph, and independent Mexico began its chaotic and violent career."[37]

Northern South America. In South America the road to independence was taking different routes. Here the royalists were better supported by Spain and the struggle more arduous. The first Venezuelan surges toward independence were led by Francisco Miranda, the *precursor*—or forerunner—of independence. Born in Caracas, he had lived for a time in the new republic of the United States where he studied the political experiments there. While in the United States he developed the vision of a Great Colombia emerging to replace the Spanish rule; later his base of operations became England. The aristocratic *criollo* Simón Bolívar, *El Libertador,* also of Caracas, was tutored there by Andres Bello, an outstanding man of letters. Bolívar's education in Europe was nurtured on the ideals of the French Enlightenment, and in Rome he vowed to dedicate his life to the freedom struggle.

Bolívar's first battle in 1812 resulted in defeat to the royalists. When General Miranda lost heart in the fighting, Bolívar and other junior officers called him a traitor and handed him over to the royalists. He was carried to Spain as a prisoner and died in a dungeon in Cadiz. Bolívar's long saga combined periods of military strategies and struggles with periods dedicated to the writing of constitutions, and with a series of retreats and exile periods. Bolívar returned to conquer Venezuela in 1813, and he set up a strong centralized government. But this venture also ended in defeat and he fled to Haiti. His next invading force in December of 1812 finally defeated the royalists, and a long chain of victorious battles ensued. The incredible march over the Andes with his army merits a book of its own. Finally, aided by more than five hundred British adventurers, the *Gran Colombia* of Venezuela, Colombia, and Ecuador established his rule. He was thirty-nine years old at the time.

The Southern Cone. Down in Argentina arose the leader José de San Martín as the Patriot. Son of a Spanish officer and trained in Spain, he returned to Buenos Aires to aid the independence movement that had already shaken off the Spanish rule. So San Martín moved his theater to Chile, leading his Army of the Andes once again over the high passes (he crossed the Andes seven times in all). In early 1817 Santiago fell and Bernardo O'Higgens (San Martín's second in command and son of an Irish-born viceroy of Peru) became the head of the new republic. San Martín then sailed up the Pacific to Peru, and in July 1821 Lima fell. This was the final disastrous blow to Spain, for the "City of the Kings" was the crown jewel of Spain's South American colonies.

The sad story repeated itself—it was easier to win a war than organize a new nation—and San Martín was unable to produce an effective government. A major summit meeting was held between him and Bolívar in Guayaquil during late July 1821. The goal was to stitch together an integrated solution to South America. But differing personalities and visions produced such conflict that the meeting ended in defeat for both men, and ultimately for Latin America. Disappointed, San Martín pulled out of the political struggle, slipping into lonely self-exile in Europe, where he died in France in 1850.

The final battles. Bolívar carried the mantle virtually alone, winning the final battles in Peru and Bolivia, and witnessing the impossible—the total political emancipation of South America from Spain. The frustrations of organizing the new nations were compounded by the conflicting dreams of the new leadership, who had scant preparation for ruling. Bolívar traveled unceasingly, smothering political fires, writing and rewriting constitutions, decreeing and forcing decisions. British historian George Pendle concludes:

> But it was a hopeless task. Gran Colombia was already breaking up into its component parts—Venezuela, Colombia, Ecuador—Bolívar himself was exhausted, ill, and disillusioned. An attempt was made on his life. Slowly he moved away towards exile, following the Colombian coast until he reached Santa Marta. He never went any farther. He died on the edge of his continent, in 1830, at the age of forty-seven. In the previous year he had written:

"There is no good faith in America, nor among the nations of America. Treaties are scraps of paper; constitutions, printed matter; elections, battles; freedom, anarchy; and life a torment."

Shortly before his death he added: "America is ungovernable. He who served a revolution ploughs the sea."[38]

International Recognition of the New Nations

Perceiving a golden moment, England in particular wished to inherit the commercial ties with Hispanic America; but the United States of America, that young and vigorous nation, also had her own designs for both trade and leadership. United States industrial growth had started, and the new republics were magnificent sources for raw materials as well as markets for finished products. While the English discussed whether to and how to recognize the countries, the United States acted. The secretary of state, John Quincy Adams, developed with President Monroe what became known as the Monroe Doctrine, propounding four basic principles:

The United States (1) would not intervene in European affairs; (2) would respect "the existing colonies or dependencies of any European Power"; (3) could not admit that the recognized republics be considered "as subjects for future colonization by any European Power"; (4) could not view "any interposition [in those republics] for the purpose of oppressing them or controlling their destiny by any European Power in any other light than as a manifestation of an unfriendly disposition towards the United States."[39]

However, this Monroe Doctrine did not stop the British from signing major trade treaties with Argentina, Colombia, and Mexico. Bolívar attempted in a Panama continental congress to foster a sense of Pan-Americanism, a dream that floundered when only four nations sent representatives. There was too much mutual distrust and internal conflict, a legacy handed down through the generations.

Brazil's Unique Path to Independence

The contrast of Portuguese-speaking Brazil with Hispanic America is astounding. Whereas the Hispanics shed blood in the battles for liberty, the Brazilian route was radically different, almost a gentle transition more in harmony with the Portuguese spirit. When the Portuguese royal family and court—some two thousand people—had escaped Napoleonic forces by fleeing to Rio de Janeiro, they simply set up court there. They had taken the gold and other valuables, and British ships had protected them on the seas from hostile attack. Rio, as of January 1808, was now the capital of Portugal. The city had to be refurbished for royalty, and the British continued their commercial involvement.

By 1815 Brazil was declared equal to Portugal in status and Dom Joao became the king over both. He returned to Portugal in 1821 to reclaim his European throne, and he left his son Dom Pedro as regent.

As it became increasingly apparent that the Lisbon government planned to reduce Brazil to its former colonial status, Dom Pedro, in September 1822, with the encouragement of Brazilian patriots, uttered the historic cry: "Independence or death!" Before the end of the year he was proclaimed Pedro I, Emperor of independent Brazil.[40]

Without bloodshed Brazil gained her emancipation and the royalist troops returned home. "From the beginning of independence the country possessed trained administrators, and it was peculiarly happy in the character of its second emperor, Pedro II, who governed constitutionally and wisely, until in 1889 the monarchy withered away and the republican era began."[41] It truly stands in stark contrast with the Spanish republics.

THE PROCESS OF ORGANIZATION AND DEVELOPMENT OF THE NEW REPUBLICS: 1824-1880

The Situation

The map was drawn. By 1824 the former Spanish colonies had produced seven new republics: Mexico, the United Provinces of Central America, Colombia, Peru, Chile, Paraguay, and the Provinces of the Rio de la Plata. The latter became Argentina, and in 1830 when Gran Colombia came apart, four others emerged: Bolivia, Uruguay, Ecuador, and Venezuela. Add Brazil to the list and the modern map was basically drawn.

The republics were in crisis. Octavio Paz, contemporary Mexican writer, perceptively discusses the meaning of independence to the new nations. He juxtaposes the conquest with the independence. Both "seem like moments of flux and reflux in a great historical wave that gathered in the fifteenth century, flooded over America, attained a brief but splendid equilibrium in the sixteenth and seventeenth centuries, and finally receded after collapsing into a thousand fragments."[42] He goes on to affirm that

> the independence movement in South America began with a continent-wide victory: San Martín liberated half the continent, Bolívar the other half. They created great states and confederations. They thought that emancipation from Spain would not bring about the dismemberment of the Hispanic world. In a short while, however, reality shattered all their projects. The process of disintegration in the Spanish Empire proved stronger than Bolívar's clairvoyance.[43]

North Americans misunderstand Latin America when they assume that the two independence movements were similar. Although there are major parallels—both colonies sought freedom from the mother country—the differences are structural. In North America the patriots led a people who had been geared to independence through a greater percentage of involved electorate, as well as internal development and infrastructure, years of discussion and public arguments, minimal class and ethnic variants, and decades of experience in governing. Spanish America was different. There had not been a real desire to change the social structures of the colonies. The power and wealth simply passed from one elite to another. Even though the international independence vocabulary was similar, its particular definitions were not. Paz concludes:

> Among ourselves . . . the ruling classes consolidated themselves, once Independence was achieved, as heirs of the old Spanish order. They broke with Spain, but they proved incapable of creating a modern society. It could not have been otherwise, because the groups that headed the Independence movement did not represent new social forces, merely a prolongation of the feudal system.

> The newness of the new Spanish-American nations is deceptive: in reality, they were decadent or static societies, fragments and survivals of a shattered whole.[44]

The new nations struggled with the internal issues as they organized themselves. No unanimous spirit had guided their vision of what the republics would become upon gaining their liberty. The political experimentation moved across the spectrum. Provisional constitutions, treaties, pacts, statutes were written and seldom, if ever, applied. The federalists struggled against the unitarists. "The former supported a system of loose confederation between the different provinces or, perhaps more accurately, between the caudillos, whereas the latter wanted a unified state."[45] Another tension came between the urban and the rural inhabitants. In Argentina the *porteños* of Buenos Aires violently fought against the *provincianos* of the interior. Conservatives clamored for authoritarian regimes, and the liberals apparently wanted to eliminate all kinds of absolutism. A major battle swirled around clericalism, for "Latin America had inherited from the days of Spanish sovereignty a clergy accustomed to playing a political role, and possessing great wealth besides. Separation of Church and State, distribution of Church property, and elimination of the clergy's political influence were the issues on which Latin American statesmen were deeply divided."[46]

Some statesmen wanted a monarchy; and Mexico, for example, tried that option twice, with disastrous results. Parliamentary government was experimented with—and the results were dubious. But what emerged was the need for strong central authority. The United States constitution had been used as an original model for the Latin American ones, with very limited success. Now that same foreign document was used to justify the move toward centralization with democratic respectability. The regime of presidential dominance became the central political model for the new republics.

The *Caudillos* Emerge to Take Power

The young Bolívar had cried out in Europe: "I swear that I will not die until I have driven the last Spaniard out of America." But the dying *Libertador* lamented, "Many tyrants will arise on my tomb." And that is what happened. The Spanish yoke had been discarded; but the structures of society were unchanged, and the lofty and noble ideals stumbled on the colonial hangovers: ignorance, apathy, poverty, illiteracy, class and racial struggles, clerical domination, land control by a few wealthy families, a closed mentality to new ideas, mercantilism, and an exploitative economy. The new nations were unprepared for a representative democracy, and into the vacuum of power emerged the *caudillos*, those strong, charismatic men who embodied the frustrated aspirations of the masses. Freedom had been transformed into a millstone, and the national identity crises cried for relief.

These strong leaders evolved from the *caciques* (*coroneis* in Brazil): the more-localized chiefs of *latifundios*, tribes, regional armies, *gauchos*, and even outlaws. The relationship of a *cacique* to his men was a feudal relationship in which the *cacique* gave his followers protection and they in turn served him with loyalty. The supreme virtue was loyalty, not patriotism. Generosity and atrocity enforced the relationship. Conquest by power was key. Now the *caudillo* was the only one capable of controlling the *caciques*, and national power in Latin America was assumed by the *caudillos*, who brushed aside the vaccillating politicians of the capital cities.

All of the social strata of Latin America have been represented among the caudillos: Francia (1811–1840) in Paraguay was a cultivated, paternalistic aristocrat; Santa Anna (1824–1844) in Mexico was a wealthy Creole, charming and volatile, who dreamed of military glory; Santa Cruz (1829–1839) in Bolivia was a professional officer, honest but conceited, who believed himself heir of the Incas through his mother's line; Portales (1830–1837) in Chile was a rich businessman, concerned with order and prosperity; Rafael Carrera (1836–1865) in Guatemala was a mystical and illiterate Indian; Juárez (1857–1872) in Mexico was also an Indian, but highly educated and liberal; Melgarejo (1864–1871) in Bolivia was an illiterate, alcoholic mestizo; García Moreno (1869–1875) in Ecuador was a very learned and pious professor; Rufino Barrios (1872–1895) in Guatemala was a general, but Fulgencio Batista (1934–1959) in Cuba was a noncommissioned officer in revolt against the generals; Gusman Blanco (1870–1890) in Venezuela was a cultivated gentleman, but Cipriano Castro (1899–1908), who succeeded him, was an illiterate cowboy.[47]

The *caudillos* marked a transitional period of Latin American history. In some countries, such as Venezuela, they provided a chain of rulers for the period 1830–1935. Some of them, such as the national hero Benito Juárez—defender of the Indians and the liberator of Mexico—served their countries well. Others were barbarian megalomaniacs, such as Melgarejo of Bolivia and Francia "El Supremo" of Paraguay. Yet others such as Porfirio Díaz, who followed Juárez, introduced, at great national price, modernization to Mexico.

The *caudillos* marked the history of Latin America in singular manners. Not all of them were negative influences, for the republics needed strong, central leadership. They lasted long decades, overlapping into the twentieth century and their values persist even today in Peru and Cuba. But the transition was being made to other political structures as the society evolved and matured in its search for greater stability and continuity.

Brazil was writing her own chapter in history as a new republic. That nation had advanced economically under the monarchy of Pedro II, originally developing the plantations. Later, industry began to emerge along with the railroads. Territorial expansionism and disputes led to what Pendle calls "the greatest international war in Latin American history."[48] Paraguay's dictator Solano López disastrously lost the war, and Brazil annexed much of the neighbor's land. Independence came in 1889 and a republican constitution was published in 1891, although the military controlled real power. The classic continental struggle showed itself—how to apply new rules to old colonial structures. Yet the nation held together based on crucial compromises. Millions of European immigrants arrived to fuel development—Italians, Portuguese, Spaniards, and Germans. Sugar, coffee, rubber, and cattle came from the land, but it was industry that gradually set the pace in the powerful cities, particularly Sao Paulo.

THE PERIOD OF RELATIVE PEACE AND NATIONAL DEVELOPMENT: 1880-1930

As we move into study of this period, it becomes increasingly difficult to deal with Latin America as a whole entity. Each country now developed its own identity; each one had its particular historical dynamics. Nevertheless some tentative generalizations can be made that provide a continental perspective. Lambert, a French Latin Americanist, calls the nineteenth century a "wasted one" for the area. His lament comes because the republics missed the opportunity during that century to pass from chaos into solid models of development. The natural and human resources of Latin America were greater than those of Europe and at least matched those of the United States. But, "compared to fast-growing Western Europe and Anglo-America, Latin America had turned into an underdeveloped continent."[49]

The Changing Context of Latin America

General social changes. During this period Latin American society experienced a gamut of changes and shifts, some minor, others major, all combining to transform the face of these cultures. The black slaves were finally freed in Cuba (1886) and Brazil (1889), although this did not have the major impact on those societies that the emancipation of the North American slaves had had. National infrastructures were developed, primarily with foreign investments and corresponding monopolies. Significantly, though, the infrastructure was not geared to bring the republics together, which would have fostered trade and interaction with each other. The system followed the colonial patterns—they were designed for international export.

Thousands of railroad lines were laid to develop the interior primarily for agricultural export and industrial projects. This was true in Central America for coffee and bananas, and in the Southern Cone it opened the Pampas for agricultural and cattle programs. Mining interests were supported by the new lines in Mexico and South America. Latin America was gearing itself for major exports in agriculture (sugar, coffee, cacao, grains, rubber, lumber, tobacco), metals (silver, tin, copper), and other products (guano, nitrates, hides).

These commercial changes began to modify the traditional class structures, particularly as a small but significant middle class emerged between the wealthy landed elites and the *mestizo*-Indian masses. The new class, however, did not have any particular interest in aiding those on the underside of history. The conflicts were exacerbated, adding yet another fuse to the social time bomb.

"To progress is to populate" became a slogan in Argentina, and the doors were opened up to millions of European immigrants. Other nations feeling the impact of the new citizens were Chile, Brazil, and Uruguay.

Land changes. Another tragic internal change unleashed a wave of violence between and among Latin American countries. Many Latin Americans today tend to speak of the peaceful manner in which they have solved their internal social and international problems. The opposite is really the truth. Pendle observes:

> In addition to numerous lesser conflicts in the area,
> the South American republics have been involved in five

major wars among themselves: Argentina against Brazil, 1825–8; Argentina against Uruguay and then Brazil, 1842–52; Paraguay against Argentina, Uruguay, and Brazil, 1864–70; Chile against Peru and Bolivia, 1879–83; Bolivia against Paraguay (the Chaco War), 1932–5. In all those wars the purpose of one side was to obtain control over a neighbouring country or else to seize some part of a neighbour's territory.[50]

Paraguay lost almost all of its adult male population in the battles against the Triple Alliance. In the 1898 Spanish-American War the United States with a heavy hand gained control of Cuba—giving it formal independence. Puerto Rico was ceded to the United States by Spain and then maintained as a semi-colony. Mexico lost land to the United States after a series of bloody battles, which included the Texan loss of the Alamo and the subsequent defeat of Santa Anna's army at San Jacinto. This led to the independence of Texas. Both England and Mexico wanted to keep Texas from annexation into the United States. But by 1848 Mexico's territory had been mutilated and drastically reduced as the United States excised land that swept from the Rio Grande to California—the current southwest United States.[51]

Other pressure groups. National armed forces developed, and during this period began to flex their iron power. Their multiplied interventions into national life have not been motivated at root by national interest; rather, the interventions came from the military's drive to perpetuate its power and selfishness. The *mestizos* in the officer corps realized that they could retaliate against the entrenched aristocracy by military action. In some cases the military was trained by Europeans, such as the German reorganization of Chile's army. Germany also advised the military in Argentina and Bolivia, while France did the same in Brazil, Ecuador, Peru, and Paraguay.[52] Latin America's armed forces have intervened throughout the last century in governments. The results have primarily been negative; producing instability as political institutions were undermined, leading to more cruelty, torture, anarchy, and disorder; permitting military control of national coffers, leaving them bankrupt many times as a result of hardware expenditures and blatant corruption. On the other side, some military interventions did accelerate positive change of social institutions. But the pattern was set: the military generally brokered elections and was prepared to subvert civilian authority.

Other pressure groups that emerged during this period were the university students and organized labor. The *Reforma Universitaria* of 1918 sparked in Cordoba, Argentina, a movement that spread throughout the continent. Students exploded, protesting archaic educational structures and demanding a governing role in their universities. This modernization movement has generally affected higher education in positive ways, although extreme student power has weakened the university in some cases. The revolutionary role of the university student in national society became evident in this period also, and has extended down to the present. Organized labor gradually developed to a point that permitted banding together to seek common interests and benefits, which started breaking down the power elites who controlled wealth.

Models and Experiments for Socio-Political Change

The latter part of the nineteenth century had found Latin America searching for a consistent political and economic structure to provide cohesiveness. Utilitariansism—the dream that virtue should consist in utility, thus providing the greatest amount of happiness for the greatest number of people—was briefly experimented with. But it was too limited to serve the multi-faceted needs of Latin America.

The rise of positivism. Latin American political thought continued to seek European models to solve its problems, and thus the theories of Comte and Spencer surged to the fore. Positivism—affirming the power of science and order to solve problems and excluding questions of ultimate causes and spiritual values—swept into the continent. Order would bring progress after the chaos of the *caudillos* and the military debacles. Mexico, Argentina, Chile, Uruguay, Peru, Bolivia, Cuba, and Brazil saw their solutions in positivism.

> Between 1880 and 1890, a new Spanish America seemed to be emerging—a group of countries which seemed to have nothing in common with the Spanish America that had arisen after political independence. A new order was developing in every country; not the colonial order but one which was based on the concepts of progress and science; an order which appeared to be giving thought to the education and the material comfort of its citizens. Political liberties were sacrificed for the sake of this order, since they were considered to be superfluous and a source of unrest. In every country, oligarchies came forward to take responsibility for the new order and for its reflection in the field of politics.[53]

But it was Mexico and Brazil that provided clear examples of this sociopolitical experimentation. Mexico, bordering on the "Great Colossus of the North" (the United States), sensed even further threats to its national sovereignty. In order to compete, Mexico would have to industrialize with speed. The dictatorial government of Porfirio Díaz unleashed the *tecnócratas, Los Científicos,* to solve national problems. Massive financial investment from the United States led Mexico to launch her industrialization. But a high price was paid, and

> during the so-called *Pax Porfiriana* foreigners attained a position of such importance that they dominated the Mexican economy, and they were duly appreciative of the regime that so favoured them. United States and British investors owned the oilfields, the mines, and the public utilities, and U.S. citizens acquired millions of acres in the north of the country. It has been said that the Díaz administration was "mother of the foreigner and stepmother of the Mexicans." Certainly the mass of the people derived little benefit from the dictator's economic achievements, and his courting of the outsider was to be the cause of the violent storm of xenophobia which broke out after his downfall. It is felt that he had gone too far; he is supposed to have exclaimed: *"Pobre Méjico, tan lejos de Dios, y tan cerca de los Estados Unidos!"* ("Poor Mexico, so far from God, and so near the United States!").[54]

Mexican positivism unraveled and the nation exploded in the 1910–1920 revolution. Brazil's pattern was quite different; there, positivism guided evolution toward change. The Brazilian *fazendeiro* power had been weakened by the emerging Sao Paulo industrial power. The monarchy had vanished, slavery had been abolished, but the church and the Freemasons had to be checked. The military school at Rio then became the center of positivism, and the new Brazilian flag bore Comte's motto, "Order and Progress." The new philosophy was applied to society, but disintegrated because of internal schisms that went to the extreme of creating the Brazilian Positivist Church. Nevertheless, positivism permanently marked Brazil.

Two models for structural change. Uruguay had had such a history of violent unrest and civil conflict that even one of its military dictators, Latorre, had in 1880 resigned, "declaring that the people were 'ungovernable.'" Yet it was Uruguay, during the first decades of this century, that under the leadership of a former newspaper owner and editor, José Batlle y Ordóñez, moved peacefully into a national structural modification of the entire society. As a first-term president he had crushed a revolution, and his authority was unquestioned. He actually obeyed the constitution by not running for a second term. During later years he studied European political institutions, and then returned to be elected a second time. His programs were peaceful yet radical, calling for honest civil servants, new laws that would assure orderly transitions, and the institution of labor and other welfare reforms. Amazingly, the changes endured into the 1960s.

Mexico, on the other hand, found violence necessary to produce structural changes. When Díaz and his New Creoles fell after thirty-four years of power, Mexico faced abysmal social crises with some one thousand families owning most of the country—and foreigners owning a quarter of the land. Real wages had shrunk, productivity was dropping, and the repressed *mestizos* and Indians were ready to explode. Following a short term of a new, incompetent president, the drive for land reform lit the fuse and the Revolution of 1910–1920 was on. Rivals for power led their own regional armies, including the legendary Emiliano Zapata in the south and Pancho Villa in the north. The country was in chaos, and destruction was the norm. Over a million persons died and the infrastructure was ruined by a revolution with no central leadership or philosophy. The *criollos* had lost permanently and the *mestizos* were in to stay, but it took many years before the country settled down and a new constitution was implemented under a one-party system. The Catholic church lost much of its position, power, and wealth because the revolution disenfranchised all religious organizations. Mexico became a secular state, and anticlericalism remained high among government leaders.

The Struggle for Intellectual Emancipation in Latin America

The ongoing search for self-identity continued among Latin American intellectuals. Both *peninsulares* and *criollos* had largely been replaced by *mestizos* in the struggle for political independence. Yet Latin Americans did not *feel* free. Leopoldo Zea, prominent Mexican writer, points to the Iberian heritage as the apparent root of Latin America's problems. He states that the liberal ideas of independence had not extinguished the hangover of the Spanish spirit. Others affirmed that freedom divided instead of uniting. The solution for these negative attitudes was "education . . . to liberate the Spanish-American peoples from their intellectual subservience to Spain, and to Europe in general."[55]

It was this intellectual subservience that grated the most, and the Latin American writers began addressing these issues. I will give three examples, all appearing near the turn of this century. Ruben Dario, Latin America's foremost poet, rose from the soil of a small Nicaraguan village to become the spokesman for modernism. This was a revolutionary form that attacked traditional Castilian literature; and although it was indebted to French style, it was an original expression of the new, proud attitudes of Latin American independence. It even seriously influenced Spanish literature, as well as showing a religious ethos:

Christ walks, thin and feeble through the streets.
Barabbas keeps his slaves, his toadies lick his shoes.
And the land of the Chibcha, Cuzco and Palenque,
Has seen the panthers sleek and in their prime.[56]

José Martí, the Cuban patriot, offers another example of nationalist writing. Known as "The Apostle," he revolutionized poetry not only in style but in content. His vision was *Nuestra América*, "Our America," with a Pan-Americanist vision, and he died in Cuba fighting for its independence. He wrote with full freedom on North American soil, free to condemn his host's imperialism. The two Americas fascinated him, but he made his choice:

However great this America may be, and however consecrated it may be to the free men of the America in which Lincoln was born, to us in the depths of our hearts, the America in which Juárez was born is greater, and no one can blame us for it, nor think ill of us for it, because it is ours, and because it has been more unfortunate.[57]

It was José Enrique Rodó, the Uruguayan, who in 1900 wrote *Ariel*,[58] an essay on Latin American spiritual values. He contrasted Caliban, the brutish, materialistic, ugly North American dedicated to pragmatism and technology, with Ariel, the idealistic, spiritual, and graceful man of Latin America. Rodó argued that to be different did not mean to be inferior, that Latin America's own values provided beauty, worth, and high self-esteem.

The Controversial Continental Role of the United States

North American expansionism sought to establish a general hegemony over the Western Hemisphere, which was further evidence of the United States's emergence as a major world power desiring political, military, and commercial security. While Britain still sustained great influence—lasting nearly a century—and valuable trade privileges with Latin America, the United States demanded a greater monopoly of raw materials for its voracious industrial appetite. New markets were sought for finished products, and during the last decades of the nineteenth century commerce and investment grew rapidly.

The United States was flexing its military muscle and wrestling territory from Mexico and Spain. Between 1846 and 1848 the United States and Mexico were at war, resulting in Mexico's loss of California, New Mexico, and Arizona. As a result of the Spanish-American War, the United States took possession of Puerto Rico, and Cuba gained nominal independence from Spain. Many United States leaders at that time displayed the disturbing attitude that the United States should ultimately control all the Latin American republics. One writer spoke arrogantly of the responsibility to impose "civilization" on Latin America: "The United States is in honor bound to maintain law and order in South America, and we may just as well take complete control of several of the countries, and establish decent governments while we are about it."[59]

"Dollar Diplomacy," the "Big Stick" combined with the Roosevelt Corollary to the Monroe Doctrine, and the many military interventions generated a tense relationship between the United States and Latin America.

> In the period between 1898 and 1934, the United States intervened militarily in Cuba, Mexico, Guatemala, Honduras, Nicaragua, Panama, Colombia, Haiti, and the Dominican Republic. In some nations, such as Honduras, Panama, and Cuba, the interventions occurred repeatedly. In others, like Haiti, the Dominican Republic, and Nicaragua, they lasted for years, even decades. In Haiti, for example, the marines landed in 1915 and did not depart until 1934.[60]

The events surrounding the creation of both the Panama Canal and the Republic of Panama clearly indict North American intrigue. When the Panamanians seceded (with obvious North American encouragement) in 1903 from Colombia, American gunboats blocked Colombian ships, and Panama was rapidly recognized as a sovereign nation by the United States. North America was granted control "in perpetuity" over a ten-mile swath across the nation. The canal was completed in 1914 after a decade of exhausting labor. Ironically, the Panama Canal decades later led to one of the wisest and most just North American foreign policy decisions in Latin America—the 1978 treaty returning the Canal Zone to complete Panamanian ownership and direction by 1999.

An objective analysis of the entire picture clearly proves that North American diplomacy was not guided by good-will ambassadors. While the Latin Americans continued their love-hate relationship with the American way of life, the Northern world power was building up a debt of mistrust and antipathy that would be hard to pay off in the future.

This negative attitude toward the United States became evident during World War I when many Latin American republics resisted pressure to support the Allied powers. Historian Donald M. Dozer explains the tension: "Bound to the Allied Powers by strong ties of consanguinity and culture they were nevertheless subjected to a persistent pressure from the Central Powers. Almost all the individual American governments issued neutrality proclamations in accordance with the Hague conventions."[61] The eventual breakdown was as follows. Declaring war against Germany were Brazil, Costa Rica, Cuba, Guatemala, Honduras, Nicaragua, Panama. Severing relationship: Bolivia, Dominican Republic, Ecuador, Peru, Uruguay. Maintaining neutrality: Argentina, Chile, Colombia, Mexico, Paraguay, El Salvador, Venezuela. Many of the nations who stayed out of the war had been heavily influenced by their large colonies of German residents.

The United States Central Intelligence Agency (CIA) now acknowledges its crucial role in the overthrow of Guatemalan President Jacobo Arbenz in 1954. It also coordinated the flawed 1961 Bay of Pigs invasion that attempted to overthrow Fidel Castro. Again in 1965 the United States invaded the Dominican Republic, and in Chile the CIA encouraged the 1973 overthrow of President Allende. In 1984 the CIA mined the harbors of Nicaragua; and the entire Contra movement would have been impossible without United States aid and guidance. The portrait of North American relations with Latin America is not very attractive, and unfortunately overshadows some of the better chapters of this tenuous relationship—such as the Alliance for Progress established under President Kennedy in 1961.

The North American legacy in Latin America is checkered at best, and this partially explains the love-hate relationship that Latins have toward the United States. It is a complex world of conflicts that fortunately can be bridged on a personal basis and certainly on truly biblical values of justice, national autonomy, and the rich tapestry of cultural beauty in each people.

The Roman Catholic Church

During this period of fifty years the established church suffered significant changes. The centuries of religious hegemony over civilian authorities was fast fading. The church had consistently identified with either Spain and the colonial government, or with the landed aristocracy, the military, or even German interests in World War I. The church opposed social change, and certainly opposed legislation or shifts that would affect her prestige and societal control. The increasing shortage of clergy led millions of Latin Americans to slip into cultural Catholicism, which encouraged nominal or public participation in ceremonies but was void of personal conviction. Extreme power loss came in Mexico when the church's vast properties were expropriated by the secular state, and even to this day all religious properties legally belong to the government. The Catholic clergy were not allowed to wear clerical garb in public, and a host of other limitations curbed public church power and influence.

Freedom of worship had been generally prohibited in Latin America until the latter quarter of the nineteenth century. Protestant evangelical missionaries began appearing in Latin America during those years because of the new affirmations of the legal religious liberty. However, "in all Spanish America in 1900 there were only 5,246 communicants and in Brazil only 11,376. The shadow of the Inquisition lay heavy on Latin America: even when the law permitted Protestantism, local public opinion did not; and the Church often pressed persecution long after the legislature had abolished it."[62]

Conclusions to the Period 1880-1930

While on the continental scale it appeared that Latin America was finally emerging into the twentieth century, it was an uneasy time. The colonial heritage still could not be completely shaken, and governments remained unsteady or changed with sad regularity. The more change of governments, the less social change could truly be accomplished. Industrialization seemed to provide some kind of road of progress and development, even though positivism had been generally discredited. At least the age of the *caudillos* appeared to be over, with singular exceptions. But would consistent stability and development characterize the republics? Would progress come to affect the underside of history, the disenfranchised masses now growing in number and poverty? Only time would tell.

THE ECONOMIC AND POLITICAL CRISES OF INSTABILITY: 1930 TO THE PRESENT

Why does Latin America continue to incarnate so much crisis and instability? And why so when it has such impressive natural resources, with knowledge and technology available, and where Christianity has been on the scene for so many years?

Risking a simplistic answer, I suggest that the root cause combines at least four major elements: the colonial heritage; a particular cultural attitude toward "development" and socio-economic change; the complex national drive for autonomy and independence interacting with international pressures; and the problems derived from the sinful nature of humanity, complicated by the supernatural "principalities and powers" at work over the nations.

In a sense only the Christian can understand the complete and authentic "why" behind Latin American instability. It is ridiculously facile for North American conservative capitalists simply to declare that Latin America needs an "American-style free-market-pro-democratic-anti-Marxist" social structure. This would be absurd; it ignores history and is doomed to failure. The dynamics of Latin America today are complex and appear humanly unsolvable. The Christian must constantly look to the sovereign God, the Word of God, and the people of God contextualized within their own socio-cultural soil.

The Economic Changes Provoking Crises

The Great Depression of the 1930s bottomed out Latin American hopes for stability. The international debts were called in; and with capital shrunk to near invisibility, nations had few options. The British salvaged their interests in Argentina with creative financing, but it was an exception. Nations whose economies were geared to agricultural export, primarily those with single-crop economies, such as Cuba with sugar and others with coffee, found markets disappearing. Economies geared to copper or tin, such as Chile and Bolivia, had similar experiences. Those were hard times for Latin America.

Following the Depression some of the larger nations imagined their solution lay in rapid industrialization. Argentina under Perón did so, but it was an overly ambitious program that foundered under poor planning, internal chaos, and corruption. Brazil in the south and Mexico in the north later emerged as growing industrial powers, but both had major and ongoing problems.

When massive deposits of oil were discovered, international companies began to exploit the reserves. But the profits went mainly to the transnational companies, and this later provoked the nationalization of the petroleum companies, as well as other industries. Mexico led the way, with other countries, such as Peru, following. However, in recent years the oil boom has turned into an oil bust. International banking concerns loaned billions of dollars at high interest, but when the oil market collapsed, the countries were left with major internal conflicts as well as the overwhelming international debts to be paid.

The Social Changes

Much of this material will be discussed in the following chapter, so only a few items need to be mentioned. The rush to industrialize produced a massive exodus from both the rural areas and the smaller cities. Most of the countries concentrated the factories in the capital city, though Brazil and Mexico attempted to decentralize industry. The flood to the cities produced a rural and agricultural vacuum. Some countries that had been exporters of agricultural products, such as Argentina, faced the tremendous crisis of spending hard cash to import food. The social dislocation produced terrible crises in the very fabric of the family as the traditional cultural infrastructure disintegrated.

On the more positive side of the ledger, basic literacy, education, and medical services became available to a greater number of people. But many social-aid programs did not have national support, and the programs seemed more like palliatives. Latin American population was beginning to explode in number, and the societies were not prepared for so many more people. Whereas in the past sickness and infant mortality had kept the birth rate down, now increased medical care meant that more babies of the poor classes would live. While upper and middle classes limited the number of their own children, the poor reproduced with joy and sorrow. The popular saying *Cada niño nace con su pan bajo el brazo* ("Every child is born with a loaf of bread under his arm") was proving insufficient. Sadly, the children are too many, and the loaf of bread too small.

The colonial period had structured the social classes of Latin America, and these persevered into the twentieth century. At the very top was a minuscule upper class, the landed gentry. At the other end, in varying scales of welfare and poverty, were the masses of illiterate *mestizos,* Indians and blacks who served the upper class. In the middle was a small group of merchants and immigrants with limited economic power. But in the twentieth century the structure began to change. A new upper and upper-middle class, those now powerful through political, commercial, and industrial activities, challenged the traditional elites, although they would imitate the values and life-style of the wealthy. At the same time, from the lower classes emerged an upper-lower to lower-middle class of labor workers, many as members of unions both in industry and agriculture. And a small but growing middle class of white-collar business and government workers joined the new university-graduate professionals. Nevertheless, the sector of the population that grew the most was the group locked into poverty, disenfranchised, and excluded from material benefits and hope.

The Internal Struggles and Political Flux

There is space only to list the litany of problems which beset Latin America:

Military conflicts. The Chaco War of 1932–1935 pitted Bolivia against Paraguay. Both contested the Chaco area, harrassing each other for nearly a century; but when oil was discovered tensions heated up and the two poor nations went to war. Bolivia was thrashed, lost both the war and much of its territory, and then plunged into severe self-analysis. Who was at fault? Some blamed the international oil companies, with the result that Bolivia led the continent in the expropriation of the Standard Oil Company of Bolivia in 1937. Others turned to socialism and Marxism for answers. The Bolivians could not face the reality that perhaps they were to blame.

Negative self-analysis. The Bolivian writer Alcides Arguedas had first published his disturbing book *Pueblo Enfermo (Sick People)* in 1909.[63] I have a copy of the third edition that came after the Chaco disaster. Arguedas pessimistically speaks of national geography that seemed to conspire against his nation, of a race that suffered almost a genetic flaw, a nation broken by vices, a people incapable of governing themselves, a people condemned to mediocrity, a military and political set of rulers committed to the rape of the land. When Arguedas finishes his book there seems to be absolutely no hope.

Other writers began analyzing the Latin American situation, with Mexican intellectuals leading the way. Among them are Octavio Paz, José Vasconcelos, Samuel Ramos, and Leopoldo Zea—all of whom have been mentioned before in this book. Although the four come from the same country, they have continental experience and much of what they write can be applied to the larger context of Latin America.

The many constitutions. Citizens of the United States are accustomed to accepting as normal a government of more than two hundred years under one long-lasting constitution of 1787. But not in Latin America. Lambert has attempted to document the number of constitutions in Latin America for the period 1811–1961.[64] The figure comes close to 190, with fifty-three written before 1850 (when the nations were working through their first years), and 127 after 1950. Most of those constitutions were written for the smaller nations. Guatemala recently finished going through the process of writing another detailed constitution following the long period of military misrule. But the new document had no surprises. It seemed like just another time-consuming legal exercise in apparent political decision-making.

Agrarian reform. Agrarian reform has always been one of the most sensitive hot potatoes in Latin America. Its roots return to the colonial era, when the land was divided into the *latifundios*. Many of these massive tracts of land have been owned and exploited by the same aristocratic families whose bloodlines may be traced back to Spain. In other cases the land barons are of relatively recent vintage, but in most cases the correct word to describe life on these estates is "feudalism." Mexico in its revolution had instituted a massive program of land reform with limited success. Bolivia as part of its 1953 revolution faced the striking phenomenon of Indians invading in mass to possess large estates. Legal land reform followed soon after. Guatemala during the early 1950s under Jacobo Arbenz attempted land reform. But when some of the United Fruit Company territory was seized, the United States in 1954 moved to undermine the government by supporting the CIA-sponsored "invasion" from El Salvador. Admittedly, Arbenz had allowed a disturbing number of Marxists into his government, but it would be naive to assume that Guatemala had gone Communist.

A recent controversial case focusing on land reform comes from El Salvador. The administration of the late Napoleon Duarte tried to introduce peaceful structural change. But the radical right and left despised him and his policies, and the North American press weighed in against him also. The right attacked him because he threatened their traditional power, and they accused him of being a Marxist. The left hated Duarte because he had co-opted much of their agenda, and to them his changes were not radical enough. Both wanted to assassinate him, and both hindered sane policies for that densely populated country.

Critics of land reform point to the loss of productivity of the land after the "reforms." That is true, particularly where the government does not provide the technical aid and financial support to institute the reforms effectively. Burns responds:

> Students of agrarian reform point out that the peasants tend to sell less of their product because they are able for the first time to eat better. Cold statistics also ignore the immeasurable psychological results and benefits for the nation. Land ownership turns the rural proletariat into responsible citizens; it bestows dignity reflected in the peasants' new pride in self and country. It redistributes power.[65]

The Marxist options. During the twentieth century the Marxist political alternative came to Latin America. It came because of two primary reasons. First, Marxism is essentially messianic and international. As a secular and all-encompassing religion it offers a total package: a source of authority, a concept of man, a way of salvation, an eschatological promise. Secondly, it came because of the inhuman conditions of oppression and poverty in Latin America. Marxism did not cause these conditions, it has taken advantage of them. The universities became fermenting centers of leftist ideology as the social consciences of students were radicalized to conclude that Marxism offered the best option.

The first country to experiment with Marxism was Mexico. Her twentieth-century revolution took place at the same time as the Russian one. Many Mexican leaders expressed open admiration for Communism, particularly its socialistic elements, some of which were institutionalized in Mexico. But ideological Marxism did not win the power struggle with the Mexican nationalists.

Cuba became the first sovereign nation in Latin America to move entirely into the Marxist camp. This island has had a unique history very different from the other countries. It belonged to Spain until 1898, when it technically gained its independence. But actually the United States maintained it as a protectorate until the Cuban constitution of 1940, a significant document that included major social-structural change. The corrupt dictatorship of Fulgencio Batista collapsed when Fidel Castro and his revolutionary forces entered Havana in triumph on January 1, 1959. Had Castro always been a Marxist, or even a crypto-Marxist? Or did he become one when the United States turned against him and his radical policies—many based on the 1940 constitution? Arguments heat up on both sides, and the reader will have to decide for himself. What is clear today, however, is that Cuba had traded one colonialist dependency for another one. While most Cuban Christians find it impossible to support an atheistic Marxist system, the revolution has brought another set of "human rights" and improved many areas.

Although some Cuban Catholic and Protestant leaders have identified the faith with the revolution, most evangelical leaders today have struck a middle path and generally come to grips with their national reality and understand that the church belongs to Jesus Christ and that his promises are valid for his people in every socio-political structure.

In all political cases there is a trade off. The Cuban revolution

> had eradicated illiteracy, hunger, destitution, and unemployment. It had diminished racial and sexual discrimination. Conformity, limits on freedom of expression, and the economy's overdependence on sugar and Soviet aid headed the list of criticisms. Certainly the life styles of the former elite and middle class have been reduced, but, at the other end of the spectrum, those of the once impoverished have been improved.[66]

At the same time other basic liberties have been greatly limited: freedom of speech, travel, press and writing, freedom to be educated without Marxist indoctrination, freedom to unionize or to work according to interests, ability, and opportunity. Religious freedom is increasingly available, though with clear restrictions, harrassment, and in some cases persecution.

Chile became the first nation in history to elect a Marxist president, albeit controversially. When Salvador Allende won in 1970 with the significant support of evangelicals who identified with his populist platform—he immediately moved to transform Chile into a socialist society. He worked mainly within the constitutional powers available to him, but there was no doubt as to his goals, and the change would be radical. His drastic social and economic policies included the nationalization of the foreign-owned copper mines and banks, agrarian reform, and major salary increases for the labor classes. Internal and international conflicts exploded, and a class warfare seemed imminent. The military—which had a history of political non-intervention—finally acted in September 1973, bombing the presidential palace and killing Allende in the process. General Pinochet violently took over, instituted a repressive regime, and is still a power, although his designs have now been eliminated by democratic elections.

In the United States the topic of Nicaragua heats up any discussion, with the hostile camps simplistically reduced to two alternatives. We

were left with either the Contras (killers or freedom fighters) or the Sandinistas (misinterpreted nationalists or Communist-expansionist guerillas). I reject this reductionism. Fortunately there are many sources to
read in North America that will force us to consider all sides—and there
are more than just two.[67]

Nicaragua represented the most recent example of a country in the
Marxist camp, with government, party, and army fused into one united
body. Undoubtedly the nine-man junta had long been personally identified with the Marxist vision for its country. Its ideology, forged over
decades of conflict, produced an extraordinary vision and discipline that
guided the Sandinista's struggle. Victory came after terrible bloodshed in
July 1979. By early 1979 few Nicaraguans had wanted the Somoza dynasty to remain in power, though many suspected the designs of the Sandinistas. For that reason they identified with the slogan *"Ni Sandino ni
Somoza"* ("Neither Sandino nor Somoza").

The Sandinistas led the war with the goal to rule; and when the middle classes joined the coalition during the final stages of the struggle, it
was just a matter of time before Somoza either was killed or fled. He fled
in July 1979 with his coterie, leaving thousands killed, the coffers
stripped, and the nation demolished. Some have suggested that if Somoza
had left even three months earlier the current regime would not be in
power. The Sandinistas took over and began the radical restructuring of
the nation, a process resembling the Cuban model.

North Americans cannot understand Nicaragua unless they remember the repeated U.S. Marine invasions and occupations. Sandino,
the guerilla martyr after whom the Sandinista movement was named, had
not been a Marxist himself. He was an anti-American nationalist, whose
spirit and name have effectively been used by the Sandinistas. Credit
must be given to the Sandinistas: they carried out great literacy campaigns, expanded medical care, distributed some land to the peasants,
opened up higher education, and generally aided those who needed help
the most. They also wanted to determine Nicaragua's own national destiny, a decision that also inherently had an anti-North American component as well as a rewriting of the rules of politics. All these changes
were accomplished at great expense to other liberties: free speech, free
press, free labor unions. Religious liberty was curtailed in various cases,
but it would be unfair to accuse the Sandinistas of systematic persecution, in spite of what some say. The fact is that every day brought
news of a Nicaragua in flux. And the Arias peace plan (which may be
passé next week) merited respect and support.

The United States as of late 1988 continued to seek a military solution, sinking millions of dollars into the Contras' fight against the Sandinista regime; but there was little hope for a Contra victory. They were seriously divided internally, the military leadership inextricably tied to Somoza interests, their record on human rights atrocious, and they were not able to communicate a positive alternative to Nicaraguan government. It would behoove us to listen to the Nicaraguan opposition resident in the country and less to the exiles. Will there be more democratic change in Nicaragua that would please the United States? Probably not, until the astonishing electoral defeat of the Sandinistas!

The options for change. We have already discussed the violent revolutionary alternative. The Christian Democrats in Chile, Venezuela, El Salvador, and Guatemala offer another option: structural change without violence—an alternative to violent revolution, reactionary conservatism, or mere liberal tinkering with the socio-political machine. The essential ideology of the Christian Democrats comes from the Catholic parties of West Germany, and was first introduced in Chile and Venezuela as the solution to Latin America. West Germany has invested vast sums in Latin America to cultivate this new Christianizing vision of government and social change, a political philosophy with a clear ideology.[68] It was an option that went substantially beyond the "liberal democratic" tinkering with the politico-economic machinery. Nevertheless I foresee the continental and even national pendulum moving in the future from authoritarian regimes of left and right to more democratic ones. I do not see long-term stability under the present circumstances.

Civil war. Central America is the current example of the tragic conflicts that can destroy a small area. I was born and brought up in Central America, and never in my wildest imagination did I dream that these small countries would be a focal point of war and world attention. Why such conflicts? Simply—or complicatedly—because of the long-term social injustice that Marxist elements have taken advantage of. The United States's continuing to seek a military solution has transformed Honduras into a military base. A Honduran joke asks, "What's the name of the new North American aircraft carrier?" Answer: "Why the USS Honduras, of course!"

All the countries fester with conflict: Guatemala, El Salvador, Honduras, Nicaragua, and even Costa Rica. The United States is justly concerned about the situation because it is so close to home and it affects the national security doctrine. The republics have been considered hippocket nations that acted in constant obedience to *El Norte.* "Banana republics" has been the unfortunate sobriquet, but no longer will simplistic solutions solve complex issues. While North American foreign policy gropes for coherence, perhaps it will be the Central Americans themselves who will find their solution. Costa Rican President Oscar Arias Sánchez, 1987 Nobel Peace Prize winner, put his reputation on the line with a promising solution that demanded sacrifice of all.

The United States and Latin America

Through the work of the Franklin D. Roosevelt Good Neighbor Policy (1933–1948) a new attitude of respect was communicated by the Northern Giant to its southern neighbors. One tangible result was that all the Latin American nations cooperated with the United States in World War II. Eventually all of them came into the war, though in South America many sympathized with Germany and Italy—again the result of the massive earlier immigrations to Argentina, Uruguay, Chile, and Brazil. Because of that sympathy many Nazi leaders found refuge in those four countries. Following the war the United States pumped billions of dollars into Latin America, cementing the lopsided commercial relationships. "In 1960 Latin America took one-fifth of our exports and furnished one-third of our imports. Investments of United States citizens were responsible for one-third of all the exports of the Latin American countries."[69]

When John F. Kennedy took office he sensed the need for a new policy toward Latin America. But though the Alliance for Progress might have had good motives, it was fatally flawed. The liberal political thesis prevalent in Washington was simple: pump massive capital into Latin America, force internal political and tax reform, recommend new management techniques, sell new technology and hardware, industrialize and promote new agricultural models. The obvious result, they boasted: Latin America will develop and wealth will flow to the masses and thus transform society and in the process neutralize the Marxist mystique. Did it work? After the billions of dollars invested, today the ledger presents a confused deficit. For too many Latin Americans, the dream of rising expectations foundered on the unrealistic theories which ignored the major role that history and culture play in "development and progress."

Today it is virtually impossible to speak of Latin America without having to refer to the United States. Their current situation and futures are inextricably interwoven—for better or for worse. North American foreign policy, like that of every country, is not based on the fruit of the Holy Spirit. It is based on self-interest. Apparent benevolence is either merely apparent, or perhaps the result of some honestly philanthropic individuals who make and apply foreign policy. Significantly, Jimmy Carter is highly respected in many South American nations for his commitment to human rights. That, probably more than any other international element, pushed former totalitarian regimes to allow honest elections that swept into power democratic leadership. On the other hand, rightists accused Carter of being a "pinko," soft on the Communists. The United States considers Latin America primarily in secular terms: national military security, raw materials, cheap labor, and a market for finished products. North Americans have not respected Latin America; and their relationships are paternalistic toward Latin Americans, a prevailing attitude sadly projected even by North American evangelicals. Latins are justly sensitive to criticism and may lash out in retaliation; theirs is a love-hate relationship with the Colossus of the North.

A BRIEF CONCLUSION TO THIS HISTORY

Loving understanding of Latin America comes when her particular history is evaluated within its context. Too many North Americans—to say nothing about peoples of other non-Latin nations—have made sweeping generalizations about Latin America, reducing complex issues to simplistic slogans. Yet others have chosen to ignore the past, a flaw observed in many missionaries who conclude: "There are only two types of people—those with Christ and those without. My only task is to present the Gospel and get people to move from darkness to light." While there is truth in their simplistic conclusion, the reductionism stunts understanding and limits their ultimate impact on Latin America.

Latin American history is unique, rich in textures and at the same time tragic in essence and proportion. Her history continues today in complexities beyond the scope of this survey. The future is not very encouraging, a reality noted by both secular and Christian observers. E. Bradford Burns writes at the conclusion of his book:

> Well-defined institutions from the past, enshrined by the elites and middle classes and which rely on the strength of the military, still prevail.... If history does in fact suggest "lessons" on which we can draw, then it teaches that change of any fundamental nature will not be achieved easily. Eventually it will probably result from this dialectic of violence so long a characteristic of Latin America.... As we have seen, it is much easier to maintain the present system than to bring about authentic change.... The enigma remains: poor people inhabit rich lands.[70]

A short time ago a leading Latin American evangelical lawyer said to me: "Latin America has experimented with the political solution. It has experimented with the economic solution. It has experimented with the violent solution. None of them has worked. The only thing left for us is the spiritual solution."

NOTES

1. These authors represent the spectrum: Britisher, George Pendle, *A History of Latin America* (Middlesex, England: Penguin, 1971). Frenchman, Jacques Lambert, trans. Helen Katel, *Latin America: Social Structures and Political Institutions* (Berkeley, CA: University of California, 1971). American, Donald Marquand Dozer, *Latin America: An Interpretive History,* rev. ed. (Tempe, AZ: Center for Latin American Studies, Arizona State University, 1979). American, E. Bradford Burns, *Latin America: A Concise Interpretive History,* 4th ed. (Englewood Cliffs, NJ: Prentice-Hall, 1986). Columbian, German Archiniegas, trans. Joan MacLean, *Latin America: A Cultural History* (New York: Alfred A. Knopf, 1972). Bolivian Methodists, Esther and Mortimer Arias, *The Cry of My People* (New York: Friendship Press, 1980). Marxist South American, Eduardo Galeano, *Open Veins of Latin America,* trans. Cedric Belfrage (New York: Monthly Review Press, 1973).

2. H. B. Johnson, Jr., *From Reconquest to Empire* (New York: Alfred A. Knopf, 1970), p. 5.

3. Ibid., pp. 24-25.

4. J. Edwin Orr, Evangelical Awakenings in Latin America (Minneapolis: Bethany Fellowship, 1978),p.1.

5. Bartolomé de las Casas, *History of the Indies,* trans. and ed. Andree M. Collard (New York: Harper & Row, 1971), p. 106.

6. Joseph Judge, "Our Search for the True Columbus Landfall," *National Geographic,* vol. 170, no. 5, November 1986, pp. 566-71.

7. Ibid., p. 572.

8. Dozer, *Latin America,* p. 37.

9. Ibid.

10. Arciniegas, *Latin America,* p. 3.

11. Walter Alva, "Discovering the New World's Richest Unlooted Tomb," *National Geographic,* vol. 174, no. 4, October 1988, pp. 510-55.

12. Burns, *Latin America*, p. 7.

13. Ibid.

14. G. C. Vaillant, *Aztecs of Mexico*, rev. ed. (Middlesex, England: Penguin, 1966), p. 176.

15. Ibid., p. 208.

16. Burns, *Latin America*, p. 7.

17. John MacKay, *The Other Spanish Christ* (New York: MacMillan, 1932), pp. 30-31.

18. Ibid., pp. 35-36.

19. Ibid., p. 37

20. Miguel León-Portilla, "The Aztecs," in Sheldon B. Liss and Peggy Liss, eds., *Man, State and Society in Latin American History* (New York: Praeger, 1972), p. 19.

21. Gordon Young, "Chile: Republic on a Shoestring," *National Geographic*, vol. 144, no. 4, October 1973, p. 439.

22. Galeano, *Open Veins*, p. 25.

23. Both Dozer and Burns develop these institutions fully in their histories of Latin America. Burns has a very helpful glossary of Spanish terms.

24. Burns, *Latin America*, pp. 28-29.

25. Liss and Liss, *Man, State and Society*, p. 61.

26. *Encyclopedia Americana*, s.v. "Latin America."

27. Burns, *Latin America*, p. 66.

28. Ibid., p. 64.

29. For an excellent study of the colonial university see John Tate Lanning, *Academic Culture in the Spanish Colonies* (New York: Oxford University, 1940).

30. Michael Novak, *The Spirit of Democratic Capitalism* (New York: Touchstone Books, American Enterprise Institute/Simon & Schuster, 1982), p. 277.

31. Arciniegas, *Latin America*, pp. xxiii-xxiv.

32. Ibid., pp. 38-63.

33. Ibid., p. 287.

34. Pendle, *A History of Latin America*, pp. 76-83.

35. *Encyclopedia Americana*, s.v. "Latin America."

36. Dozer, *Latin America*, p. 190.

37. Pendle, *A History*, p. 95.

38. Ibid., p. 109.

39. Ibid., p. 113.

40. Ibid., p. 123.

41. Ibid., p. 124.

42. Octavio Paz, "The Meaning of Independence," in Liss and Liss, *Man, State and Society*, p. 172.

43. Ibid., p. 173.

44. Ibid.

45. Lambert, *Latin America*, pp. 264-66.

46. Ibid., pp. 265-66.

47. Ibid., pp. 160-61.

48. Pendle, *A History*, p. 153.

49. Lambert, *Latin America*, p. 3.

50. Pendle, *A History*, p. 115.

51. Dozer, *Latin America*, pp. 285-91, deals with the Mexican loss of territory to the United States.

52. Lambert, *Latin America*, pp. 228-56.

53. Leopoldo Zea, "The Struggle for Intellectual Emancipation," in Liss and Liss, *Man, State and Society*, p. 272.

54. Pendle, *A History*, pp. 163-64.

55. Leopoldo Zea, "The Struggle," p. 267.

56. Arciniegas, *Latin America*, pp. 263-65.

57. Ibid., p. 466.

58. José Enrique Rodó, *Ariel* (Mexico: Editorial Porrua, S.A., 1970). English translations of this book are available also.

59. Burns, *Latin America*, p. 179.

60. Ibid., p. 180.

61. Dozer, *Latin America*, p. 473.

62. William R. Reed, Victor M. Monterroso, Harmon A. Johnson, *Latin American
Church Growth* (Grand Rapids: Eerdmans, 1969), p. 37.

63. Alcides Arguedas, *Pueblo Enfermo* (La Paz, Bolivia: Libreria Editorial "Juventud,"
1982).

64. Lambert, *Latin America*, pp. 257-62.

65. Burns, *Latin America*, p. 283.

66. Ibid., p. 297.

67. The literature on Nicaragua is currently vast, but here are a few recommended items
showing different perspectives. An extreme left perspective comes with Walter La-
Feber, *Inevitable Revolutions: The United States in Central America* (New York: W.
W. Norton, 1983). An excellent volume detailing unfortunate United States involvement in Nicaragua comes from evangelical historian Richard Millet, *Guar-
dians of the Dynasty: A History of the U.S. Created Guardia Nacional de Nicaragua
and the Somoza Family* (Maryknoll, N.Y.: Orbis Books, 1977). Millet's perspective
is increasingly valuable because of his current evaluation of the ongoing Nicaraguan crisis. A former Sandinista who is now in exile, charismatic Catholic Hum-
berto Belli has written *Breaking Faith: The Sandinista Revolution and Its Impact on
Freedom and Christian Faith in Nicaragua* (Westchester, IL: Crossway Books/The
Puebla Institute, 1982). For a solid eye-witness account read Shirley Christian, *Nicaragua: Revolution in the Family* (New York: Random House, 1985). Evangelicals
for Social Action (ESA) publishes frequent bulletins on the Central American situation with a preference toward the Sandinista regime (P.O. Box 76560, Washington,
DC 20013).

68. Georgie Anne Geyer, *The New Latins: Fateful Change in South and Central America* (Garden City, NY: Doubleday, 1970), pp. 155-71. For a more personal, and perhaps less objective, point of view, see the struggles of José Napoleón Duarte, *Duarte: My Story*, with Diana Page (New York: Putnam's, 1986).

69. Dozer, *Latin America*, p. 23.

70. Burns, *Latin America*, p. 352.

3

Latin America's Human Crises

The staggering contrasts of Latin America are overwhelming to the thoughtful visitor, the long-term resident, and the reflective Latin American. The first one because he or she simply has never experienced such an assault on senses and value systems. The other two perhaps because after years of study and understanding of the entire Latin American picture there does not seem to be much hope for the future—at least humanly speaking. Our previous review of history now brings us to confront the contemporary realities, *La Situación* (The Situation), as we say in Spanish.

A Personal Perspective

Our entire family sat outside doña Miria's home—actually a former storeroom converted into a little two-room abode. There was no way we would all fit inside, and the weather was pleasant that evening in Guatemala City. Sweet doña Miria, a lovely sister in Christ, a single mother of seven children, was finishing with her two youngest daughters the preparation of a feast of appreciation for us simply because we, the guest families, had helped her escape from the slum room she had existed in for too long. Her feast: charbroiled meat, vegetables, warm Coca Cola, and hot tortillas. She was spending a fortune, but it surged from her grateful heart. As we prayed before eating, my mind flashed back to the plush hotel where I had eaten lunch that noon. A good friend had met me there for the famous buffet: beef, poultry, seafood, salads, fruits, vegetables, multiple desserts. We had enough food to stuff us, and the left-overs were dumped. It had been culinary paradise, served by a cultured staff who could take orders in five languages. Guatemala's elite swirled around us. It was a heady, luxurious atmosphere.

But the contrast was almost too much for me that cool evening. As we ate, I mentally saw the uncounted thousands of workers jamming into buses, some literally hanging from the door handles as they jostled their way home. Others rode bicycles, the more fortunate had motorcycles, and the privileged had some kind of car. Dusk gathered around our little party as I silently struggled with the crisis of Latin America. Another day wound down, a day of desperation for too many, fighting to survive, to maintain their sense of values and the integrity of their families. Where was God? Where was the God of Habakkuk? Why did He make us see oppression, twisted justice, cruelty, personal and structural sin? How long would this last? The answers did not come quickly; rather they came as they had to the prophets: "Look at the nations and watch—and be utterly amazed. For I am going to do something in your days that you would not believe, even if you were told" (Hab. 1:5, NIV). It was not an encouraging message for Habakkuk; it was one of imminent judgment and yet one of hope as God established himself as the sovereign of history. He was not absent; he heard the lament of his people. He was acting in history, and he would bring all to a glorious culmination—in his time. I had to weep, rest, and trust that night as we banqueted at doña Miria's.

Latin America, Member of the Third World, Two-Thirds World, South

I have brainstormed with some of my students at Trinity Evangelical Divinity School about the various ways to categorize the world. Some of these differentiations are based on political, economic, or geographical concepts, and others on population distribution. The most common one speaks of the three Worlds: First, Second, Third. The First groups the nations of the "West"—Europe, North America, Japan; the Second refers to the former Soviet Union and Communist Europe; while the Third refers to Latin America, Africa, and the rest of Asia. But who made this up, and why in that order? The categories come from the United Nations' economic orientation. They also project an attitude of superiority for the "First" world. For various reasons, many of the so-called "Third World" nations reject the model. What is more, there is also a "Fourth World," composed of the most destitute nations of the globe. Nevertheless we will continue to use these terms.

There are other ways of categorizing the world: East versus West (Marxist versus non-Marxist nations); Democratic/Non-Democratic; Free/Non-Free; Aligned/Non-Aligned (with many of the "non" actually identified with the Marxist bloc); Developed/Developing/Non-Developed/Never-to-Develop; More Developed/Less Developed; Haves/Have-nots; Two-Thirds World/Rest of World. Perhaps one of the best categorizations today would be North/South, North generally referring to the nations of North America, Europe, the Soviet Union, and Japan, as well as Australia and New Zealand (which are in the south but are yet "North"), and South speaking of the countries of Latin America, the Caribbean, the Middle East, the South Pacific, Asia, and Africa that struggle with history and economic development. One of the newest models is also economic, speaking of the NICS (Newly Industrializing Countries), with first members including two from Latin America and the rest from Asia: Mexico, Brazil, Singapore, Hong Kong, Taiwan, and South Korea. No categorization is perfect, and most are useful at different times. The key is to avoid oversimplification.

WHY IS LATIN AMERICA WHERE IT IS TODAY?

Regardless of the categorizations, Latin America is a full member of the underside of history, of the Third World, of the Two-Thirds World, of the South. The nineteen nations of our study all suffer in varying degrees from chronic underdevelopment, bulky administrative bureaucracy, endemic corruption. Admittedly there is a great variation in terms of Latin American development and national wealth, from Bolivia and Honduras at the bottom to Venezuela and Brazil at the top. Yet the entire continent is rich with natural resources, there is a partial heritage of democratic values, and Christianity has been present for five centuries. Why is the picture so somber?

We have referred to some of the causes in the previous chapter, but it might be good to lay the options out. We must carefully make our analysis, with full utilization of the data: historical, socio-anthropological, cultural, statistical, economical, and spiritual. Above all we must attempt to interpret the scenario from a Christian perspective, a difficult and risky task at best. Nobody is totally objective.

The Problem of Racial Psychology

Es que tenemos mala sangre ("It's just that we have bad blood." Or,

"Well, we have the government we deserve—rotten!") We have already referred to this destructive attitude that has echoed throughout Latin America for centuries. It is produced by a mentality that judges racial mixtures as genetically destructive, for some affirmed that "the blend of these races through interbreeding would doom Latin America to an alternation of anarchy and dictatorship, or even to their coexistence. Some pessimists, even among Latin Americans . . . believe that nothing can mitigate the results of this racial inheritance."[1] The great Argentine leader Sarmiento even hoped that the infusion of Saxon blood into his country would somehow improve the race and give hope for a better future. We remember the Bolivian Arguedas' dark analysis of a "sick people."[2]

Although there is no doubt that the continental search for identity is compounded by the racial element, it is simplistic to proffer this as *the* cause of Latin America's problems. An analysis of other nations and regions shows that racial combination per se does not doom a people to cycles of underdevelopment and instability. And certainly biblical evidence does not support this option.

The Dependency Theory

Widely accepted by many international experts, members of the intellectual and academic community, Marxists, and liberation theologians, the dependency theory is the most challenging of the explanations. Four examples of writers who vehemently sustain this position are the Marxist historian Galeano; Protestant liberationist José Míguez-Bonino; Gustavo Gutiérrez, the Roman Catholic "systematizer" of liberation theology; and the Catholic church historian Dussel, a liberationist.[3]

A definition. Burns gives us a workable description of the dependency theory.

> Dependency describes a situation in which the economic well-being, or lack of it, of one nation, colony, or area results from the consequences of decisions made elsewhere. Latin America was first dependent on the Iberian motherlands, then in the nineteenth century on England, and in the twentieth on the United States, whose decisions and policies directly influenced, or influence, its economic prosperity or poverty. Obviously to the degree a nation is dependent, it will lack "independence" of action.[4]

The United States. Currently the United States appears as the cause of Latin American underdevelopment. The "Decade of Development" introduced with so much fanfare by the United Nations, coupled with the Kennedy administration's Alliance for Progress, simply did not match the promises. Dependency theorists accuse the United States of tightly controlling the economic world, setting prices and determining markets, loaning massive capital at unbearably high interest rates, and at the same time imperialistically imposing a free-enterprise economy on Latin America. Critics of developmentalism say that the only thing to develop has been the development of underdevelopment.

Undoubtedly there is a measure of truth in the accusations, and it must be recognized that the capitalistic mentality is not known primarily for its philanthropic policies. For all the "Christian" justifications of capitalism as the biblical model, they suffer from the problem of human nature—greed as a major root of capitalism. While free enterprise has its values, in Latin America too many individuals and governments have allowed a destructive variety of capitalism and "free enterprise" to prosper. Without the pressures and protections for the "little guys," without the balance of counterpressures, capitalism founders on original sin. Yes, any nation that can will attempt to establish prices to favor its own economy—whether in the "West" or the former Marxist nations. Many of the liberationists refuse to acknowledge the overwhelming dependency in which Cuba finds itself today, a colony of Marxist imperialism.

Its handicaps. The dependency theory has its merits and its demerits. North American neo-conservatives Michael Novak (a Catholic) and Peter L. Berger (a Lutheran) are two of the most insightful critics of dependency theory, and the reader who wishes to study this more carefully can seek the cited sources.[5] What are some of the limitations of the dependency theory? They include: an ignorance of the role played by the value system and the mercantilist economic policies of the colonial era; a glossing over by some of the role of the Catholic church in Latin America as it supported mercantilism and blocked reforms; an almost blind trust in socialism to generate development with justice and liberty, ignoring its legacy of failure in Russia, Eastern Europe, Africa, Asia, and Cuba; the difficulty dependency theory has in explaining the "success" stories of Singapore, Hong Kong, Taiwan, and South Korea; and the fact that it turns a blind eye to the fundamental flaw in human nature—the sinful characteristic of humanity so evident from grassroots life all the way up to governmental relations.

As I write, *The Cry of My People* by Esther and Mortimer Arias sits next to the keyboard. Theirs is not a tourist book on Latin America, nor is it simply a historical review; it is a passionate perspective with an agenda, subtitled *Out of Captivity in Latin America*. The Bolivian Methodist bishop and his wife are identified with the historic denominations of Protestantism as well as the moderate wing of liberation theology. The book is must reading—either in English or in Spanish—for evangelicals who would minister within the context of Latin America, but it will require a careful critique. Many evangelicals will appreciate the book's eloquence in presenting the human face of the continent in crisis. The authors engage us in appreciating why we must study Latin America: because all of us *Americans* are in the same boat. "A few of us travel first class, many of us second or third class, but millions of us are living in the galleys of this continental boat.... We will sail together or we will sink together . . . and to ignore each other is a non-permissible, suicidal luxury."[6] The most important contribution of the book is found in its attempt to be a Christian perspective. Perhaps the major weakness of the book is its reductionism—the problems of this continent seem to be traced simply to dependency coming from North American exploitation. Unfortunately, even the Ariases shift the primary blame to others. It is just too simple a conclusion.

The East-West Conflict

The East-West conflict is a popular explanation found in radically contrasting political camps. On the one side, the Marxists defended their "scientific" analysis: Latin America's problems are class oriented, and these problems provoke the conflict. Historic oppression and injustice will be corrected only when a socialist regime is implanted. This may in rare cases come through the ballot boxes, but in all probability it will come as a result of bullets and bombs. The Marxists were perhaps the most committed to the ideological cause of historic materialism, and their hard-core cadres have the discipline to struggle and prepare for the day of redemption. But Marxism is a secular religion, flawed both in its analysis of humanity as well as in its economic theory. Nevertheless, why was it such an attractive alternative in Latin America, particularly to the restless university students? The reasons are partially obvious and partially subtle: the ideology reduces complex issues to simpler solutions, and this appeals to many; it is a violent revolutionary option, and many conclude that this is the *only* option; it is also a spiritual deception that promises but cannot produce. Georgie Anne Geyer, having spent extended time with Guatemalan guerillas, concludes: "Marxism offered them the only coherent, fully integrated, total ideology by which to transform their societies from feudalism to modernism.... That they would form another authoritarian structure does not concern them—they believed it would be a genuine authority because it would be of 'the masses of the people.'"[7]

It is in the United States that we find those who reduce Latin America's problems merely to the Marxists. They tend to say: "The Communists have caused all the unrest in Latin America. There were not so many revolutions before the Commies came in and provoked the explosions. The answer is to wipe them out militarily!" Many North American evangelicals have fallen into this reductionism. It is so handy. But it is wrong. The Marxists only capitalized on a *pre-existing* situation, aggravated it with their promising scenarios, and perhaps set the match to the bomb for the social explosion. But the context of poverty, oppression, and injustice was there long before Marxism exploded on the world community. This anti-Communist, reductionistic reasoning is also simplistic.

A "Spiritual" Explanation

The alternative of a "spiritual" explanation is intriguing. The most basic explanation for Christians is to reduce all the problems of human existence—personal, familial, national, societal—to one truth: all humans are sinners. Therefore the only answer is to lead people to Christ; and once they have accepted Christ, they and the society will change. This is a tricky one to respond to. On the one hand, it is a biblical truth, but it also is too easy. Most Latin American evangelicals have been at best apolitical, and most still are antipolitical. Only in recent years has this attitude changed, primarily because of the number of evangelical intellectuals who are spearheading a major study of the Scriptures and the impact of the believer in society. Latin evangelicals are beginning to discover in the Word the social implications of the gospel, and it would behoove expatriate missionaries to listen to the insights their Latin colleagues are receiving from Scripture.

A second "Christian" perspective is seen primarily in North American evangelicals who conclude that free enterprise and capitalism are *God's economic policy*. The solution for Latin America, they suggest, is double: lead people to Christ and then teach them that capitalism is the only biblical answer to underdevelopment. Unfortunately, this is the message of some North American television evangelists who invested massive sums to communicate this heretical double-gospel.[8]

The Broader Cultural-Heritage Explanation

The problems of any society are complex, combining economic, political, social, cultural, historical, racial, and spiritual elements. This is true of Latin America; and perhaps the best alternative to the *why* being discussed is to combine the suggestions, thus avoiding a reductionism. The reason each of the positions is argued is because each one has a dimension of validity, in particular certain elements of the dependency theory. But taken alone, none answers the problem.

The Mexican intellectual Leopoldo Zea interacts with the cultural-heritage problem and quotes Andres Bello (1781-1865):

> "We snatched the sceptor from the monarch, but we did not rid ourselves of the Spanish spirit: our congresses obeyed, without knowing it, Gothic inspiration.... Even our soldiers, adhering to the special code, which was in opposition to the principle of equality before the law, revealed the predominance of the ideas of the same Spain whose banner they had trampled."[9]

Mexican Samuel Ramos has argued eloquently that the main problem of the Latin American personality is caused by the conceptual transplantation from Europe, and later the United States.[10] If this is true, then who is responsible for accepting the transplant?

Again I recommend that the reader study some of the writings of Michael Novak alongside the Arias book. Novak has his presuppositions with their respective limitations. Some champion him as the important defender of capitalism; others attack him, but they miss some of his more significant emphases: the need for a *democratic* capitalism, the need for compassion regarding the root and manifestations of poverty and structural injustice, and the imperative to understand the historical and cultural causes for the creation of Latin poverty.

The publication by the Harvard Center for International Affairs bears comment. Lawrence E. Harrison, after twenty years in an international-aid career, has developed a most significant thesis in his book *Underdevelopment Is a State of Mind*. His major contribution places a finger on the problems of underdevelopment, particularly the cultural dimensions. He defines progress as improvement in human well-being. Although he acknowledges the role that other factors play in the lack of progress—such as resource endowment, geography and market proximity, government policies, the vagaries of history, the international forces, and even "luck"—he argues for something different:

> I believe that the creative capacity of human beings
> is at the heart of the development process. What makes
> development happen is our ability to imagine, theorize,
> conceptualize, experiment, invest, articulate, organize,
> manage, solve problems, and do a hundred other things
> with our minds and hands that contribute to the progress
> of the individual and of humankind.[11]

Harrison develops his thesis primarily by juxtaposing a series of national case studies (Nicaragua and Costa Rica, the Dominican Republic and Haiti, Barbados and Haiti, Argentina and Australia, Spain and Spanish America, Spanish America and the United States). He writes fully armed with the necessary conceptual and statistical data, and concludes that in the case of Latin America "we see a cultural pattern, derivative of traditional Hispanic culture, that is anti-democratic, anti-social, anti-progress, anti-entrepreneurial, and, at least among the elite, anti-work."[12]

His portrait is not altogether flattering. But Latin America will never move out of its cycles of crisis and underdevelopment unless the national and international Latin leadership stops resorting to the classic "passing the buck." Harrison's observations are not racial in focus—not based on genetic superiority and inferiority. Neither is he a North American supremacist. His final challenges are specific, directed to Latin American intellectuals and leaders, calling them to self-analysis and self-responsibility. Only this way will the desired change come about.

Fortunately there is a core of Latin American leaders who understand that *Latin America* is largely responsible for its problems, and the sooner the entire region acknowledges this, the sooner development will occur. Nevertheless, it seems to me that ultimately the structural change so necessary may come from another route—that of the emerging young evangelicals who sense that God has given them a political vocation. This is already being experienced in a number of countries such as Brazil, Venezuela, the Dominican Republic, Argentina, Peru, and Guatemala. As the evangelical population grows numerically, it will also become a politically sensitive group that has the capacity to rally around competent, gifted, eloquent, and honest believers who see that God has raised them to national prominence. They must anticipate accusations of causing a religious war, the "Irelandization" syndrome that pits Roman Catholics against Protestants. The Catholic church is very sensitive to evangelical growth—at Roman expense—and has already agitated the sensitive nerve of the religious war. Such new, truly Christian, national leaders must also be seen as representative voices of the entire nation, not merely as members of a historically religious minority.

SOME OF LATIN AMERICA'S HUMAN CRISES

Our survey of the problems of Latin America must sweep the continent, for entire volumes have been written on just each one. While statistics may be given for some of the issues, in other cases the focus is personal.

There Are Positive Signs

I am tempted to slide into total negativism when studying the Latin American picture; care must be taken to acknowledge the tangible signs of improvement in human well-being—even though the distribution of the benefits has been unequal. Traveling through Latin America, one is impressed by the external signs of progress: massive highway systems, urban communications, hydroelectric plants, high-rise apartment complexes, the ubiquitous computer, the development of new agricultural products primarily for export, the presence of small and large industries, new schools springing up (from primary through college), modern cities and government buildings, plush hotels and exquisite restaurants, world-class airports, exclusive tourist centers. In just about every category there is progress. Two specific areas of encouragement deserve mention.

Health. Medical care has been extended to serve more and more people. This is proved by the declines in death rates and the rising percentage of children who continue to live beyond the critical first year. In 1930 "life expectancy was about 35 years, a level attained by Northwestern Europe before 1850 and by the rest of Europe by 1900."[13] By 1985 the Latin American average of life expectancy was sixty-five years. This is a most significant improvement for that one category.

In 1984 Colombia was able to mount a health campaign that immunized in three days some 800,000 young children against five major diseases. More than 120,000 volunteers were mobilized in 10,000 posts. The care went beyond this one-time event, for "every parent bringing a child for immunization has been given a growth chart with the child's immunization record—plus advice on breast-feeding, nutrition, and the treatment of diarrheal illness."[14] In Brazil during 1983 a similar campaign "virtually wiped out poliomyelitis among Brazil's 19 million under-fives."[15] In 1984 some 90,000 immunization posts were manned and it was announced that "2 million under-twos have been vaccinated against measles and 1.5 million against diphtheria, whooping cough and tetanus."[16] At the same time one prevailing truth must be mentioned: infants and young children from poor homes keep the negative statistics at a high level. And the children from these homes are less likely to attend school beyond the minimal first one to three years—if they go at all.

Education. There have been remarkable gains in education in recent years, though the differences from country to country remain significant. In republics such as Costa Rica, Panama, Argentina, Uruguay, and Chile there has been a history of high investment in formal education. This has not been the case in others, where the budget restrictions demonstrate shortsightedness in national planning. Some countries, such as Guatemala, face a polyglot reality, with more than twenty-two major language groups.

The percentage of children in formal schooling has increased, with fifty-eight percent enrollment of children ages six to eleven in 1960, but a jump to eighty-four percent in 1985. The rate of enrollment for those aged twelve to seventeen soared in the same period from thirty-six to seventy-one percent. The gender differences in enrollment in Latin America are not significant, in contrast with Africa and Asia, and in both the above-age categories girls trailed boys by only one percent.[17]

The Underside of History in Latin America

The litany of Latin America's tragedy stares into our faces, inhuman conditions that stoke a conflagration. Some of the problems are the product of a colonial heritage, others are the result of personal sin, yet others come from structural injustice, and some even come as a result of modern technology. We must see people—hungry, malnourished people, some with permanent brain damage caused by infant malnourishment; we must see hopeless eyes, people without a future beyond desperate subsistence, individuals also bound by destructive habits, persons enveloped in sin, and even demonic spirits.

The population explosion. The following two tables demonstrate another perspective on Latin American growth.[18] It is crucial to observe growth over decades, particularly the average annual growth rates as they vary from country to country. For example, note the difference between Uruguay and Paraguay, between Cuba and Honduras. In short, Latin American population is exploding, but unevenly. What these tables do not show is the population "doubling time," the number of years it will take to double the national population—at current rates of growth. For Latin America as a whole, it will take thirty-six years, whereas for the United States it will take 105 years (if at all). Honduras will double in twenty-five years, Guatemala in twenty-two years, and Nicaragua in twenty-six. It will take Argentina fifty-five years to double, and Uruguay 102.[19]

Some of Latin America's problems are caused by the population explosion, others accompany it or parallel its growth. It is the Christian who is called to see beyond the numbing statistics, to peer into human eyes that are represented by the sterilizing and mind-boggling facts, to see people as Christ sees them—helpless and harassed sheep without a shepherd. The sensitive Christian can take these numbers and go to prayer, perhaps even staining the pages with tears.

Less food to eat. North Americans complain about inflation, but they cannot conceive of inflation that literally cuts the family diet in half. This is the scenario faced by many of the destitute poor in Latin America. Some estimates suggest that 100 million Latin Americans are undernourished, a fact easy to believe when visiting the shantytowns of any city. The United Nations Childrens' Fund (UNICEF) defines malnutrition poignantly: "when a child doesn't eat sufficiently to have the energy necessary to play."[20]

More sickness. In spite of the advances in health care in Latin America, the tragic list of sickness is increasing. In some Central American countries the vast majority of medical doctors and dentists live and practice in the capital city, avoiding the rural areas. "Undernourished children are less resistant to disease. The World Health Organization says 119 children die daily in Peru from malnutrition and preventable diseases: measles, tetanus, polio, whooping cough and diptheria."[21] In Bolivia two-thirds of the people do not have access to clean drinking water and health care. And forty-five percent of the people do not consume the minimum calories to maintain health. The Population Reference Bureau observes that "Bolivia is more similar to many sub-Saharan African countries than to its Latin American neighbors."[22]

Less formal education. "A government report of 1982 states that half of Rio de Janeiro's *favela* children, more than a million, could not get into schools and dropout rates were 'astronomical' for those who did."[23] Mexico City faces a similiar crisis, with an estimated two million children having no access to any kind of school. Compounding the problem is the prevalence of child labor, whether in rural or urban areas. Children must work, either in the fields or in town. Indian children face an even more critical situation, for many times they are forced into schools that teach only the national language, not their mother tongue. The Indian girls face almost insurmountable odds—tradition favors schooling for the boys, and girls are to stay at home, work, marry, and bear children.

POPULATION PROJECTIONS: 1985-2025
(Numbers in thousands)

Subregion and country	Total Population			Population ages 15-24		
	1985	2000	2025	1985	2000	2025
Total	404,806	546,395	778,662	81,934	103,731	127,467
South America						
Argentina	30,564	37,197	47,421	4,770	6,635	7,395
Bolivia	6,371	9,742	18,294	1,207	1,890	3,686
Brazil	135,564	179,487	245,809	27,566	33,671	38,854
Chile	12,038	14,792	18,301	2,455	2,380	2,639
Colombia	28,714	37,999	51,718	6,261	7,192	8,259
Ecuador	9,378	13,939	22,910	1,913	2,695	4,017
Paraguay	3,681	5,405	8,552	750	1,074	1,519
Peru	19,698	27,952	41,006	3,989	5,454	6,828
Uruguay	3,012	3,364	3,975	486	536	563
Venezuela	17,317	24,715	37,999	3,550	4,794	6,407
Mexico and Central America						
Costa Rica	2,600	3,596	5,099	561	676	812
El Salvador	5,552	8,708	15,048	1,105	1,738	2,799
Guatemala	7,963	12,222	21,668	1,541	2,479	4,228
Honduras	4,372	6,978	13,293	864	1,433	2,680
Mexico	78,996	109,180	154,085	16,552	22,095	24,666
Nicaragua	3,272	5,261	9,219	656	1,066	1,752
Panama	2,180	2,893	3,862	460	536	593
Caribbean						
Cuba	10,038	11,718	13,575	2,251	1,555	1,750
Dominican Republic	6,243	8,407	12,154	1,388	1,621	1,957
Guyana	953	1,196	1,562	214	234	220
Haiti	6,585	9,860	18,312	1,293	1,929	3,677
Jamaica	2,336	2,880	3,704	570	534	519
Puerto Rico	3,451	4,185	5,121	674	690	700
Suriname	375	469	625	90	89	91
Trinidad and Tobago	1,185	1,473	1,897	255	265	267
Others	2,368	2,795	3,553	517	471	500

Some years ago K. S. Silvert reported some disturbing information about education in Mexico. Even though the statistics are not fresh, they illustrate the frustrating task of educators in Latin America.

> According to recent information, of every thousand children who manage to put their feet on the first rung of primary school (on the same base, 460 never get even that far), only one reaches the last grade of the professional school.... During the course of the first six grades ... no fewer than 886 are left on the road. Only 59 get to the threshold of secondary education; but of these, 32 drop out during the three scholastic grades of secondary, prevocational, and special education, who added to the previous ones give us the figure of 973. Only nine arrive at the bachillerato, vocational education, and the professional cycle of primary normal instruction, of whom three drop out in the two or three grades involved . . . with whom the total of desertion rises to 994. And, finally, only six get to higher education, but of these five drop out.... In summary, through the course of the sixteen grades that comprise a complete educational scale 999 abandon their studies and only one finishes. To this we must add the alarming circumstance that 471 abandon school . . . in the first grade.[24]

The job shortage. As late as 1950 about half of Latin America's labor force was involved in agriculture, but by 1980 this was true only in Guatemala, Honduras, and Haiti. However, the switch to industry and manufacturing did not guarantee jobs for all, because much of the new employment was capital intensive and technological, not labor intensive. Too many vast new tracts opened up for agricultural export were developed with machinery, not people. Consequently, people sought jobs elsewhere, primarily in the cities. This has produced a massive underemployment in the "informal sector": legions of street vendors, errand runners, handyman jobs, and other work performed on an irregular basis. This sector shows a mixed ledger: on the one hand it does provide some kind of job; but on the other hand most of these people are bereft of social-security benefits, wage contracts, and job security —and the gap between the haves and the have-nots widens dramatically.

Significantly, Peruvian novelist-politician Mario Vargas Llosa argues for the recognition of the value of the underground economy as evidence of human ingenuity and persistence. While the stifling bureaucracies destroy creativity and foment underdevelopment, the underground holds answers.[25] But then, what kinds of answers are these?

The housing shortage. The social groups with adequate housing in Latin America are the middle and upper classes, representing at most twenty percent of the population. The crisis is palpable in the cities. During a recent trip to Sao Paulo, a leading architect told me that in his city ninety percent of present housing construction was dedicated to only ten percent of the population—the higher class. That means that ninety percent of the population—the less fortunate majority—must compete for a mere ten percent of construction of homes.

The crisis leaps out at you as you walk through any of the countless shantytowns that rim or lace the large urban centers. "Here, cut off from the city's economic mainstream and many of its services, the urban poor live in makeshift shelters of cardboard, wood scraps, corrugated plastic, even mud. Nearly half (46 percent) of Mexico City's population lived in shantytowns or other slums in 1970; . . . in Caracas, Venezuela, the proportion was 42 percent, and in Bogota, Colombia, 60 percent."[26]

I have seen some of these *villas de miseria* erected overnight (literally) to establish a "safety in numbers" mass against the absent landowner—who may also be the government. I have seen the police dismantle the same *callampas* (mushrooms) in short days. The shantytown inhabitants exist in grinding poverty and are prey to floods, mudslides, disease resulting from the absence of basic sanitary provisions, prostitution, drugs, violence, and crime. In the providence of God the gospel is present in these *barrios* where you will find many evangelical churches with dedicated workers attempting to improve the people's lot and dignify human life. Just in Mexico City's famous largest slum, Nezahualcóyotl, with 2.5 million people, there were 191 local churches in 1988.

The dream of owning one's little *casita* is coming true only for those who have either the funds or the connections in order to benefit from the newer housing developments. Some of these are governmental, others private. All tend to offer long-term loans at varying prices, depending on the size and location of the new home. The families will pass the debt on to their children, but at least they have something that is theirs. At long last they are legal landowners. That does provide status in Latin America.

The family disintegration. Family disintegration is perhaps the saddest crisis. Individuals flooding to the cities many times abandon the relatively stable structures of the rural and small-town world. For example: a young woman travels to the city to work as a maid, earning a minimal

salary plus room and board, getting perhaps Sunday off (at most) for lei-
sure and personal time. What does she do that day? Perhaps visit other
family and friends in the city, perhaps go to the park with acquaintances,
or even to the dance hall. She meets men on the search for naive girls,
and she is pressured into a sexual relationship. Pregnant, she faces a crisis both on the job (she will be fired) and back home (disgrace to the
family) and is forced to seek lodging and another job in town. All too often she takes the path to prostitution—easy but shameful money, and personal destruction.

"Rural emigration, poverty and unemployment tear at the fabric of
the family. Single parent households are common in the poor barrios. An
estimated 35 million children in Latin America have weak or absolutely
no family ties."[27] I was recently told in Brazil that Sao Paulo has an estimated 2.5 million abandoned children, only 50,000 receive any help
from government agencies, and the entire nation has 16 million street
kids. Too many of these children are the human castoffs of the disintegrated family, and too many will be sucked into the vortex of crime
and drug abuse. Just in Bolivia there is tragic evidence of small children
addicted to drugs who pay for their own addiction by selling marijuana
and cocaine.

THE CRISIS OF THE LAND

Who owns the land? For what purpose? How is it used? Can there
be peaceful land reform? Why so little aid and counsel to complete land
reform laws and programs? And how long have the distribution patterns
been as they are today?

Another Colonial Heritage

From early colonial years the land has been concentrated in the
hands of a minority. The *latifundios,* massive estates, were distributed
and owned by a few families. Some scholars estimate that even today ten
percent of the population owns ninety percent of the land.[28] Too much of
the time land has been utilized inefficiently; and in many cases landlords
are absent, living in comfort in the city. In some countries the estates are
owned by families whose name derives from colonial days. A recent
trend in agricultural lands is to develop crops for exportation, projects
that are machine intensive and use few laborers. In other cases grain
products are used more to fatten beef than for human consumption, with

the anomalous result being nations that previously exported food are now transformed into food importers.

Land Reform: The Hot Potato

One of the quickest ways to cause a coup in Latin America is to accuse the regime of surreptitiously scheming for land reform. This injects fear into powerful landowners and fuels the political parties that have traditionally defended the old aristocracies. During the years since independence, many short-lived governments have attempted land reform. A few nations have seen the reforms only partially implemented. El Salvador is a fascinating contemporary case study. The Christian Democrat Party of the late Napoleón Duarte finally instituted the long-promised land reforms—a necessary step in structural change and national development. However, two antagonistic groups stymied ongoing implementation of the land reforms. On the one hand Marxist guerillas violently sabotaged the land project because it undercut their own promises. On the other hand the right wing sabotaged it through political pressures and even death squads. Land reform is destined to disaster if it is not accompanied by financial credit, agricultural counsel, market coordination, and political power. Obviously, large farms can be run more *efficiently* than myriad smaller ones. But the benefits and pride of personal ownership outweigh serfdom, and smaller farms have the potential of meeting national needs.

Countries where major land reforms have been introduced and sustained include Cuba, Nicaragua, Bolivia, Mexico, Venezuela, and Peru. In Venezuela, land reform expropriated the largest estates and compensated the owner. In Peru the land reform progressed without production decline. During the 1950s the Guatemalan government of Jacobo Arbenz initiated land reform; but local elites, the United States (North American fruit companies lost land), and even the Catholic hierarchy coalesced to back a CIA-sponsored invasion from El Salvador. Arbenz was overthrown (there was solid evidence of Communist infiltration into his government), but a series of military regimes systematically bankrupted the nation and helped create the cycle of violence from which Guatemala is only now beginning to emerge. Ironically, a quietly developed program of land reform emerged as one of the factors in Guatemala that motivated the 1983 military coup that removed the evangelical head of state, General Efraín Ríos Montt.

THE URBAN/RURAL DICHOTOMY

Again a Colonial Heritage

Spanish authorities in particular set the pattern from the very beginning: stress the cities and use the interior only to fortify the cities. All benefits of the new culture were concentrated in the major urban centers: education, health care, government, church hierarchy, import-export structures, and significant employment. The future was in the city. The notable exception is seen in Brazil, where at the beginning the Portuguese empire had little interest in developing anything. However, when the monarchy fled into exile and set up court in Rio de Janeiro things began to change. But even then, power was concentrated in the enormous estates where export crops were grown and an entire culture evolved around the manor house—somewhat similar to the American South and its plantation life. In the eighteenth century Argentina faced a long, violent struggle between elitist Buenos Aires and the *gaucho*-led interior. Finally the city won, but the *gaucho* became an immortal piece of Argentine history and ethos.

The Two Worlds

Today in every Latin American country one sees the drastic contrast between the large cities and the rest of the country. Within brief minutes the traveler leaves the twentieth century and plunges into a world long disappeared from North American society. The pace of life changes, "proofs of modernity" are gone, with perhaps two exceptions—the ubiquitous transistor radio and the digital wristwatch. Modes of travel contrast: motorized high speed versus oxen, pack animals, and laden humans. It is a world of the soil, of the land. In some areas the land is fertile, gratefully bearing century after century, with occasional improvements in technique, seed, and fertilizer. In others it is a desperate battle to eke out an existence, tilling sterile or overworked land, fighting pestilence, drought, exhaustion, and despair.

These two worlds coexist, each with advantages and disadvantages. Prestige, power, higher education, and better jobs are found in the cities. But the city's magnetic and almost mythical attraction transforms rural stability into chaos. The *favelas* disintegrate known social fabric. In many cases, families who thought the city would improve their lot found that back "home" did have advantages: there was less hunger, the choices were limited, life was more simple, and the family network provided daily support.

GROWTH OF LATIN AMERICA'S TWELVE
LARGEST CITIES: 1950-2000

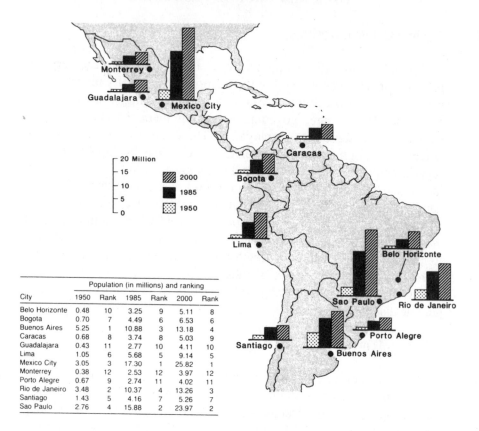

City	Population (in millions) and ranking					
	1950	Rank	1985	Rank	2000	Rank
Belo Horizonte	0.48	10	3.25	9	5.11	8
Bogota	0.70	7	4.49	6	6.53	6
Buenos Aires	5.25	1	10.88	3	13.18	4
Caracas	0.68	8	3.74	8	5.03	9
Guadalajara	0.43	11	2.77	10	4.11	10
Lima	1.05	6	5.68	5	9.14	5
Mexico City	3.05	3	17.30	1	25.82	1
Monterrey	0.38	12	2.53	12	3.97	12
Porto Alegre	0.67	9	2.74	11	4.02	11
Rio de Janeiro	3.48	2	10.37	4	13.26	3
Santiago	1.43	5	4.16	7	5.26	7
Sao Paulo	2.76	4	15.88	2	23.97	2

The Growth of the Cities

In spite of all the destructive elements of the cities, people continue to stream in at incredible rates. Rural bus terminals are jammed with families with meager possessions, risking all to stake out a future in the city. As of 1995, seventy percent of Latin America was classified as urban, with the highest in Uruguay (ninety percent) and Argentina (eighty-seven percent), and the lowest in Guatemala (thirty-eight percent).[29] The following figure illustrates the phenomenal development of Latin America's dozen giant cities.[30]

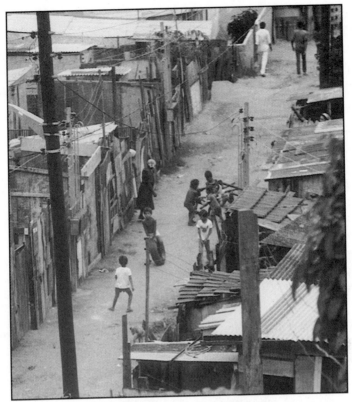

Life on the Underside of History

THE ECONOMIC CRISES

Latin America's economic future is bleak. Each week new statistics pour in: the international debt rises to the critical point where interest payments are suspended, as in Brazil and Ecuador. Mexico continues to be bailed out with more loans and refinancing, and both Peru and Argentina threaten default. Raw materials and other products are channeled to exportation, and nations with single crops or minerals—Cuba with sugar and Bolivia with tin—cannot develop OPEC-style cartels to protect their own interests. The oil boom has busted, and economic planning geared to future rising petroleum value has brought chaos, particularly to Mexico. Ecuador's 1987 earthquakes and massive mudslides not only killed thousands of people but temporarily destroyed the national oil industry. Brazil's vaunted *Cruzado* plan of early 1986 disintegrated in less than a year into triple-digit inflation, and interest payment on its 108 billion dollar debt jolted to a stop. One major Sao Paulo business magazine printed in 1987 the headline "GENERAL CONFUSION," with an upside-down map of the country.

Few items monopolize international headlines on Latin America like the debt crisis. The figures are astronomical and unrelenting, and every government struggles with the pressures to reform economic policy while avoiding a military coup or political loss in the next elections. Here are a few of the current debtors, as of November 1987 records.[31]

Country	Debt (Billions of Dollars)	Debt Per Capita
Argentina	48.40	$1,484.00
Brazil	107.00	713.00
Costa Rica	4.20	1,448.00
Ecuador	9.20	860.00
Mexico	97.40	1,094.00
Panama	4.70	1,958.00
Peru	13.70	665.00
Venezuela	32.10	1,637.00

One new political bloc emerging in Latin America to deal with this debt problem—among others—is the "Group of Eight": Mexico, Panama, Colombia, Venezuela, Brazil, Argentina, Peru, and Uruguay. Their most recent summit in Mexico, held without the presence of the United

Life for the Privileged Few

States, which is pointedly not a member of the group, attempted to recommend solutions to renegotiate debt. About thirty to forty percent of Latin American government spending goes only for interest payments, further fostering the various governments' own social crises.[32]

Topping that off, systematic and institutionalized corruption bled the nations, inadequate tax systems generated even less income and more evasion, and poor administration and shortsighted planning assured an uneasy future. The newest experiment in creative financing became the debt-equity conversion, allowing foreign banks to sell or buy bad debts at reduced prices. These were exchanged for local currency and required to be invested in local businesses. On the negative side, this fosters a loss of national sovereignty over national business and natural resources, but on the positive side it encourages investment and development. *South* magazine dedicated a major section to discussion of this swap-market boom.[33]

A Final Word on the Economic Crisis

Latin America confronts a sustained, hopeless economic future. Millions of citizens conclude that their only alternative is to emigrate, even from some of the more prosperous nations. Argentina has experienced the dramatic exodus of more than 600,000 people just since 1960, departparting for the United States, Brazil, Spain, Venezuela, Australia, and Canada.[34] It is significant to note that not all are leaving for the United States. At the same time, uncounted thousands of Central Americans are flooding illegally into the United States, fleeing both political and economic chaos. And Mexico will continue to use its northern border as a safety valve for its own unemployment and economic crises. Meanwhile the economic crises of Mexico grow even more grim. *South* reports:

> Rising prices are adding to the agony of Mexico's poor. By mid-December the minimum daily wage in Mexico City—5,626 pesos, or just under US$2.50—was worth only 50 percent of its 1981 equivalent. The basic basket of goods such as beans, rice, sugar and maize now costs 14 percent more than the minimum wage.[35]

SOCIAL STRATIFICATION IN LATIN AMERICA

Latin America's class structure is centuries old. Today it is difficult to give accurate figures for each country, and each nation has different figures. However, I estimate the following: perhaps two percent at the top, at most eighteen percent in the middle, and eighty percent on the bottom. A disturbing pattern emerges in the new members of the rising middle class. Most of them have come from families which a generation ago formed part of the "popular classes." You would expect that they, having risen on the scale, would be more sensitive to those who remain on the underside. Why have they experienced rapid upward social mobility without a keen social consciousness toward the less fortunate? Would they not be natural promotors of justice and change? The "new rich" have short memories and readily adopt the value systems of the elite, forgetting their roots. Richard Adams observes that "the apparently new middle group is only an extension of the traditional upper class, both in terms of economic position and basic values."[36]

Indians on the same rising ladder find the odds stacked against them. While back in their indigenous communities they might have been local elites, once they step into *mestizo* society they automatically drop a few notches on the national social scale. A medical, law, or engineering degree does open doors to limited upward social mobility. Racial prejudice is prevalent toward Indian peoples. Because they are different from the dominant society, many times they are judged dumb and unprepared for modern society. In other countries prejudice is directed against the black populations. One Central American country had a constitutional prohibition against blacks gaining permanent residence. While Brazil is justly proud of its racial blending, even there prejudice is present. Examine the faces of national politicians, army generals, and top businessmen to discover how many are black.

THE POLITICAL CRISIS OF LATIN AMERICA

I have written enough in previous chapters to underline Latin America's disturbing political uncertainty. Latin America was the locus of a political ferment that both experimented with and criticized hard-line Marxism, socialism, and free-enterprise capitalism. No system has been able to produce stability and still guarantee peace, justice, and liberty. The law is all too many times chilled, serving the ruling class. As the *gaucho* Martin Fierro said: "The law is like the knife, it does not cut the one holding the handle." The prophet Habakkuk would understand Latin America well.

Radomiro Tomic, former Chilean presidential candidate for the Christian Democrat Party, diagnosed Latin America's problems in a

Mexico City--One of the Exploding Ninevehs

closed seminar I attended some years ago at the University of Texas, Austin. He affirmed that the problems are threefold: internal poverty, internal disintegration, and external dependency. To him the key questions were: Who rules? How do they rule? Why do they rule? For whose benefit do they rule? Latin American nations reminded him of "tragic abortions, miscarried by capitalism, born before their time." Although he had lost the election to Allende, he concluded that the overthrow of his opponent's Marxist government was the "ultimate example of the incompatibility of representative democracy and social order."

During the mid-1970s Peru experimented with a hybrid brand of nationalistic socialism. It was touted as a Peruvian Renaissance, and a "new man" was being molded for the nation. The Indian language Quechua was spoken with pride, land reform was instituted, and the future seemed to glow with promise. Ismael Frías, a leftist journalist, wrote at the time that the expulsion and expropriation of a North American oil company had been the first step to affirming national sovereignty. "In that moment, truly historical Peru not only rescued one of its primary natural resources, but something of incomparably higher value: its own national dignity violated for more than forty years by an imperialistic potency." The political alternative would not be Marxist, and Frías scored that system because "it represents a regime of exploitation of work, of political oppression and of imperialism as unlivable as capitalism in its worst forms." The new system would be socialistic, but with a Latin face. Frías concluded: "This is the way in which the Peruvian Revolution has developed from a nationalism to a socialism that is humanist, libertarian, and culturally immersed in the Christian tradition; and it will be national, patriotic, Peruvian above all things, and in this sense irreconcilably anti-imperialistic."[37] Yet even that experiment foundered on the shoals of internal and international opposition.

Today it is hard to locate a country with a year-long track record of economic stability. At least the decades of military totalitarianisms have ended, for now. However, the military, one of Latin America's most powerful elite, sits backstage, brokering governments and assuring that its military power is not threatened. Mexico is a country with a professional and nonpolitical military, and Costa Rica continues its non-military tradition. Only in Argentina has the backlash following the Falkland Island debacle allowed a civilian government to judge and jail former military presidents, although the 1989 Peronist government tried to make peace with both military and Catholic hierarchy. But in the other countries the military is making sure it is not treated as its Argentine colleagues were.

Democracy sustains its illusive nature. One Mexican politician recently observed with sardonic humor, "Democracy is like the Holy Grail. Everyone talks about it, but nobody has really seen it." As of 1995, most Latin American governments were experimenting with some variety of a democratic system, but it was an uneasy truce. Central America is convulsed with bitter, contrasting political alternatives. The acid test for the future will be to determine which of the options has both an ideology and a discipline to create and prevail in the maelstrom of societal turmoil. And is it too much to dream for an honest administration in Latin America?

The heroes of the left have been apotheosized: Camilo Torres, Che Guevara, Salvador Allende. Independence heroes such as Bolívar are immortal, and each country has its particular set of personages who have marked national history. But democracy does not yet seem to have a hero to apotheosize. Do Latin American democracies lack both a political ideology as well as deep commitment to their values? What options do Latin Americans have today? Most of them will stay in their countries, loving their patriotic symbols, and hoping in hope; some will emigrate legally or illegally, either within Latin America or to the "promised land," *El Norte* of mythical proportions and broken dreams.

THE LOVE-HATE RELATIONSHIP WITH THE UNITED STATES

From the pre-independence years to the present, Latin Americans have struggled with their attitude toward the United States. Previous chapters have underlined some of the early positive attitudes toward this northern neighbor, to the point of modeling the first constitutions after that of the United States. For about one hundred years Latin Americans looked on the United States with a kind of pride, laced with envy that a newer nation would progress so rapidly. But the love affair deteriorated close to the turn of this century. By then the United States had embarked on its own imperialistic expansion and heavy-handed diplomacy: Cuba, Puerto Rico, Panama, Mexico, the interventions in the Caribbean and Central America. These all contributed to a dramatic change in attitude: "That gigantic neighbor to the North truly does not love us. Our love is unilateral. The land of democracy and liberty does not respect the democracy and liberty of other countries."

I have already mentioned the Latin American intellectuals who rose to defend Hispanic values and culture. José Enrique Rodó's *Ariel*[38] lauded the familial, Christian, and moral values of beauty and idealism and criticized North America's cold pragmatism. But it was Nicaraguan poet Ruben Darío who penned his eloquent "Ode to Roosevelt," a biting critique in the spirit of Rodó.

The voice that would reach you, Hunter, must speak
in Biblical tones, or in the poetry of Walt Whitman.
You are primitive and modern, simple and complex;
you are one part George Washington and one part Nimrod.
    You are the United States,
future invader of our naive America
with its Indian blood, an America
that still prays to Christ and still speaks Spanish.
You are a strong, proud model of your race;
you are cultured and able; you oppose Tolstoy.
You are an Alexander-Nebuchadnezzar,
breaking horses and murdering tigers.

(You are a Professor of Energy,
as the current lunatics say).

You think that life is a fire,
that progress is an irruption,
that the future is wherever
your bullet strikes.

No.

The United States is grand and powerful.
Whenever it trembles, a profound shudder
runs down the enormous backbone of the Andes.
If it shouts, the sound is like the roar of a lion.
And Hugo said to Grant: "The stars are yours."
(The dawning sun of the Argentine barely shines;
the star of Chile is rising . . .) A wealthy country,
joining the cult of Mammon to the cult of Hercules;
while Liberty, lighting the path
to easy conquest, raises her torch in New York.

But our own America, which has had poets
since the ancient times of Nezahualcóyotl;
which preserved the footprints of great Bacchus,
and learned the Panic alphabet once,
and consulted the stars; which also knew Atlantis
(whose name comes ringing down to us in Plato)
and has lived, since the earliest moments of its life,
in light, in fire, in fragrance, and in love—
the America of Moctezuma and Atahualpa,
the aromatic America of Colombus,
Catholic America, Spanish America,
the America where noble Cuauhtémoc said:
"I am not on a bed of roses"—our America,
trembling with hurricanes, trembling with Love:
O men with Saxon eyes and barbarous souls,
our America lives. And dreams. And loves.
And it is the daughter of the Sun. Be careful.
Long live Spanish America!
A thousand cubs of the Spanish lion are roaming free.
Roosevelt, you must become, by God's own will,

the deadly Rifleman and the dreadful Hunter
before you can clutch us in your iron claws.

And though you have everything, you are lacking one thing:
    God![39]

The Guatemalan intellectual, social democrat, and former president of the nation, Juan José Arévalo, wrote a symbolic book, *The Shark and the Sardines,* in which he spoke of the United States as the shark and Latin America the sardines. His polemic may disturb some readers, but it merits pondering in order for understanding to emerge.

> In our resistance to the business man mentality, we are still Spanish, stubbornly Spanish. Also, we have not left off being Catholic, nor have we left off being romantic and we cannot conceive of private life without enlightening ideals. If you want to be our friends, you will have to accept us as we are. Do not attempt to remodel us after your image. Mechanical civilization, material progress, industrial techniques, fiduciary wealth, comfort, hobbies—all these figure in your programs of work and enjoyment of life. But for us, the essence of human life does not lie in such things.[40]

I spoke with Dr. Arévalo one day in Guatemala City. He was a gracious and dignified gentleman in his late seventies, and he had been a true liberal revolutionary in Guatemala, freely elected with great dreams and hopes following a long and violent dictatorship. When I asked him about *The Shark and the Sardines,* he was quick to assure me that he fully respected North Americans and the United States but felt that at that moment in history a strong word had to be said about all kinds of sharks in the world who fed their appetites at the expense of the sardines.

More recently the United States has transmitted a confused signal to Latin America. On the one hand Franklin Delano Roosevelt and John F. Kennedy have gone down on the record as men who respected Latin America. Kennedy died and was apotheosized to the point that his support of the invasion of the Bay of Pigs in Cuba, as well as his Alliance for Progress, has escaped serious judgment. In the 1970s it was a combination of Watergate, Vietnam, the CIA scandals, and the multimillion dollar bribes of transnational corporations that led the distinguished Spaniard, Salvador deMadariaga, to write of the "vertical fall of all moral authority of the United States."[41]

Military Power of the Left

Military Power of the Right

Latin Americans had a rough time sifting out the foreign policies of Jimmy Carter and Ronald Reagan. Carter has been vilified by the right but appreciated by the progressives. Reagan has experienced the opposite. The return of the Panama Canal to the Panamanians during the Carter administration was the only *just* thing to do, and that bold act generated good will toward the United States. But the Reagan administration's support of the British in the 1982 Malvinas-Falkland Islands war created a storm of opposition. The United States had reneged on its treaty agreements with Latin America and had openly supported the British. The Reagan attitude toward Nicaragua was another example of dangerous military games. While Congress deserves absolutely no credit for its vacillations, many serious observers wonder if there is *any* North American policy for Central America. The Bush and Clinton administrations may stand for a more sensitive Latin American policy, but only time will tell.

This love-hate relationship with the United States takes on a variety of manifestations today. On the one hand, most Latin Americans will generally admire the North American life-style—actually coveting it— and are generally friendly to the individual *Gringo-Yankee-norteamericano*. At the same time they struggle with the imitation of foreign life-styles, and they are frustrated with North American foreign policy—often so heavy-handed, shortsighted, and self-serving. There will always be a powerful minority that virulently attacks the United States.

Yet there is a growing group of Latin Americans who are trying to face their own realities head-on. The late Carlos Rangel, a Venezuelan, was one such spokesman. He wrote insightfully in *The Latin Americans: Their Love-Hate Relationships with the United States.* He was not a servile Americanophile, and he articulated a serious, objective critique of the United States. But more significantly, he was also fearless in judging Latin Americans who blame all their problems on the United States. He refused to avoid responsibility by merely accepting the dependency theory, afraid that "by echoing this line of thought, we Latin Americans are starting on a new cycle in our self-delusion over the causes of our frustration. We are once again refusing to admit that the reasons for North American success and Latin American failure are to be found in the qualities of North Americans and in the defects of Latin Americans."[42] Such writers deserve much more serious study.

IN CONCLUSION

The colonial heritage, compounded by the post-independence experimentations, the *caudillo* era, the years of the technocrats, the centuries of imitation, the disenfranchised masses, the unequal social and class structure, international dependency and internal oppression, Marxism and selfish capitalism, personal and structural sin, even demonic principalities, all of these have conspired against Latin America. Again we reaffirm our faith in a sovereign God who not only knows where history is going, but is also in control. Jesus Christ from the beginning clarified that his church would be built in the context of spiritual warfare, not peace, prosperity, position, and power. Certainly Latin America is a test case of conflict, where the crises force its magnificent people to seek ultimate answers in the person of the virile and powerful Victor, Jesus Christ. At the same time the church has been left on planet Earth to fulfill her cultural mandate. Increasing numbers of Latin evangelical leaders— godly and committed, competent and honest, tried and experienced— must enter the public arena by election or appointment in the name of Christ and in service to their fellow citizens. May this day come soon! Meanwhile, our Quiche proverb for "crisis" continues ever so relevant.

NOTES

1.   Jacques Lambert, *Latin America: Social Structures and Political Institutions*, trans. Helen Katel (Berkeley, CA: University of California, 1971), pp. 109-10.

2.   Alcides Arguedas, *Pueblo Enfermo* (La Paz, Bolivia: Libreria Editorial "Juventud," 1982).

3.   Eduardo Galeano, *Open Veins of Latin America*, trans. Cedric Belfrage (New York: Monthly Review Press, 1973). José Míguez Bonino, *Doing Theology in a Revolutionary Situation* (Philadelphia: Fortress, 1975). Gustavo Gutiérrez, *A Theology of Liberation: History, Politics and Salvation*, trans. and ed. Sister Caridad Inda and John Eagleson (Maryknoll, NY: Orbis, 1986). Enrique Dussel, *A History of the Church in Latin America: Colonialism to Liberation*, trans. anbd rev. Alan Neely (Grand Rapids, MI: Eerdmans, 1981). All of these authors subscribe to liberation theology and the dependency theory.

4.   E. Bradford Burns, *Latin America: A Concise Interpretive History*, 4th ed. (Englewood Cliffs, NJ: Prentice-Hall, 1986), p. 297.

5.   Michael Novak, *The Spirit of Democratic Capitalism* (New York: A Touchstone Book, American Enterprise Institute/Simon and Schuster, 1982). Novak, *Will It Liberate? Questions About Liberation Theology* (New York: Paulist, 1986). Peter Berger and Michael Novak, *Speaking to the Third World: Essays on Democracy and Development* (Washington, DC: American Enterprise Institute for Public Policy Research, 1985). Michael Novak, ed., *Liberation South, Liberation North* (Washington,

DC: American Enterprise Institute for Public Policy Research, 1981).

6. Esther and Mortimer Arias, *The Cry of My People* (New York: Friendship Press, 1980), pp. viii-ix.

7. Georgie Ann Geyer, *The New Latins: Fateful Change in South and Central America* (Garden City, NY: Doubleday, 1970), p. 210.

8. Gustav Niebuhr, "Born Again, Latin Style." The *Austin American-Statesman* (Texas) published a five-part series starting March 15, 1987, detailing the growth of evangelicals in Latin America. Of particular interest is the article entitled "Born-Again Christians, 'Kingdom Theology' Versus Communists" (March 17, 1987), which develops the linkage between the gospel and conservative American-style politics. It is a dangerous mix and frankly a heresy that could seriously damage the churches.

9. Leopoldo Zea, *The Latin American Mind,* trans. James H. Abbott and Lowell Dunham (Norman, OK: University of Oklahoma, 1963), p. 37.

10. Samuel Ramos, *Profile of Man and Culture in Mexico,* trans. Peter G. Earle (Austin, TX: University of Texas, 1962). Of particular interest are chapter 1–3.

11. Lawrence E. Harrison, *Underdevelopment Is a State of Mind: The Latin American Case* (Boston: The Center for International Affairs, Harvard University and University Press of America, 1985), p. 2.

12. Ibid., p. 165.

13. Thomas W. Merrick, "Population Pressures in Latin America," *Population Bulletin,* vol. 41, no. 3, July 1986, p. 11.

14. UNICEF, *The State of the World's Children: 1985* (Oxford: Oxford University, 1984), p. 2.

15. Ibid., p. 37.

16. Ibid., p. 39.

17. Merrick, "Population Pressures," p. 33.

18. Ibid., p. 29.

19. Population Reference Bureau, Inc. *1995 World Population Data Sheet.*

20. John Maust, "The Plight of Latin American Children: What Can Be Done for Them?" *Latin America Evangelist,* July-September 1985, p. 5.

21. Ibid.

22. Paola Scommegna, "Bolivia," *Population Today,* vol. 14, no. 3, March 1986, p. 12.

23. Merrick, "Population Pressures," p. 29.

24. K. S. Silvert, "The University Student," in John J. Johnson, ed., *Continuity and Change in Lain America* (Stanford, CA: Stanford University, 1964), p. 208.

25. Mario Vargas Llosa, "In Defense of the Black Market," *The New York Times Magazine,* February 22, 1987.

26. Merrick, "Population Pressures," p. 28.

27. Maust, "The Plight," p. 5.

28. Burns, *Latin America: A Concise Interpretive History,* 3d ed. (Englewood Cliffs, NJ: Prentice-Hall, 1982), pp. 288-89.

29. *1995 World Population Data Sheet.*

30. Merrick, "Population Pressures," p. 25.

31. Gary Lewis, "Strategic Survey 1988," *South,* November 1987, pp. 50-51.

32. "Latin America," *South,* January 1988, pp. 17-29.

33. "*South* on Latin America," Special section of *South,* October 1987, pp. 1-9.

34. "Argentina Looks to Stem the Flow of Emigrants," *Wall Street Journal,* March 20, 1987.

35. Richard Lapper, "Mexico: Running Out of Options," *South,* February 1988, pp. 23-24.

36. Richard N. Adams, "Political Power and Social Structure," in Claudio Veliz, ed., *The Politics of Conformity in Latin America* (London: Oxford University, 1967), p. 7.

37. Ismael Frías, *Visión,* April 30, 1975, p. 25.

38. José Enrique Rodó, *Ariel* (Mexico: Editorial Porrua, S.A., 1970).

39. Ruben Darío, "To Roosevelt," in Sheldon B. Liss and Peggy K. Liss, eds., *Man, State, and Society in Latin American History* (New York: Praeger, 1972), pp. 294-95.

40. Geyer, *The New Latins,* p. 116.

41. *Visión,* p. 25.

42. Carlos Rangel, *The Latin Americans: Their Love-hate Relationship with the United States,* translated from the French by Ivan Kats (New York: Harcourt Brace Jovanovich, 1976), p. 44.

4

Spiritual Dimensions of Latin America

"Es que somos un pueblo religioso, y la espiritualidad fluye en nuestras venas." ("It's just that we
are a religious people, and spirituality flows in our
veins.")

—A Latin American

Ever since I had the use of reason, the name Jesus
Christ was one of the most familiar in my house and in
school during my infancy and adolescence. I never saw a
contradiction between the ideas that sustain me and the
ideas of that symbol, of that extraordinary figure.[1]

—Fidel Castro

Latin America's racial rainbow is matched by its religious mosaic,
with overlapping pieces that can periodically confuse the observer. The
original continental religions were practiced by the Indian peoples. Those
religions were animisms that continue to permeate the Indians' worldview to this day. The Spaniards and Portuguese later brought a Christ,
the *other* Spanish Christ, the hybrid conceived from Moorish medieval
seeds and imported with conviction and force. In many ways that Christ
was blended into the animistic beliefs, producing a syncretism evident today throughout the continent and particularly witnessed in popular Catholicism. At other times the hybrid Christ demonstrated his own severe,

suffering Spanish identity—an agent of mystery, miracle, and authority. The third major spiritual piece of the mosaic came with the importation of Africans to the New World. Catholicism was the official creed of the colonial rulers, but the black peoples injected into it a belief system appealing more to their own ethos, and reflecting their own spiritual traditions—spiritism. This produced another brand of syncretism particularly experienced in Brazil today, where perhaps thirty percent of the population would call themselves both Catholic and spiritist.

In the late nineteenth century a more biblical Christ made his appearance to Latin American republics. In those early years he arrived under adverse conditions, and at times dressed in Anglo-Saxon clothing. But nevertheless the Scriptures spoke with their own power, for this Christ was the supernatural one who transforms people. For decades the evangelical population has existed with a minority complex, even a catacomb mentality. But lately these churches have exploded with a virile growth that surprised both religious and secular observers. There is a quickening pulse beating in the heart of Latin evangelicals. Lives *are* being changed; hope surges through the continent. Of course, not all the signs of life are biblically healthy. Many of the churches suffer from diseases similar to those of their Anglo-Saxon counterparts, and others breed their own national viruses. Many churches and denominations are large, but that does not necessarily mean they are all healthy churches. Too many of them suffer from doctrinal deadness, or insufficient biblical teaching, or from emotional overdoses. An analytical eye needs to examine carefully the evangelical churches of Latin America.[2]

For decades animism, Catholicism, spiritism, and evangelical Protestantism presented the only significant spiritual alternatives. Then the other groups invaded the scenario. The cults have sent thousands of missionaries and made converts. The Bahai have scored heavily among, of all groups, the Bolivian Indian populations, where three percent of that country's population profess the Bahai faith. Jim Jones made tragic history in Guyana, the Oriental and mystical groups offer their alternative, and even gnosticism has its peculiar appeal. The secular religions of Marxist materialism and consumer materialism seduce with terrible consequences; and even atheism makes its mark in some lands. In Uruguay, for example, atheism claims thirty-seven percent of the population, and in Cuba it claims forty-four percent of the populace.[3]

Today Latin Americans seem to open their hearts and lives to whatever spiritual message comes with emotion, conviction, and the offer of personal change. It is obviously a time of harvest in almost every country, and this means it is a time of crisis. Will the strong, virile, resurrected Christ reign on this continent, bringing even national transformation, or will the evangelicals miss this historical moment?

THE HOLY APOSTOLIC ROMAN CATHOLIC CHURCH IN LATIN AMERICA

Latin American history confirms the thesis that when Christianity enters a culture, both culture and Christianity change. What kind of Christianity was imported to the New World? How did it change and how was it changed? MacKay's unequaled classic, *The Other Spanish Christ,* indicts the Conquest Christ, arguing that this one was not the authentic One.

> However much overshadowed by His Mother, Christ too came to America. Journeying from Bethlehem and Calvary, He passed through Africa and Spain, on His long westward journey to the Pampas and Cordilleras. And yet, was it really He Who came, or another religious figure with His name and some of His works? Methinks the Christ, as He sojourned westward, went to prison in Spain, while another who took His name embarked with the Spanish crusaders for the New World, a Christ who was not born in Bethlehem but in North Africa. This Christ became naturalized in the Iberian colonies of America, while Mary's Son and Lord has been little else than a stranger and sojourner in these lands from Columbus's day to this.[4]

In Latin America, Christ represents the tragic victim, the focus of a cult of death, an expiatory creature who had neither personality nor power. He came to show people not how to live, but how to die. MacKay continues to evaluate this Christ as

> a Christ known in life as an infant and in death as a corpse, over whose helpless childhood and tragic fate the Virgin Mother presides; a Christ who became man in the interests of eschatology, whose permanent reality resides in a magic wafer bestowing immortality; a Virgin Mother who by not tasting death, became the Queen of Life— that is the Christ and that the Virgin who came to America! He came as Lord of Death and of the life that is to

be; she came as Sovereign Lady of the life that now is.[5]

José Míguez Bonino agrees that "Latin America was never 'Christian' in the sense that Europe or even North America can be said to be so. What took place here was a colossal transplantation—the basic ecclesiastical structures, disciplines, and ministries were brought wholesale from Spain and were expected to function as a Christian order; a tremendous form without substance."[6] And traveling with this dark Christ came the darkness of the Inquisition, inspired by Torquemada's vision of a pure Roman church. Visit the Museum of the Inquisition in downtown Lima and sense the reality of that tortured technology.

The Black Legend merits comment here. The Spaniards accuse the English of perpetrating this legend, which essentially argues that all of the Spanish influence in the New World was negative, that no good at all came of the colonial era, and that Spain is to blame for all the evils of Hispanic America. The British retort that such accusations are false; that it was not a British creation, that history must speak for itself. I refer to this Black Legend because to some readers my own conclusions seem black. I do not fully subscribe to the Black Legend, though Spain—political and religious—must bear responsibility for her imported institutions, many benevolent, while others were destructive. Ironically, it was the Spanish friar Bartolomé de las Casas whose heated indictments of Spain gave much credence to the Black Legend.

Post-revolutionary Catholicism in Latin America suffered major changes. Although the political battles themselves did not have religious discontent at their core—actually in Mexico and Brazil priests led the revolutionary struggle—Bolívar was convinced of the necessity of separation of church and state. But he did not advocate the totally secularized French model. In actuality the new republics instituted Catholicism as the state religion—the only faith they had ever really known. But the tensions between church and state soon broke open. The Spanish crown during the colonial period had exercised the power to name bishops, and it wished to continue doing so. It was rejected in the new Americas. The papacy had earlier appealed to faithful Catholics to fight for Spain. The plea was rejected also. Later violent anticlerical actions swept through some of the new countries, and the church was disestablished in several of them.[7]

Catholicism as an Institution Facing Crisis and Change

The Roman Catholic church of Latin America finds itself today in a historic and multifaceted crisis. For centuries she had operated on the basis of the dogma formulated in the Council of Trent. She was the One, Holy, Roman, Apostolic, Catholic church, indivisible, exercising tremendous temporal power; at times on center stage, but very adept at behind-the-curtains influence. For centuries it was the medieval triad of miracle, mystery, and authority, with the Bible unavailable to the masses.

Over the decades, the Catholic church of Latin America experienced a variety of changes from different sources. But it was Vatican Council II (1962-1965) that caused the tremendous upheaval that rocked the church. "Pope John XXIII's encyclicals *Mater et Magistra* and especially *Pacen in Terris* called for an end to ghetto Catholicism and cooperation with men of diverse persuasions in meeting the crises of the modern world."[8] Because Dr. Núñez deals with these matters, my treatment will be very general; and the following are my personal observations.

This new church has made a radical and renewed commitment to socio-political activism. Today's social crises had festered in the hearts of the younger leaders of the Latin church, many of whom had served in the poor parishes. So when the Catholic bishops of Latin America met in Medellín in September 1968 the continent was recast in theo-political categories. There seemed to be two strands of the new focus, one centrist and the other radical. However, Medellín was not the first time in recent years that the Catholic church awoke to her perceived role in modern Latin America. Houtart and Emile Pin had written and actively worked in the mid-1960s,[9] and others had published extensively on the topic. The more moderate perspective was expressed by Ivan Vallier, who argue Roman Catholicism's "international character provides it with a special potential for articulating and symbolizing universal values. . . . Instead of using their office and prestige as bases for promoting confessional goals and mobilizing commitments to sacramental participation, the stress has been on the problem of the poor, the importance of human freedom and dignity, and the sacredness of the value of social justice."[10]

However, it was at Medellín that Gustavo Gutiérrez, first systematizer of liberation theology, emerged as a *periti*—advisor to his bishops. His perspective was radical. It was revolutionary both in theology and praxis. He compared Vatican II with Medellín in the following manner:

At Medellín, the Latin American Church . . . realitically perceived the world in which it was and clearly saw its place in that world. In short, it began to be aware of its own coming of age and to take the reins of its own destiny. Vatican II speaks of the underdevelopment of peoples, of the developed countries and what they can and should do about this underdevelopment; Medellín tries to deal with the problem from the standpoint of the poor countries, characterizing them as subjected to a new kind of colonialism. Vatican II talks about a Church in the world and describes the relationship in a way which tends to neutralize the conflicts; Medellín demonstrates that the world in which the Latin American Church ought to be present is in full revolution. Vatican II sketches a general outline for Church renewal; Medellín provides guidelines for a transformation of the Church in terms of its presence on a continent of misery and injustice.[11]

Bishop Elder Cámara of northeast Brazil has been accused of being the "red bishop"; but he rejects violence, urging the pursuit of a peaceful revolution. Nevertheless he is forthright: "Our objective is the integration of Latin America without external nor internal imperialism. We have no desire to simply exchange masters (*patrones*). The United States, Russia, China. They are all *patrones*."[12]

Today's Latin American Catholic hierarchy is not united, following one single position. Nevertheless, the church clearly is moving aggressively into the sphere of socio-ethical leadership. Pope John Paul II has attempted to rein in the Jesuits and the extreme liberationists—with moderate success—but he has called the church to play a public role in the transformation of society, with a preferential option for the poor and without ideological identification with leftist political parties. The countries where the Christian Democrat Parties have won national elections for the presidency exemplify this public role. These parties, advised by Catholic ideologues, attempt to steer a progressive course between doctrinaire socialism and nondemocratic capitalism. Chilean Christian Democrats received multiple millions of German marks to stop Marxism, failing when Allende was elected to office; at that time the Christian Democrats were discredited and demoralized.

Medellín also underscored the crucial role of the national, regional, and continental Catholic conferences, particularly so in the Latin American Episcopal Council (CELAM). This collective body harkens back to the activist role of Vatican II; and although the clarion calls of Medellín are partially muted by the 1979 Council in Puebla, the commitment to influence the public life will continue. Of critical importance to both evangelicals and Catholics will be the day when top *evangelical* political candidates emerge for the presidency of a nation. A sour foretaste of that has already been experienced tice in Guatemala.

Catholicism has renewed its attempts to attract and keep its laity, particularly the key ones. The quality and quantity of literature is formidable, and meets specific needs. The very effective *cursillos*—intensive seminars—have drawn together chosen leaders for fellowship, training, and devotional exercises. The Christian Family Movement has extensive weekend retreats to fortify the home. The Opus Dei, a highly select and disciplined order, has elevated the role of consecrated laity within the Catholic church. It has a network of groups in Latin America, and also provides scholarships to qualified young people to study in universities and live in special residence halls run by the Opus Dei. During my last trip to Central America I was surprised by one Catholic parish church that was offering special workshops on how to study the Bible and lead Bible groups. Catholic liturgy has more recently borrowed elements of evangelical churches: guitars, informal singing of gospel songs, flannelgraphs for children's ministries, parish church and home Bible studies, and other methods that attract and keep the faithful.

Evangelical Samuel Escobar gives a fascinating historical note. When the Catholic bishops met in Rio de Janeiro in 1955 to discuss matters of their concern, one high priority item dealt with the "Protestant danger." They called on the Roman church to send to Latin America those missionaries who had been forced to leave their fields due to the rise of Communism. This would enable the Latin American Catholics to stem the rising influence of evangelicals. This concern has continued and even motivated aspects of their pastoral renewal.[13]

Of particular importance has been the development of the *Comunidades Eclesiales de Base* (CEB), Base Ecclesial Communities, in the last twenty years—with an estimated 150,000–180,000 groups in Latin America, and up to 100,000 just in Brazil. What are they? One Catholic report says the following:"Typically, a CEB is a grouping of a dozen to 50 or more persons, accompanied occasionally by a priest or pastoral agent, who meet to pray and reflect on their everyday lives in the light of the Bible, and to celebrate their faith."[14] Ironically, this aptly describes many things that evangelicals in Latin America have been trying to do for some one hundred years.

The uniqueness *and* importance of the CEB movement for Catholicism is seen in numerous ways: it is a discovery of the laity even in the face of hierarchical criticism; it is an experimentation with new forms of being the church, a novel ecclesiology; it is an expression of pastoral concern to meet personal needs of the faithful in light of a desperate dearth of clergy—in some parishes there is one priest for every ten thousand people; it is a forum for individuals to express their social concerns, and even to channel them into some kind of formal political expression of protest; it is also a means by which Marxist liberation theology penetrated the bases of Catholicism; it is an approach that gives the poor an outlet to share and convey their faith and convictions—many times in the context of oppression and conflict; it is a means of re-evangelization of a continent perceived as Catholic but not practicing its faith; it is a very effective counter to Protestant conversion methodology, thus stemming the spiritual hemorrhage that has so worried the hierarchy. In essence, the CEB movement is a new challenge for the Roman Catholic church as well as evangelicals in Latin America. Whether or not these groups will prosper under hierarchical blessing waits to be seen, but they were there to stay.[15]

The Catholic church historically has committed itself to education on all levels. Many different religious orders today maintain a fully developed system of education. Generally they have focused on the secondary level and in recent decades have established high quality universities. And whereas the national autonomous universities go on strike after strike, the Catholic universities continually produce graduates to serve both church and country.

Christo-paganism in Latin America

Catholicism in Multi-Faceted Church Perspective

The once-monolithic church is no longer a reality acknowledged even by Catholic leaders. Recent battles between the Vatican and certain liberation theologians illustrates only one facet of the schisms. There are different groups that exercise particular influence and pull for their positions. I remind the reader that I am evaluating *Latin American* Roman Catholicism and not North American or North European Catholicism. Whatever we say must be guided by Scripture within today's context. Also, it is important to study two dimensions: official Vatican-hierarchy statements in harmony-tension with grassroots Catholicism. In this regard I recommend the study of the World Evangelical Fellowship statement on Roman Catholicism. This document is based on the current official teachings of Rome, not on the particular characteristics of Catholicism in North America or Northern Europe.[16]

First, the old-line conservatives. Some years ago journalist Georgie Anne Geyer interviewed Colombian Cardinal Luis Concha Córdoba, then seventy-six years old. Colombia at that time had been the scenario of conflict between old and young priests.

> Aging, retired, and feeling set aside, the cardinal sat in the quiet and lonely splendor of his red brick mansion and mused over the Church that had been torn apart by the division.
> I asked him whether he had seen many changes in his fifty-two years as a priest—years that had encompassed the Vatican Councils, Pope John and the entire trauma of the revolution in the social doctrine of the Church "No great changes," he answered slowly, his aged hands resting in his lap on the black cassock that had changed little in centuries. "But there has been an improvement in spiritual life. To me it seems that the religious life here is very good. In all the churches of Bogota, there are masses from morning to night. The churches are filled with people. Every day things are better and better."[17]

Clearly not all conservatives in the Catholic church perceive reality in the same way. They lament many changes that have threatened their position of authority. They would harken to the days before Vatican II, with a doctrine closer to the Council of Trent. And amazingly, their day

Cult Explosion in Latin America

seems to be returning even in the last years of this decade. Pope John Paul II has emphasized many doctrines that were cardianl to the conservatives. A chief one is his profound commitment to Mary's place in the life of the churhc. The documents of Puebla reaffirm this very clearly; and Mary even appears to replace the role of the Holy Spirit, for she presides over a new Pentecost. She can replace the work of Christ—the document states that she reigns and intercedes for humans. She is the Queen of the apostles, reigning over all nations. And the pope has made it clear that he has unlimited confidence in her.[18]

Liberation theology. This cultural theology (now in great flux) is an authentic expression that emerges from the underside of history, from the context of poverty and oppression. At the same time it borrows constructs from European theological presuppositions. Many liberationists are radical in their exegesis of the biblical text, preferring to substitute the contemporary context as their authority in matters of faith and praxis. Dr. Núñez deals fully with this issue in his major text on the subject, and surveys it later in this book.[19] Liberation theology is still a challenge to every faith found in Latin America. To Catholicism it says, "We've been here about five hundred years and what have we done that has transformed peoples and eliminated poverty? Precious little! Our option now must be radical and political." Sensitive evangelicals recognize that liberationists have challenged them to search the social implications of a biblical gospel for its politico-social applications to life. Unfortunately, a few keen young evangelicals have been seduced by liberation theology's radical response to transformation—ultimately a dead end when it disregards the Word and the Spirit. Emerging from the effervescence of liberationist thinking comes the *Iglesia Popular,* the "Popular Church." One currently well-known variety is active today in Nicaragua. This movement professes independence from the Nicaraguan Catholic hierarchy (accusing it of abandoning the "people" and compliance with North American interventionism) and commitment both to biblical themes of socio-political revolution and the Sandinista revolution.[20] In other countries this *Iglesia Popular* is seen in the dynamic of the Basic Ecclesiastical Communities.

The biblical movements. As far back as 1979 some evangelicals noted a biblical renewal movement within Catholicism, coming particularly on the heels of Vatican II.[21] It heralded a return to the Scriptures, which for most Catholics means a first-time encounter with the Word of God in their own language. Today we see an amazing openness among Catholics to possess and read the Scriptures with understanding. Many priests and bishops encourage their people to purchase the Bible, even the "Protestant" versions.

This rapidly growing group also provides serious Bible study materials, helping even evangelical seminaries as they stock their libraries. Sadly, evangelical publishers, who take their cue from North American markets, tend to translate and distribute best sellers that have made money in the United States, or more popular, lightweight books. Catholic scholars have dedicated themselves to a study of the Word of God. One word of caution must be expressed about this biblical-theology movement—its weakness in terms of higher criticism regarding the Word. Many Catholic scholars were trained in seminaries and universities that accepted theologically liberal presuppositions. This obviously requires evangelical alertness and discernment.

The charismatic Catholics. The charismatic Catholics in many ways emerge as nonhierarchical, interconfessional, at times preferring to call themselves simply "Christians," "renewed Catholics," or even "evangel-

A View of the Other Spanish Christ

ical Catholics." The Vatican has struggled for some time with this dynamic movement, attempting to control it. On the one hand here are Catholics finally excited about personal Christian faith; but on the other hand many of them dangerously flirt with *Protestantes,* the evangelical "sects." Many Catholics, upon studying the Holy Spirit, are developing a thirst for more Bible study, which leads some to a personal religious crisis: either stay within their mother church or leave it and probably identify as new believers in Christ with the evangelicals. A measured response has been to permit, and even guide, the charismatic experience, teaching Catholics that such spiritual intuition stimulates them to greater devotion to the mother church, its sacraments, and the Blessed Holy Virgin.

Many "renewed Catholics" have opted to remain within their church as a force for biblical change. In 1987 I sat in a Guatemalan restaurant with a friend but could not avoid overhearing the conversation at the next table. Four men were discussing a series of spiritual retreats, seminars, prayer breakfasts, and home Bible studies. At one point they paused to pray for the food and their plans. Wondering who they might be, the question was resolved when they made the sign of the cross and later mentioned something about their priest. Evangelical charismatics tread dangerous ground when they assume that since Catholics and others have had the "same Pentecostal experience" they share the same bases of fellowship and unity in the Spirit established by Scripture.

As evangelicals ponder the future of the Catholic church in Latin America some suggest that the continent may be on the eve of a new Reformation that would transform that church. The near-evangelical tone of many BECs, coupled with Catholic theologians reexamining the biblical nature of the church, mixed together with the various renewal movements—all of these have the potential for structural change. The keys will be historic Reformation themes. What will be the place of scriptural authority and the nature of saving faith? Without regeneration the changes will be stalemated.

Popular Catholicism. Popular Catholicism speaks of a generalized practice of vague spiritual commitments that comes from a religious heritage of Christendom. Behavior is guided by tradition, not conviction. Evangelical Brazilian theologian Key Yuasa offers a Catholic definition of popular religiosity as follows:

> Popular religiosity is the totality of religious convictions and practices, formed by ethnic and social groups in their confrontation with Christianity as the re-

ligion of the dominators. It is an attempt to conserve their identity and existence as a people. They know that in religions and their ritual celebrations they can affirm their way of being human and Christian.[22]

A greater percentage of Latin Americans practice Popular Catholicism. They might find their bases of faith reflected in the Spanish fable *The Faith of the Charcoal Seller*. When asked, "And what do you believe?" The charcoal seller replied, "I believe what the Church believes." Second question: "And what does the Church believe?" His final answer: "Ah, it believes what I believe." In other words, it is a faith devoid of content beyond tradition and emotion. Ignorant of the essence of their faith, Latin American Catholics are Catholics by birth certificate and baptism and are left to practice a folk religion riddled with syncretism, superstition, and spiritism. Notwithstanding the massive outpourings of fervor during Holy Week processions, the essence of faith that saves and works is absent from daily life.

MacKay records the words of that great Spanish writer-philosopher-Christian, Miguel de Unamuno, regarding cultural Christianity, with surprising conclusions.

He identifies the popular faith of the African Moslem and the Spanish Catholic. . . . Their living popular religion is the same as ours. Our peasants believe in God and in the immortality of the soul, in a heaven in which they will take up again their earthly life, only far from misery, and in which there will be fairs and pilgrimages. All that goes beyond this simple creed they simply admit as ornament. And the substance of this faith is the same as the Moors'. Nothing has any value for us except the doctrines we live by; and our people live by no doctrine but this. All the business of the *filioque,* and even of the Trinity, are for the Spaniard nothing but theology, science, that is to say, irony and scepticism, an ethical device to aid mental economy. His aesthetic demands are met by the tragedy of the Passion, which pierces his soul because it is a tragedy. And this tragedy strengthens his faith in immortality, a faith which has a tragic basis.[23]

Ironically, Catholic documents coming from both Medellín and Puebla supported the need to sustain popular religiosity among the masses.

They understood this option to be the only one that would allow millions of nominal "believers" to remain both Latin American and Catholic. But it also gives the people a spiritual sensitivity that allows them to consider a biblical and vital life-changing faith. The Catholic leadership knows this, and is launching itself to re-evangelization methodology.

Nominal Catholicism. Nominal Catholicism is similar to Popular Catholicism but speaks of those who are Catholic simply because they are not evangelical, Jewish, or Muslim. They are Catholics by tradition, by baptism and perhaps by first communion, but without personal commitment even to the externals of the religion. Their culture calls them Catholic, but in fact they are secular. Probably the majority of Latin Americans are nominal in faith, and perhaps only ten percent of the total population practices its faith. Token demonstrations of religiosity at best emerge when required at weddings and funerals. This group represents a serious challenge to Catholic leadership, as well as to evangelicals, who must proclaim a Christ who transform both life and society.

Catholics and Evangelicals in Latin America

When my parents as young missionaries sailed to Costa Rica in 1938 on a banana boat, relationships between Catholics and *Protestantes* were tense. It was the polemical era with battles of ideology and theology and years of hostile persecution. In some countries such as Colombia, evangelicals faced a terrible decade of open persecution from 1948 to 1958. Evangelicals in other lands lived with harassment. When thirty years later my wife and I drove by land to Costa Rica, relationships between the two religious bodies were characterized by a more formal and gracious spirit, which was nevertheless a bit suspicious. Some well-known evangelical leaders—expatriate and national—were lauding the new spirit of Vatican II and its "biblical ecumenism." This euphoria of idealism was not shared by all Christian leaders, some of whom suspected that not all was as rosy as it was painted.

Latin American Catholicism has experienced major changes in the last half-century, changes that have permanently marked the church. W. Dayton Roberts, veteran missionary to Costa Rica, suggests key terms to describe these changes: in the 1940s and 1950s the word was *self-awareness* as the church realized the need for spiritual re-evangelization of the continent; the 1960s were years of awakening *social reform* spearheaded by Vatican II and Medellín; during the last years of that decade *renewal* caught fire, particularly in the charismatic movement, which fostered some interconfessional activities; *liberation* then moved to the forefront. Roberts concludes: "By 1980, however, both the charismatic renewal and the theology of liberation had leveled off. Pope John II was firmly in the saddle, and theological innovation was discouraged."[24] Today veteran evangelical leaders observe a historical reversal of attitudes, with the conservative Catholic hierarchy returning to a polemic stance again.[25] Before Vatican II evangelicals were "sects," then they were warmly described as "separated brethren," and now they are back to "sects" again.[26] The Catholic hierarchy has been encouraged by the current pope—who demonstrates suspicion of evangelicals and seldom refers to them. One clear example comes from Venezuela, where in January 1988 the National Council of Catholic Bishops published its report on evangelicals in the country. They were "sects, aggressive and fanatical." The only Protestant exceptions to this condemnation were the "historical groups": Lutherans, Orthodox, Anglicans, and Armenians. The article is laced with strong accusations against evangelicals: they foment division and confusion among the people; they defame the church and scorn Catholic worship, the Virgin Mary, the saints, and even God; they use the Bible in a simplistic and "fundamentalist" manner; they use fear to win converts by preaching about the last judgment. At the same time, it is recognized that these sects are challenging the church pastorally to strengthen the liturgy and popular religiosity and to encourage a missionary outreach.[27]

Why such an attitudinal change in Latin American Catholicism? Perhaps there are many reasons, but I will mention only a few. For a time it seemed that a select group of Catholic leaders really thought there might be some kind of union between Rome and the evangelicals, or at least with the more liberal Protestants of Latin America. They thought that unity could start with certain cooperative activities. Of course, it would be on Rome's terms. Liberal Protestants *have* merged with liberal Catholics in liberation theology, but both groups have lost biblical moorings and are cast adrift on the sea of the human context. There *are* some examples of grassroots interconfessional cooperation, as seen in the UCELAM (United Group of Roman Catholics and Evangelicals for the Evanglization of Latin America) and in charismatic ecumenism—witnessed particularly in Mexico, Central America, Peru, and Brazil.[28] But any significant unity with Rome is currently impossible, a fact well recognized by Catholics.

Secondly, the pope's attitude toward evangelical growth in Latin America has led his church toward a harder line, calling for a reconversion of former Catholics, calling for national and continental "evangelism crusades," inviting evangelicals to return and embrace the only mother church. Catholic charismatics have been warned that they may have their experience, but they must remain Apostolic and Roman Catholic. Bible study may be encouraged by the church, but always within the framework of Roman theology and affiliation. The lines are drawn much harder now, and this is forcing people to define themselves spiritually.

Thirdly, the change in attitude comes from Pope John Paul II's profound devotion to and veneration of Mary. It is with difficulty that North American Catholics understand Latin American Catholicism. They must remember that Latin American Catholicism did not come from northern Europe. It came from Mediterranean Europe and, hence, is radically different. The Pope's Polish heritage, with Mary the patron saint of his own country, has again injected and reinforced Latin American Catholicism with the worship of Mary. Last year in Central America I saw two evidences of the renewed commitment to Mary. One was a huge billboard along the highway affirming, "Pray to Jesus and the Virgin Mary for

Guatemala," and other posters announcing the celebration of "2,000 years with Jesus and the Virgin." This worship by definition divides evangelicals and Catholics on the ground of authority: either the Scriptures alone, or tradition interpreting the Scriptures.

A Final Statement on Roman Catholicism

Latin America might have been "Christianized" but it is certainly not Christian, a reality Catholics also acknowledge. If the true gospel is to touch and transform people's lives and nations it must come as a movement of the Holy Spirit utilizing the unsheathed Bible. If the Catholic church were to free its members to an open study of the Word, trusting the Holy Spirit to act, the continent could be radically changed. This historic church is experiencing tectonic changes within its own structure, and the original monolith will probably never be restored. Perhaps a holy minority from within the church will appeal to the Word, leading people to a saving faith in the powerful Christ of Resurrection Sunday.

THE EVANGELICALS OF LATIN AMERICA

I was an infant when first taken to our local *Iglesia Centroamericana* in Turrialba, Costa Rica. My parents were pioneer church-planting missionaries in rural areas, and they imbued me with a love for Christ, his church, and Latin America. At one time my folks traded in our milk cow for a horse so Dad could travel into more remote areas. I grew up in evangelical churches in Costa Rica, Nicaragua, and Guatemala. They are part of my fiber, and I thank God for the privilege of being a part of those churches. The highlight of my own missionary career in Guatemala came from the joy of working with a team to plant a church in the capital, a church that continues strong, with a vibrant outreach and singular world-missions commitment. Our three children were baptized in that church. Our memories are warm and powerful. It still is our home church from which *we* were commissioned in 1985 as part of *their* missionary outreach. That congregation is but one of multiplied evangelical churches of all shapes, colors, structures, ecclesiologies, and sizes in Latin America.

But where did these churches come from? Who are the evangelicals? How many churches and believers are there in latin America? What are their characteristics and the challenges they face? What follows is my personal perspective on the evangelicals of Latin America. Many others have written from different perspectives: socio-anthropological, theologically liberal, or biblically conservative.[29] The reader must investigate these sources for a fuller picture, but nothing will put flesh on perspective like years immersed in the life and pulse of these churches within the concrete world of Latin America.

An Historical Overview of the Evangelicals of Latin America

The following survey merely indicates some of the highlights in the development of today's Latin American evangelicals. Facing opposition from state, populace, and Catholic church, all Protestant-evangelicals operated in an uneasy context up until the early 1990s. "The shadow of the Inquisition lay heavy on Latin America: even when the law permitted Protestantism, local public opinion did not, and the Church often pressed persecution long after the legislature had abolished it."[30] Another important note: few historians have given significant importance to the history of Christianity in Latin America, which reflects a particular prejudgment regarding important information of the church in the world.

The first roots and limited fruit. A few major strands intertwine to introduce Protestantism in Latin America. Initiating the arrival of the Protestant faith were various disparate groups during the colonial era. Deiros writes that probably the first was the short-lived Lutheran Welser colony that settled in Venezuela from 1528 to 1546.[31] French Huguenot immigrants, fleeing persecution back home, tried to establish from 1555 to 1567 a Brazilian base from which they could also evangelize the Indians. They were soon forced out. Dutch Protestants attempted a theocratic colony in Brazil from 1624 to 1654 and controlled a significant segment of northern Brazil for about thirty years. They also had the vision of evangelizing the Indians of their areas and, unique to the continent, gave religious freedom to Jews and Roman Catholics. They were driven out by the Roman Catholic Portuguese authorities.

In the latter 1700s Dutch, English, and French groups—led mainly by pirates, some professing Protestantism—took over northern South American territory and settled what became the three Guianas. "It was during this period that the Moravians began missionary work among West Indian slaves; the Congregational and Methodist missionary societies also began in this area and in the Guianas in the early 1800s when the British and Dutch were in control."[32]

A second strand is woven in not so much as a result of colonization by European Protestants, but by their presence in foreign coastal enclaves. Some were sailors in the ports; but most were merchants, for the

British in particular had commercial interests in the Buenos Aires vicinity. Others came for business but decided to remain in the New World. Brazil was the first to sign an agreement with England that allowed Protestant establishments. These Protestant foreign citizens had permission to celebrate worship for themselves, but not to reach out to the nationals. The truth is that few of them were really interested in evangelizing the "locals."

A glorious chapter in the advance of the gospel—leaving permanent though costly fruit—in Latin America was written in blood by the Bible colporteurs, agents of British and American Bible Societies. MacKay writes: "To the British and Foreign Bible Society belongs the honour of having introduced South America to the perennial source of Christian thought and experience. Not with a sword, but with a Book, did the new Christians appear. Between 1804 and 1807 the Bible Society published twenty thousand copies of the New Testament in Portuguese."[33]

The Inquisition had blocked every possible attempt to import Bibles, although some copies of the historica *Biblia del Oso* (the first translation of the Scriptures into Spanish from Hebrew and Greek) slipped through customs agents—the first Bible smuggling of the Americas. Other Bibles came during the early 1800s, when "the American and British Bible societies shipped Bibles to merchants who were living in towns along both sides of the continent."[34]

The Scottish Baptist pastor James Diego Thomson, agent of the British and Foreign Bible Societies as well as of the Lancasterian Educational Society, covered the coasts of western South America and all of Central America with Bibles in his luggage. He landed in Buenos Aires on October 6, 1818; and while his passion was that people come to know Christ, he opened doors for the gospel as an expert of the Lancastrian monitorial education. He was warmly welcomed in Argentina in 1818; and the government appointed him director of a primary school, paying him a salary of 1,000 pesos. Soon he had about one hundred of these schools in operation.[35] His prime text? The Bible. And his impact was felt not only in Argentina, but also in Uruguay, Chile, Peru, and Colombia through his schools. Significantly, in these countries Thomson was invited by the patriots of Spanish-American independence—Bolívar, Miranda, O'Higgins, and San Martín. Although his educational activities were later stymied by Catholic opposition, his Bible distribution projects spread copies of the Scriptures from Argentina to Mexico to the Carribean. He later even served in Spain, and died in England in 1854 after an outstanding career of service to his Lord.

During the 1820s, Luke Matthews traveled in Bolivia as a col-

porteur and was martyred in the Andes in 1831. In 1877 Joseph Mon-
guiardino penetrated the same area and was stoned to death. Francisco
Penzotti (1851–1925) ranks highest among Latin American evangelicals
for his commitment to the distribution of the Word and his evangelistic
zeal. This indefatigable gospel pioneer had emigrated from Italy to Montevideo, where he came to Christ through the reading of the gospel of
John. Originally working with the outreach of his Methodist church,
from 1883 to 1908 he dedicated himself to the broadest promotion of the
Bible. Obstacles were his daily bread. Traveling on foot, mounted, or
sailing, he met harassment and persecution as common events. He was
jailed various times; in Callao, Peru, he spent nine months incarcerated,
convicted for Scripture distribution. In 1892 he chose Guatemala as a
strategic base for northern Latin America, and the last seventeen years of
his life he served as the main agent of the American Bible Society in
Buenos Aires.[36]

The first expatriate missionaries and churches. Before we continue,
it might be wise to pause and ponder some of the factors that made possible the Protestant penetration into the new Latin America republics that
were gradually developing politically. Deiros underscores some of the
key elements: the impact of the French and North American revolutionary philosophers with their emphasis on the "rights of man"; the new
Latin American independence and the elimination of the Inquisition; the
Latin American contact with Protestant nations of England and the United States for commerce and diplomacy; the European immigration designed to develop the new lands; the political liberalism and anticlericalism of some of the highest political leaders; and finally the
linkage between the Spanish crown and Roman Catholicism. All these
contributed to the preparation of the ground for the soon-coming wave of
Protestantism.[37]

Latourette reports that "as early as 1833–1834 an effort was made
by the American Board of Commissioners for Foreign Missions to explore the possibilities for missions to the Indians of Patagonia. . . . Two
men were sent to investigate, but after hearing their report the Board decided not to pursue the project."[38] During the first decades of Protestant
penetration the Europeans led the way, particularly in South America,
where the British especially had commercial concerns. By the mid-
1800s, in spite of opposition, beachheads were established. Capt. Allen
Gardiner and his parties, serving under the Patagonian Missionary Society (later the South American Missionary Society), attempted three
times to pioneer ministries in Patagonia, Bolivia. "At mid-century, as one
of a party of seven, Gardiner landed on the shores of Tierra del Fuego,

but within a few months the whole party died of starvation and exposure."[39] I encourage the reader to appreciate the providence of God at work in SAMS, the Latin American missionary arm of the Church of England. Its renewed commitment to church planting in Latin American countries has resulted in a surge of growth for this Anglican denomination.

In 1845 the second pioneer, David Trumbull, was sent to Chile by the Evangelical Foreign Society. He became the true founder of Spanish work in Chile in 1868. The Anglican Bishop of the Falklands, with jurisdiction throughout South America, W. H. Sterling, covered the republics in an outreach to Indians as well as supervised Anglican chaplaincies that served British expatriates. The major non-Christian target of those early years was the Indian populations, not so much the Spanish- and Portuguese-speaking peoples. Others started first with expatriates, then tentatively moved out into an inevitable ministry to the national populations. Gradually efforts were expended to consolidate these new works. The Scottish physician Robert R. Kelly pioneered in 1855 a work that later became part of the Congregational Union of Churches. Deiros says: "Kelly is the precursor of the evangelizing missionary who attempted to carry the message above all to nationals."[40] The Moravians had initiated missionary work in Central America in 1849. "The period from 1855 onward witnessed the entrance, in rapid succession, of evangelical missionaries and missionary societies in the different Latin American countries."[41]

The Plymouth Brethren assemblies arrived in Argentina in the 1880s. Other denominational churches were established when the flood of European immigrants—many of them Protestants and others nominal believers—reached South America, a case particularly witnessed among the German-Brazilian Lutherans at the turn of the century. These Lutherans later began reaching out to the rest of the Brazilians.

Three North American denominations manifested priority outreach to Latin America: the Presbyterians, Methodists, and Baptists. As best as I can get the dates, here are the years of first arrivals of these three denominations so committed to evangelization and church planting.[42]

The Presbyterians:	Argentina	1823
	Colombia	1856
	Brazil	1859
	Mexico	1871
	Guatemala	1882

The Methodists:	(See next page)

The Methodists:	Brazil	1835
	Argentina	1835
	Uruguay	1835
	Mexico	1872
	Chile	1877
	Bolivia	1901
The Baptists:	Mexico	1870
	Brazil	1881
	Argentina	1881
	Bolivia	1895

We must underscore the fact that some liberal Latin American politicians favored Protestantism for political motives. The Ariases write that,

> particularly the new elite . . . was looking to the Protestant European countries and the United States for new models of "modernization." Latin American intellectuals and anti-clerical freemasons—who stressed freedom over against the backward Catholic clergy's dogmatism—looked to the Anglo-Saxon world as their model and to Protestantism (the religion of freedom and responsibility) as a timely ally against religious and political conservative forces.[43]

Guatemala illustrates the Ariases's point, for in 1882 the Presbyterians began their work at the invitation of liberal president Justo Rufino Barrios, who saw them as an instrument to weaken Catholic hegemony.

The faith missions. Surprising things happened in Latin America at the close of the last century. In 1894 D. L. Moody and Ira Sankey visited Mexico City, speaking to 140 workers at the first General Missionary Conference. Moody also preached the gospel in the Teatro Nacional, a historic first. In 1890 C. I. Scofield and others founded the Central American Mission, with the vision to reach this close but closed "Samaria." That year the first base was opened in Costa Rica by the pioneers Mr. and Mrs. W. W. McConnell, and shortly thereafter outposts were opened in the other Central American republics.[44]

By the end of the last century God was moving in the entire continent, and such is the wealth of information that each country has to write its own evangelical church history. Although in the pioneer years the majority of missionaries had come from Great Britain and the European continent, by 1900 it was the churches of North America—historic and newer denominations, and the faith missions—that were pouring in new personnel. Nevertheless, the historic denominations had now begun to shift their emphasis away from evangelism to education and socio-political concerns. This directly affected the numerical growth of members. The newer agencies filled the vacuum. A significant number of these agencies came right after World War II. Some of them were more specialized in their original charter, such as the Latin America Evangelistic Crusade (later the Latin America Mission) under that indomitable couple Harry and Susan Strachan. The major growth of the faith missions came between 1930 and 1950. However, though their missionary force continued to rise, the number of national evangelical members did not rise accordingly. Explosive growth was to come first from churches with Pentecostal distinctives.

The beginnings of the Pentecostal movement. Historic events for Pentecostals are the Topeka Revival (Topeka, Kansas, 1901) and the Azusa Street Revival (Los Angeles, 1906). Brazilian and Mexican Pentecostals fix Azusa and 1906 as the start of such works in their countries. Pentecostal flames were lighted in Chile about the same time; however, it was a split among the Methodist churches—producing the Methodist Pentecostal Church of Chile—that led to the tremendous Chilean Pentecostal growth. In a short time all Latin American Countries had Pentecostal denominations. Some of them were offshoots of North American groups, but many from the beginning were completely autonomous national movements. Their proliferation and growth—many times as a result of unhappy divisions—is truly astonishing, and later I shall try to evaluate this growth.

The Consolidation of Evangelical Growth: 1900–1930

By the beginning of the present Century most Latin American republics permitted at least partial religious freedom, though harassment and persecution were still a possibility. Brazil experienced in 1905 a special "awakening" of the Lord that produced some twenty years of sustained growth among Presbyterians, Baptists, and Methodists. Argentina in the same year had a similar movement, with special growth among the Plymouth Brethren, Baptists, and the Christian and Missionary Alliance. Bible distribution continued to be the spearhead for evangelism and church planting. Read, Monterroso and Johnson observe:

The years from 1900 to 1916 marked a new kind of growth for the young Churches. These were years of missionary mobility into the interior of the continent despite isolation, poor communications, bad roads, and primitive living conditions. Heavy responsibilities were placed immediately upon willing, able, and enthusiastic converts, encouraging the emergence of national leadership.[45]

The Panama Conference of 1916. The Panama Conference of 1916, an historic event in the life of Latin American evangelicals, came in part as a reaction to the 1909 World Missionary Conference in Edinburgh, when the organizers did not allow representation from Latin American agencies. Why? Because this continent was still considered "Christian" and hence not a mission field. Edinburgh focused only on "pagan" nations. However, some North Americans at Edinburgh decided to have a Latin American Congress and began planning for that occasion. It was held in Panama, "Crossroads of the World," in 1916. "A total of 304 delegates from forty-four mission boards and societies in the United States; one from Canada; two from Jamaica; and three from Great Britain met with 204 auditors in Panama."[46] The Panama Congress is a watershed of Latin American evangelical missiology because of the serious analyses and extensive reports on the nature of evangelical churches in Latin America. The Panama congress reported a total membership of 126,000 in Latin America, up from 50,000 in 1900. However, it was dominated by North Americans, with English the official language, and the agenda carrying items of particular interest to expatriate missionaries.

Post-Panama events. The Congress of Christian Work in South America was held in Montevideo in 1925. At that time half the participants and leaders were Latin Americans, Spanish the official language, and the Congress a true expression of Latin American evangelicalism. The growth of the churches was evident from the report that the number of believers had doubled in number since 1916. Their figures speak of communicant membership, not total Protestant community. The broader community includes nonbaptized believers as well as members of Christian households. These are categories utilized even today when we study the size of churches in Latin America. If we used a ratio of three in the evangelical community to each member the figures would surge as follows:

Year	Communicants	Total Community
1900	?	50,000 (Arias)
1916	126,000	378,000
1925	252,000 (?)	450,000 to 756,000 (?)
	(Deiros: 125,000)	

However, following the Montevideo Congress the focus in some of the Protestant denominations shifted from evangelism and church planting to educational and developmental projects. This significant change gave even more justification to the influx of new faith missions and thousands of North American missionaries with a passion for evangelism.

A number of positive results with continental impact arose from the Panama Congress. One was the decision by denominations and faith missions to operate on the basis of comity agreements whereby they would distribute national territory to avoid duplication and competition. For example, in Argentina the ministry boundaries were drawn up following the railroad lines. In Guatemala the country was divided along both geographical and tribal lines. Comity worked until the Baptists, Pentecostals, and other newer groups arrived after the territorial division had been forged. They never felt bound to those agreements and worked as they wished.

Latin American Evangelical Praise

Formal Christian schooling received great impulse after Panama, including both primary and secondary schools as well as ministerial training institutions. In 1900 it was estimated that seventy-five percent of Latin America was illiterate, and this encouraged evangelicals to found Christian schools that would also reach the more learned classes in Latin America for Christ. Some of those institutions became nationally famous and continue to this day, perhaps not with the same Christian value and philosophy of education. Others gradually became purely secular schools. This project of "indirect evangelism" continued for some thirty years.

The Bible institute movement had profoundly affected North American evangelicals, and most of the newer missionaries were graduates of those schools. Thus they also established Bible institutes all through Latin America—with North American staff, curriculum, and administrative policies. It was but one example of benign importation of cultural structures that later would cause tensions. A serious evangelical vision for university-level theological training would not come until decades later, sadly lagging far behind liberal Protestant seminary training. One singular exception was the *Seminario Biblico Latinoamericanao* in Costa Rica. Founded by the Latin American Mission, it met a great need for years, until more recently as an independent, nationalized institution it separated itself from its historical biblical moorings and moved into a liberationist focus.

Relationships with Catholics. Having already addressed the issue of the relationship between Roman Catholics and evangelicals, I will underscore simply that these were tough years for evangelicals—years of harassment, controversy, and polemics. Aggressive opposition from the Catholic church—hierarchy and grassroots—was common. The Catholic church was "Constantinized," compromised by its political involvement as an "official church." Protestants were people of the Book, a book generally closed to Catholics.

The Continuation of Evangelical Growth: 1930–1950

The evaluation of the period 1930–1950 is mixed. On the one hand new and creative specialized missions emerged, with a particular focus on evangelistic crusades. New and strong national leaders were emerging into positions of responsibility. Many of them were graduates of the Bible institute movement and other leadership training programs. But more of them simply surged ahead spontaneously without much formal biblical training. There was little time for theological reflection. Contextualization was not something to be discussed, simply because the term had not yet been coined. Action was required.

But on the other hand those young churches faced and fought new and tough tensions. One major bone of contention was the issue of the indigenous church, specifically the salary subsidy of pastors and the entire process of what was then called "indigenization." Some missions terminated the salary subsidy rather abruptly as a result of the Great Depression, others tapered it off gradually, and yet others today still pay part or all of their national pastors' salaries. The "three selfs" of self-propagating, self-governing, and self-supporting swirled through the churches.

The indigenization issue—still hot today—rippled through all levels of expatriate-national relationships but basically revolved around the questions: Who controlled the churches? Who controlled the foreign missions and the missionaries? Who controlled the purse strings? Who controlled the institutions? Who controlled the agenda, discussion, and decisions? Some historic denominations solved the issue by withdrawing their personnel, others moved into a "fraternal worker" mode, yet others opted for "separate but equal" coparticipation, some chose merger of church and mission, and still others maintained the foreign dominance.

Nevertheless those churches continued to grow, and by 1936 there were about 2.4 million evangelical *members* in Latin America. "While the population only grew three percent annually, the evangelical membership grew 10 percent, doubling itself every ten years."[47] The faith missions represented about 25 percent of the total North American missionary force in Latin America—5,431 out of 20,970. However, their national church growth entered a period of stagnation. Growth was evident in the Pentecostal groups, and by 1930 the Assemblies of God had thirty thousand members in Brazil alone.[48]

The Explosive Growth: 1950–1988

Phenomenal evangelical growth took place during the period 1950–1988. Read, Monterroso and Johnson have amply documented the information, and by 1967 they estimated a total evangelical membership of 4.9 million. The same formula would give a total evangelical community of 14.7 million, about six percent of the Latin American population.[49] The Ariases report a total community figure for 1973 of twenty million, about seven and on half percent of the total population. Pentecostals accounted for seventy-five percent of the evangelical population. They

Evangelical Population of Latin America

Year	Communicants	Total Community	Percent of Population
1900	?	50,000 (Arias)	
1916	126,000	378,000	
1925	252,000 (?)	756,000 (?)	
1936	2,400,000	7,200,000	
1967	4,915,400	14,746,200	6.0
1973	6,666,666	20,000,000	7.5
1987	11,635,666 (?)	37,432,000	8.8
2000	26,666,666 (?)	80,000,000 (P. Johnstone, est.)	15.0

Evangelicals in Latin America by Country

Country	1988 Population (millions)	Density (persons per square mile)	Evangelicals in 1967 (thousands)	Evangelicals in 1988 (thousands)	Evangelical Percentage of 1988 Population	Number of Missionaries in 1988
Argentina	32.0	30	748.5	1,920	6.0	590
Bolivia	6.9	16	136.2	449	6.5	650
Brazil	144.4	44	9,939.6	23,104	16.0	2,741
Chile	12.6	43	1,315.1	2,722	21.6	440
Colombia	30.6	70	221.7	734	2.4	1,150
Costa Rica	2.9	148	42.6	464	16.0	330
Cuba	10.4	242	—	260	2.5	6
Dominican Republic	6.9	365	—	324	4.7	190
Ecuador	10.2	93	37.8	326	3.2	822
El Salvador	5.4	652	107.4	691	12.8	43
Guatemala	8.7	206	231.6	2,175	25.0	457
Honduras	4.8	111	56.4	528	11.0	405
Mexico	83.5	110	1,289.7	2,589	3.1	1,700
Nicaragua	3.6	72	59.4	450	12.5	60
Panama	2.3	78	112.5	276	12.0	210
Paraguay	4.4	28	45.6	110	2.5	235
Peru	21.3	43	185.7	639	3.0	890
Uruguay	3.0	44	65.4	57	1.9	115
Venezuela	18.8	53	46.9	545	2.9	510
Totals	403.9	48	14,735.9	37,432	8.8	11,544

were exploding in numbers. The Ariases suggest a cluster of reasons for the Pentecostal growth: spiritual facts—the free action of the Spirit; anthropological reasons—hunger for God; sociological elements—they provided a sure sense of shelter, security, identity, and community in the hostile world; pastoral methodology—lay participation; psychological and cultural factions—freedom of worship and emotion, use of folk music and instruments.

> The fact is that they are large, self-supporting, self-governed and self-multiplying churches, rooted among the poor masses, while the historical Protestant churches are confined to middle-class enclaves. Pentecostals do not lack problems of leadership, education, division and social alienation, but there is no doubt that they have a significant place in the future of Christianity in Latin America.[50]

There are notable Pentecostal shortcomings, some of which they themselves acknowledge: a serious lack of trained leadership, the problem of numerical growth without biblical teaching and discipleship, the tendency to center power in authoritarian leaders, artificial spirituality, lively but routine liturgy, and a spirit of legalism in the Christian life.

What happened to the churches that came out of the faith missions? Some of them just stopped growing, and the reasons are varied but very sobering. Others have held their own, and yet others have experienced notable growth, an example being the *Iglesias Centroamericanas* of Guatemala, historically related to the CAM International ministries, and currently one of the largest denominations in that land. Why are some of these non-charismatic churches growing at a clip equal to the Pentecostals? Probably because they are aggressively moving out in evangelism and church planting, a ministry led almost entirely by nationals themselves.

During this period the continent witnessed a tremendous proliferation of evangelical groups, and by 1988 just in Guatemala alone there were more than one hundred ten different denominations for some eight thousand churches. Ecuador, with a much smaller evangelical population, had forty-seven denominations and church groups for only sixteen hundred local churches and congregations.[51] The specialized missions grew, with a particular emphasis on radio—the most famous being HCJB—Christian bookstores, missionary aviation, and other ministries. How many evangelicals are there now? For a numerical review, let us bring together the figures previously given, remembering that the statistics vary in reliability; I have thus simply combined the sources and tried to harmonize them.[52] Only God really knows how many there are, and I doubt that the exact figure is as important to him as it tends to be for us. (Read my update chapter for recent numbers.)

Exact figures on evangelical churches for all the countries of Latin America do not exist yet. My data comes from various sources: Read, Monterroso and Johnson; Patrick Johnstone; the *Atlas de COMIBAM*; and my own information, with percentages and figures updated according to the *1988 World Population Data Sheet* of the Population Reference Bureau. All statistics are estimates, up to twenty percent low or twenty percent high. The total ranges from thirty-seven to forty-five million. I prefer to err on the side of conservative figures.

A Personal Perspective of the Evangelicals of Latin America

This final section reflects my personal evaluation, resulting from my own experience and reflection. The reader must seek other sources—written and living—to complete the picture. But before we get into the major points, a few items must be clarified. The terms *Protestant* and *evangelical* must be defined. Latin American *Evangélicos* want to be called just that, a cordial term that speaks of their commitment to the Bible, Christ, and the good news of personal salvation by faith alone. *Protestant* is a broader religious category to describe the Reformation branch of Christianity. Catholics and much of the secular press will use either *Protestante* or even *sectas* to refer to the evangelicals. This is because they use terms and categories coming from the sociology of religion.

In the United States there is a clearer demarcation between Protestant and evangelical, the latter referring to those who affirm the inspiration and authority of the Bible and hold to a personal, saving experience with Christ. The former term speaks more of the historic mainline denominations that may or may not be biblically conservative in theology. The overwhelming majority of non-Catholic Christians in Latin America are evangelical. Patrick Johnstone states that 10.2 percent of Latin America is Protestant and 9.1 percent is evangelical. (The COMIBAM data drop the total to 8.8 percent). That means that 1.1 percent would be less conservative doctrinally, belonging primarily to the historic mainline denominations that have lost biblical moorings even in Latin America. We run the risk of nominal Protestantism in Latin America already.

Also, Latin American evangelicals must be understood in terms of their particular continental history. Anglo-Saxon Christians tend to impute their own particular historico-cultural religious experience to Latin Americans.

This is inadequate and wrong. Therefore the expatriate must come to a comprehension of Latin American history and culture in order fully to appreciate what God is doing there. And now let me give my evaluation of the evangelical church in Latin America.

First: Rapid numerical growth. The statistics are clear; and although we can quibble over the figures, the record demonstrates unprecedented evangelical growth.[53] About seventy-five percent of these evangelicals are Pentecostals. While the general population grows at an annual rate of 2.2 percent, evangelicals grow at a rate at least twice that clip and in some countries three times as fast. This truly is a movement of the Spirit of God, and we rejoice in it. It is also growth with few financial resources, mostly lay participation, relatively few paid pastors, and the generally scarce formal preparation of those pastors.

Growth rates vary from country to country, with some more resistant to the gospel, such as Paraguay, Uruguay, and Venezuela. On the other hand the Central American republics, Chile, and Brazil enjoy phenomenal growth—enough to alert politicians to a new bloc and disturb the Catholic hierarchy. Johnstone notes that "there are, in fact, more evangelical Christians in Brazil than in the whole of Europe, excluding the USSR!"[54] Brazilian evangelicals now outnumber practicing Roman Catholics according to Johnstone—twenty-two million to seventeen million. Significantly, when the Latin American nations produce a population census they no longer include the religion factor. Although official statements play up the "objective and secular" reasons, the fact is that Catholic leadership is fearful of such religious information becoming public news.

Just about every European and North American strand of Protestant church can be found in Latin America, as well as uncounted autochthonous varieties. North Americans are accused of exporting their Yankee individualism and ecclesiastical-theological splinters to Latin America. But that is only part of the story. The fact is that fierce Latin American individualistic nationalism does not subject itself to any kind of united evangelical movement, either foreign or local.

A recent and disturbing phenomenon in Latin America merits careful study: the television blitz of made-in-the-USA programs dubbed into Spanish. Whether it is the Spanish PTL, 700 Club, or Jimmy Swaggart (whose moral collapse disillusioned so many Latin Americans), with far-reaching implications as to the authenticity of the evangelical gospel proclamation, there is now an electronic and foreign church, geared to media standards. Unfortunately it projects in many cases a message that combines and confuses the gospel with anti-communistic capitalism— the American Way of Christian Prosperity. This has given the secular and Catholic press ammunition to charge that evangelical growth in Latin America is simply the result of millions of imported dollars and high television budgets. The accusation is largely false, but does Latin America really need this high-budget, high-tech methodology? Most sensitive evangelical leaders seriously question this, while at the same time recognizing that programs like Swaggart's have penetrated all levels of society, and in some countries captured seventy percent of the television audience.[55]

Historically most of the growth has taken place among the lower classes of Latin America. These churches are proletarian, they *are* the poor and disinherited masses who have received much: identity as children of the King, personal transformation and victory over sin, and title to a heavenly mansion.

But in recent years the gospel has begun to penetrate the middle classes of Latin America, and second- to third-generation evangelicals have experienced their own upward social mobility. Some members of the most powerful classes are coming to Christ. Luis Palau, Argentine-born evangelist with a global ministry, has seen doors open to the highest elites of Latin America through his television call-in programs. Unfortunately, most local churches have not been able to integrate and conserve the fruits of such a ministry. Palau's crusades in general have been instruments to bring evangelicals together for mass events, with varied impact in local church growth.

Today again some churches are experiencing harassment, persecution, and even martyrdom. Costa Rican evangelicals face a hostile press and Catholic leadership, with indirect legal pressures and visa controls on new missionaries. Other countries multiply the red tape for missionary visas. Mexico has been the scene for violent persecution of believers in small towns; and bombs have exploded in the Summer Institute of Linguistics' (SIL) Mexico City center. The Mexican press has sustained a tremendous barrage against the SIL work in the country. In Peru, El Salvador, Nicaragua, and Guatemala evangelicals suffer as they are caught in the crossfires between subversives and government troops. In Venezuela the New Tribes Mission continues to face hostile opposition from a coalition of opponents.

One of the most amazing current stories of evangelical growth comes from Argentina, a nation proud of its "Europeanness," exuding superiority over its neighbors. With one of the highest literacy rates—matched by one of the highest inflation rates—Argentinians have also been proud of their secularism and along with Uruguay have had the highest percentage of agnostics and atheists. It has been hard territory for the gospel. But disillusionment hit the nation from a variety of sources: the humiliating defeat in the Malvinas ("Falklands" to the English-speaking worlds); the subsequent popular rejection of the disgraced military regime in which a democratic election put progressive Raul Alfonsín into the presidency; the unprecedented trials that convicted and jailed former heads of state; the ongoing economic crises; the hunger for some kind of permanent message of hope. All these contributed to an historic movement of the Spirit—a story amply documented in other sources.[56]

Significantly, the growth is coming on multiple fronts, with churches of many denominations growing. "I would say the church has grown more in the last two years than in the last twenty," says one Pentecostal leader whose churches are growing at forty percent a year. Other groups report an annual growth rate of about fifteen percent. The Argentinian revival is not without its critics, who are concerned over theology (the validity of supernatural manifestations) and practical issues (the desperate shortage of equipped leaders to handle the growth). Yet tougher opposition comes from the secular and Catholic press which attacks evangelicals as "Reagan's sects." The false cults are also exploiting the situation, particularly the Mormons (who are planning to send twenty thousand young missionaries) and the Jehovah's Witnesses. Spiritism imported from Brazil also flourishes in the climate of spiritual hunger and personal emptiness.

Yet the story of Latin American church growth must be scrutinized. Years ago I spoke with Ecuadorian evangelical theologian and author René Padilla about these stories of growth. He said, "Ah, Guillermo, we must ask our church-growth friends two questions: What is church? What is growth?" In other words, mere numerical growth is not sufficient to measure the biblical church. Latin American church growth fascinates the number-hunters of North America who see size as the prime measure of growth. Some emphasize the need only for homogeneous churches, but the reality of Latin America is that sociological and anthropological categories cannot become our guidelines. Many churches are large, but they are perhaps obese, not healthy. As one church leader told me this year, "We have more births than midwives in our country."

Numerical growth has far outstripped the capacity to minister to the babes in Christ. Other questions must be asked: What is repentance?

What is true conversion? What is the security of the believer that frees him or her from Protestant legalism or the constant fear of losing salvation? Where is the internal transformation that produces authentic external changes of private and public values and behavior? What is biblical discipleship?

And these tough questions lead us to a second characteristic. Sadly, many evangelical churches and denominations are so institutionalized that they cannot minister effectively. They are stagnant internally, leadership is not renewed as *caudillos* solidify their power base; youth are slipping out the side door; and services are routine, predictable, and lethargic. Ongoing spiritual complacency will bear tragic fruit in successive generations of nominal, cultural evangelicals. Too many theological institutions are producing young graduates unable to minister in humility, with inadequate pastoral gifts, and without leadership skills. Some Latin church leaders reflect a subtle dependency upon the Anglo-Saxon leaders, funds, and ideas.

Second: Evangelicals love the Bible but are biblically illiterate. Evangelicals are known as people of the "Book," or actually two books: on Sunday you can identify the evangelicals on the streets because they are carrying their precious Bible and hymnbook. Their love for God's Word is seen in the names they give their own local congregations—a delightful variety of biblical names, geographical places, and even theological concepts. Yes, they love the Word of God, but they have a superficial working knowledge of it. Hence there is a poor integration of biblical truth to the problems of life. Some Pentecostal groups reject even books that would aid Bible study. A theologican friend of mine was leading a workshop on Bible study and exposition. When he asked the class to use the New Testament commentary in an assignment, one woman, a university professor, vehemently objected: "These human writings aren't inspired by the Spirit! All we need is the Bible and the Holy Spirit."

A number of acute evangelical observers are deeply troubled with the lack of internalization of biblical values. Secular "virtues" such as *machismo,* the sexual double standard for men, dangerously characterize too many believers.[57] On one occasion I had spoken on the Christian concept of sex to a large youth group in an evangelical church. Afterward I chatted with the president of the group. "Memo," I asked, "how many of the guys in this group have had premarital sex?" He laughed and said, "Oh, perhaps ninety percent!" Was he exaggerating or speaking the truth? A similar cavalier attitude condones too much cheating and general lying. On one trip I made from the United States to Central America a local church leader asked me to bring him a TV, and he "would take care of the customs agent." One delegate to a continental evangelical congress returned to his country loaded with undeclared items, tried to slip them through customs, was caught and jailed.

Some would call these items superficial, but they point to underlying problems—a lack of dynamic and systematic teaching of the Word of God contextualized and applied to daily lives. Serious questions emerge about evangelical attitudes in times of crisis. If people come from an animistic or spiritist background before conversion, and after this new relationship find themselves facing a major crisis, do they return to the spirit world for help? Studies need to be made for Latin America like those that have been done in Africa.[58] But the growing evidence from Latin America is disquieting in this area of spiritual warfare.

Doctrinal distinctives in Latin America do not always carry the same degree of importance that they do for North Americans—a fact that causes conflict between Christian leaders of the two areas. Church members tend to minimize some of the theological variants, calling them irrelevant. This may be true, but a more dangerous problem lies underneath—the ignorance of even basic doctrines. One Dominican student of mine at the Central American Theological Seminary in Guatemala City wrote her thesis comparing doctrinal convictions among Presbyterians, *Centroamericanos,* and Pentecostals. Of particular interest to her was the doctrine of eternal security—firmly taught in the first two churches but not in the latter. The results surprised her: even the official teaching differed, individuals in all three groups defended the *insecurity* of the believer.

Yet another disturbing element is seen in the evangelical upward social mobility. Most of the evangelicals have come to Christ from the lower socio-economic sectors. Their commitment to Christ and the power of the Spirit has given them victory over past vices—primarily women and alcohol—which has in turn freed up money and motivation to serve family needs, to work harder, to plan for the future, to assure a higher education for their kids. And when they "arrive" in the lower middle class, do they remember their lower roots? No, and this does not seem to bother them. It is a characteristic of the secular society that has permeated the evangelical mindset regarding society's needs.

Who is responsible for the lack of biblical teaching among Latin American evangelicals? All who have exercised leadership: pioneer missionaries whose emphasis was solely evangelistic, current expatriate and national leaders who evade serious Bible study and teaching, theological institutions that produced leaders unprepared to meet the deeper needs of the churches, and Christian publishers who push translated best-sellers.

And beyond lies the cultural heritage: five centuries of a superficial religion, a Latin American mindset that concerns itself with the existential *now,* an emotional penchant that minimizes the intellectual discipline of biblical study. Although the emphasis on numerical church growth is fine, more enthusiasm should be placed on internal church growth—Christian maturity within the context of Latin America. It will become even more acute with the historical development of third-, fourth-, and fifth-generation evangelicals. Will the original fires stay hot, or will the passage of time produce generations of cultural evangelicals similar in value and life-style to the cultural Catholics?

Third: A critical shortage of biblically trained leaders. There is a critical shortage of biblically trained leaders. By this I do not necessarily mean graduates of formal or nonformal institutions, residence or extension. I mean men and women who know the Scriptures thoroughly, who know how to teach the Bible and apply it wisely in their own historico-cultural context. My observation is that church leaders in Latin America emerge from two major sources: the formally trained ones (Bible institute, seminary, university, or a combination) and the self-taught ones (who "surge" into positions of leadership and power). Some of the latter may have studies in a nonformal theological program.

Many times the self-taught leaders are godly individuals with attractive personalities; but all too often their knowledge of the Word is shallow. On the other hand formal theological training runs the risk of domesticating gifted believers, narrowing their vision, and communicating to them that leadership must be accompanied by all the formal trappings of the ministry. The fact is that Latin American evangelicals desperately need committed, creative, passionate, and biblically trained leaders. Some years ago there were many highly trained but theologically liberal Protestant leaders who had an international platform. Their crisis was simple: they had few people listening within the ranks. On the other hand, the masses of believers were evangelicals, but without qualified leaders. This led Antonio Núñez to say to me once that liberals are "generals without an army," and conservatives are an "army without generals."

In the providence of God this picture is changing, manifested by a number of international forums for evangelical Latin leaders. One is the Latin Americal Theological Fraternity (FTL), a broadly-based fellowship, founded in 1970 and composed of a select group of men and women who share a commitment to the Word applied in the Latin American context.[59] This Latin voice many times makes North American evangelicals most uncomfortable, primarily because the Latins are courageous enough to speak out on prickly issues, including church and society, and relationships between the United States and Latin America. Some of the better-known names are Pedro Arana (Peru); Orlando Costas (Puerto Rico), who died in November 1987; Samuel Escobar (Peru); Rolando Gutiérrez (Nicaragua and Mexico); Emilio Antonio Núñez (El Salvador and Guatemala); and René Padilla (Ecuador and Argentina). These men represent the older generation of evangelical thinkers and writers, and now we must pray for the younger leaders who will receive the torch.

One of the FTL's major contributions has been in the publication of the papers from theological conferences. One of the most recent books, edited by Pablo Alberto Deiros, *Los Evangélicos y el Poder Político en América Latina (Evangelicals and Political Power in Latin America)*, is published by Eerdman's Spanish division, *Nueva Creación*. It is the result of an FTL consultation held in the Dominican Republic to study political power from the perspective of both social sciences and Scripture, and it offers a major treatise designed to guide the Christian social conscience of evangelicals as they play an increasingly larger role in their national societies. Another book, edited by C. René Padilla and published by Nueva Creación, deals with theological education themes, *Nuevas Alternativas de Educación Teológica (New Theological Education Alternatives)*.

But the FTL is not charged alone to engender a new generation of gifted Latin expositors of the Word, a generation of men and women with vision and authentic Latin pride capable of bringing the church to maturity. The Bible institute movement (generally on a high school level or lower) in Latin America produced an effective generation for its time, but the times are changing. The evangelical seminaries of Latin America (generally on a college level, with a few giving the equivalent of an M.A. in theology, the "licenciatura") that sustain high academic standards are relatively small in size. More seminaries must study the model of renewal and transformation of the Central American Theological Seminary in Guatemala City. It has broadened its programs to meet the needs of a changing church and society, albeit with a very specific non-charismatic and relatively separatistic stance. From a school that primarily offered a residence program, it now offers seven different ministry-training programs, with a total 1989 enrollment of 835 students.

But too many of these institutions operate on specific and limited theological platforms. Either they are non-Pentecostal and hence close their doors to the seventy-five percent of evangelicals, or they promote Pentecostal distinctives to the point that the non-Pentecostal does not feel comfortable. These centers carry out their ministries largely unrelated to each other unless there are denominational ties, and even then the relationships can be tenuous. With the exception of Caribbean Evangelical Theological Association and the recent Brazilian one, AETTE, most of these institutions remain independent of a global association such as the International Council for Accrediting Agencies (ICAA) of the World Evangelical Fellowship. Spanish America has two non-ICAA analogous bodies, ALIET in the northern area and ASIT in the Southern Cone; but these have not coalesced on the continental evangelical level as movements to stimulate renewal, contextualization, and accreditation.

Another problem is that too many theological institutions continue to operate on a purely North American model that has not come to grips with contextualization issues in Latin America. There is a desperate need for Latins who have studies matters deeply—both theological and secular—in order to apply the Word of God in its fullness to Latin America. They will be able to produce a contextualized theology and ecclesiology that are both biblical and Latin. They will be the writers whose books will forge values (and one hopes the North American-based publishers will print and distribute these books, not merely translate into Spanish works that do not scratch where Latins itch). They will be the leaders of the next generation of Latin American evangelicals.

I am greatly encouraged by a newer phenomenon in Latin American evangelicals; young university graduates committed to Christ and his church who are seeking the highest quality biblical training for ministry. Most will do their biblio-theological studies within their own cultures, a very few will travel to North America, Europe or Asia. Yet others will become self-trained leaders. If they study outside of Latin America, pray that their financial aid will come from evangelical sources and not from organizations that would undermine their biblical foundations. Here I see tremendous need for substantial scholarship programs from the North that will stimulate progressive contextualization, as well as pastoral care that enables Latin students to keep their return-home-target after graduation.

These men and women offer unusual gifts, leadership and administrative skills, depth of perception and study, pastoral passion, and psychological abilities. They should enable the churches to enter the next century, meeting the challenges of wholistic church growth. They also are the keys to reaching the upper class, the university worlds, the intellectuals, the Marxists, and the secular humanists. A good number may become cross-cultural missionaries. But I wonder if North Americans and Europeans are capable of working in full partnership with this creative new generation of leaders who do not feel inferior to or threatened by their Anglo-Saxon counterparts.

Fourth: A need to express Latin evangelical unity in Christ. Protestant ecumenism is not new to Latin America, as the 1916 Panama Congress demonstrated. Over the years the more ecumenical and liberal sector of Protestantism has developed its own organizations and relationships. Most of them would find representation in CLAI (*Consejo Latinoamericano de Iglesias,* the Latin American Council of Churches), which was established in Mexico in 1978. But in the 1960s three bodies came into being. The first was ISAL (*Isglesia y Sociedad en América Latina,* Church and Society in Latin America), which was born with an ecumenical and interconfessional commitment to liberation theology. The other groups are CELADEC (*Comision Evangélica Latinoamericana de Educación Cristiana,* the Latin American Christian Education Evangelical Commission), and UNELAM (*Unidad Evangélica en América Latina,* Latin American Evangelical Unity).

But now evangelicals are beginning to express the desire for a more biblical expression of their unity in Christ. Often I have heard it said: "We evangelicals must stand united." But the fact is that the Spanish proverb is right: *"Cada Cuál jala agua para su propio molina"* ("Each one carries water to his own mill"). That is, the calls for unity are there, but each one wants it on his terms. This is the result in part of the extreme Latin spirit of independence. One Costa Rican educator told me, "Our educational system has taught us that 'I have my own rights,' and *that* makes it so difficult for us to get along with each other on a broader base." Ironically it is when the entire community of churches faces a united outside enemy that the churches bond together. This has been experienced recently in a number of countries.

Hopefully, two evangelical associations of recent vintage are providing some expression of evangelical unity, though neither one enjoys full support. The first organization is CONELA (Confraternity of Evangelicals of Latin America), founded in 1982 with a more ecclesiastical vision than the FTL. Conceived in the format of both the World Evangelical Fellowship and the Lausanne movement, it adopted the Lausanne Covenant as its doctrinal statement. In its first years CONELA was characterized by some as an extension of the promoters of evangelistic crusades and hence did not enjoy a broad reception. Lately, however, large and small church bodies of all theological stripes—Pentecostal and non-Pentecostal—as well as many other institutions, have become members. CONELA, in time and with godly, respected leadership, has the potential of becoming a viable voice for Latin American evangelicals.

A specifically focused movement that in its recent history enjoyed even a broader though temporary reception among evangelicals was CO-MIBAM (The Congress of Iberoamerican Missions), established in Mexico in late 1984.[60] Initially led by Argentine Luis Bush, COMIBAM's first meeting was called under the auspices of CONELA, but the movement rapidly extended its arms to take in the widest representation in Latin America. While the original COMIBAM spoke of the Sao Paulo Congress held in November 1987, the ongoing vision is the *Comission* of Iberoamerican Missions which will further the cross-cultural missionary vision sweeping through the continent. It is also responsible for producing the most significant body of cross-cultural missionary literature for the churches ever seen yet. Although COMIBAM is not an ecclesiastical body designed to bring evangelicals together in Latin America, nevertheless it has served the church of Christ in bringing together for a common cause groups and individuals that would not have cooperated in other programs. COMIBAM's missiology must develop and strengthen into a more holistic and contextualized mission of the church if it wants to avoid the charge of shallow theology and activism.

Fifth: Historically weak in social conscience, but now changing. At best evangelicals have been apolitical, and most of them harbor a deep suspicion of Latin American politics—well deserved—that causes them to be against involvement in this dimension of local and national life. They have not been so concerned with life on this planet; and that is understandable if we remember the socio-economic strata from which most of these believers have come—the lower ranks. What political options did they have in a semi-feudal world? Jesus provided the answer with eternal salvation, and praise God for this message! The hymnbooks are laced with songs that speak of the glorious future, and most speak only of spiritual responsibilities on earth coupled with celestial promises. Why have evangelicals been so unconcerned about their social responsibility, demonstrating little commitment to the poor? Steve Sywulka explains part of the reason in *Transformation:*

> Evangelicals have been "base" and abased from the beginning. They have been historically, and vast numbers still are, the poor and powerless, the alienated and marginalized.
>
> One could say that evangelicals don't get excited about a "preference for the poor": they *are* the poor. Nevertheless, there is an obvious and visible danger that as evangelicals move up the scale and get into the middle-class structures, they forget their roots.[61]

Evangelicals have generally preferred the more conservative political options, most often voting—if they vote at all—for the rightist, law-and-order candidates, many of them military officers. Evangelicals tend to operate more comfortably in right-wing regimes, even dictatorships. When Castro took power in 1959 a majority of Christian leaders fled the island, leaving the evangelicals bereft of trained shepherds. Nicaraguan evangelicals did not ommit the same mistake, and most came to terms with the ongoing revolutionary process—even though for many their personal political preference was not Sandinista.

Yet evangelicals are slow and inexorably changing in terms of social conscience. This results from a combination of reasons. In the first place, the newer Catholic "preferential option for the poor" combined with the Base Ecclesial Communities and liberation theology has affected many evangelical circles. Secondly, evangelicals, led primarily by the FTL, have come to a newer understanding of their biblical duties as citizens, even under hopeless conditions. These studies and recommendations for action come as a crucially needed response to the passionate challenges of a liberation theology, which challenges diregard biblical authority. Evangelicals must counter with biblical teaching on poverty and society that does not capitulate to a noncritical acceptance of any particular ideology or economic system. This means a critique of Marxism, socialism, and capitalism.

The rising number of evangelical university students and graduates has called for a more reasoned study of the Word as it applies to concrete human issues. In some countries a vanguard of young and restless evangelical thinkers is emerging, independent of older leaders and very critical of United States policies and Latin evangelical conservatism. Not incidentally, in a number of countries—such as Peru, Bolivia, Dominican Republic, El Salvador, and Guatemala—evangelicals have opened their own Christian universities. However, this does not mean that they function with a fully Christian philosophy of education that affects the total life and ethos of the school—objectives, board, faculty, students, curriculum, and pedagogical emphases that relate all truth to a Christian worldview.

Whether evangelicals like it or not they are targets for political manipulation. A case in point is Chile where the Marxist Allende captured overwhelming support from evangelicals. Why? Because he offered them something, an escape from grinding poverty. And many of those same leaders later expressed support for Pinochet. Rightist dictators and totalitarian military leaders have courted support by questionable means. I personally know one Central American pastor who was asked by the

Evangelical Brothers and Sisters on the Underside

A Sample from 250,000 Church Signs

Proclaiming the Gospel by All Means

Hope for the Future--Emerging Latin Evangelical Leaders

government if his church would appreciate cement and other building materials to finish off the educational unit for a new Christian school. Believers in Latin America must stay alert lest similar manipulation neutralize their voice.

Finally, the course of history is forcing evangelicals to participate in the political process. In a number of countries evangelicals have run for local, regional, and national offices. In Guatemala during the 1985 presidential election the candidate registering a respectable third place was an evangelical engineer, the most competent and honest of that lot. He awaits his turn for the next national campaign. Venezuela has a similar situation. Others across the continent are already running for political office; and as the evangelical population grows, its political clout will also increase. One danger I see is the rise of evangelical political parties. They are unfortunate and ultimately self-defeating because their base is so limited, and they are polarizing the body politic into religious adversaries we do not need in Latin America. Probably the best option is for gifted evangelicals to enter established parties that stand for justice and liberty and which have a chance of winning elections. This requires a high level of pastoral care. In 1988 thirty-four of the five hundred congressmen in Brazil and ten percent of the members of the Guatemalan congress were evangelical, but few had adequate pastoral care or saw their task with a solid biblical foundation for social participation.

From March 1982 through August 1983, Guatemalans experienced a unique moment in history—the "presidential" leadership of General José Efraín Rios Montt. That period also forced evangelicals to come to grips wtih the biblical basis of political participation, a process that continues to the present. As far as I can tell, very little serious evaluation of that period has been made, although authors have argued in favor and against Rios Montt's person and administration. I am not the best analyst of this period but believe that some observations must be made.

Guatemala was experiencing a desperate time of violence, corruption, and spiritual darkness. The powers of the Evil One were unleashed, and the disintegration of the nation's social fiber was evident by fear, death, and general hopelessness. The corrupt military was losing battles on the international scene, to say nothing about the internal crises in the battles against the growing Marxist movements. Junior officers, one whom I met and spoke with at length, led the surprising coup that brought about the changes, including the blow to army hierarchy. When those junior officers called on the radio for Rios Montt to take the leadership, they did not know about Rios Montt's conversion to Christ. They had known him during this period as director of the military academy and respected his high moral leadership. They also remembered that in 1972 Rios Montt had run on the Christian Democratic presidential ticket and was well known in the country as a man with convictions.

When Rios Montt, whom I know personally, took over he surprised everybody on that first evening television appearance. And he launched the nation into unique history. How should we evaluate him and his administration? Here are some observations made by thoughtful Guatemalan Christian leaders.

- Rios Montt was a good general but not the best politician. He gave orders, but the nation could not work by military rules. He offended some people who deserved to be attacked, but gradually he alienated all the national power blocs—the media, civil servants, chambers of industry, agriculture, and commerce, international powers, the U.S. State Department (for his positive neutrality on Nicaragua), and the Catholic church (although his brother is a bishop).
- He was well advised by some; but others did not counsel him wisely; and he himself made wrong decisions.
- While he wanted Christian counselors, he made the mistake of moving two other pastor-elders of his church into the presidential palace as prime leaders. Evangelicals would not like a Catholic president to bring two priests into the palace and appoint them to high positions.
- Evangelicals in the United States made mistakes by visiting Guatemala and then making too many public pronouncements for personal gain and publicity.
- His spiritual shepherds developed a theonomic structure to guide Rios Montt, the "Nehemiah" of Guatemala, confusing Old Testament practice with universal principles for a pluralistic society.
- Rios Montt restructured the army internally and for the battle against the subversives—both of the right and particularly of the left. In the war, thousands of people died, too many innocently. But it is wrong to accuse him of genocide.
- Unfortunately he did not try in the courts military officers whose guilt was unquestioned.
- His personal morality was untouched by corruption, and even his enemies do not attempt to accuse him in this area.
- He is one of the very few former Latin American heads of state who today calmly drives his own car and walks the streets. The vast majority have become rich through corruption and do not dare live as Rios Montt does.
- He set a high ethical standard for political office that has not been

matched in Guatemala, a fact acknowledged more and more today in that country.

• Although some dispute this, he truly set in motion the process that led to the democratically elected government ruling today.

• His seventeen-month rule gave invaluable political lessons for evangelicals in all Latin America.

Rios Montt, a true believer and brother in Christ, a rather quixotic and at times unpredictable individual, also serves his church as a pastor-elder. The last time I saw him was in a Christian bookstore, purchasing materials for the church leadership program he was directing.

Another example of evangelicals involved in the search for reconciliation, peace, and justice is the Peruvian organization "Peace and Hope." An outreach of the National Evangelical Council of Peru, it has national support from evangelicals as well as respect by the government. The organization emerged after believers were caught in the brutal crossfires between army and Shining Light guerillas. Christians have been killed by guerillas and by the army, and gripping fear paralyzed the emergency zones. Peace and Hope met the needs of the Christian population through every possible means, including relief, developmental projects, and the resettlement of refugees into lands that can be cultivated in peace. It also provided legal representation before the authorities to assure evangelicals of their just rights as citizens.[62]

Sixth: A move toward contextualization. The need in Latin America is for evangelicals to establish their own identity as a Latin body, cognizant of their own multiracial, cultural, and spiritual heritage. And this heritage must be expressed in evangelism, worship, music, leadership styles, decision-making processes, administrative policies, architecture, and ultimate authority over the church. This will not come quickly or easily, but it is coming. Part of the lack of contextualization comes from the foreign influence—the missionary and the general cultural invasion from abroad. But national leaders are also at fault, particularly those who find it comfortable to operate with the foreign models or who are even "more North American than the North Americans" themselves. This may be in part the result of the Latin sense of inferiority about things Latin and the excessive admiration for things foreign. This North Americanization also happens because of a fear of losing employment in evangelical ministries with North American funds.

Commitment must arise for a creative breakthrough on the part of national evangelical leaders to pursue the ongoing task of contextualization—that dynamic process by which the Scriptures are released in a culture in order to have maximum impact and expression within that culture.[63]

Much has been said about the Pentecostal freedom of worship as a contextualized use of Latin emotions. This is probably true, and unfortunately some very conservative Latin and expatriate missionaries confuse liturgical expression with theological conviction. Clapping or lifting the hands is not theology. It manifests praise and worship if done in the Spirit. Clearly there can be false and wrong motivated emotionalism; not every song lends itself to the same purpose; there are times to be quiet before God; church services should respect the rights of the neighborhood; not everything that is called worship is really worship. Nevertheless, even non-Pentecostal churches are being freed up to new and warm manifestations of worship. And all the churches need both solid biblical exposition and uplifting praise that reflect Latin America's cultural and spiritual mosaic.

A special word of appreciation for its commitment to contextualization goes to *Misión* magazine. Edited and nurtured by René Padilla, today in Latin America it is the prime periodical with continental distribution that challenges the churches and leaders to serious application of the Scriptures in the Latin context.[64] Readers may not agree with some of the positions, but all are stirred to serious reflection.

Seventh: Struggling with complex theological issues. Space permits only a general listing of the complex theological issues with which evangelicals must struggle, some of which I have already discussed. First let us consider that cluster of issues that combines liberation theology with Marxism-socialism-capitalism, with poverty and development, with personal and structural sin. Obviously not all evangelicals are concerned to the same degree about these issues. But they clearly affect the entire fabric of Latin American society, the top, middle, and bottom of the social pyramid; and they simply cannot be ignored. Some proposed suggestions and solutions may not meet the approval of North American missionaries and agencies. What we need is true confidence in the Holy Spirit to guide his Latin servants to make decisions within their cultures in humble submission to the authority of the Word of God.

A second category deals with the forms and structures of evangelical churches and institutions which have come from abroad. Latins do not want to toss the institutional baby out with the bathwater. But they do respectfully request permission to make decisions as Latin evangelicals. Mission boards working in this continent must have Latin members to give them an accurate reflection of Latin opinion. Expatriates cannot do this, even if they speak good Spanish or Portuguese and have identified well with the Latin Americans during their careers on the field. There is nothing like the honest and brave counsel of the national who will have to speak English to be understood fully.

Still other issues deal with the rapidly shifting religious panorama of Latin America: Roman Catholicism, spiritism, animism, syncretism, ecumenism, and the plethora of false cults invading the scene.

Eighth: Struggling with issues of the secular society. Evangelicals must struggle with issues raised by their secular society. The first of these is secularism, defined as the "secular spirit or tendency, a system of political or social philosophy that rejects all forms of religious faith and worship." Although Latin America offers a unique religious context where a God mentality has traditionally pervaded life, secularism is nevertheless changing the religious horizon. The drive for material possessions furthers the ethos of secularism. Competitive capitalism and Marxism share blame, for both preach that a person consists of the abundance of things she or he possesses. Evangelicals have tended to view secularism as a liberalizing influence, further weakening Catholic hegemony. But evangelicals are now challenged to think differently, particularly as Latin America makes the transition from a "religious" to a "modern world," one operating without spiritual values.

Happiness is marketed in Latin America just as in the United States (and many times the English language is used in advertising to create a false "international" pleasure). Everything can be bought on credit—from shirts to autos. The poor pay weekly, and the middle to upper class monthly as they flash credit cards. Evangelicals are not exempt from the secularizing forces, and their value systems have invisibly been infiltrated. The neglect of the poorer classes, or blindness to their own former status, can be tied to this spirit of selfishness. Marxists and "Christian Socialists" correctly criticize evangelicals on this latter point, even though leftist ideologies have no real alternative answer because they ignore the biblical analyses and solutions.

Another matter evangelicals continue to confront is totalitarianism, either of the left or the right. The former is found in Cuba; the latter is found at present in Peru, but latently in so many other countries where the military continues as the prime power broker or where death squads murder at will. We must pray for Christians in these tense situations, and we must take steps to aid them in whatever way possible. The entire gamut of the population explosion and its impact provides a baffling set of thorny issues for Christians. Urbanization and industrialization with all of their destabilizing effects are others. In other words, all that has been said in the chapter on the crises of Latin America must be lived day in and day out by our brothers and sisters.

Ninth: Grappling with a newly adversarial Catholic church. I have referred to this previously, and the reader might desire to return to that section in light of the changing Roman Catholic church in Latin America. These shifts call for tremendous evangelical sensitivity, wisdom, and the careful use of prayer and public pressure to assure full constitutional rights. No evangelical wants a religious war in Latin America, but there must be mutual respect and graciousness in the public arena of vibrant Christian witness to the changing continent.

Tenth: Facing their own missionary challenge. Perhaps one of the most moving characteristics of today's Latin American church is the way in which it is facing its own missionary challenge. A movement sparked by the Holy Spirit is sweeping the continent, and surely there will be an excessive emotional response by some. But time will test and purify motives, and emotions will be balanced by realism. COMIBAM will continue, even though certain individuals and groups will follow their own different missiological route. Yet not all Latin evangelicals are pleased with the COMIBAM missiology, feeling that it still lacks theological content and that some emphases are unbalanced.[65]

One of the best signs of missionary maturity is the rise of national missionary agencies with Brazil leading the way. Brazil has economic

World Mission From Latin America

power and a large evangelical population to support a global missionary outreach. National, regional, and international missionary conferences have been held in recent years, and they will increase in number and importance. Ironically those with the highest enthusiasm for cross-cultural missions are the youth and the young professional-business class. Many pastors are threatened by their lack of control and by a potentially weakened economic base. Even some expatriate missionaries have doubted the emerging missionary movement. Ironically, Latin America has, as do Asia and Africa, expatriate missionaries incapable of seeing that the missionary vision must also belong to the young churches. Praise God for those missionaries who have been touched by the Spirit and are participating fully as co-partners.

Latin America offers a world of unreached peoples. But the cities must be given the first place of evangelism, church planting, and leadership training. If Mexico City is only *one percent* evangelical, then the challenge is mammoth; and the Mexicans cannot do it alone. Help is needed from the outside, but it should be sensitive and cooperative missionary help that is willing to enter into partnership relationships with existing Mexican churches instead of merely starting an uncounted flock of new denominations.

Other unreached peoples include Latin America's economic elites[66]; the university students and faculty, the university graduates, the schoolteachers, the military in their enclaves, the labor-union officials, the new urban and industrial middle classes, the untouchable upper classes, the Indian and peasant leaders, the media, and others. At the opposite end of the economic spectrum of under-reached peoples are the slum inhabitants, those who live off the garbage dumps, those locked into hopelessly grinding poverty. Latin missiology must deal with all of these.

The tribes of Latin America continue with their unique contextaul needs—reachable, but requiring missionaries with language and cross-cultural training. The Asian people in Latin America require a special approach; and we thank God for what he is already doing throughout the continent, where Asian missionaries are working with their own diaspora people. Muslims (0.11 percent of the population) are moving into Latin America, and the Jews (0.28 percent) have been there for long decades. Traditional evangelism will not touch these two groups.

One major question comes to my mind: Is there room for the North American or European missionary in Latin America? Yes, of course. *But,* he or she must be a missionary who comes devoid of even latent paternalism, one ready to learn from Latin ministry partners, one who has talents and training but is also humble, one who will learn the language with the highest proficiency possible, and one who will understand and come to love the history and cultural mosaic that makes Latin America what it truly is and can become by God's grace.

A FINAL WORD ON THE SPIRITUAL DIMENSIONS OF LATIN AMERICA

Much ground has been covered in these pages. Latin America is a continent infused with a religious ethos—animist, spiritist, cultic, Jewish, Muslim, Catholic, and evangelical. All these faiths have a message and invite people to come to them. But which one truly is biblical and truly meets people's deepest longings? That is the faith that ultimately must win the spiritual warfare of Latin America.

The history and socio-economic crises of Latin America frankly discourage me many times, and I cannot always conceal my pessimism. But my confidence must be in God and not in history. He is working in amazing, even in peculiar, ways in Latin America. Our vision is focused on this sovereign God of history, the Lord of time and eternity.

NOTES

1. Richard N. Ostling, "Castro Looks at Christianity," *Time,* December 30, 1985, p. 71.

2. I am speaking from my own experience: born in Costa Rica of missionary parents, having lived thirty years in Latin America, seventeen of them as a missionary based at the Central American Theological Seminary in Guatemala City.

3. *Atlas de COMIBAM,* Sao Paulo, Brazil, November 1987. This unique trilingual volume (Spanish, Portuguese, and English) had the most updated statistics from Iberoamerica.

4. John MacKay, *The Other Spanish Christ* (New York: MacMillan, 1932), p. 95.

5. Ibid., p. 102.
6. José Míguez Bonino, in *The Prospects of Christianity Throughout the World,* eds. M Searle Bates and Wilhelm Pauck (New York: Scribner's, 1964), p. 168.

7. Kenneth Scott Latourette, *A History of the Expansion of Christianity,* vol. 3, *Three Centuries of Advance* (Grand Rapids, MI: Zondervan, 1970), pp. 70ff. Latourette has one of the best treatments of this period from a Christian perspective, dedicating

three chapters to the topic.

8. Karl Schmitt, *The Roman Catholic Church in Modern Latin America* (New York: Alfred A. Knopf, 1971), p. 22.

9. Francois Houtart and Emile Pin, *The Church and the Latin American Revolution,* trans. Gilbert Barth (New York: Sheed and Ward, 1965). See also John J. Considine, M. M., ed, *The Religious Dimension in the New Latin America* (Notre Dame, IN: Fides Publishers, 1966). These two books exemplify the pre-liberation theology analysis of Latin America that favored social transformation through the political process.

10. Ivan Vallier, *Catholicism, Social Control, and Modernization in Latin America* (Englewood Cliffs, NJ: Prentice-Hall, 1970), p. 85.

11. Gustavo Gutiérrez, *A Theology of Liberation: History, Politics and Salvation,* trans. and ed. Sister Caridad Inda and John Eagleson (Maryknoll, NY: Orbis, 1986), p. 134.

12. David Mutchler, *The Church as a Political Factor in Latin America* (New York: Praeger, 1971), p. 119.

13. Samuel Escobar, *La Fe Evangélica y las Teologías de la liberación* (El Paso, TX: Casa Bautista de Publicaciones, 1978), p. 34. This is the best work today on the topic. I hope it will be published in English.

14. *Transformation,* vol. 3, no. 3, July-September 1986. This entire issue is dedicated to the Base Ecclesial Communities, from an interconfessional perspective.

15. Guillermo Cook, *The Expectation of the Poor: Latin American Basic Ecclesial Communities in Protestant Perspective* (Maryknoll, NY: Orbis, 1985). This is the most comprehensive and sympathetic treatment of the CEB. For a Catholic perspective see José Maríns y Equipo, *Misión Evangelizadora de la Comunidad Eclesial* (Bogotá: Ediciones Paulinas, 1976). I also have a set of six different study guides in Spanish for the CEB on various topics: alienations, personalization (human virtue and sin), socialization (society and the kingdom), Jesus Christ, God, and the church. They are edited and distributed by Indo American Press Service, Apartado aereo 53274, Chapinero, Bogotá, Colombia (1978).

16. "Contemporary Evangelical Perspective on Roman Catholicism," World Evangelical Fellowship, 1976. This document is important because it takes official Catholic teaching on major doctrines of particular concern to evangelicals around the world. Copies can be purchased from World Evangelical Fellowship, P.O. Box WEF, Wheaton, IL 60189.

17. Georgie Anne Geyer, *The New Latins: Fateful Change in South and Central America* (Garden City, NY: Doubleday, 1970).

18. Key Yuasa, "The Holy Spirit and Popular Religiosity: A Study from a Brazilian and

Evangelical Perspective," a paper given at a theological consultation of the Latin American Theological Fraternity, Mexico, June 1984, pp. 23-24. See also John Eagleson and Philip Scharper, eds., *Puebla and Beyond: Documentation and Commentary,* trans. John Drury (Maryknoll, NY: Orbis, 1980). Note the significant section on popular religiosity, pp. 184-88.

19. Emilio Antonio Núñez, *Liberation Theology* (Chicago: Moody, 1985). See also Escobar, *Fe Evangélica.*

20. Gordon Spykman, Guillermo Cook, Michael Dodson, Lance Grahn, Sidney Rooy, John Stam, *Let My People Live: Faith and Struggle in Central America* (Grand Rapids, MI: Eerdmans, 1988).

21. Escobar, *Fe Evangélica,* p. 74.

22. Yuasa, p. 3.

23. MacKay, *The Other Spanish Christ,* pp. 95-96.

24. W. Dayton Roberts, "Roman Catholicism Never the Same Again," *Latin America Evangelist,* April-June 1987, pp. 10-11.

25. I have had ample opportunity to speak during major consultations and meetings in Latin America with key evangelical leaders from Latin America about the new Catholic emphases.

26. José Antonio Guevara, S.D.B., *Defiende Tu Fe,* San Salvador, 1983. This fascinating handbook of 209 pages gives Catholics a wealth of information: how to treat the "separated brethren," the essence of Protestantism, its denominations and Central American groups of churches, the cults and all sorts of questions a good Catholic must be able to answer.

27. Rosita Caldera, "El Episcopado acusa a las sectas de agresivas y fanáticas," *El Nacional,* January 14, 1988. I was in Venezuela at that time and was able to sense the initial impact of those attacks.

28. Samuel Escobar, "Future Trends: Roman Catholicism in Latin America," *Latin America Evangelist,* April-June 1987, pp. 6-9.

29. Two classic studies by social scientists of evangelicals in Latin America include: Emilio Willems, *Followers of the New Faith: Culture Change and the Rise of Protestantism in Brazil and Chile* (Nashville: Vanderbilt, University, 1967) and Christian Lalive De'Epinay, *Haven of the Masses: A Study of the Pentecostal Movement in Chile,* trans. Marjorie Sandle (London: Lutterworth, 1969). An evangelical perspective comes from the writings of Orlando Costas, *Christ Outside the Gate: Mission Beyond Christendom* (Maryknoll, NY: Orbis, 1982); Costas, *The Church and Its Mission: A Shattering Critique* (Wheaton, IL: Tyndale House, 1974); and Costas, *Theology of the Crossroads in Latin America* (Amsterdam: Editions Rodopoi, 1976). For information on Brazil, see William R. Read and Frank A. Ineson, *Brazil 1980: The Protestant Handbook* (Monrovia, CA: MARC, 1973).

30. William R. Read, Victor M. Monterroso, Harmon A. Johnson, *Latin American Church Growth* (Grand Rapids, MI: Eerdmans, 1969), p. 37.

31. Pablo Alberto Deiros, *Historia del Cristianismo* (El Paso, TX: Casa Bautista de Publicaciones, 1980), p. 230. I have translated the items from the Spanish.

32. Read, Monterroso, Johnson, *Latin American*, p. 36.

33. MacKay, *The Other Spanish Christ*, p. 232.

34. Read, Monterros, Johnson, *Latin American*, p. 38.

35. J. Edwin Orr, *Evangelical Awakenings in Latin America* (Minneapolis: Bethany Fellowship, 1978), p. 10.

36. Eugenio Campos and William Taylor, *Misiones Mundiales,* Estudios CLASE, Central American Theological Seminary, Guatemala, 1984, pp. 27-28.

37. Deiros, *Historia*, pp. 233-235.

38. Latourette, *A History*, p. 102.

39. Orr, *Evangelical Awakenings*, p. 16.

40. Deiros, *Historia*, p. 243.

41. Ibid.

42. Ibid.

43. Esther and Mortimer Arias, *The Cry of My People: Out of Captivity in Latin America* (New York: Friendship Press, 1980), p. 6.

44. Mildred W. Spain, *And in Samaria* (Dallas: Central American Mission, 1954), pp. 9-10.

45. Read, Monterroso, Johnson, *Latin American*, p. 40.

46. Ibid., p. 43.

47. Arias, *The Cry,* pp. 7-8.

48. Deiros, *Historia*, p. 262.
49. Read, Monterroso, Johnson, *Latin American*, p. 49.

50. Arias, *The Cry*, p. 8.

51. *Directorio de Iglesias, Organizaciones y Ministerios del Movimento Protestante:*

Guatemala (Costa Rica: INDEF, Guatemala: SEPAL 1981). *Directorio de la Iglesia Evangélica del Ecuador* (Quito: Comité Interdenominacional Pro-Directorio, 1985).

52. Patrick Johnstone, *Operation World* (Bromley, England: Operation Mobilisation, 4th ed., 1978), pp. 62-67.

53. The data come from a variety of sources, but primarily from Read, Monterroso, and Johnson, *Latin American Church Growth,* and the *COMIBAM Atlas.* I have also utilized other unpublished sources.

54. Johnstone, *Operation World,* p. 65.

55. Gustav Niebuhr, "Born Again, Latin Style." The *Austin American-Stateman* (Texas) published a five-part series that started March 15, 1987, detailing the growth of evangelicals in Latin America and the Spanish-version television programming of North American evangelists. They were written long before Swaggart's moral collapse.

56. Daniel E. Wray, "Revive, Argentina!" *Eternity,* July-August 1987, pp. 22-26.

57. William David Taylor, *Worlds in Conflict: The Impact of the University Social Structure on Protestant Students in the National University of Guatemala,* Ph.D. diss., the University of Texas, Austin, December 1976.

58. Loren Entz, "Challenges to Abou's Jesus," *Evangelical Missions Quarterly,* January 1986, pp. 46-50.

59. I have been a member of the Latin American Theological Fraternity since 1974, and it has been one of the most challenging groups in the contextualization process.

60. I was a member of the continental COMIBAM committee because I was executive secretary of the World Evangelical Fellowship Missions Commission. It was also my privilege to be a plenary speaker, as well as to give three seminars.

61. Stephen Sywulka, "A Latin American Evangelical View of Base Communities," *Transformation,* vol 3., no. 3, July-September 1986, p. 29.

62. *Paz y Esperanza,* Bulletin of the Peace and Hope Commission of the National Council of Peru, 1985.

63. A number of works have been written on the subject of contextualization. Here is one excellent book: John R.W. Stott and Robert T. Coote, eds., *Gospel and Culture* (Pasadena, CA: William Carey Library, 1979). Note in particular the essay by René Padilla.

64. *Misión* can be ordered from Apartado 133-2300, Curridabat, Costa Rica. See also the book of essays by C. René Padilla, *Mission Between the Times* (Grand Rapids, MI: Eerdmans, 1985). Padilla here deals with a series of topics having particular application to Latin America and the mission of the church.

65. *Consulta Nacional Sobre in Misión de la Iglesia,* Concilio Nacional Evangélico del Peru, Lima, 1987.

66. Seymour Martin Lipset, Aldo Solari, eds., *Elites in Latin America* (Oxford: Oxford University, 1967).

5

A Personal Perspective of the Latin American People

This chapter, clearly the most subjective one to write, is based on my impressions of the particular ethos (the essential spirit or characteristic of a people) and cultures that make up the Latin American personality. Admittedly my perceptions are not only personal, they are limited to the interactions I as an individual have had during nearly thirty years of life in Latin America. Just as there is no single Latin American culture, so there is no single, unique Latin American personality. Nevertheless, I shall make generalizations that I hope will reflect both profound respect and love for my friends who make up the glorious mosaic of Latin America.

Unfortunately too many missionaries have served Christ in Latin America without much serious interaction with what makes Latin Americans special and even different from the Anglo-Saxon peoples. There has been a cavalier attitude toward the psychological and cultural elements that affect a people. Again, we evangelicals have reduced people to either "Christian or non-Christian" and glossed over the rich cultural dimensions. And from an evangelical perspective we rightly continue to read Nida's classic, *Understanding Latin Americans*.[1] Nida, a magnificent evangelical student of Latin America as well as a linguist and anthropologist, is at his best when he places primary Latin characteristics in tension. He sees similarities and contrasts in the three areas of authoritarianism and individualism, idealism and realism, *machismo* and *hem-*

brismo. These in turn are applied to religion, philosophy, politics, aesthetics, society, and family life. A secular evaluation of the Latin American can be seen in Geyer's *The New Latins,* where she discusses topics such as the importance of form, authoritarianism, individualism, personalism, *machismo* and so many other elements which color the continent so vividly.[2]

A singular group of Latin Americans have analyzed their own culture, and in particular I would like to recommend four of them.[3] Samuel Ramos wrote *Profile of Man and Culture in Mexico,* which despite the mention of his own nation has great applications for the entire continent. Carlos Rangel, a Venezuelan journalist-essayist, wrote *The Latin Americans: Their Love-Hate Relationship with the United States* with particular reference to the North-South dialogue of understanding we so desperately need. Octavio Paz, a multigifted Mexican essayist-playwright-editor-diplomat-poet, has many books; but I recommend the penetrating *Labyrinth of Solitude: Life and Thought in Mexico.* The sweeping and painful evaluation of his own people overlaps with the continental experience. Leopoldo Zea, another Mexican, deliberately writes for all Latin America in his *Latin American Mind.* This work primarily evaluates romanticism and positivism as the two philosophical systems that Zea feels have profoundly affected Latin America. Many other Latin Americans have written about their culture, and the careful student of these peoples will seek out sources that make particular sense within each culture and country.

DIFFERING IDEOLOGIES HAVE AFFECTED LATIN AMERICA

My professor of Latin American studies at the University of Texas, Austin, suggested to me that there are particular periods in the history of Latin American formal thinking. I present these five stages in order for the reader to develop a historical flow that provides a context for greater contemporary understanding. Although the years given are flexible estimates, nevertheless they guide our thinking so that we can better evaluate the currents of philosophy that controlled the dominant societies of the period, determined educational curricula, and influenced the worlds of politics, economics, and culture. Here is a sweeping panorama.

The World of Scholasticism (1492-1770)

The Latin American colonies, like the Iberian Peninsula, suffered greatly from the extremely limited impact of both the Renaissance and the Reformation. For that reason Scholasticism—a worldview which combined religious dogma with intuitive philosophy—dominated the colonial mindset and controlled theories of state, economics, theology, and law. By the sixteenth century most of Europe had said farewell to this perspective but not Spain, that great defender of tradition and the faith. Spanish universities, led by Salamanca, protected the nation and colonies from all kinds of heterodoxy —religious, spiritual, ideological, scientific. In the New World, Scholasticism also enthroned theology as the queen of the sciences and used the syllogism as the prime method of analyzing and teaching reality. This Aristotelian hierarchicalism pervaded the entire society and was particularly taught in the schools and universities of the era.

The World of the Enlightenment (1770-1830)

The Enlightenment had rejected revelation and all vestiges of Scholasticism. Rationalism, liberalism, and progress were now enthroned and even worshiped. The new appreciation of nature and the rational dimension of humanity came to the fore, since reason was considered humanity's superior instrument. Liberalism introduced the concept of political change, and progress opened the door to higher advances in humanity and society. The "Gospel of the Enlightenment" proclaimed the good news of natural rights, popular sovereignty, and egalitarianism.

While the European continent drank heavily of this radical thinking regarding law, society, and even religion, very few individuals in the New World imbibed these heady doctrines. This was because of the Spanish and Portuguese intellectual boycott of new ideas that might destabilize their colonial empire. Nevertheless these radical ideas were smuggled across the Atlantic and had their prime impact on the emerging group of intellectual *criollos*. Other *criollos* studied the same concepts during their stay both in the new United States and Europe. Hence the independence movement exploded mentally before any steps were taken to start a revolution. Although the Enlightenment ideas never filtered down below the restless upper classes, they still affected the entire region when the drive for independence emerged and radically changed history.

The World of Romanticism (1830-1860)

Romanticism was particularly held by the children of the independence movement, influencing both politics and literature and emerging to affirm the independence of the spirit in Spanish America. Even more serious, it was a search for the spirit of the Latin American people, who for three centuries had lived in complete dependence upon the mother countries. It is Leopoldo Zea who most eloquently documents this period and the role it played on the new nations that sought their intellectual autonomy from Europe. To him, the Liberators had not anticipated the post-independence era.

> Like good men of the Enlightenment, they executed plans by which they intended to remake and orient the liberated peoples. They looked upon the latter as clay easy to mold. The Hispanic-American people understood that they were still not prepared to enjoy the fruits of their liberty, but that their liberators, now turned governors, would assume the responsibility of preparing them. Enlightened despotism was the redeeming formula. The American peoples were to be taught by force to be free. In the name of liberty Bolivar imposed his power upon the peoples whom he had liberated. O'Higgins did the same in Chile, Iturbide in Mexico, Rivadavia in Argentina and Dr. Francia in Paraguay.[4]

The early optimism degenerated into profound pessimism. And the search led to the rejection of Enlightenment rationalism; but then Romanticism began to inspire the new Spanish American dream. Its implications were not only personal but national and continental as its proponents talked of developing a new culture, a new literature, even a new grammar, a new ethos. Yet an ambivalence persisted. Elements of Romanticism were borrowed from the same Europe that was being rejected as a model. The new spirit was felt on the individual level and particularly seen in the new literature. But it was not only poetry and essays. It was an attitude, a style of life, a personal philosophy. It was opposed to cold rationalism. "The heart has reasons that the mind is ignorant of," said its spokesmen. This new spirit rippled through the entire continent and fostered a sense of continental interdependence, a feeling that the new nations were all part of something valuable.

The World of Positivism (1860-1910)

Yet humanity could not live by Romanticism alone, and the search opened up again for more concrete solutions to Latin America's problems. It was a pendulum movement, for following a brief experimentation with utilitarianism, Positivism—another European system of thought—captured the imagination of key Latin American leaders. The teachings of August Comte, the father of sociology, and Herbert Spencer perhaps would bring political and economic order out of chaos and uncertainty. Positivism, rejecting theology and metaphysics as outdated and irrelevant to modern society, theorized that positive knowledge is based on empirical studies, evolution, social Darwinism, and the scientific method. These would in turn naturally produce "order and progress"— the Positivistic slogan that later was emblazoned on the Brazilian flag.

Widespread acceptance of the new transforming message stimulated many nations to attempt to implement Positivisim and, in some cases, to modify it, giving it a Latin face as did Sarmiento in Argentina. For some this meant a firm rejection of the past, including the powerful Roman church. Social Darwinism also permitted a sad display of racial rejection of the Indians, who were deemed inferior and parasitic in some countries. Fortunately this was not so in all of Latin America, as Peruvian Positivism attested. Countries working hard to apply the new order of progress were Argentina, Uruguay, Chile, Bolivia, Peru, Cuba, Brazil, and Mexico. It was in the latter two countries that the Positivistic experiment was put to its greatest test. And probably that is one reason that today Brazil and Mexico are considered as members of the NICs—Newly Industrialized Countries. Let us look at the Mexican case from the perspective of Mexican writer Leopoldo Zea.

> Education was the best instrument for carrying out this transformation of the Mexicans. But to accomplish the deed there must be a doctrine, an ideology, an instrument of thought which would effect this change. Positivistic doctrine was the adequate instrument. Positivisim was a doctrine for practical men, for men like the Anglo-Saxons who had forged their countries into great nations. The same doctrine, it was thought, would endow the Mexicans with a series of qualities without which neither authentic liberty nor an authentic democracy was possible.[5]

The Comtian motto emerged in a Mexican form calling for greater order, progress, and peace, even at the expense of fewer rights and liberties. The generation of *Los Científicos*, the technocrats, took over the country. During this time the famous Polytecnic University was founded.

And power was handed to the *caudillo* Porfirio Díaz who ruled from 1884 until 1911.

The Post-Positivistic Era (1910-The Present)

What legacy did Positivism bestow on Latin America? It was mixed at best, and today is seen as a past phase. The pendulum was to begin swinging again, bringing a variety of reactions as Latin American leaders continued searching for their answer. The Latins reacted against the materialistic bias of a Positivism that neglected the metaphysical realities and had borrowed so much again from Europe. Ideological dependence was hard to shake.

For a time poets and writers were drawn to modernism, seeking truth in the pale princesses and majestic swans of their imaginations. It was also an escape from reality. Bergsonian intuitionism had its day, but today stronger currents sweep through the continent. Dialectical Marxist materialism battled with conviction and commitment against its enemy, existentialism laced with metaphysics. Marxism cried that the world is not here to be contemplated, but to be changed. Existentialism values the essence of humanity, the present, the now, and in the center of that now is the reality of one's personal existence. However, it seems to me that Marxism's attraction was mostly among the intellectual elite as well as among militant worker and revolutionary movements. Perhaps the strongest growing force today in Latin America is secularism, a perspective that rejects the place religious values must have in one's life. Over the centuries the pendulum of ideological systems has swung from one side to another. It is a challenge to the true church of Christ to analyze the current Latin American mentality and seek to present the powerful life-and-society-changing Jesus Christ as the One to provide true transformation.

A LATIN AMERICAN SELF-EVALUATION

A second dimension of the personal perspective comes from a group of young university-age students of mine. A number of years ago during one of my classes at the Central American Theological Seminary in Guatemala, I challenged the students—of seven nationalities—to a serious evaluation of their own countries and cultures. I asked them to consider the positive and negative aspects they could observe within their own Latin American context. The discussions were lively and even heated as students argued for their perspective; seldom was there unanimity. Here is the result of that discussion, modified by different groups of students and friends over a period of five years. The first eleven points are presented in contrast, with the remaining ones standing alone.[6]

THE EVALUATION OF LATIN AMERICAN PEOPLES

Positive Values

Negative Values

1. Sensibility, seen in the capacity to perceive small details, as well as allowing oneself to be carried away from emotions of compassion and tenderness.

1. We are very suspicious, touchy, and easily offended.

2. No strict subjection to time. In other words, flexibility in terms of formal schedule.

2. Irresponsible in terms of time, with an exaggerated flexibility of schedule.

3. High prizing of intellectual work, particularly in the world of ideas.

3. A dislike for manual labor, which is seen in the lack of workers for the manual and technical vocations and an excess of people in the so-called intellectual and white-collar office jobs.

4. Very high appreciation of the heritage of cultural traditions.

4. Extreme traditionalism that rejects change and an incapacity to solve basic problems of illiteracy.

5. A sense of national pride, placing high value on patriotic symbols such as the national hymn (memorizing from childhood all the stanzas of the hymn, not just the first one, as do the North Americans), the flag, the na-

5. Fanatical nationalism that leads to conflict with peoples of other countries. And at the same time almost a need to be dependent on foreign ideas. Also a heritage of corrupt politicians and incompetent economists.

tional bird and flower, as well as other symbols of national sovereignty.

6. A religious mentality that appreciates the spiritual dimensions. A belief in a creator God who is powerful. There is a sense of personal faith in Latin America.

6. A religious mentality that accepts supersitition and fanatically rejects new ideas.

7. An emphasis on idealism that seeks metaphysical values and spiritual dimensions of the soul and personal being.

7. An idealism that allows one to live in a dream world and does not want to face reality. There is much talking and too little production.

8. The capacity to improvise and to "fix things as we go along the way."

8. A difficulty in planning, and if planning is done, a second problem in the inability to transform the plan into action.

9. An emotional commitment to liberty, observed in the content of the national hymns and the willingness to give sacrificially when it comes time to defend those liberties.

9. Difficulty in resolving problems democratically, which in turn allows the rise of dictatorial power in either the *cacique,* or the *caudillo* (the dictator).

10. An emphasis on what is human and humanitarian, rejecting the dry and mechanistic emphasis of the industrialized nations.

10. A desire to progress and to live well without much cost to one personally. Also an excess of individualism, with the corresponding lack of community commitment in a kind of Latin American social contract.

11. A great concept of the family: parents, children, uncles, grandparents, grandparents of cousins, uncles by marriage, first cousins, and cousins of all grades

11. The problem of *machismo* and *hembrismo.* The first focuses on the dominant man, very *macho* and unfaithful to his wife. The second focuses on the passive

of blood and family relation.

and dependent woman. Other problems were seen in the fact that the man is a great romantic lover but not necessarily a good husband and father.

12. A concept of respect and honor for parents, particularly as they grow older. We do not like to see our parents in old folks' homes.

12. The ability to allow oneself to be carried away by various elements of foreign cultures—ideas, customs—in such a way that the foreign is overestimated, and the national products and values are not appreciated. This contributes to a sense of Latin American inferiority.

13. The way we identify with the social needs of the Latin American peoples.

13. An inability to take care of what we have, or poor maintenance. Therefore we can mistreat and destroy what we possess.

14. The way we relate to other people: friendly, positive, charged with a good sense of humor.

14. A marked class division, which is seen also in the existence of extremely poor people.

Something significant happened to the group that developed these comparative values: it was very easy for them to discover the negative factors of their culture and quite difficult to appreciate positive dimensions. One class came up with twenty positives and thirty-one negatives. We discussed *this* problem also, and they concluded that persons in the Latin American cultures had spent all their lives comparing themselves to others—Spain, Europe, the United States—to the point that their own culture was laced more with negatives than positives. This conclusion was painful for these emerging Christian leaders, who were struggling with the task of thinking "Christianly" and not merely reacting as children of their own culture.

The discussion then flowed to an analysis of the paragraph on culture in the Lausanne Covenant and its applications to Latin American realities, a task that even yet has not been undertaken with seriousness. Of particular interest was this section and its implications for Latin America:

Culture must always be tested and judged by Scripture. Because man is God's creature, some of his culture is rich in beauty and goodness. Because he has fallen, all of it is tainted with sin and some of it is demonic. The Gospel does not presuppose the superiority of any culture to another, but evaluates all cultures according to its own criteria of truth and righteousness, and insists on moral absolutes in every culture.[7]

PERSONAL IMPRESSIONS OF THE LATIN AMERICAN ETHOS

I now enter potentially explosive territory, and I thank my close Latin friends for their gracious forbearance, which I trust they will extend. Before going into specifics, let me clarify again some important matters. These are personal impressions, based less on research and documentation than on my nearly thirty years of living with and studying Latin American peoples. I am limited to a primary contact with the *ladino* and the *mestizo*. Whatever is said about them is spoken with love and appreciation. In a sense I am "burning my boats" as I write, a saying that comes from Hernan Cortés's action of literally burning his boats after he and his *conquistadores* landed on the eastern coast of Mexico. The English equivalent is "burning your bridges." Both proverbs advise me that I really cannot go back now.

Latin America is *different* from North America, but different does not mean inferior or bad; it just means "different." As the Lausanne Covenant affirms, all cultures have positive and negative dimensions, and all demonstrate evidence of the demonic at work. Latin America is different because of the historical factors that converged to make it what it is today. Significantly, there is a cultural value-sharing between the French Canadians and Latin America as Seymour Martin Lipset argues.[8] Both are populated by peoples from a European Catholic culture, they demonstrate a history of democratic instability, they value authoritarianism in spiritual matters, they have brought a hierarchical organization of social classes, and they share similar attitudes toward economic development.

The Latin Is Known for Personal Warmth, Responsiveness, and Emotion

The fundamental characteristic of Latin warmth, responsiveness, and emotion demonstrates itself in both positive and negative ways. The visitor to and long-term resident of Latin America is struck by this characteristic, particularly if he or she comes from "cooler climates" of human relations. I have seen North American tourists and new missionaries literally freeze when they realize that they are about to be enveloped in a bear hug, the famous *abrazo*. Throughout Latin America there is much more physical contact between people—children, youth, adults, and up and down the age spectrum. Anglo-Saxons and Asians tend to shy away from such contact; but, incidentally, the Africans understand it better, for it reflects some of their own cultural values. This *abrazo* is only one of many body gestures that communicate so much, and each country and culture has its particular variants.

I have observed the behavior of friends who meet on a downtown street: initial verbal greetings, strong handshaking or patting on the arm or shoulder (the *abrazo* may come then, or when they have not seen each other in a long time). There will be a series of questions about respective families and other personal matters, and when the time comes to terminate the brief encounter, it may come after at least two full handshakes. Phone calls between family and friends inevitably are loaded with preliminaries, inquiry, warmth, and information that the foreigner would think insignificant.

The youth subcultures develop their own systems of greetings and communications, and many times they will seep into adult behavior also. When my kids became part of the youth group at our church, they were initiated into the casual-kiss greeting—either a peck on the cheek or a half-missed kiss into the air on the side of the cheek. To some this did not seem very appropriate for Christians. But it became a beautiful way to express warm feeling, and I was a willing participant in the process. Our family received a whiplash on this touching dynamic when we returned to live in the United States. Some *Gringos,* or *Yankees* (by the way, all North Americans are both—to the chagrin of the United States Southerner who does not like to be called a Yankee), had a terrible time with the variety of bodily contact. My son in eighth grade was called a homosexual simply because he congratulated a race-winning buddy with a warm hug. It was a deep blow to David, who did not understand how football pros could celebrate touchdowns that way, but he could not. "David," I stated, "these North Americans don't like to be touched, so let's both be wary of this."

Edward T. Hall's beautiful book *The Silent Language* is laced with illustration after illustration of the way people "talk" with each other without words. He writes of the relationship between personal space and

warmth and speaks of the differences between Latin America and the
United States.

> In Latin America the interaction distance is much
> less than it is in the United States. Indeed, people cannot
> talk comfortably with one another unless they are very
> close to the distance that evokes either sexual or hostile
> feelings in the North American. The result is that when
> they move close, we withdraw and back away. As a con-
> sequence, they think we are distant or cold, withdrawn
> and unfriendly. We, on the other hand, are constantly ac-
> cusing them of breathing down our necks, crowding us,
> and spraying our faces.
>
> Americans who have spent some time in Latin
> America without learning these space considerations
> make other adaptations, like barricading themselves be-
> hind their desks, using chairs and typewriter tables to
> keep the Latin American at what is to us a comfortable
> distance. The result is that the Latin American may even
> climb over the obstacles until he has achieved a distance
> at which he can comfortably talk.[9]

There is another side to this projection of warmth that must be mentioned. In some ways this is a first-level warmth that so impresses the
visitor. The careful student of Latin America will note that quite frequently the warmth is tied up in careful restraints. The marvelous graciousness and friendliness carefully guard deeper emotions, more profound penetration into the personal life, or even visits to the home. If you
are a member of the extended family or a good friend of a family member, or have earned the right to be accepted and even loved by the inner
family, *then* the doors open beyond comparison. In a sense, cultural appreciation and understanding are like preparing an artichoke for dinner—
the delicate feast is there before you, but you must be careful of the
spines, and you have to peel the leaves and enjoy the meal little by little.

Yes, Latins are hot-blooded people, and passions run close to the
surface. They can dissolve in side-splitting laughter on a downtown
boulevard or at meal time. Seldom are emotions expressed with Anglo-
Saxon or Oriental moderation. The Latin sense of humor has its par-
ticularities, and often I have sat in a joking group; but I find the jokes different from most North American ones. Many times the Latin humor
starts with a brief story or pun, or a complete joke, but then another per-

son present takes the same story, builds on it with his own touch of humor, yet another adds his own humorous insight, and finally, after all have participated, the entire group collapses in laughter. The unique feature is the progressive build-up of the original joke or pun, ending perhaps with a conclusion totally different from the start.

At times the emotional explosion is tragic and devastating, such as in soccer competitions. Geyer reports one of the most terrible events, which occurred in Lima in May 1964.[10] Peru played Argentina in the Lima stadium and bitterly lost as a result of a controversial call by the Uruguayan umpire. In the melee that followed, 319 people were killed in the stampede to the locked gates. And in the self-analysis that followed, the popular explanation for the tragedy was in itself sadly simple: Peru had lost because of an anti-Peruvian foreigner who was the "intellectual author of the massacre." It was another example of placing the blame elsewhere rather than recognizing that perhaps the umpire might have judged correctly.

In 1968 El Salvador and Honduras fought a bloody and deadly conflict unfortunately dubbed by the press as the "soccer war." It started after a hotly contested match in El Salvador. However, that game riot that sparked the war was simply the proverbial straw that broke the camel's back; the two countries were at flash point as a result of long-lasting hostilities. Yet, Latin Americans are not the only ones who take soccer with serious passion, as the European litany of soccer riots and deaths attests.

On the humorous side, I remember a soccer story from my years at the seminary in Guatemala. Games were played with passion on our seminary field also, and over the years certain matches excited the students. One such game was fought on a cool afternoon. I got to the game late and chatted with our goalie, at that moment resting since the action was at the other end of the playing field. "Jeremías," I asked, "how are we doing?" The response was classic: "We are losing five to one, but you should have seen our goal. It was a beautiful one, easily worth five of theirs!" Ah, the importance of form, so many times covering the lack of substance—at least something is done with a flair.

Emotions and words are graphically expressed in the Latin's ability to use his hands. One day I was driving behind a car with two Latin men. To my amazement the driver ahead seemed to manage without hands on wheel, simply because he needed both hands to gesticulate to his friend. Hand gestures are part of the silent language of the culture. Early in my career in Latin America I received a beautiful class in culture. During one visit to a rural area I sat with some *campesinos,* chatting the evening away. Somehow we got on to different hand gestures. They proceeded to instruct me on what gesture to use for different things: how to measure the size of a fish, a snake, a chicken, a boy, a box, a pig, a child—all with the hands. Never should I use a gesture for a child that is designed for an animal. I never forgot the lesson—an experience that enriched my teaching by using these and so many other gestures.

The Struggle with the Inferiority Complex

Any evaluation of the Latin American personality must come to grips with a down-side dimension: the struggle with the inferiority complex. Samuel Ramos argues that this complex is caused by the heavy imitation of foreign forms, resulting in a serious lack of personal and national sense of authenticity.[11] Octavio Paz discusses similar themes in his books, especially *The Labyrinth of Solitude*. He gives a graphic yet painful illustration of this sense of inferiority when he analyzes the Mexican cry, *"Viva Mexico, hijos de la chingada!"*—basically a cheer that combines praise to a Mexico composed of illegitimate Mexicans.[12] Arciniegas suggests that the Latin problem is that of the *mestizo* mixture: "The *mestizo* received no more than half of the things that came from Europe—everything about him is by halves. He is a native product, and an illegitimate one to boot, born of the contact between the white man and the Indian woman, an under-the-counter product, as it were."[13] Sarmiento cried once of the "disease in our blood," a lament I have heard from Christian leaders who in their attempt to explain why failures occur in Latin America shrug their shoulders and say, "It is just that we have bad blood."

The white North American missionary to Latin America generally is oblivious of this deep psychological conflict, primarily because he comes from a culture that has prided itself on being a "melting pot" of the nations and peoples. And because this missionary has not lived such an internal conflict, it "just does not exist in others." But it *does* exist, and it colors the entire Latin mindset. Different groups blame other ones for their own limitations—either racial, geographic, or cultural. The lower classes emulate and blame the middle ones, and they in turn do the same with the elite. This problem of identity requires sensitive research on the part of Christians, both Latin and expatriate. There is a tremendous need to underscore the biblical concept of personhood, especially the new person, regardless of racial combinations or social classifications. Evangelicals in Latin America could carefully evaluate a "Christianization" of Paulo Freire's process of "conscientization." Such an evaluation can stimulate the creation of a positive valuing of oneself as a priceless creation of God—in spite of crippling oppression or low self-esteem.

A People Known for Their Social Commitment. But—

The Latin social commitment ripples through many discussions, oral and literary, for the Latin American is an expert in social analysis. These, the "true issues of life," as I was once told, are crucial to the Latin American personality. The Latin arts—literature, drama, art—are "committed arts," also known as "witnesses to the truth." The university student is famous for protest, a characteristic found all through the region.[14] They are especially active in criticism, change, and overthrow. Student years are presupposed to be times of political expression and vocal— even violent—discontent. Many of the national universities are also "autonomous," that is, neither government nor military forces have the right to invade the campus. And that permits and even encourages the spirit of criticism, or even armed revolt. Many universities have been used to hide subversive propaganda or even arms.

However, the closer the student comes to graduation and entrance into the society at large, the more the rhetoric tones down and the more attitudes begin to adapt that will aid the graduate in the marketplace. The university students, "in spite of their vociferous radicalism, slide with surprising ease into the well-worn channels of orthodox behavior."[15]

I have already discussed some aspects of this Latin social ambivalence, a reality witnessed to within the evangelicals as well. Social commitment for most in the past has been a nonexistent reality, although that is changing today. Yet for many it still is a theoretical priority, and "certainly must not get in the way of personal fulfillment and upward social mobility." Anglo-Saxon missionaries have not contributed much to change this mindset, simply because they come from societies where structural change or revolution is distant history, where Christian social commitment, if seen at all, is geared to personal ethical problems such as abortion, pornography, and homosexual rights.

I have studied the patriotic words of the national hymns of Latin American countries, invariably set to majestic and inspiring music. Children in first grade memorize all lyrical stanzas and can sing them on special occasions with formal solemnity. In contrast to the North American national-hymn singing, there is no clapping or cheering afterwards. That would be national blasphemy. But the hymns reflect this tension between theoretical and real commitment to social change. Pedro Arana speaks of a "disposition of surrender to a noble cause, that fullness of healthy and good intentions. All this is very positive. But the big question which arises and accuses us is this: How long will this feeling of generosity which often leads to heroism last?" Arana goes on to affirm that the Latin American has, in the words of the well-known proverb, "his heart in his hand, but he has more heart than brains."[16]

The Centrality of the Family

There is a positive side. The North American nuclear family differs from the basic Latin American family unit. The Latin unit is the extended family that includes mother, father, children, grandparents on both sides, aunts and uncles and their children, cousins of all stripes and colors, and relatives by marriage. One friend of mine in Sao Paulo has 150 known members of his extended family. It is an incredible net, many times with a central and dominant member in the middle, such as a strong grandmother. This family provides the major outlet for social life and cares for the welfare of its members, particularly those in some kind of personal, legal, or economic crisis. Evangelical missionaries must study anew the significance of the extended family, for it provides a most crucial key to family evangelism. When one member trusts Christ as Savior this opens the door to the entire extended family. Unfortunately, national and foreign Christian leaders have tended to cut the new believer away from the "negative influences of his family," and in the process have eliminated entrance to the family. The extended family is a fertile area to evaluate in terms of outreach and church growth, particularly in the tough urban sectors.

There are other beautiful aspects of the Latin family. One is the respect that children demonstrate toward adults: parents, grandparents, and other older people. Politeness is ingrained as a virtue. I have observed this virtue in all strata of society, not only the middle and upper classes. Children at a very young age are taught to greet visitors and other people. Babies and the young are loved by all ages. We were struck time after time by observing young people coming up to our children, talking with them, playing with them, and engaging them in conversation. It was a far cry from the North American cult of youth that encourages them to ignore or treat with disdain all not in their own age bracket.

Another fascinating dimension in Latin America is the concept of physical beauty, particularly when compared to the North American values. The United States holds to a specific image of the "beautiful woman": she is to be tallish and extremely lean, with muscular definition, long legs akin to a filly's; she is not to be very curvy, though the mythical hourglass figure is still a high priority for many. In Latin America the vision is different, and many consider North American women undernourished and excessively preoccupied with weight loss. I well remember the advertisements in the Guatemalan press when national holidays saw thousands heading for the beach. The papers touted special clinics where women could add pounds. "Don't be a skinny woman!!! Put on some weight so you will not be embarrassed on the beach." Latin American upper-middle-class women now are beginning to strive for the slender figure, but this is relatively unusual. It is common to hear a husband introduce his wife as *Mi Gordita,* "My chubby one." A Latin male will admire a very hefty woman and say *Qué hermosa,* "How lovely."

Expatriates at first are confused by the way Latin Americans use their names, especially the last ones. This happened to me in my first year of teaching in Guatemala. I took roll, requesting the students to fill out a card with their complete name and other data. When I received the cards and began to read them, I could not understand. For example, if one student was called José María Gonzalez Martínez, I wanted to know which was his last name. He responded, "*Profe,* both are my last name." I soon understood that the first last name referred to his father's side and the second one his mother's side. Then it became so clear to me that names were crucial to determine legitimacy of birth. When a student showed up with only one last name, it generally indicated that he was born out of wedlock, and the shame was expressed in the shorter last name. One student changed names during his years of study because of an unusual phenomenon—his natural father had finally legally recognized him as a son, even though this did not mean that the son would have the care of a father. It was legal only, but a very important act that changed his self-image and personal pride.

When a Latin American girl marries, she does not lose her last name, as North American women tend to do. My daughters born in Guatemala liked this because they would be able to keep their names if they married in Latin America. When a man marries he carries both of his last names, his wife takes on his paternal last name, and the children take a last name from each of the parents. When a girl marries in Latin America, her maiden last name is dropped, and she picks up the husband's first last name. For example, if María Guadalupe Cortéz López marries José María Marín Gutiérrez, she becomes María Guadalupe Cortéz de (of) Marín. By the way, these are two good Catholic names, and most Latin American names have traditionally come from the Bible, with Mary and Joseph being top favorites, followed by the names of special saints. I have had students whose names are prophets, kings of Judah, apostles, or names of other biblical figures; some have been picked out of obscure biblical genealogical lists.

There is a negative side. I mentioned that the extended family generally has a strong central-authority figure, and perhaps in most of the cases it may appear to be the father. But in actuality it seems as if it is either a mother or grandmother who provides the stability and even controls the family net. Why so in a male-dominated society?

This leads us to discuss the *machismo-hembrismo* characteristic of Latin America. Yes, the father is the external symbol of power, and to him belongs the task of economic provision, the *machete* of the family as he is called in rural areas—he is the man who takes care of the material needs. It is also he who rules and arbitrates major struggles, who decides many times autocratically where the family will live, and who determines what it will do for recreation and vocation. He decides how much money the wife will have for the household expenses. He is the titular head of the family.

However, Nida observes that

> Strong emphasis on *machismo* inevitably produces the complementary *hembrismo,* or extreme female passivity and dependence. At the same time *machismo,* though catering to male dominance, also implies considerable dependence on females, who must constitute the "stage" upon which the male acts out his dominant role. Being constantly motivated to exhibit his dominance also produces a measure of insecurity in the male—an aspect of the two-edged sword of values.[17]

But it is the mother who is given the overwhelming responsibility for taking care of the home as well as providing the care and discipline and education of the children. She is the heart of the family, the center of emotions, the sacrificing woman who gives her entire life to advance the future of her children. She will scrimp on what the father gives—assuming there *is* a father present—making ends meet as is possible. She will get what she wants out of him, perhaps by manipulation—subtle or obvious. She is also the religious parent, sensing in the parish priest the true model of manhood—the pure, gentle man of God who does not stoop to sexual relationships and whose eyes are fixed on higher spiritual values. Her husband, she suspects or knows, is unfaithful to her. If she knows, she has two options: make a scandal or keep it quiet. Perhaps she will bargain with her husband, saying essentially, "I know what you are doing. Just don't embarrass me and I won't embarrass you, and above all keep it from the children. I won't tell them, if you behave." In subtle ways she may manipulate her children as they grow: "I am the one who has given my life for you; I have laid down my rights to help you. And I know that when you are grown and I am old and grey-headed you won't forget me. You will take care of me in my waning years." And they probably will not forget; they will take care of her.

The preceding cases speak of homes where both parents live; but the reality in Latin America is all too often a dramatic tragedy in which the man has fatherer or sired, like a stud horse, uncounted numbers of children. On one plane trip to Latin America with my family I sat next to a Latin military officer. I thought I might witness to him and opened the conversation on the family side of things. He asked about my children and I pointed them out on the plane—not too hard to do with three red-heads. I asked him how many he had and he sardonically remarked, "At home I have five, but on the streets, only God knows how many there are!" A close friend of mine has two brothers and sisters by both parents, but has traced down about twenty-seven half-brothers and half-sisters, all a result of his father's sexual desires. Pedro Arana wrote in Guatemala some years ago the following statement on love and lust in Latin America:

> The most widely spread idea of love in our lands has as its symbol, the bed, the archetype of man in our lands continues being a Don Juan, the sexual athlete who lives exclusively for the satisfaction of his glands. And it is precisely because of that class of pseudo-man that our societies have a high percentage of illegitimate sons, unmarried mothers and children virtually abandoned.[18]

Nida and Geyer are two North American authors who deal directly with the *machismo* factor. One writes from a Christian perspective, the other from a secular one. But both put a finger on the double standard in sexual and marital ethics that favors the male in every respect. Many Latin men prohibit the wife's use of birth-control methods because they simply distrust the wife; they suspect that the woman will be unfaithful if given a chance, but that the threat of pregnancy will keep her circumspect. However, it is expected that the man will be sexually promiscuous before and after marriage. One study done in Chile years ago revealed that the women considered it normal that a man have sexual experience before marriage, and many thought it good that the man have experience in sexual behavior before marriage. Geyer is biting in her judgment: "There is the wife for child-bearing and raising, and there are the women outside the family for carnal pleasures, for the symbolic ripping open. He is the ultimate man of appetite—but ironically he probably is a man who rarely enjoys that appetite because it always must serve his own ego."[19]

Do these attitudes surface within the evangelical church? Yes, they sadly do, for culture is the mother that forges family values. Two good Christian friends of mine, one a doctor and the other a psychologist, have been approached by evangelical mothers with a request similar to this: "Doctor, my son is going to turn sixteen, and I know he is looking for a sexual experience. But I don't want him to get a disease. Could you please recommend a good clean woman for him?" Each friend's response was truly Christian, and they explained why such a request was out of place for a believer. At the same time my own research has led me to believe that the majority of true Christians live a sexual ethic that is different from the non-Christian population.[20]

Nevertheless the problem of sexual ethics crops up in the youth of the churches. Who are their male models? The dominant *macho* father (even many Christians) lives with the submissive and servile wife, exemplifying anything but the New Testament example of a Christian home. If the father is a nonbeliever the example will probably be a negative one; and many non-Christian fathers will introduce their sons to a prostitute, the unwilling maid, or a willing woman for the first sexual experience. If the father has been unfaithful, this is the mentoring the son receives. If the mother expects unfaithfulness and is resigned to it, then the children will grow up expecting the same. Ironically, whereas the young man will have his sexual adventures before marriage, he feels it is important to marry a virgin.

Many times the sons grow up as pampered little babies who can do no wrong: protected by the father, babied by the mother, and favored by the entire family, particularly if the son is either the first or the last child. These values are also seen in too many evangelical homes, where they form the substrata of family attitudes. The fact is that few Latin American men are prepared adequately for marriage, including evangelicals. Premarital counseling is almost unheard of among pastors whose training has been so limited. The dearth of Christian literature written for the context of Latin America (and not translations of English-language best sellers) is marked. For that reason, after fourteen years of research and teaching on the topic, I ventured into writing a book *for and from* that context.[21]

A Different Rhythm of Life

Latin America has a bad reputation as the land of "Mañana," the world of "tomorrow." This is a caricature; but it does reflect a historically particular attitude toward time, an attitude that is often such an irritant for the Anglo-Saxon. The Latin cultures place a different value on time, and time is not really gold to them. People are more important. Time is a servant, not the master.

Hall states that "time talks. It speaks more plainly than words." This I have seen time and time again as I wait in government offices. Many times I have been told to come for the appointment at a certain time. I used to arrive a bit early, "just in case." I learned quickly that regardless of the time I showed up, I would wait. So I always took along something to read. One observer noted that when the Latin spends a night in a hotel and needs to be awakened in the morning he might say, "Wake me up *somewhere* between six and six-thirty A.M." And most appointments between friends have this delightful flexibility of scheduling, allowing always for the inevitable delays, some uncontrolled and many others designed.

Hall writes that "as a rule, Americans think of time as a road or a ribbon stretching into the future, along which one progresses. The road has segments or compartments which are to be kept discrete ('one thing at a time')."[22] But not Latin Americans. A common sight finds many things going on at the same time in the same room or office. "Good grief! How can you get *anything* done here?" But the Latin can flex more with such situations in which many relationships are being worked on at the same time.

The Latin American calendar is loaded with holidays: international, national, state, city or local, secular, and religious. Every village, town, and city has its own patron saint who guarantees another holiday. And Catholic hierarchy with influence will also seek an annual holiday in honor of the Virgin Mary. Labor laws give many days off with full pay, and the government will schedule many holidays to provide long weekends. The roads will be jammed out of the city at the start and end of these "weekend bridges." Christians have learned to plan church schedules and special activities around these holidays, particularly events that emphasize family activities.

Fiestas and holidays break the deadening rhythm of life. Mexican poet and philosopher Octavio Paz writes that Mexicans at the local fiesta escape drudgery; and when an angry or excited Mexican party-goer "discharges his pistol into the air, he discharges his soul." There is a catharsis in the party, too many times accompanied by drunkenness and immorality. The annual calendar is guided by the rhythm of fiestas and holidays. Perhaps the continental epitome of celebration is Rio de Janeiro's pre-Lenten four-day festival of flesh and fantasy, ironically a show put on by the city's poor and black for the whole world—the destitute and the wealthy. Samba clubs compete ferociously for the annual prizes; but after the festival, life sinks back to deadening routine. In many countries no significant government business can be taken care of during the last two weeks of December or even the first one of January. It is a time to have parties, to celebrate, to escape. For the Christian it is a marvelous time to evaluate the past and seek God's blessing for the future.

For that reason most evangelical churches have a solid series of church activities during the Christmas and New Year's season. As far as I can remember—from my childhood through to the last new year we celebrated in Guatemala—the New Year's service was special. It would start about 7:30 P.M. and end after midnight, sometimes celebrating the Lord's Table with special poignancy. Our Guatemalan church would conclude shortly before midnight for a magnificent time of blowing off fireworks, a costly but meaningful national custom.

The Prizing of Detailed Laws

From the Iberian legacy comes the Latin prizing of detailed laws. Colonial America in 1635 had some four hundred thousand edicts on the law books at the same time. One major difference between North America and Latin America can be observed in the legal traditions that have forged these civilizations. North America practices common law, which came from England and is based on historical precedents. Law is constantly being made and even changed by ongoing rulings. Latin American law is Spanish, Roman law, civil law, law of written codes—penal, civil, and many other. To study law requires the student to memorize the codes. It is a legalistic society. One simple difference can be seen between "Innocent until proven guilty," North American law; and, on the other side, "Guilty until proven innocent," Latin American law.

One South American proverb speaks volumes: "The law is to be acknowledged but not obeyed." What does this mean? Well, even though the laws are on the books and should be obeyed by most people, there are times when circumstances call for "flexibility" in the application of the law. There is a ready ability—sometimes delightful, sometimes questionable, other times blatantly illegal—to transcend those laws through different connections of family, friends, or cash payment. Clearly it is not a matter of *what* you know but *whom* you know, a reality demonstrated from the lowest legal levels up through the supreme courts. Those without the connections fatalistically resign themselves to whatever comes, and many become ripe for radical political change.

Hall discusses this flexible attitude toward law, particularly noting the interaction between the formal law and the family's role in protecting its members.

> If something should happen or if something is wanted in a Latin-American country, families are apt to be better at handling the affair than the government. This informal tradition is associated with a different concept of law from our own. Law in Latin America is enforced technically (by the book), but it is mediated by family relationships.[23]

Latin evangelicals demonstrate this love for detailed law with extremely complex constitutions and bylaws of churches and other Christian organizations. The appeal of ecclesiastical bureaucracy shows itself in the bestowal of important titles and in the desire to obtain and exercise power, and it is compounded by the sacerdotal mentality of both the clergy and the laity. All too often one sees within Christian leaders the willingness to bend laws, to pressure for special privileges, even to lie and cheat. Built into the culture is a fundamental distrust of other people, particularly those outside the family network. In numerous cases I have seen Anglo-Saxon missionaries elected treasurers of organizations simply because they are trusted. They also are assumed to have no need to pilfer from the coffer because of their foreign support.

When a Latin is caught cheating—for example, on an examination in a seminary class—many times guilt is limited. What is felt is shame for having been caught, shame for having embarrassed oneself, one's family, or the teacher. In many sad ways Latin evangelicals reflect the lower standard of the secular society when it comes to the matter of truth. This fundamental flaw must be dealt with by serious and applied teaching of the Scriptures. If evangelicals are to be elected to the highest office of the land, qualified, honest, and committed fellow-believers must emerge to share the task of governing the land.

The Combination of Authoritarianism and Individualism

Nida has done an excellent job in juxtaposing authoritarianism and individualism. Let us follow his definitions within the Latin context:

> Authoritarianism stands for a structured control of society from some "top" or "center." The avowed pur-

pose of authoritarian control is unity, and generally the proclaimed basis is some doctrinaire concern for tradition. In any event the society (as expressed in and through its leadership) takes priority over the individual.

Individualism, on the other hand, may be described as expressing itself primarily in terms of personal reaction and revolt against the status quo, with strong appeals to liberty and a tendency to radicalism (or break with tradition) in politics, religion, and art.[24]

The authoritarian strand was built into Latin American society from even before the conquest and colonization. Spain in particular ruled with a rod of iron; and the church backed the cross with miracle, mystery, and authority. The political history resonates with the ongoing *caudillos,* and family life never doubts the authority of the father. While authoritarianism is not peculiar to Latin American society, it is ironic that both the political left and right have their *caudillos.* A number of sensitive authors have criticized this Latin penchant for building the power base from which to exercise personal authority.

This characteristic is very visible among evangelical leaders, whether on a small scale in a little church, in the megachurches of the large cities, in the denominational bureaucracies, in the various para-ecclesiastical organizations, or other ministries. The concentration and abuse of personal power among Latin evangelicals simply reflects the larger secular society, for most of them have not seen the biblical servant-leader modeled. This becomes a most significant challenge for true biblical teaching and Christian discipleship in Latin America.

One fascinating demonstration of individualism crops up in the Latin's signature, a unique mark of *that* person. From early childhood the Latin begins working on a particular signature that later will become a written fingerprint of identity. It is so interesting to observe children developing their own formations of letters with added swirls, cutting lines, and special angles. By the time adulthood comes, that signature belongs to only one person in the world; and it will be the mark on all correspondence, bank accounts, legal documents, passports, or other personal-identity papers. That indecipherable squiggle probably has precious little resemblance to the typed name, but it is *his,* it is *hers.* It is unique.

Individualism allows the Latin to cope creatively with authoritarianism. Here again he or she can jump the legal barriers and resort to personal or family connections to neutralize the abuse of power. *Per-*

sonalismo is a similar term, speaking of the intense focus on the *yo*, the "me first and foremost" of the society. You clearly see it in the Latin soccer style, one that rewards the brilliant individual player, not necessarily the team player. *Personalismo* also allows the individual to exert his personality and assume personal power, and from there it is a short trip to some variety of the strongman.[25]

Latin individualism is also epitomized in the *yo* ("me") demonstration. The Spanish author-philosopher Miguel de Unamuno was once asked, "Sir, to what political party do you belong?" He responded, "To Unamuno's party, and to the dissident wing!" Only a Latin can understand this fully. I shall never forget the Spanish cartoon entitled "I have rights!" It portrayed a small boy urinating in a public site. I also well remember the times in Costa Rica when, standing in line at a government office, a person would cut into the line, affirming proudly, *"Tengo derecho"* ("I have rights"). One Latin American educator told me that the national educational system of her country was designed to produce individualistic persons, not members of the larger society.

A Particular Attitude Toward Work

The Spanish mentality, heavily influenced by Moorish thought and blessed by Catholic theology, denigrated physical labor and idealized those who "used their brains." Lipset writes in *Elites in Latin America*: "Those sent over from Spain or Portugal held the predominant positions, and in the colonies 'ostentatiously proclaimed their lack of association with manual, productive labor or any kind of vile employment.'"[26] The historic attitude has been that a few are born to rule, and the rest are born to serve those who rule. Hernán Cortés, conqueror of Mexico, expressed the Spanish attitude well: "I came for gold, not to till the land like a peasant."

Related to this is the importance given to an education that bestows diplomas, degrees, and formal titles. The simple title *Don* or *Doña* (Mr. and Mrs.) gives a category to a person and becomes an important part of the name. Other titles include, "Professor," "Licenciate," "Doctor," and all convey status and power. These are historically related to the ancient custom of bestowing upon a person a title of some kind. Manual labor is generally looked down upon, even by many who have to do it for a living. It is common to find craftsmen who produce beautiful work but who feel that their job is cursed because it is not "brain power." A Latin prefers to get some kind of white-collar job, even if it pays less than a manual or technical one. Rarely do you see a middle-class homeowner or a professional working in his yard or home. Few of them have any kinds of tools to work with, much less a tool shed or personal shop.

This work ethic can be observed in all aspects of the society, including the evangelical church. Once a believer moves vocationally beyond the point of physical labor, he never returns willingly to it. I have seen this in Bible institutes and seminaries. A young person from the lower laboring class who acquires a basic Bible training will have a most difficult time accepting that he might have to work again with his hands in the ministry. Thankfully this is not always the case, particularly in those schools which operate in rural areas and where studies are geared to crop cycles. Evangelicals must teach the biblical concept of work, not because North American missionaries have come up with the Puritan ethic, but because the Word sanctifies manual and nonmanual work. It is all to be done to the glory of God, who dignifies all labor.

A Special Love for Their Spanish Language

Latins are devoted to their language. How many peoples have a royal society dedicated to the preservation and purity of their language? The Spanish do. And the truly authorized Spanish dictionary is the one produced by the Royal Spanish Academy. In literary magazines as well as in newspapers one can find articles written about particular words, or about an unusual subjunctive-mood construction, or about proverbs and sayings. These latter are the key to unlocking much of the mental processes of the Latins, and they become formidable communication tools in evangelizing, teaching, and preaching. Significantly, some six thousand Spanish words can be traced to Arabic roots.

Frustration comes for the learner of Spanish when he discovers the intricacy of the Spanish verb system or the complex uses of the second-person pronoun. In Central America this pronoun has three forms, and each changes totally the verb used in the clause. Each "you" pronoun, *usted, tu,* and *vos,* also comes with different degrees of personal intimacy. The missionary beginning his study of Spanish may begin to master the *usted* form only to discover that one prays in the *tu* form with a different verb structure. Personal relationships are controlled by this pronoun. The *usted* form keeps things at a distance and with respect, while the *tu* tends to introduce dimensions of intimacy. I have seen a teacher use the *tu* form with his students, but they are to respond in the *usted* form. He can be intimate, but they must be respectful.

The subjunctive mood bears brief comment. This language category, the "could be, perhaps, if, depending, it might be that under certain circumstances we could consider the possibility of perhaps—" is a crucial key for unlocking the subtleties and the nuances of conversation and meaning. It is very complex as well, tripping up the young and even the veteran Spanish student.

Once I listened to an entire message by a new missionary, but there was something strange. His doctrine was firm, the accent quite good, the sentences appeared to be complete, the illustrations fine. What was wrong? He was about to conclude when it dawned on me, "This man has not used the subjunctive once in the entire sermon!" I cautiously broached the topic with him later, and he confessed, "I never understood the subjunctive, and I avoid it always." To which I said, "Brother, if you do not master the subjunctive, you will never minister effectively in Spanish." The subjunctive is a sensitive element in problem solving, in evaluations, or in business meetings, particularly when something difficult has to be said to another person. The rebuke or admonition comes wrapped in subjunctive. Most Latins understand what is happening, especially if they are on the receiving end of the exhortation. But many times missionaries miss the whole point because they lose the soft subjunctive nuances. If a missionary wants to capture the love of the people, there must be a commitment to mastering the language, preferably with an excellent accent.

A Somber Dimension—The Cult of Death

Visit any Latin American cemetery and contrast it to most Anglo-Saxon ones. The cult of death is particularly visible at the end of life when families and friends demonstrate their emotions and evaluations of the deceased. The cult of death is woven into the very warp and woof of Latin society, with the apex seen in the tragic Christ of Latin America. John MacKay's masterful evaluation of this emotional set of values is penetrating, particularly as he quotes from Spanish authors, especially Miguel de Unamuno.

> In Spanish religion Christ has been the centre of a cult of death. And yet, paradoxically enough, it was the passion for fleshly life and immortality that created this interest in death. The dead Christ is an expiatory victim. The details of His earthly life are of slight importance and make relatively small appeal. He is regarded as a purely supernatural being, whose humanity, being only apparent, has little ethical bearing upon ours. This docet-

ic Christ died as the victim of human hate, and in order
to bestow immortality, that is to say, a continuation of
the present earthly, fleshly existence. The contemplation
of His passion produces a sort of catharsis . . . just as in
the bull-fight, an analogous creation of the Spanish spirit, the Spaniard sees and feels death in all its dread reality in the fate of a victim. The total sensation in-
tensifies his sense of the reality and terribleness of death;
it increases his passion for life, and, in the religous
realm, makes him cling desperately and tragically to the
dead Victim that died to give him immortality.[27]

MacKay also notes that such attitudes produce a Christianity "devoid of both intellectual and ethical content." The cult of death comes to
a climax on the annual Day of the Dead as well as during the Easter season, when the Passion Week is recreated, in some cases with literal cru-
cifixions. Sevilla, Spain, and Antigua, Guatemala, are two of the prime
examples of the Passion fervor; for weeks before Good Friday, processions slowly wind through the city streets. But the pinnacle of faith
and death comes on Friday when the full re-enactment is completed and
passionate emotions are played out. And Sunday, what happens? Will
there be majestic resurrection processions? No. There may be a small and
symbolic ceremony, but nothing compared to the death on Friday. MacK-
ay again:

A Christ known in life as an infant and in death as a
corpse, over whose helpless childhood and tragic fate the
Virgin Mother presides; a Christ who became man in the
interests of eschatology, whose permanent reality resides
in a magic wafer bestowing immortality; a Virgin Mother who by not tasting death, became the Queen of Life—
that is the Christ and that the Virgin who came to America! He came as Lord of Death and of the life that is to
be; she came as sovereign Lady of the life that now is.[28]

CONCLUSION

These are but a few of the characteristics of the Latin American personality that I perhaps understand in part. Others could be mentioned,
such as the Latin joy of living, the exuberant attitude toward existence

tempered by a profound sense of fatalism. Another is the idealism-realism combination, where the Latin is part Don Quixote and part Sancho Panza—the dreamer and the realist. Never underestimate the place of the Spanish novel *Don Quixote* in the formation of the Spanish mind and heart.

Yet another dimension is expressed eloquently in the terms *ganas* and *sensibilidad*. The first literally means "desire," but it goes deeper than that word, referring to a gut-level drive to accomplish something or to feel something. It can be used in either a positive or negative sense. *Sensibilidad* touches again on that tender, sensitive spirit that responds with deep emotion, many times openly, to the entire spectrum of feeling. It is generally a positive term, referring to the emotional reaction to many things: tragedy, beauty, patriotism, family, sports, and others.

The few qualities I have discussed come from years of living in Latin America. However, my love goes deeper, based on a growing acceptance of the way God has allowed these cultures to evolve, as well as his desire that they experience his culture-changing power through the vibrant resurrected Christ.

NOTES

1. Eugene Nida, *Understanding Latin Americans: With Special Reference to Religious Values and Movements* (South Pasadena, CA: William Carey Library, 1974).

2. Georgie Anne Geyer, *The New Latins: Fateful Changes in South and Central America* (Garden City, NY: Doubleday, 1970).

3. Sarnuel Ramos, *Profile of Man and Culture in Mexico,* trans. Peter G. Earle (Austin, TX: University of Texas, 1962). Carlos Rangel, *The Latin Americans: Their Love-Hate Relationship with the United States,* trans. from the French by Ivan Kats (New York: Harcourt, Brace Jovanovich, 1976). Octavio Paz, *The Labyrinth of Solitude: Life and Thought in Mexico,* trans. Lysander Kemp (New York: Grove Press, 1961). Leopoldo Zea, *The Latin American Mind,* trans. James H. Abbott and Lowell Dunham (Norman, OK: University of Oklahoma, 1963).

4. Zea, *The Latin American Mind,* pp. 16-17.

5. Ibid., p. 270.

6. Gene Getz, *Refinemos la Perspectiva de la Iglesia,* trans. Guillermo Serrano (Miami: Editorial Caribe, 1981), pp. 270-71. The chapters on history and culture were adapted to Latin America by William D. Taylor and Esther L. de Cajas, faculty of the Central American Theological Seminary in Guatemala City.

7. J. D. Douglas, ed., *Let the Earth Hear His Voice: International Congress on World Evangelization, Lausanne, Switzerland* (Minneapolis: World Wide Publications, 1975), pp. 6-7.

8. Seymour Martin Lipset, "Values, Education and Entrepreneurship," in Seymour Martin Lipset and Aldo Solari, eds., *Elites in Latin America* (London: Oxford University, p. 1976), pp. 11-12.

9. Edward T. Hall, *The Silent Language* (Greenwich, CT: Fawcett, 1959), p. 164.

10. Geyer, *The New Latins*, pp. 27-32.

11. Ramos, *Profile*, p. 53.

12. Paz, *The Labyrinth*, p. 54.

13. Germán Arciniegas, *Latin America: A Cultural History* (New York: Alfred A. Knopf, 1972), p. 55.

14. William D. Taylor, *Worlds in Conflict: The Impact of the University Social Structure on Protestant Students in the National University of Guatemala*, Ph.D. diss. University of Texas, Austin, 1967.

15. Claudio Veliz, ed., *The Politics of Conformity in Latin America* (London: Oxford University, 1967), p. 7.

16. Pedro Arana Quiróz, "The Spiritual Diagnosis of Latin America," Guatemala City, n.d., p. 2.

17. Nida, *Understanding Latin Americans*, p. 56.

18. Ibid., p. 7.

19. Geyer, *The New Latins*, p. 58.

20. Taylor, *Worlds in Conflict*. The sections dealing with sexual ethics among evangelical youth are pertinent.

21. Guillermo (William) D. Taylor, *La Familia Autenticamente Cristiana* (Grand Rapids, MI: Publicaciones Portavóz Evangélico, 1983). The manuscript was written in Spanish, from and for Latin America.

22. Hall, *The Silent Language*, p. 19.

23. Ibid., p. 81.

24. Nida, *Understanding Latin Americans*, p. 15.

25. Luis Mercier Vega, *Roads to Power in Latin America* (New York: Praeger, 1969).

26. Lipset and Solari, *Elites,* p. 8.

27. John MacKay, *The Other Spanish Christ* (New York: MacMillan, 1932), p. 98.

28. Ibid., p. 102.

Part Two

Critical Issues for Evangelicals in Latin America

Emilio Antonio Núñez

Introduction
to Part Two

The Introduction to this book gives a brief survey to Emilio Antonio Núñez's series of essays, which the reader might want to review before reading on. Writing from close to sixty years of experience as a Christian, with a Latin American as well as a global perspective, Dr. Núñez will introduce you to some of the weighty but crucial theological themes pertinent to Latin America.

Some of the essays, generated from a variety of contexts and now edited or rewritten for this book, were first presented in the context of Latin America's secular universities. Others were given in theological seminaries as lecture series, and yet others came as a result of Núñez's participation in international theological consultations. Some came in part from his role in the Theological Commission of the World Evangelical Fellowship, as well as from his role as a founder and current leader of the Latin American Theological Fraternity. And part of this section was created expressly for this work. All of the essays were written originally in Spanish and then translated into English.

Various major strands interweave to produce this scholarly tapestry of Latin American themes. One demonstrates Núñez's concern that Latin American evangelicals themselves speak to the contemporary issues that wrench their cultures and nations. His drive is to speak from a biblical perspective, yet at the same time to be sensitive to the social sciences and other disciplines. It is only too easy for some spokespersons to claim that *their perspective is the only valid one.* All opinions must be held under the scrutiny of God's Word, and at the same time be aware of the historical context of Latin America. Núñez encourages us to evaluate him also.

Secondly, Núñez writes from the perspective of the universal church of Christ as well as that of the local evangelical churches of Latin America. He is not only a scholar, a professor of theology, an international speaker and member of numerous global organizations. But he is also a pastor, and the founding spirit and teacher of a new and creative congregation in Guatemala City. His touch, therefore, is pastoral.

Third, Núñez writes from a long-term perspective of militancy in the Christian ministry. Shortly after his conversion (and in the process meeting the young woman whom he would marry) in El Salvador decades ago as a young school teacher, he was led of the Spirit to prepare for and enter the ministry. His experience is vast and heterogeneous. In the early years of his international ministry some Latin evangelical leaders did not consider his voice one that merited much attention. He won their respect not with eloquence or power, but by his humility, gracious spirit, the capacity to learn from others, pastoral heart, and unquestioned competence in the Scriptures and contemporary theology.

Fourth, he writes very much aware of his changing Latin America, including the reality that the "older guard" of evangelical thinkers of his continent must pass on the torch to their Timothys. For that reason one will find him constantly surrounded by a group of disciples, who interact listening, learning, questioning, and dialoguing with him. He encourages them to think creatively, pushing them to break new biblical ground, to stake out a wider horizon, to write and publish, to probe the mission of the church within the context of contemporary Latin America, to serve with humility and a pastoral heart. Would to God that Latin America had more leaders of this timbre.

So as you read, listen to the voice of a veteran, interact with him, stretch your world, disagree creatively and biblically with him. You are not required to accept everything you read, but you are challenged to examine everything and hold fast to that which is true. May God give you insight as you read, ponder, and apply these thoughts to Latin America and to your own life as well.

6

The Hispano-American Christs

About Spain the poet has sung, "The Spanish race is ready and prepared. Captain Cervantes is at the helm, and the banner of Christ floats on high." It has also been said that the simple American of Indian blood "still prays to Christ and still speaks Spanish." This latter is certainly undeniable; the reign of Cervantes continues among us, although we are not all his most loyal subjects. The point about praying to Christ raises certain questions, one of which is, To which Christ do the Latin Americans pray? For the truth is that, although there are many Christs of humnan fabrication, there is only one true, authentic Christ who lies hidden behind altars that could well bear the legend, "To the Unknown Christ," because there are thousands upon thousands who worship him without knowing him.[1]

THE SPANISH CHRIST

It is true that Christ came to us via Spain—that Spain which, endowed with a sense of mission, a singular mystique of the Iberian spirit, conquered and colonized a large part of the New World. "For the first and last time in the history of Christianity," says John MacKay, "the sword and cross formed an offensive alliance for the purpose of taking Christianity—or at least that which was considered to be such—to foreign lands."[2]

Heading up the enterprise was Christopher Columbus, the admiral

227

from Genoa who, capitalizing on the tradition surrounding his historical namesake, claimed to be a true "bearer of Christ." But to the question, Which Christ? the reply must be: none other than the one of austere medieval garb, the one of the cold and inflexible Scholastics, the Christ of Spain.

How strange the conquerors' Christ must have seemed to the aboriginal Americans: the white God who dies for all humanity establishes a religion with its supreme authority in Rome and with the king of Spain among its devotees—the same king who sends a group of his warlike subjects to discover and subjugate mysterious and distant lands on the other side of the ocean. In the name of God and of the king, these men from Castille—ruddy as the sun and riding spirited steeds—slay Indians right and left, rob their lands, rape their women, and transform those who survive the slaughter into slaves of the pope and of the great Spanish empire.

"In many cases," states Sante Uberto Barbieri, "the spirit of the sword was stronger and more powerful than the spirit of the cross. For many, Christ was not a savior who had given his life for them, but a celestial tyrant who destroyed lives for his glory, through the conquest of the lands of others."[3]

With the exception of the works of charity on the part of some missionary priests—such as the well-known Fray Bartolomé de las Casas—the colonizer did extremely little in the social and economic spheres, efforts that would have helped erase the negative impressions acquired by the Indians in their first encounter with the Christ in whose name they lost everything, including their liberty. And not only the Indians, but also the new race that grew out of the union of the two peoples, were objects of persistent oppression and humiliation on the part of the followers and defenders of this Christ.

This most certainly was not the Christ that had been announced in golden trumpet tones by the Reformers of the sixteenth century. No, he had been left behind in Spain to be attacked unrelentingly by Ignacio de Loyola, crushed by Charles V and Philip II, and consumed in the implacable flames of the *autos de fe*. Although other European countries were able to shake off their centuries-old lethargy in the convulsive awakening of the Reformation, Spain remained undisturbed and inert, its religion failing to experience the labor pains of a new era.

"The other Spanish Christ," of whom the great Spanish mystics such as San Juan de la Cruz and Fray Luis de Granada sang in magnificent poems, was very slow in making his pilgrimage to the new continent. If he did in fact have followers here from the beginning of the colonial period, his influence was insufficient to counteract that of the Christ of tradition.

Still and all, the missionaries labored long and hard to make their Christ acceptable to the mentality of the oppressed race; but in their zeal to adapt to the Indian culture they were unable to avoid the emergence of religious syncretism. They tolerated and even stimulated the mixture of Spanish Christianity with the beliefs and practices of the local religion. Christ, the Virgin, and the saints merely swelled the ranks of the deities of the American pantheon, while countless numbers of Indians continued to worship their former gods in the images brought by Catholicism. Behind these saints with white skin and blue eyes, the magical and powerful presence of regional gods and goddesses arose, unrestrained and unchallenged in the religious experience of their worshipers.

THE IMAGE CHRIST

Images of Christ, already very prominent in the religion of the colonizers, proved very useful to the church in its task of indoctrination in the Americas. It was much easier to display a statue than elucidate a dogma; to replace native idols with European images than uproot centuries-old religious beliefs. And once again, religious syncretism manifested itself, for it was not difficult to give the image a New World likeness in the sculptures and paintings of a Christ who, although retaining European features, was dark in color. There are many *mestizo*—and even black—Christs in our Hispanic America today.

Here Christ became wood or stone, canvas or paper—often magnificent art—carving and painting, visible in splendid altars, in special niches in homes, in monastic cells, at the junctions of roads, and on the tops of mountains. The shadows of the image Christ fell across an entire continent.

The ubiquitous figure of Christ awakened deep sympathies in the people: after all, Christ is little more than a helpless infant in the protective arms of his mother—as sweet and inoffensive as any tiny child. How could he possibly be a tyrant or despot? Although he may not be able to free the people from their ominous chains, he is equally incapable of having forged the chains with his weak little hands.

He is the child that cannot talk; only Mary, who holds and protects him, can at times understand his infant babblings. This tiny infant God is most incapable of scolding the white masters of their abuse of power, their boundless greed and lust, or their overwhelming injustices perpetrated against the conquered and humiliated people. Deprived of the wonderful gift of speech, he poses no threat to anyone, whether powerful, or weak, or small. There is nothing he can do to stop either one from sinning: he is merely the image of a child that forever smiles, indifferent to the enormous tragedy going on around him. While a new race and a new world are being forcibly constructed under the heavy hand of despots, the child Christ remains serenely silent.

Hence, the simple Indian, subjugated by the white power brokers and treated like a child by his conquerors, consciously or unconsciously identifies himself with the child Christ and flees to seek refuge in the arms of the tender and loving mother. It is not surprising that the veneration of Mary came to enjoy a more prominent position than the worship of Christ. The oppressed seek the mother, Mary, and not her son, Jesus.

Another prevalent image is that of the suffering Christ. A principal feature of Hispano-American Catholicism has been that of the Nazarene who suffers pain, crucifixion, and death. one feature of the "Christianization" of this part of the Americas was the extensive implantation of the cross—the religious symbol employed by the Spanish in the conquest of the consciences of their new subjects. It was the religion of the crucifix, of the Christ that dies, powerless, nailed to an ignominious cross. While it is true that official dogma affirms the resurrection of Christ, that teaching seems not to reach the masses: the high point of the church year is not Easter Sunday, but Good Friday, when Christ is seen as the prisoner, flogged, crowned with thorns, nailed to the cross, and laid in a casket where he reposes year after year, for centuries.

The image Christ is a vanquished Christ. The Indians flee from him in terror and the new race, an admixture of two bloodlines, is born in defeat.

Hispano-America has not only wept *with* Christ; it has also—and to greater degree—wept *for* him: His words on the Calvary road have long since been forgotten: "Daughters of Jerusalem, do not weep for me; weep rather for yourselves and for your children."

Nevertheless, and for all its apparent contradictions, it is from the image Christ that favors are sought. He is at once pitied and feared, inspiring compassion and faith. In dire emergencies it is possible to turn to the image Christ, though it is better if the petition can be directed to one of the more miraculous ones. In his novel *El Señor Presidente,* Miguel Angel Asturias paints a vivid picture of the faith of the Latin American masses in the image Christ when he puts the following words into the mouth of a poor woman:

> I feel very sorry for you, so I went to ask a favor of the
> Jesus of Mercy. Maybe he'll work a miracle for you. Just

this mornin', before goin' to the penitentiary, I went to light a candle to him and tell him, "Look, black man, here I am with you and it ain't for nothin' you're the Daddy of us all so you listen up, now. You have the power to make sure that girl don't die and I asked the Virgin for this favor before I even got up this mornin' and now I'm botherin' you for the same thing, so here's a prayer candle, and I'm goin' now, and I'm countin' on your power, but I'll be back to remind you of my prayer."[4]

This woman's prayer could hardly be more sincere, nor her confidence stronger. This is how our people pray; this is how they have prayed for centuries to a Christ that is crucified, dead, and buried.

THE CHRIST OF THE MINORITIES

The Christ that is a stranger to the masses has not fared any better with the minority groups of our continent.

Not a few rich and powerful have found it very comfortable to believe in the image Christ that patiently suffers on the cross, all the while maintaining total silence in the face of the suffering of the poverty-stricken masses around them. For four hundred years their lips have been sealed, never uttering a word of what the people are waiting to hear.

It is quite easy to tolerate a Jesus of Nazareth who does not irritate his worshipers by calling attention to their sins or pricking their consciences calloused by evil ways. All that is required is to toss him a few alms from time to time and carry him on their shoulders once a year in the Holy Week processions, where all can see. He is safely nailed to the cross, sealed in the sepulcher, kept behind church walls, locked in a glass coffin, or reduced to impotence in the safety of the convent or monastery. He is not to be found in the intimacy of homes or becoming involved in the lives of others. His world is the sanctuary, his tomb-like peace being disturbed only when, on rare occasions, he is taken out to be admired, pitied, and wept for by the multitudes.

In intellectual circles, Christ is easily transformed into a mere symbol or figure of speech. He is observed from a variety of angles and presented as a spiritual leader, a teacher or philosopher, a social reformer, or perhaps as a misguided visionary who took the wrong road in his sincere desire to liberate humanity.

Some respect and admire him, proffering thousands of compliments, whereas others pass him by with utter indifference or mockery. Many merely tolerate him, manifesting an attitude of solicitous paternalism. They feel sorry for him because they see him, as Ruben Darío would put it, still wandering through the streets, "scrawny and frail." For them he is the Christ who, according to Amado Nervo, knocks in vain on the doors, seeking a place where he can rest:

> Christ: from everywhere,
> Modern science casts you out
> Without compassion. You
> Have nowhere to live, Lord!
>
> (Hospitalidad)

As always, there are those who deny the reality of Christ's existence. Of course, they are not involved in any quests for the historical Jesus. For others, he might possibly pertain to the past but not to the present, and certainly not to the future. They believe they live in a post-Christian era and do not see in Christ the answer to the anguish of contemporary humans.

THE CHRIST OF PROTESTANTISM

If the Roman Catholic Christ came to us via Spain, the Protestant Christ came from other European countries—such as England, Germany, France, and the Netherlands—and from the United States. As a consequence, many have come to identify Protestantism with western imperialist or capitalist systems—a topic well worth separate study.

From now on and in general terms, suffice it to say that the Protestant Christ was inherited from the religious Reformers of the sixteenth century—thjough he did not originate with them, nor was he mediated by them.

The Reformers regard the sacred Scriptures as their final authority, referring to them exclusively in all questions of faith and placing them before and above the authority of the church. Their battle cry was: "The Scriptures alone, Christ alone, grace alone, and faith alone as the means of justification before God."

Rather than seeking Christ in the shadow of altars, in ancient parchment of ecclesiastical tradition, or in the philosophical-theological writings of the Scholastics, they turned to the Sacred Text. The Reformation was a return to the Bible, a determined effort to rediscover the Christ of the New Testament.

This suggests the second main theme of the Reformation: the salvation message that has as its center and circumference the person and work of Jesus Christ. He is lifted to the place preeminence, not only in theology, but in the life and worship of the church as well. He is the Christ who, through the incarnation, participates in the history and experience of humanity. Clothed in human flesh and blood, he lives with humans, identifying himself completely with them, suffering with and for them and, in the end, dying for them. But he is also the Christ of the resurrection; consequently, emphasis is on the Christ who lives forever and who, transcending time and space, is nevertheless present in his redemptive work in the world today.

A third characteristic of the Reformation was its tendency to individualism. The Reformers strove for the liberty of conscience, proclaiming that every person possessed the unrestricted fight to the free consideration of all questions having to do with matters of faith. The teaching of the universal priesthood of believers emphasized the freedom of the individual to seek God and approach his word without the intervention of human authority. The Reformation left the individual alone with God in the santuary of his conscience, guided by the light of divine revelation.

This Protestant individualism is also manifested in the secular dimension of the Christian for whom—conscious of her or his personal dignity before God, the church, and the state—all vocations are sacred. Thus, the individual can and should glorify God in any honorable job or profession, not only in the isolation of the convent cell. Nor does the priesthood have a monopoly on the sacred: in the eyes of the Creator, all vocations are holy.

Also, it was to be expected that this individualism would produce a variety of Protestant groups. But, by the same token, it should not be surprising, the monolithic structure of the medieval church having been fractured, that those who for the first time breathed the fresh air of religious freedom would not want to erect another vast hierarchical structure to which to submit. Such a move would be entirely out of keeping with the spirit of the Reformation. When certain Protestant leaders, such as John Calvin, attempted to return to the earlier authoritarianism, they encountered determined resistance from those who had been enlightened by the new day of spiritual freedom.

Fourthly, the Reformation produced certain socio-political effects. For one thing, given the close ties that had existed between the church and civil jurisdiction, it was inevitable that conflicts between the latter and the reform movement should develop: to oppose the church was to

oppose secular authority as well. Consequently, certain political and social changes were very quickly effected in those countries where the Reformation succeeded, bringing along with them seeds of liberty that one
day would germinate and grow, to the benefit of our civilization.

Having been known through the Scriptures, the Christ of the majority of Latin American Protestants is, without doubt, a biblical one. Hispano-American Protestants are a community of the Book—the Bible—
and their doctrine is profoundly Christological: Christ is preeminent in
theology, liturgy, and service. In their worship, the cross and tomb are
empty, for he is the Lord of life and conqueror of death, the Lord who
lives now and forever, the only mediator between God and humanity.
"Only Christ Saves," "Christ is the Answer," and "Christ the Only Hope"
have been favorite slogans of the Protestants in their evangelistic efforts
throughout the continent.

The Latin American Protestant's individualism is also reflected in
his experience: in the light of his conscience and under the searchlight of
the divine world, Protestant believers enjoy freedom from ecclesiastical
and hierarchical entanglements in the pursuit of communion with their
God. Their faith does not depend on human authority. Their relationship
with Christ is deep and intensely personal. Hence, Protestant groups pro-
liferate in Ibero-America; but the erection of a huge hierarchical edifice
for the purpose of bringing together and governing all the various Protestant communions would contradict the very spirit of Latin American
Protestantism. The disadvantages of disjunction are to be preferred to
those that a centralized church government would bring.

That historical and social factors have generally served to accentu-
ate the individualistic approach to social responsibility on the part of the
Latin American Protestant is undeniable (yet another very interesting
topic for subsequent research). The truth is that, particularly among the
more conservative elements of Protestantism in Hispan-America, there
has been an attitude of indifference in the face of the serious problems
that keep these so-called "developing countries" in turmoil.

Up to now, when social problems came into focus the Christ of
many Ibero-American Protestants has been merely eschatological—in
the narrow sense of the term. With their apparent attitude of indifference
toward the conflicts that afflict our society, these Christians could well
have left the impression that, for them, all socio-economic difficulties
should be left for Christ to resolve in the next life, and that little or nothing should be done now to improve the world in which they live.

Fortunately, new breezes have begun to blow that promise a change
in this posture of social negligence. Even the Christ of conservative Prot-

estantism has begun to open his mouth to say what for so long was kept quiet regarding the social problems of the Latin Americans. It is high time he be allowed to speak.

THE CHRIST OF THE NEW THEOLOGY

One of the most widespread reactions to the silence of the traditional Christ is that which is now beginning to manifest itself in both Catholic and Protestant theological circles of the political left of Latin America.

Impatient and rebellious, and with a mystique capable of totally controlling certain personality types, the new theologians raise their cry for social justice.

The Christ they proclaim is anthropological and sociological; a capable economist and skilled statistician; mass psychologist, expert in foreign and domestic politics, revolutionary theoretician, and social reformer. He is the nonconformist Christ, the activist, the rebel (even violent) who dresses like a common laborer and speaks the complicated language of the technologists of our time.

The theology of this Christ—if it can be called theology—is definitely anthropocentric. It comes from humans, is for humans, and does not go beyond humans. It sets up its priorities within the material order and seeks a kingdom which is of this world, consisting of meat and drink that are separate from the spirit. Its supreme objective is the transformation of social structures, even though the individual remains unchanged.

In contrst to the individualist Christ or traditional Ibero-America Protestantism, this Christ of the leftist theologians is so furiously collectivist, so obsessed with the masses, that he is in danger of losing sight of the individual. In a way, this Christ is a product of our ultramodern civilization that depersonalizes the individual, crushing him or her beneath its enormous socio-economic machinery.

We should not be surprised, therefore, at the presence of the leftist Christ in Latin America. It was inevitable that, sooner or later, the socially inactive Christ would have his centuries-long sleep interrupted by the coming of another Christ who was anxious to speak out and to act. Whether the newcomer is genuine and authentic, however, needs to be made clear in the light of the New Testament.

Why in the light of the New Testament? Simply because there are no documents that speak with greater authority than they about the true

Christ. It is in the New Testament where, for the first time in the history of humanity, the person and work of Jesus of Nazareth are described. The testimony of men who walked with him and knew him intimately is found in its ancient pages—the source of Christianity, the spring from which we assimilate the lessons of its teacher and founder. For this reason, the New Testament is the norm or standard that determines the authenticity or falseness of our Christs, the light that reveals the truth or error of our Christianity, the flaming sword that separates those who belong to the true Christ from those who do not.

A new sign of hope is now visible on the horizon of our Hispanic America: there is a return to the reading of the Bible in various ecclesiastical communities. As a result, the Book of yesterday, today, and forever is in the hands of many, being devoured by eyes that are hungry for spiritual understanding. In response to the quest for faith, the majestic figure of the historical, living, and true Christ is bound to stand forth from its sacred pages.

The time has come for the moral courage to set the false Christs aside and embrace the true one, the one known by the writers of the New Testament: Peter, Paul, Matthew, John, Mark, and Luke, and the rest. Let us abandon the Spanish or Anglo-Saxon Christ, the blond or black Christ, *mestizo* or native-born. Let us rid ourselves of the Christ of our superstitious fears or our intellectual pride, and let us sign our spiritual declaration of independence by turning to the Christ who said, "The truth will make you free. . . . If the Son makes you free, you will be truly free."

NOTES

1.   This chapter is the text of a paper read in the main auditorium of the National University of San Carlos, Guatemala, in response to a request from the University Evangelical Group. It was published in 1972 in vol. 12, no. 47, of *Certeza,* of Buenos Aires, Argentina. (The style has been slightly edited for use in this volume.)

2.   John MacKay, *El Otro Cristo Español* (México: CUO, 1952), p. 41.

3.   Sante Uberto Barbieri, *El Pais de Eldorado* (Buenos Aires: La Aurora, 1962).

4.   Miguel Angel Asturias, *El Señor Presidente* (Buenos Aires: Ed. Losada), pp. 262-63.

Post-Conciliar Catholicism
in Latin America

7

Introduction
The Search for Renewal

Until World War II it was relatively easy to give a general description of Roman Catholicism in our Latin American countries. The Catholic church, at least institutionally, seemed to be a monolithic whole, with neither external fissures nor internal disturbances. The massive solidity of its cathedrals was like a symbol of its centuries-old stability.

Beginning in the 1940s, however, Latin America began to experience, much more intensely than in other periods, profound political and social questionings. Our economic dependence, precarious political liberty, and the misery of our situation all became more evident in the light of those noble ideals for which so many died in the war against the dictatorial Axis powers.

Latin America had been the empire of national and international colonialism. Dictatorships were our daily bread, and militarism reigned in several countries of this continent. In this atmosphere of oppression and misery it was ridiculous and paradoxical that Latin American governments of "El Señor Presidente" or of the current dictator should have declared war on Nazi Germany.While they obviously did this to keep in line with the United States government, the proclamation of democracy against Hitler's totalitarianism acted as a boomerang in some Latin American dictatorships. The Atlantic Charter and the Declaration of Human Rights, and other documents, encouraged Latin Americans in their search for freedom.

Roman Catholicism had allied itself with political conservatism and could not remain exempt from the attack launched against oppression by

239

the forces of change. The church had been, generally speaking, the property of the powerful, and the oppressed masses began to turn their back on it in political and social matters. The church did not have a relevant message for the hour in which our oppressed peoples had their great awakening. In order to find this message, she herself had to change.

The transformation of society, and the effort of the church to adapt herself to a changing world, have produced division among the clergy and laypeople in Roman Catholicism. There is no more just one Roman Catholic church in Latin America. It is now necessary to explain what kind of Catholicism we have in mind when we are dealing with the Catholic phenomenon in these countries.

Catholics used to boast about four main characteristics that they attributed to their church: apostolicity, catholicity, sanctity, and unity. As never before, unity is lacking in Roman Catholicism around the world. (It is not the purpose of this essay to discuss the other characteristics.) For instance, in Latin America we have the archconservative church and the revolutionary church; the church of popular religiosity and of the avant-garde theologians; the church of the hierarchy and "the people's church." Such a diversity is unknown to many evangelical leaders in other latitudes. Consequently they are surprised by the attitude taken by most of us Latin American evangelicals toward Roman Catholicism. But they have also to realize that in countries where the Roman Catholic church is in the minority, surrounded by another world religion, or by secularism, she is more ecumenical than in Latin America. Traditionally, Roman Catholicism has claimed the Latin American countries as its "area of influence" or missionary territory on the basis of history and culture, forgetting that the gospel is above culture, transforming culture, and that we are living no more in colonial times.

To know Roman Catholicism from the Latin American perspective, apart from any naive analysis of our religious situation, is indispensable for a relevant preaching of the gospel and for a real contextualization of evangelical theology in this subcontinent.

THE SEARCH FOR RENEWAL

From the beginning of this century there had been within Catholicism certain efforts to respond to the social problems of Latin America, most notable those based in the *Rerum novarum* encyclical of Leo XIII (1891).[1] From 1903 to 1923 movements were established in Mexico and Argentina that were precursors of Acción Católica (Catholic Action).[2] According to José Míguez Bonino, the widely known Protestant theologian from Argentina, "the different currents of renewal in European Catholicism—biblical, liturgical, ecumenical, social"—have since 1950 made headway in Latin America.[3] This, of course, occurs only within very select circles of Latin American Catholicism and not at the mass level. The masses continue to wander "like sheep without a shepherd."

The thousands of young people and workers involved in Acción Católica were a small minority of the millions of Catholics who remained alienated from the ethical orientation of the church. In the meantime, the institutional church continued to be tied to its traditional practices in political and social areas. John XXIII, who was aware of the economic, social, political, and moral challenges of the postwar world, asked for an "aggiornamento,"namely, an updating, a renewal, an awakening, a "fresh air" in the medieval atmosphere of the church.

Vatican II (1962-1965)

The importance of the Second Vatican Council cannot be exaggerated. Now it is absolutely necessary to speak of the preconciliar and postconciliar church. It is evident that since the days of Vatican II the Catholic church has been in the process of change. The theological profundity of this change may be questioned, but not so the reality of what has happened and continues to happen in contemporary Catholicism. Consider, for example, the new interest in the Bible, the liturgical renaissance, the declaration of religious freedom, the ecumenical openness toward other churches and religions, the new approach to the church's responsibility in the modern world, the crisis of authority in the clerical structures, the presence of theologians eager to reinterpret traditional dogma, and the apparent veering of Medellín toward the left in its analysis of the continent's social and political problems.[4] All these point to the transformation that is taking place in Catholicism today.

Medellín (1968)

The Second Latin American Episcopal Conference held in Medellín, Colombia, in 1968 was a sequel to the Second Vatican Council. Míguez Bonino has called the Medellín assembly "the Vatican II of Latin America."[5] The Latin American bishops dealt with the transformation of Latin America in the light of the Council and established guidelines for a new Latin American pastoral work.[6] Monsignor Alfonso López Trujillo, general secretary of the Latin American Episcopal Council (CELAM), the sponsoring organism of Medellín, has said that this conference presented a series of options as the foundation of a new era for the Catholic church in Latin America. One of these options is the one for the total person, for the Latin American people, for the poor, and for total liberation.[7]

Bishop Alisio Lorscheider, president of CELAM, points out that this council has promoted the development of autochthonous pastoral thought, that it has advocated a more just society in our continent, and that it has helped to discover the genuine image of the church in Latin America, "a poor church with an inescapable mandate to accomplish a mission of liberation."[8] According to Enrique Dussel, a Catholic scholar from Argentina, "CELAM will develop the theology of liberation as its own theology."[9] And regarding the conference at Medellín he comments: "At any rate Medellín opens the door for a clear class commitment, and it allows the taking of positions in defense of the interests of workers, peasants and those who have no voice in society."[10] In the opinion of the Catholic writer Roberto Oliveros Maqueo, the fundamental contribution of Medellín was to reflect on the faith from the context of misery and injustice under which large groups of Latin Americans are suffering.[11]

It is worth keeping in mind that Gustavo Gutiérrez, without a doubt the best known of the theologians of liberation, was one of the theological consultants for CELAM, and at Medellín he was a member of one of the most important task forces, the Peace Commission.[12] It can be said that Medellín officially opened the door to the theology of liberation.

Dealing with the concept of liberation according to his understanding of the conference of Medellín and its documents, Monsignor López Trujillo says:

> The liberating pastoral option demands a spirit of true reconciliation. . . . Social conflicts are neither denied nor unrecognized. . . . It does not identify itself with an attitude of traditional pacifism. . . . It has to be present in the struggle for justice. . . . It opposes a form of class struggle which is proper to Marxist analysis. . . . The occurrences of class consciousness are not denied. . . . There are forms of class struggle in which the Christian may, and in some occasions should, participate . . . without enmity or mutual hatred . . . based in the Love for justice.[13]

Even that moderate evaluation of the meaning of Medellín can open the way for Latin American theological liberationism.

Puebla (1979)

The third Latin American Episcopal Conference, sponsored by CELAM, was held in Puebla, Mexico, in February 1979. When the time for this transcendental event was approaching, many questions were asked in Latin America and in other parts of the world. Some observers of the ecclesiastical scene were wondering about the attitude that the Puebla Conference would assume toward some critical issues—for example, liberation theology, the political involvement of members of the clergy in the Latin American revolution, the extreme poverty of the masses and the excessive wealth of the few, the conflict between capitalism and Marxism, and the church of the poor.

Would Puebla mean a setback in the transformation promoted by Medellín? Or would Puebla move forward in the revolutionary process that Medellín encouraged? The presence of a new pope was also a motive of concern. Would John Paul II try to suffocate the revolutionary spirit within the Roman Catholic church, or would he follow the path of his predecessors John XXIII and Paul VI?

Generally speaking, the Medellín Conference meant, in a sense, the end of the centuries-old alliance of the Catholic church with the conservative political powers ruling Latin America. Moreover, Medellín motivated the political involvement of Catholics—members of the clergy included—in the struggle for social change. Since Medellín, hundreds of priests, monks, and nuns have been persecuted, arrested and tortured, and a number of them have been killed, as a result of the revolutionary situation prevailing in some Latin American countries. It was natural to ask what the pope and the Puebla Conference would say about the mission of the Catholic church in a context of social turmoil and change.

If the theme of Medellín was "The Church in the Present Transformation of Latin America in the Light of the Counbcil," Puebla dealt with "The Evangelization in the Present and Future of Latin America." To some extent the emphasis has changed. The main purpose is now the "evangelization" of Latin America. But most of the bishops considered Medellín as a *fait accompli*. And from the neo-Catholic point of view, "evangelization" includes political action to liberate the poor.

In Puebla the pope was quite conservative and gave a new thrust to popular religiosity, including the excesses in the veneration of Mary. With respect to social change in Latin America, both the pope and the conference were in the tradition of Medellín, but in a moderate way. The pope opposed the political involvement of the priests, but he did not condemn liberation theology. The conference did not approve capitalism or

Marxism. Instead, it offered a broad opening for other historical alternatives in favor of social transformation. The "preferential option for the poor" was supported and promoted. The Puebla Documents seem to be a special effort to integrate the new message on social justice and liberation into the theological framework of traditional Catholicism.

NOTES

1. In *Ocho Grandes Mensajes* (Madrid: Biblioteca de Autores Cristianos, 1973), pp. 13-56.

2. Enrique Dussel, *Historia de la Iglesia en América Latina* (Barcelona, Spain: Editorial Nova Terra, 1972), pp. 126-27.

3. José Míguez Bonino, "El Nuevo Catolicismo," *Fe Cristiana y Latinoamérica Hoy,* C. René Padilla, ed. (Buenos Aires, Argentina: Ediciones Certeza, 1974), pp. 84-90. See also Dussel, pp. 129-33.

4. *La Iglesia en la Actual Transformación de América Latina a la Luz del Concilio,* 2 vols. (Bogotá, Secretariado General del CELAM, 1969).

5. Míguez Bonino, "El Nuevo Catolicismo," p. 91.

6. Emilio A. Núñez, "Posición de la Iglesia Evangélica frente al Aggiornamento," *Acción en Cristo para un Continente en Crisis* (San José, Costa Rica: Editorial Caribe, 1970), pp. 39-40.

7. Alfonso López Trujillo, "Medellín una mirada global," *La Iglesia en la actual transformación de América Latina a la luz del Concilio,* 1:12.

8. Monsignor Alisio Lorscheider, "Qué es el CELAM" (What is CELAM), *Medellín: Reflexiones en el CELAM* (Madrid: Biblioteca de Autores Cristianos, 1977), pp. 8-10.

9. Enrique D. Dussel, "Un análisis contextual de la Iglesia Católica en América Latina (1968-1969)," *Pastoralia* (San José, Costa Rica) 2, 3 (September 1979), pp. 31-81.

10. Ibid., pp. 38-39.

11. Roberto Oliveros Maqueo, *Liberación y Teología* (Mexico City: Ediciones Centro de Reflexión Teológica, 1977), p. 120.

12. Dussel, "Un análisis contextual," p. 38.

13. López Trujillo, "Medellín: una mirada global," pp. 17-22.

8

Revolutionary Ferment:
Liberation Theology

In one way or another, directly or indirectly, the documents of Vatican II and Medellín, and the social doctrine of John XXIII and Paul VI encouraged the revolutionary spirit in various sectors of Latin American Catholicism. The encyclical *Pacem in terris* (1963) of John XXIII was carrying within itself the revolutionary seed for those peoples who had not found a solution for their problems in the thesis of development, although the pope affirms that salvation and justice are not in revolution but in economic and social evolution.[1] In his encyclical *Populorum progressio* (1967), Paul VI advocates also development, but he comes to the point of justifying a revolutionary uprising "where there is manifest, long-standing tyranny which would do great damage to fundamental personal rights and dangerous harm to the common good of the country."[2] Later on he tried to be an element of balance among the warring ideological factions within the Catholic church. For example, in Colombia in 1968 he told the peasants not to put their confidence in violence or in revolution, because "such an attitude is contrary to the Christian spirit and may also delay rather than promote the social advancement to which you legitimately aspire."[3] Seven years later, in his encyclical "The Evangelization of the Contemporary World" (*Evangelii nuntiandi*), Paul VI declared that the Church "cannot accept violence."[4] However, there already had been an awakening of the revolutionary consciousness within the Catholic church, and it seemed impossible that it could in any way reverse its own history.

Revolution is now present in Latin America in theory and in practice, in the sphere of ideas and in the field of action; in passive resistance and in the outburst of violence by those who seek a rapid and complete change in the social order. The revolutionary spirit is seen, for example, in the writings and actions of the pacifist bishop Helder Camara, in the educator Pablo Freire, in the poet and monk Ernesto Cardenal, in the martyr priest Camilo Torres, who opted for violent revolution, in liberation theologians like Gustavo Gutiérrez, in the priests who have adopted a new pastoral model among the Latin American masses, and in the Roman Catholics who belong to the armed groups that fight for a radical change in our social structures.

VIOLENT REVOLUTION

It is very easy to move from the pulpit or the lecture room to street demonstrations, to the public plazas where the masses form to protest against the established order, or even to the trenches where the stammering of the machine guns is much louder than the voice of reason and emotions.

In a certain sense this was the pilgrimage made by Father Camilo Torres, who has become the symbol of those Latin American Catholics who are willing to take their revolutionary commitment to its ultimate consequences.

There are those who hold that Camilo opted for his retreat to the mountains "not because he believed in guerrilla warfare, its effectiveness or its methods" but only because it was there that "he felt secure."[5] It is also said that he did not die with a gun in his hands and, in fact, never had one and never pressed the trigger to kill anyone. It is admitted, however, that he was in the guerrilla movement and in combat with the army. "But he never shot at anybody, nor did he ever kill anybody."

What is certain is that for one reason or another Camilo felt impelled to follow the way of the guerrillas, which is the way of violent action in a revolutionary praxis. It was his opinion that in the poor countries the Christian not only could but should commit himself to structural changes that would benefit the masses.[6] He finally came to the profound conviction that "the way of armed action" is the only one which is open to "any sincere revolutionary."[7] His proclamation to Colombians on January 7, 1966, ends with the words "Liberation or death!"[8] And death he found on February 15, 1967, "facing heaven, facing Colombia, and facing this Indian and mestizo America. Face to face with the conscience of free men," according to the words of one of his biographers.[9]

Camilo found theological justification for revolutionary commitment in the nature of love for one's neighbor. After requesting his reduction to lay status, he made a public declaration in which the following words appear:

> I opted for Christianity because I felt that I found in it the purest form of serving my neighbor. I was elected by Christ to be a priest eternally, motivated by the desire to give myself full time to my fellow men. As a sociologist, I have desired that love be effective through technology and science; in analyzing Colombian society I have become aware of the need for a revolution to be able to feed the hungry, to give drink to the thirsty, to clothe the naked and to bring about the welfare of the majority of our people. I believe that the revolutionary struggle is a Christian and priestly struggle, and that only through this struggle, in the concrete circumstances of our country, can we put into practice the love that men ought to have for their neighbors.[10]

In his message to the Christian public on August 26, 1966, he declared:

> The most important element in Catholicism is love for one's neighbor. "He who loves his neighbor has fulfilled the law" (St. Paul, Romans 13:8). In order for this love to be effective it must seek to be effective.... It is necessary, therefore, to take the power away from the privileged minorities in order to give it to the poor masses.... The revolution is not only permissible but rather obligatory for those Christians who see in it the only way which is both effective and broad enough to practice love toward all.... I believe that I have given myself to the revolution for love of my neighbor.[11]

Such language had to sound subversive to the powerful, and there has been no lack of those who identity Camilo with Communism. However, in his "Message to Communists" on September 2, 1965, he declared that neither as a Colombian, nor as a sociologist, nor as a Christian, nor as a priest, was he, or would he be, a Communist. At the same time he denied that he was anti-Communist and stated his willingness to fight alongside the Communists, without being one of them, "for common objectives; against the oligarchy and the dominion of the United States, and for the people's acquisition of power."[12] His hope was "to build socialism without destroying what is essential in Christianity."[13] He dreamed of fomenting a revolution that would be socialistic but also nationalistic, "without falling completely within the Soviet bloc," but maintaining a neutral stance toward the competition between the great world powers.[14] Although the Catholic church may not have approved of Camilo's radically revolutionary choice, he never renounced his Catholic faith.

He seems to incarnate, with his heroic self-denial and his martyr's sense of renunciation, the spirit of suffering, indignation, and rebellion that is either latent or manifest in thousands and thousands of Catholics in our underdeveloped countries.

The name of Father Camilo Torres, along with his message and his complete surrender to the cause of the liberation of the oppressed classes, form without a doubt part of postconciliar Latin American Catholicism.

PACIFIST REVOLUTION

In sharp contrast to Camilo Torres's desperate and violent response to the Latin American dilemma, the firm but peaceful voice of Helder Camara also speaks from the heart of postconciliar Catholicism. Camara has been called "the red archbishop of Brazil" and "Lenin in cassock" because of his persistent fight on behalf of the poor. His concern is to speak in the name of those who cannot speak for themselves.[15]

Following the path marked out by the great pacifists Mahatma Gandhi and Martin Luther King, Helder Camara neither closes his eyes nor holds his tongue in the face of the tragic helplessness of the oppressed and exploited, those who live on the edge of Brazil's opulent society and of other societies, especially in the Third World. Along with his pacifist heroes, Bishop Camara rejects the idea that violence will be the remedy for the evils that surround us: "He does not believe in the force of arms and he hates war; he considers himself a pilgrim of peace and trusts in the effectiveness of non-violence, expecting no solution from governments, which are almost always docile instruments employed in the service of the big powers."[16]

Dom Helder maintains that violence engenders violence without solving the problems of the oppressed masses. He speaks of three kinds of violence. The first is the violence that the weak suffer under the yoke of the powerful. Injustice is "the first of all kinds of violence, violence number one."[17] As a reaction to this violence there is the revolution of the oppressed or "of the youth dedicated to fighting for a more just world."[18] Following this comes the repression of the authorities in order to preserve or restore public order. This is violence number three. "The conclusion is clear," says Camara; "there is a very real danger that the world will enter into an escalation of violence, that it may fall into a spiral of violence."[19]

If, however, Camara does not believe in the force of arms, what is the solution to the problem facing the oppressed? In a lecture given at Rome on December 1, 1965, Dom Helder said, "I have the fraternal confidence to suggest that within each Latin American country the hierarchy may, without in any way forgetting its directly pastoral work, offer its moral support, if the case so demands it, to a movement of non-violent action which will be able to stimulate the weakness of the patrons who still live in the Middle Ages."[20]

According to Camara this will be an action of "justice and peace" that will bring about a liberating moral pressure that will help in a peaceful and effective way to change the economic-social and political-cultural structures of the underdeveloped countries, and to induce the developed countries radically to change their policies regarding international commerce with the underdeveloped countries.[21]

The call of the "Bishop of the poor" to an "action of justice and peace" is ecumenical in nature. It is directed to all men, regardless of racial, linguistic, geographic, or religious barriers, calling them to unite in the task of peacefully demanding "justice as a prerequisite for peace."[22]

Camara makes a special call to young people to form "Abrahamic minorities," that is, a movement of men and women of good will who hope and trust in the triumph of peace and justice.[23] Hoping to gain their support, Dom Helder does not condemn the youth; on the contrary, he makes an effort to understand them, and even to flatter and cajole them. He uses moral persuasion, inviting them to participate in constructive dialogues and a broad and sincere discussion of his proposition to exert a liberating and moral pressure in order to achieve a more just and human world.[24]

Helder Camara is not blind to the tremendous obstacles that stand in the way of nonviolence; but he trusts that "time is in favor of Gandhi" and the pacifist movement that he initiated. "Before long," he affirms, "Gandhi will be recognized as a prophet."[25] One reason for maintaining such an inspiring hope is that humans will come to realize the absurdity of war. Moreover, there exist minorities who oppose the forces of hatred and violence, knowing full well that all this evil in no way promotes peace among humans and that "the only real answer to violence lies in the courage to face the injustices which constitute violence number one."[26]

In view of the brutal violence that surrounds us in our America shaken by hate, and in view of the desperation of those who, whether from the left or the right, can only respond to violence with more violence, Bishop Camara's message is a consolation. It proves once again that there are still select spirits among us who are enemies of violence and lovers of that justice which leads to peace. Whether Dom Helder's pacifist world can find echo in the hearts of those who do not have peace with God through Jesus Christ and therefore cannot be at peace with their neighbors is a subject worthy of considering separately. The prophet Isaiah says of the sinners who are far from God, "the way of peace they do not know" (Isa. 59:8, NIV; cf. Rom. 3:17).

Which economic and political system does Camara propose as a substitute for the present situation of injustice and violence? He finds no solution for the underdeveloped countries, neither in capitalism, nor in neocapitalism, nor in existing socialism; neither from Cuba, nor from Russia, nor from China. He says: "If you wish, you may say socialism, but a socialism that respects in reality—not only in theory—the human person, and that doesn't fall into dictatorship. Not a government dictatorship or a party dictatorship."[27] In other words, Dom Helder proposes that the solution should be sought in a form of socialization, or a "personalist socialism, to which Christians can offer a mystique of universal fraternity and incomparable hope far more comprehensive than the narrow mystique of historic materialism."[28]

Of course, there are those who question Bishop Camara's teaching and attitude. They say that he argues for nonviolent violence, since nonviolent resistance also disturbs the established order. What is undeniable is that sixteen years after the publication in French of Camara's now famous book *Spiral of Violence,* the fertile soil of Latin America continues to be dampened with the blood shed by those who are guilty of the violence that "the Bishop of the poor" condemns.

POETIC REVOLUTION

It may seem strange to some that we deal here with a poetic revolution, but this revolution is found in postconciliar Latin American Catholicism in "protest" poems, and in a very special way in the works of the Nicaraguan poet-priest Ernesto Cardenal. He has written poems like the following, a daring paraphrase of the Psalms of Israel:

Liberate us
(Psalm 11)

Free us Lord
because their political parties will not free us
They deceive one another
and they exploit one another
Their lies are repeated on a thousand radios
and their slander in all the newspapers.
They have special offices to create lies
Those who say: "We will rule with Propaganda.
Propaganda is with us."
For the oppression of the poor
For the cry of the exploited
Even now will I rise up
says the Lord
I will give them freedom because they sigh.
But the words of the Lord are clean words
and not Propaganda.
Their armaments are everywhere
Their machine guns and their tanks surround us
The assassins with their decorations insult us
and those who offer toasts in their clubs
while we weep in our hovels
they spend their lives in cocktail parties.[29]

Who is Ernesto Cardenal? He was born in Granada, Nicaragua, in 1925 and studied philosophy and letters at the Universidad Autónoma of Mexico, later doing postgraduate studies at Columbia University. After being persecuted for participating in a resistance movement, he experienced a great change in his life in 1956. He retired to the Monastery of Gethsemane in Kentucky, where he had the poet-monk Thomas Merton for a teacher. Because the Kentucky climate was not good for him he moved first to Cuernavaca, Mexico, and later to Medellín, Colombia, to finish his theological studies. He returned to Nicaragua in 1965 and was ordained priest in the cathedral of Managua. In the island of Solentiname in the Great Lake of Nicaragua he formed a community of reflection and service that helped the islanders through a school and a clinic. In a book entitled *El Evangelio de Solentiname* (The Solentiname Gospel),[30] Cardenal has compiled ideas expressed by his brothers in response to the reading of the gospels.

In reference to the experience in Solentiname, Cardenal explained: "the contemplative or semi-contemplative life which we live there has also led us to the revolution, to revolutionary solidarity. Our path has led from contemplation to Revolution and from the Gospel to Marxism."[31]

In an interview televised on Channel 11 in Guatemala on September 25, 1978, Cardenal admitted that he was a member of the Sandinista National Liberation Front and affirmed that he did not see a dichotomy between the gospel and politics, because the gospel is political. He clarified that he had not participated in the armed struggle because his age did not allow it, but his struggle was being carried out "with poetry and preaching." By that time the international news media were already calling Cardenal "the ideologist of the Sandinista Movement in Nicaragua." At the present time Cardenal is a member of the revolutionary cabinet in his country. He has been head of the Ministry of Culture since the triumph of the revolution that overthrew President Somoza. In September 1979 he declared to the press:

> This is a Christian revolution. The people of Nicaragua are, in the great majority, Christian, and that is why the people carried out the revolution . . . The church never condemned recourse to weapons for a just cause. Pope Paul VI said that armed struggle and violence were legitimately moral in the case of evident and prolonged dictatorship—and ours was truly prolonged.[32]

According to José Ramón Enriquez, "one cannot say that Cardenal is first and foremost a poet or a Christian or a revolutionary . . .; he is a poet, Catholic priest and revolutionary all at the same time and for the same reasons."[33] In response to the question, "What is Christianity for you?" put to Cardenal by José Steinsleger in an interview, the poet-priest affirmed:

> For me Christianity is the Christianity of the Gospels, a Christianity which has been disfigured down through the ages but which in its essence is authentically revolutionary. In Latin America now a number of us who are

priests, theologians or religious workers have come to understand that Christianity and Marxism are not incompatible; on the contrary, they have a common goal: what the Gospels call the Kingdom of God on earth and what Marxism calls the perfect communist society.[34]

Although during the last three decades there has been enthusiasm in some sectors of Roman Catholicism about the Christian-Marxist dialogue, many Catholics are in disagreement with Ernesto Cardenal in his attitude toward Marxism. In the *Puebla Document* (issued by the Second Episcopal Conference held in Puebla, Mexico, 1979), the Latin American bishops did not take sides with capitalism, nor with socialism, nor with the thesis of "national security." But apart from any discussion on the so-called coincidences between Christianity and Marxism, it is a fact that in Cardenal's poetry we find expressed the revolutionary spirit of contemporary Catholicism in Latin America. Through the alchemy of his poetic gift, Cardenal converts this spirit into a message that is an angry and choleric cry for the pain of his people; a voice of anguished protest for the tears of the afflicted; a triumphal song anticipating the overthrow of tyranny.

Cardenal conceives of God only as the one who intervenes to defend the poor and to judge the oppressors. For him there is no other true church than that which identifies itself with the cause of the disinherited of the earth.[35]

The voice of the poet-priest is basically the same as that of the guerrilla-priest who dies with his face to the sky in the Colombian mountains. The one speaks by playing the poetic lyre, while the other died with a machine gun in his hand. Both claim to seek the liberation of Latin America.

PEDAGOGICAL REVOLUTION

In our description of postconciliar Catholicism, we dare not fail to mention the influence of Paulo Freire, the Brazilian Catholic educator,[36] upon Latin American theological thought. Although he is not a theologian (in the strictest sense of the word), Freire enters the field of theology, as when he counsels a young theologian with these words:

Since the Word became flesh, it is only possible to approach it through man, so therefore the starting point for theology should be anthropology. In this way, a utopian theology must be associated with cultural action for liberation, by means of which men should substitute for their naive conception of God as an alienating myth a new concept: God as a Presence in history which does not impede man in any way from making the history of his liberation.[37]

The Jesuit theologian José I. Gonzáles-Faus sees that the ethical, anthropological, and philosophical principles upon which Freire's pedagogy rests "have a very close relationship with theology."[38] That even though Freire himself does not claim to be a theologian.

Freire has become particularly known for his method of teaching adults to read, which he formally developed in 1961. He created "circles of culture" and "centers of popular culture" in all of Brazil. He was in charge of the Department of Adult Literacy of the Ministry of Education and Culture of Brazil before the military coup of 1964, when he was forced to emigrate to Chile.[39]

In 1963 Freire published an article in *Revista de Cultura* of the University of Recife, Pernambuco, in which he joins the concept of "conscientization" to that of literacy. His book *The Pedagogy of the Oppressed* appeared in Portuguese in 1967. Its first Spanish edition was published in 1970. Hugo Assmann, Brazilian liberation theologian, mentions that the document on Medellín on "Liberating Education" fundamentally took its inspiration from the ideas of Paul Freire.[40]

Without a doubt, the method and message of Freire fit very well with the aspirations of the revolutionary movements of the Latin American continent.

Freire writes from the basis of his thinking and experiences as an educator of adults. His motto might be "education as the practice of freedom." His method is that of educating by "conscientizing" and "problem-posing." According to Freire, society is divided into oppressors and oppressed. The latter have within themselves the image of the oppressor, and it is not strange that they should see liberation as the possibility of becoming like their oppressors, of living as the oppressors of today live and becoming themselves tomorrow's oppressors.

At the same time, "the oppressed, who have adapted to the structure of domination in which they are immersed, and have become resigned to it, are inhibited from waging the struggle of freedom as long as they feel incapable of running the risks it requires."[41] The problem becomes more acute because of the fear of freedom that the oppressed feel, the fear of losing their sense of oppression and of having to assume as free men full responsibility for themselves. The oppressed are the only ones responsible for and capable of liberating themselves and of liberating the oppressor.

What must be done so that the oppressed can be liberated? It is imperative that they assume a radical attitude in order to transform their oppressive situation. The oppressed must commit themselves to a praxis, "which is man's reflection upon and action in the world in order to transform it."[42] Without that praxis it is impossible to overcome the oppressor-oppressed dichotomy.

How can the oppressed be brought to that liberating praxis? The answer is found in "the pedagogy of the oppressed, which is the pedagogy of men engaged in the fight for their own liberation." According to Freire, there are two types of education: the first is "banking," which consists in the mere depositing of knowledge in the mind of the one that is being educated, leaving him or her in his or her state of oppression. The other is "problem-posing," which "conscientizes" the one being educated regarding the "myths" she or he has received from the oppressor. Liberating education seeks to transform the oppressive situation and not only to transform the mentality of the oppressed.[43]

The initial purpose of that education is to overcome the educator-educated dichotomy, so that both may become, simultaneously, educators and educated. That could be called an educational fellowship, in which thosee who educate are at the same time being educated, in a liberating, pedagogical process. Problem-posing education is "dialogical" and liberating, in contrast to banking education, which is "antidialogical" and serves the interests of oppression.

Authentic liberating action does not seek to conquer the common people but rather to cooperate with them in their liberation; it does not divide people, it unites them; it does not manipulate them, it organizes them; it is not cultural invasion, it is a cultural "dialogical" action that leads to "cultural revolution" and "the participation of the people in power."[44] It is little wonder, therefore, that Gonzáles-Faus says that the work of Freire, more than a "pedagogy of the oppressed," is a pedagogy of the revolutionary leader.[45] Freire does not believe that there can be a profound and radical transformation in the educational system unless society itself also becomes radically transformed.

A concrete proposal for action is Freire's method of adult literacy. Ivan Illich explains that "the effectiveness of this program is built around key words which are loaded with political meaning."[46] The adults who become interested in the political problems of their community can learn to read and write in six weeks of night classes. But Illich is quick to point out that the program has its difficulties also.

More important than the method of dialogue and "conscientization" is the goal that Freire pursues: social revolution. His major interest is found in humanization. He has great confidence and hope in the human being; he believes that human beings can change themselves and change the world; he accepts the Marxist analysis of society and history. His optimism sometimes sounds exaggerated.

The evangelical Christian is concerned when he sees that Freirean anthropology assigns no proper place to the Scriptures and that humanity does not appear as sinners. Dehumanization is, according to Freire, only the result of an unjust social order. In Freire's program, "the point of departure of theology has to be anthropology" and "the theologian has to take as a point of departure his reflection on the history of mankind."[47] Biblical anthropology and the biblical concept of history are, in theory and practice, out of Freire's system of thought.

THEOLOGICAL REVOLUTION

We have already said that the revolutionary spirit of postconciliar Catholicism is present in Latin America in theory and practice, in the sphere of ideas and in the field of action. There is a theology of revolution and a revolution in theology.

In Roman Catholic as well as in Protestant circles, theology in Latin America has historically been simply a repetition of what has been said in Europe and the United States. The Latin American churches have only echoed the theology formed in other cultures, rather than contributing in a significant way to the development of Christian thought. But this situation has begun to change, especially since the 1960s. For the first time in the history of Christianity, a theological movement is coming out of Latin America that has awakened the interest of the experts in those countries that seemed to have a monopoly on the science of theology.

That the so-called "Latin America theology" is not totally original is obvious. What theology could be original after nearly twenty centuries of Christian thought? If the Latin American theologians have anything original, it is their effort to relate their concept of Christianity to the Latin culture.

The Latin American theological current best known outside the continent is no doubt the already-famous "theology of liberation." There are several theologies of liberation. For instance, black liberation theology, feminist liberation theology, and Latin American liberation theology—not to mention the different shades that the last one has acquired through the years.

Segundo Galilea, a Roman Catholic theologian from Chile, says there are four tendencies he sees in liberation theology at the present time. The first tendency emphasizes the biblical notion of liberation and the application of this concept to our society. The second tendency takes as a point of departure Latin American history and culture and the liberating potential possessed by the people in these countries. The emphasis of the third tendency is on economics, on class struggle, and the ideologies confronted by the Christian faith. In this variety of liberation theology there are points of contact with the Marxist analysis of society. But this analysis is used only insofar as it is valid for the social sciences today. The fourth tendency is, according to Galilea, more an ideology than a theology, and it is definitely under the influence of Marxism. Galilea declares that in this case we are not any more on theological grounds, and there is no reason to speak of a theology of liberation.[48]

In practice, it may be quite difficult to distinguish one kind of liberation theology from another; but it is possible to say that the first three tendencies are represented in the kind of liberation theology that is becoming popular among Catholics and some Protestants today. There is a strong emphasis on history as a process of liberation: there is an extensive use of Marxist interpretation of society, and there is an effort to find liberation theology in the biblical text. We evangelicals have problems, of course, with the hermeneutics employed by liberation theologians and with their low view of biblical authority. Some evangelical theologians are talking about the need of doing a biblical theology of liberation.

The purpose of this section in our description of postconciliar Catholicism in Latin America is to deal with the kind of liberation theology that is becoming widely known in academic circles around the world, namely, the theology of Roman Catholic writers like Gustavo Gutiérrez, Hugo Assmann, Jon Sobrino, and Leonardo Boff.

The Social Context of Liberation Theology

Simply stated, the theology of liberation is "a new way of doing theology." Its point of departure and hermeneutical norm are not the written revelation of God, but the social context of Latin America and the revolutionary praxis striving to create there a "new man" and a "new society" within a socialist system as a supposed manifestation of the kingdom of God.

Liberation theology is a good example of the tremendous influence exercised by the social sciences on contemporary theological thinking. Even if we trace liberation theology to its European sources, we shall discover that theologians like Dietrich Bonhoeffer, J.B. Metz, and Jürgen Moltmann were deeply concerned about social problems, although they were doing theology in a cultural context that is quite different from ours in Latin America.

The existential hermeneutics of Rudolf Bultmann, the secular approach of Bonhoeffer to Christianity, the political hermeneutics of Metz, for example, have been influenced to a large extent on liberation theology. Of course, the representatives of this theological system are not eager to admit their dependence on a foreign theology. They argue that European theologians are doing their work in a capitalistic society, for people who enjoy the material advantage of a highly developed country. By contrast, they say, liberation theology has emerged from a situation of poverty, in countries that are underdeveloped because they are dependent on Western capitalism and neocolonialism. For the same reason they believe to have gone, in their theological thinking, beyond vanguard theologians like Rahner and Küng, who belong also to an affluent society.[49]

Liberation theology claims to be a theology produced in Latin America, by and for Latin Americans. It is the attempt to contextualize the Christian message according to the particular needs of men and women who live in a social context that is crying for radical changes. The motivation, method, and goals of this theology demand, to some extent, a different approach from the one we use in evaluating other theological systems. For instance, it is indispensable to give serious consideration to the social milieu in which liberation theology is framed.

We cannot achieve a proper understanding of liberation theology unless we are aware of the particular social problems confronting Latin Americans today. I am not talking of approving, or accepting, this theology, but about understanding its motivation, its method, and purposes. As evangelicals educated according to the principles and ideals of American Protestantism, it is usually difficult for us Latin Americans (I include myself because theologically I am a creature of American evangelicalism) to think in categories that are different from those in which we have been trained to think. For instance, some evangelicals, here at home and abroad, have believed that if you are on behalf of social reforms you are already a Communist, or at least you are foolishly helping the cause of international Communism. They may also classify you as anti-American. Some evangelicals have also left the impression that in their minds they are equating the gospel with capitalism, more or less in the same way in which some revolutionaries in Latin America are trying to equate the gospel with Communism, or at least with socialism. Forty years ago some evangelicals wanted us to wear Uncle Sam's hat as a distinctive of our faith; and now some leftist leaders come asking us to wear Fidel Castro's beret as the symbol of our loyalty to the gospel of Christ. This is a symbolic way to speak about the tendency to identify the gospel with a political system, whatever it may be.

It is also evident that to have a proper understanding of liberation theology we need to take seriously into consideration the extenuating circumstances in which millions of Latin Americans live. Luis Marchand, the Peruvian ambassador to the Organization of American States, reported in 1979 that about forty-three percent of the Latin American people lived in extreme poverty. At least one million babies died every year because of lack of medical care or undernourishment. One hundred million Latin Americans were at that time illiterate. Of this group of people who could not read, fifty-six percent were under fifteen years of age. There were no schools for them. From 125 million to 130 million Latin Americans had no drinkable water, and 150 million Latin Americans lacked sanitary facilities. At least twenty percent of the population merely subsisted. It was a miracle that they were still alive.[50]

To a large extent this is still reality today south of the border. According to figures published on August 10, 1987, by *Prensa Libre* (Free Press), the widely read Guatemalan newspaper, that Central American country has forty percent of the people living in extreme poverty. They barely survive. This is the highest rate of poverty in Central America. More than fifty percent of the people are illiterate. The students' enrollment in both public and private schools is in proportion to the number of inhabitants—the lowest in Latin America. Because of the financial situation only twenty-five percent of the children are able to finish elementary school. Not all of them graduate from high school; only thirty-six percent of the ones enrolled in high school complete their studies to get their diploma.[51] The same newspaper said in 1983 that eighty percent of the Guatemalan children were undernourished.[52]

If you goes to Central America and associates yourself with the masses, not with upper-class or middle-class people only, you will understand better the theology of liberation. And if you are a Latin American and born and reared as the child of a poor family, you may have a better understanding of the motivations behind this theological system. Because of the vast majority of the people who belong to the low classes of society, liberation theology may exercise a strong influence on the future of Latin American countries and on the future of the so-called Third World as a whole. Liberation theology continues to be a favorite subject of discussion all over Latin America.

In evaluating liberation theology, we Latin American Christians have to be sincere in asking ourselves if we are really concerned about the gospel of Christ or about a particular political system. Are we defending the gospel or capitalism? Or, are we more enthusiastic about socialism than about New Testament Christianity? Our political convictions may play an important role in our evaluation of liberation theology, because this is a political theology, based to a large extent on the Marxist analysis of society. It is therefore natural for conservatives to reject liberation theology just on the basis of political conviction. On the other hand, it is also natural for a liberal-minded citizen in the United States or somewhere else to be in sympathy with the viewpoint of theologians who emphasize the need for a radical change in the social structures of the Third World.

We Latin American evangelicals should not be indifferent to our own social reality. On the contrary, we are supposed to identify ourselves with our people in their sufferings and longing for freedom. And we have to admit that traditional capitalism has not been able to solve our problems; that generally speaking the rich are getting richer and the poor, poorer in Latin American society. Industrialization is creating new problems, which in many respects may be more difficult than the ones we had when our economy depended almost completely on agriculture. But we have also the right to ask whether socialism, as it is preached today, shall succeed where capitalism has failed.

We conservative evangelicals in Latin America have usually been concerned only about the individual, without taking into consideration his or her social context. We have been preaching about the spiritual element in humans without really paying attention to their physical and material needs. We have been preaching about heaven and hell without declaring the totality of the counsel of God in relation to life this side of the grave. We have been denouncing the sinfulness of the individual, but not the evils of society as a whole. Our message has not been a threat to the people in the wealthy class, in government, in the military.

We conservative evangelicals in Latin America have been known as "good people" because we do not interfere in political affairs and do not make the people aware of the possibility of a better life in this world. Dictators loved us, and even protected us for almost a century in Central America, because of our noninvolvement in politics. Of course, our noninvolvement has been a political option, by which we have contributed to the preservation of the status quo in Latin American society.

Now, with liberation theology the pendulum has swung to the left. We are told that to be authentic Christians we must be concerned about poverty and be willing to do something about it; that we have to find Jesus in the poor; that political action is included in the gospel; that we have to identify ourselves with the cause of the oppressed and fight the oppressors; that God is active in history on behalf of the poor and against the wealthy; that the mission of the church is to help to change social structures in the process of establishing the kingdom of God on earth by means of socialism; that the future is always open for Christian thought and action; and that we should see God's hand in any revolutionary movement that claims to be striving for the economic, social, and political liberation of humanity.

Without closing our eyes to our own socio-economic reality, and without establishing a dichotomy between our Christian faith and our social responsibility, we Latin American evangelicals have to approach liberation theology from a biblical standpoint. Our highest authority has to be the written Word of God. Any ideology, or system of human thought, or socio-political movement is imperfect and transitory. But the Word of God is perfect and remains forever. If we are faithful to our evangelical inheritance, we will let God say the first and final word about our social problems in Latin America.

The Immediate Origin of Liberation Theology

In a sense the theology of liberation is a result of the upheavals that have occurred within the Roman Catholic church, especially since World War II. This church had been serving the dominant classes, and common people were turning their backs on it politically and socially. Catholicism was losing ground in the minds and hearts of the Latin American people. Leftist ideologies had found here a well-fertilized field for their propagation. At the same time, some ecclesiastical leaders began to realize that the so-called Christianization of Latin America was an unfinished task. The Roman Catholic church was facing one of its most critical hours in these countries and in the whole

It was in that crucial moment that the kindly figure of Pope John XXIII appeared with his decision to convene the Second Vatican Council in order to bring about the ecclesiastical transformation that the postwar world demanded. Without producing fundamental changes in the distinctive doctrines of the Roman church, the council has introduced currents of renewal to Catholicism. Two examples of this renewal are the openness of the Catholic church toward other churches and religions and its new attitude toward socio-economic problems.

A sequel to Vatican II was the Conference of Latin American Bishops, held in Medellín, Colombia, in 1968. In contrast to the Catholic conservatism of the preconciliar period, Medellín seems to be a turn toward the left in regard to the problems of underdevelopment in Latin America. Consciously or unconsciously, the bishops were opening the door for a free expression of liberationist theology in the heart of Latin American Catholicism. There seems to be a consensus among scholars that liberation theology began to make itself explicit especially after Medellín.

We have already suggested in this chapter that liberation theology has deep roots in European philosophy and theology. The influence of Karl Marx is evident. European theologians like J. B. Metz and Jürgen Moltmann have also been influential on this system of thought. But liberation theologians assume a critical stance in relation to the work of these European theologians. For instance, they consider European political theology deficient in its analysis of the contemporary situation and inadequate for Latin American reality.[53] Both relation and rupture exist between European theologians and their Latin American counterparts regarding the formulation of a theology that aspires to be liberating. Liberation theology's radicalism, which is born with the consciousness of the state of oppression in which our people live and of the need to break away from all dehumanizing systems, is in opposition to development schemes.

One of the principal characteristics of liberation theology is the effort of its authors to make an in-depth study of Latin American social problems. To that end they avail themselves of the social sciences. At the same time they take for granted that the best economic and social analysis comes from Karl Marx, although they admit that in a certain sense it is necessary to adapt Marxist thought to the concrete situation of Latin America. They conclude that underdevelopment is a product of the economic dependence of the poor countries on rich countries. The development of the rich countries depends on the underdevelopment of the poor countries.

The thesis of dependency is accompanied in liberation theology by a total rejection of developmentalism as an answer to the Latin American problem. For them, developmentalism has a negative connotation; it has become a synonym of reformism and modernization and does not attack the roots of the problem. They see the Alliance for Progress of the early 1960s as a complete failure. They reject the idea that a capitalistic culture is a model of development for Latin America. The failure of developmentalism is due, say liberation theologians, to the capitalistic system of economic production and to the way in which our society is structured. As a result, what is needed is not development or evolution, but rather revolution, the radical change of social structures and the establishment of socialism in Latin America.

Enrique D. Dussel, a Catholic intellectual from Argentina, describes three recent periods in the development of Latin American theology. In the first period Latin American professors from seminaries and faculties of theology went to study in Europe. In the second period courses of study were organized for the purpose of understanding in depth the Latin American reality. The emphasis at that point was not so much theological as sociological. "The third stage, that is, the 'birth' of theology not 'in' Latin America nor 'with' sociographical Latin American themes, but a 'Latin American' theology, will come only when . . . the political relations . . . are seen."[54]

According to Dussel, liberation theology came when the dialectic of dominator-oppressed became understood. In that way the church progressed from conservatism to liberalism, then to developmentalism, finally opening itself "to a posture of liberation." One of the greatest differences between European political theology and Latin American liberation theology, says Dussel, is that the second movement views the dialectic of oppressor-oppressed on the international level.[55]

During the formative years of liberation theology there was some cooperation between some Catholic theologians and a Protestant ecumenical movement called "Church and Society in Latin America" (Iglesia y Sociedad en América Latina: ISAL). One of the elements that helped to shape the Isaline thought was the Catholic-Protestant dialogue. At the same time, that dialogue allowed for a Protestant contribution to the development of the Latin American theology of liberation.[56] But the final product is basically a creature of Roman Catholicism in Latin America. In 1971, Gustavo Gutiérrez published in Lima, Peru, the first edition of his now-famous book *Liberation Theology: Perspectives*.[57] Gutiérrez has been called "the systematizer of liberation theology."

The Method of Liberation Theology

Gustavo Gutiérrez explains that he is not suggesting new theological themes but "a new way of doing theology." Segundo Galilea says that there are three ways of doing theology: (1) the spiritual study of the Scriptures (the emphasis here is devotional); (2) systematic or scientific theology, which—according to Galilea—is the attempt to relate faith and reason in the study of divine revelation; and (3) pastoral theology, with the point of departure being the church, the pastoral ministry, the social action of Christians, the social context in which the church carries on its mission.[58] Liberation theology belongs to this last category. It goes from the social context to the biblical text. Hugo Assmann affirms:

> We must not forget that "liberation theology" is to be understood as a critical reflection upon the present historical praxis in all its intensity and concrete complexity. The "text," we repeat, is our situation, our "primary theological reference point." . . . Now the traditional perspective of those exegetes who "work with the sacred text" is no longer sufficient, because we want "to work with today's reality."[59]

The context, analyzed sociologically with the help of some Marxist presuppositions, is the point of departure for theological reflection. For Assmann, the analysis of the Latin American reality in the light of the human sciences is more important than biblical exegesis. These sciences make the biblical text speak, not only applying it to the concrete situation but also determining its fundamental meaning. Scripture must give way to the rule of the social sciences and to liberationist praxis.[60] Assmann recognizes that even the analytical instruments provided by the social sciences "easily conceal ideological presuppositions." This leaves him without any criteria in which he can confide; however, he does not seek an answer in submission to the Word of God, but rather in the effort to liberate in the midst of the praxis to which he is committed, he devises his own criteria. In the final analysis his political ideology and sociopolitical action determine the kind of theology he will proclaim.

Liberation theology begins with "the scientific analysis" of the socioeconomic-political reality of our continent. It is a movement that goes "from society to theology," questioning established theological or ethical principles. We evangelicals have to ask if the social analysis made by liberation theologians is in harmony with reality, and most of all if this analysis is in agreement with the biblical concept of humanity. We are not supposed to stop thinking in the presence of the Marxist analysis of society just because the defenders of Marxism use the adjective "scientific." Marxist dogmatism has been questioned on scientific grounds, and Marxist reductionism does not explain the total problem of the person in Latin America.

Answering to the objection that liberation theology is "sociologism" because of its overemphasis on the social sciences, Galilea indicates that theology has always used auxiliary sciences; for instance, philosophy was extensively used by theologians in the past.[61] But when we read liberation theology we discover that the social sciences are not only instruments in the hands of the liberation theologian, but the dominant element in his or her system of thought. The basic presuppositions are not biblical but sociological. This criticism does not mean that we should say that Latin American liberationism is sociology instead of theology. We speak of "liberal theology" even though that system of thought is to a large extent a product of philosophy and other intellectual disciplines. We are in profound disagreement with liberalism, but we call it "liberal theology." Liberation theologians speak of "a new way of doing theology," not of "a new way of doing sociology," even though they admit that their current of thought goes from the social context to the biblical text, from sociology to theology.

The point of departure for liberation theology is not just the sociological analysis and theological reflection. It is also the participation in the struggle of the poor to liberate themselves from their oppressors. To do theology in Latin America today it is indispensable, in the opinion of liberation theologians, to take sides with the poor in their praxis of liberation. Praxis precedes reflection. Theology is "the second act" in the drama of liberation. Revolutionary praxis is the point of departure for liberation theology. Action is supreme over reflection.

What is the hermeneutical norm in liberation theology? Gutiérrez has said that liberation theology is a reflection upon praxis in the light of faith, or in the light of the gospel. Assmann affirms that a "critical reflection on liberating historical praxis" is theology because it is carried out "in light of faith" or "in light of the Word of God."[62]

Liberation theologians have made the effort to give biblical clothing to the socio-theological structure that they themselves have raised. Biblical subjects like salvation, the exodus, the new human, justice, love, the kingdom of God, and hope are continually repeated as models of liberation given in God's special revelation. The hermeneutic used in the explanation of these concepts and their application to the Latin American reality is, of course, still open to question.[63] In the view of evangelical hermeneutics, liberationism has been weighed in the balance and found wanting.

We evangelicals are also in disagreement with the Catholic concept of divine revelation. This concept is much broader than that of Protestantism. In Catholic teaching, normative revelation for the church includes tradition as well as the Holy Scriptures, which according to Catholicism have more than sixty-six books. The idea of revelation is already a serious problem for the dialogue between the Catholic theologians of liberation and evangelicals.

Moreover, it is well known that Vatican II's concept of biblical inspiration is not as high as that of conservative evangelicals. Vanguard Catholic theologians seem to be more willing to submit themselves to the dictates of rationalistic criticism than to the authority of the Bible. It is a fact that Roman Catholicism does not have the same view of Scripture that evangelicals have.

For Hugo Assmann, neither the Bible, nor theology, nor the human sciences are sure sources of criteria. The hermeneutical criterion for liberation theologians is not to be found in the written Word of God—that is, the Bible in and of itself. The final criterion rather is revolutionary praxis, or the ideology that moves that praxis. We are supposed to do theology in the process of identifying ourselves with the poor in their struggle of liberation. But praxis by itself cannot offer a final criterion either. There are no norms or criteria already established except the ones provided by the ideology endorsed by the theologians of liberation. Liberation theology as such is a theology on the way. "Traveler, there is no road; the road is made by walking." Gutierrez says that the authentic theology of liberation will come when the ones who are oppressed will be able to speak freely in society and in the fellowship of the people of God.[64]

Some Fundamental Themes of Liberation Theology

In this general description and evaluation of liberation theology it is impossible to deal in depth with some of the fundamental Christian doctrines incorporated in one way or another in this system of thought; but it is necessary to say at least something about anthropology, soteriology, Christology, ecclesiology, and eschatology in relation to liberationism, and in the light of the Word of God.

Anthropoloy. Liberation theologians do not deny that humanity is created by God. Because of sin, humans are alienated from God, and in a very special way from their fellow-humans. The emphasis is not on sinful individuals, however, but on evil social structures. Gutiérrez explains the sin that is the concern of liberation theology:

> But in the liberation approach sin is not considered as an individual, private, or merely interior reality—asserted just enough to necessitate a "spiritual" redemption which does not challenge the order in which we live. Sin is re-

garded as a social, historical fact, the absence of brotherhood and love in relationships among men, the breach
of friendship with God and with other men and, therefore, an interior, personal fracture. When it is considered
in this way, the collective dimensions of sin are re-
discovered . . . Sin is evident in oppressive structures, in
the exploitation of man by man, in the domination and
slavery of peoples, races, and social classes. Sin appears,
therefore, as the fundamental alienation, the root of a situation of injustice and exploitation.[65]

Liberation theologians tend to overlook the doctrine of the sinfulness of all humans. They strongly denounce the capitalist system, international and national colonialism, the wealthy classes, the military and
the civil rulers who, using the doctrine of national security as a pretext,
permit the exploitation of the masses by foreign and native oppressors.
But these theologians deemphasize the sinfulness of the poor. Reading
their argument we may get the impression that the rich are sinners just
because they are rich and that the poor are not sinners just because they
are poor.

There seems not to be a concern for the eternal consequences of sin
or for the responsibility of the oppressed before the justice of God. The
fact is overlooked that in the sight of God there is "none righteous, not
even one," whether rich or poor, oppressor or oppressed, and that no one
on his or her own attains to the measure of divine righteousness.

As is natural in Roman Catholic thought, there is no room in liberation theology for the total depravity of humanity. Humans are enslaved,
but not to the extent that they cannot become aware of their slavery and
free themselves from the forces that oppress them. Gutiérrez says that humans know they are entering a new era, a world fashioned by their own
hands. "We live on the verge of man's epiphany."[66] In contrast to evangelicals, who expect a theophany—the return of the Lord—Gutiérrez
expects an "anthrophany," a glorious manifestation of humanity.[67]

And yet the interest of the liberationist theologians in the "new
man" indicates that for them humanity is not what they could and should
be. This theme is not new for the diligent reader of the Bible. But it is to
be regretted that we Latin American evangelicals have not proclaimed
more forcefully and perseveringly that the promise of a totally transformed "new man" comes from the gospel, and that this promise can become a reality only in the ideal Man, "the man Christ Jesus."

Soteriology. Gustavo Gutiérrez affirms that the work of creation is the first salvific act. God creates people to be his children. Salvation has to do also with the transformation of nature and society. Humans cooperate with God in the saving process. Nature is transformed by means of human labor. Society is transformed by means of political action. According to Gutiérrez, salvation is intrahistorical. It takes place here and now, in the world and in the present time. It is a reality that occurs within history. There are not two histories, one sacred and the other profane, whether parallel or related to each other, but only one. God and humanity are working together in history.

Salvation, Gutiérrez says, is qualitative. The quantitative emphasis has to do with numerical concerns (how many and who are saved); the qualitative emphasis puts aside the distinction between the sacred and the profane; it abandons the tendency to make out of salvation a concept that belongs to the other world, to the hereafter; it sees humans in their totality; and it emphasizes the fact that salvation is universal.

> Man is saved if he opens himself to God and to others, even if he is not clearly aware that he is doing so. This is valid for Christians and non-Christians alike—for all people. To speak about the presence of grace—whether accepted or rejected—in all people implies, on the other hand, to value from a Christian standpoint the very roots of human activity. We can no longer speak properly of a profane world.[68]

Gutierréz makes other statements that also leave him open to the possibility of being interpreted in universalist terms, as when he says that any person is a temple of God: "The 'profane,' that which is located outside the temple, no longer exists."[69] The emphasis of liberation theology does not fall on the perdition of some but rather on the salvation of all, because that which is profane no longer exists.

Salvation is eschatological. In the section dealing with the kingdom of God, we shall make some comments on the intrahistorical future aspect of salvation.

Gutiérrez clarifies that salvation is Christological. The struggle against misery and exploitation is already a part of the saving action. And the work of Christ "forms part of this movement and brings it to complete fulfillment."[70] Nevertheless, the major emphasis is on the active participation of humanity in the creation of such a society, in the creation of the new person.

Salvation is the work of God and the work of humanity in a synergism of faith and works. That notion is not foreign to Roman Catholic soteriology, which serves Gutiérrez very well in supporting his unitarian thesis of salvation. Salvation is social, universal, intrahistorical, eschatological, Christological, and, in the final analysis, human. Insufficient attention is given to the redemptive significance of the sacrifices of Christ and to the ministry of the Holy Spirit and the Word of God in the salvation of the sinner. There is no emphasis on repentance toward God or on faith that lays hold of salvation. The doctrine of the new birth as evangelicals perceive it is noticeably absent. In his philosophy of history Gutiérrez, like other liberation theologians, does not take into account the demonic forces at work in the universe. These forces are in opposition to the purpose of the Creator and the best efforts of humanity. What stands out in liberation theology is not the action of God, but that of humans.

Christology. The man Jesus of Nazareth is the point of departure and the center of special interest for the Christology of the liberationist theologians under consideration in this chapter. Their Christology is mainly "from below," not "from above." In other words they are more interested in the humanity than in the deity of Christ. There is not a clear and forceful declaration of His deity. Jon Sobrino has opened himself to the suspicion of adoptionism.[71] In his answer to this suspicion, Sobriono does not emphasize "the reality of Christ himself" but that which he becomes in the consciousness of the church through time.[72]

Liberation theologians seem to accept without reservation the opinions of modern textual criticism. For Leonardo Boff, belief in the deity of Christ is a product of the postresurrection Christological reflection of Christians in the first century. The climactic point in this process of Christological reflection and elaboration was reached by the Hellenistic Christians who believed that Jesus of Nazareth is the only begotten of God and God himself. Thus when the New Testament speaks of the deity of Christ it reflects a belief of the Hellenistic Christians, not necessarily that of the other traditions that appear on the pages of the New Testament. It is not so much a matter of revelation and divine inspiration as of human reflection.

There is in liberation theology a great interest in the earthly ministry of the Son of God, in order to emphasize his "relation to the political world."[73] Gutierrez takes a special interest in the attitude of Jesus toward the political situation of his time, and he affirms that the ministry of Christ had a political aspect. He sees differences and areas of agreement between Jesus and the Zealots. Jesus opposed politically powerful Jews, and the reasons of the Sanhedrin for condemning him were both religious and political. It is of course undeniable that the presence, message, and attitude of Jesus had political implications, but not to the extent that some want to see today.

Both Sobrino and Boff insist that Jesus did not come to preach concerning himself, but to announce the kingdom of God. The announcement of the kingdom could have been interpreted as a challenge to the power of the Roman Empire. The word kingdom is loaded with political meaning. According to Sobrino, in the first stage of his ministry, before the "Galilean crisis," Jesus announced that the kingdom of God was near. But then came the "Galilean crisis," in which Jesus realized that he had failed in his mission as he had previously understood it. As a result of this crisis there is a significant change in his ministry. Now he presents himself as the suffering Servant of Jehovah. At the same time, the kingdom of God became universal and radical. There was a break with Jewish orthodoxy. The norm of the kingdom became Jesus himself. His kingdom would be entered not by means of orthodoxy but by "orthopraxis," that is, by following Jesus with all the perilous social, personal, and political implications involved.[74]

With regard to the things Jesus did to promote the kingdom of God, it is significant that in spite of the political implications of his ministry he did not enter into the party struggles for political power in Palestine. He never appealed to violence in order to establish his kingdom. He did not show his love to enemies by fighting them, as some liberation theologians claim should be done today in the name of freedom. One does not have to be a radical pacifist to seriously question this idea. No matter how many exegetical acrobatics are done with the biblical text, the fact remains that Jesus did not love his enemies in that way. His love was not seditious in the political sense that some want to give it today; He did not try to change the structures of power in the society of his time by means of violence.

According to Boff, Jesus himself did not think about dying at the beginning of his ministry. He did not want death; he did not seek it, although he was willing to obey the Father in everything and was aware of the tragic end that a faithful prophet might expect. He slowly began to warn that what was coming was not the kingdom, but the death of Messiah upon the cross. Boff does not deny outright the transcendent meaning of the death of Christ (expiation, propitiation, justification, etc.), but neither does he give it all the importance it deserves. Moreover, he believes that this meaning is a product more of human reflection, after the resurrection of Jesus, than of divine revelation.

The discrepancy between Latin American evangelicalism and the liberation theologians quoted in this work goes far beyond the political and ecclesiastical; it transcends the conflict between capitalism and socialism and touches the very foundations of our faith, as can be seen in the case of Christology. On the other hand, we may take liberation theology as a challenge to recuperate the balance we have often lost in relation to the person and work of the Son of God. For example, we have strongly afffirmed his deity, underemphasizing his humanity in our teaching and praxis. And we have often overlooked his example and teachings in the area of human needs that are not of a spiritual nature.

Ecclesiology. In liberation theology the church is defined not so much on the basis of what it is as on the basis of what it does in relation to social problems. In the scheme of liberation ecclesiology the nature and mission of the church go hand in hand. The most important ecclesiological question is, *What does it mean to be a church today* in a revolutionary context, a context of extreme poverty and social injustice?

Liberation theologians like Gustavo Gutiérrez and Leonardo Boff deal with some themes related to the nature of the church—for instance, its universality and unity. It has been a teaching of Roman Catholicism that the church is "the universal sacrament of salvation." Gutiérrez interprets the sacramentality of the church in the sense of an "uncentering" of the church, by which it "must cease considering itself as the exclusive place of salvation and orient itself towards a new and radical service of people."[75] We have already mentioned that Gutiérrez is opposed to the separation of the natural order from the supernatural order, or the sacred from the profane. But in the attempt to go beyond traditional "ecclesiocentrism," the dividing line between the church and the world vanishes.

According to Leonardo Boff, the church becomes universal when it confronts universal causes; for example, in the case of Latin America, the liberation of the exploited.[76] Consequently the church does not renounce its universality when it chooses on behalf of the poor. Boff sees a link between universal mission and concrete liberation.

Liberation theologians do not see the unity of the church apart from social reality. Class struggle, they say, is a reality that divides the church itself. Therefore, it is impossible to manifest the true unity of the church without taking the side of the oppressed class for the achievement of a more just society in which authentic brotherhood may reign.

It greatly troubles us evangelicals that liberation theology does not make use of serious biblical exegesis in discussing a subject of such great importance as the unity of the church. We miss in the ecclesiology of liberation fundamental biblical truths like those expressed in the high priestly prayer of Christ (John 17).

With regard to the mission of the church, liberation theologians strongly believe that the church has to recognize the existence of class struggle and the need of taking sides with the poor against the oppressors. The church should become converted to the poor and become poor in order to speak from the situation of those who suffer social injustice. Only in solidarity with the exploited classes can we understand the gospel and make it understood.

Taking sides with the poor is the first step in accomplishing the mission of the church. The next step is publicly to denounce the oppressors. Gutiérrez suggests three traits of prophetic denunciation. First, prophetic denunciation is global. It includes "every dehumanizing situation . . ., every sacralization of oppressive structures to which the church itself might have contributed."[77] Second, the prophetic denunciation is radical. It goes to the very causes of injustice and oppression. Third, prophetic denunciation is "praxiological." It does not remain on the merely verbal level.

Prophetic denunciation should be accompanied by the announcement of the Kingdom of God. This message is not simply spiritual and futuristic. It is a "conscientizing" and "politicizing" announcement. Inevitably, the "conscientized" people look for political avenues to liberate themselves. No wonder that Gutiérrez says that the church "politicizes by evangelizing." The gospel "has an inescapable political dimension."[78] Liberating praxis is not carried out in a political vacuum; it implies a political option. Gutiérrez and other theologians of liberation have opted for socialism as a political channel for their faith. They hope that the revolutionary movements in Latin America will produce a unique kind of socialism inspired by liberation theology. Their ideal is "to build a socialist society, more just, free, and human, and not a society of superficial and false reconciliation and equality."[79]

Liberation theologians recognize that liberating praxis can reach the point of physical violence, but they do not see a contradiction between the universal love of God and the violent struggle against oppressors who must be loved by fighting yet not hating them. Gutiérrez says:

> One loves the oppressors by liberating them from their inhuman condition as oppressors; by liberating them from themselves. But this cannot be achieved except by resolutely opting for the oppressed, that is, by combating the oppressive class. It must be a real and effective combat; not hate. This is the challenge, as new as the Gospel; to love our enemies.[80]

If one adopts the conviction of Gutiérrez, one will not hate the enemy but will combat the enemy while loving him or her. Is the mission of the church, and of the Christian individually, to show love to the enemies of the gospel by combating them? The example and the teachings of Jesus of Nazareth in his earthly ministry present a very difficult problem for those who advocate a "Christian violence."

In the opinion of liberation theologians, the mission of the church is not limited to what we call spiritual and eternal, and it should not be defined in abstract terms. The mission of the church consists of becoming conscious of social injustice, taking the side of the poor, and assuming a posture of serious and irrevocable commitment in the revolutionary process to liberate them.

Liberation ecclesiology is supported more by the sociological and theological reflection of its exponents than by a serious, careful exegesis of biblical ecclesiological texts. But the exponents do not take advantage of the abundant ecclesiological material in the New Testament to give a biblical foundation to their thought regarding the nature and mission of the church.

Eschatology. Salvation is also a liberating movement that changes history, leading it to a glorious consummation. The goal is the establishment of a better world, a new person, a new humanity, a socialist society, "more just, free, and human." It is a historical project that can mobilize and transform history.

Liberation theologians profess to have great confidence in the future. Evident in their eschatological view is the influence of Jürgen Moltmann's *Theology of Hope* and of the Christian-Marxist dialogue, especially in relation to the work of Ernst Bloch. In *The Hope Principle,* Bloch follows Karl Marx in the conviction that it is imperative to change the world, not only to explain it, and he presents hope as an element that becomes subversive to the present order of things.

To speak of the future in biblical terms, Gutiérrez uses the category of "promise." In liberation theology Bloch's "hope principle" becomes "eschatological promise." The fundamental promise was made initially to Abraham, and it will reach its complete fulfillment in Christ. In the meanwhile this promise is developing its potential in the promises that God has made throughout history. The promise is not exhausted by these promises or by their fulfillment. There is an *already* and a *not yet.*

The partial and total fulfillment of the eschatological promises has to do primarily with social transformation, not with individual salvation. The fulfillment takes place where the cause of the oppressed is being defended. At the same time, Gutiérrez does not limit the fulfillment to a particular process or revolutionary movement. There is an *already* and a *not yet.*

The kingdom of God is, of course, one of the most important themes in the eschatology of liberation. The kingdom of God does not belong only to the future, nor is it simply other-worldly. God's kingdom is here and now as "a process which becomes closely related to the constant dynamic of the historical process"[81] and is moving toward its consummation. Gutiérrez affirms:

> The growth of the Kingdom is a process which occurs historically in liberation, insofar as liberation means a greater fulfillment of man. Liberation is a precondition for the new society, but this is not all it is. While liberation is implemented in historical events, it also denounces their limitation and ambiguities, proclaims their fulfillment, and impels them effectively towards total communion.[82]

According to Gutiérrez the kingdom is a gift of God and a work of humanity. Socio-political liberation is a human achievement and a manifestation of the kingdom. Without the liberation that humans attains by themselves there is no growth of the kingdom. But Gutiérrez wants to avoid fully identifying the kingdom with a particular political system:

> The process of liberation will not have conquered the very roots of oppression and the exploitation of man by man without the coming of the Kingdom, which is above all a gift. Moreover, we can say that the historical, political liberating event is the growth of the Kingdom and is a salvific event; but it is not the coming of the Kingdom, not all of salvation.[83]

Assmann does the same when he says that the kingdom is always open to what is ahead, in "constant futurization, even in its conquests."[84] Nevertheless, the total panorama of liberationist theology is that of a commitment to leftist ideologies, although the liberationists would resist admitting that their option might be equivalent to a "sanctifying" of the socio-political system, which they have chosen as the most adequate means in this historical moment for the liberation of the Latin American people.

In liberationist eschatology salvation consists also in the progress of the kingdom, a fact that implies in turn the search for a radical break with the status quo, in order to begin the formation of a new society that one day will have completely suppressed the class system and produced a totally new humanity. It is suggested that this hope is not based on archaic messianism, but rather on scientific rationality, on a historical, scientific analysis of reality. It is a liberation carried out by and for the oppressed masses.

In this view, the Christian must become involved in the revolutionary process. The Christian faith has a political dimension. This dimension is not simply a complementary aspect of the faith; it is "the act of faith as such in its concrete context of historical praxis."[85] Gutiérrez affirms that just as Pius XII said that the church civilizes by evangelizing, so now in the Latin American context "it would be necessary to say that the Church should politicize by evangelizing,"[86] in the sense that it should manifest the political dimension of the gospel.

The emphasis of the church's mission falls definitely on social action. "In Latin America to be Church today means to take a clear position regarding both the present state of social injustice and the revolutionary process which is attempting to abolish that injustice and build a more human order.[87]

There are, of course, questions to be asked of liberation theologians. No Latin American who knows firsthand and feels the anguish of his or her people opposes the cause of the poor, but even on the political plane it must be asked whether or not the option of the liberation theologians is the only valid one for our countries. It is also natural to ask if that political option will liberate and really do justice to the oppressed, or if it will result in another dictatorship that will brutally frustrate the hope of liberation for the individual and society.

A Roman Catholic Evaluation of Liberation Theology

In a gathering sponsored by CELAM (Consejo Episcopal Latinoamericano) in Bogotá, Colombia, in November 1973, Friar Buenaventura Kloppenburg referred to the "temptations" of liberation theology. Among those that he mentioned, it is worthwhile quoting the following: the primacy of the situation over the gospel, the belittling of the ontological aspect of theology (because of an inordinate emphasis upon the existential aspect), the reduction of theology to politology, the devaluation of personal and individual sin, the exclusivistic linking of the gospel with socialism, the ignoring of the eschatological reserve (that is, ignoring the fact that now history has a goal that the Lord has already stipulated), the emergence of a new kind of clericalism (the clergy claims to assume the role of the laity in politics), and resorting to violence.[88]

This is only one example among many of the negative reactions of Catholic theologians to a system of thought that is many respects is the fruit of Latin American catholicism.

Challenges to Liberation Theology

From the point of view of conservative Latin American evangelical, liberation theology is far from being, strictly speaking, a biblical theology and is therefore not satisfactory for those who have the Scriptures as their supreme rule of faith. It is a relativistic theology because it takes lightly the firm foundation of biblical authority, because its hermeneutical criterion is a political ideology, and because its proponents opt for the insecurity of a future that is always open.

Nevertheless, liberation theology is not only a problem to us; it is also in a sense a challenge that we cannot avoid. This challenge confronts us in the following ways.

1.   It is a challenge to study the basic presuppositons of this system of thought, in the light of the Scriptures, in interaction with our Latin American reality. All of our pastors and evangelists should know the basic contents of liberation theology. They should not be satisfied with some of the superficial interpretations given to liberation theology by the political right. They should not limit themselves to repeating these interpretations in the pulpit. It is not necessary to be naive to oppose liberation theology. But on the other hand we do not have to be naive, non-critical, and at the service of the political left.

2.   It is a challenge to study our Bible afresh, under the ministry of the Holy Spirit, in fellowship with the church, in response to the needs and problems of our social context.

3.   It is a challenge either to discover, or to recuperate, those elements of divine revelation that we have often overlooked in our teaching and preaching ministry—for instance, the unity of humanity as a product of divine creation. The dichotomy we have frequently established in our gospel preaching between soul and body does not exist in the Scriptures. The human being is a unity. Spirit, soul, and body are included in the work of redemption. Our evangelistic message has to be addressed to the total human being.

4.   It is a challenge to announce "the whole purpose of God" (Acts 20:27). This purpose includes our life beyond the grave and our life this side of the grave. It includes the individual, the family, the church, the

state. God's revelation has to do with the evils of society—for instance, social injustice, oppression, violence. We should not limit ourselves to mentioning those evils as an illustration "to communicate the gospel in a relevant way." We should be truly concerned about the sufferings of our own people. We should encourage the church to serve the people and to pray for "the peace of the city," a peace that is not possible for the nation where injustice reigns.

5.   It is a challenge to realize that according to the Scriptures our mission is not supposed to be limited to the oral communication of the gospel. Social responsibility is included in the mission of the church. On the other hand, it is necessary to remember that the mission of the church is not to strive for political power. Its mission is not to manipulate the people on behalf of a particular political ideology, to achieve political power, or to maintain ecclesiastical privileges in the nation. The church must everywhere have a ministry of reconciliation. Its message is never supposed to be a call to violence.

As the moral conscience of the nation, the church has to remind the people again and again of the spiritual dimension of the social problems. The Lord Jesus Christ came to the world to deal primarily with humanity as a problem, not just with the problems of humanity. Humans are sinners, and their main problem is deep in their own heart. It is from the inside, from a person's heart, that the evil ideas and practices come. A radical transformation is needed deep in the human heart. This is the work that only the Holy Spirit can do, as he applies the Word and the benefits of the work of the Son of God to the repentant sinner who receives by faith the Lord Jesus Christ as Savior. It is absolutely necessary to be born again. A transformation of the social structures may be necessary and urgent, but such a transformation is not enough to solve our personal and social problems.

6.   It is a challenge to evaluate one's own life, to see if we are really committed to the Lord, and to serve the people in his name. Even in the most difficult circumstances confronting the nation, individual Christians and the church can serve the people in one way or another.

Finally, we have to evaluate ourselves in the light of the Word of God, in submission to the Holy Spirit, to see if we are living according to the demands of Christian discipleship. The best response to the ideological and theological challenges of our day is a life transformed by the power of the Holy Spirit and dedicated to serving the Kingdom of God.

PASTORAL REVOLUTION

The revolutionary ideas have not remained secluded in the "ivory tower" of some theologians who are isolated from our social reality; nor are those ideas limited to some idealistic thinkers or lyric writers who do not dare to enter into revolutionary action. The Catholic revolution is not reduced to either the heroic example of a few guerrilla priests like Camilo Torres or the political activism of Ernesto Cardenal and Father D'Escoto, the foreign relations secretary in the Sandinista cabinet in Nicaragua. There is a pastoral revolution going on in the Roman Catholic church.

Revolutionary Catholic Priests

Liberation theology has permeated the minds and the hearts of a number of priests, monks, and nuns who reside among the peasants and urban workers. The priests, who are determined to work as priests for the transformation of "oppressive structures," are many. Some of them have been willing to join the "guerrillas," following the example of Father Camilo Torres. Others have opted for staying in the cities, or in the countryside, awakening the consciences of the people to the possibility of liberating themselves by means of the revolutionary praxis.

Rutilio Grande. Father Rutilio Grande, assassinated in El Salvador in 1977, is one of the representatives of the pastoral revolution in Latin American Catholicism.

He was born in 1928 in a semirural area of that country. He was still a child when he felt that God was calling him to the priesthood. At the age of seventeen he entered the Jesuit order as a novice. He studied philosophy and theology in Venezuela, Ecuador, and Spain from 1955 through 1960. After two years as a professor in the San José de la Montaña Seminary in San Salvador, El Salvador, he went back to Spain in 1962 to complete his studies as a Jesuit. From October 1963 through June 1964 he studied at the International Institute of Pastoral Studies *Lumen Vitae* in Belgium. There he learned the most advanced European methods of pastoral work. It seems that it was at that institution where he became deeply interested in a pastoral renovation. When he went back to the seminary in San Salvador he tried to introduce some changes in the formation of the future priests.

Then in the Latin American Pastoral Institute in Quito, Ecuador, he experienced a profound transformation in his life. "That was a time of pastoral reflection having as a point of departure the Latin American context. It was a challenge to update in the concrete situation of Latin America the European pastoral schemes and his own experience of past years."[89] Moreover, he had the opportunity to work with the Riobamba Bishop Monsignor Proaño, who was putting into practice the theoretical principles taught at the Latin American Pastoral Institute. It was also at that time that Father Grande learned the method of Paulo Freire and decided to dedicate his life to the new pastoral strategies in Latin America. No wonder that when he returned to El Salvador in 1972, instead of reassuming his position as a seminary professor, he became a member of a missionary team to work in the small town of Aguilares, in the Salvadorian countryside. This assignment was the greatest work of his life.

Evidently, Rutilio's way of thinking was under the influence of Vatican II, Medellín, and the theology of liberation. In the general conference of Central American Jesuits, held in December 1969, he grasped the main intuitions of liberation theology. According to his own testimony, it was the assimilation of the liberationist ideas that forced him to act in a firm and conflictive manner during the pastoral week of the Salvadorian clergy in July 1970. With regard to conclusions that the participants reached at the end of that week, and the resulting alarm, Rutilio advocated a serious consideration of the documents of Vatican II and Medellín.[90]

In November of the same year, in the monthly meeting of the Salvadoran clergy, Father Grande made some comments on the events of that pastoral week. In relation to the discrepancy about the attempt to implement Vatican II and Medellín in El Salvador, he said that the crisis confronting the clergy was a gift from God and a call to repentance. He believed that the crisis was caused by the deficient education received by the priests. The basis of this education was a philosophy isolated from the reality of this world.

Rutilio asked for a change of emphasis in the pastoral work. He suggested that the clergy should change from an almost magical pastoral ministry that emphasizes sacramental salvation to a more dynamic ministry in which preeminence would be given to the Word of God and evangelization as the total liberation of humanity and the universe.[91] According to Rutilio, the answer to the crisis of the church is in God and the clergy. Before starting to apply the new pastoral strategies, it was necessary for one to experience a personal conversion that would destroy any false sense of security, to be free to look for that which is new, to wait for the spirit that will open new avenues for pastoral action.[92] He concluded by saying that "for the fulfillment of its apostolic mission the Church was called to give absolute priority to the social problem."[93]

In a sermon preached at the Metropolitan Cathedral in San Salvador in the presence of the nation's president and other dignitaries, Father Grande asked for repentance and conversion and advocated a "Christian revolution based on the Gospel, the Gospel which in its very essence is love, and excludes nobody."[94]

Motivated by his new ideas, Rutilio started his pastoral labors in Aguilares. His "primary and fundamental option" included the effort to make the people aware of their own social problems, hoping to promote in this way economic and social changes at the national level. To achieve this purpose, team work was indispensable in a communal setting that would make possible collective study, reflection, dialogue, evaluation, and action. They would live and work together on behalf of the project.

The team tried to establish dynamic communities which, being awakened to social reality, would be willing to become agents of social change. In the effort to awaken the social awareness of the people, Paulo Freire's influence was evident. The so-called generative themes for dialogue were collected in house-to-house visitation and in personal interviews with urban workers and peasants.

The work took as its point of departure the people's traditional religiosity. But they were led to a socio-political dialogue on the basis of the social implications of the gospel. Rutilio used to say: "I took their rosaries away, and got the people into Bible reading with commentaries, as the preachers do."[95] In the adult meetings a prominent place was given to the reading of the gospels. The ones who were leaders by nature emerged from those meetings to become the lay agents of pastoral renovation.

The catechists of the base communities were elected by the people. They served as a link between the community and the parochial church. At the beginning each catechist represented four or five people. The members of the missionary team dedicated themselves especially to the formation of these lay preachers of the Word ("delegados de la Palabra"). In a way the catechists would function as priests in their communities. The movement was characterized by the direct participation of lay people in the ministry of the Word. The emphasis was on the common people. There was no monopoly of the pastoral ministry by the clergy.

> The people were trained to use the Bible spontaneously in close relationship with daily events. Although the emphasis was on evangelization, there were political consequences. It was not necessary to tell the peasants that they were oppressed, and who were their oppressors. This situation was evident. But they came to understand clearly that the oppression they suffered was anti-

Christian, and that the Gospel instead of teaching resignation was asking them to fight for their own liberation.[96]

The awakening of the social conscience of the people produced almost immediate results. Eight months after the arrival of the missionary team to Aguilares, the first strike broke out in one of the sugar-cane plantations in that region. The workers demanded higher salaries. The movement spread to other plantations in the neighborhood. It was not difficult to associate the labor unrest with the base communities in the local Catholic church. Rutilio became the symbol of the labor movement.[97] The accusation of "Communist priests" did not take much time to come. Rutilio's explanation that he was not a politician but a religious leader was in vain:

> l am a religious leader, and I do not belong to any political party. I plead that no political faction enrolls me in its official membership, because I owe myself to all the people. My vocation is to serve eternal values which correspond to fundamental human values. These eternal values are not the exclusive possession of a particular group or faction. The Gospel of Christ proclaims them, and defends them in the concrete situation of the world, and immortalizes them with that transcendency of the hereafter.[98]

Father Grande knew that he was not allowed to participate in the struggle for political power, but his idea of politics was broad enough to see political action as a commitment and service to the people, especially in a situation of social injustice and violation of human rights. He did not want to evade this responsibility. At the same time he rejected the idea of becoming himself a political agitator.

To the people in general, and particularly in the eyes of those who were interested in maintaining the status quo, there was ambiguity, or ambivalence, in Rutilio's attitude. The situation became more complicated than ever when political groups and labor unions started a movement in different parts of the country asking for higher salaries and better labor conditions. Popular unrest and political ambition seemed to be growing everywhere in El Salvador. Public authorities and those who opposed social change easily associated the "liberationist priests" with the restlessness of the workers. Of course it would not be surprising that professional politicians could take advantage of Rutilio's ideas and work to achieve their selfish purposes, although he and his colleagues were not willing to enter into political alliances.

The persecution against the priests who were involved in pastoral renewal was increasing. Mario Bernal, a Colombian priest who was working in the small town of Apopa, was expelled from the country. On February 13, 1977, Rutilio and other priests got together to celebrate Mass as a protest against the expulsion of their colleague. Rutilio's words on that particular occasion were a direct challenge to the enemies of social change:

> I am afraid, my dear brothers and friends, that in a short time to bring Bibles to our country will be illegal. We will receive just the covers, because all of its pages are subversive. They are subversive, of course, against sin.... If Jesus of Nazareth were to come back, as in the first century, going down from Galilee to Judea, I mean from Chalatenango to San Salvador, I dare to say that he would not get, with his preaching and good works, even to the town of Apopa. They would stop him, and put him in jail, and he would be taken to court, to be accused of trying to subvert the Constitutional order.... He would be accused of being a foreign Jew, agitator, and propagator of exotic ideas, which are against God and Democracy.... They would crucify him again.... We prefer a Christ of grave-diggers . . ., a voiceless Christ, to take him in our processions . . ., a Christ made by ourselves, to serve our selfish interests. Some people do not want a Christ that would bother their conscience . . ., a questioning Christ. They prefer a God who is up there in heaven, far away from earthly things. In Christian discipleship one has to be willing to sacrifice his life for a just social order, for the salvation of others, for the values of the Gospel.[99]

A month later, on March 12, Rutilio was ambushed and shot to death in a sugar-cane plantation. He was on his way to say Mass in a neighboring town. Up to now it is unknown what persons were directly involved in the crime. Rutilio paid the price for his "primary and fundamental option" in a social context in which, according to his own words, "it is dangerous to be a Christian."[100]

He translated into simple and familiar words, but with great conviction, the revolutionary message of Gutiérrez, Assmann, Helder Cámara, Paulo Freire, Ernesto Cardenal, and other Catholics who in their own way have advocated the total liberation of the Latin American people.

Rogelio Ponceele. Another example of priests who are deeply involved in the "revolutionary process" is Father Rogelio Ponceele, who was born in Belgium in 1939. After completing his seminary studies he was ordained a priest at the age of twenty-five. In 1970 he went as a missionary to El Salvador, Central America, where he started immediately doing pastoral work and learning simultaneously the Spanish language in one of the proletarian sections of the capital city, San Salvador. He worked also among the people in the slums, where he knew firsthand the drama of extreme poverty.

At the very beginning of his ministry he spoke against violence. One of the factors to change his mind was his interaction with Salvadorans who had already opted for revolution as the answer to the social problem in their own country. He worked for ten years in San Salvador, helping to organize basic ecclesial communities for Bible study in response to spiritual and social needs and for political indoctrination. He became a personal friend of Monsignor Oscar Romero, the Catholic archbishop who was assassinated when he was saying Mass in one of the churches of the capital city in 1980.

Father Ponceele says that the governmental repression of the people who were asking for a better life opened his eyes. He decided to take sides with the revolutionary movement. Because so many members of the clergy had become involved in politics, the Catholic church was in serious conflict with the national government. In 1980 Father Ponceele realized that his life was in danger. He and his colleagues had already organized many "communities" that were deeply committed to subverting the status quo.[101] Close to the end of 1980, he felt that he had only two alternatives left: to abandon the country or to join the "guerrillas" in the countryside, far away from the capital city. He opted for staying in El Salvador as a priest of the revolutionary army.

At the present time Father Ponceele is in the eastern section of that country, where the "guerrillas" have military camps. He ministers to the members of the revolutionary army and to the peasants in that area. According to his own testimony, he is not there as a soldier, to combat the national army, but as a priest. He did not accept a weapon when he arrived at the camp. He has no military assignments. He is working only as a priest.[102]

However, he strongly believes in what the revolutionaries are doing. He is an enthusiastic apologist of the revolution. In the first Mass he celebrated at the camp, he told his comrades: "You do not have a rifle because you are violent by nature, or because you enjoy killing your fellow men. In your hands the rifle has become a sacred weapon to liberate the people."[103] He is optimistic enough to think that the revolutionaries are willing to fight but not to hate. Consequently, he sees no reason to exhort them to forgive.[104]

One of the reasons he does not have a gun is because he wants to remind the people that the ideal is not to resort to violence—although violence is painfully necessary.[105] On the other hand, it is his conviction that "violence is not a moral problem, but first of all a political problem."[106]

As a pastor he is really trying to identify himself with the people in their sufferings and longings and in their revolutionary praxis. He confesses that when he is close to a dying man, he limits himself to being there, holding his hand; but in those solemn moments he almost never speaks of God. He feels it is too cheap to tell him: "be confident, because God...."[107]

Nevertheless, he realizes that the peasants believe in God. They believe he is in action, helping them in their struggle for freedom. And he wants them to exercise faith, because they deserve to be happy. He says that in the revolutionary praxis Christians and Marxists have come together on behalf of the people. All of them are looking for the same values. The triumph of the revolution will not bring Christian values to an end. A revolution within the revolution will be always necessary. God is always ahead of us, inviting us to move forward.[108]

With regard to the officers of the revolutionary army, Father Ponceele prefers not to discuss whether they are really Christian believers or not. He feels that "they are more Christian than we are, because of their total dedication to serve others. And that is the meaning of being a Christian."[109]

He stays with the people because he is convinced that his main responsibility as a pastor is to give hope. The presence of a priest among the people is a sign that God goes with them.[110]

Such is the testimony of Rogelio Ponceele, a Catholic priest who has opted for the pastoral revolution in Latin America.

Base Ecclesial Communities

On May 7, 1979, *Time* magazine reported, under the title "The Church of the Poor," that the *comunidades de base* (base communities) are "the most influential movement among Latin America's 300 million faithful.... There may be as many as 150,000 comunidades, 80,000 in Brazil alone, chiefly in the destitute states of that country's north and northeast."[111]

History. According to Frei Betto, the Brazilian *comunidades* started around the year 1960 by the initiative of laymen, priests, or bishops.[112] Many of the communities were started by foreign missionary priests working among the poor, as in the already-mentioned case of Father Rogelio Ponceele, who helped to establish politically-oriented base communities in the capital city of El Salvador.

Definition. The base communities are groups of Catholics who usually belong to the low strata of society. They organize themselves to edify one another in their faith and to help each other in the struggle for life. In their meetings they may have Bible study, discussion of local and national problems, and even political indoctrination. The majority of these communities are rural and on the outskirts of the big towns. Each community may be led by a layman. A priest assists the coordination of a large number of communities.

The Second Latin American Episcopal Conference, held in Medellín in 1968, defines the base ecclesial communities as follows:

> Thus the Base Christian Community is the primary and fundamental ecclesial nucleus which on its own level must take responsibility for the resources and spread of the faith as well as for the worship which is its expression. It is therefore the initial cell of the Church structures and the source of evangelization, and at the present time the primordial factor of human advancement and development.[113]

At Medellín, the base communities were encouraged to continue playing an important role, under the leadership of a renewed pastoral action, for the transformation of Latin America.

Enrique Dussel points out that at the Third Latin American Episcopal Conference, held in 1979 in Puebla, Mexico, the groups that wanted to condemn the base communities, or the Church of the Poor, and liberation theology were not able to achieve their purpose. "The doors stayed open for Christians to continue identifying themselves with the poor, and working for the interests of the oppressed."[114] Puebla is in the tradition of Medellín.

The final document of Puebla says that the base ecclesial communities express the preferential love of the church for the poor. "In these communities there is the possibility for the common people to participate in the mission of the Church, in the commitment to transform the world."[115]

In February 1980, the Fourth International Ecumenical Congress on Theology was held in Sao Paulo, Brazil. One hundred eighty participants from forty-two countries, representing Africa, Asia, the United States (ethnic minorities), Europe, the Caribbean, and Latin America, reflected on "The Ecclesiology of the Popular Christian Communities," with special emphasis on Latin America.

Base communities and politics. The Sao Paulo Document points out that the number of Christians committed to social change within the movements of liberation is growing. Many of these Christians belong to the base communities, which have also been an instrument of renewal for the church.[116] In other words, the poor are exercising a profound influence on politics and the church. Jose Marins explains that in the base communities emphasis is given to social commitment, without assuming a specific political line. "Greater stress is laid on the concern of the communities to awaken people's awareness, leading them to make their own socio-political commitment, not in the name of the community but in the name of faith."[117]

Leonardo Boff sees the base communities "as a true ecclesiogenesis" that becomes a reality among the poor.[118] In the opinion of Gustavo Gutiérrez, only those communities emerging from the oppressed people are capable of living and proclaiming the kingdom values in a real identification with the people who are struggling for their own liberation.[119] "The base ecclesial communities participated in the Nicaraguan revolution, the church committed itself to the anti-Somoza 'war.'"[120]

There are, of course, base communities that concentrate on spiritual and cultural activities like reading, Bible study, and the training of lay leaders to perform some priestly functions in areas that the clergy does not reach regularly. They are also interested in economic and social development, adopting specific projects to improve their neighborhood.

However, theologians like Frei Betto, who has worked with base communities in Brazil for a number of years, realize that these ecclesial groups "are open to the popular revolutionary movement, helping to create or strengthen new organizations which are autonomous, independent from the State and the Church,"[121] although the base communities themselves are not officially separated from Roman Catholicism.

"The word liberation is prominent in the vocabulary of the base communities."[122] Volta Redonda Bishop Waldyr Calheiros de Novais observes: "The *comunidades* are the theology of liberation put into practice."[123] On the other hand we have to keep in mind that chronologically the base communities precede liberation theology, and they helped to develop this system of thought. Gustavo Gutiérrez says:

> One characteristic of my kind of theology is precisely my relationship with the basic church communities. I could say that the real subject of Liberation Theology is those communities and the insights which they develop as they reflect on their Christian life and commitment and open themselves to the input of God's Word. It is their thinking about communion, about faith, about hope, which brings theology to the surface.
>
> . . . It has been necessary for others to articulate that theology. But it is no coincidence that the basic church communities—by whatever name they may be called—emerged just before the Theology of Liberation came into being and found in it their own affirmation. The experience of faith and the commitment to church and society appeared hand in hand.[124]

Betto declares that "political involvement is an essential part of the evangelistic mission of the Church."[125] The Sao Paulo Document affirms that a community is Christian because it evangelizes; but to evangelize means "to announce the God who enters into a covenant with the oppressed to defend their cause; it is to announce the God who liberates his people from social injustice, from oppression, and sin."[126]

When the people's social awareness is awakened, it is not difficult for them to make a socio-political commitment in response to the indoctrination given by the leader of the community. Frei Betto says that in practice it is not unusual for the members of the base community to see no conflict between prayer and action, between faith in God and political activity, between pastoral work and labor-union activities. They do not seem to have any problem with a pastoral praxis complemented by a political praxis.[127] Betto himself is not afraid that active involvement in a political party would neutralize or nullify the pastoral praxis; but he is also concerned about maintaining the pastoral identity in the midst of political involvement. He sees the danger of secularization in the Liberation process. In regard to the pastoral agents, he suggests that because of the many demands for immediate action, they may not have time to pray. It is not easy to join pastoral praxis and a life of prayer. The pastoral agent has to learn how to relate political rationality to spirituality.[128]

Base communities and spirituality. Spirituality is precisely emphasized in the Sao Paulo Document in relation to the base communities. It is declared that the base communities "are not a political movement, or power, parallel to the people's organizations, and that the base communities are not either trying to legitimate these organizations."[129] According to the Document, "the spirituality of liberaton" has to be practiced in the base communities:[130]

> It is imperative to revitalize, and in some cases to recuperate, Christian spirituality as the original experience that drives the individual Christian and people's communities into an evangelistic and political commitment, and theological reflection.... We reaffirm the evangelistic and liberating efficacy of prayer, for us and the people.[131]

However, it is valid to ask whether the spirituality of liberation will be able to counteract in the base communities the danger of losing their ecclesiastical identity in the effort to identify themselves with a political movement that would sacralize or absolutize a particular political ideology.

The pastoral revolution is creating tension inside and outside the Catholic church. In some places there seems to be in practice a separation between "the Church of the Poor" and the hierarchy of official Catholicism. The Nicaraguan situation is a case in point. Outside observers may see not much difference between a base ecclesial community deeply involved in political praxis and the popular movement of liberation.

The challenge to us. Since the beginning of our history we evangelicals have used to some extent the "base community" method. We have gone also to the countryside and to the outskirts of the big towns to evangelize the low strata of society. In reality most evangelicals have belonged to "base evangelical communities," if we analyze the evangelical community as a whole from a sociological standpoint. But, of course, we have not demanded social changes, we have avoided politics. Our message has been criticized as too individualistic, dualistic, and futuristic.

A change is taking place among evangelicals in regard to social responsibility. It is a healthy change, if we take into serious consideration the totality of God's written revelation. Nevertheless, we have to learn from the experience of the Catholic base communities that once the social conscience of the people is awakened the danger of losing our Christian identity is present. On the basis of his own experience with the base communities in El Salvador, Father Rogelio Ponceele says: "It is dangerous to take the people to a certain point [in the awakening of their social awareness], because then they may lead us beyond that point."[132] This is an important lesson to learn.

If we are going to continue emphasizing our social responsibility as evangelicals, we have to be spiritually, theologically, and technically prepared to lead the way instead of being led to a situation in which we may not be any more salt of the earth or light of the world.

The cleavage between "the Church of the Poor" and traditional Catholicism is another lesson to learn. The base community movement challenges us to study our ecclesiology anew, on the basis of the Word of God, in submission to the Holy Spirit, and in response to our social and ecclesiastical context. What does it mean to be the church of Jesus Christ today? This is a question we have to answer in an evangelical ecclesiology written in Latin America for Latin America.

THEOLOGY BY THE PEOPLE

Closely related to liberation theology is "the theology by the people," a new modality in theological education today.

The base community has been used in many cases to encourage the people to get involved in the process of doing theology. One of the best-known examples of this theological method is the one provided by Ernesto Cardenal, the secretary of culture of the Nicaraguan Sandinista government. Several years ago, Cardenal motivated people, especially poor people, peasants, and proletarians, to do theology by themselves in the island of Solentiname, in the Great Lake of Nicaragua. In his book *The Gospel of Solentiname*,[133] Cardenal reports on the reactions of the people to the reading of the Scriptures.

The "theology by the people" has been considered "a new phenomenon" in the area of theological education. Briefly explained, this theology means that the people are the subjects, not simply the objects, of theological reflection. We have to listen to the people, especially the poor, and let them do their own theology. It is not any more a theology *for* the people, written for them, but a theology *by* the people.[134]

Tracing the history of the "theology by the people," we may start with the philosophy of the Brazilian educator Paulo Freire. We have already mentioned that in his book *The Pedagogy of the Oppressed* he proposes a renewal of education by which the student and the teacher are deeply involved in the process of discovering truth. But we should not think that the student is completely free from indoctrination to do his own thinking. The "dialogical method" is also a "method of conscientization"—namely, a method for making the student aware of his social and political situation and for encouraging him to liberate himself from his oppression. Freire's commitment to the political left is evident. One of the documents of Church and Society in Latin America (ISAL) says: "The Church, then, should give attention to the formulation of a 'theology of the people,' and not a 'theology for the people.'"[135]

At the end of his book *Liberation Theology,* Gustavo Gutiérrez declares: "But in the last instance we will have an authentic theology of liberation only when the oppressed themselves can freely raise their voice and express themselves directly and creatively in society and in the heart of the People of God . . ., when they are the protagonists of their own liberation."[136]

Under the sponsorship of the World Council of Churches, the "theology by the people" is trying to attract the attention of educators, pastors, and other evangelical leaders in Latin America. A consultation on this subject was sponsored by the World Council of Churches in Mexico two years ago. The papers read on that occasion have been published under the title *Theology by the People: Reflections on Doing Theology in Community.*[137] In May 1986 a consultation sponsored by the Latin American Association of Theological Institutions was held in Guatemala, with the participation of at least one representative of the WCC. The main subject of the consultation was "theology by the people."

It is natural to ask for the meaning of *people* in this new modality of theological education. Definitely, it is not the meaning given by the New Testament to the word *people* in the phrase "the people of God" (2 Pet. 2). The editors of the book *Theology by the People* say that "when used in the Latin American theological context people (*pueblo*) refers to the poor people, especially the oppressed, exploited people. People refers to more than the oppressed class, it is a social block of the oppressed of the nation."[138]

The word *people* has in this context an ideological meaning. It is not the people of God, the church. It is the people of the political left. Jorge C. Bravo, a Methodist educator from Peru, says that the "theology by the people" has to be biblical, dialogical, and for the service of Christian and cultural identity. But he underscores that the doing of theology must be committed to the poor.[139]

We evangelicals realize that the pulpit provides a great opportunity to do theology at the level of the people. We believe that the local congregation has to be a hermeneutical community in which the people of God interact with their leaders to learn what the written Word of God has to tell them about their Christian life and service in their own social context. A hermeneutical community would be a real help in contextualizing the gospel. But the advocates of the "theology by the people" seem to be limiting the privilege of doing theology to a particular segment of society.

We cannot deny that the Christian poor and oppressed have also the Word of God and the Holy Spirit to lead them into the truth. We need their contribution in the process of doing theology. This affirmation is in harmony with the teaching on the universal priesthood of the believers. On the other hand, according to the Scriptures, in Christ there is no Jew or Gentile, male or female, servant or free person. The ideal is not a theology by the poor, or a theology by the rich, but a theology by the people of God on the basis of the Scriptures, under the illumination of the Holy Spirit, in response to human need.

From the New Testament we learn also that the gifts of the Holy Spirit are not given only to a particular class of people in the body of Christ. Consequently, doing theology cannot be an exclusive privilege of a particular social segment in the universal church. It is possible to say that the one who desires to do theology should be willing to become poor on behalf of the kingdom of God, if the King leads him or her to do so. It is also possible to say that we cannot do a relevant theology in the Third World, or in any region of the world, if we isolate ourselves from the poor. The Lord Jesus Christ lived among the poor, as one of them. But it is interesting to take note that not all the theologians who are talking a great deal about the "theology by the poor" are living among the poor in Latin America.

Freire has also written the book *Education as a Practice of Freedom*. It remains to be seen whether the poor will be really free in the process of doing theology, or whether they will be manipulated to serve the purposes of the political left. The orientation given by the teacher in the educational process will determine to a large extent the kind of theology that the oppressed will produce. There is still much of the "banking method" in the educational philosophy of Freire. He is trying to deposit in our minds his educational thesis by means of his writings. The fact is that there is always knowledge to communicate, to deposit into the mind of the student. In evangelical theological education we insist that we have to communicate faithfully the doctrine we have received from God's written revelation, through the ministry of our teachers (2 Tim. 2:1-2). It is understood that this communication is not supposed to be limited to a process of indoctrination, memorization, and naive or blind repetition. But from the evangelical standpoint, the ones doing theology has to submit themselves to the authority of the Word of God and the authority of the Holy Spirit. Moreover, the theologian has to be in close fellowship with the Christian community, the people of God.

The editors of the book *Theology by the People* confess that the chapters "are not themselves theological reflection by the people, they are reflections of theologians on 'theology by the people.'"[140] The fact is that the poor do not seem to be ready yet to do theology. Once again, bourgeois leaders have to design, promote, and direct a proletarian revolution, this time a revolution in theological education.

Jorge C. Bravo, whose paper we have already quoted, indicates that "theology by the people" must be biblical, but he immediately explains that "opting for the poor and marginalized is a result of a rereading of the biblical message in response to the irruption of the poor and marginalized in the heart of the church, which in turn is caused by the situation of death and oppression in which our Latin American continent lives."[141]

It is not necessary to reread the Bible to discover the interest of God in the orphan, the widow, the foreigner, the prisoner, the poor. As the defender of the oppressed, he demands the practice of justice in the relationship between each other. It is not necessary to reread the Scriptures to discover that the Lord Jesus acted in behalf of poor and marginalized people. He made himself poor to be the Savior of the world. The rereading asked by Bravo may be necessary to inject a political ideology into the Scriptures. It may be necessary for a social class within the church. In reality a "theology by the poor" would have to depend always on the presence of class struggle to be considered relevant. New Testament theology is valid for all cultural, social, and ecclesiastical situations. It is not a social-class theology. It is the theology of the people's God for God's people. It is a strong denunciation of social injustice, a clear demand for repentance, an urgent call to reconciliation between God and humanity, and between one human and another. It is a proclamation of peace, the peace that is based on that justice revealed by God in his written Word. This justice is far superior to the one proclaimed by a non-Christian, an anti-Christian, ideology.

In Latin America it is our responsibility to give the people of God the opportunity to participate in one way or another in our theological reflection, to produce a contextualized theology, a theology relevant to our own society. In a sense we are not just going to educate the people; we are also going to be educated by the people in our interaction with them. There should be no room any more for a paternalistic attitude ("the people are ignorant; we come to teach them").

But if we also believe that the people should have a say in the task of doing theology, what is the difference between our concept of the church as a theological community and the "theology by the people" proposed by some educators in Latin America? There is a great difference because we have a high view of biblical inspiration and a high respect for biblical authority. We believe in the finality of the Scriptures in all matters of faith and practice. We believe in the illumination of the Holy Spirit. We believe in the freedom of the Holy Spirit to confer his gifts apart from any social discrimination. We do not take the word *people* in a political sense. We believe in doing theology with all the people of God, the community of those who are born again by the power of the Holy Spirit because they have believed in the Lord Jesus Christ. Finally, we do not believe in doing theology with the people to serve the purposes of a political ideology, whatever this ideology may be. Our duty and privilege is to do theology in subjection to the Word of God, under the illumination of the Holy Spirit, in fellowship with the evangelical community, in response to the needs of the individual and society.

NOTES

1. Juan XXIII, "Introduction to Pacem in Terris," in *Ocho Grandes Mensajes* (Madrid: Biblioteca de Autores Christianos, 1973), p. 204.

2. Paul Vl, "Populorum Progression," in *Ocho Grandes Mensajes*, p. 57.

3. Paul Vl, "Mensaje a los campesinos colombianos," Bogota, August 23, 1968, in *La Iglesia en la Actual Transformación de América Latin a la luz del Concilio*, 2 vols. (Bogotá, Secretariado General del CELAM, 1969), 1:252-53.

4. Paul Vl, *La Evangelización del mundo contemporáneo* (Evangelii nuntiandi), arts. 35-37.

5. "Camilo Torres: Sacerdote Guerrillero?" in *Protesta* (Caracas: EPLA, Number 20).

6. Camilo Torres, *Cristianismo y Revolución* (México: Ediciones Era, 1972), p. 341.

7. Ibid., p. 571.

8. Ibid.

294 CRISIS AND HOPE IN LATIN AMERICA

9. Germán Guzmán Campos, *El Padre Camilo Torres* (México: Siglo 21, 1969), p. 263.

10. Camilo Torres, *Cristianismo y Revolución,* p. 376.

11. Ibid., pp. 525-26.

12. Ibid., p. 527.

13. Ibid., p. 528.

14. Ibid., pp. 429, 527-28.

15. Feliciano Blázquez, *Helder Camara: El Grito del Pobre* (Madrid: Sígueme, 1972), p. 12.

16. Ibid., p. 120.

17. Helder Camara, *Espiral de Violencia* (Salamanca: Ediciones Slgueme, 1970), p. 18.

18. Ibid., p. 19.

19. Ibid., p. 30.

20. Blázquez, p. 121.

21. Camara, p. 59.

22. Ibid., p. 55.

23. Ibid., p. 65.

24. Ibid., pp. 75-81.

25. Ibid., p. 47

26. Ibid., pp. 47-48.

27. Blázquez, pp. 38-39.

28. Enrique D. Dussel, *A History of the Church in Latin America: Colonialism to Liberation (1492–1979).* trans. Alan Neely (Grand Rapids: Eerdmans, 1971), pp. 163-64.

29. Ernesto Cardenal, *Salmos* (Buenos Aires: Ediciones Carlos Lohlé, 1971), p. 21.

30. Ernesto Cardenal, *El Evangelio de Solentiname* (Salamanca: Ediciones Sigueme, 1975).

31. José Steinsleger, "La Meta Común del Cristianismo y el Marxismo," *La Hora Dominical,* Guatemala, March 7, 1976.

32. *Prensa Libre,* Guatemala, September 14, 1979.

33. José Ramón Enríquez, "Ernesto Cardenal: Nuestro Delito es Anunciar un Paraíso," *La Hora Dominical,* Guatemala, May 23, 1976.

34. Steinsleger.

35. Ibid.

36. "Paulo Freire por sí mismo," *Concientización* (Bogotá: Departamento de Educación del CELAM, 1974), pp. 15-18.

37. "Carta a un joven teólogo," *Selecciones de Teología* (Barcelona: Facultad de Teología de San Francisco de Borja, vol. 13, no. 50, April-June 1974), p. 180.

38. José 1. Gonzalez-Faus, "La teología latinoamericana de la liberación," *Actualidad Bibliográfica* (Barcelona: Facultad de Teología de San Francisco Borja, vol. 10, no. 20, July-December 1973), p. 429.

39. Hugo Assmann, "Bibliografía de y sobre Paulo Freire," appendix to Paulo Freire, *Pedagogía del Oprimido* (Montevideo: Tierra Nueva, 1970), pp. 244-50.

40. Ibid., p. 247.

41. Paulo Freire, *Pedagogy of the Oppressed,* trans. Myra Bergman Ramos (New York: Herder & Herder, 1970), p. 32. Spanish edition, *Pedagogía del Oprimido* (Montevideo: Tierra Nueva, 1970).

42. Ibid., p. 36.

43. Ibid., pp. 39, 60.

44. Ibid., p. 158.

45. González-Faus, p. 434.

46. Ivan Illich, *¿En América Latina, Para qué sirve la escuela?* (Buenos Aires: Ediciones Búsqueda, 1974), p. 30.

47. Freire, "Carta a un joven teólogo," p. 180.

48. Segundo Galilea, *Teología de Liberación. Ensayo de Síntesis* (Colombia: Indo-American Press Service, 1976), pp. 27-28.

49. Hugo Assmann, *Teología desde la Praxis de la Liberación* (Salamanca: Ediciones Sígueme, 1973), pp. 16-20, 23-25, 44, 76-89.

50. *Prensa Libre,* Guatemala, January 30, 1979.

51. Ibid., August 10, 1987.

52. Ibid., June 29, 1983.

53. Hugo Assmann, *Opresión-Liberación, Desafío a los Cristianos* (Montevideo: Tierra Nueva, 1971), pp. 39-40, 1 15-22.

54. Enrique D. Dussel, pp. 244-45.

55. Ibid., p. 245.

56. Assmann, *Teología desde la Praxis,* p. 79.

57. Gustavo Gutiérrez, *A Theology of Liberation: History, Politics and Salvation,* trans. and ed. Caridad Inda and John Eagleson (Maryknoll, NY: Orbis, 1973).

58. Galilea, pp. 14-16.

59. Assmann, *Opresión-Liberación,* p. 141.

60. Ibid., pp. 67-68.

61. Galilea, pp. 17-18.

62. Hugo Assmann, *Theology for a Nomad Church,* trans. Paul Burns (Maryknoll, NY: Orbis, 1975),p.62.

63. J. Mervin Breneman O., "El Exodo como tema de Interpretación Teológica," *Liberación, Exodo y Biblia* (Miami: Editoral Caribe, 1975), pp. 11-52. Andrew Kirk, "La Biblia y su hermenéutica en relación con la teología protestante en América Latina," *El Debate Contemporáneo sobre la Biblia* (Barcelona: Ediciones Evangelicas Europeas, 1972), pp. 155-213.

64. Gustavo Gutiérrez expresses this thought at the very end of his book *A Theology of Liberation Theology.*

65. Ibid., pp. 175-76.

66. Ibid., p. 2 13.

67. Ibid.

68. Ibid., p. 151.

69. Ibid., pp. 151, 194.

70. Ibid., pp. 158-60.

71. "New Debate Over Jesus' Divinity," *Time,* February 27, 1978.

72. Jon Sobrino, *Jesús en América Latina* (Santander, Spain: Sal Terrae, 1982), pp. 47, 80.

73. Gutiérrez, pp. 225-32.

74. Sobrino, *Jesús en América Latina,* pp. 58, 93, 60.

75. Gutierrez, pp. 151, 194, 196-203, 256.

76. Leonardo Boff, *La fe en la periferia del mundo* (Santander, Spain: Sal Terrae, 1981), p. 145.

77. Gutierrez, p. 267.

78. Ibid., pp. 269-70.

79. Ibid., pp. 274-75.

80. Ibid., pp. 273, 276.

81. Assmann, *Opresión-Liberación,* pp. 163-64.

82. Gutiérrez, p. 177.

83. Ibid.

84. Assman, *Opresión-Liberación,* p. 164.

85. Ibid., p. 20.

86. Gutiérrez, p. 296.

87. Ibid., p. 265.

88. Buenaventura Kloppenburg, "Las Tentaciones de la Teología de la Liberación," *Liberación: Diálogos en el CELAM* (Bogatá, Colombia: Secretariado General del CELAM, 1974), pp.401-15.

89. The information on the life and work of Rutilio Grande is taken from the book *Rutilio Grande: Mártir de la Evangelización Rural en El Salvador,* published by Universidad Centroamericana, San Salvador, El Salvador, 1978.

90. Ibid., p. 38.

91. Ibid., p. 39.

92. Ibid., p. 40.

93. Ibid., p. 41.

94. Ibid., p. 43.

95. Ibid., p. 33.

96. Ibid., p. 80.

97. Ibid., p. 83.

98. Ibid., p. 101.

99. Ibid., pp. 108-9.

100. Ibid., p. 108.

101. María López Vigil, *Muerte y Vida en Morazón* (San Salvador, El Salvador: Universidad Centroamericana Editores, 1987). This book is actually the testimony of the Catholic priest Rogelio Ponceele. The information given in this chapter on Father Ponceele comes from his own account. P. 44.

102. Ibid., pp. 49, 60.

103. Ibid., p. 51.

104. Ibid., p. 59.

105. Ibid., p. 87.

106. Ibid., p. 81.

107. Ibid., p. 76.

108. Ibid., pp. 120-21.

109. Ibid., p. 8 1 .

110. Ibid., p. 122.

111. "The Church of the Poor," *Time*, May 7, 1979. For a comprehensive treatment of the base ecclesial communities, see Guillermo Cook, *The Expectation of the Poor: Latin American Base Ecclesial Communities in Protestant Perspective* (Maryknoll, NY: Orbis, 1985), pp. xix, 316. See also the special issue of *Transformation* on this subject, July-September 1986, vol. 3, no. 3.

112. Frei Betto, *¿Qué es la Comunidad Ecclesial de Base?* (Managua, Nicaragua: Centro Ecuménico Antonio Valdivieso, n.d.), p. 10.

113. José Marins, "Basic Ecclesial Communities in Latin America," *International Review of Missions*, July 1969. Translated from the Portuguese by the Language Service, WCC.

114. Enrique Dussel, "La Iglesia Latinoamencana en la Actual Coyuntura" (1972-1980), *Teología de la Liberación y Comunidades Cristianas de Base,* ed. Sergio Torres (Salamanca, Spain: Ediciones Sígueme, 1983), pp. 116-17.

115. *Documentos.* Third Latin American Episcopal Conference. Puebla 1979 (Bogotá, Colombia: CELAM, 1979), para. 643.

116. "Documento Final del Congreso Internacional Ecuménico de Teología" (Sao Paulo, 20 de febrero—2 de marzo 1980), *Teología de la Liberación y Comunidades Cristianas de Base,* ed. Sergio Torres (Salamanca, Spain: Ediciones Sigueme, 1983), p. 229.

117. Marins.

118. Leonardo Boff, "Notas Teológicas de la Iglesia de Base," *Teología de la Liberación y Comunidades Cristianas de Base,* ed. Sergio Torres (Salamanca, Spain: Ediciones Sígueme, 1983), p.154.

119. Gustavo Gutiérrez, "La Irrupción del Pobre en América Latina y las Comunidades Cristianas Populares," *Teología de la Liberación y Comunidades Cristianas de Base,* ed. Sergio Torres (Salamanca, Spain: Ediciones Sígueme, 1983), p. 136.

120. Dussel, "La Iglesia Lationamericana," p. 112.

121. Betto, *¿Qué es la Comunidad Ecclesial de Base?*, p. 13.

122. Idem.

123. "The Church of the Poor," *Time,* May 7, 1979.

124. Gustavo Gutiérrez, in an interview published by *Together,* World Vision International, April-June 1986, pp. 33-35.

125. Betto, *¿Qué es la Comunidad Ecclesial de Base?*, p. 49.

126. "Sao Paulo Document," *Teología de la Liberación y Comunidades de Base,* p. 237.

127. Betto, *¿Qué es la Comunidad Eclesial de Base?*, p. 45.

128. Frei Betto, "La Oración: Una Exigencia (también) Politica," *Espiritualidad y Liberación en América Latina* (San José, Costa Rica: Departamento Ecuménico de Investigaciones, 1982), pp. 16-20.

129.
"Sao Paulo Document," pp. 233-34.

130. Ibid., p. 241.

131. Ibid.

132. María López Vigil, p. 46.

133. Ernesto Cardenal, *The Gospel of Solentiname,* 3 vols. (Maryknoll, NY: Orbis, 1979).

134. Paulo Freire, *Pedagogy of the Oppressed,* trans. Myra Bergman Ramos (New York: Seabury, 1970).

135. *América Latina: Movilización Popular y Fe Cristiana* (Montevideo, Uruguay: Iglesia y Sociedad en América Latina, ISAL, Documents of the Fourth Continental Assembly, Nana, Peru, July 1971), p. 150.

136. Gutiérrez, *Teología de la Liberación,* p. 307.

137. Samuel Amirtham and John S. Pobee, *Theology by the People: Reflections on Doing Theology in Community* (Geneva: World Council of Churches, 1986).

138. Ibid., p. 10.

139. Jorge C. Bravo, "Perspectives from Latin America," *Theology by the People: Reflections on Doing Theology in Community,* pp. 109-12.

140. Amirtham and Pobee, *Theology by the People,* pp. ix-x.

141. Bravo, p. 109.

9

The Charismatic Movement

A Guatemalan lady who was a very well-known writer in the public press, and by her own confession an agnostic, admitted some years ago that she did not know what to do with "mystic people" who are not related to traditional Christianity, nor to violent revolution, and who speak joyfully of love as the only answer to the problems of mankind. This lady had been analyzing idealistic and materialistic people on the philosophical level. She had apparently adopted a self-sufficient attitude toward religion in general. But now she was incapable of evaluating the "mystics." In a sense she surrendered herself to them. After all, she was a sensible lady, and her heart had been moved by the message of brotherly love.[1]

I am afraid that this has been, basically, the experience of many people in response to the challenge of the charismatic movement. Even many conservative evangelicals have been taken by surprise by this movement. People have stopped *thinking*, to start *feeling*. We have to admit that it is difficult to pass judgment on the experiences of people who come telling you enthusiastically about the blessing of the Holy Spirit and their love for the Lord Jesus Christ and his people. It is not easy to deal with a movement that claims a great success in winning souls for Christ. But it is our responsibility to see this movement not only in the light of experience, but especially under the authority of the written Word of God. On this occasion I am going to emphasize a missiological approach to the charismatic movement, especially from the Latin American standpoint. The emphasis will be on Catholic charismatism, because Catholics are the vast majority in Latin America, and, to some extent, charismatism is changing the image of the Catholic church in those countries and exercising some influence on Protestants who belong to different denominations. This movement is a real challenge to us in our evangelistic effort among Latin American Catholics today.

ORIGIN AND DEVELOPMENT OF THE CHARISMATIC MOVEMENT

It is very well known that the modern charismatic movement among Catholics was born in Pittsburgh, Pennsylvania, in 1966.[2] Kevin and Dorothy Ranaghan say that the experience of the baptism of the Holy Spirit, followed by the gifts and fruits of the Spirit and recognized and organized as such, was unknown in American Catholicism until 1967.[3]

Edward D. O'Connor, an American charismatic priest, says that the Catholic mind has always been kept open to the charismatic through the experiences of the saints as well as through the miracles in sacred places like Lourdes.[4] The Second Vatican Council (1962-1965) understands that all the gifts of the Holy Spirit are present in the church today. It exhorts the faithful not to seek only the spectacular gifts.[5] A footnote in one of the English versions of the council documents explains that Vatican II makes clear that charisms should not necessarily be identified with "extraordinary and spectacular phenomena, which are by their very nature rare."[6] But it is also true that the council exhorts the ecclesiastical leaders not to extinguish the Spirit, suggesting in this injunction that all the gifts should be freely manifested in the congregation.[7]

Charles Moeller, one of the theologians of the Second Vatican Council, says that "charisms are neither reserved to the hierarchy, nor limited to ancient times; they are constantly present in the life of the Church; they animate this dimension of salvation history which the ecclesiology of Vatican II recovered."[8] Consequently, charismatics find strong support in that council for their doctrines and practices.

In ten years the movement multiplied itself from a handful of people to hundreds of thousands of adherents. Many would call this a tremendous success. In September 1972, Catholic Pentecostal leaders claimed sixty thousand participants in their movement.[9] The First Charismatic Congress was held in Notre Dame, Indiana, in 1967. Only ninety people attended that congress.[10] But the attendance went up to thirty-five thousand in the Second International Congress of the Charismatic Movement, held in Notre Dame again in 1974.[11]

For the Third International Congress, more than ten thousand charismatic Catholics from sixty different nations went to Rome to participate at the same time in the activities of the Holy Year in 1975. It has been reported that one million charismatic Catholics were represented in that congress.[12] Cardinal Suenens, from Belgium, the outstanding leader of the movement, celebrated Mass at the main altar of St. Peter's Basilica on the day of Pentecost. For his part, the pope blessed the charismatic movement, saying that the Holy Spirit is renewing the church and that charismatism is an evidence of this work of the Spirit. At the same time he exhorted the charismatics to be obedient to the hierarchy, to be loyal to the authentic doctrines of the Roman Catholic church, to be faithful in the practice of the sacraments, and to remember that Christian love is more important than the charisms of the Spirit.[13] Charismatics left Rome with the assurance that the pope had approved their movement.

In August 1970, denominational Pentecostals and charismatic Catholics met together in Salamanca, Spain, for the Third Congress of the International Ecumenical Fellowship.[14] In 1977, a big ecumenical Conference on Charismatic Renewal took place in Kansas City. At least fifty thousand people attended that conference. Cardenal Suenens was one of the speakers. Kevin Ranaghan, a Roman Catholic, was the president of the planning committee.[15]

In 1987, the Latin American Charismatic Convention held in Cordoba, Argentina, April 12-16, was attended by 1,550 people. There were delegates from several Latin American countries, the United States, England, and Sweden. The same month there was a charismatic gathering in San José, Costa Rica. Several hundred people were present there. Catholic and Protestant leaders had an opportunity for fellowship in a meeting especially prepared for them.[16]

According to René Laurentin, a French Catholic theologian, there were from two to four million participants in the charismatic movement around the world in 1975. Seven per cent of the forty-seven million Catholics in the United States had been related to this movement in one way or another in 1975. This means there were more than three million Charismatic Catholics, and perhaps only one or two million active participants in American Catholicism. At that time charismatism was already established in one hundred countries.[17] In 1976 there were seventy Catholic charismatic communities in Spain.[18]

In the summer of 1987 the North American Congress on the Holy Spirit and World Evangelization was held in New Orleans, Lousiana, marking the twentieth anniversary of the organization of the charismatic Catholic movement, which had taken place at Pittsburgh's Duquesne

University in February 1967. A total of thirty-five thousand Christians—Protestant, Catholic, Orthodox, messianic Jewish, and Pentecostal—attended the congress. Roman Catholics made up fifty-one percent of the participants. The number attending fell fifteen thousand short of the attendance at the 1977 Kansas City conference. There have been divisions in the movement, and the split was felt in one way or another at the congress. The two main charismatic branches in North America are the Word of God community in Ann Arbor, Michigan, and the People of Praise community in South Bend, Indiana. But according to David Barrett, editor of the World Christian Encyclopedia (Oxford), "The worldwide charismatic movement has tripled in the past 10 years to total 227 million adherents worldwide. Third World Christians are rapidly joining the ranks of the charismatics, including 29 million in China alone."[19]

Charismatism is also growing in Latin America and transcending denominational barriers. There are charismatics in the Catholic church, in the big Protestant denominations, in the Pentecostal churches, and even in churches established by the so-called "faith mission."

GENERAL CHARACTERISTICS OF THE
CHARISMATIC MOVEMENT

Catholic Charismatism as a Dependent Movement

First of all, we have to recognize that there is a charismatic movement that is strictly speaking Catholic, in complete dependence on the hierarchy. In their book *Catholic Pentecostals,* Kevin and Dorothy Ranaghan mention the influence exercised by the books of David Wilkerson and John Sherrill on the pioneers of the movement in Pittsburgh.[20] But they also explain that the charismatic movement within the Catholic church was not started by Protestant Pentecostals.[21] They are right in saying so. On the other hand, it is evident that there are points of contact between Catholic charismatism and traditional Pentecostalism.

O'Connor admits that from a historical and phenomenological point of view, Catholic charismatism "is only one branch of a much larger movement affecting all Christian churches."[22] Nevertheless, it would be a mistake to identify Catholic charismatism with denominational Pentecostalism. In Central America there are many Pentecostals who are in profound disagreement with the charismatic movement, and many Catholic charismatics who prefer not to identify themselves with Protestants in general, much less with Pentecostals.

According to O'Connor, "there are not statistics on the number of people who have left their church due to the influence of the Pentecostal movement. So far as Catholics are concerned, the number is certainly not great to be alarming."[23] It is his hope that the charismatic movement will restore faith in the Catholic church. The Ranaghans believe that instead of separating people from the Catholic church, this movement has revived their love for it.[24]

The tendency is for Catholic charismatics to emphasize their loyalty to Roman Catholicism in order to avoid a negative reaction on the part of the hierarchy. For this reason they make a great deal of personal testimonies in which this loyalty is emphasized. For instance: "I used time to say the Rosary, a practice I started after my baptism by the Holy Spirit."[25] "Now I feel a profound reverence for the Virgin Mary.... This is something I could not do before the baptism of the Holy Spirit."[26] "The sacraments have now a new meaning for us, especially the sacrament of Penance."[27] "The Catholic Mass has now more meaning, and I love and understand better our priests."[28] "I will continue praying to Mary, who is the example of those who worship God in Spirit and Truth."[29] "Our love for the Church has been revived."[30]

On their part, the leaders of the Catholic church are trying to keep the Catholic charismatics within the church. Serafino Falvo, an Italian theologian, explains: "Charismatism is not a movement to modify the structures of the Church, to substitute for them charismatic structures.... It is not a movement that pretends to live an autonomous life, independently from the hierarchy, or what it would be worst, in opposition to it."[31]

The charismatic movement may also help to keep non-charismatic Catholics within the church; at least it may help to avoid these Catholics' leaving the church to join another group. In Central America there are many Catholics who are quite confused because of the similarities between Catholic charismatism and Protestant Pentecostalism. Because for the average Latin American it is difficult to distinguish one Protestant group from another, they see no difference now between charismatic Catholicism and Protestantism. Charismatics read and study the Bible, organize prayer groups, use Protestant songs or choruses, participate in interconfessional meetings, emphasize fraternal love, proclaim the name of the Lord Jesus Christ.

In many respects they seem to be another Protestant group. But they are still Catholics, and many of them are more Catholic than ever. For example, they have not abandoned their concept of divine revelation, which according to the official teaching of the Roman Catholic church includes human tradition on the same level with the Scriptures. They have not given up completely their synergistic doctrine of salvation. Their soteriology is sacramental. Water baptism is the basis for becoming a member of the Body of Christ.

It is beyond any doubt that many charismatics have been saved as a result of being exposed to the written Word of God. They claim to accept the lordship of Christ in their lives and give great emphasis to the ministry of the Holy Spirit. They even speak of receiving Jesus as their personal Savior and give him an important place in their doctrine and worship. But it seems that most Catholic charismatics have not abandoned their Marian devotion. They continue to believe in their love for Mary. They venerate her as never before. She is considered to be the highest example of a charismatic person. On the day of Pentecost she was baptized in the Spirit and spoke in tongues.[32]

However, it is also true that in their spiritual life many Catholic charismatics are eager to believe God, taking his promises by faith. They represent a strong pietistic movement within the Roman Catholic church. Evidently, the charismatic experience has produced significant changes in the lives of many people who have discovered the joy of addressing themselves directly to God in spontaneous prayer. But serious doctrinal differences between charismatics and conservative evangelicals persist.

It is a common belief among charismatics that the baptism of the Holy Spirit is an experience subsequent to the sacrament of baptism. O'Connor affirms, "besides the hidden communication of the Holy Spirit which occurs through the sacrament of baptism, there is also a manifest communication that may occur late, and which is here vividly described as the Holy Spirit 'falling upon' a person."[33] O'Connor makes clear that "to be baptized in the Holy Spirit does not mean to receive the sacrament of baptism through the pouring of water over one's head.... The baptism in the Holy Spirit is something that happens to them often many years after they have been sacramentally baptized."[34] It is O'Connor's conviction that "the expression 'baptism in the Holy Spirit' does not imply that the Spirit was not given through the sacrament of baptism."[35]

The British pastor Michael Harper, who is enthusiastic about Pentecostals and Catholic charismatics, makes reference in his book *Three Sisters* to the distinction made by a Catholic writer between the theological use of the phrase "baptism of the Holy Spirit" (which indicates that all Christians have been baptized by the Holy Spirit) and the charismatic emphasis on the experience produced in the ones who are renewed by the Spirit.[36] Because of the strong testimony of 1 Corinthians 12:13 to the fact that all newborn Christians are already baptized by the

Holy Spirit, there are charismatics who say that all believers have that baptism by the Spirit, but not all of them have experienced the baptism in the Spirit.[37]

Father José María Delgado Varela, a Catholic charismatic leader in Guatemala, sees relationship and at the same time difference between the sacrament of baptism and the baptism by the Holy Spirit. By water baptism the one who is baptized is placed into the Body of Christ. The Holy Spirit is also communicated in a sacramental way. The one who is christianized receives the Holy Spirit and is entitled to possess all of his gifts and virtues.[38]

The second sacrament of initiation is called confirmation. By this sacrament the new life communicated by the Spirit in baptism is strengthened in the believer. The sacraments of baptism and confirmation are different from the baptism by the Holy Spirit. Water baptism is received once and forever; the baptism by the Holy Spirit can be repeated. The sacramental reality of confirmation is contained in the meaning of the baptism of the Holy Spirit. But this baptism is not equivalent to confirmation.[39]

The third sacrament discussed by Delgado Varela in conjunction with the baptism by the Holy Spirit is holy communion. He states that in the teachings of Jesus on the eucharist, the promises on the ministry by the Holy Spirit are abundant. The eucharist is the sacrament of fellowship with God and with one another in Christ. This fellowship is experienced in a more intensive way by the one who has been baptized by the Holy Spirit.[40]

According to Delgado Varela the baptism by the Holy Spirit is subsequent to the sacraments of baptism and confirmation. It is a new effusion of the Holy Spirit. To experience this baptism it is indispensable to reject Satan and to surrender oneself to Christ, believing that he is the King of kings and Lord of lords. It requires an act of faith, renunciation, and obedience.[41]

Delgado Varela brings to an end his discussion on the baptism by the Holy Spirit by saying that Mary, the mother of Jesus, is the perfect model of a person who is under the power of the Holy Spirit. She is the first charismatic person, the first one in whom the Holy Spirit manifests himself as a person, without any limitation.[42] Mary is the first and most important charismatic person in history.[43]

In general, charismatics believe that the baptism by the Holy Spirit may be manifested by the reception of some charism, especially the gift of tongues. Some charismatics are more emphatic than others in this regard, but all of them seem to be open to the possibility that the baptism by the Holy Spirit may result immediately in speaking in tongues.

On the basis established by Vatican II for a Catholic dialogue with other Christians, Catholic charismatics are ecumenical. For all practical purposes, they have actually accomplished more on behalf of the ecumenical cause in Latin America than the ecumenical movement represented by the World Council of Churches.

Catholic Charismatism as an Independent Movement

There are some charismatic Catholics who are more or less isolated from their church. Some of them abandon the characteristic dogmas of the Roman Catholic church. They are even critical of traditional Catholicism and are not in complete agreement with the charismatic movement controlled by the hierarchy. They may have their own meetings without the assistance of a Catholic priest. They may invite a Protestant leader to help them in their Bible study. These groups give a tremendous opportunity for a real evangelical witness.

The Protestant Charismatic Movement

With regard to Protestant charismatics it would also be a mistake to identify them with traditional Pentecostals, although there are Pentecostals who are charismatic.

Orlando Costas, a late Latin American missiologist, indicates that the theological emphasis of charismatism is different from that of historical Pentecostalism. For example, charismatics emphasize the ecumenicity of the Holy Spirit, who is also given to other Christian groups. They insist that the greatest evidence of the pentecostal experience is not speaking in tongues but love. Charismatics emphasize the Lordship of Christ. They have a christological basis for their pentecostal experience, instead of limiting themselves to a pneumatological foundation, as traditional Pentecostals do. According to Costas, the liturgy is the result of a more serious theological reflection, in contrast to the liturgy in traditional Pentecostalism.[44] Ecumenism is one of the most distinctive marks of the charismatic movement. At the same time, charismatism has been a divisive element in many Protestant churches in Latin America.

It is undeniable that the charismatic experience has transformed the lives of many people. Christians who had played only a passive role in their congregations have now become superactive in telling other Christians about the blessing of the Holy Spirit or in witnessing to unsaved people about the gospel of Christ. Broken marriages have been restored to happy relationships, and young people testify that they were saved in a charismatic meeting. The largest Protestant churches in Guatemala City are charismatic. Old-line Pentecostal churches have been left behind as far as numerical growth is concerned.

GENERAL EVALUATION OF THE CHARISMATIC MOVEMENT

Roman Catholic Evaluation

The Declaration of the American Catholic Bishops. The Declaration of the American Catholic Bishops (1975) starts by quoting Vatican II on the subject of spiritual gifts: "Extraordinary gifts are not to be rashly sought after nor are the fruits of apostolic labor to be presumptuously expected from them. In any case, judgment as to their genuiness and proper use belongs to those who preside over the Church, and to whose special competence it belongs, not indeed to extinguish the Spirit, but to test all things and hold fast to that which is good."[45]

The bishops declare that the gifts of the Holy Spirit have always been present in the church since the beginning; but to be sure that some manifestations come from the Holy Spirit it is necessary to be in fellowship with the pastors of the church and to take into consideration the Word of God and the permanent teaching of the church. It is possible for Christians to be deceived in regard to these gifts. The authentic gifts of the Spirit are given for the edification of the church in unity and love. Love is the most important sign of the genuine manifestation of the Holy Spirit. But it has to be the kind of love described by Paul in 1 Corinthians 13. Another sign of the work of the Spirit is that he always gives testimony to Jesus (John 14:26; 16:13-14).

The charismatic movement seems to be one of the greatest manifestations of the Spirit in our times. There are many positive elements in this movement. Some of those elements are, for instance, a solid and deeply rooted faith in Jesus Christ as Lord; a new interest in prayer, both private and public; a greater appreciation of spiritual values; a special awareness of the action of the Holy Spirit; a joyful desire to praise the Lord; and a personal commitment to Christ. Many charismatics are more interested than ever in the sacraments; their devotion to Mary is more meaningful than in the past; and they feel close to the church in a special way.

But the bishops add that as in any other movement there are problems in the charismatic renewal. Charismatism is inclined to become exclusive. One of the results of elitism is the tendency to consider the charismatic group as a privileged class, creating division instead of unity in the church. There is also the tendency to ignore the intellectual and doctrinal contents of the Catholic faith. In this case faith is reduced to an emotional religious experience. Anti-intellectualism is another danger confronting the charismatic movement.

The American bishops recommend that the faithful be cautious in relation to spectacular gifts like healing, prophecy, and speaking in tongues. These activities may be genuine manifestations of the Holy Spirit, but they have to be carefully examined, and their importance should not be exaggerated.

The charismatic renewal is supposed to be related to the total life of the church. A close relationship has to be established between the clergy and the lay leaders of the charismatic movement.

A matter of special concern for the bishops is the existence of charismatic groups that include both Catholics and other Christians. It is the opinion of the bishops that a frequent or exclusive participation in ecumenical groups may dilute the sense of Catholic identity. On the other hand, an occasional participation in ecumenical prayer groups may be profitable. But those Catholics who take part in ecumenical activities must be mature persons in their faith. They need to be deeply committed to the teachings of the Catholic church.

It is possible to say that in general the American bishops did not seem to be enthusiastic about the charismatic movement. Their declaration emphasizes the duty of Catholic charismatics to remain loyal to their church and the responsibility of the clergy to keep charismatism under ecclesiastical control.[46]

CELAM and the charismatic movement. In response to the request of many priests and other Catholic leaders, the Latin American Episcopal Council (Consejo Episcopal Latinoamericano; CELAM), sponsored an in-depth study on the charismatic movement. A book was published in 1977, including some of the papers written for that purpose. That book does not seem to be an official and definitive declaration of CELAM on the charismatic renewal. The editors say that it is expected that the pastors will read the papers in a critical way.[47]

In the prologue Monsignor Alfonso López Trujillo, at that time executive secretary of CELAM, gives some criteria for the charismatic movement to follow. In the first place he is concerned about the unity of the church and the authority of the ecclesiastical hierarchy. He feels that the charismatic movement may give the impression that there is no power in the ecclesiastical function of the hierarchy. There is the danger of opposing "the church of the Spirit" to "the church of the bishops."

A criterion to be followed is that of making a distinction between *accidental* and *essential* elements in the faith and life of the church. For instance, it is possible to give the gift of tongues an excessive importance, from the functional point of view. It is also indispensable, according to Monsignor López Trujillo, to discern between that which is intellectual and that which is experiential. There is the ever-present danger of subjectivism in the charismatic renewal. It is necessary to emphasize the fruit more than the gifts of the Spirit. Quoting Augustine, he says, "Not your gifts, oh Lord, but you." Christians are supposed to concentrate their attention not on the gifts but on the Giver.

Monsignor López Trujillo warns against the dangers of interpreting the baptism by the Holy Spirit as a new baptism that has in itself a liturgical value. This interpretation may create confusion in the minds of the faithful. Moreover, the impression may be given that those who have not had a particular experience are not Christians or that they are second-class Christians. He also makes reference to the scant social concern in the charismatic movement. Charismatics do not seem to be be interested in committing themselves to social action.

The last words of the executive secretary of CELAM are characterized by caution and moderation. He advises the leaders of Latin American Catholicism to be open to a dialogue that would allow for a plurality of experiences in the church.

In the final chapter of the book, it is stated that in general the charismatic renewal has produced positive results. Exaggerations and abuses are the exception, not the rule. The number of bishops, priests, and lay-people participating in the movement is increasing every day. This participation is a guarantee of the spiritual stability and strength of Roman Catholic charismatism.

Instruction of the Guatemalan Episcopal Council. In April 1986 the Guatemalan Episcopal Council of the Roman Catholic church published a *Pastoral Instruction on the Charismatic Renewal.*[48] In the introduction of this document the bishops quote briefly Pope Paul VI's message to the Charismatic World Congress of 1975 and the address of John Paul II in 1981 to six hundred Catholic leaders who represented the charismatic renewal at the worldwide level. The pontiff exhorted those leaders to take into consideration three principles: (1) faithfulness to the authentic doctrine of the church, (2) emphasis on the most important gifts of the Spirit, and (3) love as the only virtue that can lead the Christian believer to perfection, according to Colossians 3:14.

Discussing the theology of the gifts of the Spirit, the Guatemalan bishops affirm that the source of all gifts is Jesus Christ, that they are given for personal sanctification and the edification of the Body of Christ, and that not all of them have the same importance. There is no opposition between the *charisma* and hierarchical authority. The charismatic renewal has to be at the service of the church. Because the charismatic renewal is a product of Vatican II, it is expected that this movement will also be, in a particular way, loyal to the conciliar teachings. A movement that would set aside Vatican II would not be an authentic renewal from the Spirit.

Mary, the mother of Jesus, could not be left out of the episcopal *Instruction* on charismatism. Mention is made that the desire of Pope John Paul II is that Mary should be at the heart of the charismatic renewal because she is the most capable person to lead this movement. It is when the faithful follow Mary's example that she can help them to submit themselves to the Holy Spirit and to live under his power to grow in holiness.

After the doctrinal exhortations, the bishops mention some of the positive results of Charismatism—for example, a revival in the prayer life of many people in the church; a growth in fraternal love; a spiritual transformation in the lives of priests and members of monastic orders; a spiritual awakening in the laity; a greater love than in the past for the Bible; a new interest in announcing the mighty works of God; a new sense of fellowship with the Lord; and a new experience of the power of the Holy Spirit.

On the other hand, the Guatemalan bishops point out some of the dangers in the charismatic movement. There is the danger of falling into serious "aberrations" in public prayer. Some Catholic charismatics condition their participation in the eucharist on a particular form of charismatic liturgy. There is also the danger of forgetting that "the effusion of the Holy Spirit is given through the sacraments." Some people may want to follow a teaching that they suppose is directly from the Spirit instead of an official teaching of the church. A false sense of autonomy has been created in some charismatic groups, promoting an attitude of self-sufficiency and a false concept of the priestly ministry. They do not ask for the assistance of a priest.

The so-called "baptism in the Spirit" seems to undermine the importance of the sacrament of baptism, "which is the only true baptism in water and in the Spirit." Some charismatic groups give an excessive importance to the emotional aspect of their experience. They easily fall into subjectivism and a kind of illuminism, which are extremely dangerous for the faithful personally and for the church in general.

There also may be excesses in the "prayers for divine healing." The Catholic church has established the sacrament of extreme unction, which has produced healing, both spiritually and physically, through centuries. But both the clergy and the laity must pray on the basis of the Lord's promises for those who are ill. The sacrament of extreme unction is the exclusive responsibility of the clergy.

In the final section of the *Instruction* the bishops give some special recommendations to the priests and other Catholic leaders. There is a great concern for the unity of the church, the authority of the hierarchy, the sacramental ministry of the church, the devotion to Mary and the saints. Marian veneration is considered as "a guarantee of orthodoxy, and of abundant mercies from God." The *Instruction* ends with a prayer to Mary, asking her to help Catholics to be faithful to the Holy Spirit for the renewal of the church.

The Guatemalan bishops do not oppose the charismatic renewal, but they are trying to keep this movement under hierarchical control. They want nothing less than a Roman Catholic renewal.

Protestant Evaluation

Gospel and Spirit: A Joint Statement. October 1977 saw the publication of "Gospel and Spirit: A Joint Statement." This document is the product of four valuable day-long conferences held over a period of eighteen months by groups nominated by the Church of England Evangelical Council and the Fountain Trust.[49] John Stott and J. I. Packer, who are known in Latin America through their writings (Dr. Stott has also visited several Latin American countries), were among the participants in those meetings.

According to the *Statement,* the purpose of the conferences was "to try to articulate widely held and representative attitudes among the so-called charismatic and non-charismatic leaders of Anglican evangelicalism and to bring both to the bar of Holy Scripture. We have sought to understand each other's views better, and to achieve closer harmony and correspondence through examining them all in the light of Biblical teaching."

They affirm that "the Charismatic Movement in the United Kingdom has Evangelical roots, but is now both trans-denominational and trans-traditional, and embraces a very wide spectrum of views, attitudes and practices." At the same time they rejoice too that renewal of spiritual life is manifestly not confined to "charismatic" circles and churches. But they also recognize that "the main concern of the Charismatic renewal, at least until recently, has been experiential rather than theological."

In regard to the "baptism in the Holy Spirit," it is declared that the New Testament usage of the words *baptize* and especially *baptize into* refers "to Christian initiation, rather than to a later enrichment of Christian experience." Consequently, this usage "must not be employed in a way which would question the reality of the work of the Spirit in regeneration and the real difference that this brings in experience from the outset." But this affirmation does not have the purpose of denying "the possibility or reality of subsequent experiences of the grace of God which have deep and transforming significance."

Is speaking in tongues the evidence of having received the gift of the Spirit? The participants answer this question by saying that "the New Testament will not allow us to make it either the only, or the universal, or an indubitable evidence that this gift has been given." However, they admit that one of the evidences of having received the Spirit is "the joyful spontaneous praise of God (whether in one's own tongue or another)." They are open to receiving any spiritual gifts that are consonant with the New Testament, "and see no reason why such gifts should not be given and exercised today." With respect to speaking in tongues it is declared:

> Most of us would accept that some tongues-speaking, though not necessarily a heavenly language, is nevertheless divinely given and has spiritual and psychological value. We are also aware that a similar phenomenon can occur under occult/demonic influence, and that some such utterances may be merely psychological in origin and not necessarily edifying or beneficial at all. Opinions also vary as to the value of this gift to the individual, and (with interpretation) to the church. We consider it necessary to hold to the balance of the New Testament in our general attitude to it, in accordance with I Corinthians 14, neither exalting it above all other gifts, nor despising it and forbidding its exercise (though always with interpretation if in public).

Of special interest for us Latin American evangelicals is also what our Anglican brothers say about Roman Catholics and renewal. They rejoice in the fact that Christians of different backgrounds have fellowship together in the charismatic movement, but they recognize at the same time the existence of some dangers:

   (i) A unity based on experience at the expense of doctrine would be less than the unity envisaged in the
New Testament, and would be dangerous in the long
term.

  (ii) Personal (and even corporate) renewal has not always meant the dropping of all anti-Biblical or sub-
Biblical traditions and practices. We see need to
pray for and to encourage reformation by God's
Word as well as by renewal by his Spirit in all
churches. In the case of the Roman Catholic Church,
however, a massive international community which
has only recently begun to question its own historic
stances, we recognize that God calls us to be realistic
in our expectations and to allow time (how long is
not for us to say) for the forces of reformation and
renewal to operate widely enough for changes in official formulations and interpretations of doctrine to
become possible, where they are necessary.

The Anglican *Statement* is the product of dialogue between two
groups of Christians who belong to the same ecclesiastical tradition. The
purpose of seeking understanding and closer harmony may have been
achieved to a large extent. The *Statement* is respectful, open-minded,
irenic, and positive. Negative elements are not emphasized, much less
overemphasized. This document has to be read taking into consideration
the social and ecclesiastical context of British evangelicalism.

James I. Packer, who participated in that dialogue, has taken a long,
hard look at charismatism in his book *Keep in Step with the Spirit,*[50]
pointing out negative and positive aspects of this movement. According
to Packer, positive aspects are Christ-centeredness, Spirit-empowered
living, emotion finding expression, prayerfulness, joyfulness, every-heart
involvement in the worship of God, every-member ministry in the Body
of Christ, missionary zeal, small-group ministry, a balanced attitude toward church structures, communal living, and generous giving. Among
the negative aspects he mentions are elitism, emotionalism, anti-
intellectualism, illuminism "charismania," "supernaturalism," eudaemon-
ism ("the belief that God means us to spend our time in this fallen world
feeling well and in a state of euphoria based on that fact"), demon obsession, and conformism ("group pressure is tyrannical"). Dr. Packer tries to
be objective and positive in his approach to charismatism. His book is
very helpful for a more personal and detailed evaluation of this movement from an Anglican point of view.

A Latin American perspective. We evangelicals in Latin America have to rejoice also in the positive aspects of the charismatic movement. It is a blessing to see that many charismatics have come to a personal knowledge of the Lord Jesus Christ through a serious study of God's written revelation, in submission to the illuminating ministry of the Holy Spirit. They have experienced a radical transformation as a result of their conversion to the Lord Jesus Christ. It is evident that the Holy Spirit is doing a special work in the lives of many Roman Catholics in Latin America today, not necessarily because they are Catholic charismatics but because they have been open to the witness of the Spirit and his Word. We have to realize that especially after Vatican II the Scriptures have been freely distributed, read, and studied by Catholics in those countries. The Word of God, widely disseminated by both evangelicals and Catholics, is bearing fruit as never before in the lives of large numbers of Latin Americans, even within the Roman Catholic church.

We also rejoice when we see the spiritual and moral change experienced by evangelicals who through the years did not seem to be really committed to serving the Lord Jesus Christ in any capacity. But now they claim that the Holy Spirit has done a special work in them, and they are full of joy and enthusiasm, assuming their Christian responsibilities in their family lives and doing whatever they can in their local churches for the greater progress of the gospel.

We cannot deny, much less oppose, the positive results of the charismatic movement. We praise the Lord for these results. But at the same time we realize that, generally speaking, the main concern of the charismatic renewal has been experiential rather than theological. Emotions have played the most important role in this movement. The general tendency has been to emphasize experiences instead of the knowledge of the Scriptures. There is, consequently, the danger of subjectivism. The inward voice of the heart speaks louder than the external voice of the written Word of God.

When experiences or spectacular gifts are overemphasized, there is the danger of pride. It seems that the tremendous charismatic experience has not been able to overcome in many people the "I am better than you" spirit. There is in many charismatics a superiority complex—"I have something you do not have." A year ago we were having a home Bible study when a Christian lady gave a personal testimony. She started by saying that she had recently had "the charismatic experience." Now she realized that all the churches in the country were carnal and dead. What she had learned at her local church and at a Bible school was of no spiritual value. But because of her "new experience" she now had total victory over sin in her own life and a new joy in her heart.

Such an attitude has been responsible, to a large extent, for the divisive nature of the charismatic movement in Latin America. This tendency is paradoxical in view of the ecumenical propensity of charismatism. Some years ago, Orlando E. Costas reported that in Brazil new denominations had been organized as a result of the charismatic influence on historical Protestant bodies in that country.[51] Nevertheless, with regard to the Roman Catholic church, Protestant charismatism is ecumenical. The Anglican *Joint Statement,* already mentioned, recognizes the danger of a "unity based on experience at the expense of doctrine." Catholic leaders see the same danger for their church. The majority of evangelicals are concerned about the ecumenical tendency of charismatism, especially when they realize that most Catholic charismatics remain loyal to the distinctive doctrines of their church and that the conservative bishops and priests are determined to keep the movement under their control. We are not called to antagonize Catholic charismatics but to love them in the Lord. But neither are we supposed to be naive, believing that just because they are charismatic all of them are already evangelical, in the doctrinal and practical sense of this word.

The extremes to which some people may go in their desire to have supernatural experiences is also a motive of serious concern. They may even try to manipulate the Godhead to see a miracle. Dr. Cecilio Arrastía, a Cuban pastor and theologian, has said that neo-Pentecostalism is in danger of having a Greek concept of the Holy Spirit—considering him not as a person, but as a substance that can be manipulated by humans. Arrastía sees also in charismatism a form of occultism—the tendency to produce supernatural experiences as if these experiences were the goal of the Christian life.[52]

From a sociological standpoint, it has been pointed out that the charismatic movement is strongly individualistic, isolated from Latin American socio-political reality. Charismatics may speak a great deal about the kingdom of God as a present reality, but they are still secluding themselves in their super-spiritual experiences. It is interesting to notice that, generally speaking, charismatism started as a middle-class movement in Latin America. This is especially true among Catholics. Writing in 1977, Pedro A. Riverio de Oliveira, a Roman Catholic from Brazil, says that the participants in the charismatic renewal were, relatively speaking, people who enjoyed a high social status. Some of the first charismatic meetings in Guatemala City were held in fine restaurants or hotels.

Charismatic meetings may become a way to escape from the complicated problems of our society. Because of their middle-class mentality, many charismatics identify their new spiritual experience with financial success. To some extent "the gospel of prosperity" has permeated their minds. If the Lord is able to heal the bodies, he can also give material wealth to those who really believe his promises.

We have to admit that the charismatic movement is a real challenge to the Roman Catholic church, to the mainline Protestant denominations, to classic or historical Pentecostalism, and to us evangelicals in the so-called biblical movement. We have to answer this challenge on exegetical grounds, with an open Bible in our hands, but also on a practical level. Our biblical knowledge and orthodoxy are basic in dealing with this movement. But we have also to answer the challenge with our lives. For instance, do we really believe God? Do we really trust him in our daily lives? Or is he only a far away person, reduced to our theological thinking? We know he is personal, we know he has wonderful attributes, we know he is the creator, the God of providence, God the redeemer, and God the consummator. We know he is the only living and true God. But, do we know him in action in our daily walks? We have to demonstrate in one way or another that he is real to us, not only in our books of theology, but also in our own day-to-day experience. Some people go to the charismatic movement because they feel they are spiritually empty; they have not seen God as a reality in their lives or in our congregations.

Many of our churches are agonizing. They have Bible study, Sunday school, women's fellowship, youth meetings, vacation Bible schools, and you name it, but they are not really alive. There is not a real difference between the environment outside the church and the atmosphere inside the congregation. There is not a real worship. There is not a joyful praise to the Lord. The Scriptures may be explained in a technical way, when they are really explained, but the people do not feel the impact of the Word. Their hearts are not warmed by the Scriptures. It seems that we are missing something. We do not have just to blame charismatism if the people leave our agonizing churches to go somewhere else, perhaps back to the world. Are we not supposed to take seriously in our own lives and ministry the New Testament teaching on the person and work of the Holy Spirit?

NOTES

1. Irma Flaquer, "Qué Haré con los Misticos," *La Nación,* Guatemala, October 10, 1975.

2. Kevin and Dorothy Ranaghan, *Pentecosales Católicos* (Plainfield, NJ: Logos International, 1971), p. x.

3. Ibid., p. 217.

4. Edward D. O'Connor, *The Pentecostal Movement* (Notre Dame, IN: Ave Maria Press, 1971), p. 251 .

5. "Dogmatic Constitution on the Church," *The Documents of Vatican II* (New York: Guild Press, 1966), p. 30.

6. Ibid.

7. Ibid.

8. Charles Moeller, "History of Lumen Gentium's Structure and Ideas," *Vatican II: An Interfaith Appraisal* (Notre Dame, IN: University of Notre Dame, 1966), pp. 128-29.

9. *The Church Around the World* (Wheaton, IL: Tyndale House Publishers), September 1972.

10. Rene Laurentin, *Pentecostalismo Católico* (Madrid: Propaganda Popular Católica, 1975), p. 292.

11. Ibid., p. 293.

12. Ibid., p. 293. *Pregonero de Justicia,* Fallbrook, CA, vol. I, no. 3, p. 30.

13. Laurentin, pp. 298-304.

14. Ibid., p. 292.

15. *Vino Nuevo,* San José, Costa Rica, May-June 1978, p. 3.

16. Ibid., p. 31.

17. Laurentin, p. 37.

18. Ibid., p. 13 .

19. "The Holy Spirit and World Evangelization," *Christianity Today,* September 4, 1987.

20. Ranaghan, pp. 4-5.

21. Ibid., p. 127.

22. O'Connor, p. 28.

23. Ibid., p. 252.

24. Ranaghan, p. 44.

25. Ibid., p. 55.

26. Ibid., p. 57.

27. Ibid., p. 72.

28. Ibid., p. 81.

29. José María Delgado Varela, *Bautizados en el Espíritu Santo* (Guatemala: Instituto Teológico Salesiano, 1975), p. 32.

30. Ranaghan, p. 72.

31. Serafino Falvo, *¿Creemos en el Espíritu?* (Madrid: Ediciones Paulina, 1976, 1976), pp. 81-82.

32. Delgado Varela, pp. 341-42.

33. O'Connor, pp. 131-36.

34. Ibid., p. 183.

35. Ibid., p. 132.

36. Michael Harper, *Las Tres Hermanas* (Tarrassa, Barcelona: Libros CLIE, 1983), pp. 75-76. English edition: *Three Sisters,* Wheaton, IL: Tyndale House.

37. Charles C. Ryrie, *Basic Theology* (Wheaton, IL: Victor Books, 1986), p. 365.

38. Delgado Varela, p. 262.

39. Ibid., pp. 289-90.

40. Ibid., p. 303.

41. Ibid., pp. 264-65.

42. Ibid., pp. 326, 333.

43. Ibid., pp. 341-42.

44. Orlando E. Costas, *La Realidad de la Iglesia Evangélica Latinoamericana,* mimeographed paper, Buenos Aires, Argentina: Agencia de Promoción Misiológica, n. d.

45. Salvador Carrillo Alday, "Declaración del Episcopado Americano, 1975," *Renovación Cristiana en el Espírtu Santo* (México: Instituto de Sagrada Escritura, 1975), pp. 131-39.

46. Ibid.

47. Alfonso López Trujillo, "Prólogo: La Renovación en el Espírtu," *Movimientos Carismáticos en América Latina* (Bogotá, Colombia: Secretariado General del Consejo Episcopal Latinoamericano, CELAM, 1977), pp. ix-xxvii.

48. *Instrucción Pastoral Colectiva de los Obispos de Guatemala sobre la Renovación Carismática,* 1986.

49. "Gospel and Spirit: A Joint Statement," *Evangelical Review of Theology,* World Evangelical Fellowship, New Delhi, India, no. 1, October 1977, pp. 125-39.

50. J. I. Packer, *Keep in Step with the Spirit* (Leicester, England: InterVarsity, 1984), pp. 185-97.

51. Orlando E. Costas, *La Realidad de la Iglesia Evangélica Lainoamericana,* mimeographed paper, distributed by APOYO, Agencia de Promoción Misiológica, Casilla 46, Suc. 24, 142 Buenos Aires, C. F. Argentina. *Desafíos al Protestantismo—1949 al presente El Movimiento de Renovación Carismática.* San José, Costa Rica: Centro Evangélico Latinoamericano de Estudios Pastorales, 1976. Mimeographed paper.

52. Cecilio Arrastía. *El Movimiento Carismárico o Neopentecostal.* Mimeographed paper. N.d.

10

Resistance to Change

Within the diversity of postconciliar Catholicism in Latin America there is also a resistance to any critical change in the ideas, attitudes, and practices that are deeply rooted in five hundred years of Catholic presence in those countries. Since the Iberian discovery of America, our history and culture have been shaped to a large extent by medieval and colonial Catholicism. Generally speaking, before Vatican II the Roman Catholic Church, especially in the most undeveloped Latin American countries, had not officially experienced profound changes in its teaching, liturgy, and pastoral ministry, nor in its attitude toward the problems of society.

In view of this long history of traditional Catholicism in our Latin American soil, it is not surprising that even today there are clergy and lay people who tenaciously oppose the forces of ecclesiastical and social change.

Apparently, the vast majority of people have not yet received the impact of the *aggiornamento* in their religious beliefs and practices. They still express their faith by means of a "popular religiosity" (or "popular piety") that in many cases is a clear example of religious syncretism.

On the other hand, traditional Catholicism is also represented by the millions of Latin Americans who as far as their private lives are concerned are indifferent to any form of religion. They may still profess to be Catholic because they were born in a so-called Catholic country, in a home that perhaps follows a long-standing religious tradition or for social convenience claims to be Catholic. But they would not be concerned about church renewal, as long as this renewal would not affect their personal interests. From a personal standpoint and for all practical purposes they have no religion to renew.

We will take a look at these groups of people who are not really involved in the transformation of Roman Catholicism in Latin America.

THE CONSERVATIVE CHURCH

We must not forget that in institutional terms, Rome continues to be basically and officially unchanged in its dogma. It was not the Second Vatican Council's purpose to change the "deposit of faith," but rather to explain it in language relevant to modern humanity and in a way that would be acceptable to "integrationists" and "progressives" within the church.[1]

The authority of tradition (on an equal footing with Scripture), the primacy and infallibility of the pope, synergism in the order of salvation, traditional Mariology, and the sacramental system still maintain their status.[2]

Rome has not changed its hierarchical organization or its caste spirit, the idea that it has an inalienable right over lives and haciendas in our pain-ridden Latin America. Samuel Escobar warns that it is necessary always to relate the theological and institutional aspects of Catholicism, and notes that "the old Constantinianism" still persists along with "that paternalism which has marked the Catholic Church's politics toward the indigenous minorities in various countries; 'the Indians are ours.' All this comes wrapped up in a leftist liberationist rhetoric."[3]

There still exists in Latin America that hierarchical Catholicism that is at home in government and diplomatic circles and in the so-called high society, and which defends its own interests and those of the ruling classes. For these hierarchs it is as though Vatican II and the Medellín Conference had never been held.[4] They seem to long for the preconciliar era, when they lived peacefully in their palaces and did not hear the cry of those Catholics who demand a change in the ecclesiastical and social structures.

In some parishes the archconservative priests have the unqualified support of the ultramontane hierarchy. This hierarchy in turn takes refuge in the piety of thousands and thousands of sincere Catholics and in the religiosity of those who, led only by tradition or social convenience, continue to profess the faith of their forebears and to participate in the rites of the church. This is the sleeping church that the Jesuit Freizede wants to awaken.[5]

The spirit of the archconservative bishop Marcel Lefebvre is also present in Latin America. There is in Mexico a group of Catholics who endorse his movement of protest against the reforms proclaimed by Vatican II. The name of that group is *Trent*.[6] This is the name of the Italian city in which a general council was held in the years 1546-1563 to counteract the Protestant Reformation by means of dogmatic formulations and some internal reforms in the Catholic church. For us evangelicals in Latin America, Trent is a symbol of the church that in colonial times took sides with the ruling class in our countries, at the service of the Spanish crown. It is a symbol of the doctrine disseminated by the Catholic church this side of the Atlantic through more than four hundred years of our history—the anti-Protestant theology promulgated by Trent and confirmed by Vatican I (1870). The purpose of Monsignor Lefebvre and his followers is to restore Tridentine Catholicism around the world.

It would be unfair to readers in other parts of the world if we were to skip over this facet of the Catholic church in the description we are trying to present. Unfortunately, this antiquated, fossilized, hierarchical, and dominating Catholicism still exists in Latin America, no matter how much we would like to hide the fact, whether motivated by an ingenuous or nearsighted ecumenism or dazzled by progressive Catholicism.

But the whole picture includes other facets of a church whose monolithic unity has been fractured. We are face to face with the reality of a multifaceted Catholicism that is deeply divided.

NOMINAL CATHOLICS

It is universally recognized that in our Latin American countries millions are Catholic by heritage and convenience, not by conviction. When the moment comes for these people to declare their religious affiliation, they answer "Catholic." They were baptized Catholic, their family is Catholic, and everyone (or almost everyone) in their circle of friends is Catholic. In the society in which they live it is normal to be "Catholic."

Nominal Catholics abound in the middle and upper classes. Many come from families who have a long history of membership in militant Catholicism. They attended the best nuns' and monks' schools and fulfilled the rites of initiation in the Roman church. They have established their own homes with the blessing of the ecclesiastical hierarchy and send their children to a good Catholic school where they will learn the indispensable moral principles necessary for relating to important people.

Beyond these family and social conveniences, however, it does not matter to them what happens in the church just as long as it does not upset their status quo. In private conversation these nominal Catholics can be biting critics of the church and may boast of their broad-mindedness in regard to religious phenomena. They claim to respect all religions, but do not commit themselves to any one of them. They go to the Catholic churches for baptisms, weddings, funerals, and other special occasions that social convenience demands.

To be sure, they recognize that the church may exert a moral influence upon the masses to keep them from rising up against the established order—that is, against the interests of the ruling class—and they are alarmed by the new ideas of the priest of the vanguard. These nominal Catholics have a utilitarian sense of religion; they are willing to make use of it but not serve it. Whether consciously or unconsciously, this kind of person has helped the Catholic church to be a useful tool in preventing changes in the underdeveloped countries.

The group of nominal Catholics also includes those proletarians—both rural and urban—and students who live outside the church but do not irrevocably renounce it. In other words, they say they are Catholic but do not practice their faith, and they resist the idea of being "church people." They are not active Catholics, but they are still included within Latin American Catholicism. Many of them, particularly in student circles, feel that the church has been left behind in the process of change in these countries, and they tend toward the political left, outside the ecclesiastical circle.

We mention the nominal Catholics not only because they form part of the church but also because a partial or even ingenuous description of post-conciliar Latin American Catholicism might leave the mistaken impression that all Catholics in these countries are, under the direction of the ecclesiastical hierarchy, directly involved in the process of change initiated by Vatican II and nourished by the conferences of Medellín (1968) and Puebla (1979). Nothing could be further from the truth. It is one thing to examine contemporary Catholicism in the light of the teachings of avant-garde theologians, but it is very different to live among Catholics and to observe firsthand the tremendous contrasts within the church as a whole in our Latin American countries. Perhaps the following illustrates this most clearly.

POPULAR RELIGIOSITY

In the company of a Latin American friend, we visited one of the most famous sanctuaries of Central America. We arrived at the back of the principal altar, where there is a small staircase the pilgrims ascend in order to be near the image of Jesus—which is considered very miraculous—and to kiss the heel while they recite a prayer. We said to our friend: "This, too, is Latin American Catholicism." It seems that the strong winds of Medellín and Vatican II have not blown here yet. The angry and revolutionary voices of Camilo Torres and Ernesto Cardenal go unheard, as do the theological reflections of Gutiérrez and Assmann, and Bishop Cámara's call for the transformation of existing structures through moral pressure.

Catholicism of the vanguard exists in Latin America, but it exists alongside the Catholicism of those who pray before the tomb of a monk who died years ago. Those Catholics reach out their trembling hands to touch the door of the sepulchre, in the hope that that monk will hear them and perform "a miracle" for them. Catholicism is also the multitudes who reverently participate in the massive Holy Week processions; it is those who walk upon their bloody knees to the altar of the Virgin of Guadalupe in Mexico; it is the Indians of the central Guatemalan highlands who, in a now-famous case of religious syncretism, combine the faith of the *conquistadores* with the adoration of the ancient Mayan gods—all this more than twenty years after Vatican II. Catholicism also includes those who mix the faith of the church with spiritism. In these days when there is a tremendous growth in the occult sciences, the so-called Catholic-spiritist or spiritist-Catholic church is present.

It is no wonder that in Catholic circles today there is so much talk of "evangelizing" our continent once again.

CONCLUSION

In general terms, then, this is the mosaic that post-conciliar Latin American Catholicism presents to even the most superficial observer. It cannot be denied that within the categories mentioned here, and between groups, there is a whole spectrum of convictions, attitudes, and practices that could not even be mentioned in a work of this sort. There are other categories that were not even included—for example, the Catholicism of *Opus Dei* and similar movements that wish to raise their rightist or centrist flags upon the battlements of the church and carry out their political maneuverings in the shadow of the sanctuary.

It remains for the careful investigator to deepen the socio-religious analysis of the Catholic phenomenon in Latin America. We have only indicated anew some well-known guidelines that if followed with the tools provided by theology and the social sciences can lead us to a broader comprehension of Latin American Catholicism before venturing to emit unilateral judgments or exceedingly optimistic evaluations of the Catholic situation in our countries.

NOTES

1. "Alocución de Juan XXIII en la ceremonia de apertura del Concilio, Octubre 1962," *Vaticano II* (Barcelona: Editorial Regina, S.A., 1967), p. 1042. See also José Miguez Bonino, *Concilio Abierto* (Buenos Aires, Editorial La Aurora, 1967), p. 66.

2. Emillo A. Núñez, "Posición de la Iglesia Evangélica frente al Aggiornamento," *Acción en Cristo para un Continente en Crisis* (San José, Costa Rica: Editorial Garibe, 1970), pp. 40-41.

3. Samuel Escobar, "El Futuro: Búsqueda de Identidad y de Misión." Consultation of the Commission on the Life and Mission of the Church in Latin America. Latin American Theological Fraternity, Buenos Aires, Argentina, March 1976. Mimeographed paper, pp. 27-28.

4. "The great hopes which Medellín raised have disappeared like a mere illusion." Orlando E. Costas, *Theology of the Crossroads in Contemporary Latin America* (Amsterdam: Rodopi, 1976), p. 212. It was not until July 1976 that the Guatemalan Episcopal Council published a message that endeavored to reflect the spirit of Medellín: *Unidos en la Esperanza* (Guatemala: Secretariado de Medios de Comunicacion Social del Episcopado de Guatemala, July 1976).

5. S. Freixedo, *Mi Iglesia Duerme* (Río Piedras, Puerto Rico: Editorial ISLA, 1969).

6. Raul Macin, *Monseñor Lefebvre, el Obispo Maldito* (México: Editorial Posada, S.A., 1977).

Evangelical Self-Theologizing
in Latin America

11

Doing Theology in Latin America:
Contextualization

During at least the last twenty years there has been a great deal of theological and missiological discussion about the idea of encouraging the churches in the Two-Thirds World to produce their own evangelical theology in response to their own needs, in their particular cultural and social context. There have been both positive and negative reactions to this idea. For instance, the suggestion of having a theology written in Latin America for Latin Americans has created a sense of uneasiness, suspicion, and even fear at home and abroad.

Some years ago in a theological consultation held at Guatemala, a dear Christian lady was so concerned and disturbed by the discussion of the possibility of doing evangelical theology in Latin America that she asked, "Are you planning to write another Bible? My Bible is good enough for me." Other people say: "We have already an evangelical theology. There is no need for another one." Some evangelical leaders are afraid of any attempt to go beyond our predecessors in biblical and theological research. To them, evangelical theology is a finished product that admits no new forms of expression that would be more relevant to our society. They make no distinction between God's written revelation as such and theology as a human reflection that has been going on through almost two thousand years of church history. The leaders of the Protestant Reformation made that distinction. Martin Luther said that a gen-

331

eral council as well as a pope may err, and thus neither had a right to impose any article of faith not founded in the Scriptures. Theological systems may change, at least in their forms: only the Word of God remains forever.

There may be, however, some justification for the immediate negative response to the idea of doing a regional theology. From the evangelical standpoint, it is always risky to explore new territories in the attempt to theologize, especially if the scholar is not deeply grounded in God's written revelation, if he or she has not strong evangelical convictions, if he or she is not in close fellowship with the Lord and his church. Evangelical theology has to be done on the basis of the Scriptures, in subjection to the Holy Spirit, in "the communion of the saints," in a respectful and constant dialogue with the evangelical theology of yesterday and today, in a meaningful and discerning interaction with the cultural and social context.

We need a Latin American theology, as evangelicals in the United States need a theology to meet their needs and the spiritual and ethical needs of their country. The gospel brought to North America by the British, the Dutch, and other immigrants is contextualized in American reality. What American and European evangelicals are doing, we Latin Americans are supposed to do—to contextualize the gospel in our cultural and social situation.

THE MEANING OF CONTEXTUALIZATION

The very well-known illustration of the seed and the flowerpot, as given by Dr. D. T. Niles, a Methodist preacher of Sri Lanka, comes immediately to mind when we speak of indigenization and contextualization. According to Dr. Niles,

> the Gospel is like a seed, and you have to sow it. When you sow the seed of the Gospel in Palestine, a plant that can be called Palestinian Christianity grows. When you sow it in Rome, a plant of Roman Christianity grows. You sow the Gospel in Great Britain and you get British Christianity. The seed of the Gospel is later brought to America, and a plant grows of American Christianity. Now, when the missionaries came to our lands they brought not only the seed of the Gospel, but their own plant of Christianity, flowerpot included! So, what we have to do is to break the flowerpot, take out the seed of

the Gospel, sow it in our own cultural soil, and let our own version of Christianity grow.[1]

It is evident that the flowerpot has not been broken in many mission fields. In Latin America, for example, there are churches that have tried to be a Xerox copy of churches in the United States. We have seen in many cases a translation of the North American evangelical culture into our own culture. Some young preachers have gone to the extreme of imitating the foreign missionary in the pulpit.

Indigenization and Contextualization

In 1885 John L. Nevius published a series of articles on missiological methodology. These papers were developed into the book *Planting and Development of Missionary Churches*.[2] The Nevius Method became widely known in relation to the subject of "indigenization." The *Willowbank Report* on gospel and culture points out that even in the middle of the last century "pioneer missionary thinkers like Henry Venn and Rufus Anderson . . . popularized the concept of 'indigenous' churches, which would be 'self-governing, self-supporting and self-propagating.'"[3] Roland Allen did the same earlier in this century. But in the "three-self approach" the principle of self-theologizing was lacking. Theology continued to be, to a large extent, the imported theology from the West. There were other areas in which indigenization was also necessary—for instance, liturgy, methods of preaching, church government, and even church architecture.

In 1928 the Jerusalem Conference of the International Missionary Council, which was an outcome of the now-famous missionary conference held in Edinburgh in 1910, gave serious attention to the urgent need for developing truly indigenous churches. The conference called for churches "which expressed in worship, customs, art and architecture the best characteristics of a people, but at the same time preserved the inheritance of the church of every land and of every age."[4]

In January 1949, Professor H. Richard Niebuhr gave a series of lectures on the subject of Christ and culture at Austin Presbyterian Theological Seminary. His book *Christ and Culture*,[5] based on those lectures, has become widely known and quoted in missiological literature. Professor Niebuhr is dealing with a difficult problem faced by Christians: In what way, or degree, is Christ relevant to the situation in which the individual Christian and the church are called to fulfill their mission? It is actually a book on basic Christian social ethics. Five alternative ways to relate the gospel to culture are given:

> (1) "Christ against culture," or the counterculture approach, is illustrated by Tertullian, medieval mystics, and several conservative groups in our contemporary world. (2) The second kind of approach is called "the Christ of culture," or the accommodationist approach, as illustrated by Gnosticism and Abelard, "culture Protestantism," Albrecht Ritschlo, and others. (3) The "Christ above culture" approach, or the synthesis of Christ and culture, is represented by Clement of Alexandria and Thomas Aquinas, "who is probably the greatest of all the synthesists in Christian history."[6] (4) The dualistic approach of "Christ and culture in Paradox" was taken by Luther, Kierkegaard, Troeltsch, and others. (5) "Christ the transformer of culture" is the fifth view. Among the representatives of the conversionist model, Niebuhr mentions Augustine, Calvin, and F. D. Maurice.

In the last paragraph of his book, Niebuhr says:

> To make our decisions in faith is to make them in view of the fact that no single man or group or historical time is the church; but that there is a church of faith in which we do our partial, relative work and on which we count. It is to make them in view of the fact that Christ is risen from the dead, and is not only the head of the church but the redeemer of the world. It is to make them in view of the fact that the world of culture—man's achievement—exists within the world of grace—God's Kingdom.[7]

In other words, there is no contradiction between gospel and culture in the kingdom of God.

In relation to the missionary task, Peter Savage indicates that some Catholic missiologists have talked of "accommodation to culture" (Luzbetak). Protestants have preferred to speak of "adaptation to culture" (Kraemer, first director of the WCC Ecumenical Institute), "possession of culture" (the classical Reformed posture, defended by Peter Beyerhaus), and "transformation of culture" (Charles H. Kraft). Savage discusses briefly these four concepts in his paper "Discipleship in Context: The Challenge of 'Contextualization.'" Luzbetak proposes "accommodation" in the sense of a "respectful, prudent, scientifically and theologically sound adjustment of the Church to the native culture in attitude, outward behavior, and practical apostolic approach," with the idea of permeating the whole of culture with the gospel, without compromising the essentials of faith.[8]

"Adaptation" differs from "accommodation" in that "it strives not for assimilation of cultural elements but for *expression* of the Gospel through familiar cultural forms and ideas." The example given is that of the apostle John who uses the logos idea to express incarnation.[9]

The concept of "possession" is based on Psalm 2:8: "Ask of me, and I will make the nations your heritage, and the ends of the earth your possession." "Possession" is a cosmic process. But according to Beyerhaus, this approach to indigenization is primarily concerned "with the personal allegiance of people, based on a change of mind, a metaphysical liberation and a spiritual regeneration."[10]

In the "transformation" approach God is seen "above culture but as employing culture as the vehicle for his interaction with man."[11] The role of the individual Christian is emphasized for cultural change, but attention is also given to the social context in which the individual is located. "When processes of individual transformation take place, they influence both the individual internal culture—his psychology—and his use of his external culture."[12]

At the present time even among evangelicals in different parts of the world there is the tendency to go beyond indigenization to contextualization both in theory and practice, although it has been pointed out that this tendency came originally from the World Council of Churches. It is a fact that a consultation on "Dogmatic or Contextual Theology?" was held by the Ecumenical Institute of the World Council of Churches at Bossey, Switzerland, in 1971. In that conference the guidelines were laid down for contextualizing the gospel in accord with the Theological Education Fund (TEF) of the World Council of Churches. Bruce C. G. Fleming writes that "the term 'contextualization' first surfaced publicly in 1972 with the publication of *Ministry in Context* by the Theological Education Fund."[13] Explaining the meaning of contextualization, this book says:

> It [contextualization] means all that is implied in the familiar term "indigenization" and yet seeks to press beyond. Contextualization has to do with how we assess the peculiarity of third world context. Indigenization tends to be used in the sense of responding to the Gospel

in terms of a traditional culture. Contextualization, while not ignoring this, takes into account the process of secularity, technology, and the struggle for human justice, which characterize the historical moment of nations in the Third World.[14]

According to this view, in contrast to traditional indigenization, *contextualization is open to social change:* it is aware of the revolutionary situation in which we live; it is concerned about the movements for social justice in the Third World; it is future oriented. Contextualization has to do not only with traditional cultural values—language, customs, arts— but also with new economic and political concepts.

Contextualization comes to remind us Latin American evangelicals that we belong to a social and cultural context, and that we are not supposed to close our eyes to the sufferings of our own people; that the gospel message is not only for life after death, but also for life this side of the grave. Contextualization has come to tell us, in emphatic terms, that the gospel itself was originally given in a social context; that the biblical writers did not speak in a social vacuum, and that we do not read the Word of God in a social vacuum.

A difference between theoretical indigenization and contextualization is seen perhaps in the traditional attitude of evangelical missions toward the Indian culture in Latin America and the new missionary approach to the Indian problem in those countries. For instance, Indian culture in Latin America is in many ways beautiful. Our Indians have cultural values that must be preserved. But as the same time most of the Indian people live miserable lives from the spiritual, moral, educational, and economic standpoint. Their standard of living is in many cases subhuman. They have been deprived of their land and have to work for wealthy farmers who may treat them as slaves. Hundreds of Indians— men, women, and children—are taken in big trucks to coffee, sugar-cane, and cotton plantations where they live in very sad conditions, work hard, and are given the lowest possible salaries. Some people may ask whether we should go on trying to indigenize the gospel according to traditional cultural values in a social context that is crying for a radical change.

It seems to me that, generally speaking, traditional indigenization was not concerned about the social problem of the Latin American Indians. For some missiological reasons, traditional indigenization has been enthusiastic about preserving our Indian culture, especially the Indian dialects. This indigenization has been to a large extent romantic, in the sense of looking to the past and glorifying the noble savage without seriously taking into consideration the present, much less the future. Contextualization is asking for the incarnation of the gospel, not in a traditional and static culture, but in the struggle and agony of the people in their search for a new culture, namely, a better way of life for them and their children.

The Problems of Contextualization

As Latin American Christians we have to admit the need for an application of the gospel to the totality of humanity. The Lord Jesus Christ has come to liberate humans completely; not only to prepare them for heaven, but also to give them a new quality of life here on earth. At the same time, we have to be faithful to the gospel itself, to submit ourselves to the final authority of God's written revelation. We have to be wise, depending on the light of the Scriptures and on the leading of the Holy Spirit, to avoid any distortion of the gospel in our lives and ministries. In other words, we have to be aware of *the problems of contextualization.*

In the final analysis, contextualization is closely related to hermeneutics—hermeneutics not only as exegesis, but also as interpretation in the light of our social context. In exegesis we may stop in the culture in which divine revelation was given. We may become experts in the study of the Middle Eastern culture and Mediterranean culture of biblical times without being really concerned about the social and cultural problems of our contemporaries.

To solve the problem of exegetical isolation from the realities of daily life, we speak of application as a necessary step in the process. Once we have determined the meaning of the text in the light of the context (grammatical, historical, and cultural), we apply it to ourselves and to other people's experience. The meaning of the biblical text is not determined by our social context, which is subject to change. We do not want to relativize the truth of God's written revelation. The Word of God remains forever, far above the ever-changing social context. The Scriptures sit in judgment on all economic, social, and political ideologies. We also believe in the ministry of the Holy Spirit, who leads us into the mind of God as we study his Word. We also believe that the written Word and the Holy Spirit have spoken to other holy persons in past centuries and in our own time. Therefore, we believe that the church has a body of sound doctrine that we have the privilege of using as a safeguard against theological deviations in our hermeneutical task.

In contrast to our way of interpreting and applying the Scriptures in our ministries, there is a great deal of existential and political hermeneutics going on in contemporary theology. According to the new hermeneutics, the interpreter goes from oneself or from one's social context to the Scriptures. It is a movement from psychology, or from sociology, to theology. Contextualization may easily become an instrument for religious syncretism or political ideology. The Uruguayan theologian Mortimer Arias, who has been a lecturer in evangelism at Perkins School of Theology, recognizes that "Contextualization may become mere accommodation, acculturation, domestication, or absorption of the Gospel as in syncretism or culture religion."[15]

Syncretism has always been a threat to the Christian church. There was syncretism in the early centuries of Christianity, especially when Christianism became a legal religion in the Roman Empire and ecclesiastical leaders began to use pagan means and methods to communicate the gospel of Christ. There is syncretism in the religion of the Indian peoples who were supposedly "evangelized" by the Roman Catholic priests and monks in Latin America four centuries ago. In missiological literature a distinction has been established between "easy accommodation" and "prophetic accommodation." Nevertheless the dividing line between accommodation and syncretism is always too thin to be kept clear and distinctive in the performing of the missionary task.

There is today a strong syncretistic tendency among ecumenical theologians around the world. Speaking on "Contextualization and Asian Theology," Bong Rin Ro says:

> There are Christian theologians and other religious thinkers who have tried to syncretize Christianity with a national religion (Hinduism, Buddhism, or Islam) in an attempt to contextualie theology into the national situation. The Commission of World Mission and Evangelism of the World Council of Churches has sponsored a number of religious dialogues with the leaders of other living religions. Many of these dialogues have resulted in a mutual acceptance of each other's beliefs. The scope of Hinduism and Buddhism is large enough to accommodate all other religions, including Christianity.[16]

In Latin America we are confronted at the present time by what may be called "socio-Christian syncretism"—a mixture of social sciences and some Christian principles under the guiding star of leftist ideologies to promote structural changes in our society. We have come to the point at which some people think that we are not contextualizing the gospel correctly unless we are active in the political left. Others are pushing us to take an extreme conservative position against any change in our social structures. It is undeniable that all of us have opted for something in the area of politics, even if our option is noninvolvement. But we are, above all, Christians, and our political options are not supposed to have a final character. Jesus Christ is the Lord. Any socio-political system is imperfect and temporary. But the Word of the Lord remains forever. For us evangelical Christians, contextualization does not mean compromise with contemporary philosophy or theology, or current ideology.

In an article published in the *International Bulletin of Missionary Research,* Dr. Paul G. Hiebert expresses some of his concerns about embracing "an uncritical contextualization." He asks: "If the gospel is contextualized, what are the checks against biblical and theological distortion? Where are the absolutes?" Another problem is "the ahistorical nature of most discussions on contextualization." Dr. Hiebert explains:

> Contemporary cultural contexts are taken seriously, but historical contexts are largely ignored. In each culture Christians face new questions for which they must find biblical answers. But in many things, particularly in developing their biblical and systematic theologies . . . they can learn much from church history. Exegesis and hermeneutics are not the rights of individuals but of the church as an exegetical and hermeneutical community. And that community includes not only the saints within our cultural context, and even the saints outside our culture, but also the saints down through history.

Closely related to this problem is the fact, according to Dr. Hiebert, that "uncritical contextualization, at least in its more extreme forms, provides us with no means for working toward the unity of churches in different cultures." There is no basis for mutual understanding, no common foundation of faith.[17]

Taking into consideration the problems, or dangers, of contextualization, including the influence exercised by political theologies and ideologies in some efforts of contextualization, in which the context becomes the content, Fleming advocates what he calls "context-indigenization." He explains that this term "truly means all that is meant in the traditional understanding of the term indigenization. Yet it seeks to press beyond it by implementing insights of anthropology, among other things. At the same time, however, these insights are subjected to the judgment of Scripture."[18] In his conclusion, he says: "Properly speaking, evangelicals do not, and should not, contextualize the gospel. The indigenizing, or more properly, the context-indigenizing of the gospel, should be the method of evangelical work."[19]

In the *Willowbank Report* notice is taken of some dangers like heresy, provincialism, and syncretism, but the contextual approach is emphasized for understanding God's Word today because this approach "takes seriously the cultural context of the contemporary readers as well as of the biblical text, and recognizes that a dialogue must develop between the two."[20]

> It is the need for this dynamic interplay between text and the interpreters which we wish to emphasize .... In this process of interaction our knowledge of God and our response to his will are continuously being deepened. . . . It is this continuous growth in knowledge, love and obedience which is the purpose and profit of the "contextual" approach. Out of the context in which his word was originally given, we hear God speaking to us in our contemporary context, and we find it a transforming experience. This process is a kind of upward spiral in which Scripture remains always central and normative.[21]

In Latin America "indigenization" does not seem to be used today as a basic concept for doing evangelical missiology. In some quarters this term may even have a negative connotation. Our theologians or missiologists prefer to speak of contextualization. But it is necessary to make a distinction between noncritical contextualizers and critical contextualizers.

A Latin American Perspective

Contextualization is, generally speaking, the effort to make relevant the meaning of the biblical text to our contemporary social context. It is in a sense the transculturization of the text from the times of the biblical writers to our own times.

The word *contextualization* can suggest to us the content, context, and communication of our message to contemporary people.

In conservative evangelical circles, there is definite agreement on the fact that the essential content of our proclamation is the written Word of God. Paul exhorts us to preach the Word (*Keruxon ton logon*, 2 Tim.

4:2). We are heralds who publicly proclaim the message that comes from the King of kings and the Lord of lords. His will has been expressed clearly and finally in the propositions of the Scriptures. We do not make a difference between the container and the content. For us the Bible is the Word of God. This is the sacred trust that has been committed to us in order that we might transmit it faithfully to trustworthy people who will be able to teach others also (2 Tim. 2:2).

When it comes to passing on the treasure of written revelation, our educational system has to be in a sense a "banking" one,[22] since we are not to formulate our own revelation, nor encourage others to formulate theirs. "For I delivered unto you first of all that which I also received" (1 Cor. 15:3, KJV). "The things that thou hast heard of me among many witnesses, the same commit thou" (2 Tim. 2:2, KJV).

The content of revelation has already been given to us by the Lord (Jude 3). Now it simply has to be transmitted in a process that belongs to the authentic Christian tradition. For us there is no additional revelation. We are not prophets or apostles, in the strict sense of the terms. It is our privilege simply to communicate what God has indicated in his written Word. For this reason, when it comes to the essential content of our message, our interest is not so much in the theology of the First World, or of the Second, or of the Third World as it is in that which God has communicated in his written Word.

In expressing this conviction we take upon ourselves the enormous responsibility of knowing in as far as it is possible God's written revelation in order to submit ourselves to its sovereign demands. We have the sacred obligation of studying, obeying, and proclaiming "the whole counsel of God," not only those portions of Scripture that particularly appeal to us. There is no place here for theological or missiological hobby horses or for interpretations that are designed to support a certain ecclesiastical or political system, whatever that system might be. The Word of God must always stand above every human-made theology and above every socio-political ideology.

One of the great dangers in the current emphasis on contextualization is that of seeking to exalt what humanity says over that which God has already said. Some people are itching to hear teachers who will talk to them along the lines of their own political inclinations. For these people, we are not contextualizing the evangelical message correctly unless we align ourselves with the political cause they have undertaken and consider to be the only alternative for solving the grave problems that burden us in Latin America.

We understand, of course, that in every aspect of their lives evangelical Christians should be characterized by their love for liberty. This does not mean, however, that they should become involved with a political doctrine—whether of the right or of the left—to the point where they convert that doctrine into their message or impose it on the content of the gospel. Any socio-political system, no matter how sincere and noble it may appear in its liberating purposes, is imperfect and temporary. But the Word of the Lord remains forever. If the written Word of God is for us the supreme authority in all that relates to our lives (and every Christian has opted for something in the area of politics, even if it is non-involvement), our political options do not have a final character. Jesus Christ is the Lord. He has spoken not the next to the last word, but the last, the final word, for those who believe in his name. Biblically speaking, contextualization does not mean compromise with philosophy or theology or current ideology. What we need to do is not change the message or disfigure it, but apply it correctly to the needs of our own culture.

Contextualization takes us into the field of hermeneutics. At the present time hermeneutics is no longer limited to a set of rules or principles for the correct interpretation of the biblical text. It is said that the interpreter, as a child of his or her own culture and as a member of a social and ecclesiastical context, comes to the Bible with her or his own presuppositions. His or her own way of interpreting life and the world, and her or his own social and ecclesiastical background may determine for him or her, to a large extent, the meaning of the Scriptures. Biblical interpretation, it is said, does not take place in a cultural vacuum. In this case, hermeneutics is much more than interpretation and application as we evangelicals are used to saying.

For a theologian with little or no respect whatsoever for the authority of the Bible, the meaning of the text may be determined by personal choice, by the ever-changing social context, or by a political ideology, whatever it might be. There is the ever-present danger of injecting meaning into Holy Scripture, instead of struggling to discover the meaning given by the writer to the words of the text under the inspiration of the Holy Spirit.

We have to admit, of course, that basically the same danger may exist in our conservative evangelical hermeneutics. We may have been guilty of imposing upon the text a meaning of our own choice. In the Latin American Protestant community there are a variety of "final authorities" in biblical interpretation—for instance, the authority of human reason, the authority of emotional experience, the authority of denominational tradition, the authority of an inflexible theological system, the authority of a political option. In all of these cases human authority is above the authority of the written Word of God, although we enthusiastically profess the Protestant principle of *sola Scriptura*. In the midst of political turmoil and social change, contextualization may become a pretext for a distortion of the gospel at the service of a political ideology.

Contextualization may be used as a pretext for misinterpreting the biblical text. But, on the other hand, contextualization is now a subject of serious study almost everywhere in the theological world. Contextualization is not a passing fad. It is indispensable to know this concept in order to interact intelligently with contemporary theology. Above all, we need to know and use contextualization in order to present the gospel in such a way that our contemporaries will see the relevance of this message for their personal and social needs. We cannot afford to leave contextualization out of our theological concern, especially if we are trying to do theology in the Third World.

On the basis of our strong conviction that God has already given us his written revelation and that this revelation has a definite meaning of its own, we have to affirm again and again the need for a sound biblical exegesis apart from any tendency to impose on the Scriptures an exotic, non-biblical meaning. Contextualization does not have to mean the attempt to change the contents of the Bible. We have already suggested that contextualization is the effort to get to the real meaning of the Scriptures, having in view both our personal needs and the needs of our social context.

The big question is whether the Bible has something to tell us Latin American evangelicals concerning the particular problems of our society. But we have to look for the biblical meaning without the lenses of political ideologies that are trying to capture the Latin American mind. Some theology professors in Latin America believe they are contextualizing the gospel when in reality what they are doing is contextualizing the democratic capitalism of the Roman Catholic scholar Michael Novak. The same may be said in regard to those professors who are contextualizing the liberation theology of the Peruvian Jesuit Gustavo Gutiérrez.

A careful study of the Scriptures teaches us that written revelation was also transmitted within a cultural context. In order to communicate with us God spoke in human language through people who were immersed in a given culture. The culture we find in the Old Testament is not the same as the culture reflected in the New Testament. And there are differences in the cultural contexts of the various writers in both Testaments. But although the sacred writers wrote in terms that were meaningful in their own cultures, the message itself is a revelation of God and not simply a product of cultural accommodation.

It is interesting to observe that the writers of the New Testament do not change the message of the Old to please the Greeks and Romans. They do not submit themselves to the dictates of their contemporaries. The culture serves the message, rather than the message serving the culture. Both the writers of the Old Testament and those of the New pass on for their own time and for future generations a message that sits in judgment on all cultures.

It should be kept in mind also that the experience of those "holy men of God" was unique in the history of the Creator's self-communication. They were involved, so to speak, in the revelatory task. Guided by the Holy Spirit, they faithfully contextualized the divine revelation in the infallible pages of the Bible. We need to contextualize, in our own culture, the Word contextualized by them in their times. But we cannot do exactly what they did under the impulse of the Spirit. We are not called to write a special revelation for the culture of the twentieth century.

Neither can we imitate completely the Lord Jesus—the Word made flesh—the Word contextualized in the Palestinian culture of those days. He is not simply an interpreter of the Word, but the very Word of God. He does not only pronounce the Word; he is the Word, and he does not cease being the Word upon taking to himself humanity and living among humans. Strictly speaking, the incarnation is possible only for the Son of God.

Nevertheless, in our effort to contextualize the gospel we will do well to keep always in mind that the Son of God identified himself with the culture of his time, although without becoming a slave to it. In reality, he brought the culture of his time under judgment, as he does every culture.

Even though our contextualization is different from that of Christ and from that of the biblical writers, we can learn much from the ways in which God has spoken to humanity throughout history. For example, he takes the initiative in revelation, speaks in human language, and comes to humans where they are. The gospel is for every culture and for each individual, and it adequately meets the needs of people in any cultural context.

We should ask ourselves if the problem of contextualization is not more missiological than theological. Although every missionary may become "an agent of cultural change," the divine mandate has to do with the proclamation of the gospel as it is found in the Scriptures and not with efforts to impose a foreign culture on the recipients of the message.

Nevertheless, in the process of establishing the church in different regions of the world, it has been impossible for the messengers to avoid leaving their cultural mark on the Christian communities that they have founded.

In the light of this reality, some evangelical leaders insist that we strip off the Anglo-Saxon robe from the gospel and that we contextualize it in the Latin American culture. This idea is certainly welcome if by contextualization we understand the proclamation of the good news in terms meaningful to our culture and the building up of a church that is able adequately to respond to the needs of the Latin American people.

If we understand the context as we should, we still have to decide whether it is more important than the text: whether the gospel will be over the culture, under it, against it, or in agreement with it. Our Latin American culture has great values that we certainly do not want to lose, but like any other culture it is imperfect. There are elements in it that do not deserve to be preserved and with which even the avant-garde Catholics who make much of contextualization do not want to be identified, even though in general this is a culture with strong Roman Catholic roots. We are referring to influences from across the Atlantic, from Rome, from faraway Europe, which conquered us with the cross and the sword and mixed our blood, our myths, and our customs with the imported culture in the name of God, the pope, and the king. When we evangelicals speak of taking off the Anglo-Saxon robe, have we thought of also taking off the Roman tunic?

When we are sure of the biblical text and the cultural context, we still have the enormous task of bringing together both elements in the carrying out of our missionary commitment. Knowing the gospel and the culture is not enough. The theological content and the cultural context must be joined by means of effective communication. In a certain sense this is the most critical aspect of contextualization. It is here where we have failed many times in our effort to get across the message.

In the United States, the missionary enterprise has developed in a society dominated by the middle class. In Latin America, the lower classes form the majority. Nevertheless, we have imported North American missionary methods without making in many cases the necessary adaptations. The result has been that our preaching and even our music are characterized generally by the strong foreign flavor, estranged from the feelings of the Latin American masses.

Certain themes should be given more attention in order to achieve better communication. One is the effect the Latin American concept of family solidarity should have on the methodology of Christian education as applied to the Sunday school and the other agencies of the local church.

As Latin Americans, we place great emphasis on personal relationships and courtesy. Therefore, a second theme would be the way these characteristics should affect evangelism and the concept of the ministry.

Current affairs and background form a third theme. Here, the attitude of the missionary is crucial. How many are reading about Latin America's history, culture, literature, and social and political struggles? Far too many are not conversant with current issues because they do not regularly read the local newspapers.

The word *contextualization* causes us to consider especially the fact that we have not applied the Word of God in a broad and penetrating way to the great needs of the developing nations and, in some cases, greatly underdeveloped nations.

In these countries we find ourselves face to face with many and serious problems concerning which we as evangelical Christians will have to express ourselves sooner or later. Some of these problems are peculiar to our region, whereas others are found also outside Latin America—for example, the demographic explosion; air pollution; the progressive depletion of natural resources; the threat of hunger; increasing industrialization and the profound cultural changes that it produces; the new attitude toward the family and the community—including courtship, extramarital sexual relations, family planning, abortion, divorce, education of children, respect for parents and care of the aged, and woman's degradation; geographical and social mobility; *machismo*; syncretism in the indigenous cultures as well as in the refined atmosphere of those who pretend to mix the gospel with "isms" of a religious or socio-political character; nationalism that is nothing more than xenophobia; *caudillismo*; the great economic and social inequalities; erroneous concepts about private property; the wrong idea regarding work, which was willed to us by the Iberian conquerors and traditional Roman Catholicism; the racial inferiority complex that leads us to look down on that which is indigenous and exalt that which is foreign to us, without the proper evaluation of our own culture. These and other problems cry out for an eminently biblical consideration.

It may be said that a serious effort in contextualization is only beginning among us. Without any doubt the most important element in this effort, from the human point of view, is the communicator, the person responsible for applying the immutable message of the gospel to the changing cultural situation.

In Latin America we are far behind in the training of leaders capable of carrying out contextualization: leaders rooted deeply in the Word of God and fully identified with their own culture; leaders who know well the text and the context and can unite both in theological reflection and in the proclamation of the gospel. It may not be necessary to speak of "a Latin American theology," but it is important that we seek a pre-eminently biblical theology expressed by and for Latin Americans.

To contextualize is not to change the message but rather to apply it to every dimension of one's personality and to all the relationships in one's life.

THE CHALLENGE OF CONTEXTUALIZATION

Generally speaking, we conservative evangelicals in Latin America have been behind schedule in our theological work. Our under-development is also theological. Some of us have finally become interested in doing theology; but we are reacting to some challenges that we cannot avoid any more in our social and ecclesiastical context. Our theology is a theology in reaction. We did not take the initiative to produce an evangelical theology on the basis of the Scriptures in response to our social situation. We have been forced to enter into the theological arena by the social turmoil in which we live and by the non-biblical or anti-biblical answers that some theologians are giving to the problems of the Latin American people. And in this process of reflection, the challenge of the Scriptures has been greater than the one coming from social reality and from the new trends in Latin American theology. Consequently, it is indispensable to go back to the example of God's written revelation to deal with the subject of this chapter.

The Challenge of Contextualization
Comes From the Gospel Itself

Since the beginning it was demonstrated that the gospel was designed to grow and flourish in different cultural situations. The incarnation of the Son of God is, of course, in a sense the greatest example of contextualization. The Logos "became flesh." It does not say that he became a Jew, nor a Gentile, but "a human being" *(Good News Bible).* Moreover, the incarnate Logos was born in a proletarian family; he became a carpenter, living and suffering among his own people, especially among those who were the poor and despised by society. The incarnate

Word and the written Word demonstrate God's willingness to come where we are, to reveal himself to us in a condescending and relevant way. We understand him because he became like one of us, living among his contemporaries and expressing himself in human language. No wonder that the gospel has the power to germinate, grow, and bear fruit everywhere in the world.

The gospel is a message addressed to all peoples on earth. God wants to meet men and women in their own cultural and social situations. The apostles had to understand the distinctive universal character of the gospel. It was not easy for them to come to this understanding. But the time came when they perceived that the Christian message was for both Jews and Gentiles, that the new *ekklesia* was designed to be different from Judaism. They had to abandon the Temple and the synagogue as their main places of learning and worship. New Christian assemblies were established all over Palestine. Then the gospel invaded the Gentile world. But the new *ekklesia* was not just another gathering of Gentiles, nor was it a group of proselytes to Judaism. It was an entirely new thing. Jews and Gentiles could get together as one people —God's people—in the name of the Lord Jesus Christ.

The apostles were not sent to spread Judaism. Because of their race and culture they could not avoid being Jews, and there were Jewish elements in the church established by them in the Gentile world. But they came to realize that above anything else they were supposed to be Christian, and they did not try to impose Judaism on the Gentiles or "paganism" on the Jews. It was not a crusade to implant Jewish culture, or Greek culture, or Roman culture. This was a very important lesson that both Hebrew and Gentile Christians had to learn at the very beginning of Christian missions. Their responsibility was to demonstrate that the gospel was able to incarnate itself in any kind of culture without losing its own identity.

When the time came to produce the New Testament books, the gospel was written in a particular context, to a particular people, in a particular time, by particular servants of God. So to speak, the Holy Spirit contextualized the gospel through the ministry of those holy people who were moved by him to write the New Testament revelation.

In a sense the message of the New Testament, like that of the Old Testament, is a result of contextualization. The New Testament writers were responding, under the inspiration of the Holy Spirit, both to the particular needs of the first-century people and to the fundamental needs of all human beings. In other words, the New Testament was born out of the interaction between gospel and culture, under the control of the Holy

Spirit. In a unique way New Testament theology is contextualized theology. It is indispensable to say "in a unique way," because divine revelation written under the inspiration of the Holy Spirit is closed, and our contextualization has to do precisely with interpreting this revelation that "once for all God has given to His people." It is possible for us to contextualize the New Testament because the gospel is addressed to all cultures on earth. The New Testament challenges us to write a biblical and contextualized theology.

The Challenge to Contextualize the Gospel
Comes from Cultural Diversity

Many of us Central American evangelicals received the gospel through the personal ministry of North American missionaries or through the testimony of churches established by them. The American influence is evident in our theology, liturgy, church government, evangelistic methods and strategies, and personal ministry. The American political ideology and the American way of life have determined to some extent the nature of evangelical Christianity in our countries. In the United States, American individualism and the idea of bigness and terrestrial success have permeated in one way or another the evangelistic enterprise, especially in the so-called electronic church and in the massive campaigns conducted by some American evangelists south of the border. Such is the American image many Central Americans have perceived. It is so easy to forget that the best American export is not U.S.-made political ideas and ideals or the American way of life, American industrial and military power or American foreign aid, but the Christian gospel, for which we are deeply grateful to our American brothers and sisters who in different ways have contributed to taking the message to the Latin American people.

In doing theology and determining missionary methods and strategies for Latin America, we have to take into consideration the great cultural differences between Anglo America and Latin America.

One of the best ways to understand those differences is a historical comparison between the United States and Latin America. The history of the European discovery and colonization of North America and of the creation, geographical expansion, and economic development of the United States is enough to see the vast cultural differences between that nation and our Latin American countries.

Even if we reject the "black legend" in describing the Iberian conquest and colonization of our subcontinent, we still have to recognize that we inherited more vices than virtues from the ones who created the Ibero-American culture. Many of the serious problems confronting Latin America today have their basic explanations in the economic, social, political, and religious systems established by the Iberian in our countries.

There is not, of course, a perfect culture anywhere. Anglo-American culture is not an exception to this rule. We have already affirmed that our Latin American culture, like any other culture, is human and consequently imperfect and transitory. We are convinced that not all which is Latin American is good simply because it is Latin American. And we do not want to become worshipers of our own culture. We need to guard ourselves from falling into *culturolatry* (if I may use that term), although we see in our culture positive elements like the ones mentioned in the preceding chapter.

We have been a religious people by nature and by our Amerindian-Iberian heritage. We are a "theistic" nation, although the God and Father of our Lord Jesus Christ, the true and living God, is yet unknown on the personal level to millions of Latin Americans.

We realize that the gospel has not come to destroy any positive cultural elements. In this sense, the gospel is not against culture. But the gospel is not supposed to be in subjection to culture, much less to be absorbed by it. As God's revelation of his justice and mercy, the gospel is in judgment above culture. However, this message has also the power to produce positive cultural changes through the lives of those who surrender themselves to the Lord Jesus Christ—whether we like it or not. Christ is, in one way or another, the transformer of the culture of those who receive him and serve him as Savior and Lord. National Christians and expatriate missionaries are expected to be representatives of the gospel contraculture and agents of cultural change.

The Challenge to Contextualize the Gospel Comes from Our Social Problems

In doing evangelical theology in Latin America we have to take into consideration our complex social problems, including, of course, social injustice and the extreme poverty in which millions of Latin Americans live. There is no point of comparison between the affluent middle class in North America and the impoverished masses in Latin America. In contrast to North America, our middle class is not yet the largest segment of society. But especially in our big cities we have tried, consciously or unconsciously, to establish churches on the basis of North American middle-class values in a context of economic, social, and political underdevelopment, and we may be preaching a middle-class gospel in countries where most of the people belong to the low strata of society.

Evangelical theology for Latin America is not supposed to be a middle-class theology isolated from the masses, but a biblical theology contextualized in our cultural and social reality. To achieve this goal, it is indispensable to know the Word of God by means of sound exegesis and to know as much as possible our own cultural identity.

During my most recent visit to West Germany, an evangelical friend asked me: "How is Guatemala?" My prompt answer was: "Population growth is up, inflation is up, taxes are up, unemployment is up, delinquency on the streets is up, so, we are at the top."

I am sure that you know a good deal on Latin American poverty: our undernourishment and illiteracy (fifty percent in Guatemala); our big deficit in housing, schools, and hospitals; our lack of adequate care for the orphans, the handicapped, and the elderly.

Millions of Latin Americans have not had a real opportunity to improve their economic situation. They have not found a way out of extreme poverty, although they have spent their entire lives working hard in the fields or in the big urban centers. The mechanization of agriculture and the industrial growth in the cities have not really meant a better life for millions of Latin American workers. Some observers say that as a result of the Alliance for Progress, sponsored by the Kennedy administration, the Latin American rich became richer and the poor poorer. It seems that the structure of economic and political power did not permit the masses to have their share in the benefits of economic development.

You may ask for statistics to support these comments. The experts have their answer. We who are close to the people do not need sociological data to see the tragic situation in which so many of them live.

Why are so many Central Americans coming to the United States? Many of them are political refugees; most of them come for the simple reason that they do not have a job; they have no hope of a better life in their own country. America is the land of promise for them, as it was for all the immigrants who built that great nation under the blessing of God.

At the same time we have to realize that Latin American society is experiencing change in many respects. For instance, in many places we have seen change from a provincial culture to a modern way of life. The neighborhood where almost everybody knew everybody is disappearing to make room for new housing projects or commercial buildings. Moral values are also changing, especially in the big urban centers. There is a deterioration in family relationships. The old generation may feel that the changes are coming too soon. We certainly are not prepared for this cultural shock. Even the church is not any more a haven for the old way of life. Changes in society have to produce sooner or later changes in the church.

Social change in Latin America means much more than social evolution. Many Latin Americans are asking for revolution, the radical transformation of our social structures. One of the greatest differences between the social problem in North America and our social problem is that most Latin Americans live in extreme poverty, and we are already in a revolutionary situation. Evangelicals in Nicaragua and El Salvador are already experiencing the tragedy of a civil war. All of us in Latin America are in the midst of an ideological confrontation. Two economic and political systems are asking for our adherence and loyalty: neocapitalism and socialism. Some theologians have already chosen one of these two systems. They have the right to do so. But they are trying to impose their political option on their biblical interpretation. As citizens of this world we have to make political decisions. The question is whether we are going to be at the service of a particular ideology in our theological work or at the service of God and his purpose in history. This question is in itself a challenge to do biblical and contextualized theology in Latin America.

The Challenge to Contextualize the Gospel Comes from Revolutionary Theologies

We are challenged to contextualize our theology in Latin America by the gospel itself, by the simple fact of cultural diversity, and by our complex social problems. Some Latin American theologians have been working hard to respond to those challenges, and their theologizing is another challenge to us in regard to our responsibility of doing a Latin American evangelical theology.

Roman Catholic liberation theology. In a preceding chapter we have already made a brief description and evaluation of Roman Catholic liberation theology. This theology is a serious attempt to do Christian theology in response to the problems of the Latin American cultural and social context. Unfortunately, there are more negative than positive elements in liberation theology from our evangelical standpoint. We are deeply concerned about what liberation theologians do *to* the Scriptures and about what they do *with* the Scriptures to support a particular ideology.

Liberation theologians propose that Latin America needs a special type of socialism. It has to be an authentic Latin American socialism. Beyond any doubt they are on the political left. Their option is for socialism against capitalism and for revolution against "developmentalism." Liberation theology is a clear example of an effort to politicise the gospel. We know, of course, that the same can be said of those theologies that seem to have the tendency to protect the interest of the political right.

Latin American society, like other societies around the world, is deeply divided by racial, social, and religious discrimination. It is also deeply divided by social injustice. Liberation theologians are now producing more polarization in our society and even in the church in the name of their special branch of Christianity. They claim that to be the authentic church of Jesus Christ today we as a church are supposed to take sides ideologically and politically with the oppressed in their struggle against the oppressors. A new divisive element is being introduced into Latin American Christianity. The day may come when Christians may accuse other Christians on the basis of a political ideology. This painful situation was experienced in continental China many years ago. It may also happen among us as a result of uncontrolled political passion.

As evangelicals we must be in favor of social justice, in harmony with the teachings of the Scriptures. It is undeniable that a society cannot have peace, even in a relative way, apart from the practice of social justice. At the same time we believe that the gospel of Christ has to be in judgment above any political system. It is one thing to speak on justice in the name of the Lord on the basis of his written revelation and quite another matter to promote a political cause in the name of an ideology, whatever it might be. If in the past many of us Latin American evangelicals were consciously or unconsciously at the service of the political right, we do not now have to be naive, serving as church the interests of the political left just to make up for our past mistakes in the political arena.

In view of the political option of liberation theologians, to criticize their way of thinking may be dangerous in Latin America. In the opinion of some people, to be critical of the radical left means to support what they call American imperialism. For these people there is not a third or middle way in politics. We have to choose either American capitalism or the kind of socialism proposed by Latin American revolutionary groups, their strategies for radical social change included. The middle ground is ruled out. We must decide as churches to be for the oppressed or for the oppressors.

We evangelicals prefer to believe that the church as church is not called to take sides in the political struggles of our day and thus make enemies on the basis of an ideological option and renounce the privilege and responsibility of ministering to all people in the name of the Lord Jesus Christ. If the church as church advocates class struggle even to the

354 CRISIS AND HOPE IN LATIN AMERICA

extreme of psychological and physical violence, what institution is going to speak of love, justice, reconciliation, and peace in the name of the Lord Jesus Christ? The church has to be always open to receive those who in times of social peace or in the midst of social conflict are looking for spiritual help. Even in an ideologically divided nation, all the people, apart from any political option, have spiritual and moral needs that only the Christian message can meet. But a politicized gospel may become like salt that, having lost its taste, is good for nothing from the biblical standpoint.

The theological task before us is gigantic. In response to the challenge of liberation theology it is our responsibility to affirm that we are not against the oppressed or on the side of the oppressor. We want social justice to prevail, especially for those millions of Latin Americans who are unable to exercise their fundamental human rights, such as their right to be respected as human beings created in the image of God, their right to work, their right to education and social promotion, their right to vote and to be elected to public offices, their right to speak and worship according to the dictates of their own consciences, their right to move wherever they want, their right to expect at least basic financial support and medical care for their last years on earth.

At the same time we have to declare the supreme authority of the Word of God, realizing that it is our inescapable duty and privilege to renew unconditional obedience to him under any form of human government. Some governments may give us more "freedom" than others. But we have to consider the nature of that "freedom" and the price we are supposed to pay for it. For example, some Latin American dictators have been friendly to evangelicals, but the price has been our silence on social issues.

Dictatorships are always bad for the people. It does not matter whether the dictator belongs to the left or to the right. The dictator is always against freedom and paralyzes the growth of genuine democracy. There is a great deal of talk about democracy all over the world. Dictators of the political right and dictators of the political left claim to be building "democracy" in their countries. Etymologically, *democracy* means that the people are preeminent in the government of the state. But as the highly respected Mexican writer and poet Octavio Paz has said: "Democracy without freedom is the tyranny of the majority."[23]

The concept of human dignity and the idea of freedom come from the Scriptures. A theology that sacrifices these biblical ideas and ideals on the altar of a political idol does not deserve to be called a theology of freedom but a theology of human slavery and dehumanization.

We are commanded by the Scriptures to obey human governments (Rom. 13:1-8; Titus 3:1; 1 Pet. 2 17). On the other hand we are also taught by the Bible that the authority of the rulers of this world comes from God (Dan. 2:21; John 19:10-11). This authority is not absolute but relative. The Scripture does not deify the emperor. Only God is sovereign, the supreme ruler of the world and history. King of kings and Lord of lords, today and forever. This teaching has to transpire in our theology and in our Christian experience as citizens of two worlds.

We are not called to do a rightist theology or a leftist one, but a biblical and contextualized theology in response to the needs of the individual and to the challenges of our society. This theology has to be faithful to God's written revelation. It has to be concerned for the spiritual, physical, and material well-being of the people. It has to evaluate both the political left and the political right in the light of the Scriptures. It has to be critical of those theologies that are serving the purposes of a political system instead of submitting themselves to the authority of the Word of God.

It is not easy to do such theology in the midst of revolutionary passion and political turmoil. We should have done it years ago. Theological liberationism is now offering to fill the void that the preconciliar Catholic church and traditional evangelical hermeneutics had left in Latin American Christianity. Unfortunately, liberation theology is in subjection to a social-political ideology. But from a Latin American evangelical perspective, the problem with this system of thought is not only ideological but theological as well.

Church and society in Latin America. On the Protestant side there also have been some attempts to formulate a contextualized theology for Latin America. The best-known movement dealing with social issues from a sociological and theological perspective, apart from an evangelical approach to the Scriptures, is *Church and Society in Latin America* (Iglesia y Sociedad en America Latina, ISAL).

Thirty years ago a group of Protestant intellectuals were already making in South America a serious effort to analyze sociologically our Latin American reality in the name of Christianity. From social analysis they moved themselves into theological reflection. Under their leadership the theological movement known as Iglesia y Sociedad en América Latina was born, sponsored by the World Council of Churches. As an ecumenical organization, ISAL was open to the exchange of ideas with some Catholic theologians even before the Second Vatican Council was held (1962-1965). Vatican II decided in favor of the official participation of the Roman Catholic church in the ecumenical cause. Orlando Costas, a

Latin American theologian, has said that ISAL was "the most consistent-ly radical Protestant ecumenical organization in Latin America."[24]

In regard to a solution to the social problem, the ISAL leaders gave some consideration at the beginning to the idea of development, or social evolution; but afterwards they opted for a socialist revolution.[25]

ISAL became a radical leftist movement, isolated from the church-es. For all practical purposes, the Isaline leaders lost their Protestant identity. In 1966 they came to the conclusion that it was necessary to go from dialogue to direct participation in the revolutionary struggle.[26] In other words, they decided to be revolutionaries under the leading star of radical socialism. Because of their strong ideological commitment, they continued to separate themselves from the larger sector of Latin American Protestantism. In 1969, an evangelical leader from Argentina said that "ISAL was a group of generals without an army and the Latin American evangelical community an army without generals" because of the ecclesiastical isolation of the Isaline movement and the lack of evangelical leadership in the Latin American theological arena.

The Church and Society leaders were aware of the isolation into which they had fallen and decided to change their strategy. In 1967 they realized that it was necessary to infiltrate the churches in order to in-doctrinate and mobilize people for revolutionary action. In 1971 the churches were the first target of the Isaline strategy. It was obvious that "a change of the old ecclesiastical structures" was necessary if the churches were going to cooperate in the struggle for social change.

The ISAL movement had turned furiously radical in its ideological commitment to the left; but at the fall and death of President Salvador Allende in Chile, the group had to disband and reorganize, losing much of its cohesion and strength. Nevertheless, ISAL has a place in the his-tory of Latin American theology.

A theological journal (Cristianismo y Sociedad) and several books were published in the 1960s and early 1970s. The Isaline message did not descend to the level of the vast majority of evangelical pastors, much less to the people in the pews. But it was influential in the lives of some young evangelical leaders who could never be the same again once they had been exposed to the challenge of this revolutionary theology.

The Isaline influence was deeply felt at the World Conference on Church and Society, held in Geneva in July 1966 under the auspices of the World Council of Churches. On that occasion the ecumenical move-ment gave more emphasis than ever to direct action for radical social change. It was taken for granted that the church should become involved in contemporary revolutionary movements, including the possibility of

Christian participation in violent revolution to overthrow unjust regimes.

I have also suggested that ISAL participated in the origins of Roman Catholic liberation theology. According to Hugo Assmann and other Catholic writers, Protestant theologians like the Brazilian Presbyterian Ruben Alves made a significant contribution in the formative years of this system of thought.[27] Alves was deeply involved in the Isaline movement. Some of the fundamental ideas of ISAL are still heard in the theology of liberation.

As an effort to formulate a theology that would be relevant to our Latin American reality, ISAL has stimulated us Protestants to read the Scriptures anew in order to find what the Lord would have to say to us regarding our social problems. We have also to recognize that more than a few of ISAL's criticisms of the church are valid, and it is our duty to respond to those criticisms, making the necessary changes in the fulfillment of our mission.

On the other hand ISAL is a solemn warning concerning the danger of subjecting the gospel to an ideology in the effort of theological contextualization.[28] ISAL has serious problems in its theology and praxis. The hermeneutical criteria are not found in the Word of God but in human reflection and in historical events. Biblical interpretation is left at the mercy of historical changes and subjectivism. In a sense, Marxism becomes the criterion for the interpretation of the Scriptures. In regard to personal freedom, the leaders of ISAL came to the point of making a distinction between bourgeois freedom and socialist freedom. The traditional view of the individual rights of the intellectuals is rejected. Freedom has to be conceived of in terms of socialist progress.[29] It is suggested that on the political plane only the Marxist option is valid for the Christian. Intellectual suicide seems to be demanded on behalf of socialism.

The Challenge to Contextualize the Gospel
Comes from Missionary Expansion

Up to recent times, Western theologians were the best-known representatives of evangelical missionary thought. The theology of mission used to come from the North Atlantic world. This situation is changing. A few years ago, a distinguished American theologian said that in the near future some of the leading voices in evangelical theology may come from Africa, Asia, and Latin America as a result of the vitality of the church in the Third World. He added that the emerging of this new leadership in evangelical theology should not be surprising if we remember that in the early centuries of Christianity there were outstanding theologians like Origen, Tertullian, and Augustine in North Africa.

There is in fact a Latin American evangelical theology in the making. This theological activity is not surprising, for the concern about doing a regional and relevant theology is found all over the Third World. There is an interaction between theology and mission. The missionary movement is in many respects the outcome of theology; but this movement exercises a great influence on theology, and produces theology. Some of the most important theological issues in our day come from the world of missions.

One of the purposes of Third World seminaries has always been to produce at least some graduates proficient in theology. The number of well-educated Third World theologians is constantly growing, and there are now more opportunities than ever for non-Western theologians to express themselves on exceedingly important doctrinal issues in congresses and consultations sponsored by the worldwide evangelical community. Even the "nationals" from underdeveloped countries are no longer reduced to playing the role of "exhibit one" (an African), "exhibit two" (an Asian), and "exhibit three" (a Latin American) in some of the missionary conferences held in the West.

Third World theologians have started to contribute in a significant way to theological reflection at the international level. Their theological and missiological thought is evident in documents like the Lausanne Covenant (1974), one of the most important declarations of twentieth-century evangelicalism. Professor Samuel Escobar, honorary chairman of the Latin American Fraternity and a very well-known theologian from Peru was a member of the drafting committee.

The opportunity to do theology in fellowship with evangelical leaders from all over the world is a serious responsibility that our Latin American theologians must assume with a deep sense of humility and dedication to their task.

It is encouraging to see the beginnings of an evangelical theological movement in Latin America. We have to clarify, of course, that the interest in doing a regional and relevant theology is not necessarily the natural or spontaneous outcome of church growth in our countries. The Latin American church is one of the fastest-growing evangelical communities in the world. However, the vast majority of our churches or congregations have not been interested in theological reflection, much less in doing a Latin American theology. We are grateful to our missionary pioneers and their disciples for the theology they taught us to memorize and communicate; but they did not encourage us to be creative in our theologizing in order to meet the needs of our social context.

The challenge to contextualize the gospel is unavoidable. It comes from the Scripture itself, from our cultural identity, from our complex social problems, from a growing church confronted by a revolutionary situation, from a new generation of evangelical leaders who are aware of the social implications of the gospel.

LATIN AMERICAN EVANGELICALISM AND CONTEXTUALIZATION

The Latin American challenge is not an insignificant one. It has produced a theological turbulence around the world. And it seems to be destined to continue exercising a considerable influence on Christianity for many years to come. Furthermore, the theological commotion does not come just from Latin America; it is shaking the Two-Thirds World. Christian thought has not been the same since the day when the people in the underdeveloped countries started to express themselves on theological issues in response to their own social problems. The time has come when the ones who were voiceless are speaking freely and loudly. We cannot afford to close our ears to their message. We have to respond to their challenge. Shall we try to answer this challenge by communicating our evangelical theology the same way we have been doing it through so many years, or shall we try to do a biblical and contextualized theology in Latin America for Latin Americans?

Traditional Evangelical Theology in Latin America

Generally speaking, most of our theology has come from Anglo-Saxon missionaries in the nineteenth and twentieth centuries. It is not surprising that this theology does not deal with our particular social problems. And we have no right to expect European and North American theologians to deal specifically with these problems. They were doing theology for their own social context. They were speaking to their own generation in their own cultural milieu. It is possible that they did not imagine that some of their writings or books would be translated into Spanish. They may not have imagined that Latin American students would read those works in English. We are grateful for what we have learned from the theology produced in other latitudes, in other segments of world Christianity. We exist as an evangelical church in Latin America because of our theological heritage. And we cannot abandon this doctrinal treasure without losing our own identity. Personally, I am grateful to my teachers, both in Central America and in the United States, for the training they gave me in the Word of God for the ministry. To a large extent it is because of that solid and basic training that I have been able to continue doing theological research and participating in several theological events without losing my evangelical identity. I praise the Lord for my teachers and for the theological books written by theologians in other parts of the world. This theology belongs to the doctrinal treasure of the universal church. And the theologians who faithfully communicate the sacred deposit of the written Word of God are a gift of the Holy Spirit to build up the church.

On the other hand we have to admit that after more than one hundred years of evangelical presence in Latin America we have limited ourselves to translating theology instead of doing theology. An Argentinian theologian has said that we have been no more than a distribution center of foreign theology. According to our critics, this theology is individualistic, dualistic, futuristic, and pessimistic.

They say that our evangelical theology is individualistic because it is not really concerned about society and the relationship of the individual Christian with his or her social context. They see our theology as a creature of American individualism. In answer to this criticism we have to realize that the Scriptures see the human being as an individual and as a member of society. But in the past many of us Latin American evangelicals were not led to attain the biblical balance in our theological reflection. We were not aware of our social responsibility. Our tendency was to make a distinction between civic and spiritual life. Even today the participation of Christians as candidates for public office is considered sinful by some evangelical leaders in Latin America. They have their own reasons for opposing political involvement on the part of Christians. The problem is that we may go now to the other extreme in our desire to escape from our excessive individualism. Once again we may lose the biblical balance in our theology.

Our critics affirm that our evangelical theology is dualistic because it makes a deep and wide separation between soul and body, in a neoplatonic fashion. The result of this dichotomy, they say, is an overemphasis on that which is spiritual and a lack of concern for the physical and material needs of humanity. This theological dualism determines to a large extent our concept of Christian mission. If we are interested only in spiritual and eternal salvation, then we do not include social responsibility in the mission of the church. We are just concerned for the eternal destiny of humanity. But, on the other hand, we may overemphasize physical and material needs, losing the balance in our soteriological message.

By a futuristic theology our critics mean the tendency to jump over the present to the future, in a sort of escapism from the problems confronting society. In their opinion this theology is also pessimistic because the emphasis is on the future destruction of the world and because the critics are given to understand that in this theology there is no need to worry about social evils. These evils may be mentioned in the pulpit as an evidence of human sinfulness or as a sign of the impending judgment of God over the world, but not as a challenge to assume our social responsibility.

These criticisms are another reason to do evangelical theology in Latin America. But more important than answering the arguments of our critics is the recuperation of the biblical balance in our missionary theology and praxis. There are in the Scriptures some elements that we need to emphasize more than ever in Latin America—for example, the teaching in both Testaments on the unity and dignity of humanity, the important place of the human body in the plan of redemption; the humanity of Christ and his ministry to people in physical and material need; the New Testament teaching on good works; the example of the first-century church in the area of social responsibility; the social implications of the gospel in relation to the dignity of woman, the nature and purpose of human government, and our Christian behavior as members of the civil community; the biblical concept of labor and social justice; peace as the result of the practice of justice; love as the key word in our human relations; the present lordship of Christ over creation and history; his final triumph over the forces of evil in this world; the cosmic renovation as the final chapter in his redemptive program on earth.

More biblical and theological work is needed at the local church level to deal with the subject of social responsibility on the basis of the Scriptures. Many evangelical leaders in Latin America have not yet read documents like the Lausanne Covenant and the Grand Rapids Declaration on Evangelism and Social Responsibility. They have not had the opportunity to reflect on the social implications of the gospel. No wonder that they are taken by surprise by the idea that the mission of the church includes much more than the public communication of the gospel in a big evangelistic campaign or the use of personal testimony to win people for Christ.

In the area of biblical and systematic theology we are grateful for those theologians whose works have been translated into Spanish. More translation has to be done. But this literature has to be complemented by the one produced in Latin America from a Latin American perspective. For example, we need a Christology written on the basis of the Word of God, in interaction with the Christological thought of the universal church, in the light of our history and culture, in a serious dialogue with the Christologies recently produced in Latin America, in response to the questions, longings, and hope of our own people.

It is possible to say the same in regard to ecclesiology and other subjects of systematic theology. The theological volumes written outside Latin America, or the ones produced in Latin America but from a perspective that is not Latin American, are of a great value for us, but they have to be complemented by a biblical theology contextualized in our reality.

And contextualize means much more than doing exegesis of the biblical text and working hard on the ancient culture and languages of the biblical world. Sound exegesis is exceedingly important and indispensable for doing biblical theology. We can be outstanding exegetes in Chicago, New Delhi, Singapore, Nairobi, Mexico City, or somewhere else without being relevant to the social situation in which we are interpreting the biblical text. We can be living in a foreign country without really getting related to the culture of the people. In our hermeneutics we would not be able to address ourselves to the particular problems of the social context. We would be dealing with the culture of the Assyrians of the eighth century B.C., or with the culture of the Romans and Greeks of the first century of the Christian era, or perhaps with American culture; but in regard to our Latin American reality we would be doing exegesis in a social vacuum, isolated from our contemporaries.

Contemporary Evangelical Theology in Latin America

The Latin American Theological Fraternity. It was not until the First Continental Congress on Evangelization, Bogotá, Colombia, November 1969, that I came to know more about the movement called Church and Society in Latin America. I had to realize that I knew very little about contemporary Latin American theology. I was not the only one to be concerned about the new theological developments in Central and South America. In that congress Peter Wagner's book *Latin American Theology* was circulated. I was deeply impressed when I read in that book that in a bibliographical work published in the United States there was not a single entry of a theological work written by a Latin American conservative evangelical. This meant that there were no Latin American theologians articulating their faith by writing on the academic level as an expression of conservative evangelicalism in Latin America.

A small group of evangelicals got together in one of the hotels of Bogota and decided to take the necessary steps to start a theological fraternity. In November 1970 the Latin American Theological Fraternity (LATF) was born in Cochabamba, Bolivia. The Fraternity is not an association of churches but of individuals. Nor is it an association of theological institutions. It is international and nondenominational. Among the members of LATF, Samuel Escobar, G. Rene Padilla, Orlando E. Costas (who went to be with the Lord November 6, 1987), and Andrew Kirk have also become widely known in the English-speaking Christian community through their publication in English.

The nature of the Fraternity gives us a great deal of freedom for theological reflection under the authority of the Scriptures. A variety of Protestant traditions are represented. The purpose of this association is to reflect on God's written revelation in response to the needs of the Latin American people. We want to be in dialogue with our own history, with the church, with the social context. Up to now the Fraternity has published several books and booklets and several issues of a theological bulletin, both in Spanish and English.

The Latin American Theological Fraternity has provided an interdenominational and international forum in which conservative evangelicals feel free to express themselves at a continental level, apart from any compromising relationship that would hinder their ministries in the evangelical churches. To a large extent LATF has become known to the worldwide evangelical community. Doctoral dissertations have been written in the United States on this theological movement.

Of course, for some evangelical leaders LATF is under suspicion because on several occasions it has assumed a critical attitude in its evaluation of our evangelical reality. It is unavoidable for a theological movement like this, in a situation like ours, to sound negative, especially at the beginning. But criticism is necessary for a renewal of the church, as long as the motivation is right and the criticism is done in humility and love.

A general evaluation of the work done by LATF would indicate that not very much has been achieved in the area of Bible exegesis; but the ground is prepared for a young generation of exegetes who will wrestle with the Latin American problems in the light of the biblical text. I dream of the day when a Bible commentary written in Latin America for Latin America will be published. We also need a systematic theology deeply grounded in the Scriptures, but written with our Latin American reality in view.

It is evident that LATF has been trying to help Latin American evangelicals recuperate in their faith and praxis the social dimension of the gospel. Some of the members of the Fraternity have contributed in a significant way to the formulation of a theology of mission on the basis of the Scriptures and in response to the Latin American context, church and state. Theological education and different aspects of the pastoral ministry, including evangelization, church growth, youth work, the family, and counseling, have been the subjects of serious study in consultations held at the regional and continental levels.

Theological education. To a large extent the answer to the need for Latin American biblical theology is in theological education. A great deal depends on our seminaries, Bible schools, short-term institutes, and extension programs. It is there, especially at the seminary level, where we see the difference between limiting ourselves to the transmission of theology, usually a translated theology, and leading our students to become interested in doing biblical and contextualized theology.

Because of the diversity of gifts and vocations in our student body and because we have to do the best we can to give our students the opportunity to develop their gifts and follow their vocations in life, a diversification is necessary in our academic program. The straitjacket curriculum does not take into consideration the variety of gifts and vocations. Several seminaries and Bible schools have only one curriculum for all the students. The reasons for this situation have to do with our underdevelopment—usually we do not have the human and financial resources to diversify the program. But there is also another reason—tradition. This is the way we have done it, and this is the way we are supposed to do it. This conservatism in theological education has also to do with our tendency to imitate, to be a Xerox copy of, seminaries and Bible schools abroad. But there is a great different between the United States and El Salvador, or Bolivia, or whatever other underdeveloped country in Latin America.

Nevertheless, we can do something with the limited resources we have to help those students who are inclined to doing theology in Latin America for Latin America.

To train servant leaders who will do evangelical theology in Latin America for Latin America we need material resources—a good library is indispensable. But many of our evangelical institutions do not have respectable libraries, from the standpoint of the First World. However, we can still be interested in discovering theological vocations in our student body and encouraging these vocations for the benefit of the church in Latin America.

The most important elements in a theological school are the teachers and the students. The building may be impressive in the eyes of the visitor, but what makes the institution is people—students, teachers, and staff.

For the task of doing theology we need students with a theological mentality. I am not speaking of IQ necessarily. I used to tell my students that I do not believe the student in the department of theology is necessarily more intelligent than the one who prefers the department of practical theology (pastoral ministries, evangelism, and missions). It is a matter of mentality, and most of all it is a matter of gifts of the Holy Spirit. Whatever our call may be in the ministry, we need a good portion of brains to succeed, for the glory of God and for the benefit of the people.

Definitely, to do theology in Latin America we need some students with theological mentality. And the more training these students have in the secular sciences, especially in the so-called human sciences, the better.

To do evangelical theology we need students who are born again by the power of the Holy Spirit, students who have seen in Christ the Light of the World, students who have received the eternal life in him—newborn Christians, deeply committed to the Lord and his work; newborn Christians, deeply committed to their own people. The heart of the genuine Christian theologian is evangelistic and pastoral. To do an authentic evangelical theology for Latin America it is indispensable to love Latin Americans. Only genuine Christian love gets to the minds and to the hearts of the people. If we love Latin Americans we want to know them better—their history, their culture, their psychology, their way of life. If we love Latin Americans we will suffer and rejoice with them, we will feel that we belong to them, and humanly speaking we will feel proud of our Latin American identity. We will respect and admire other cultures without despising our own. We will pray and cry for our people, for their salvation in Christ. Then we will want to do theology with them and for them, a theology that will come out of our own hearts, not just from our minds.

To do theology we need students with a theological mentality and with evangelistic and pastoral hearts. If these students are going to make a serious contribution to our Latin American theology, sooner or later they may go for further studies abroad. But they will go because they are committed to serving their own people. They will go knowing what they want to do, having a purpose in their hearts. Their purpose will not be to improve their own image, to attain a better position in life, to receive the glory of this world. The splendor of an affluent society in North America or Europe will not fascinate them and cause them to stay there. They will not surrender themselves to the temptation of abandoning their own people to live somewhere else. I am not saying that the Holy Spirit cannot call leaders from the Two-Thirds World to serve in the First World. What I am saying is that to do evangelical theology for Latin America or for the Two-Thirds World we have to be identified, closely identified, with our own people, suffering with them, rejoicing with them. Otherwise our theology would be foreign to them. To send them our theology by mail is not enough. We have to do our theology among them, with them, for them.

In a 1985 consultation on new alternatives in theological education sponsored by the Latin American Theological Fraternity in Quito, Ecuador, we came to the conclusion that theologians should start their training at the local church level. They have to learn to love the church. Otherwise they may go to the extreme of doing theology in total isolation from the people of God. Actually, in most cases students should complete their basic theological training in their home country before going abroad for other degrees. Noncontextualized theologians produce a noncontextualized theology.

Praise the Lord for the new generation of theologians that is coming up in Latin America. Praise the Lord for the young theologians who have gone abroad to study and have come back to us. May the Lord strengthen them in their vocation to serve him and their people.

Now, what about the teachers? We need Latin American professors of theology, and we need professors from other cultures.

I take seriously the New Testament teaching on the Body of Christ. The church is universal. The church is one, and the Holy Spirit is providing his gifts for the edification of the church around the world. More than ever we need fellowship and cooperation at the international level. The world is becoming smaller because of the modern means of communication. We are closer to each other than in the past. We can say that almost everybody is our neighbor in the geographical sense. When I was president of the seminary in Guatemala City I had a dream. I was daydreaming about the time when we would have in our seminary not only professors from Latin and North America, but also professors from other continents, from other cultures.

The day for foreign missions has not come to an end. It is starting with a new dimension, with a renewed vision. In Latin America we are experiencing an awakening of our interest in the worldwide mission of the church. A large congress on missions was held in Sao Paulo, Brazil, in November 1987 to promote the involvement of the Latin American church in foreign missions. In our seminary in Guatemala we have sponsored two major missionary conferences in the last six years. The positive results of these conferences are evident. There is now a missionary agency in Guatemala to recruit, train, send, and support transcultural missionaries. There are missionary agencies in other Latin American countries. In other words, before the end of the twentieth century a significant number of Latin American missionaries may go to other cultures, to other continents. The day of foreign missions is starting with a new dimension, the Third-World dimension, the Latin American dimension. But if we are planning to send missionaries, this means we are willing, and in some cases eager, to receive missionaries.

We need in Latin America professors in the different areas of the biblical and theological sciences. Of course, there are special requirements for the expatriate missionary who is going as a teacher to Latin America. Some of the requirements are those that are applicable to the student of theology. For instance, the missionary has to be a born-again Christian; he or must have mature, deep, evangelical convictions; she or he must be willing to live among the people, to work with the people and for the people. He or she has to come to the point of loving the people. She or he will want to know more about the people: their history, their culture, their social problems, their longings, and their hopes. He or she will have a high view of culture, but his or her view of Scripture will be higher than his or her concept of culture. She or he will know that in any culture the people are able to detect our pride—and to feel our love for them.

The new generation of expatriate missionaries has, generally speaking, more training than many of the missionaries in the past. This is excellent. But the new missionaries have to be more open than their predecessors to learning from the people on the field. The relationship between expatriate missionary and national brothers and sisters is changing dramatically. The romantic view of missions is fading away, especially in our urban centers. The foreign missionary stands or falls on her or his own merits or demerits. The missionary has to demonstrate that he or she is willing and able to work, or as some people say, to perform. I can assure you that in Central America most evangelicals are open to receiving foreign missionaries and to giving them the opportunity to work.

But the missionary of this last part of the twentieth century has to be willing to listen, to pay attention to what the nationals have to say. One of the major problems is precisely the natural difficulty the average North American leader has in taking seriously the suggestions given by a national leader, unless the suggestions are in harmony with the missionary's way of thinking.

There are books on how to succeed as a public speaker; all of us need to read a book on how to be a good listener in private and in public—how to listen to the Lord and how to listen to our fellow human beings or to our colleagues.

The professor of theology in this new era of missions in Latin America has to communciate knowledge and lead his or her students on the path to doing theology on the basis of the Word of God in response to their own culture. To do this the missionary has to be much more than a technician who is there for just a short while teaching an intensive course to a group of students. We need visiting professors, but we also need permanent professors. Short-term missionaries are welcome; but for this task of doing theology we need longterm missionaries, men and women who would be willing to spend their lives, if necessary, in this ministry.

With regard to evangelical seminaries in the United States, I would like to say that their educational programs as well have to be Third-World oriented. Because these seminaries are deeply involved in training missionaries for the Third World, their programs of study have to take into serious consideration contemporary theological trends in the Two-Thirds World.

Problems. As in any other region of the world, we are confronted by many problems on the road toward a contextualized theology. One of these problems is the lack of financial resources to strengthen the faculty in our theological institutions with personnel qualified to teach at a high academic level. We also need more funds to enlarge our libraries, to give scholarships to needy students, to help our professors continue their training in their own fields of specialization, and to give them time and financial assistance for research and writing.

Most of our Latin leaders who are good writers do not have time for the Christian literature ministry. They are always too busy teaching, preaching, pastoring, and attending board meetings, consultations, or congresses at home and abroad.

Another problem is that the market for theological works is very limited in the Spanish-speaking world. Most of the pastors are not trained to read this kind of literature. Consequently, bookstore managers do not order books that their average customer would not buy. The increase in the costs of production complicates the problem. The vast majority of our leaders cannot afford to buy an expensive theological book.

Moreover, evangelicals in general have not been enthusiastic about theology. They prefer emotion and action to reflection. They are looking for activists who would be able to get immediate and measurable results. Evangelical pragmatism and "functionalism" exist. The obsession for numerical growth seems also to be invading the field of theological education. We are asked to train activists. Very few people are conscious of the need for training people who have a theological vocation.

The charismatic movement and its overemphasis on the emotional aspect of the Christian life may not encourage people to think theologically. If in the numerical-growth movement there is the danger of overemphasizing action, in the charismatic movement passion may substitute for reflection. We need, of course, balance in our Christian lives and ministries. Intelletual achievement is not enough. Theology also has to be a matter of the heart. And theology has to lead us into action.

We have to recognize that one of the biggest problems on the road of contexualization has been our traditional Latin American evangelical mentality. We have been afraid of exploring new territory, of abandoning the safety that we feel in the theology we have received from other latitudes. We have been reluctant to take a good look at our own social context and then do theology in interaction with the questions and longings of the Latin American people. But as has been suggested in this book, there is certainly an evangelical Latin American theology in the making. Theologians like C. René Padilla, Samuel Escobar, Orlando E. Costas, and others have made a significant contribution to the advancement of contextualized theology at the worldwide level. And a new generation of young theologians is coming up in our subcontinent. It is possible to hope for better times in regard to an evangelical biblical theology written in Latin America for Latin America, written to the glory of God, and written for the benefit of his people in this area of the world.

NOTES

1. As quoted by Mortimer Arias in "Contextual Evangelization in Latin America: Between Accommodation and Confrontation," *Occasional Bulletin,* January 1978, pp. 19-28.

2. John L. Nevius, *Planting and Development of Missionary Churches,* 4th ed. (Philadelphia: Presbyterian & Reformed, 1958).

3. *The Willowbank Repott on Gospel and Culture.* Consultation held at Willowbank, Somerset Bridge, Bermuda, January 6-13, 1978, sponsored by the Lausanne Theology and Education Group. P. 23.

4. Peter Savage, "Discipleship in Context: The Challenge of 'Contextualization.'" Mimeographed material.

5. H. Richard Niebuhr, *Christ and Culture* (New York: Harper Torchbooks, 1951).

6. Ibid., p. 128.

7. Ibid., p. 256.

8. Savage, "Discipleship in Context." Louis I. Luzbetak, *The Church and Cultures* (Techny, IL: Divine Word Publications, 1963), as quoted by Savage.

9. Savage.

10. Ibid.

11. Ibid.

12. Ibid. See also Charles H. Kraft, *Christianity in Culture* (Maryknoll, NY: Orbis, 1980).

13. Bruce C. G. Fleming, *Contextualization of Theology: An Evangelical Assessment* (Pasadena, CA: William Carey Library, 1980), p. 4.

14. *Ministry in Context* (Bromley, Kent, England: New Life Press, 1972). The Theological Education Fund is sponsored by the World Council of Churches.

15. Arias, "Contextual Evangelization."

16. Bong Rin Ro, mimeographed material.

17. Paul G. Hiebert, "Critical Contextualization," *International Bulletin of Missionary Research*, July 1987.

18. Fleming, p. 53.

19. Ibid., p. 78.

20. *Willowbank Report*, p. 11.

21. Ibid.

22. Pablo Freire uses this term to describe the traditional educational approach, as opposed to the concept he endorses—that education is "conscientization." *Pedagogy of the Oppressed*, trans. Myra Bergman Ramos (New York: Seabury, 1970).

23. "Entrevista con Octavio Paz," *Gente y Actualidad*, Buenos Aires, November 1981.

24. Orlando E. Costas, *Theology of the Crossroads in Contemporary Latin America* (Amsterdam: Rodopi, 1976), p. 199.

25. José Míguez Bonino, *Doing Theology in a Revolutionary Situation* (Philadelphia: Fortress, 1975), pp.54-55.

26. "Documents from the Second Latin American Consultation on Church and Society," *América Hoy* (Montevideo, Uruguay: ISAL, 1966).

27. Hugo Assmann, *Opresión-Liberación: Desafío a los Cristianos* (Montevideo: Tierra Nueva, 1971), p. 79ff. Roberto Oliveros Maqueo, *Liberación y Teología* (Mexico: Centro de Reflexión Teológica, 1977), pp. 155-75.

28. José Míguez Bonino, "Visión del Cambio Social y sus Tareas desde las Iglesias Cristianas No-Católicas," *Fe Cristiana y Cambio Social en América Latina* (Salamanca, Spain: 1973), pp.201-2.

29. *América Latina: Movilización Popular y Fe Cristiana* (Montevideo: ISAL, 1971), p. 160.

12

Latin American Evangelicals and Social Responsibility: A Case Study

This chapter, when originally written as an article, was titled "Protestantism and Guatemala's Social-Historical Development." Was that title a good one? In order to be able to address a variety of topics, while at the same time avoiding sweeping generalizations on a potentially controversial subject, it probably would be better to recast that original title in the form of a question to begin this discussion: Has Protestantism had an influence in the social-historical development of Guatemala?[1]

The phrase "historical development" immediately defines history not as the mere chronicle of past events but as a process that begins in the past and unfolds in the present, producing changes in the social scene along the way. There is a history that is past, and there is a history that is in the process of development—although some scholars maintain that, strictly speaking, history does not exist until it has been written.

As to whether or not Protestantism has had an influence in Guatemala's history, it should be kept in mind that there is a difference between recounting history and living it, between having a history and "making history," be that at a regional, national, or international level. Although both individuals and institutions have their own histories, not all of them participate in the shaping of history: not all of them par-

372

ticipate in directing the historical process of their own peoples or nations. That is, in one way or another we all are carried along in the current of history, but only a few have succeeded in changing its course. But even though one's personal history be ever so insignificant, it is nevertheless unavoidably a part of what one's country has written over the centuries. We are committed to the historical process: history belongs to us, and we to it.

Has the Protestant sector had an influence on the unfolding drama of Guatemala's history? While some would respond to that question in the negative, alleging that Protestants have separated themselves from the socio-political currents of their own nation, and others would say that Protestantism is at least partly responsible for the spread of neo-colonialism in Guatemala, many Protestant leaders would claim that the movement has had a moral and spiritual influence in the country's history, mentioning as well a number of purely social programs that have been carried out under Protestant aegis. These three viewpoints provide the outline for this chapter, which is to be considered only a beginning point in the examination of the question at hand.

PROTESTANT DETACHMENT

A great deal has been said and written over the last decade about the isolation that has characterized Latin American Protestants vis-a-vis the deep socio-economic problems of the area. For example, in his analysis of Chilean Pentecostalism in the years 1965-1966, Christian Lalive D'Epinay discovered, among other things, that the majority of pastors believed that the gospel should not be mixed with politics and that the Protestant church should not concern itself with the socio-political problems of the country, to the point of not even talking about them.

Pentecostal thinking reflects a polarization between the spiritual and the material, the church and the world, Christ and society. Pentecostalism rejects the present world in order to enjoy the anticipation of the future one.[2]

In general, accusations of Protestant detachment would not be entirely without support in Guatemala as well. In his book *Cien Años de Presencia Protestante en Centroamerica (One Hundred Years of Protestant Presence in Central America)*, sociologist-economist Domingo Alcántara Matos argues that Guatemalan Protestantism is a closed society, cut off from social reality.[3]

In a study done for the Institute of Latin American Studies of the University of Texas, Bryan Roberts, a sociologist at the University of

374 CRISIS AND HOPE IN LATIN AMERICA

Manchester, researched two areas of Guatemala City, one of them a poor squatter settlement, the other one a middle-class area. Roberts wanted to study the manner in which Protestants resolved the problems of city living.

The total sampling consisted of sixty-four families in the middle-class area, of which thirteen were Protestant, and one hundred two in the poor area, of which twenty were Protestant. The study seems to be rather narrowly based, however, because there are over four hundred different Protestant churches in Guatemala City. Further, although Roberts obviously focused his research more on the Pentecostal sector than on any other Protestant group, he believes that "the features as described bear a marked similarity to the great majority of the denominations represented in the two colonies."[4]

According to Roberts, when the economic picture provides little hope of improvement, the Protestant approach to life "can lead to an emphasis on spiritual well-being at the expense of concern in the material affairs of the individual."[5] At the end of his study, he states:

> As a consequence, Protestantism in this city, instead of being a faith which helps the individual to dominate the urban environment which surrounds him, has assumed the social characteristics of a faith which isolates the individual from that environment. Although this statement most accurately describes the more fundamentalist groups of both colonies, it is also applicable to the majority of the Protestants that live in the two areas.[6]

It has also been pointed out that as a result of the social mobility sought by Protestants, many of them have moved into the middle class, which, according to some sociologists, is characterized by its resistance to changes in the structure of society and by its ambition to emulate the life-style of the oligarchy.[7] Contrary to the predictions of those who expected that the middle class would become an instigator of fundamental changes in Latin America, it has assumed instead a very conservative posture.

Our point of view, as expressed elsewhere already, is that we Protestants, while recognizing the various senses of the word *world* in the New Testament, have not translated those differences into daily life.[8] In emphasizing the antithesis of church versus world, we have chosen a position of deep and apparently irreconcilable antagonism between Christ and society, between Christ and culture.[9] We have perhaps not yet experienced the death agony of which Unamuno writes: "But Christianity—Protestant Christianity—has nothing to do with civilization. Nor with culture.... And thus, since it is impossible for Christianity to live without culture, here lies the agony of Christianity."[10] That struggle, or tension, is the one occasioned by being in the world but not of the world (John 17).

If, therefore, for whatever reasons, the tendency of the Protestants has been to isolate themselves from socio-economic problems, could it be expected that they would have had any significant influence in the social-historical development of Guatemala? The above data would suggest a negative response to that question, especially if what is in focus is the sort of radical change that is being demanded on behalf of Latin American society today. Hence, it is possible to conclude that, because of his absence from the political scene, the Protestant Christian could well have contributed, consciously or unconsciously, to the maintenance of a given socio-economic system.

It is no secret that, because of an extreme apolitical posture, the average Protestant has not properly questioned the established order. Nevertheless, there are other replies to the question regarding the part Protestantism may have played in Guatemala's historical process, and they, along with other aspects of the Protestant phenomenon, merit consideration as well.

PROTESTANTISM AND IMPERIALISM

There has never been a lack of those who claim that, in Guatemala, Protestantism has been the handmaiden of Anglo-Saxon capitalism. Just as the alliance of religion with arms in the Spanish conquest is reflected in the well-known phrase *"la cruz y el arcabuz"* ("the cross and the musket"), so have the terms *Protestant missions* and *imperialist expansionism* come to be closely linked with each other. Alcántara Matos suggests that Central American Protestantism has played the role of creating the "subjective conditions" for the establishment and dominance of imperialism in these countries.[11] Denton states that "from time to time the accusation is heard that the Protestant movement is as much a part of the United States' imperialist offensive in Latin America as the C.I.A."[12]

Max Weber's thesis that Calvinistic Protestantism has been a major force in the development of capitalism is well known.[13] On the other hand, Andre Bieler argues that Weber's analysis is based on a Calvinism that had changed since its inception, and that "if Weber had studied sixteenth century Calvinism instead of that of the eighteenth century, he would have arrived at different conclusions."[14] Herbert M. Zorn points out that Christianity came to the vast majority of Third-World countries as a concomitant of the imperialisit movement—that the gospel was not brought there by a rejected and persecuted minority that confessed Christ in martyrdom, but rather by those who enjoyed the tacit or expressed approval of the dominant powers or of a nation of worldwide influence at that time.[15]

It is evident, of course, that the formal establishment of Protestant missions in Guatemala (1882-1916) coincides with an era of North American economic and military expansion. Nor can it be denied that beginning around the middle of the nineteenth century many North Americans enthusiastically embraced the idea that their country had been divinely predestined ("Manifest Destiny") to dominate all of North America and to extend its might and influence to other nations. They felt called to export their system of government and to assume control of certain regions, including Central America and the Caribbean, where they could develop the slave system. At least such was the dream of many who possessed extensive landholdings in the southern United States. The persistence of the expansionist spirit is demonstrated in its revival following the Civil War, sparked to a large degree by the abolition of slavery—a question that had deeply divided the North American people.[16]

It is equally undeniable that the mentality of the Protestant pioneers who had been sent from the United States to Guatemala was, generally speaking, formed by the ideals of traditional capitalism: they would have been classified at that time within the United States as political and religious conservatives. And it is only natural that they would be loyal citizens, proud of the North American system, convinced that these countries should follow the example of the Colossus of the North in order to overcome the state of underdevelopment in which they lived. It is altogether possible that, upon observing the contrast between the economic advancement of the United States and the underdevelopment of Central America, they should feel a great deal of admiration for North American democracy.

Whatever the case, inasmuch as the advance of Anglo-Saxon imperialism and the establishment of the Protestant church in Guatemala took place within the same time frame, it is imperative to examine if the Protestant pioneers were sent to this country by Anglo-Saxon expansionist forces in order to prepare the way for capitalism, or if they merely contributed indirectly to that expansionism. It is an intriguing question, but the present study is perforce limited to mentioning its importance

while offering some ideas that we hope will lead to a deeper understanding of the topic. For one thing, it must not be forgotten that the phenomenon of colonialism existed in this part of the world long before the
Protestant church was established in Guatemala. Jean-Loup Herbert
states it well when he observes that colonial expansion "began with the
Spanish, grew more intense under the English, and reached its culmination under the Americans."[17]

The Forerunners

Although history attests that the principal role in the establishment
of Protestantism in Guatemala was played by North Americans, the very
first Protestants on the scene were British subjects. For all we know,
there were no formal attempts to establish the Protestant church in Guatemala prior to independence (1821). During the period of the Spanish
colonies some individuals were accused of "Protestantism" or "Lu-
theranism" by the Inquisition, but as Chinchilla Aguilar notes:

> This does not mean, in any sense, that in the interior of
> Guatemala or of its wider provincial area there were nu-
> merous manifestations of Protestantism, or that Prot-
> estant nuclei were established in the area under the ju-
> risdictional control of its authorities. While there were
> some border contacts of a commercial nature, Prot-
> estantism did not realize any gains beyond what had al-
> ready been in place. That is to say that at the end of the
> eighteenth century, the situation had not appreciably
> changed from one of a few isolated cases which were
> easily controlled by the Inquisition.[18]

The "contacts" mentioned here were on the Atlantic coast, where there
were some British colonists.

An English Baptist by the name of Bourne came to Guatemalan territory in 1822, visiting the region of Lake Izabal in 1824. In the same
year, two businessmen from Belize visited Guatemala City in order to
study the possibilities of establishing a Protestant work there.[19]

For twelve months during 1827-1828 an Anglican priest, Henry
Dunn, lived in the capital, devoting himself to the distribution of Bibles,
Testaments, and other literature that he sold through various stores and
establishments of the city; but as he himself said, "It was quite obvious
that there was no demand for books of this sort."[20]

The next in the line of Protestant forerunners in Guatemala is Frederick Crowe, also a British subject, born in Belgium. Arriving in Guatemala City in 1843, Crowe was the first to establish a Protestant work here, though it was doomed from the outset by Roman Catholic intolerance. Crowe founded a school and shared his faith with many—including students from the National University and persons from the upper echelons of Guatemalan society. He even presented a Bible along with copies of other books of high spiritual value to President Carrera. But as a result of pressures brought to bear on the government by the ecclesiastical hierarchy, Crowe was expelled from Guatemala in 1846. Among other things, he was accused of pursuing "political" ends and of being in the service of English espionage. Although Crowe sought protection from his country's representative, the exasperated consul declined to give it to him, asking him impatiently to abandon the consulate.[21]

Any research regarding the claim that Protestant missions spearheaded the Anglo-Saxon Colonial cause in Guatemala must not ignore the case of Frederick Crowe.

As can be seen, Guatemala was practically closed to Protestantism until the triumph in 1871 of the reform movement led by Justo Rufino Barrios and Miguel García Granados. During the last century, the liberal reformation was second only to independence in degree of importance for Guatemala, though the Guatemalan writer Mario Monteforte Toledo ascribes it even higher status when he says, "Historically, in spite of all its limitations, deviations, and frustrations, liberalism was the most important political and socio-economic reform movement in Mesoamerica from the conquest until the nineteenth century."[22]

The Guatemalan Liberals

Moving further back in history to the early nineteenth century, we discover that one of the causes of the Latin American independence movements of that time was the intellectual ferment that had begun to appear on this side of the Atlantic. The ideas of such thinkers as Montesquieu, Locke, Rousseau, and Voltaire were hardly unknown in the Americas, and the successes of the French Revolution and North American independence provided impetus to the ideals of liberty that fanned the spirit of independence in the Spanish colonies.[23]

Without denying that the United States exercised some influence in the area, Monteforte Toledo insists that "the roots of nineteenth century Hispanic liberal thought must be sought in France," claiming that the antecedents of Central American liberalism are to be found in the activities of the Economic Society of the Friends of the Nation, founded in Guatemala toward the end of the eighteenth century.[24]

According to the memoirs *(Memorias)* of Miguel García Granados, even "the liberales—or those infected with independence fever—were determined to imitate the United States in the establishment of a federal system."[25] But the Central Americans were not alone. For example, Carlos Rangel observes that the Argentine constitution of 1853 "is copied so closely from that of the United States, that the Argentine judges are able to refer to North American jurisprudence for interpreting it."[26]

Alberto Rembao states:

> Following the winning of independence in our countries, the Hispano-American constitutional systems were little more than a carbon copy of the North American Protestant scheme of Philadelphia. After three centuries of European domination, the newly independent Spanish colonies had to look to others for models of government: they had neither developed their own, nor inherited one from a Spain that had no tradition of liberty to bequeath to its political offspring.[27]

The foregoing all suggests a close ideological relationship at that time between the Hispano-American liberals and the United States.

Upon gaining its independence under the guidance of a group of *criollos* (a racial term referring to the offspring of European immigrants with no admixture of New World native blood)[28] Central America was confronted with the serious problem of the lack of unity among its five states. In Guatemala, as in other Hispano-American republics, opinions became polarized between the conservatives and liberals, and from the days of the United Provinces of Central America (1823) until the days of Jorge Ubico (1931-1944), Guatemalan history abounds with accounts of the perennial conflict between these two socio-political groups.

In the last century the conservatives, whose leaders were generally *criollo* aristocrats, lent their support to the continuance of the extensive political privileges that the church enjoyed, while the liberals argued for a radical rupture with the past, demanding the separation of church and state. Monteforte Toledo comments:

> The most outstanding Liberal contributions were the separation of Church and State, and the abolition of the economic power of the Church as well as the practice of

holding vast tracts of land without putting them into production. No less important were the results of these
measures within the economic order: the establishment
of conditions which were intended to steer Me-
soamerican development towards modern capitalism.[29]

It requires little study to perceive that there was a certain affinity between the Guatemalan liberalism of the reform movement of the last
three decades of the nineteenth century and the North American system.
While the archconservatives Carrera and Cerna apparently were not
pleasing to Washington,[30] the North Americans must certainly have rejoiced in the triumph of the so-called revolution of 1871, knowing that its
leaders were in sympathy with the socio-political system of the United
States. Proof of this sympathy can be found in the famous booklet *Un
Dualismo Imposible (An Impossible Dualism)* written by Lorenzo Montufar, one of the champions of Guatemalan liberalism.

The kind of government that the North Americans enjoyed profoundly impressed Montufar, and commenting specifically on the subject
of the separation of church and state, he concludes: "Imitation of the
United States is indispensable. Their system grants liberty to all."[31] Modern writers frequently criticize the liberal movement for its docile accommodation to North American expansionist policies. Enrique D. Dussel claims that Justo Rufino Barrios (Guatemalan president, 1873-1875)
and Manuel Estrada Cabrera (Guatemalan dictator, 1898-1920), along
with subsequent government, "open[ed] the doors to the North American
capital ventures, International Railways of Central America, and especially the United Fruit Company."[32]

Liberalism and Protestantism

It is obvious that, to a degree, Guatemalan liberals were sympathetic
toward Protestantism. Frederick Crowe enjoyed the hospitality of don
Antonio Valdez, "a well-to-do native son, businessman, and ardent liberal,"[33] and it was especially liberals who, in spite of the clerical opposition and persecution Crowe faced, supported him in his educational
work. Crowe says that "some businessmen and two or three top liberal
leaders" sent their children to the school he founded,[34] and that when it
was shut down by an order from city hall, "don Felix Solano, a gentle-
men of this country, owner of a distillery, and well-known liberal,"
called him to ask if he would spend "some hours every day teaching
three of his children *in his own home*."[35] It is reported that Dr. Lorenzo

Montufar was one of Crowe's followers,[36] but further historical research is required to prove this.

The most compelling evidence of liberal support of Protestants is the fact that the Presbyterian missionary who launched the first permanent Protestant effort in Guatemala came in response to a petition from the country's own president, General Justo Rufino Barrios. Dr. Paul Burgess asserts that "Barrios was a determining factor in the establishment of Protestantism in his country" and that the invitation could well have been sent to the Presbyterian Board of Missions in New York "by the hand of his emissary in Washington, Dr. Lorenzo Montufar."[37]

Of course, one of the principal reasons for the official openness to the Protestant cause was the anticlerical posture of the government that came into power in 1871. What J. Lloyd Mecham states regarding the Hispano-American anticlericalists of 1820-1830 can be applied as well to the Guatemalan liberals of the Barrios era: "The reasons for the opposition to the Roman Catholic organization—not to the Catholic religion as such—were in large measure political."[38]

The conflict of 1871 was not theological, but socio-political. The liberals had no intention whatever of reproducing the Reformation of the sixteenth century on Guatemalan soil, even though they certainly recognized the benefits of that movement; what they did seek was to correct the abuses of the church and to free the state from its bondage to ecclesiastical authority. Nor were they interested in abandoning the Catholic fold—at least not externally—or, much less, in converting to Protestantism. Justo Rufino Barrios was a long way from being the Henry VIII of Guatemala. Burgess states:

> When the Presbyterian mission founded a private school, President Barrios sent his children there and urged his ministers to do likewise. Nevertheless, in spite of his opposition to the Catholic Church, he never separated himself from it.... In Guatemala, as in all Latin America, the liberal party has favored Protestant missions, not because of the religious convictions of its leaders or party members in general, but rather because they see in these missions an effective means for breaking the power the Catholic clergy holds over the masses. This quasi sponsorship has had certain effects. The fact, admitted generally by both friends and opponents, that it was General Barrios who brought Protestant missions to Guatemala, has endowed them with a certain amount of privilege

and a degree of prestige that have contributed, partly, to their remarkable success.[39]

But it would be all too hasty to conclude that the liberals were appreciative only of the anticlerical aspects of Protestantism while ignoring or forgetting the fundamental characteristics of the movement—for example, the concept of the dignity and equality of all people in the eyes of the Creator, the deep love of liberty, the emphasis on public education, and the desire for progress in all aspects of life. In the pursuit of these and other social benefits, teh militants of liberalism, who truly sought the best for their country, would feel that they walked hand-in-hand with the Protestants.

It could be suggested that there was an intrinsic affinity between the Guatemalan liberalism of the end of the nineteenth century and Protestantism, even though there were neither Guatemalan nor foreign Protestants to influence directly the liberal leaders of that time. According to Alberto Rembao, "cultural Protestantism was already present in the countries of Latin America when the bearers of religious Protestantism arrived there."[40] He goes on:

By cultural Protestantism is meant the spirit of progress, the notion of giving free rein to recognized ability, the optimistic view of the future, the attitude of the strong man of robust spirit: the entire spectrum of those social forces which, throughout the centuries, have challenged the backward-looking attitude of the Altar and Throne.[41]

Of course, the great social principles of Protestantism—those principles that are worthy of the respect and admiration of everyone who loves liberty, justice, and peace—find their origin in those biblical precepts that have influenced, either directly or indirectly, the great liberating movements of the modern world. The Scriptures have always been a source of inspiritation for that authentic humanism which, in Jesus Christ, elevates humans in their relationship to God and their neighbor.

One of the major contributions of Guatemalan liberalism to the cause of human rights in this continent was the decree of religious liberty that was proclaimed by Barrios on March 15, 1873. For more than a hundred years Guatemala has been able to hold its head high with legitimate pride, especially in the face of those regimes of force which, even in the twentieth century, have trampled freedom of worship underfoot—nations which, given their degree of cultural development, should have been at the forefront in defending this inalienable right. Under the protection of the law that was proclaimed by liberalism, the Guatemalan Protestant church has experienced such vigorous growth that it has attained a place of honor in the eyes of worldwide Protestantism.

As to whether or not Protestant missionaries were sent for the purpose of advancing capitalistic interests in Central America, the answer remains to be shown. Further, it would be necessary, in any study addressing that issue, to avoid the mere application of a given socio-economic theory to the Guatemalan situation, researching instead the histories of both Guatemala and the Anglo-Saxon countries, examining the archives both of the missionary societies that initiated the Protestant effort in Guatemala and of the foreign corporations that have had extensive economic interests here, and analyzing the correspondence of the early Protestant missionaries in this country.[42]

But even if it were to be proved that Protestant missions and North American corporations pursued the same ends, it would still be necessary to inquire as to what degree Protestantism succeeded in achieving its "colonialist" aims, or if perhaps it had nothing more than an indirect influence on the development of North American capitalism in Guatemala. Another question would be that of whether or not this socio-economic system would have grown in this environment quite without the feeble support of an incipient Protestantism whose influence was limited to a minority of Guatemalans. Enrique D. Dussel reports that the number of Protestants in all of Central America and Panama in 1916 was 18,564.[43] In that same year, a Protestant congress held in Panama reported the number of Protestants on the church rolls in all of Central America as being no greater than 10,442.[44] Twenty years prior to that, therefore, it is not unreasonable to estimate the number of Protestants in the entire Central American isthmus at around six thousand, which would imply that there was only a very small group of Guatemalan Protestants at that time.

Could those few Protestants have been able to create the necessary "subjective conditions" for the establishment and expansion of North American capitalism in Guatemala? Who were the outstanding Protestant political figures and intellectuals of the late nineteenth and early twentieth centuries? Who were the persuasive Protestant congressmen who would have influenced the legislature on behalf of neo-colonialism in those days? Who were the Protestant writers and journalists who, through the printed page, would have endeavored to mold public opinion in favor of neo-colonialism? Which were the Protestant pressure groups in congress, the executive branch, industry, banking, commerce, the university, or labor? The fact is that prior to World War II the Protestant presence in Guatemala was barely noticeable, and it was not until the electoral campaign of 1969 that politicians endeavored to manipulate the Protestant vote by means of advertisements in the press.

It is well known that North American industrial might, together with the *crillo* oligarchy, the media—press, radio, motion pictures, television—and the growth of tourism, have all done much more to "Americanize" our culture than have all the Protestants put together. Nevertheless, if historical and social research should prove that in one way or another Protestantism has been a determining factor in the development of neo-colonialism in Guatemala, the response to the original question (Has Protestantism had an influence in the social-historical development of Guatemala?) must then be in the affirmative, even though that influence be considered detrimental for Guatemalan society.

THE ACHIEVEMENTS OF PROTESTANTISM

The third approach to the question about Protestantism's possible influence on Guatemala is to point out, first of all, the positive moral and spiritual benefits that it has brought to many Guatemalans and, secondly, the programs of social benefit in which it has been involved.

When the history of Guatemala is compared with that of other countries where, even in recent years, religious intolerance has gone unchecked, it is impossible not to recognize the substantial advantages that the Guatemalan Protestant church has enjoyed throughout its one-hundred-five-year existence, beginning with the arrival of Reverend Hill, pioneer Presbyterian missionary in this country, in November of 1882.

This does not mean, of course, that Protestantism has not suffered persecution in Guatemala. There have been many instances in which religious fanaticism has overflowed into violence in its attempt to impede the establishment of Protestant work in some areas or to destroy what had already been begun in others. There are also Guatemalan heroes and heroines of the faith: men and women who dedicated their lives totally to the service of the Lord Jesus Christ and who were ready to suffer for their love of him. The names of these champions of the gospel are to be found written in heaven, where they will shine for eternity.

But thanks to the law of religious freedom, many Protestant groups have come to Guatemala and have, within the framework of the law, been able to pursue their religious activities without government intervention. Past abuses of power directed against Protestantism were the exception rather than the rule, and Protestant institutions have been allowed to function without limitations other than those established by the laws of the land.

The climate of liberty of conscience, inaugurated by Barrios and continued by his successors in the presidency, has contributed greatly to the formation of a tolerant viewpoint among the Guatemalan people regarding questions of religion. In general, and in contrast to what has happened in other countries, Guatemalans do not equate nationalism with loyalty to Roman Catholicism. It is not necessary to be a Catholic in order to be a good Guatemalan citizen. In the eyes of society, no one ceases to be patriotic for having subscribed to a religious creed that is different from that of the traditional church.

In missionary terms, a remarkable receptivity to the gospel exists among the Guatemalan people, resulting in one of the highest rates of Protestant growth in the entire continent. We have confirmed this through visits to other countries where, in some instances, Protestants continue to be a barely perceptible minority on the social scene.

While it is true that in the eyes of the general public the Protestant church has remained silent in the face of the serious social problems that afflict us, it is also true that, within its own limitations, the Protestant church has held high the ideals of the Reformation of the sixteenth century through the proclamation of the message of freedom in Christ and through worthwhile efforts on behalf of the culture and welfare of the peoples of Guatemala. Evidence in support of this is the educational contribution of Christian schools, the delivery of medical aid in distant rural areas, and the quiet but effective work being done in the various ethnic groups—work that includes the reducing of native Guatemalan languages to writing, the translation of the New Testament into those languages, and the teaching of reading and writing to thousands of Guatemalans who have been excluded from the benefits of literacy. In other sectors of the population, not a few have found in the gospel a powerful incentive for personal growth and development.

From a small handful of men and women, belittled by the forces of traditionalism and intolerance, Guatemalan Protestants have grown into a sizable group that includes outstanding men and women in various spheres of national life—scholarship, the arts, commerce, industry, and so forth—who contribute to the growth and well-being of Guatemala.

Although it would appear as though Protestantism has not played an important role in determining the directions that Guatemalan history has taken, it nevertheless is a part of that history, occupying a place of honor there. In analyzing Guatemalan reality, historians and sociologists can no longer enjoy the luxury of ignoring the Protestant phenomenon. The

Protestant church is an inseparable component of Guatemala's historical-social picture.

CONCLUSION

First, it is undeniable that, generally speaking, Guatemalan Protestantism has not been in the mainstream of socio-political reform movements. That the separation of the gospel from politics has become proverbial in the Guatemalan context can probably be traced to the early Protestants in our country who, being foreigners, were obliged to abstain from any and all local political activity, thus projecting this attitude to the congregations they founded. The theology they propounded insisted on the separation of the Christian from everything having to do with the "world"—to the point that in some cases Protestants were denied communion for having participated in politics. The ethical problems of local "dirty politics" seemed to justify this Protestant isolationism.

Of course, party politics yet today is a dangerous enough game to play, and many who prefer to live in peace avoid its entanglements. But as a consequence of their isolationism, Protestants have generally limited their political participation to the ballot box, although their votes are not always well-reasoned—not always based on an analysis of social reality or growing out of a desire to integrate their faith into that reality.

It is not at all strange that some should claim that Protestants, rather than being a factor of social change, have been one of preservation of the established order. It is argued that their touted apolitical posture has resulted in an attitude that favors those forces that oppose social change, so that when all is said and done, Protestants have not been politically neutral at all. From that point of view, Protestant influence in Guatemala's historical-social development has been clearly conservative. However, there have been changes over the past decades, so that not all Protestants are scandalized now when one of their number participates, on a personal level, in political activities.

Second, the convergence in time of a period of United States economic expansionism with the initial stages of Protestant missions in Guatemala cannot be denied. It is also evident that there was a certain ideological affinity between Protestantism and Guatemalan liberalism. However, the claim that the pioneer missionaries were sent out in order to establish favorable conditions for the development of Anglo-Saxon capitalism demands serious and unbiased research of the historical records and a commitment to accept without reservation the verdict of history, whatever it be, regarding the origin and development of Protestantism in Guatemala. The field is open to the serious, careful, and—to whatever degree possible—impartial researcher.

A question must also be raised regarding what truly motivated the Protestant pioneers in their work in this country. The sincere researcher will need to take into account the personal testimony of those who never doubted their having received an eminently spiritual calling from God. Above and beyond all else, they considered themselves ambassadors of Jesus Christ, and not of London or Washington. The words of Crowe regarding his expulsion are most moving:

> I was quite certain that my absence from Guatemala would not be for long—at the most just a few months—but the blow was heavy and the conflict of emotions and sentiments of that day drained all my strength. Sitting down, I placed my aching head in my hands and silently let the tears overflow.[45]

Such is the testimony of a foreign missionary who knew how to weep for Guatemala because he loved it in the name of Christ; and imbued with like spirit were and are many others who have followed Crowe in the worthy task of planting the gospel in Guatemalan soil.

Third, it is equally undeniable that the Protestant church has had a profound moral and spiritual influence on the lives of hundreds of thousands of Guatemalans. Also, the efforts expended by Protestants on behalf of the progress of the country are open for all to see. This contribution, albeit modest, has been effective in the economic, social, and cultural development of Guatemala.

It is altogether true that much more could have been done. When we reflect upon the marvelous ways in which the Guatemalan Protestant church has been favored by divine providence since its first days in 1882, we must ask ourselves if we have always lived in accordance with the privileges we have enjoyed and if we have taken proper advantage of all our opportunities.

History and experience teach us that when the church becomes established and has grown, it runs the risk of stagnation, of falling into routines, of resisting any and all change, and of closing its eyes to the clear challenges of the present and the future. It is easy to forget that, although the gospel does not change, the Protestant church with a true Reformation spirit must, in the light of the immutable gospel, continue to reform itself. We also must remember that there is no excuse for deterring that process. Yesterday's victories are insufficient for winning today's battles. Today's questions are seldom the ones of fifty years ago or more, and we have no right to think that the traditional operational methods must always be as efficient in responding to the exigencies of today's world. The church, in the power of the Holy Spirit and in the light of the written Word of God, must be in a state of continual renewal.

The nature of this renewal demands, of course, that we remain faithful to the spiritual heritage of our forebears. We need a historical continuity that is characterized fundamentally by a doctrinal continuity: "What you have heard from me keep as the pattern of sound teaching.... Guard the good deposit that was entrusted to you . . . with the help of the Holy Spirit who lives in us.... And the things you have heard me say in the presence of many witnesses entrust to reliable men who will also be qualified to teach others" (2 Tim 1:13, 14; 2:2, NIV).

Finally, it will be to our advantage to follow the example of servanthood set us by the Protestant pioneers who came to our country, so that we may take courage in the discharge of our task of seeking the salvation (body, soul, and spirit) of many Guatemalans and of working for the general welfare of Guatemala.

NOTES

1. This chapter was translated from the Spanish by David Oltrogge.

2. Christian Lalive D'Epinay, *El Refugio de las Masas*, trans. from the French by Narciso Amanillo (Santiago de Chile: Editorial del Pacífico, 1968), p. 157.

3. Domingo Alcántara, *Cien Años de Presencia Protestante en Centroamerica* (Santiago de Chile: ISAL).

4. Bryan Roberts, *El Protestantismo en dos Barrios Marginales de Guatemala* (Guatemala: Seminario de Integración Social Guatemalteca, Ministerio de Educación, 1967), p. 9.

5. Ibid.

6. Ibid., pp. 21-22.

7. Charles F. Denton, "La Mentalidad Protestante: Un Enfoque Sociológico," *Fe Cristiana y Latinoamerica Hoy*, C. René Padilla, comp. (Buenos Aires: Ediciones Certeza, 1974), pp. 67-69.

8. Paper read at the 10th Congress of Central American Churches, December 1972. See also my book *Caminos de Renovación* (Barcelona: El Portavoz Evangélico, 1974).

9. H. Richard Niebuhr, *Christ and Culture* (New York: Harper & Row, 1956), pp. 45-82. Niebuhr talks about five kinds of Christian ethics: Christ against culture, Christ of culture, Christ above culture, Christ and culture in paradox, and Christ the transformer of culture.

10. Miguel de Unamuno, *La agonía del Cristianismo* (Buenos Aires: Editorial Losada, 1973), p. 81.

11. Matos, in *Fe Cristiana y Latinoamerica Hoy.*

12. Denton, ibid., p. 76.

13. Max Weber, *La Etica Protestante y el Espíritu del Capitalismo* (Madrid: Editorial Revista Derecho Privado, 1955).

14. Andre Bieler, *El Humanismo Social de Calvino* (Buenos Aires: Editorial Escaton, 1973), pp. 67-68.

15. Herbert M. Zorn, *Viability in Context* (England: The Theological Education Fund, The World Council of Churches, 1975), p. 41.

16. T. Harry Williams, R. N. Current, Frank Freidel, *A History of the United States* (New York: Alfred A. Knopf, 1959), 1:434, 511.

17. Jean-Loup Herbert, "Ensayo de explicación teórica sobre la realidad social guatemalteca," *Guatemala: Una Interpretación Histórico-social* (Mexico: Siglo Veintiuno Editores, 1972), p. 54.

18. Chinchilla Aguilar, *La Inqusición en Guatemala* (Guatemala: Editorial del Ministerio de Educación Pública, 1953), p. 163.

19. Kenneth G. Grubb, *Religion in Central America* (London: World Dominion Press, 1973), p. 31.

20. *Henry Dunn, Cómo era Guatemala Hace 133 años.* Original title in English: *Guatemala or the United Provinces of Central America.* 1827, 1829. Translation by Ricardo de Leon (Guatemala: Tipografia Nacional, 1960), pp. 88-89.

21. Juan C. Varetto, *Federico Crowe en Guatemala* (Buenos Aires: Junta Bautista de Publicaciones, 1940) .

22. Mario Monteforte Toledo, *Mirada sobre Lationoamérica* (San José, Costa Rica: Editorial Universitaria Centroamericana, 1975, p. 115.

23. Alejandro Marure, Bosquejo *Histórico de las Revoluciones de Centroamerica* (Guatemala: Biblioteca Guatemalteca de Cultura Popular. Ministerio de Educación Pública, 1960), 1:41-42. Mariano Zecena, *La Revolución de 1871 y sus Caudillos* (Guatemala: Editorial José Pineda Ibarra, 1971), p. 26. Miguel García Granados, *Memorias* (Guatemala: Editorial del Ministerio de Educación Pública, 1952), 1:60-63.

24. Toledo, pp. 93, 96.

25. Granados, 1:60-63.

26. Carlos Rangel, *Del Buen Salvaje al Buen Revolucionario* (Barcelona: Libros de Monte Avila, 1976), p. 54.

27. Alberto Rembao, *Discurso a la Nación Evangélica* (Buenos Aires: Editorial La Aurora, 1949), p. 76.

28. Severo Martínez Pelaez, *La Patria del Criollo* (San José, Costa Rica: Editorial Universitaria Centroamericana, 1975).

29. Toledo, p. 114.

30. Jorge Skinner-Klee, *Revolución y Derecho* (Guatemala: Editorial José de Pineda Ibarra, 1971), p. 71 .

31. Lorenzo Montufar, *Un Dualismo Imposible* (Cristobal, Zona del Canal de Panama: Reproducido de *El Centinela*, la Revista Interamericana, n. d.

32. Enrique D. Dussel, *Historia de la Iglesia en América Latina* (Barcelona: Editorial Nova Terra, 1972),pp. 118-19.

33. Varetto, p. 44.

34. Ibid., pp. 67, 68.

35. Ibid., p. 79.

36. *Historia de la Obra Evangélica Presbiteriana* (Quezaltenango: "El Noticiero Evangélico," 1957), p. 13.

37. Pablo Burgess, *Justino Rufino Barrios*, trans. from the English by Ricardo

Letona E. (Guatemala: Editorial Universitaria de Guatemala, 1972), pp. 328-29.

38. J. Lloyd Mecham, "A Survey of the Church-State Conflict in Latin America During the First Century of Independence," in *The Conflict Between Church and State in Latin America*, ed. Frederick B. Pike (New York: Alfred A. Knopf, 1967), p. 165.

39. Burgess, pp. 329-30.

40. Rembao, p. 75.

41. Ibid.

42. For example: *Historia de la Obra Evangélica Presbiteriana* (Quezaltenango: "El Noticiero Evangelico," 1957). *The Central American Bulletin* (Dallas, Tex.), especially the numbers having to do with the first decades of the history of the Central American Mission. Wilkins B. Win, "A History of the Central American Mission Seen in the Work of Albert E. Bishop, 1896-1922" (Ph. D. diss., University of Alabama, 1963).

43. Dussel, p. 323. By the same author, *Hipótesis para una Historia de la Iglesia en América Latina* (Barcelona: Editorial Estela, 1967), p. 191.

44. W. R. Reed, V. M. Monterroso, H. A. Johnson, *Avance Evangélico en la America Latina* (El Paso, TX: Casa Bautista de Publicaciones, 1970), p. 20.

45. Varetto, p. 71.

13

The Awakening of Our Evangelical Social Conscience

The social isolation of most evangelicals in Latin America has become more evident than ever in the light of the revolutionary situation in which many people live, the strong emphasis given to social responsibility by both conciliar or ecumenical Protestantism and neo-Catholicism, and the social concern of many evangelical leaders around the world. But as a result of the challenges of our times, we are witnessing even in Latin America what may be called the awakening of our evangelical social conscience.

The purpose of this chapter is to discuss the meaning of social responsibility in contemporary theological thought, the testimony of the Scriptures, the causes of our evangelical social isolation, the development of a theology of social concern in the worldwide evangelical community, and the interaction of Latin American evangelicals with that theological trend.

THE MEANING OF SOCIAL RESPONSIBILITY

We who belong to the older generation of Latin American evangelicals have usually answered the criticism of our social alienation by saying that we have done social work in the areas of education, health, and development. We have also said that the proclamation of the gospel has produced positive results in society through the life and work of those who have been radically transformed by the Lord Jesus Christ. Without denying these and other blessings that the gospel has brought to our society, some Protestant leaders are not completely satisfied with our answer because, among other reasons, they understand that the New Testament gospel is not just an individualistic, other-worldly message. They consider humans as social beings, having material, physical, and spiritual needs, and they see no significant social changes produced by our evangelistic efforts, even in countries where the evangelical church is experiencing an explosive growth. According to this social analysis, most evangelicals, because of their individualistic approach to the Scriptures and their supposed political neutrality, have been consciously or unconsciously at the service of the status quo.

Moreoever, a distinction is now made between social responsibility as *social assistance* or *service,* and social responsibility as *social action* to change economic and political structures.[1] It has been said that social assistance deals only with the *effects* of our underdevelopment, whereas social and political action is the serious attempt to deal with the *causes* of our social problems. In this view, literacy crusades, educational efforts at the elementary and high school levels, medical assistance, all-encompassing projects in urban areas and in the countryside, and other ministries designed to improve the economic and social condition of the people are good in themselves, but in the final analysis they do not go far enough on the road of social change, they do not get to the real causes of our social problems. We need more than some palliatives, critics say; a radical transformation of society is imperative.

It is undeniable that millions of Latin Americans are in extreme poverty. It is depressing to see the subhuman conditions in which so many people live in the slums of the gigantic urban centers and in the countryside. Almost five hundred years of social injustice have fertilized the soil for the seed of foreign ideologies that claim to possess the answer for our complex social problems. The dialogue between these ideologies and a particular kind of Christianity has resulted in a theology that endorses a radical, and even violent, social change in the name of the gospel. The theology of the political left is one of the greatest challenges to the evangelical church in Latin America today.

On the other hand, there are among us some evangelical leaders who are still discussing whether the church is really supposed to get involved in helping those who are in material or physical need outside the local congregation. They are asking if the mission of the church has to be limited to the oral communication of the gospel, or if it should include "good works" for the benefit of the unbelievers. This discussion is, of course, unnecessary after a cursory reading of biblical texts like Matthew 5:13-16, Galatians 6:10, and Romans 12:20. More important than arguing about *social assistance* is to pay serious attention to the fact that to other leaders in some ecclesiastical quarters, Christian social responsibility means the involvement of the church as church in the radical transformation of the economic and political structures of society.

THE TESTIMONY OF THE SCRIPTURES

Basically we are dealing in this chapter with the mission of the church, and we have to ask the Word of God for instruction on our social responsibility.

The Old Testament Testimony

The Old Testament revelation deals with the total person, without overlooking his or her physical and material needs and without isolating him or her from society. Even in their prelapsarian condition, Adam and Eve had a variety of responsibilities. In obedience to the cultural mandate, they had to take care of each other, laying the foundations for the human family and society.

In the Old Testament theocracy, a person is seen as a being who is spiritual and physical and who is related to a family, to a tribe, to a nation, and to humankind as a whole. For the Israelite, her or his religion had to do with all the elements of her or his own personality and with all her or his relationships in society. Pagan people had different gods for different situations in human life, although in reality those gods were not capable of meeting any need of their worshipers. The Israelites had one God—the only true and living God—who had the ability to supply every need of his people, and the right to demand everything from them.

For the Israelite, the fullness of Jehovah's blessing meant to have spiritual, physical, and material well-being. The messianic hope included the restitution of all things (Jer. 31:12; Ezek. 34:24-27; Joel 2:21-27; Amos 9;13-14; cf. Acts 3:21; Rom. 8:20-23).

In the expectation of this new era and in obedience to the law, the Israelites were responsible to honor God, living according to the principles of love and justice in relation to their fellow humans. The law goes even to specifics in dealing with the social responsibilities of the chosen people of God—for instance, the care for the widows, the orphans, and the foreigners who lived in Israel.

In times of spiritual and moral declension, the prophets denounced the idolatry, the apostasy, the rebellion of the people against Jehovah and their injustices against humanity. The prophetic denunciation had to do with both personal sin and social evil. It was a severe condemnation of the transgressions of the common people and of the iniquities of the ruling class—the king, the royal family, the priests. The entire life of the nation was under divine judgment. There was no dichotomy in Israel between spiritual life and social responsibility.

The New Testament Testimony

There was not such a dichotomy between spiritual life and social responsibility for the people of God in the New Testament either. Actually, although a new era was inaugurated in the history of salvation by the incarnation and ministry of the Son of God, by the descent of the Holy Spirit, and by the birth of the church on the Day of Pentecost (Acts 2), there is continuity between the Old and the New Testaments in many respects. One of the elements of unity in both major sections of God's written revelation is the emphasis on the total person, and on the social responsibility of the people of God.

The Lord Jesus did not spiritualize his view of humanity to the extent of overlooking, much less denying, the physical, material, and social needs of humankind. His teaching had a great deal to do with the practice of justice in human relations (Matthew 5-7). He did not see men and women as if they were isolated from society, but deeply immersed in it.

He was really concerned about the spiritual, physical, and material needs of the people. His prayer in Matthew 6:9-13 is a beautiful example of this concern. We are taught by him to ask the heavenly Father for our daily bread. His miracles were signs, credentials, of his kingship; but they were also tangible proofs of his compassion. Although the emphasis of his earthly ministry was on teaching and preaching, he also ministered to the physical needs of men and women everywhere. He did not limit his social action to the circle of his disciples, nor to the people of Israel. He showed mercy to a Samaritan leper and to a Phoenician woman. In this sense, social action was an important part of his work. He saw no dichotomy between social action and evangelization. At the same time, he did not help needy people just as a means for converting them into proselytes. On the contrary, he rebuked those who followed him for a selfish purpose after they had seen a great miracle (John 6:26-27).

The apostolic church got into social action in a very spontaneous way, as a result of a genuine Christian love (Acts 2:43-47; 4:32-37; 11:26-30). Nobody was forced to give up material possessions for the benefit of the newborn community (Acts 5:3-4). Nobody was forced to get into a program of social action. It seems that at the beginning there was no program at all. The believers were not organized as a philanthropic movement, much less as a political party. But it was natural to them to help each other, to be concerned about the widows, the orphans, the needy people in their congregation and even outside the Christian assembly. Paul says that Christians are supposed to feed even their enemies (Rom. 12:20-21); and when he exhorts the Galatians to continue doing what is good, especially "to them who are of the household of faith" (Gal. 6:10), he leads us to understand that the Galatians were also responsible for helping those outside the family of God ("we should do good to everyone").

James teaches that true religion means to control our tongues, to visit orphans and widows in their afflictions, and to keep ourselves morally clean in this world (James 1:26-27). Genuine, saving faith is demonstrated by works (James 2:14-26). At the very beginning of the church, Christians took care of widows (Acts 6). According to 1 Timothy 5, this was still the practice of the church many years later. At the end of the apostolic age, John the beloved disciple taught that love is also manifested by sharing material things with a brother (1 John 3:17).

In regard to social issues like the general tendency among Jews and Gentiles to look down upon women and deny them their fundamental human rights, the problem of slavery, and the relation of the Christian to the state, the New Testament teaches some principles for the daily conduct of the disciples and proclaims ideas that for those times were revolutionary. Some examples are the immense value attributed to human life on the basis of creation and redemption (Matt. 6:25-34; Luke 12:22-31; 1 Cor. 6:19-20; 1 Pet. 3:7); the high view of human freedom (John 8:31-36); the dignity of all human beings because they were created in the image of God (James 3:9); the dignification and regulation of labor (Eph. 4:28; 6:5-9; 1 Thess. 4 12; 2 Thess. 3:10); the statement that in Christ there is no difference between Jews and Gentiles, between slaves and free men, between men and women (Gal. 3:28); no discrimination on the basis of race, culture, social status, sex; the intimation that freedom, not slavery, is the divine ideal for all human beings (1 Cor. 7:20-24; Philemon); the lordship of Christ over all creation (Matt. 28:18; Acts 2:29-36; Phil. 2:5-11), including his sovereign power over the rulers of this world (John 19:11; Rev. 11:15). There is no room in the New Testament for the deification of the emperor. Jesus of Nazareth, not Caesar, has been declared *Kurios,* the King of kings and Lord of lords.

Jesus and his disciples planted in the minds and hearts of their listeners powerful seeds of authentic freedom for all the peoples on earth. Jesus taught that the roots of evil are deep in the human heart. Out of the innermost part of humanity comes that which is sinful (Mark 7:14-23). Consequently, people have to be liberated first of all in their own hearts, from their own sin, before attempting the liberation of their fellow human beings. The revolution has to start deep in their own inner beings (John 3:3-13; 8:36; 2 Cor. 5:17).

The gospel is the power of God for the transformation of the individual and of society. The New Testament teaches also that the Messiah will bring a total renovation to this world (Rom. 8:18-25). But the church strategy for change is supposed to be different from the revolutionary strategy of humans. Jesus and his apostles did not promote a bloody uprising of the masses to overthrow the Roman emperor and to destroy the slave owners, the oppressors of the poor. Had they called the people to fight the imperial army, Christianity would have been destroyed and remembered as just another violent and unfortunate rebellion against the empire. The Lord of Sabaoth, the Captain of the heavenly armies, does not summon his church on earth to lead a violent revolutionary movement. His missionary mandate is to make disciples who will turn the world upside-down by communicating, in the power of the Holy Spirit, the transforming message of Christ.

In the light of the New Testament it is possible to conclude that the mission of the church is, first of all, to be present in the world, in the very scene where social conflicts take place. But the church has to maintain always its Christian identity, whatever the cost may be, remembering that it does not belong to the world and that the Father is able to keep it from evil (John 17).

Secondly, the church has to proclaim faithfully "the whole will of God" (Acts 20:27, NIV). To preach the gospel is much more than giving "five things you have to know to get to heaven." The emphasis on repentance is indispensable. But we cannot preach genuine repentance apart from a clear and concrete denunciation of sin as a serious offense against God's holiness and justice (Psalm 51). Sin is a devastating demonic force that breaks our fellowship with God and with our fellow humans. We sin against God when we sin against humans. And we must not limit this denunciation to the sins of the poor, nor to personal or private sins. In our countries, as in other parts of the world, sin is not only intimate; it is also social. Individual sinners have produced evil social structures that deserve God's judgment. Repentance according to the divine demands of social justice is also imperative in the case of the ones who are responsible for the existence and function of those structures.

John the Baptist preached repentance to the people, to the religious leaders, to the soldiers, and to Herod the king (Luke 3). The Lord Jesus Christ called the people to repent, to turn away from their sins, at the very beginning of his earthly ministry (Matt. 4:17) and on other occasions before his death on the cross (Matt. 12:41; Luke 5:32; 13:1-5; 15:7, 10; 17:3). After his resurrection he sent his disciples to preach in his name the message about repentance and forgiveness of sins to all nations, beginning in Jerusalem (Luke 24:47). Simon Peter demanded repentance from the Jews on the Day of Pentecost (Acts 2:38). Later on he said to both the people and the leaders of the nation: "Repent, then, and turn to God, so that your sins may be wiped out" (Acts 3:19, NIV). They had to repent from their regicide. Paul the apostle preached repentance to the philosophers in Athens (Acts 17). They believed themselves to be wise, but in reality they were fools in the eyes of God (Rom. 1:22). Their intellectual pride did not make them acceptable to the Lord. They had to repent of their sins to escape divine judgment.

To preach the gospel is much more than giving biblical and theological information. It is much more than entertaining an audience which is eager to enjoy "a good religious show" or listen to preachers who will tell them what they are itching to hear (2 Tim. 4:3). Men and women must be confronted with the claims of Christ and asked to make a decision in response to the gospel.

Thirdly, to fulfill her mission the church has to live out the gospel in the power of the Holy Spirit. The world has to listen to the gospel, but it has also to *see* it in action in the lives of those who profess to be Christians. The church is called to be the community in which the signs of the kingdom of God are present—the signs of love, joy, justice, peace, and power in the Holy Spirit.

To live the gospel means in a very special way to serve our fellow humans, especially those who are in spiritual and material destitution, the poor of the land. The divine blueprint for the church is not a big institution, rich and powerful according to the standards and ideals of humanity. The mission of the church is not to take advantage of the people and exercise a leadership that the Chief Shepherd would never approve of. As the servant par excellence, the Lord Jesus Christ has given us the highest example of service in the spirit of humility and love.

The mission of the church is to glorify the Lord by being present in society, living among men and women as the incarnate Logos did; by announcing "the whole will of God"; by living in obedience to the gospel, as salt of the earth and light of the world; by doing "good works," especially for the benefit of the most needy ones, and remembering that a "good work" can also be everything we may do to make life more human, here and now, to the glory of God.

CHRISTIAN SOCIAL RESPONSIBILITY IN POST-BIBLICAL TIMES

The apostolic and post-apostolic Fathers testify that in those days church leaders encouraged the people of God to be concerned about the sick and the poor.[2]

Through the centuries, Christians have felt their social responsibility in different degrees and have been involved in different ways in solving the problems of society. In the Middle Ages there was a serious distortion of the doctrine of faith and works when the Roman Catholic church taught a synergistic way of salvation—faith plus works. Philanthropy was considered by many people as a basis for salvation. Nevertheless, whatever the motivation they may have had for their social work, we cannot deny that a great deal of good was done for the needy, especially by some monastic orders, in the name of Christianity.

Emphasizing the doctrine of justification by faith alone, the Reformers reacted against Romanism and declared that good works are the result of salvation, but not the source or basis of it. This teaching was revolutionary in those times. Rome counterattacked, saying that the Reformers were preaching a gospel deprived of good works and opening the door for all sort of abuses in morals. This attack, of course, was unjust.

History tells us that Protestantism, in general, became a dynamic movement that produced profound transformations in Western society. It is a commonplace to speak of the powerful influence exercised by Protestantism in our civilization. We could mention the social concern of the Anabaptists, Methodists, and other Protestant groups that not only performed philanthropic works but also got involved in social action to change society. For John Wesley there was not a dichotomy between evangelization and social action. For William Wilberforce there was not a dichotomy between his Christian faith and his social responsibility in the British Parliament. On the contrary, because he was a Christian he felt it was his inescapable duty to fight slavery in the British Empire. A Catholic theologian says that even the great evangelical scholar B. F. Wescott was a mediator in labor conflicts in his home country. He was deeply concerned about social problems, and wrote a paper on social aspects of Christianity (1887).[3] Apparently, there was not a dichotomy for him between Christian scholarship and social responsibility.

The modern Protestant missionary movement, which began in the days of William Carey—toward the end of the eighteenth century—was not entirely lacking in social concern. Even in Latin America there were some missionaries like Diego Thomson, who worked in Argentina and in other South American countries as the agent of the British and Foreign Bible Society. He arrived in Argentina in 1818. His main responsibility was to distribute the Bible, but he also dedicated himself to teaching a new method of education for the benefit of society. His contribution to social progress was so deeply appreciated that the Argentinian government granted him honorary citizenship in that country.

THE GREAT REVERSAL IN AMERICAN EVANGELICALISM

The founding fathers of the United States came to America to establish a society on the basis of their Christian beliefs. Those Protestant leaders did not see a dichotomy between their faith and their social responsibility. Protestantism exercised a great influence on the shaping of American culture. It was natural for the individual Christian and for the church as an institution to get involved in the discussion of social issues and in the solution of social problems. On the other hand, it is undeniable that later on many Protestants did not assume as they should their social responsibility.

George M. Marsden points out that "social concern may emphasize one or both of the following: (1) political means to promote the welfare of society, especially of the poor and the oppressed, and (2) reliance on private charity to meet such needs."[4] He adds:

> Although before the Civil War many evangelicals displayed neither type of social concern, many others emphasized both. The ensuing transition came in two stages. From 1865 to about 1900 interest in political action diminished, though it did not disappear, among revivalist evangelicals.... The lessening of political concern ... did not in itself signify a "Great Reversal" in social concern.... The "Great Reversal" took place from about 1900 to about 1930, when all progressive social concern, whether political or private, became suspect among re-

vivalist evangelicals and was relegated to a very minor
role.[5]

The causes of that "reversal" are a very interesting subject of discussion for the students of the social and ecclesiastical context of those
times in America.

In his paper on evangelical views of history and eschatology which
he read at the Consultation on the Relationship Between Evangelism and
Social Responsibility (Grand Rapids, Michigan, 1982), Dr. Peter Kuzmic
concurs with Timothy Weber, who "came to the conclusion that Pre-
millennalism, and especially its dispensational variety, had a negative effect upon social attitudes."[6] In other words, premillennialism is closely
tied in with "the Great Reversal." Other authors have arrived at the same
conclusion.

It cannot be denied that premillennialism has been used and abused
in contemporary evangelicalism around the world. No wonder that this
eschatological view has been described by some of its critics as pessimistic, fatalistic, and excessively futuristic. At the same time, they have
to admit the strong evangelistic emphasis and the worldwide missionary
vision of the premillennialist movement. But they add, of course, that the
spread of premillennialism "explains why evangelical Christianity in so
many third-world countries suffers from the same and similar di-
chotomies and distortions as in the West."[7]

Without attempting a justification of some of the ways in which so
many teachers and preachers have used premillennarist eschatology, it is
necessary to say that from the standpoint of social responsibility and the
effort to eradicate the causes of social evils, other eschatological views
have also lacked social concern. No scholar would say that all the defenders of slavery in North America were premillenarian. The church
that took sides with the oppressors in Latin America for more than four
hundred years is not premillenarian but amillenarian. This church is responsible to a large extent for the system of social injustice established in
the Latin American countries almost five centuries ago. We who belonged to Roman Catholicism four decades ago were not made aware of
the social injustice prevailing in our subcontinent since colonial times.
We perceived that the church was the kingdom. However, the kingdom
we saw was the kingdom of the wealthy families and the clergy, not the
Kingdom of God, much less the kingdom of the masses living in subhuman conditions.

We admit without any hesitation that premillennialism had to do
with "the Great Reversal" in American evangelicalism and that we in the

Third World have inherited the use and abuse of that system of biblical interpretation. It is our duty to be aware of our problems and to put in order our own house, making the necessary refinements in our eschatological view. Many of the criticisms made of popular dispensational premillennialism are well taken, although some critics are still generalizing too much. They do not give enough emphasis to the fact that many of us reject the excesses of old-time premillenarian writers and preachers. In the revolutionary situation of Latin America, we are trying to do a theology that is biblical in its foundations and relevant to our own people.

Students of American evangelicalism see other causes, besides premillennialism, for "the Great Reversal." For instance, pietism has been mentioned as one of the factors contributing to the tendency of many American evangelicals to be indifferent to social issues and to retreat from social action, especially during the first three decades of the twentieth century. George M. Marsden sees that although outstanding evangelical leaders like A. J. Gordon, A. C. Dixon, James M. Gray, and others had been interested in social issues and advocated social work among the poor, the time came when there was "a shift in Evangelical pietism toward a more 'private' view of Christianity."[8] Marsden recognizes that the basic causes of "the Great Reversal" seem to be "broader than simply the rise of the new dispensationalist or holiness views," although these two movements "were contributing causes of the 'reversal.'"[9]

Many of the American missionaries who came to Latin America from about 1900 to about 1940 were premillenarian in eschatology, pietistic in their view of Christianity, and separatistic in their basic attitude toward other ecclesiastical bodies and toward society in general. One of the main characteristics of "faith missions" in our countries, generally speaking, was their reluctance to assume their social responsibility. They were a product, to a large extent, of "the Great Reversal" in American evangelicalism.

The cultural and social situation in our Latin American countries strengthened the separatistic attitude of those American missionary pioneers. As foreigners and as members of an evangelical minority in countries dominated by Roman Catholicism, they had to be extra careful in regard to social problems. They had no other choice, if they wanted to stay in their mission field and continue their work. In Guatemala, as in other foreign countries, it was illegal for foreigners, priests, and pastors to participate in politics. But political noninvolvement became the watchword even for laymen in the evangelical church. They were imitating their missionary teachers. In Latin America, politics has been a dangerous game, and usually a dirty game. Therefore, evangelical leaders could not see how a Christian could be a politician and at the same time keep a good testimony for the Lord. Ecclesiastical excommunication was applied in some churches to those who dared to go into politics. But non-involvement has meant for most evangelicals in Central America a complete isolation from politics and an almost total indifference to social issues. Very few understand that noninvolvement is, in the final analysis, a political option. It is the policy of silent approval for the status quo.

Pentecostalism is a product, or by-product, of the American holiness movement that grew and acquired several characteristics in different churches during the last part of the nineteenth century. According to L. Grant McClung, Jr., a Pentecostal writer, "the event that preceded Azusa Street by five years and actually precipitated the revival in Los Angeles began at the outset of the century in a student atmosphere . . . in a Bible School, in Topeka, Kansas."[10] Pentecostalism is strongly pietistic.

It has been said that more than seventy percent of Latin American evangelicals are Pentecostal. This figure means that Pentecostals have been the most visible evangelical force in our subcontinent; but they are widely known for their tendency to retreat from the "world." Latin American Pentecostalism has been considered to be "The Haven of the Masses."[11] It is said that Pentecostals find in their new faith a sort of compensation for their social alienation; they become indifferent to social issues and staunch opponents of political involvement. By nature, Pentecostalism is strongly individualistic (in regard to social issues) and intensively emotional. But as in any religious movement, there are exceptions to the general attitude of its members. There are signs of change among the younger leadership of Latin American Pentecostalism.

Marsden concludes: "The factor crucial to understanding the 'Great Reversal,' and especially in explaining its timing and exact shape, is the fundamentalist reaction to the liberal Social Gospel after 1900."[12] This is the main theological and historical explanation that some of us evangelicals in Latin America had already given for our lack of social concern. It is interesting to notice that the era of consolidation of the evangelical missionary enterprise in Latin America coincides to some extent with the period in which liberalism and fundamentalism were fighting their battles in the United States. In those days the social gospel, considered a fruit of liberal theology, was a symbol of humanistic, anthropocentric Protestantism.

No wonder that pioneer American evangelical missionaries in Central America were afraid of falling into the trap of liberalism if they got involved in social work. They wanted to be loyal, and rightly so, to their spiritual vocation. They did not want to betray the gospel message and preach instead the improvement of the individual by means of the improvement of society. Their hope was not in human progress, but in the Lord's return. They preferred not to invest time, money, and human resources in establishing big institutions. The experience of some historical Protestant denominations, which dedicated their main efforts in the mission field to institutional work with little success in the area of church growth, was a negative lesson to the pioneers working under faith missions.

Those devoted and beloved pioneers seemed to endorse the saying of some missionaries in other latitudes: "We are in the mission field to evangelize, not to educate." More than thirty years ago, a dear American missionary lady was giving herself full-time as principal and teacher in a Christian grade school in a semirural Guatemalan town. One day, with tears in her eyes she said that some of her American colleagues were asking her when she was really going to get into business as a missionary. In reality she was doing a magnificent job for the Lord and his church in Central America. Many children were saved through the ministry of the school, and several of them came into positions of leadership in the church or in the society.

Early in my ministry a group of Guatemalan brothers and sisters and I became quite interested in establishing a Christian grade school for humanitarian purposes. It was at that time that I became acquainted on a practical level with the debate on evangelization versus social responsibility. I could justify, of course, our project by saying that the school could also be used to win children to Christ. But a dear American missionary asked me, "Do you really believe that all the children attending your school will be saved?" I answered, "Do you really believe that all the people listening to your evangelistic sermons are saved?" The school was finally established in 1952. It is still in existence, and many children have been saved by the Lord.

A misunderstanding of the Protestant emphasis on the New Testament teaching that we are not saved "by works" has also been a cause of our social alienation in Latin American. The doctrine of justification by faith alone produced a profound change in my religious convictions. The Roman Catholic church had encouraged me to work hard for my own salvation; I had to accumulate merits in preparation for the Day of Judgment. Then, in the evangelical church I came to understand, through the New Testament message, that I was supposed to do nothing but receive the gift of God to be saved. Good works receded from the picture. The emphasis was now on faith, not on works. I had to believe. It was not a matter of doing.

I did not perceive, as I should have, that we are not saved *by* works, but *for* good works. I did not know the old Protestant saying that "we are justified by faith alone, but the faith that justifies does not stay alone"—it produces works. Good works became optional in my life, so to speak. The people from whom I received the gospel were not concerned about social action. So, I understood that good works meant especially to avoid some practices—like smoking, drinking alcoholic beverages, going to movies—and to be faithful in attending church, giving money to the Lord's work, and telling people about the gospel. I was not helped to see the social implications of the gospel. Unconsciously I was separating my Christian life from my life as a member of my family and as a citizen of my country.

Outside the church there was nothing else but "the world," where I had to go once in a while to rescue some souls for Christ. My responsibility to society was to preach the gospel of spiritual and eternal salvation, hoping that those who would respond in faith to that message would become a blessing to society by telling others about the Lord Jesus Christ. I was told that the greater the number of converts to the gospel, the greater the changes that would take place in our Latin American countries. It is evident that the evangelical church has been in many respects an instrument in the hands of God for the benefit of society. But church growth by itself has not necessarily meant in Latin America a radical change in the attitude of evangelicalism toward social issues and social transformation.

Fortunately, this situation is changing around the world. As we have already said early in this chapter, there are evangelical leaders who are still asking whether *the* mission of the church should include the doing of good works on behalf of needy people inside and outside the local congregation. But the big issue in Latin America today is whether or not we should get involved as church in transforming the basic structures of society. It seems that most leaders in the worldwide evangelical community are not concerned any more about the question of the validity of *social assistance* as a dimension of the missionary task. The greatest challenge today has to do with social responsibility as *political action* to produce radical social changes.

TOWARD AN EVANGELICAL THEOLOGY
AND PRAXIS OF SOCIAL CONCERN

The awakening of the evangelical social conscience has been accelerated by the changes experienced by the world after the second major war of this century (1939-1945). Examples of those changes are the rise of the United States and the Soviet Union as the two major powers in the world; the threat of a nuclear war; the birth of new nations in territories that used to be European colonies; the demographic explosion; the ecological problem; the awakening of the masses in the underdeveloped countries to the subhuman conditions in which they live, and their cry for social justice; the amazing achievements of science and technology; the growth in interaction between people from different cultures and countries as a result of the modern means of communication; the massive migration of peoples to the gigantic urban centers; the ever-present danger of losing our individual freedom in a society that is becoming led and controlled more and more by the new class, the technocrats; the spread of socialism in the world.

On the ecclesiastical scene, the awakening of the evangelical social conscience is being accelerated by the new approach of Catholicism to the economic and social problems in the poor nations; by the social message and action of the World Council of Churches; and in a very special way by a new generation of evangelical leaders who in different parts of the world are deeply involved in the task of doing theology on the basis of the Scriptures and in response to the challenges of contemporary society.

The following pages make reference to evangelical declarations on social responsibility, covering the period 1960 through 1987. The declarations were made at the interdenominational and international level.

Congress on World Missions
Chicago, December 1960

The Congress on World Missions (Chicago, December 1960) was sponsored by the Interdenominational Foreign Mission Association. Although the main purpose of the organizers was to promote evangelization in the traditional way, some of the speakers expressed their concern about the revolutionary spirit that was already permeating the minds of many people around the world and for the responsibility of the church to respond to social needs.

Speaking on the student world and the unfinished task, Eric S. Fife, Missionary Secretary of Inter-Varsity Christian Fellowship, declared:

> We have to understand that there have been sweeping changes that have taken place in the world mind since the last World War, and these students are up against it all the time and are living in an intellectually stimulating environment. They are looking for mission boards which they feel are facing the challenge of this day and generation. They are looking for a freedom from prejudice, racial and denominational. They are looking for an open-mindedness to the Lord and His work.[13]

G. Christian Weiss, missions director in those years of the Back to the Bible Broadcast, was particularly interested in underscoring "the obligation of Christians" to train at a higher academic level national leaders who would be able "to give direction to the course of their governments." He explained:

> As I recently traveled from country to country through Africa I came to one conclusion: Unless there are some well-trained Christian men who can take their place in these governments in general areas of leadership, there is little spiritual hope for these infant nations as they one by one attain independence.... the man who has graduated only from an elementary school or from a Bible institute is not likely to find his place in the parliament of his country, or in a lawyer's office, or in a hospital, or in any other place of professional leadership.... In these new nations it is the college or university graduate who will become the leader and the man of influence. They are the men who will give direction and goal to their nations; the ones who will in fact form and enforce the policies which will control the very work in which we are engaged. There is no realistic hope for these new nations apart from Christian national leadership.[14]

Even I dared to say in a plenary message at that Congress on World Missions:

> Jesus was teaching and preaching, and He was healing.

He performed miracles to endorse His message and to
give a sign to Israel. But I believe that His aim was not
only theological. He had a humanitarian purpose as well.
He wanted to do more than just convince the people. The
purpose of His heart was also to help and to supply even
their physical needs.... He had compassion on the multi-
tude . . .; the spirit of the compassionate Christ is one of
the main characteristics of genuine Christianity. We
know that this spirit has been a real blessing to missions
around the world. On the other hand, it is necessary to
keep the balance in the emphasis which is given to the
challenge of the people's needs. There is the possibility
of giving the impression that the message of salvation is
only for the sick and the poor people of the world. The
other extreme is to be so afraid of the social gospel that
the opportunity for medical missionary work and all humanitarian enterprises are neglected.[15]

It is worth noting that my speech did not go beyond social assistance as a demonstration of Christian social responsibility. In those
days we were not discussing yet whether political action was a duty of
the Christian.

Congress on the Church's Worldwide Mission
Wheaton, Illinois, April 1966

Sponsored by the Evangelical Foreign Missions Association and the
Interdenominational Foreign Mission Association, the Congress on the
Church's Worldwide Mission was held on the campus of Wheaton College in April 1966. A significant step forward was taken in relation to evangelical social responsibility. According to the *Wheaton Declaration*,

Whereas evangelicals in the Eighteenth and Nineteenth
Centuries led in social concern, in the Twentieth Century
many have lost the biblical perspective and limited themselves only to preaching a gospel of individual salvation
without sufficient involvement in their social and community responsibilities.

When theological liberalism and humanism invaded historic Protestant churches and proclaimed a "social gos-

pel," the conviction grew among evangelicals that an antithesis existed between social involvement and gospel witness.

Today, however, evangelicals are increasingly convinced that they must involve themselves in the great social problems men are facing. They are concerned for the needs of the whole man, because of their Lord's example, His constraining love, their identity with the human race, and the challenge of their evangelical heritage.

Evangelicals look to the Scriptures for guidance as to what they should do and how far they should go in expressing this social concern, without minimizing the priority of preaching the gospel of individual salvation.

Among the conclusions on social concern, we read:

That, we reaffirm unreservedly the primacy of preaching the gospel to every creature, and we will demonstrate anew God's concern for social justice and human welfare.

That, evangelical social action will include, wherever possible, a verbal witness to Jesus Christ.

That, evangelical social action must avoid wasteful and unnecessary competition.

That, we urge all evangelicals to stand openly and firmly for racial equality, human freedom, and all forms of social justice throughout the world.[16]

The *Wheaton Declaration* is not limited to *social assistance* in these conclusions; evangelical action is recommended against social evils such as racial discrimination and against all forms of social injustice. Some observers say that this emphasis on social action was related to the presence of a good number of participants from the Two-Thirds World.[17] In contrast to the missionary congress held in Chicago five years before, a large number of Latin American leaders were present at Wheaton. Although most of them seemed to be more interested in other subjects (like ecumenism) than in social responsibility, they did not oppose the final declaration on social concern. On the contrary, it was welcomed by many of us as a necessary statement for the social context in which we had to carry on our mission. After Wheaton 1966, when an evangelical speaks on behalf of social concern, either as social assistance or as social action to deal with the evils of society, he or she is not out of step with the worldwide evangelical community.

World Congress on Evangelism
Berlin, 1966

The World Congress on Evangelism was sponsored by *Christianity Today* magazine in celebration of its tenth anniversary, from October 25 to November 4, 1966, in Berlin. The motto of the congress was: "One Race, One Gospel, One Task." There were twelve hundred participants from one hundred countries.[18] According to the Australian evangelical educator Athol Gill,

> the issue of evangelism and social concern was raised in group discussions during the Berlin Congress, but it was not adequately debated.... To be sure, the Congress statement did include a lengthy section condemning racism, but it did so in purely personal terms, and in describing the "one task" of the church it spoke only of evangelism. Of the scores of papers delivered at that Congress only one dealt with evangelism and social concern, and it was devoted almost entirely to racism as a barrier to evangelism.[19]

It is true that Paul S. Rees, the author of the paper "Evangelism and Social Concern," gave more emphasis and space to racism than to other social problems; but he added:

> Race is not the only area of social concern to which we Christians should be sensitive. Another is that of war and peace. Another is that of power—the moral management of power and of the structures of power in society.... Speaking of power, it is a terrifying thought that, in a presumably free society, abject poverty, family disorder and disintegration, job insecurity and joblessness, can erect psychological barriers to the reception of the Gos-

pel that are as real as the suppression of free speech.[20]

There were other papers dealing with some social problems, but the authors were not actually discussing the relationship between evangelism and social concern.

In his opening message of the congress, Carl F. H. Henry stated:

> For good reason we repudiate the inversion of the New Testament by current emphases on the revolutionizing of social structures rather than on the regeneration of individuals.... Lack of vital faith in the supernatural Creator and Redeemer sooner or later means the terrible loss of human dignity, of social justice, and of personal salvation. Outside a rediscovery of the Gospel of grace there now remains no long-range prospect for the survival of modern civilization, but only a guarantee of its utter collapse.[21]

Answering the question, "Why the Berlin Congress?" Billy Graham, honorary chairman of the congress, discussed at length the meaning, the motive, the message, the strategy, and the method of evangelism. On this last point he declared, "Our goal is nothing less than the penetration of the entire world." He admitted that the world "desperately needs moral reform." But he added: "If we want moral reform, the quickest and surest way is by evangelism. The transforming Gospel of Jesus Christ is the only possible way to reverse the moral trends of the present hour."

> Do we want social reform? The preaching of the Cross and the resurrection have been primarily responsible for promoting humanitarian sentiment and social concern for the last 400 years. Prison reform, the abolition of slavery, the crusade for human dignity, the struggle against exploitation—all are the outcome of great religious revivals and the conversion of individuals. The preaching of the Cross could do more to bring about social change than any other method.[22]

C. René Padilla is right when he affirms that "the question of the relationship of evangelism to social responsibility—a recurring theme in the discussion groups during the conference—was not given proper attention at the plenary sessions."[23] And the plenary sessions communicate in a very special way the spirit of the event. We came back from Berlin highly motivated to penetrate our countries with the gospel, but the issue of evangelism and social concern did not make a deep impression in our minds. It was years later that I really paid attention to the "Closing Statement of the World Congress on Evangelism," an important document quoted also by Padilla and Sugden, in which emphasis is given to racism in the light of the motto of the congress ("One Race, One Gospel, One Task"). But reference is also made to whatever is displeasing to God in our relations with one another. The Statement is against "every human barrier and prejudice."[24]

If Berlin 1966 did not mean a step forward on the way of evangelical social responsibility, it was not a setback either in the process accelerated by Wheaton 1966. But a great deal of theologizing remained to be done in regard to social concern.

Latin American Congress on Evangelism
Bogotá, Colombia, November 1969

As a sequel to the Berlin Congress, the Billy Graham Evangelistic Association sponsored several regional congresses on evangelization. The Latin American Congress on Evangelism (Bogotá, Colombia, November 1969) was one of those events.

Even before Wheaton 1966 the members of Church and Society in Latin America (ISAL) had been quite active in reflecting on the complex social problems of our own countries and on the social responsibility of the church. The evangelicals had published very little on social concern, and we had not had the opportunity at the continental level as Latin Americans in a congress like the one held in Bogotá to think on our social responsibility. It was on that historic occasion that the prominent evangelical leader Samuel Escobar, from Peru, made a great impact on Latin American evangelicalism with his paper on the social responsibility of the church.[25]

By 1969 the message of the Wheaton Declaration (1966) had not yet reached most of the evangelical leaders in Latin America. It seems that many of the leaders who participated in the Wheaton Congress had not yet assimilated the statements of that declaration on social concern. Escobar's message sounded entirely new to the vast majority of people attending the Bogotá Congress. The effect of the address was shaking and profound. Escobar made a critique of our foreign strategies and methods in evangelization and pleaded for a real incarnation of the gospel in our Latin American social context. He gave us to understand that there is no dichotomy between evangelism and social responsibility. He insisted that we evangelicals should get involved in the social order, communicating the gospel by word and deed to all the people, especially to the poor.

According to the *Evangelical Declaration of Bogotá,*

> the process of evangelization takes place in a concrete social situation. Social structures exercise a powerful influence on the Church, and on those who receive the Gospel. If this reality is not taken into consideration the Gospel is distorted, and the Christian life impoverished. Consequently, the time has come for us Evangelicals to assume our social responsibility, on the biblical foundation of our faith, and following the example of the Lord Jesus Christ to the last consequences. That example has to be incarnate in our Latin American reality—a reality of underdevelopment, social injustice, hunger, violence, and despair. Men cannot build by themselves the Kingdom of God on earth, but Evangelical social action will contribute to create a better world, as an anticipation of the one for which Christians pray daily.[26]

One of the indirect results of the Bogotá Congress was the creation of the Latin American Theological Fraternity *(Fraternidad Teológica Latinoamericana)* by a group of evangelical leaders who were concerned about the lack of evangelical reflection at the national and international level on the Latin American social context and the response that we evangelicals should give to the challenges of the hour. At noon on one of the days of the Bogotá Congress, we met in a hotel to consider the possibility of organizing a theological fraternity.

A year later (November 1970), LATF came into existence in Cochabamba, Bolivia. Its purpose was to stimulate an evangelical reflection that would be based on the Word of God and give serious consideration to the questions asked by the Latin American people. This reflection would accept the normative character of the Scriptures as God's written revelation. It would strive to listen, under the ministry of the Holy Spirit, to the biblical message in interaction with the concrete Latin American reality.[27]

To attain this goal, LATF has sponsored consultations at the local, national, and regional levels for the study of the Word of God within the Latin American context. It has encouraged its members to continue doing theology and to publish the fruit of their reflection. LATF has published books; a bulletin, both in Spanish and English; and several papers or monographs. Several of its members have published books and articles on their own initiative.[28] Since 1970 LATF has been a catalyst for the development of a contextualized evangelical thought in the areas of biblical and systematic theology, theological education, pastoral ministries, missiology, ethics, and evangelization.

International Congress on World Evangelization
Lausanne, Switzerland, 1974

"Some 4,000 Christians representing 151 countries gathered in Lausanne, Switzerland, to participate in the International Congress on World Evangelization. Their primary objective was to implement strategies and programs which would aid Christians of every nation to complete the task of the Great Commission."[29] But this task, according to the International Congress on World Evangelism (Lausanne, 1974), is not only evangelism. Social action is included in the mission of the church. In regard to this subject there is a great contrast between the emphasis of Berlin 1966 and that of Lausanne 1974.

In his message explaining why the Lausanne Congress had been convened, Billy Graham said: "We expect to reaffirm that our witness must be by both word and deed. You cannot separate the two." But he warned that we are always in danger of falling into at least three or four errors concerning social action:

> The first is to deny that we have any social responsibility as Christians.... The second error is to let social concern become our all consuming mission. . . . A third error is to identify the Gospel with any one particular political program or culture. This has been my own danger.... Perhaps there is a fourth danger for us and this the danger of trying to make all Christians act alike, regardless of where God may have placed them. Some, by the nature of your societies, are able to have a fair degree of influence. Others of you come from countries in which this is very difficult.[30]

Graham told his audience that social responsibility "is not our priority mission." "After all, humanists may heal, feed, and help, but this social presence isn't Gospel proclamation.... *Evangelism and the salvation of souls* is the vital mission of the Church."[31]

The Lausanne Congress produced one of the most significant evangelical documents of the twentieth century—the Lausanne Covenant. Athol Gill writes that "the Lausanne Covenant marked a turning point in evangelical thinking, a turning point which may well have significant consequences for all Christians."[32]

For the sake of brevity we will quote just some sentences of this covenant on the issue of evangelism and social concern:

> Here too we express penitence both for our neglect and for having sometimes regarded evangelism and social concern as mutually exclusive. Although reconciliation with man is not reconciliation with God, nor is social action evangelism, nor is political liberation salvation, nevertheless we affirm that evangelism and socio-political involvement are both part of our Christian duty. For both are necessary expressions of our doctrines of God and man, our love for our neighbor and our obedience to Jesus Christ.[33]

It is evident that the Lausanne Covenant goes beyond Wheaton 1966 in its declaration on social responsibility. The question of priorities was not debated at Lausanne, although the paragraph titled "The Church and Evangelism" declares: "In the church's mission of sacrificial service evangelism is primary." Nevertheless, many people insisted on asking which one comes first: evangelism or social responsibility. John Stott, commenting on that paragraph, says that the mission of the church "includes both evangelistic and social action, so that normally the church will not have to choose between them. But if a choice has to be made, then *evangelism is primary*."[34]

On his part, René Padilla refuses "to drive a wedge between a primary task, namely the proclamation of the Gospel, and a secondary (at best) or even optional (at worst) task of the church."[35]

The debate has not come to an end among evangelicals. Padilla admits that the Covenant "does, however, fail to answer many an important question regarding the connection between evangelism and social concern."[36] But a transitional step had been taken in clarifying the mission of the church. It is possible to say that after Lausanne 1974 most evangelical leaders have come to a point of no return in regard to social concern. But the process of reflection on this issue had to move forward at Grand Rapids 1982 and Wheaton 1984.

Another question is related to the statement that socio-political involvement is a part of our Christian duty. People have asked the "how" of such an involvement. How far are the individual Christian and the church supposed to go in their political involvement? The Covenant does not answer this question in detail, although the paragraph entitled "The Church and Evangelism" declares that the church "is the community of God's people rather than an institution, and must not be identified with any particular culture, social or political system, or human ideology."[37] As in the case of the relationship of evangelism to social responsibility, the consultation in Grand Rapids in 1982 would give more thinking on the matter of the socio-political involvement of evangelicals in their particular social contexts.

Before bringing to an end these comments on the 1974 Lausanne Congress and its Covenant, it is necessary to mention the decisive influence exercised by Third World theologians at that historic event. The Latin American Theological Fraternity was represented by some of its distinguished members, (for example, C. René Padilla, Samuel Escobar, Orlando E. Costas, and Pablo Pérez). Escobar was a member of the Drafting Committee of the Covenant. The document reflects ideas that had already been a subject of discussion in LATF.

Second Latin American Congress on Evangelization
Huampaní, Peru, November 1979

To consider anew the social situation in Latin America, to evaluate what had happened in the area of evangelization and pastoral ministries since Bogotá 1969, and to reflect on strategies for the years ahead, the Latin American Theological Fraternity convened the Second Latin American Congress on Evangelization, which was held in Huampaní, Peru, in November 1979.

The Letter of the Congress to the Church in Latin America affirms that Huampaní 1979 is in harmony with the Evangelical Declaration of Bogotá (1969) and the Lausanne Covenant (1974). The signatories declare:

> We have heard the Word of God, who speaks to us and who also hears the cry of those who suffer. We have lifted up our eyes to our own continent and have seen the drama and the tragedy that our people are living through in this moment of spiritual unrest, religious confusion, moral corruption, and social and political convulsion.

We have heard the cry of those who hunger and thirst after righteousness, of those whose most basic needs are
not being met, of the marginalized ethnic groups, of
broken families, of women denied exercise of their natural rights, of youth dedicated to vice or forced into violence, of children who suffer from hunger, abandon-
ment, ignorance and exploitation. On the other hand, we
see that many Latin Americans are dedicating their lives
to the idolatry of materialism, subordinating spiritual
values to those values imposed by the consumer society,
according to which the human being has value, not for
what he himself is, but for the abundance of what he possesses. There also are those who, in a legitimate desire to
vindicate the right to life and liberty, or in order to maintain the status quo, are following ideologies that present
only a partial analysis of the Latin American scene and
lead to different forms of totalitarianism and to the violation of human rights....

We confess that as the People of God we have not always obeyed the demands of the Gospel that we preach,
as is shown in our lack of unity and our indifference in
the face of the material and spiritual needs of our neighbour.[38]

After the congresses of Wheaton 1966, Bogotá 1969, and Lausanne
1974, the relationship of evangelism to social concern was not really a
big issue in Huampaní. It seems that it was taken for granted, at least by
the majority of leaders participating in the congress, that evangelism and
social responsibility are supposed to go together in the mission of the
church.

The Hoddesdon Consultatons
Hoddesdon, England, March 1980

Under the auspices of the Unit on Ethics and Society of the World
Evangelical Fellowship (WEF), the Consultation on the Theology of Development was held at Hoddesdon, England, on March 10-14, 1980. The
Statement of Intent issued by that consultation expresses the concern of
the participants about the social evils of contemporary society. It re-
affirms the evangelical commitment "to live out the full Christian Gospel

and to apply it to the needy situations in which we find ourselves." Moreover, the participants resolve "to encourage, by all the peaceful and constructive means available to us, the poor and oppressed who are seeking to establish a position of dignity and self-worth." For the signatories of the statement "the Bible teaches that the mission of the church includes the proclamation of the gospel and the demonstration of its relevance by working for community development and social change."[39]

We notice among other elements in this document an emphasis on the poor, on development (social assistance), and on social change (political action). Evangelical thought is moving toward a more active involvement in social transformation.

Another consultation held at Hoddesdon in March 1980, prior to the General Assembly of the World Evangelical Fellowship, dealt with the subject entitled "Simple Life Style." This consultation was jointly sponsored by the Theology and Education Group of the Lausanne Committee for World Evangelization and the aforementioned Unit on Ethics and Society of the Theological Commission of WEF.[40]

The eighty-five evangelical leaders from twenty-seven countries expressed their conviction that there is an intimate connection between the personal and social dimensions of the gospel. In their statement they see the urgent need to develop a simple lifestyle in order to contribute more generously to both relief and evangelism. Involuntary poverty is condemned as "an offense against the goodness of God." The church "must stand with God and the poor against injustice, suffer with them, and call on rulers to fulfill their God-appointed role." It is also declared that "all Christians must participate in the active struggle to create a just and responsible society."[41]

In his commentary on this document ("An Evangelical Commitment to Simple Life-Style"), Alan Nichols, an Australian participant in the consultation, explains that

> the Lausanne Committee's involvement in the Consultation on Simple Life-Style arose from the sentences in the Covenant which have already been quoted more than once. They relate the need to develop a simple life-style to three Christian duties—the quest for justice, the work of relief, and evangelism. Consequently, the second stated goal of the Consultation was "to reflect on the biblical basis and the contemporary need for a simple life-style for evangelism, relief, and justice.[42]

In other words, the Consultation was in keeping with the spirit and affirmations of Lausanne 1974. As in the case of other subjects related to Christian social concern, the simple life-style proposal has been debated in the worldwide evangelical community. But apart from any ideological inclination it is a fact that while billions of dollars are wasted in the developed countries, hundreds of millions of people live in desperate poverty and billions of human beings need to hear the gospel.

Consultation on World Evangelization
Pattaya, Thailand, June 1980

Although the Consultation on World Evangelization (Pattaya, Thailand, June 1980) was sponsored by the Lausanne Committee on World Evangelization, the nature of this event was quite different from that of Lausanne 1974. Both consultations had to do with "world evangelization," but the emphasis on the "how" of the evangelistic task was obvious in Pattaya. There seemed to be a deep concern with determining strategies for-reaching different groups or peoples with the gospel, rather than dealing with the theology of mission, much less with the issue of evangelism and social responsibility.

The organizers of Pattaya 1980 may have thought that social concern had already been discussed at Lausanne 1974. Although the debate on such an issue was not closed, Pattaya 1980 would be a complement to Lausanne 1974 in the area of strategies for world evangelization.

Nevertheless, there was a strong reaction on the part of a large group of participants in Pattaya to the lack of emphasis on social concern. A statement was written and presented to the leaders of the consultation,[43] but it was not included for discussion at a plenary session. Some observers believe that this document was influential on the final draft of The Thailand Statement, which in two of its paragraphs makes reference to evangelism and social action:

> We are also the servants of Jesus Christ who is himself both "the servant" and "the Lord." He calls us, therefore, not only to obey him as Lord in every area of our lives, but also to serve as he served. We confess that we have not sufficiently followed his example of love in identifying with the poor and hungry, the deprived and the oppressed. Yet all God's people "should share his concern for justice and reconciliation throughout human so-

ciety and for the liberation of men from every kind of oppression" (Lausanne Covenant, para. 5).

Although evangelism and social action are not identical, we gladly reaffirm our commitment to both, and we endorse the Lausanne Covenant in its entirety. It remains the basis of our common activity, and nothing it contains is beyond our concern, so long as it is clearly related to world evangelization.[44]

It was dramatized in Pattaya that there were still discrepancies among evangelicals in regard to the emphasis that should be given to social action in the fulfillment of the missionary task. There were Latin American leaders among those who signed the "Statement of Concerns on the Future of the Lausanne Committee for World Evangelization International, June 1980," which asks the LCWE "to reaffirm its commitment to all aspects of the Lausanne Covenant and in particular provide new leadership to help evangelicals to implement its call to social responsibility as well as evangelism."[45]

Quite apart from that controversy, it is necessary to admit that Pattaya 1980 produced valuable materials for reaching peoples of the world with the gospel of Christ.

**Consultation on the Relationship
Between Evangelism and Social Responsibility
Grand Rapids, Michigan, June 1982**

We have already seen that there were questions among evangelicals around the world about some of the statements of the Lausanne Covenant, particularly the ones dealing with the relationship between evangelism and social responsibility and with socio-political involvement as part of our Christian duty.

The Consultation on the Relationship Between Evangelism and Social Responsibility (Grand Rapids, Michigan, June 1982) was convened by the Theology and Education Group of the Lausanne Committee for World Evangelization and the unit on Ethics and Society of the World Evangelical Fellowship in an attempt to settle those questions that had become divisive among evangelicals. In the opinion of David M. Howard, General Director of WEF, "CRESR was the most ambitious consultation on that topic yet attempted in the evangelical world."[46]

Padilla says that the Grand Rapids Report on Evangelism and Social

Responsibility represents "A milestone in the evangelical understanding of the Christian mission in the modern world."[47] By all means, this is a document that every evangelical leader must read.

After dealing with some of the causes of the divorce of evangelism and social responsibility and discussing how in general they relate to one another, the Report concludes: "Thus, evangelism and social responsibility, while distinct from one another, are integrally related in our proclamation of and obedience to the Gospel. The partnership is, in reality, a marriage."[48]

With respect to the question of primacy, the Lausanne Covenant says that "in the church's mission of sacrificial service evangelism is primary" (Para. 6). The Grand Rapids Report explains that it is true that evangelism has a certain priority; it is not necessarily a temporal priority but a logical one. "Christian social responsibility presupposes socially responsible Christians and it can only be by evangelism and discipling that they have become such." Moreover, Christians are doing in evangelism what nobody else can do. The Report agrees with the Thailand Statement (1980) in that "of all the tragic needs of human beings none is greater than their alienation from their Creator and the terrible reality of eternal death for those who refuse to repent and believe." However, the Report says that "this fact must not make us indifferent to the degradations of human poverty and oppression. The choice, we believe, is largely conceptual" (Sec. 4).

The Report is also in agreement with the Lausanne Covenant's affirmation that "evangelism and socio-political involvement are both part of our Christian duty." It offers some guidelines for that involvement. The main question is: "Does social action belong to the mission of the church as church, or is it the prerogative of individual believers who make up the church, and of groups?"

The Report answers that there is no doubt about individuals and groups. But, "Should the church get involved in politics, or keep out?" There was a great deal of discussion of this question in Grand Rapids among the fifty evangelical leaders participating in the consultation. A distinction is made in the Report between the situation of the local church in a free society and that of the church under repression. In a free society the church has to pray, to demonstrate its love in action, and to teach the whole purpose of God, addressing itself to social issues. There are controversial issues that have to be handled carefully. "But when the church concludes that biblical faith or righteousness requires it to take a public stand on some issue, then it must obey God's Word and trust him with the consequences" (Sec. 7).

In the case of the church under repression, Christians must be true to their Lord and bear their testimony by deeds of love. When the church has to act, especially in some kind of protest, the members of the Body of Christ "must stand together . . . knowing their legal rights and defending them (like the apostle Paul), and witnessing together to Christ."

> The principle is clear. We are to obey the state (whose authority comes from God) right up to the point where obedience to it would involve us in disobedience to him. In that extreme circumstance alone, it is our Christian duty to disobey the state in order to obey God.... There are occasions of moral principle in which the church must take its stand, whatever the cost. For the church is the community of the Suffering Servant who is also the Lord, and it is called to serve and suffer with him. It is not popularity which is the authentic mark of the church, but prophetic suffering, and even martyrdom. [Sec. 7]

Of course, to be in basic agreement with the Report does not mean to forget that the church as church is not supposed to enter into the struggle for political power. To do this the church should have to take sides in the political arena, hoping to gain earthly influence and authority by means of the marriage of the throne and the altar. It has been said that when we do not study history to learn from the mistakes of the past, we repeat them. There is today a "Constantinianism" of the right and a "Constantinianism" of the left. The church as church is not supposed to be naive, allowing itself to be manipulated by a particular ideology, whether of the political left or of the political right. One of the greatest dangers for the church in Latin America today is that of attempting to politicize the gospel on behalf of a political system or party. We may suffer opposition or even persecution not because of our faithfulness to the gospel, but by serving consciously or unconsciously a political cause.

Consultation at Jarabacoa
Jarabacoa, Dominican Republic, May 1983

Convened by the Latin American Theological Fraternity, a group of evangelical Christians that included theologians and politicians of Latin America met in Jarabacoa, Dominican Republic, in May 1983 to reflect on the topic of theology and the practice of power. In other words, they dealt with evangelical social responsibility in a very specific way—the exercise of political power.

Papers read included "Christian Faith and Political Power," "Power Structures in Latin America," "Ideological Trends in Latin America," and "Models of Political Action." These papers and the Declaration of Jarabacoa have been published in book form in Spanish.[49]

The Declaration points out biblical-theological principles and concrete areas for a responsible political action on the part of evangelical Christians. In regard to politics, it is stated:

> Politics is an inescapable reality, since it is an inherent factor in the living together of any people in any society, which makes possible the full self-realization of the person as a communal being. Politics is an effective instrument for the development of truth, liberty, justice, peace, solidarity, and democracy among men. Since by its character it is a means and not an end, politics has to do with the situation, organization, competence and the rights proper to human beings in reaching goals which contribute to general welfare.[50]

In its final section the document gives "Practical Suggestions for Political Action for Christians." According to these suggestions, the evangelical community should act at the local-congregation level by praying, teaching, and serving; through associations and ecclesiastical denominations, movements, and specialized groups; and as individual believers in the social context.

The effort to articulate biblical ethics for political action in Latin America is a valuable contribution to the fulfillment of the church's mission in the area of social responsibility. It is also appreciated that a group of Latin American evangelical leaders have dealt with important subjects like human rights, economics, private property, labor relations, education, public health, communications, and international relations.

Once again, as in the case of the Lausanne Covenant (1974) and the Grand Rapids Report (1982), I would like to have seen in the Declaration of Jarabacoa a direct word of warning against the ideologization of the gospel on behalf of a particular socio-political system. We cannot overlook the fact that even dictators, both of the right and of the left, claim to be champions of democracy and human rights. But they do not practice what they preach. However, the straightforward affirmations of the evangelical leaders who met in Jarabacoa are welcomed as an expression of biblical ideals and principles for our Christian social action.

Conference on the Nature and Mission of the Church
Wheaton, Illinois, June—July 1983

The Conference on the Nature and Mission of the Church was convened by the World Evangelical Fellowship. More than three hundred fifty participants from sixty countries met at the Billy Graham Center, Wheaton, Illinois, June 20—July 1, 1983. The Conference met in three simultaneous consultations. One of them dealt with "The Church in Response to Human Need."

In the document that emerged from that consultation,[51] it is acknowledged that "only by spreading the Gospel can the most basic need of human beings be met: to have fellowship with God." But the main purpose is not to emphasize evangelism as a separate theme, because it is seen "as an integral part of the total Christian response to human need." Beside, the writers of the document felt no need to repeat what the Lausanne Covenant and the Grand Rapids Report had already expressed.

The document emphasizes social transformation. The writers and signatories do not want to be naively optimistic or pessimistic about social change. They do not believe that there is such a thing as nonpolitical involvement, for they say that "our very non-involvement lends tacit support to the existing order." Consequently, "there is no escape: either we challenge the evil structures of society or we support them."

Transformation is the key word of the document. This word was chosen to replace *development* because, among other reasons, *transformation* can be applied even to the highly-developed nations, which are also in need of radical changes in their societies.

Transformation is defined as "the change from a condition of human existence contrary to God's purposes to one in which people are able to enjoy fullness of life in harmony with God." It is added that this transformation "can only take place through the obedience of individuals and communities to the Gospel, whose power makes men and women 'new creatures in Christ.'"

The biblical doctrines of creation, the Fall, and redemption are cited in support of the thesis of transformation, whose goal is best described "by the biblical vision of the Kingdom of God."

Great emphasis is placed on the stewardship of creation. "The earth is God's gift to all generations." The stewardship of creation has to do with everybody, inside or outside the church; it has to do both with the individual and with society in general; and it has to do both with private enterprises and with the state:

> When either individuals or States claim an absolute right
> of ownership, that is rebellion against God. The meaning
> of stewardship is that the poor have equal rights to God's
> resources (Dt. 15:8-9). The meaning of transformation is
> that, as stewards of God's bountiful gifts, we do justice,
> striving together through prayer, example, representation
> and protest to have resources redistributed and the con-
> sequences of greed limited (Acts 4:32-5:11). [Para. 17]

The misuse of huge amounts of resources in the present arms race,
while millions starve to death, is denounced. There is also a strong denunciation of those churches, mission societies, and Christian relief and
development agencies that by their silence give tacit support to dehumanizing social structures.

The document affirms that poverty is not a necessary evil, but often
the result of exploitation and oppression. "Evil is not only in the human
heart but also in the social structures." Consequently, Christians must
evangelize, respond to immediate human needs, "and press for social
transformation." They are called to identify themselves with the poor,
following the example of Jesus and remembering that justice and mercy
belong together with the gospel ministry. Ways have to be sought "to
bring about change in favor of the oppressed."

The local church has to be a vehicle for social transformation. "Our
churches must also address issues of evil and social injustice in the local
community and the wider society." Aid agencies are called to help the local churches in the fulfillment of their mission. These agencies are also
exhorted "to ensure biblical integrity and genuine partnership with
churches and other agencies."

The church is also called "to infuse the world with hope, for both
this age and the next," because the kingdom of God is both present and
future. "As the community of the end-time anticipating the End, we prepare for the ultimate by getting involved in the penultimate."

Toward the end of the document there is an extremely needed affirmation: "We thus move forward, without relegating salvation merely
to an eternal future or making it synonymous with a political or social
dispensation to be achieved in the here and now."

In the opinion of C. René Padilla, "Wheaton '83 completed the process of shaping an evangelical social conscience, a process in which people from the Two-Thirds World played a decisive role. It made it evident
to evangelicals that evangelism cannot be divorced from meaningful involvement with people with all their needs."[52] But even at Wheaton 1983

there were some negative reactions to the document.

For instance, although the document explains at the beginning that evangelism is an integral part of the church's mission, some participants were concerned about what they considered to be an overemphasis on social transformation that could be detrimental to the doctrine of personal regeneration. Actually, apart from the Lausanne Covenant and the Grand Rapids Report, the document from Wheaton 1983 may seem to be out of biblical balance. But the third paragraph of the document states that its main purpose is not to emphasize evangelism and that it is not necessary to repeat what other documents have already expressed.

Perhaps more clarification was needed in the document to avoid the impression that a partial view of the church's mission is being presented instead of the full-orbed approach that the writers endorse.

It is also possible that the use of some "revolutionary" expressions like "identification with the poor," "a change in favor of the oppressed," "evil social structures," and "oppression and exploitation" in addition to the ideas on private property have been a cause of alarm to some evangelical leaders, although the context in which these expressions and ideas appear in the document is quite different from that of some contemporary theological works.

At any rate, the issue of evangelism and social responsibility continues to be controversial in the worldwide evangelical community. There are in Latin America, for example, evangelical leaders who have not yet incorporated social concern into their concept of mission. Others are still limiting social responsibility to social assistance, or service. Political involvement of evangelicals as individuals or as members of special groups is for them out of the picture.

However, a significant change is taking place among many Latin American leaders in their attitude toward social concern. The experience of having in Guatemala during the years 1982-1983 as president of the nation an evangelical general who was not ashamed of the gospel before the TV cameras, and who had at the same time a bad image in the international press, made many of us aware of how little we knew of the theology of social concern and how little experience we had to deal with the new situation. Then in 1985 an evangelical politician participated as a candidate in the presidential election. As never before we saw our great need to reflect, at all levels of the evangelical community, on the whole mission of the church. We were not really prepared, as a community, to avail ourselves of the opportunities for an effective Christian testimony to the nation in the area of social concern.

It is unfortunate that evangelical documents like the ones quoted in this chapter have not had a wide circulation among evangelicals in Latin America. Many of the leaders at the local congregation level have not read them yet. But the changing situation in which we live and the message of renewal that once in a while comes to us are producing the awakening of our evangelical social conscience.

Consultaton on Evangelical Social Responsibility
Panama City, September 1983

The Panama Consultation on Evangelical Social Responsibility (September 1983) was sponsored by the Theological Commission of the Latin American Theological Confraternity (*Confraternidad Evangélica Latinoamericana,* CONELA), an association of evangelical churches, denominations, and aid agencies in our subcontinent. Twenty evangelical leaders from different Latin American countries were invited to meet in Panama City to reflect on social concern in the light of the Scriptures and in response to our Latin American reality.

It is encouraging to see that the first consultation convened by one of the commissions of CONELA had to do with evangelical social responsibility. It is also encouraging to note that CONELA reflects on social concern under the direct influence of declarations made on this subject in congresses and consultations like Wheaton 1966, Bogotá 1969, Lausanne 1974, Grand Rapids 1982, and Wheaton 1983. The report[53] that came out of Panama 1983 follows the basic emphasis of documents that the worldwide evangelical community has produced during the last two decades on the full-orbed mission of the church,

The Panama Report is first of all an attempt to define evangelical social responsibility on the basis of the Scriptures. It is on the foundation of biblical authority that the report deals with the sovereignty of God in creation, history, and redemption; the origin, fall, and salvation of the human being; the dignity of men and women; the fundamental role of the family in society; the purpose of the state from the divine standpoint; the civic duties of the Christian, and his or her right to civil disobedience when the state attempts to violate his or her Christian conscience "either on social or religious issues."

According to the report, the church as church is not supposed to get involved in the struggle for political power; but it has to affirm and defend the rights of all human beings. As individuals and citizens of their own countries, Christians have to be free to participate in the political process, following the dictates of their own Christian consciences and exercising the talents and gifts that God has given them according to their own vocations in life.

The churches have to be willing to suffer for the Lord's sake as a result of their message and good works; but they must not be naive, provoking a suffering that may not be necessary for the cause of Christ on earth.

It is declared that the hope of the Lord's return is an incentive to continue working for him, both in the spiritual and social dimensions of the gospel ministry.

In the last section of the report some suggestions are given for implementing the principles already enunciated. For instance, it is suggested that multidisciplinary consultations be held at the local, regional, and international levels to continue reflecting on subjects like wealth and poverty, the prophetic ministry of the church, the participation of Christians in the political process, and other similar themes.

The Panama Report is a short document that emphasizes the teaching of the Scriptures; assimilates the main emphasis of the Lausanne Covenant and the Grand Rapids Report on evangelism and social concern; avoids the inflammatory language of some contemporary liberationist works; and is open to further reflection on evangelical social responsibility.

As an immediate result of Panama 1983, the Guatemalan participants went back to their country with the purpose of communicating to other leaders what they had experienced in the consultation. A few weeks later they organized an Interdenominational Committee on Evangelical Social Concern. This committee sponsored several consultations for pastors at the interdenominational level.

Consultation on Transformation
Huampaní, Peru, December 1987

The Consultation on Transformation (Huampaní, Peru, December 1987) was sponsored by the Latin American Theological Fraternity for the main purpose of reflecting on an "integral transformation" with representatives of Christian aid agencies working in Latin America. Ninety leaders from seventeen Latin American countries, including more than thirty aid agencies, participated in the consultation. We have seen that the Wheaton 1983 document dedicated several paragraphs to the role that aid agencies can play in social transformation. But the Huampaní Declaration itself says very little more than Wheaton 1983 on that subject. We have to wait for the publication of the papers read at Huampaní to know more about the reflection of the participants on the ministry of the aid agencies in our countries.

The Declaration[54] starts by acknowledging the work others have done to put into practice the missiological principles enunciated in conferences like Bogotá 1969 and Lima, Peru (CLADE II, 1979). At the same time, it is affirmed that the Holy Spirit has been working in the accomplishment of the complete mission of the church "to take us now a step further" in that task here in Latin America.

The inspiration and authority of the Scriptures are affirmed, indicating at the same time that God's written revelation has to be understood under the illumination of the Holy Spirit and taking as a point of hermeneutical departure a commitment to the complete mission of the church within the Latin American context.

The writers give the declaration a Trinitarian foundation by saying that God the Father listens to the cry of the people for justice in the midst of social injustice; that God the Son is the model of solidarity with those who suffer and the model of service to the poor; and that God the Holy Spirit produces in men and women a transformation that also affects social reality.

The church is the community through which God wants to manifest his kingdom in history. Consequently, it is necessary for the church to proclaim the Good News, to be present in society, and to do those good works that demonstrate the divine justice which is inherent in the gospel. As in the Wheaton 1983 Document, *transformation* is the key word in the Declaration of Huampaní 1987.

Reference is made to the need for evaluating in a critical way the methods employed by the aid agencies in their work. There is a strong denunciation of paternalism and other attitudes that are not in keeping with our Latin American reality. It is affirmed that the poor must participate in their own transformation. A respect for the cultural identity of our people is demanded.

The second part of the declaration indicates that it is urgent to reflect on theological models that would be relevant to the Latin American situation and to respond with concrete programs to our social realities—for example, the alienation of specific human groups, including women, children, ethnic peoples, and political dissidents; the external debt of the Latin American countries; the economic policies that increase poverty for the masses and wealth for the privileged classes of society; the violation of human rights; terrorism; and the arms race on our continent.

The people of God are exhorted to support, especially in prayer, those Christians who are working in justice and peace in their own countries. Specific mention is made of those Christian pastors and lay people who are victims of repression and terrorism in Peru and the Christians who are active on behalf of peace and democracy in Nicaragua, El Salvador, Chile, and Haiti.

The declaration wants to be relevant in a very specific way to the Latin American people in their sufferings and in their longings for freedom. We identify with the writers in their concern about the sad situation in which we live and in their desire to project the influence of the kingdom of God to all the segments of our society for a genuine and complete transformation. At the same time, we do not want to forget that if we are torchbearers for social justice, peace, and freedom in the name of Christ, we are not supposed to be partial in our evaluation of what is going on in the world. It is imperative to realize that on both sides of the ideological dividing line there are Christians, and other kinds of people, who cry for justice, peace, and democracy. Partiality in their prophetic denunciation is one of the major problems with some contemporary theologies, both in Roman Catholicism and Protestantism. But our main purpose in this chapter has been to describe the awakening process of our evangelical social conscience. An in-depth evaluation of every one of the documents on evangelical social responsibility produced in a twenty-one-year period would take much more time and space. In this historical overview only those declarations or reports that are more closely related to our evangelical social awakening in Latin America have been included.[55]

CONCLUSION

From the Chicago Congress on Missions (1960) to the Consultation on Integral Transformation in Huampaní, Peru (1987), or from the interpretation of social responsibility as merely social assistance and development to the emphasis on social transformation, the road has been long, difficult, and somehow disturbing to some evangelical leaders around the world; but it has also been rewarding to many of us Third World evangelicals.

In Latin America we have been challenged to think by ourselves, to listen to other points of view, to interact theologically with other evangelical leaders, to evaluate and re-evaluate our own theology of mission, and most of all, to go back to the Scriptures to know what the Lord is telling us and what he is leading us to say in response to the problems of society.

Because of the spirit of freedom that characterizes our evangelical faith, we cannot expect uniformity of thought among evangelicals on every missiological issue. After more than twenty years of wrestling with the relationship between evangelism and social responsibility, discrepancies still exist among us. However, there is a growing consensus on some basic points related to the full-orbed mission of the church. This consensus has been made possible especially after the consultations at Wheaton (1966), Bogotá (1969), Lausanne (1974), and Grand Rapids (1982). A new direction was given by these consultations to our thinking on the mission of the church.

For instance, it is now commonplace to affirm in international gatherings of evangelical leaders that there is no dichotomy between evangelism and social responsibility; that both proclamation and social action must go together in the gospel ministry. There is a strong conviction about the social implications of the gospel; that salvation is for the individual and for the benefit of society; that the Christian message is for life beyond the grave and life this side of the grave.

On the other hand, the emphasis on the complete mission of the church seems to be gaining ground slowly in our conservative evangelical churches. The awakening process is taking time even among pastors and other leaders; the time may be longer for the people in the pews unless a radical social change takes place in the immediate future. The so-called old-line or historical denominations do not seem to have much problem in this respect. To them it has been quite natural to think of social responsibility as part of their mission, at least in the sense of social assistance and development. Although the middle-class mentality has been strong in those churches, it has been mainly from them that the intellectual leaders of "the Protestant left" have emerged.

That there is not a demise of evangelism among us conservative evangelicals in Latin America is impressively demonstrated by seminars, consultations, and congresses dedicated to designing strategies for evangelism, church growth, and missions. The practitioners are the ones leading the way in Latin American evangelicalism.

Even in those major consultations dealing especially with social concern, evangelism has not been set aside. The final declarations or reports have adhered to the principle that both evangelism and social responsibility belong together in the mission of the church. But if evangelicals lose the biblical balance in their theology and praxis, then we would have to speak of "the battle for Latin American evangelism."

At Lausanne 1974 Billy Graham said that healing the sick, feeding the hungry, helping the needy, working for political freedom, and changing political and social structures are good, where possible, "but this is not strictly evangelism." Humanists can do all of that. Only the church has the duty and privilege of proclaiming the Lord Jesus Christ "by its presence and by trusting the Holy Spirit to use the Scriptures to persuade men to become his disciples and responsible members of his church."[56] Of course, to be a disciple of Christ and a responsible member of his church also includes showing social concern.

NOTES

1. *The Grand Rapids Report on Evangelism and Social Responsibility: An Evangelical Commitment* (Exeter, Esngland: Paternoster, 1982), pp. 43-44.

2. For instance, The First Epistle of Clement of Rome to the Corinthians, The Epistle of Barnabas, The Epistles of Ignatius, The Shepherd of Hermas, The Teaching of the Twelve Apostles, The First Apology of Justin.

3. Jose Ma. Gómez-Heras, *Teología Protestant* (Madrid: Biblioteca de Autores Cristianos, 1972), pp. 246-47.

4. George M. Marsden, Fundamentalism and American Culture (Oxford University, 1980), p. 86.

5. Ibid.

6. Peter Kuzmic, "History and Eschatology: Evangelical Views," in *In Word and Deed*, ed. Bruce J. Nicholls (Australia: Paternoster, 1985), p. 144.

7. Ibid., p. 147.

8. Marsden, pp.1 80-93.

9. Ibid., p. 90.

10. L. Grant McClung, Jr., ed. *Azusa Street and Beyond* (South Plainfield, NJ: Losos, 1986), p.5.

11. Lalive D'Epinay, *El Refugio de las Masas* (Santiago de Chile: Editorial del Pacifíco, 1968). English edition: *Haven of the Masses: A Study of the Pentecostal Movement in Chile* (London: Lutterworth, 1969).

12. Marsden, p. 91.

13. Eric S. Fife, "The Student World and the Unfinished Task," in *Facing the Unfinished Task*, comp. J. O. Percy (Grand Rapids, MI: Zondervan, 1961), p. 123.

14. G. Christian Weiss, "An Inquiry into the Obligation of Christians," in *Facing the Unfinished Task*, p. 262.

15. Emilio A. Núñez, "The Ideal Missionary," in *Facing the Unfinished Task*, pp. 173-74.

16. *The Wheaton Declaration, 1966*, in *The Church's Worldwide Mission*, ed. Harold Lindsell (Waco, TX: Word, 1966), pp. 234-35.

17. C. René Padilla, "Evangelism and Social Responsibility from Wheaton '66 to Wheaton '83," in *How Evangelicals Endorsed Social Responsibility* (Texts on Evangelical Social Ethics 1974-83, II), ed. René Padilla and Chris Sugden (Bramcote, Nottingham: Grove Books, 1985), p. 5.

18. W. Stanley Mooneyham, "Introduction"; Carl F. H. Henry, "Facing a New Day in Evangelism," in *One Race, One Gospel, One Task*, ed. Carl F. H. Henry and W. Stanley Mooneyham (Minneapolis: Worldwide Publications, 1967), 1:3-4, 12.

19. Athol Gill, "Christian Social Responsibility," in *The New Face of Evangelicalism*, ed. C. Rene Padilla (London: Hodder and Stoughton, 1976), p. 90.

20. Paul S. Rees, "Evangelism and Social Concern," in *One Race, One Gospel, One Task*, 1:306-8. The "response" by Benjamin Moraes from Brazil to Rees's paper indicates that there was already a serious reflection on social concern among evangelicals in that South American country: "I agree completely with what has been said by Dr. Paul Rees. . . . It's necessary to remind everybody that when we speak about total evangelism we mean not only the beginning of the gospel of conversion. . . , but also we mean to add the social implications of the Gospel. . . . I reject the so-called social gospel. But that does not mean that the Gospel has no social implications. It has!" 1:308.

21. Carl F. H. Henry, ibid., 1:16-17

22. Billy Graham, ibid., 1:31-32.

23. Padilla, in *How Evangelicals Endorsed Social Responsibility*, p. 6.

24. "Closing Statement of the World Congress on Evangelism," in *One Race, One Gospel, One Task*, 1:5-6.

25. Samuel Escobar, "Responsabilidad Social de la Iglesia," *Acción en Cristo para un Continente en Crisis* (San José, Costa Rica: Editorial Caribe, 1970), pp. 32-39.

26. "Declaración Evangélica de Bogotá," *Acción en Criso para un Continene en Crisis*, pp. 134-35.

27. Mimeographed Documents of the Latin American Theological Fraternity.

28. The most prolific writers of the LATF have been Orlando E. Costas, C. René Padilla, and Samuel Escobar, with several titles both in Spanish and English.

29. These data are from the book *Let the Earth Hear His Voice*. This is the official reference volume containing the papers and responses of the International Congress on World Evangelization, Lausanne, Switzerland, 1974. ed. J. D. Douglas (Minneapolis: World Wide Publications, 1975), back cover.

30. Graham, "Why Lausanne?" in *Let the Earth Hear His Voice*, pp. 29-30.

31. Ibid., pp. 29, 31.

32. Athol Gill, in *The New Face of Evangelicalism*, p. 89.

33. *Let the Earth Hear His Voice*, pp. 4-5.

34. *The Lausanne Covenant—An Exposition and Commentary by John Stott* (Minneapolis: World Wide Publications, 1975), p. 19.

35. Padilla, "Evangelism and the World," in *Let the Earth Hear His Voice*, p. 144.

36. Padilla, "Introduction," in *The New Face of Evangelicalism*, p. 12.

37. *The Lausanne Covenant*, para. 6.

38. "Letter from CLADE 11 to the Evangelical Community of Latin America," translated into English for *Texts on Evangelical Social Ethics, 1974-1983* (1). Eds. René Padilla and Chris Sugden (Bramcote, Nottingham: Grove Books, 1985), pp. 15-17.

39. "A Statement of Intent," *Evangelicals and Development: Towards a Theology of Social Change*, ed. Ronald Sider (Exeter: Paternoster, 1982), p. 9.

40. "Preface," *Lifestyle in the Eighties: An Evangelical Commitment to Simple Lifestyle*, pp. 13-19.

41. "The Commitment," *Lifestyle in the Eighties: An Evangelical Commitment to Simple Lifestyle*, pp. 13-19.

42. Alan Nichols, *An Evangelical Commitment to Simple Life Style* (Wheaton, IL: Lausanne Committee for World Evangelization, 1980), p. 27.

43. Padilla, in *How Evangelicals Endorsed Social Responsibility*, pp. 13-15.

44. Mimeographed copy distributed at Pattaya.

45. Padilla, in *How Evangelicals Endorsed Social Responsibility*, p. 14.

46. David M. Howard, *The Dream that Would Not Die* (Exeter: Paternoster, 1986), p. 168.

47. Padilla, in *How Evangelicals Endorsed Social Responsibility*, p. 15.

48. *The Grand Rapids Report on Evangelism and Social Responsibility*, p. 24.

49. Pablo Alberto Deiros, ed., *Los Evangélicos y el Poder Político en America Latina* (Grand Rapids, MI: Eerdmans, 1986).

50. *Declaration of Jarabacoa: Christians and Political Action.* Mimeographed copy.

51. *The Church in Response to Human Need.* Mimeographed copy.

52. Padilla, in *How Evangelicals Endorsed Social Responsibility*, p. 17.

53. *Informe de la Consulra Theológica Sobre la Responsabilidad Social.* Panama, September 1983.

54. *Hacia Una Transformación Integral.* Document of the Consultation in Huampani, Peru, December 1987.

55. For instance, Padilla and Sugden mention "The Chicago Declaration on Evangelical Social Concern" (November 1973) and "The Madras Declaration on Evangelical Social Action."

56. Graham, in *Let the Earth Hear His Voice*, pp. 30-31

Part Three

Updating and Concluding Perspectives for Latin America

William David Taylor
and
Emilio Antonio Núñez

14

Revisiting Latin America: A Nineties Update Looking Towards the Third Millennium

William David Taylor

PART A:
Latin American Socio-Political-Economic Realities

A GRASS-ROOTS REALITY BAPTISM

There is nothing like a Latin bus trip to give you a feeling for the grass roots, to expand your perspective on national reality. A recent long bus ride became for me a continental microcosm, allowing me to discern the current scene, and also to see Latin America in ongoing flux and change. I had recently flown into the modern airport of Guatemala City and, attempting to economize on travel costs, had taken a bus to El Salvador. From the modern, people-jammed, polluted capital city into the less-populated beauty of mountains and lush valleys in full rainy-season splendor. From a fast-paced, world-class city to the slower pace of small-town and rural realities that are familiar to most Latins. The trip was a socio-economic reality check—most Latins live close to poverty.

Admittedly, my bus was not what I called a "chicken hauler," it was relatively luxurious. But it still gave another perspective on the kaleidoscopic Latin Americas of our continent. As the driver wove through the four-lane highway (bereft of any painted lanes), dodging vehicles of all sizes and makes, animals and chuck-holes, I surveyed my fellow-travelers as well as the world outside my window. To my surprise, a father and son bowed in prayer as the bus departed the stations. "Could they be believers?" I thought; then, "How do I find out?" Well, I simply asked them if they were praying. They were, and we launched into the varied stories of our relationsh with Christ. Through the window I caught a glimpse of a bumper sticker, "A Jesus por María" (To Jesus through Mary).

The bus wove its way through eastern Guatemala and then to the border crossing into El Salvador. (Borders still represent major Latin reality for me, recalling memories of scores of similar trips in years past.) Foreigners needed passports and visas, yet most of the other people swarming around that porous border didn't seem to! Children, Latin America's most precious product, were all over the place. Everybody was working: bustling and hustling, changing currencies, charging admission for a clean toilet, selling everything from chewing gum to audio cassettes to fruit and other food, to literature, to small appliances. We were far from the global economy and information age. But, then again, were we really? Satellite dishes announced their apparent capacity to beam in signals from space; the ubiquitous military had modern armaments and communications equipment; the luxury Mercedes Benz bus was a late model. Latin America was on the move here with their major product, people, always evident: children, youth, and adults of all ages, sizes, colors and nationalities. We drove on into El Salvador, a dynamic, small, post-civil war nation in transition. I would be speaking at a missions conference in a growing urban church that was breaking new ground in terms of what it means to be "the church" in Latin America.,

Spiritual concerns evidenced themselves on that bus trip, with two samples engraved on my memory. One, the conversation with my fellow passenger and his young son. Fairly recent converts to Christ, they attended a dynamic charismatic church in San Salvador. They represented youth and adults coming to Christ from traditional Latin Christianity. Secondly, the surprising number of small evangelical churches dotting the roadside. I tried to count them but finally gave up. They were simply everywhere, from Episcopal to Pentecostal to non-charismatic to independent.

Latin America: that vast spectrum of peoples, races, geographics, socio-economic status. Latin America: not realizing for the most part what the Berlin Wall and its fall represented to them. Latin America: selling sugar cane, Coke and Pepsi. Latin America: a world of worlds. Latin America: social, political, economic, always spiritual.

Continental Socio-Political-Economic Changes

The Overarching Panorama

Since publication of the first edition of this book, significant changes have rippled, and sometimes ripped, through the continent.[1] Some of them are hopeful, while others chronicle the ongoing painful crises of this continent. We could write at length about contemporary (and dated) events in all of the nineteen nations included in this work. Let me scan ten of them:

Cuba: her uncertain future, painful present and the latest flood of refugees; Fidel the unreconstructed Marxist forced to grapple with the loss of his economic/political godfather, Russia, and the need to introduce some form of market liberalization; the USA with thousands of Cuban refugees unhappily consigned to camps in Panama until the USA returned them to Cuba.

Nicaragua: with the stunning elections of February 1990, which tossed out the Sandinistas and brought in a Mother of the nations, Mrs. Chamorro with a gilded last name; an impoverished nation with no democratic tradition.

Peru: under the Peruvian-Japanese president and authoritarian leader, Alberto Fujimori, who was elected with strong evangelical support but he then rejected them; who in spite of widespread condemnation of his "fujimoraso" self-coup, has been widely supported by the people; under whose rule the Shining Path Maoist terrorists have been profoundly wounded and its prime leaders jailed; where the drug issue is now being addressed wtih tough laws and crop-substitution; but where the president openly feuds with his estranged wife.

Ecuador: in late January 1995, needlessly slicing open an historical scar as it initiated border hostilities with Peru, with killing and wounding on both sides and the inflaming of nationalistic spirits; Ecuador attempting to regain territory (potentially rich in minerals and oil) which it claims was unjustly lost in the 1941 war between these Andean neighbors—all will lose, particularly Ecuador, again.

El Salvador: with a surprising peace treaty that dissolved the long-term civil war between Marxist guerrilla forces and a rightist government, with a peace dividend opening the door to an economic boom coupled with an explosion of common criminality.

Colombia: introducing macroeconomics that appear to bring initial benefits on a national scale; but a nation profoundly affected by a drug industry formerly headquartered in Medellín but now led by more sophisticated drug imperialists from Cali, the drug lords having found new markets in Europe and even Russia with rumors of drug money funding presidential campaigns; Colombian guerrillas jumping into the drug trade to finance their wars and extend their power.

Panama: where strongman Noriega was ousted in another American military invasion of a small Latin American nation; the same caudillo captured and transported to an American prison and court system which eventually convicted him of drug charges; and the Panama holding elections to determine how it would sink back into "business as usual" politics.

Brazil: the mega-giant, with a former president, Fernando Collor de Mello, impeached for corruption charges in 1992, tried by the Supreme Court and found innocent in late 1994, but barred from politics until the year 2001; a nation led as of January 1995 by a gifted economist and former finance minister (who early in his career was known as a left-leaning sociologist). Fernando Henrique Cardoso, who swept the opposition in the 1994 elections and has tamed the wild tiger of inflation (1,158% in 1993!).

Guatemala: with a decades-long guerrilla war possibly about to be terminated, led now by an interim president elected in the wake of the moral and political failure of so-called evangelical Serrano Elías; a small nation, yet the largest in Central America, reeling from political and economic crises, living the peace of corruption with military leaders involved in the drug trade, and with a noble Indian majority working to sustain ethnic dignity and to stay alive economically.

Argentina: a giant, led by a president of Lebanese extract, Carlos Saúl Menem, who calls himself a fatalist with regard to personal faith; a "backwoods governor turned economic messiah," creating financial stability and a kind of free-enterprise "success story" under the name of Peronism, dramatically reducing the power of the unions, privatizing state-owned entities; a survivor of scandalous charges, once locking his former wife (a Muslim) out of the presidential palace in a very public spat; but as one political wag declared, "With low inflation, Menem could wed 10 women and dance till dawn, and nobody would care."[2]

Let us choose one nation, however, to serve as an extended test case to evaluate the attempts at ongoing transformation in Latin America: *Mexico.* Even as I write at my desk today, the daily newspapers as well as European and American magazines chronicle the Mexican political and economic crises: the crash of the nascent stock market and national currency; the growing doubts about Mexican capacities to face and resolve their internal crises; a massive US $50 billion bailout cobbled together by the USA ($20 billion from the USA, the rest from the IMF, the European-oriented Bank for International Settlements, and four South American nations); it would come in loan form, but Mexico must guarantee oil revenues pledges of US $7 billion per year in return.[3] The facile analyst reviews only economics and current politics, while disregarding history and the profound tectonic social changes rumbling through Mexico—home to 92 million people (including at least 4.6 million evangelicals), most of whom are still on the underside of history. Consistent with the historical thesis of this book, the Mexican case study reminds us that contemporary Latin American must be understood in the context of over five centuries of the Latin American experiment.

From now on Mexicans approach their new year with a sense of trepidation. On January 1, 1994, the Zapatista National Liberation Army rocked the nation with a major revolt against hte central government. Based in the southern state of Chiapas with a social structure somewhat closer to feudalism than democracy, a band of rebels opened their attack, claiming the legendary name of one of Mexico's revered revolutionaries, and led by a former university professor.[4] Granmt the rebels an historic fist! With high skill they won international defenders on the Internet system—with the help of peace activists and other rebel support groups. The crisis shook national confidence and provoked erratic reactions from local, state and central Mexican officials. Rebellion has always festered like a dormant volcano that periodically blew off steam. But this time the volcano erupted, ieevocably forcing a different governmental response from the old benevolent paternalism and quiet violence once used to suppress the rebels. Early in 1995 matters had seemed to simmer down, particularly when the government appointed the progressive and controversial Catholic Bishop of Chicapas, Samuel Ruíz, as its official mediator. Then, in February 1995, the president sent the military into Chiapas to clean up the rebels, but rapidly reversed his orders. On top of these crises, Mexico in 1994 also suffered the assassination of the leading presidential candidate and other top political leaders, crimes possibly orchestrated by competing politicians in the ruling party.

Almost exactly one year later, Mexicans awoke to the news of their economic crisis with a collapsing peso, an imploding economy, and a shaken new president Ernesto Zedillo who had inherited much of the mess from his predecessor, Carlos Salinas de Gortari. Salinas had avoided a planned devaluation of the peso, partly because it would jeopardize his chances—now failed—to become the first czar of the new World Trade Organization. Mexican writer and former diplomat Carlos Fuentes feels that Salinas "was worried that an ecnomic crisis in his turf would bury his candidacy."[5] As the Spanish proverb states, Zedillo, Salinas's successor, became "the duck for the soup." Optimistic reports of a new emerging and stable Latin America crashed along with Mexico's economic crisis. NAFTA supporters were shaken and NAFTA opponents were gleeful. And Salinas fled to the USA to avoid prosecution himself.

This national case study reflects issues that must be understood in a broader context. It is one thing to tout economic reforms; and they are fine and acceptable. But when they are too rapidly grafted onto five centuries of a particular political and social culture, a crisis such as Mexico's is not surprising. What's more, much of the quick foreign investment that poured into Mexico was not geared to developing critical national infrastructure but rather to making rapid profits. Dubbed the "Tequila effect," it casts shadows on the economic and political reliability of the other emerging Latin economic giants, such as Brazil and Argentina, as well as all investment expectations for the Two-Thirds world. At the January 1995 World Economic Forum in plush Davos, Switzerland, Argentine president Menem argued that his nation was not Mexico.[6] But the Mexico case illustrates that an exodus from a culture of poverty and structural injustice (30% unemployed labor force) is not achieved simply and quickly. The battle must be engaged at a much deeper level. It is cultural, it is historic, it is bound in centuries of a particular set of behavior and values. Economic metamorphosis simply must go beyond the financial categories (fiscal restraints, reforms and market liberalization) and be accompanied by systemic transitions in the legal, political, social and educational realms. Modernity and economic reforms implemented by the younger national leaders, many of them graduates of prestigious North American universities, are not enough. Treaties like NAFTA peer into the future, for they prelude broader economic and trade reforms that will radically alter the continental, political and human landscape.

Again, Mexico is only one national example. Parallel stories can be developed for each of the Latin American nations, particularly as they attempt to transition into the broader economic worlds (regional and global) as well as into the information age of the present and future. The tensions inherent in structural change must be understood in the context of 500 years of history. Nevertheless, change is in the wind, and it is here to stay. Latin America is not what it was even ten years ago. Crisis and hope in Latin America.

Some Major Trends in Latin America

In the last eight years, and particularly since the fall of the Berlin wall, the major foreign policy, political and economic professional journals have written primarily about the former Soviet empire and Central Europe, as well as the Pacific Rim world. After the Sandinista debacle in Nicaragua, with Panama's Noriega languishing in a USA jail, and the glories of NAFTA in the bag, Latin America receded from public interest—until the recent Mexican economic crisis. However, some provocative essays have come out with application to Latin America. This continent is but one major region of our world community; it is undergoing its own transformation as it grapples with its history and the future. It probably does not yet qualify for what Kenichi Ohmae calls the "region state" of natural economic zones, whether within a nation or a grouping of them.[7] Latin America could possibly become a region state under certain circumstances, but not with nasty hostilities like Ecuador and Peru in 1995. Ohmae has also written about the economic "borderless world"; but, frankly, Latin America is not there yet. Nevertheless, the sub-regions within Latin America are definitely moving towards serious and structural economic covenants. NAFTA (which may include Chile and others) is but one example. Central America, the Southern Cone and the Andean nations are working on their own trade agreements.

What are some of the major trends of the '90s that can be observed in Latin America? I mention only a few of many.

First, the rise of democratization, coupled with the ongoing search for a political model for Latin America. One clear item of good news is that seventeen (all but Cuba and Peru) of the nineteen nations forming the core of our Latin continent now have some kind of a democratic regime. All Latin Americanists have noted this phenomenon, for every country in some measure has been impacted by political forces that generate different models of democracy. Some of the forces come from far beyond the continent, such as the imploding of European/Soviet Marxism; the economic factors that push towards a globalized economy and the technology-driven information age; or they reflect fundamental changes taking place within the continent. Example: if the Mexican dominant political party, the PRI, wants to survive, it must rewrite the rules of national governance. The Latin American military has withdrawn in failure and frustration. With only two exceptions, the strongmen are out. And even that unrepentant Marxist, Fidel Castro, is forced to modify some of this ideology, though he tinkers with economics and not his system nor his personal status.

What are the political model options? One is the "Asian Tiger" route, exemplified by Singapore, Malaysia and Korea; another is the classical North American/European form; yet another is the *caudillista* strong man; finally, the traditional politics of same old business done in the same old way. Whither Latin America? Will any one of these models guarantee a healthy transition into the new world order, level the political playing field, control corruption and transform public state structures? Of course not; it may be too much to ask. But the fact is that for the first time we observe a healthy political heterogeneity of systems on the continent. French sociologist Alain Touraine argues that Latin America stands halfway between two worlds, two continents and, in a sense, two worldviews. He ponders whether Latin America will move towards the Western democratic model or will approximate the Asian authoritarian one.

> It is particularly difficult to answer that question, because the political model which dominated during much of the time in Latin America was neither the European nor the Asiatic one, rather that of the national-popular State, which redistributed the resources, in great measure external, and at the same time possessed a nationalist and integrative character.[8]

Undoubtedly the collapse of Soviet Marxism has profoundly impacted Latin American intellectuals and leftists. They simply did not foresee that fall. But then, who could have? And now what were those warriors to do with their lives, their dreams, their political and economic systems and infrastructures, their international benefactors and naive press, their subordinates? The Mexican writer, Jorge G. Castañeda, offers a serious self-evaluation and critique in *Utopia Unarmed: The Latin American Left After the Cold War*, where he recognizes the mistakes of the left, exposes internal disagreements and suggests a future role of the left in building democracy.[9] Some unreconstructed Marxists continue to defend the tired ideology. Some of the radical movements fragmented, or their leaders simply dropped out dismayed. Yet others moved into the revised political games, so today you find former Marxist militants competing in the political process. Examples include El Salvador, Colombia, possibly Guatemala if a treaty is signed between the government and guerrilla forces. However, the left enters this game at high personal risk.

Secondly, a growing wave of opposition to traditional political parties and leades. This trend is closely related to the first one, but it applies directly to the vested interests of establishment party hacks, whether Argentine, Brazilian, Guatemalan, or Mexican. Emerging on the scene is the powerful presence of the new economic wizards (some of them now presidents) through national or state election or by administrative appointment. This is a reality in nations such as Mexico, El Salvador, Brazil and Argentina. In the past national leaders would have their symbolic crew of appointed technocrats, whose actual power and influence were limited by political realities and personal preferences. What's more, when a Latin politician made it to the top, governmental benefits and perks were presumed to flow first to family and close friends rather than qualified appointees. On the positive side, the rise of this new cadre of political leader brings an improved quality and capacity for financial planning to the nation. They want to manage countries on a corporate model—a massive challenge! On the negative side, if the poor are seen only as ciphers or percentages on statistical reports, and if the technocrats heartlessly forget their own roots in the less-advantaged past, these new political leaders will also forget the masses of poor people who must benefit as well from new policies and trade reform. Another evidence of the discreding of traditional politicians is that some of them have been charged and convicted of corruption and other crimes, an amazing feat in light of the vagaries and weaknesses of the Latin American legal system. No former Latin head of state sleeps fully at peace today, as former Paraguayan dictator Alfredo Stroessner has discovered while in exile in Brazil.[10]

Thirdly, and interrelated with politics, is the structural move to some kind of market economy. The propaganda, slogans, buzz words are unceasing; internal and international trade reform, regional treaties, economic pacts with the USA, NAFTA, currency metamorphoses and new names for old currencies, privatization, macroeconomics, and so much more. For many observers the December 1994 "Summit of the Americas" held in Miami was cosmetic, merely a chance for thirty-four new and old politicians to pose and posture together, some hoping that better public relations and pictures with more popular colleagues would improve their image and skills and longevity.[11] On the other hand, the summit leaders represented their changing Latin America.

Moises Naim writes of the continent's "post-adjustment blues" as the tension rises between Latin governments and the market-oriented reforms. The state simply is not equipped to deal effectively with the economic transformations taking place. Historically the Latin state has defended varieties of mercantilism; but it now backs the new rules. What will the future bring as state expectations engage with conflicting private and public forces? "Not one of the democratic governments that launched market-oriented reforms ran on a platform of free trade, price liberalization, and privatization. The drastic reforms of elected governments almost uniformly surprised Latin American voters."[12]

Is there a downside to the lavish and even poetic language of economic reform? Of course there is! There is the problem of new political and economic dependencies—on the International Monetary Funds and the World Bank or others like it. Even as I write, the debate rages in Mexico, for one major bone of contention over the proposed US $50 billion loan guarantee for Mexico has to do with national identity, sovereignty and pride. "Our petroleum deposits belong to us and no other!" Beyond the implications of the IMF, what will happen to the majority of Latins who live on the underside of history? So what if the World Bank predicts that Latin economies would grow by 3.4 percent annually over the next ten years if that growth does not significantly improve the life of the majority of its people. Argentine news warms the hearts of free market economists. But as one commentator writes on Menem's reforms, "The biggest risk, however, is that his program to build the free market and stimulate the economy will somehow fail to reach the 30% of Argentines who lives below the poverty line, the very people for whom Peronism always had the greatest appeal."[13] The same story applies to every single Latin nation, for everywhere you find beautiful, modern buildings, high tech transformations, new ways of doing business. But what about those millions living at subsistence level? Former Chilean President Patricio Aylwin warned, "Should such conditions persist, I have profound doubts about how stable a democracy and the open-market economic model can really be."[14] At the same time Chile boasts that one million people had already moved out of poverty in the first three years of Aylwin's term, under a highly rated antipoverty program.

A fourth trend looks at the significant and growing role of microeconomics and the non-formal economy. Read the important work by Peruvian entrepreneur Hernando de Soto, *The Other Path: The Invisible Revolution in the Third World.*[15] De Soto documents the daunting and time-consuming task faced by the "little people" in order for them to acquire legal approval for their own business as the first step to making their way out of pvoerty. On the other hand, if the same man or woman simply sets up shop—that is, dreams up the idea, gets a family loan, buys the equipment, hires a couple of relatives and starts working—the same shop is off and running in a matter of days! but it is not legal, and its precarious existence could easily be snuffed out by the beaurocrats. This is the reality of the informal economy that churns out goods and pays people for honest work, with or without legal documentation. While De Soto's database comes from Peru, the reality is continent-wide.

The private sector is now getting into the business of micro-economics and extending small loans to the "little people" making a living. For many years Christian organizations have understood how small self-help projects leverage into something much greater. I continue to praise God for organizations such as World Relief, World Vision and Opportunity International, to mention but three, who invest financial resources into wholistic ministries and come as servants of the people.[16]

Fifth, the military have for the most part retreated to their barracks. About twenty years ago Latin American regimes were dominated by the military, who cast their black military-boot shadow over the continent. But civilian authority has now reclaimed governmental control. However, this does not mean that the military has disappeared. Its work on the one hand is more professional, distanced from the political quagmire. On the other hand it is more subtle, and in some cases corrupt. The military is also restless, as in Venezuela where it recently attempted two coups—to the surprise of few Venezuelans and the surprise of many non-Venezuelans. The generals of Guatemala first backed Jorge Serrano Elías's self-proclaimed coup of May 1993, but rapidly changed their minds when they met the united front of national and international opposition. Serrano Elías (who had identified himself as an evangelical) soon fled to Panama as his "fujimoraso" collapsed. The soldiers' forays into public governance are now generally discredited, but they remain self-defined true patriots, consonant with their traditional institutional values. In some countries military involvement in the drug industry is documented: Bolivia, Colombia, Guatemala. But their greatest fear is to be tried and punished by the civil judiciary of corruption. The Argentine example where civilian authorities tried and convicted military officers brings nightmares to all corrupt Latin military forces. Their budgets have been slashed in some countries; but when the mother country calls for them in the hour of crisis, they will rise again and rule if needed.

The rise of the continental Indianist Movement has been notable. Many new publications—major articles and books—are revealing the astonishing new discoveries of pre-Columbian societies. Archaeologists have exulted in fabulous recent discoveries, from Mexico to Guatemala and down to the Andean region. The "lost empires" had been found; tombs would solve the mystery of the collapse of the Maya empire.[17]

But the Indianist Movement introduces a new dimension into the Latin equation. It has galvanized and unified the Latin America's indigenous population with a plethora of informal and formal cultural and political associations. Continental summits of Indian people have helped to celebrate a valuable heritage. The movement has contributed to legitimate pride in ethnicity, culture, language, customs, history, religion. They have discovered the power of political numbers. It is difficult to affirm just how many Indians there are. While in some countries the percentage of indigenous population is very small (Argentina 3% of 33.9 million and Brazil 1% of 155.3 million), in others they represent a significant percentage of the national total: Bolivia (66% of 8.2 million); Ecuador (21% of 10.6 million); Guatemala (50% of 10.3 million); Mexico (11% of 92 million); Peru (40% of 22.9 million); Chile (9% of 14 million).[18]

To the surprise of all, the joy of some, and the consternation of others, the Guatemalan, Quiché Indian woman, Rigoberta Menchú Tum, received the 1992 Nobel Peace Prize.[19] This astonishing international decision catapulted Rigoberta Menchú into the spotlight, and she became a foremost spokeswoman for human rights. Representing the Indian, the poor and oppressed, those on the underside of history, her story is dramatic and provocative—she lost her parents in the nasty Guatemalan civil war, fled to Mexico, and then while in exile emerged into political leadership. She is seen as a public symbol for all the Indian peoples of Latin America. To top it off, the United Nations declared the year 1993 as "International Year of Indigenous Peoples," though the Indianist leaders wanted a decade!

The Indianist Movement must also be observed in the context of the 500th anniversay of Coloumbus's first journey to the "New World." While historians, publishers, map-makers, sailors, citizens of all communities with the name "Columbus" celebrated, other voices utilized the occasion to focus on the contemporary plight of Latin indigenous peoples. And make no mistake, most of them continue at the bottom of the social pyramid. Escobar quotes Emilio Castro on these celebrations: "From a European perspective a Te Deum could be called for; from the perspective of the original inhabitants of those countries, it will be the occasion for a Requiem."[20]

All Latin Christians rejoice in the legitimatization of healthy pride and self-identity of race, culture, language. For too long prejudice and discrimination against the Indian peoples has been tolerated. However, there are aspects of the Indianist Movement that must be critiqued, not so much the political issues related to the exercise of power. Rather I allude to the spiritual dimensions of this movement. The summits and celebrations many times begin by invoking the traditional Indian spirits. The religious revival focuses on the rediscovery and practice of pre-Christian religions, with universalist emphases, worshipping nature gods and other spirits. This is not a sign of hope but rather of spiritual identity in crisis. What's more, Latin Christians face the challenge of these indigenous people groups considered unevangelized. Patrick Johnstone lists ninety-six groups, with the largest number in Brazil (31), Peru (20) and Colombia (13).

Finally, we must mention the drug industry. "Economic logic and textbook business methods have brought victory in the drug war to the illegal entrepreneurs of Colombia, and those of the city of Cali in particular. The implications are depressing for Colombia, for the inner cities of rich countries, and for prohibitionists everywhere." With these strong words *The Economist* (December 24, 1994–January 6, 1995) summarized their report on Colombia's drug business. No country in the world denies that drugs are an internal problem. Former American President Bush declared a national "war on drugs" and to date the USA has invested (spent, used, wasted) more than US $50 billion in the effort to deal with the problem. The drug (cocaine, heroin, marijuana) industry is a classic case of capitalist supply and demand. As long as people want it, need it, crave their results, and are willing to pay the price, drugs will be grown, harvested, processed, shipped and sold.

Medellín, to the chagrin of Medellín's noble citizens, used to be synonymous with drugs. Of the various groups involved, it was the Escobar family that captured the world's imagination until its leader, Pablo Escobar, was killed by anti-drug security forces. He was a ruthless, violent man who also cunningly played his political cards by building homes for the poor, providing jobs for many, owning soccer teams and politicians, thus projecting the image of a benevolent "Robin Hood." His death dealt the final blow to the Medellín gang but not to drugs in Colombia. Cali is now the headquarters of a sophisticated, business-savy conglomerate of drug lords. They have suborned or openly bought political and military leaders to protect their "business." It is not really a cartel, argues *The Economist*. Rather, it is more of an "exporters association," a "co-operative," or a commodities-style "cocaine exchange." But clearly the Colombian case augurs only evil for that country. We could also write of Peru and Bolivia as major producers, of Panama as a financial laundry center, or of Guatemala and Mexico as transshipment players. But drugs would not be big business without consumers, whether Latin, North America, Asian, European or Russian. "...new markets for cocaine have opened up across the world, especially in Europe. America's State Department notes that all major European capitals have reported a growing influx of cocaine. Last year Russian police seized more than a ton of Colombian cocaine in St. Petersburg."[21]

Can the government of Colombia, or Peru, or Bolivia do anything substantial to change matters? The Peruvian case merits comment. While a fungus affected the most densely planted areas in 1992 and thus reduced yields, the fact is that under the autocratic Fujimori progress is being made against Peruvian drug production. Terrorism has receded with singular victories over the anarchist Sendero Luminoso movement. Hyperinflation has also been brought under control. "In the last month, Peru has made its largest cocaine and opium seizures ever, dismantled one of the largest drug trafficking groups, and indicted an army general for protecting cocaine shipments."[22] While some 200,000 Peruvians cultivate the coca leaves, low prices and crop substitutions have put a major dent in this destructive industry.

This is a story of crisis and very little hope. Will the drug-consuming and producing nations realize the complexity—political, social, economic, cultural and spiritual—of this problem? Ultimately, Christians acknowledge the reality of people (children, youth and adults) bound down by their sinful nature and without a transforming knowledge of the Savior.

Significant fault lines of crisis needing hope

Latins are all too familiar with the language of earthquakes. That analogy becomes relevant as we close this brief review of these current socio-political-economic realities in the Latin continent during these recent years.What are some of the fault lines that point to the deeper elements of crisis? Whatever positive elements we observe taking place in Latin America, there are certain realities that still persist, painfully so. The rise of secularizing materialism is not necessarily good for ultimate values rooted in the Living God and his Word. Modernity has its faith-killing, dehumanizing dimensions. Latin cities face an explosion of violence, where street children are hunted and killed like wild rats—Brazil and Colombia are documented examples.[23] Wealth is not trickling (much less flowing) down rapidly enough to make substantive difference for the masses of the poor. The development of underdevelopment continues; the percentage of poor increases out of proportion to the percentage of the wealthy; family breakdown is endemic particularly in urban centers; and the fragmentation has accelerated with the move from rural to urban centers. During the last twenty-five years Latin urban population increased 216%, and there are twenty-seven Latin cities of over one million inhabitants. The values of made-in-USA entertainment industry are fundamentally destructive. The decade of the '80s was a lost one economically for the poor and even for the middle class, with per capita gross domestic product *declining* 1.2 percent during that decade. The North-South Center of the University of Miami states it eloquently:

> The number of people living in extreme poverty increased dramatically—in some nations encompassing over 75 percent of the population. At the same time, the middle class, which had grown rapidly since the 1950's, found its position threatened in the 1980's by a shrinking job market, rampant inflation, and government austerity programs. Secondary and university education, long seen as a virtual guarantor of middle-class status, no longer provided such secure opportunities, producing rising frustrations and a heightened flow of intellectual capital out of the region.[24]

That same report lists evidence of a series of relatively late political crises that evidence different fault lines: "The turmoil of recent years has largely laid to rest the simplistic view that creating and maintaining democracy could be achieved simply through holding relatively honest elections, installing civilian governments and preventing military coups."[25] The fact of the matter is that if economic reforms are not accompanied by broader reform in the executive and legislative branches as well as the judiciary, military, and education sectors, and endemic corruption addressed, then economic Band-Aids of modernity will simply cover over the historic and entrenched self-defeating political culture. History and tradition cannot be ignored in any discussion of "progress into the modern era" of a global economy and information age. The same reports calls this "the burden of history."

Crisis and hope in Latin America. I see both in tension. Only the biblical Christian has the potential to understand the times in this Latin continent, who knows what to do as a modern son and daughter of the King, and is able to boldly lay hold of the Eternal Kingdom. Concluding this section I ask myself, "Am I encouraged or discouraged by the Latin scenario?" Fundamentally, I believe in the sovereignty of the God of history; this story is his Story. On the human and concrete turf of today's Latin reality, I acknowledge a degree of optimism that goes beyond my pessimism of just eight years ago. It is a matter of hope in the midst of the ongoing crises of the continent.

And where do Latin evangelicals fit in this scenario? The continent is their world, their context, their battleground, their identity, their development, their spiritual growth and their future impact on the social structures of their continent. When tectonic political and economic forces explode through a country like Mexico, our 4.6 million Mexican brothers and sisters in Christ are directly affected. Their jobs and future are on the line, their children's education is uncertain, their political, religious and human rights are threatened. And theirs is the task to focus clearly on the overall, divine big picture—with a keen eye on the eternals but with feet rooted in the world which God loves personally and desires to transform completely.

PART B
Surveying the Latin American Spiritual Landscape

The Broad Scenario

Perhaps five vignettes can offer fresh insight into the surprising changes taking place in Latin spirituality.[26] The first one I witnessed with my son-in-law in a small Guatemalan Indian town on the edge of glorious Lake Atitlán. Cliff and I stood towards the back of the church quietly observing the service in action. The music was lively, all ages were represented, the people were involved, the speaker spoke with conviction from both the Bible and the liturgy, and when the meeting concluded church members chatted warmly until departing. It was a contemporary, small-town, Catholic service in a rapidly changing Latin America.

About three weeks later I was the invited speaker at a Salvadoran church for their world missions conference. The church had recently gone through a series of major transitions—a neighborhood move, a new name, a new shared leadership team, clear-cut vision statement, a modern auditorium-style facility. The music was vibrant and charismatic in feel, a broad basis of leadership was in training, the members were enthusiastically involved, most of the young people were recent converts, and many entire families had come to Christ through the witness of peers. This church had broken into a relatively under-reached people group, the upper middle class of El Salvador. It was a new community, a new model of church, with a broad basis of fellowship with other believers, while holding membership in a non-charismatic denomination. Something powerful and new was taking place there; history was being made.

A third facet of Latin spirituality comes from Brazil where in late 1994 Catholics and evangelicals united in an unusual way to condemn a

Brazilian television soap opera with open occultic themes:

> The Journey, a prime-time, six-night-a-week soap on
> Brazil's largest network, TV Globo, won record ratings
> during its five months on the air." The report goes on to
> state that "...the occult has a strong pull in this country of
> 160 million people. Catholicism has long coexisted or
> competed with African spirit religions, witchcraft and
> European spiritualism, and now with fast-growing fun-
> damentalist Protestant groups...A 1992 study by the Re-
> ligion Studies Institute said non-Catholic churches [Ev-
> angelical] were opening at a rate of one a day in Rio de
> Janeiro."[27]

Brazil considers itself over 92 percent Christian, although about 60
percent are involved in occult activity. Yet with almost 29 million people—attending over 149,000 churches and belonging to over 270 denominations—who call themselves evangelicals, these believers outnumber practicing Catholics. The percentage who attend mass currently
hovers around 5%, in a nation of 152 million people, and with no Catholic growth forecast.[28]

We visit Argentina. "'What do you believe in?' This question was
put by Argentina's weekly current affairs magazine. The survey found
that we believe overwhelmingly in God, followed closely by economic
stability and 'nothing and nobody.' But our God seems remote; we prefer
monetarism and privatization to economic chaos; and nothing and nobody merits our confidence." So writes Silvia Chávez, General Secretary
of the Asociación Universitaria Argentina (IFES partner).[29] Yet in this
same nation known for its agnosticism, the Spirit of God is breaking
through in marvelous ways. Nation-wide, the strong growth rate of evangelical churches continues, though probably not at the high pace of a
few years ago. Churches across the spectrum are growing, as long as they
reach out with conviction and warmth.

Finally, a double report from Cuba, that island nation of eleven million people living under a Marxist regime since Castro's victory in 1959.
The collapse of Cuba's Russian support system plunged the country into
catastrophic crises. Some 41 percent of the population call themselves
Catholic, yet only 2 percent attend mass. Evangelicals claim only 2.7 percent of the population. But something is happening on the island, and its
impact is felt in both Catholic and evangelical communities. "Cuba's
New Cardinal Leads a Bolder Church," proclaims *The New York Times*.

Jaime Cardinal Ortega y Alamino represents a key aspect of Christianity's new role in Cuba. Catholics report that attendance at masses has increased as much as 50 percent in recent years. On the evangelical side all report remarkable growth, whether in the rural areas or the cities. Congregations are growing, starting branch works, even acquiring building permits from a more flexible government. Bible schools are overwhelmed with the response to even limited theological training. Cubans are now sending young leaders to acquire formal theological studies in other Latin American countries, as well as missionaries to other nations, and many of them come with a unique credential, they speak Russian.

Every Latin Christian interviewed provides a personal window into the transforming spiritual landscape of the continent. Now let us travel rapidly and widely across the spectrum in the attempt to offer a concise update on broader spiritual realities in Latin America.

Recent Literature on Evangelical Christianity in Latin America

A most surprising thing has happened since the first edition of this book: the number of very significant publications dealing in particular with the rise and strength of the evangelical/Protestant movement in Latin America. Secular academicians are rethinking their posture in light of evangelical growth, Roman Catholic scholars are revisiting their own presuppositions, and evangelical writers have contributed other special insights and reports.[30] David Martin and David Stoll have probably done more than any others to challenge preconceptions. Both write from a sociological perspective, with focus on the social dimensions and impact of this religious phenomenon under study. Not all they write will encourage evangelicals, and Stoll periodically raises hackles; but their perspective demands respect from all.

Martin approaches Latin America from the perspective of a British sociologist of religion with strong academic credentials. With a vivid literary image, "tongues of fire," he casts his study in a context of a historical genealogical struggle between two rival civilizations, "...the four hundred year clash between the Hispanic imperium and the Anglo-Saxon imperium. On the one side are all the successor states of the Iberian Peninsula; on the other side are England and its mightiest successor state— the USA."[31]

Martin traces an ethos found in British Methodism's battle to create free religious space within the Church of England's spiritual monopoly. To him a similar momentous encounter of world views in Latin America is taking place between Protestantism and Catholicism, with the former opening up the space at the expense of the latter. The term "movement" is crucial to him.

> The new society now emerging in Latin America has to do with movement, and evangelicals constitute a movement. Evangelical Christianity is a dramatic migration of the spirit matching and accompanying a dramatic migration of bodies. In undertaking this migration, people become 'independent' not at all by building up modest securities but by the reverse: by the loss of all the ties that bind, whether these be familial, communal or ecclesial. Pentecostalism in particular renews these ties in an atmosphere of hope and anticipation rather than of despair. It provides a new cell taking over from scarred and broken tissue. Above all it renews the innermost cell of the family, and protects the woman from the ravages of male desertion and violence. A new faith is able to implant new disciplines, re-order priorities, counter corruption and destructive machismo, and reverse the indifferent and injurious hierarchies of the outside world. Within the enclosed haven of faith a fraternity can be instituted under firm leadership, which provides for release, for mutuality and warmth, and for the practice of new roles.[32]

A final eloquent word from Martin underscores the long-term implications of momentous spiritual changes rippling across Latin America. "As the sacred canopy in Latin America is rent and the all-encompassing system cracks, evangelical Christianity pours in and by its own autonomous native power creates free social space."[33]

American David Stoll comes with a different history and perspective. Known previously for his polemic criticism of Wycliffe Bible Translators,[34] when he began research on the book that asks the question, *Is Latin America Turning Protestant?*, he openly acknowledged a negative presupposition. He had earlier supposed that the cause of such Protestant growth came from the influx of funds, personnel and other material resources from the USA, particularly the fundamentalist missionary industry. Stoll is honest to confess the fallacy of his *a priori* judgment and now concludes that Latin Protestants explode in growth because they are an autochthonous movement, coming primarily from the poor. He argues that to criticize evangelicals of simplistic acceptance of a "made in the USA right-wing Gospel sect" is a reductionism that denies their personal integrity.

Both Martin and Stoll unexpectedly critique liberation theologies, saying that they never enjoyed broad support from those expected to benefit from its theory and praxis. Martin notes that liberationists primarily came from radical intellectual circles and not from "below" from the people. Stoll concurs:

> The central exercise in liberation theology, consciousness-raising, raises a tangle of issues. To begin with, there is the risk of failing to speak to the actual needs of the poor, as opposed to idealized versions of those needs. Liberation theology endeavors to come out of the day-to-day experience of the poor; when successful, maybe it does. But it also originated in the crisis of the Catholic church and its attempts to recover a popular base. Despite the struggle to build a grass-roots church, the prophets of the movement tend to be religious professionals with professional interests, a fact dramatized by their disputes with offended laities and anxious hierarchies.[35]

Stoll has cooperated with Virginia Varrard-Burnett to edit a more recent series of essays under the theme *Rethinking Protestantism in Latin America*. Just the introduction and conclusion to the book are worth the price. Stoll addresses the crisis of identity and mission within Latin Catholicism as it confronts the exploding evangelical communities, and then casts a context within the broader sociological changes wracking the continent.

> In societies whose economies are being globalized, whose traditional social structures have heaved apart, where people must fend for themselves in hostile new environments, how can a single, centralized religious hierarchy satisfy a newly individuated population whose members need to chart their own courses? For those same individuals, afflicted by new forms of personal insecurity, how can sprawling, territorially based Catholic parishes satisfy the desire for closer-knit congregational experiences? How can a religious system organized around sacraments satisfy the hunger for personal transformation? In each of these respects, the decentralized structures of Latin American Protestants, their multiple

leaders competing for followers through charisma, and their emphasis on conversion proved to be distinct advantages.[36]

Evangelicals Samuel Escobar and Guillermo Cook have interacted at length with the broad gamut of social and spiritual life in Latin America. Escobar's essays have appeared in a variety of journals and interviews, and his perspective is highly valued in sociological and religious circles. He combines an unusual insight into sociological and religious phenomenology and dynamics, while remaining faithful to Scripture as well as his Latin evangelical roots.[37] Cook has recently edited *New Face of the Church in Latin America: Between Tradition and Change*, a very profitable series of essays ranging across the ecclesiastical, theological and thematic spectrum of the continent. For him, "....the new face of the Church in Latin America is largely a Protestant story." At the same time he acknowledges that there is no single face to the Latin Church.[38]

A Status Report of Latin Evangelicalism Today

How many evangelicals are there today, particularly in comparison with our first edition? "Belgian missionary specialist Franz Damen, an advisor to the Catholic Bishops of Bolivia, reports that '...every hour in Latin America an average of 400 Catholics move to membership in Protestant sects which today represent an eighth, that is 12% of the population of the continent, but in countries like Puerto Rico and Guatemala, they constitute nothing less than 25 or even 30% of the population.'"[39] Surprisingly, Damen's figures are close to ours.

But what do current numbers report? One measure comes from comparing data in the 1993 edition of Patrick Johnstone's *Operation World* with those from his 1986 edition.[40] (See chart on page 460.) But readers beware! It is impossible to resolve differences in terminology, reports or statistics. These results represent composite data, giving more conservative totals than others. For example, COMIBAM leaders in 1992 reported a total of 65 million evangelicals, while ours give 52 million. The terms "Protestant" and "evangelical" refer to the same general population, and the 1993 general population figures come from the Population Reference Bureau.

A few comments are necessary regarding the two far-right columns. Our previous edition only listed missionaries "to" Latin America. Now we report one of the dramatic changes within the continent, the emergence of Latin America as a significant missionary-sending base and

Country	National Population (millions)	Protestant Population (thousands)		Percent Growth	Prot. % of population	Missionaries	
	1993	1986	1993	1986-93	1993	To	From
Argentina	33.5	1680	2500	49%	7.5%	911	144
Bolivia	8.0	471	681	45%	8.5%	1011	47
Brazil	152.0	24120	28815	19%	18.9%	3381	2755
Chile	13.5	2710	3662	35%	27.1%	565	102
Colombia	34.9	900	1193	33%	3.4%	946	148
Costa Rica	3.3	200	323	63%	9.8%	452	107
Cuba	11.0	244	291	19%	2.7%	2	2
Dom. Rep.	7.6	397	439	10%	5.8%	174	51
Ecuador	10.3	301	376	25%	3.7%	1116	48
El Salvador	5.2	766	1083	41%	20.8%	102	130
Guatemala	10.0	1720	2212	29%	22.1%	699	123
Honduras	5.6	435	566	30%	10.1%	384	58
Mexico	90.0	3200	4628	47%	5.1%	1891	376
Nicaragua	4.1	298	670	125%	16.3%	108	34
Panama	2.5	252	403	60%	16.1%	228	26
Paraguay	4.2	236	233	71%	5.5%	522	15
Peru	22.9	692	1563	126%	6.8%	1039	190
Puerto Rico	3.6	911	966	6%	26.8%	141	65
Uruguay	3.2	76	111	46%	3.5%	218	63
Venezuela	20.7	450	1054	134%	5.1%	637	131
TOTALS	**446.1**	**40059**	**51769**	**30%**	**11.6%**	**14527**	**4615**

force. Johnstone's numbers seem high to many Latin leaders, partly because of his broader "domestic national missionary" category working within the nation. For example, Brazilian mission researchers have identified 1,783 cross-cultural missionaries, 972 less (35%) than Johnstone's figures. COMIBAM missions leaders tend to feel more comfortable with an across-the-board reduction since they apply the missionary category to refer to cross-cultural workers serving either within their country or outside its national borders. This would suggest close to 3,000 cross-cultural Latin missionaries in current service.

EVANGELICALS IN LATIN AMERICAN SINCE 1900

Regardless of precise numbers, the facts are incontrovertible. Latin evangelicals are a major force in Latin America today, and their growth appears unstoppable. But why is Latin America turning Protestant? This is the central question posed by so many students of the continent.[41] The answer depends on the presuppositions, whether Marxist, agnostic, Catholic, spiritist, liberal Protestant or evangelical. Some growth explanations come from sociology (migration from rural to megacities and its corresponding displacement which seeks new identity and community), the political left (money-inspired conversions, fanaticism, religion as opiate),

Year	Communicants	Total Community	Percent of Population
1900	?	50,000 (Arias)	
1916	126,000	378,000	
1925	252,000 (?)	756,000 (?)	
1936	2,400,000	7,200,000	
1967	4,915,400	14,746,200	6.0
1973	6,666,666	20,000,000	7.5
1987	11,635,666	37,432,000	8.8
1993	16,177,812	51,769,000	11.6
2000	26,666,666	80,000,000 (P. Johnstone, est.)	15.0

or Catholicism (USA-funded sects, or recognized absence of Catholic pastoral presence). The reasons suggested here reflect evangelical values. Berg and Pretiz offer twelve reasons, with each one playing its own role in the conversion process.

1. A background of Christian knowledge already acquired in the Roman Catholic tradition.
2. A world view that still accepts the supernatural and is not over-rationalized.
3. Disenchantment with the Roman Catholic Church and search for alternatives.
4. Expression of religious liberty in a religious space not used in pluralism.
5. Poverty and insecurity about the future lead to search for ultimate answers.
6. Evangelical use of mass media to communicate the

message.

7. Evangelical church structure providing lay participation at all levels.
8. Mobilization of all believers in obedience to Christ.
9. Faith in God's power to perform miracles and the gifts of the Spirit.
10. Contextualization of the gospel and church community.
11. The critical mass where numbers grow like compound interest.
12. A straightforward message, "Solo Cristo Salva."[42]

Here are some other causes for evangelical growth: the structural social changes which have profoundly affected the struggle to live which in turn have opened up space for alternative spiritual choices and thus lead to significant new Christian communites; the movement from Catholicism to evangelicalism through the Catholic charismatic groups; the popular recognition that the evangelical gospel affirms many Latin cultural values through spontaneous and practical contextualization; the fact that women are drawn to the gospel because they are granted dignity as women and encouraged to take public roles in church life; the dynamic of Latin music and participatory worship, whether Quechua or Caribbean salsa style. Ultimately, it is the sovereign Spirit of God working at all levels of Latin society, drawing people to the living, resurrected and powerful Christ.

Trends within Latin Evangelicalism Today

Not all that glitters is gold! As in the first edition of this book, we raise crucial questions. What are some of the major trends moving through the continent? Here are some. *First, while the numerical growth attracts widespread attention, there is another dimension.* The growth is unevenly spread across the continent. Mexico City has proven resistant, Venezuela also, particularly Caracas. Uruguayan Christians live in a nation with a strong agnostic and atheistic heritage where Christmas is called "Family Week" and Holy Week is called "Tourism Week." You can identify through the statistical report the countries or megacities with a low percentage of evangelicals; there church growth is slow and tough. Some students of Latin evangelical church growth predict a tapering off of the growth rate in the next decade. Others suggest a darker reason for rapid growth; the mass selling of a cheap gospel that offers easy solutions to tough questions, but has little lasting power.

Do all converts to evangelical churches remain in their new churches? No. Across the continent there is growing evidence of another spiritual movement as people return to the original church—mainly Catholic—or even depart from all organized Christianity! One example that has recently jolted evangelical leaders came from Central America: "In a 1989 survey of Costa Ricans, nearly as many said they used to be evangelicals as currently identified themselves as such. Evangelicals have long boasted of their ability to convert Catholics, but we have yet to hear much about evangelicals who go back to being Catholics."[43] Why is this the case? A number of reasons could be suggested: family pressures not to depart from the "Mother Faith of our culture, from the Blessed Mother of Jesus, from the faith of our mother and grandmother"; shattered expectations when the facile gospel promises die from an aborted conversion experience; inadequate discipleship of new believers that does not prepare them for practical life or opposition. The fact is that relatively few evangelical leaders want to face the implications of this disturbing development.

Second, most of the growth—though not all of it—comes from churches belonging to what Berg and Pretiz call the "Fifth Wave." The first four growth waves refer respectively to the historic immigrant churches, the denominational missions, then the independent "faith" agencies, and finally the new denominations led by Pentecostals but including other global-expanding denominations. In these first four movements the presence of expatriate missionaries was obvious. But not so in the last one. This last wave is birthing independent evangelical churches of every size, doctrine and ecclesiastical structures, and they are nationally owned and directed. This is true indigeneity. Charismatic groups predominate here, including almost all of the younger megachurches. Whether just a store front or a new cathedral, these churches are on the move. Some of the leaders have formal theological training, but most are self-made pastors; many of them now are university graduates with a mid-life call to the ministry. Worship plays an important role in just about all Latin churches; and charismatic styles predominate. Significantly, many denominational churches or those with roots in the faith missions have adopted new worship patterns—with a Latin beat!—while maintaining their doctrinal heritage.

New Latin Christian musicians such as Marcos Witt have had continental-wide impact with albums selling over 100,000 copies. Fredy Gularte's missionary music is sung in most countries. A major new Spanish hymnbook (with Latin-style songs, guitar chords and other worship aids) has been introduced continent-wide with surprising sales and the appreciation of hundreds of congregations.[44] The Aymara hymnal has sold more than 200,000 copies in Bolivia alone! How far evangelicals have come in Latin America can be seen in this item: "Sony recently launched a Christian music line in Mexico—finding and recording Mexican evangelical Christian artists and promoting them alongside its secular artists."[45] Some might wonder whether this is good or bad news!

The megachurches bear further comment. Most of these are centered on one strong, charismatic leader and perhaps members of his extended family. He may be authoritarian or even gentle in style, but the ultimate issue of power and control is clear. This style is not generally consultative, much less democratic; and there is little accountability. Obviously this can lead to potentially grave problems when power is abused. There is a debilitating spirit of competition between strong leaders in the same city or country. Few of these caudillos build relationships with the broader Body of Christ. And since so many of them have no serious biblical or theological training, there is a tendency towards dynamic preaching with little biblical content. These churches feature pulsating worship, multiple activities for all believers, and the building of ecclesiastical mini-empires. Some of them have bought into the "health and wealth gospel" of the "word of faith" movement. The megachurches have quickly moved into mass media, either providing instant recordings of their Sunday sermons, buying radio and television time, or, in other cases, acquiring ownership of radio and television stations!

Third, Latin evangelical leaders continue to lament the dearth of a theological foundation for the churches. While evangelicals are called "people of the Book," the fact is that biblical literacy is anemic. It leads to legalism, activism, superficial discipleship, reductionism, increased loss of members, and a simplistic response to complicated issues; at the same time it opens the window to manipulation, false teaching and subtle occultism. While the number of believers and churches grows, not so the number of training programs and centers that can equip lay and vocational Christian leaders for effective ministry. Many formal and non-formal theological institutions have diversified their educational delivery systems, whether to stay alive or to meet the expanding needs. The Seminario Teológico Centroamericano in Guatemala is one school where over 1000 students from eighteen nations are enrolled. It maintains a broad spectrum of programs—day, night and weekend studies; residential and non-residential; from women's programs to lay training to master's degrees. Other programs, such as Logoi, offer a broad-band curriculum to provide direct non-formal training to many leaders who prefer this approach or who do not have access to formal schools. Larger local churches are getting in the business of starting their own training programs for internal leadership and for broader geographic expansion, which eventually converts the megachurch into a mini-denomination. Even though Christian literature production increases, too many titles are still translated from English, pricing is high (booksellers must buy stock in US dollars), and most bookstores have limited stock. Brazil undoubtedly has the strongest selection of high quality Christian literature, much of it at affordable prices.

One good piece of news since the first edition is the appearance of the AETAL (the Evangelical Association for Theological Education in Latin America), a new continental Latin partner in the International Council of Accrediting Agencies (ICAA) related to the World Evangelical Fellowship. AETAL's primary values emphasize theological education renewal, the importance of mutual encouragement and increased interaction among evangelical institutions, as well as the development of accreditation standards that will enable member schools to network and strengthen each other on a global basis.

It is necessary to register other concerns here. Up to now the term "evangelical" has been used as a broad category different from both Latin Catholics and Latin liberal Protestants. But will the term "evangelical" in Latin America continue as the prime defining term in coming years? Will the churches and leaders who claim it truly rest their authority on Scripture, on justification by faith in the finished work of Christ? Will their essential doctrines reflect the historic confessions of biblical Christians along with the call for personal holiness? Will they affirm the centrality of both Great Commission and Great Commandment? Will they be both Latin and biblical? These issues must be faced sooner rather than later so that the vitality of today's Latin evangelicalism not be diluted or wasted.

Fourth, the last decade has witnessed a very significant evangelical involvement in contextualization, including involvement in the socio-political arena. Dr. Núñez has ably dealt with issues related to contextualization, and both of us are encouraged to observe recent Latin developments in this area. Whether the topics are debated in the local church or theological institution, through the networks or the theological associations, by lay leaders or theological students or highly trained theologians and writers, the fact is that believers are coming to grips with what it means to be a Christian in the context of Latin America. They want to release the power of God's Word and his Spirit in their continent! The results are evident at the local church level, in theological literature, in creative theological training alternatives and institutional curricula in the formal schools.

One of the broadest-based evangelical events in recent years was the 1992, Third Latin American Congress on Evangelization, celebrated in Quito, Ecuador, and sponsored by the Latin American Theological Fraternity (FTL). This congress, including its origins, program, participants, and outcomes, must be evaluated from the perspective of Latin contextualization of the gospel. Under the banner "The Whole Gospel for All Peoples, from Latin America," over 1,000 youth, women, men, of all races and ecclesiastical confessions, came from twenty-six nations. The leadership of CONELA (the World Evangelical Fellowship regional partner in Latin America) and CLAI (related more to the World Council of Churches) met in a serious exchange of concerns during that congress.

A year earlier, a special group of Latins had been convened in Buenos Aires for the 1991 "Second Consultation on Evangelicals in Political Action in Latin America." Much had happened since their 1983 conference. Also convened by the FTL, this gathering drew evangelicals already committed to and participating in the broader political process. They included the Peruvian president of the Bank of Nations, the Vice-Minister of Interior of El Salvador, a black Brazilian Pentecostal woman member of the Workers Party, some politically sensitive pastors and theologians. The discussions were spirited and valuable. Relationships were established, and the network was strengthened for Christians in the political process. We can make one very clear observation about evangelical political action—no single ideological position is taken by all evangelicals. This surprises many North American observers of the political scene, who assume Latin evangelicals are all right-wing conservatives or defenders of USA policies. One secular observer notes that "[t]here is no single Protestant political paradigm in Latin America, nor is there yet a focused, articulated movement of evangelical political activism equivalent to that of the Christian right in the United States."[46]

Why are evangelicals getting involved in political action?[47] For one, they are gradually rejecting the old dichotomous pietism that cast the world as the ultimate enemy, and politics the dirty game for pagans. This shrunken worldview has been replaced by one that integrates all of life under the sovereignty of Christ. Secondly, a growing number of younger believers sense God's call upon their lives in political vocations, whether by election or appointment. For them a tough decision has to do with the choice of party. Why join a party with no chances of victory? Thirdly, believers are saying, "For such a time as this we were born, and born again!" That is, space has opened up in an increasingly pluralistic (political and religious) Latin America, and the gospel has the only true power to transform individuals, families, communities and nations. Clearly all of these factors have their pitfalls, but they reflect new commitments and action.

What about Latin evangelicals with a controversial record in the political arena? Because of our work in Guatemala, both Núñez and I are periodically asked about Efraín Ríos Montt and Jorge Serrano Elías. The first edition of this book discussed some of the Ríos Montt issues. As of this writing the charismatic leader serves a year term as president of the Guatemalan Congress. The national constitution a few years ago had been purposefully rewritten to bar candidates for the presidency who had participated in previous political coups, and the Constitutional Court had thus effectively barred him from the last presidential race. But the popular vote (including Catholics and evangelicals) elected him to Congress. Then again, by the time this book is printed he could be back in civilian life!

Serrano Elías, a proclaimed evangelical, is a more difficult case to deal with, and others have done so with thoroughness.[48] When elected president, he inherited the impossible task of governing in a context of corruption, and he himself brought no clear political ideology nor realistic program for the nation. As the nation slipped out of control he gambled and lost, having opted for an auto-coup. The promised military support evaporated and Serrano Elías soon fled into exile. A lot of good people, including Guatemalan evangelicals, were hurt by his autocracy, his lack of personal accountability and the charges of personal corruption. Significantly, Guatemalan evangelicals were not tarred with Serrano's failures, although churches and leaders were left with many unanswered questions. However, this Guatemalan case again illustrates the inadequate evangelical preparation for high political service, as well as an astonishing naiveté. One Guatemalan Christian said it well, "We have lost our innocence."

Fifth, Latin America has been transformed from a mission-sending field to a global mission-sending base. I have chosen here two voices to represent this rapidly expanding international Latin movement. Both utilize similar language, namely, "shouldn't Latin America be considered rather as a mission base, from which missionaries go as messengers of Jesus Christ to plant Christianity in other continents?"[49] This language and the corresponding paradigm shift have also undergirded the vision of COMIBAM, the Latin American interdenominational missionary movement, currently under the leadership of Rudy Girón. The two Latin representatives (Escobar a Baptist and Girón a Guatemalan Pentecostal) may disagree on matters of strategy, emphases and even missiology, but they both agree on the primacy of Scripture, on the centrality of the church, on the unity of the Body of Christ, on the potential role of Latins in world evangelization, on the need for effective pre-field training of missionaries, and on a wholistic mission of the church. They represent a healthy convergence of two major Latin currents: the theological and missiological reflection engaging with the missiological/global task yet to be done.

At least 3,000 Latin Americans have moved out in cross-cultural missions, and the numbers are projected to rise rapidly in future years. Latin missions are birthed not in the context of wealth but of poverty; not in a world of privilege but limitation; not strong in high-tech equipment but strong in zeal and the power of the Spirit; not owning passports with the clout of Europe or the USA, but they will go anyway; not capable of sustaining an expensive overseas missionary machinery but committed to sending whatever force they can. This movement is predominately a church-based one, not one primarily driven by para-church agencies. Yes, Latins are short in effective cross-cultural training programs, but that is being remedied even now. Yes, they may have borrowed some constructs from "managerial missiology," but churches around the world have borrowed terms and concepts only to modify them to fit their own understanding of Scripture and the global task. Yes, they have been rightly accused of sending missionaries ill-equipped and poorly supervised and shepherded on the field (the fault of both churches and the few agencies), but this hopefully is changing. Yes, they do have a high attrition rate, but all missionary movements in their genesis suffered from the same ills. Yes, Latin missions has been romanticized, but this will moderate rapidly with the tough realities of mission service. One Salvadoran Chrisitan musician in a North African nation was suddenly taken from his home in late 1994, interrogated, charged, imprisoned, convicted. And then early in 1995 he was expelled from that nation. This was not a romantic story but a real-life account of the price to be paid. But most Latin missionaries are willing to suffer in North Africa or anywhere else, just as their believing grandparents suffered decades ago when they converted to Christ in Latin America.

How does the younger COMIBAM Latin missionary movement relate to the older Western one, predominantly from Europe and the USA? Significantly this contemporary Latin movement was not godfathered by Anglo missionaries. In fact, relatively few Western missionaries attended the major 1987 COMIBAM congress in Brazil. The energies, creativity and personnel were and continue to be overwhelmingly Latin. And we rejoice in this, for it demonstrates their capacities. These ministries welcome partnerships with expatriate colleagues and agencies serving in Latin America. But the foreigners must come in the spirit of true servanthood, open handed even as they offer their varied services. Neopaternalism will be quickly rejected. All partners, whether Anglo or Asian (the "new missionaries" to Latin America) must also be willing to work under Latins and on a broader basis of doctrinal fellowship.

Relationship Between Evangelicals and Roman Catholics

Núñez has updated the larger issues dealing with Latin American Catholicism, so this section will specifically treat the diverse and symbiotic relationship between the two. Catholic leaders are worried, for "the percentage of professing Catholics dropped eleven points during the 1980s, from 89 percent to 78 percent at present."[50] There is a profound crisis of vocation in Latin Catholicism, and the shortage of priests and nuns for priority ministries is notable. Andrés Tapia writes:

> The Pope is concerned. In the aftermath of his second visit to Brazil, his eleventh to Latin America, it is clear that he doesn't pull people in as he used to. In Brazil—supposedly the most Catholic nation in the world—the usual throngs just did not materialize: for one scheduled event, 500,000 people were expected, but only 100,000 showed up. In contrast, on the morning of the Pope's arrival, 200,000 evangelicals packed a soccer stadium for a rally sponsored by a local church, underscoring the fact that over a half-million Brazilians are leaving the Catholic church for evangelical churches *each year*.[51]

Attitudes towards evangelicals by Latin Catholics are diverse. On the one hand you will find the traditionalist, such as Pope John Paul II himself. When meeting with the bishops in the 1992 Santo Domingo CELAM he spoke of the "sects...which are destroying the true church." A growing number of bishops recently appointed by the Pope have taken a very conservative, hierarchical line. In one interview, Guatemalan Archbishop Penados affirmed that evangelical "sects" were radicals with whom there could be no dialogue, they were enemies of tradition who reject Mary (who for Catholics is critical to faith, "the exemplary figure of following the Lord and of total commitment to others"), they buy their converts and give away both Bibles and money, they are supported by

USA funds, they are part and parcel of cults like Mormonism, they are gospel reductionists and provoke religious confusion with their thousands of sects.[52]

Other Catholic leaders reflect a different spirit, which is more self-critical of their church as they evaluate what it means to be the Roman Church in a transformed Latin spiritual landscape. The late Ignacio Ellacuría, a Spanish priest who served in El Salvador (one of six Jesuits assassinated in that country) represented this segment of the church. He evidenced greater objectivity when writing on contemporary tensions, and felt free to critique traditional church leadership, as well as Catholic liberation theologies and their practical implications.[53] Franz Damen, whom we have previously cited, is another who has directly questioned the popular Catholic "conspiracy theory" about popular Latin Protestantism (Escobar has also dealt with this new "Black Legend"[54]). Damen is willing to take on top hierarchical leaders on this issue as a result of his field research on Latin evangelical growth. We have mentioned Edward L. Cleary, another irenic Catholic scholar who writes with singular objectivity even about spiritual competition between Catholics and evangelicals.

Christians from Europe or the USA tend to judge Catholicism through their own grid, and thus have difficulty understanding the nature of Latin American Roman Catholicism. Evangelical Lutherans and Catholics in Germany openly cooperate in the distribution of Scripture; both are opposed by liberal Lutherans! British Catholics have existed in a context of Anglican historic dominance, but they have competed on a fairly level ground. In the USA Catholicism has had to adapt to a particular historical context of theological pluralism. But in Latin America the Roman Church has never wrestled with religious pluralism; rather, it has enjoyed temporal and spiritual hegemony for 500 years. It is not easy for the Latin Catholic hierarchy to open spiritual space on a voluntary basis, but until they open this arena, the tensions will remain.

During 1994, well-known North American figures Charles Colson and Fr. John Neuhaus convened a common-cause consultation in light of the avalanche of anti-Christian propaganda and destructive attacks on common virtue and Judaeo-Christian values in the United States. They published a document, "Evangelicals and Catholics Together," also called "The Christian Mission in the Third Millennium," and appended the list of prominent evangelicals and Catholics who had signed it or later endorsed it.[55] The declaration provoked a bracing debate in the USA amongst evangelicals. However, a number of observers—whether Latin, from the USA or other nations—felt that the declaration was too culture-specific; that it went beyond "co-belligerent" cooperation and moved into theology and mission; what's more, it did not clarify that it spoke exclusively for the USA context and was not to be generalized in the rest of the world.

Latin American Catholicism is unique and therefore distinct from its North American branch. It must be understood within its particular history, its context, its own religious language and values. But neither is it the monolithic force of yesteryear, for the Roman Church struggles with its own internal divisions, and its leadership is attempting to understand and respond to the major crises in their church. Meanwhile, evangelicals must demonstrate a gracious spirit to all who differ with them on foundational biblical understanding. They must guard their attitudes and public judgments against Catholics. At the same time, Latin evangelicals must not be denied "hispanidad" identity simply because they are not Catholics. Nor do they want to be called "sects" (few understand how these categories are used in the sociology of religion). But they will remain firm on the meaning and process of salvation, for it defines what it means to be "Christian." And they will not restrain their enthusiastic proclamation of the whole gospel to all who will hear the message. This is part of their spiritual genetic code. The people of the Book simply cannot be silent in spite of the crises of cultural Christians, modernity, secularization and the explosion of the occult. To them Christ *is* the answer.

Whither Latin American Evangelicals As We Approach the Third Millennium?

It is not certain what evangelicals will do with some of their internal challenges. I briefly and with broad strokes sketch a future here in a dialectic tension. These eight points bear watching over the next decades.

First, the battle between profound renewal and maturity over nominalism and cultural evangelicalism. Numerical growth is encouraging, even though statistics are imprecise. But we must ask again the hard questions, "What is church?" and "What is growth?" "What about the problem of 'former evangelicals'?" Internal weaknesses and open heresies—from other regions as well as Latin species—will seep into the churches and sap their vitality. The churches must face head-on the crisis of the Latin family and articulate better answers in light of modernity's impact. The Spirit of God must be invited to renew decaying evangelical churches.

Second, the struggle between evangelical mutual acceptance and interdependency versus isolationism and critical divisionism. There is a sad division virus loose in the Body of Christ, and it manifests itself locally and nationally. At times it is open, other times more subtle. It pits Pentecostal against Pentecostal, charismatic against charismatic, Pentecostal against charismatic, non-Pentecostal against charismatic, non-Pentecostal against non-Pentecostal, traditional denomination against Fifth Wave church. The Spanish spirit of the independent "yo!" is alive and deadly. Late in 1994, the WEF-related Confraternity of Evangelicals of Latin America (CONELA) held its fourth general assembly in Costa Rica. This movement has great promise for biblical unity. But it awaits visionary, godly and gifted leadership which understands the potential influence of national and regional fellowships, and which will set a course with bold programs geared to the life of the churches. Meanwhile, a few national movements as well as sub-regional ones will increasingly and effectively address their needs.

Third, the tension between relevancy and biblical contextualization versus the super-spiritualization of the faith. There is a hermeneutical struggle going on in every Christian community. Christians must be encouraged and equipped to face the insidious enemies filtering in through the spirit of modernity, secularization and materialism. Latin theological leaders, pastors and those preparing for ministry must be equipped for the challenge of ongoing contextualization. Expatriate missionaries and organizations have a genuine contribution to make in this regard. The church must be equipped to confront the black powers of the occult which are openly active in every Latin nation.

Fourth, effective equipping of leadership for ministry versus informal volunteerism. The models of leadership development are legion, and function at all levels. But most formal educational delivery systems are still costly to create, fund, staff, and produce graduates. They do have their strategic place and we affirm it. A very small number of schools offer degrees beyond the masters, but most Latins must yet travel "North" for doctoral study. But then, others ask, "Do we need Latins with doctoral degrees?" There are two major entry points to ministry, with one route coming through formal theological study and the other emerging "on the march." How they relate to and influence each other in the future will profoundly influence the Latin churche.s

Fifth, involvement in the crises of society and political governance versus spiritualized isolationism. The genie of evangelical political action is out of the bottle and will probably never be stuffed back in. But what forms will it take in the future? Will evangelical parties be established that have no hope of winning national victory? Too many evangelicals in politics are naive, have been manipulated or have lost their vibrant faith while in power. This latter case comes from nonexistent accountability as well as weak pastoral ministry to public servants. Who will offer stable guidance to these political activists?

Sixth, polarized polemics between Catholics and evangelicals versus mutual respect. The former know they are losing influence and space to the latter, and it makes them uneasy. Some evangelicals still suffer from the ghetto mentality of a persecuted minority. Evangelicals are still being persecuted for their faith from different opponents. The Chamula Indians of Southern Mexico (religious persecution)[55] and the Quechua believers in Peru (political persecution) are just two examples. The Catholic attitude of "hispanidad" which identifies Latins intrinsically as Catholics simply must be laid to rest.

Seventh, the tension between mono-cultural evangelization and cross-cultural mission, whether national or international, continental or inter-continental. The number of evangelical churches with cross-cultural vision is still low. This must change as they are challenged biblically and then mobilized to broader mission. In Latin America, church-based missions will continue to carry the day, but church leaders must break old molds and attitudes. Missiological literature must be developed by Latin writers and theologians, as well as by the practitioners. The imperative Latin missions infrastructure must be developed for the movement to be truly viable. This challenge focuses on three areas: the pre-candidate phase of screening, primarily by the local church; the pre-field training phase; and the field ministry phase which requires supervision, shepherding and strategizing.

Eighth, the spirit of interdependent partnership versus control and neo-paternalism by expatriate organizations. This is a word to international organizations with vested interests in Latin America, whether they be funding bodies, denominations, parachurch organizations or mission agencies. Control must pass to the grass roots, and decisions must be made by those directly affected by the decisions. In the providence of God a few more Latin leaders have been appointed to governing boards of Western agencies with ministry in Latin America. On the continent we see more and more expatriate missionaries serving under Latin leadership. But much remains to be done. Expatriate missionaries from all nations continue to be welcomed . . . if they come with the true spirit of servanthood. They may have to pay a high price, a painful reality understood by the families of the five New Tribes missionaries (two of them now martyrs) and one from Wycliffe who were kidnapped in Panama and Colombia in the last two years. We will pray until we rejoice in the release of the others.

474   CRISIS AND HOPE IN LATIN AMERICA

A Final Word

Crisis and hope are woven into this entire section. Am I hopeful now? Yes. Am I naive about Latin America's history and Christianity? I trust not. The future of Christianity in Latin America lies in its commitment to biblical truth unleashed in relevance and power. ¡Maranatha!

NOTES

1.   It was a challenge to prepare for this continental review, for it required sifting through hundreds of documents, reading the updated books, interviewing and surveying people. I am especially grateful for the *Economist Country Profiles*. Produced on a quarterly basis, they provide a singular perspective on Latin America. Also of value was Benjamin Keen's *A History of Latin Americ*. The complete information on these sources is given in the annotated bibliography. *Time Magazine*, February 20, 1995, featured Castro and Cuba as its cover story.

2.   "Menem's Miracle," *Time,* July 13, 1992, pp. 19-23.

3.   "The Rescue of Mexico," *U.S. News and World Report,* January 23, 1995, pp. 48-49. "Mexican Aid Plan Loses Support in Both Parties," *The New York Times,* February 1, 1995.

4.   "The Revolution in the Other Mexico," *U.S. News and World Report,* January 17, 1994, p. 47.

5.   Carlos Fuentes, "Peso Crisis: Mexico's problem is basically political," *The Dallas Morning News,* January 12, 1995, p. 27A. "Giving critics a place on the field," *U.S. News and World Report,* January 30, 1995, p. 45.

6.   "At Forum Peso Draws Attention," *The New York Times,* January 30, 1995, p. C3.

7.   Kenichi Ohmae, "The Rise of the Region State," *Foreign Affairs,* Spring 1993, pp. 78-87.

8.   "La elección del modelo," *Crónica,* 1 de julio de 1994, p. 53.

9.   Jorge G. Castañeda, *Utopia Unarmed: The Latin American Left After the Cold War* (Vintage Books, 1994).

10.   "Los archivos del dictador," *CAMBIO16,* 22-2-93, p. 58.

11. "Summit throws door open to trade in Americas," *USA Today,* December 12, 1994, p. 10A.

12. Moises Naim, "Latin America: Post-Adjustments Blues," *Foreign Policy,* Number 92, Fall 1993, pp. 133-150.

13. "Menem's Miracle," *Time,* July 13, 1992, pp. 19-23.

14. "Winners and Losers," *Newsweek,* June 15, 1992, p. 41.

15. Hernando De Soto, *The Other Path: The Invisible Revolution in the Third World* (Harper and Row, 1989).

16. "The Gospel comes to San Mateo," *World Vision,* February-March, 1995, pp. 19-21.

17. For only two examples see "Lost Empires of the Americas" in *U.S. News and World Report,* April 2, 1990: "Lost Secrets of the Maya—What new discoveries tell us about their world—and ours," *Time,* August 9, 1993.

18. *Austin American-Statesman,* August 30, 1992, p. G10. This article gave the percentages, but the population totals come from the *1994 Population Data Sheet,* Population Reference Bureau, Washington, D.C.

19. Rigoberta Menchú, *I, Rigoberta Menchú: An Indian Woman in Guatemala* (Verso, 1984).

20. Samuel Escobar, "Latin America," in *Toward the 21st Century in Christian Mission,* James M. Philips and Robert T. Coote, eds. (Eerdmans, 1993), pp. 125-138.

21. "Colombia's Drug Business," *The Economist,* December 24, 1994-January 6, 1995, pp. 21-24.

22. "Peru Combats Drug Traffic, Winning U.S. Team's Praise," *The New York Times,* January 23, 1995.

23. "Brazil's war on children," *World Vision,* February-March, 1992.

24. "North South Issues—Democratization," University of Miami, A North-South Center Publication, Vol. II, No. 3, p. 2.

25. *Ibid.,* p. 1.

26. In preparation for this section focusing on Latin evangelicals, I wrote letters and sent a short survey to selected colleagues on the continent. The majority graciously responded, and their reflections have been included here.

27. "Catholic Church blasts Brazilian soap for occultic theme," *Austin American Statesman,* November 25, 1994, p. A24.

28. Patrick Johnstone, "Brazil," in *Operation World* (Zondervan, 1993), pp. 128-131.

29. InterVarsity IV Link letter, September 1994.

30. Included here are some of the ones that have shaped my own thinking. They appear in the annotated bibliography at the end of the book.
     Berg, Mike, and Paul Pretiz, *The Gospel People,* MARC/LAM, 1992.
     Cleary, Edward L., and Hannah Stewart-Gambino, eds. *Conflict and Competition: The Latin American Church in a Changing Environment.* Lynne Rienner Publishers, 1992.
     Cook, Guillermo, ed. *New Face of the Church in Latin America, Between Tradition and Change.* Maryknoll: Orbis, 1994.
     Deiros, Pablo Alberto. *Historia del Cristianismo en América Latina.* Buenos Aires: Fraternidad Teológica Latinoamericana, 1992.
     Dussell, Enrique, ed. *The Church in Latin America, 1492-1992.* Maryknoll: Orbis, 1992.
     Martin, David. *Tongues of Fire: The Explosion of Protestantism in Latin America.* Blackwell, 1991.
     Stoll, David. *Is Latin America Turning Protestant? The Politics of Evangelical Growth.* University of California Press, 1990.
     Stoll, David, and Virginia Barrard-Burnett, eds. *Rethinking Protestantism in Latin America.* Temple University Press, 1993.

31. David Martin, *Tongues of Fire: The Explosion of Protestantism in Latin America* (Blackwell, 1991), p. 9.

32. *Ibid.,* p. 284.

33. *Ibid.,* p. 280.

34. David Stoll, *Is Latin America Turning Protestant? The Politics of Evangelical Growth* (University of California Press, 1990). See Guillermo Cook's review of both Martin and Stoll in *The Christian Century* , December 12, 1990.

35. *Ibid.,* p. 312.

36. David Stoll and Virginia Barrard-Burnett, eds. *Rethinking Protestantism in Latin America* (Temple University Press, 1993), pp. 5-6.

37. See "A New Reformation," *Christianity Today,* April 6, 1992, pp. 30-34; "Protestantism Explodes," *Christian History* Vol. XI, No. 3. This copy of the journal was entitled "What Happened When Columbus and Christianity Collided with the Americas?"; "Mission in Latin America: An Evangelical Perspective," *Missiology: An International Review,* April 1992, pp. 241-253; "Se revisa la nueva leyenda negra?", personal copy of essay sent to the author; "Catholicism and National Identity in Latin America," *Transformation,* July/September 1991; "Latin America," in *Toward the 21st Century in Christian Mission,* James M. Phillips and Robert T. Coote, eds. (Eerdmans, 1993), pp. 125-138.

38. Guillermo Cook, ed. *New Face of the Church in Latin America, Between Tradition and Change* (Maryknoll: Orbis, 1994), pp. xiii, 268.

39. Samuel Escobar, "Latin America," in *Toward the 21st Century in Christian Mission,* James M. Phillips and Robert T. Coote, eds. (Eerdmans, 1993), p. 125.

40. Patrick Johnstone, *Operation World* (Zondervan, 1993). See the continental report on Latin America, as well as those of individual nations.

41. "Why is Latin America Turning Protestant?" *Christianity Today,* April 6, 1992. *Christian History,* Vol. XI, No. 3. Secular papers have also given their reports. See "Protestants Create an Altered State," *Insight,* July 16, 1990, from the *Washington Times* magazine.

42. Mike Berg and Paul Pretiz, *The Gospel People* (MARC/LAM, 1992), pp. 118-120.

43. David Stoll and Virginia Barrard-Burnett, eds., *Rethinking Protestantism in Latin America* (Temple University Press, 1993), p. 9.

44. *Celebremos Su Gloria* (Celebremos/Libros Alianza, Dallas, 1992). The hymnbook won the "best book" award in the 1993 Spanish Christian book convention.

45. "Christian Music with New Beat," *Latin America Evangelist,* January-March 1994.

46. Virginia Barrard-Burnett, in *Rethinking Protestantism in Latin America,* p. 201.

47. See the entire issue of *Transformation: An International Evangelical Dialogue on Mission and Ethics,* dedicated to "Evangelicals and Politics in Latin America," July/Sept, 1992. Numerous articles have come out in *News Network International,* P.O. Box 28001, Santa Ana, CA 92799, USA. The period January-November, 1994, featured 44 articles on Latin America, with many reports of evangelicals in politics.

48. Stephen Sywulka in "Evangelical President Ousted in Power Struggle," *Christianity Today,* July 19, 1993, p. 52.

49. Samuel Escobar, "Latin America," in *Toward the 21st Century in Christian Mission,* James M. Phillips and Robert T. Coote, eds. (Eerdmans, 1993), p. 127. The CO-MIBAM literature and general language is nearly identical. See *World Pulse,* January 20, 1994, for the report on COMIBAM's continental church/agency consultation held in December 1994 in Panama.

50. David Miller, "Roman Catholicism and the New Evangelization," *News Network International,* February 1993.

51. Adrés Tapia, "Why is Latin America Turning Protestant?" *Christianity Today,* April 6, 1992, p. 28.

52. "Arzobispo Penados: El Papa llama a católicos a combatir a las sectas," *Siglo Veintiuno,* 13 December, 1992, p. 12.

53. Ignacio Ellacuría, "Esquena de interpretación de la Iglesia en Centroamérica," *Revista Latinoamericana de Teologia* 31 (1994):

54. Samuel Escobar, "The Church in Latin America After 500 Years," an unpublished paper given at the April 1992 OMSC Mission Study Group.

55. "Evangelicals and Catholics Together: A Declaration," *First Things,* May 1994, pp. 15-22. See Alister McGrath, "Do We Still Need the Reformation" and J. I. Packer, "Why I Signed It," *Christianity Today,* December 12, 1994, pp. 28-37. See also four articles in *Moody Monthly,* November 1993. In early 1995 Colson convened a special meeting of leading American evangelicals that clarified some of the misunderstandings and affirmed biblical non-negotiables for American evangelicals.

56. "Chiapas Evangelicals Have Little Faith in New Government," *Christianity Today,* February 6, 1995.

15

Catholicism and
Liberation Theology Today

Emilio Antonio Núñez C.

Some important events that have taken place both inside and outside the Roman Catholic Church deserve a few comments in this addendum to our book.

The Fall of the Berlin Wall and Liberation Theology

When the first edition of this book was published (1989), the communist system in Eastern Europe was crumbling. On November 9, 1989, the government of the German Democratic Republic decided to open the border to the West, and later on the Berlin Wall, the well-known symbol of the cold war, fell down. The collapse of Soviet power is of transcendental importance for all nations on earth. There is no peace on earth yet; but the confrontation between the Soviet Union and the United States of America for world supremacy seems to have come to an end. In the area of theological reflection, the undeniable failure of Soviet socialism has raised some interesting questions.

For instance, some people ask: Did Liberation Theology collapse with the Berlin Wall? This question seems reasonable in view of the accusation that Liberation Theology is Marxist. In fact, this accusation is made in the *Instruction on Some Aspects of Liberation Theology,* published by the Holy See, under the direction of Cardinal Ratzinger in 1984.

The use of the "Marxist analysis of society" in Liberation Theology is strongly criticized by the *Instruction*. For their part, liberation theologians argue that the use of the "Marxist analysis" does not mean that Liberation Theology accepts the whole system of Marxist thought. Juan Luis Segundo, a prominent liberation theologian from Uruguay, affirms that there is no unanimity among liberation theologians as to the extent in which they use the "Marxist analysis of society." He adds that there are no two liberation theologians who agree in regard to the degree in which the atheistic conviction is a central element of Marxism. Besides, he says, there is no liberation theologian who can be accused of being atheistic. He is not convinced of the impossibility of separating the "Marxist analysis of society" from Marxist philosophy.[1]

Some liberation theologians insist that in the academic world it is usual to make reference to Marx without accepting, for instance, his interpretation of human existence as a totality. This interpretation leaves out the reality and the demands of the Christian faith. They say that even John Paul II makes use, in his encyclical *Laborem exercens,* of Marxist categories, such as alienation, exploitation, means of production, productive relations, and praxis, although the pope is against Marxism.[2]

In a paper published in 1991, Enrique D. Dussel says that Liberation Theology was not originated by the Marxist analysis of society. It was born out of Latin American reality. It was originated by Christian praxis, by the faith of the church. "It is on the road of liberating praxis that Liberation Theology comes in touch with Marxism." Dussel explains that Liberation Theology uses "a certain type of marxism," excluding other types of this socialist system, either in an implicit or explicit way.[3] "[T]he marxism used by liberation theologians is the sociological and economic marxism that in Latin America emphasized the concept of 'dependence,' the sociology of 'dependence' in its criticism to functionalism and developmentalism in Latin America."[4] Liberation Theology is far away, according to Dussel, from Stalinist dogmatism, or from "philosophical marxism."[5] He would also say that Liberation Theology has not collapsed with the Berlin Wall. This would be also the opinion of the Chilean Jesuit P. Richard who has said that "marxism is not the big problem of Liberation Theology."[6]

Speaking of "the instrumental use of marxism," Leonardo Boff and his brother Clodovis Boff admit that liberation theologians have assumed "some methodological indications" that are valuable in understanding the universe of the oppressed. For instance, the great importance of economic factors, the emphasis on class struggle, and the deceiving power of ideologies. At the same time, the Boff brothers affirm that liberation theologians have assumed a critical attitude towards Marxism. Marx may be accepted as a "fellow traveler," not as "the leader" in the effort to liberate the poor. To liberation theologians "the materialism and atheism of Marx has not been a temptation."[7]

On the other hand, Pierre Bigó, a Jesuit priest, concludes that "the marxist analysis of society is closely related, in a symbiotic way, to the global theory . . . To respect the analysis is to swallow the theory. The attempt to separate from the theory the analysis, would require a change so radical in the analysis, that this one would be marxist only in an equivocal way."[8]

It is evident that liberation theologians, such as Gustavo Gutiérrez M., have admiration for Marx, and they see a Latin American socialistic system as the answer to our economical, social and political problems. He says that the new insights coming from Marx enabled humankind to have initiatives which

> ought to assure the change from the capitalistic mode of production to the socialistic mode, that is to say, to one oriented towards a society in which persons can begin to live freely and humanly. They will have controlled nature, created the conditions for a socialized production of wealth, done away with private acquisition of excessive wealth, and established socialism.[9]

Gutiérrez seems to quote with approval the declarations made by radical leftist priests in Latin America. For instance, he cites the Mexican bishop Sergio Méndez Arceo, who asserted:

> Only socialism can enable Latin America to achieve true development . . . I believe that a socialist system is more in accord with the Christian principles of true fellowship, justice, and peace . . . I do not know what kind of socialism, but this is the direction Latin America should go. For myself, I believe it should be a democratic socialism.[10]

Of course, Gutiérrez agrees with the Argentinian priests who propose "a Latin American socialism that will promote the advent of the New Humanity."[11]

Gutiérrez has made some changes in his way of analyzing our Latin

American reality. For example, in the Introduction to the new edition of his Theology of Liberation (1988), he says:

> It is clear, for example, that the theory of dependence, which was so extensively used in the early years of our encounter with the Latin American world, is now an inadequate tool, because it does not take sufficient account of the internal dynamics of each country or of the vast dimensions of the world of the poor. In addition, Latin American social scientists are increasingly alert to factors of which they were not conscious earlier and which show that the world economy has evolved.

He has also confessed that he and other liberation theologians were in danger of initially adopting a "simplistic position,"[12] in analyzing the situation of poverty.

For the new edition of his book, Gutiérrez has "rewritten" the section that in the first edition was entitled "Christian Fellowship and Class Struggle." Gutiérrez says that this section, which included some of his most radical statements, "gave rise to misunderstandings that I want to clear up. I have rewritten the text in the light of new documents of the magisterium and by taking other aspects of the subject into account."[13] The title of the new section is "Faith and Social Conflict." Pierre Bigó points out that the orientation of Gutiérrez's introductory words to the new edition of *Liberation Theology* is different from the rest of the book, except in the section on social conflict. "There is no evidence of the marxist tendency in the 'Introduction.' Gustavo Gutiérrez is now defending democracy . . . But he does not subject to criticism the marxist system as a whole."[14]

On September 30, 1991, news came from Brazil that Leonardo Boff had decided to give up Liberation Theology, because of the pressure exercised upon him by the Vatican, through the Congregation for the Defence of the Faith. It is said that Boff sent his letter of resignation to the prelate of the Franciscan order, Hermann Schalueck. Boff has been a member of this monastic order. A version of the letter was published by the Spaniard newspaper *El País,* and then reproduced by the *Journal do Brasil.*[15]

Up to now we do not have a declaration by Boff himself about this report. But it is widely known that on June, 1992, he announced his decision to leave the Catholic priesthood. Since 1972 he had been questioned by the Vatican because of his book *Jesus Christ the Liberator.*

The publication of his work entitled *Church: Charism and Power* (1981) aroused the anger of the hierarchy. He had to meet with the Sacred Congregation in Rome in 1984 to answer questions about his writings. It seems that the major concern of the hierarchy is that in that book Boff challenges the validity of the ecclesiastical structures. It was decided to consign him to "silence" for "an opportune period." From then on he was supposed to submit his writing to censorship before publication. Boff has declared that the Catholic Church is under a dictatorship that has been trying to oppress him for the last twenty years. But he is leaving the priesthood, not the church. He remains in the church as a layman, "to continue his theological activity in freedom."[16] This freedom includes rebellion in his personal life against celibacy. The Brazilian magazine *Revista da Folha*, November 1993, reveals that Boff has had a romance with his secretary, Marcia Miranda, since 1982. She is legally separated from her husband; but she cannot get married again in the Catholic Church.

The last five years have been quite difficult for liberation theologians. Boff had to leave the priesthood because of his radical views on the institutional church. Ignacio Ellacuría and five of his Jesuit colleagues were assassinated in El Salvador in November 1989, because of their ideological and radical identification with the revolutionary army of that country. At that time, Soviet socialism had started to crumble. Of course, it is possible to say that in some respects Liberation Theology did not collapse with the Berlin Wall.

Twenty-three years ago, Gustavo Gutiérrez M. said that his theology was "a theology of the road." It was not a final system of theological thought; it was an unfinished process, open to change. Some of its chapters would be written later on. And Gutiérrez has demonstrated his willingness to make some adjustments in his way of thinking.

On the other hand, it is undeniable that after the failure of the Soviet system, the socialistic inclination of theologians like Gustavo Gutiérrez is questioned more than ever by those who are deeply concerned about the political mediation proposed by Liberation Theology to solve our social problems. And if the political mediation cannot be separated from the philosophical and metaphysical aspects of Marxism, then the foundation of Liberation Theology is badly deteriorated. But liberation theologians believe that such a separation is possible, as we have seen above.

In a book published in 1991, Jon Sobrino, one of the outstanding liberation theologians in Latin America, affirms:

> In some circles Liberation Theology is explained as a
> passing fad . . . Unfortunately, it is not a passing fad . . .

> Liberation Theology is contextual, and the context de-
> mands more liberation than ever . . . In our continent we
> are still under oppression, and the statistics indicate that
> this oppression in the form of unjust poverty is in-
> creasing.[17]

The Preferential Option for the Poor

Definitely, Liberation Theology is not a passing fad; but an inescapable challenge to us evangelicals to consider our social reality and
to contextualize the gospel in Latin America. At the same time we have
to be alert to another attempt to impose a political ideology on the biblical text. After the collapse of Soviet socialism, some people in the
northern part of our continent started to speak about "A New 'Liberation
Theology' for the World." K. E. Grubbs, Jr., Editorial and Commentary
Director, *Orange County Register,* presents two arguments:

> First, that the fall of communism in Central and Eastern
> Europe, Nicaragua and elsewhere around the world must
> be attributed to faith and the promise of the free market.
> Second, that these are precisely the things that lead to
> 'moral prosperity' and the true liberation for all men.[18]

It is obvious that if we accept this "new liberation theology" we would
go back to the times when consciously or unconsciously we applied the
ideology of capitalism to the interpretation of Holy Scriptures. From the
hermeneutical standpoint, we have problems with the socialistic ideology
of liberation theologians, and with the free market ideology of the heralds of "A New Liberation Theology. "The authority of God, revealed in
the Bible, is far above all human systems of thought.
  Liberation Theology is alive in Roman Catholicism, especially in
the version accepted by the hierarchy, with emphasis on the preferential
option for the poor. Roman Catholics have always given the poor a place
in their soteriological thinking. The beggars at the entrance of the imposing cathedral were quite convenient to gain heaven in exchange for
the alms given to them. It was a soteriology of human merits. But in
practice that was not really designed to liberate the poor from social injustice and oppression. Liberation theologians were able to see beyond
the symptoms of poverty to its causes, and proposed a change in our social structures to liberate the poor.
  At a congress of Dominican fathers in Salamanca, Spain, April

1989, Gustavo Gutiérrez said that in his speeches previous to Vatican II, Pope John XXIII discussed three important themes: (1) the openness of the church toward the world; (2) ecumenism, namely the openness toward other Christian confessions; and (3) the church of the poor. The pope said: "In the presence of the underdeveloped countries, the Church is and wants to be the Church for all, and especially the Church of the poor."[19] At the Third Conference of Latin American Bishops, held in Puebla, Mexico, in 1979, Liberation Theology was not condemned; but the Documents of Puebla speak of "total liberation," and "the preferential option for the poor." The bishops who participated in the 1992 Fourth Conference of Latin American Bishops, in Santo Domingo, Dominican Republic, assumed "with renewed zeal the evangelical and preferential option for the poor, in continuity with Medellín (1968) and Puebla (1979)."[20]

In his encyclical *Centesimus annus* (on the centennial of the *Rerum novarum,* of Leo XIII), John Paul II says:

> The crisis of the marxist system (1989) does not elim-
> inate the problems of social injustice and oppression . . .
> To those seeking a new and authentic theory and praxis
> of liberation, the Church offers not just its social doc-
> trine and, in general, its teachings on the redeemed per-
> son by Jesus Christ, but also the concrete commitment to
> help in the struggle against margination and suffering.[21]

In his social encyclicals, John Paul II has been emphatic in declaring that the social doctrine of the church *is not* a "third option" between "liberal capitalism" and "marxist collectivism." The model of a free market society has demonstrated the failure of Marxism in the effort to build a new and better society, but coincides with Marxism in reducing humans totally to the sphere of economics, and to the satisfaction of material needs.

In his message to the Fourth Conference of Latin American Bishops in Santo Domingo, October 1992, the pope said:

> In continuity with the Conferences of Medellín (1968)
> and Puebla (1979), the Church reaffirms *the preferential
> option for the poor*. This is an option based essentially
> on the Word of God, not on human sciences or ideol-
> ogies, which frequently reduce the poor to socio-
> economic and abstract categories. It is a firm and ir-
> revocable option . . . The authentic praxis of liberation

has to be always inspired by the doctrine of the Church, as this doctrine is exposed in the two Instructions of the Congregation for the Doctrine of the Faith *(Libertatis nuntius, 1984; Libertatis conscientia, 1986),* which has to be taken into consideration when dealing with the subject of the theologies of liberation.[22]

The New Evangelization

The basic document for the Conference of Latin American Bishops in Puebla, 1979, was the exhortation *Evangelii Nuntiandi*, written by Paul VI to promote the evangelization of the world by the Catholic Church. The *Document of Puebla* affirms that Holy Scriptures are supposed to be "the soul of evangelization." But the Word of God is revealed both in the Bible and in the living tradition of the church, particularly expressed in the symbols or professions of faith and dogmas of the church. The Scriptures must be read and interpreted under the living faith of the church. The meaning of the Scriptures, of the symbols and dogmatic declarations of the past does not come out only from the text itself, but from the faith of the church.[23]

The Catholic bishops who met at Santo Domingo to participate in their Fourth Conference (1992), took the opportunity to declare that the Catholic Church has been evangelizing in Latin America for the last 500 years. They explain in chapter 1 of their *Conclusions* that the new evangelization does not mean that the first evangelization is invalidated, or fruitless. It does not mean the proposal of a new gospel, different from the first and only gospel of Christ. It does not mean to disregard the first evangelization. It is the answer to the problems of our continent, in which there is a divorce between faith and life, to the point of producing painful situations of injustice, social inequality and violence. It is especially a call to conversion. It is to have the gospel in active dialogue with modernity and post-modernity. It is the effort to inculturate the gospel.[24]

According to the Latin American bishops, the goal of the new evangelization is to form people and communities deeply grounded in their faith, and to respond to the new situation in which the Latin American people live as a result of the social and cultural changes of modernity. Attention must be given to the problems of urbanization, poverty, margination, materialism, the culture of death, the invasion of the sects, and religious proposals from different sources.[25]

The "new evangelization" has meant that we evangelicals suffer again unjust criticism and even subtle defamation from some Catholic hierarchs. There is no doubt that the Catholic Church is alarmed by the significant growth of the evangelical community in Latin America. Their "new evangelization" is also an effort to neutralize that growth, and, if possible, to recuperate lost ground in these countries. To this end, they are also imitating some of our evangelistic strategies. For example, public preaching, door-to-door visitation, singing of evangelical choruses, and, most significant of all, home Bible study. The Word of God is powerful to convert the soul, and many Catholics have come to know the Lord Jesus Christ as their only Savior as a result of having read and studied the Scriptures. But we know cases of Catholics who have also discovered, in their Bible study, that some cardinal doctrines of Roman Catholicism are not in keeping with God's written revelation.

On the other hand, "the new evangelization" means also a reinforcement of popular religiosity, which includes, of course, centuries-old practices of the Catholic Church in Latin America. It is also evident in the great emphasis given to Mary, mother of Jesus of Nazareth. The cult of Mary is deeply rooted in the heart of many Latin Americans, and in the heart of John Paul II,who takes every opportunity to express his Marian devotion. To many people in Latin America, Marian devotion is the greatest distinctive of Catholicism. The theologians of the Catholic Church know this aspect of popular religiosity, and they try to reinforce it both in their doctrine and in their liturgy. On a TV program in Guatemala City, behind the preacher there is an image of Mary, as a reminder that the broadcast is Catholic. The preacher uses the Bible a great deal in his sermons, and some people may think that he is a Protestant evangelist.

John Paul II usually does not finish his sermons, speeches, encyclicals and other writings without honoring Mary. In reality, the motto he chose for his pontificate is *Totus Tuus,* which literally means "all belongs to you"; and in the case of the pope, "I belong to you, Mary," with no reservation whatsoever. In *Crossing the Threshold of Hope,* his international best-selling 1994 book, he explains his Marian devotion as a total surrender to Mary, since the days of his youth. He says that genuine devotion to Mary "is Christocentric; even more, it is deeply rooted in the Trinitarian mystery of God, and in the mysteries of the Incarnation and Redemption."[26] His sincerity, his profound spirituality, and his strong religious convictions deserve our respect; but in this book which reveals his innermost being he does not appeal directly to the Scriptures to support his Marian devotion. His argument is theological and existential. He depends on a theological deduction, and on the memories of his early youth.

Evidently, in the pontificate of John Paul II, the mother of Jesus is "the star of the evangelization," according to the desire expressed by Paul VI in his encyclical *Evangelii Nuntiandi* (1975).

The Ecumenism of John Paul II

On more than one occasion we may have asked ourselves whether the strongly conservative John Paul II is really following the steps of his predecessors John XXIII and Paul VI in his attitude toward the ecumenical cause. The final answer to this question will be given, after his death, by those historians who will evaluate his pontificate. For the time being, he has not been really enthusiastic in promoting the ecumenical cause in Latin America. At least, when he visited Central America eleven years ago, ecumenism was not one of his favorite subjects. On the occasion of his first visit to Mexico in 1979, news came about the disappointment experienced by some Protestant leaders when they saw the extreme form of Marianism displayed by the pontiff to please the multitudes.

Nevertheless, it is undeniable that John Paul II is ecumenical, in complete agreement with Vatican II. In regard to the relationship of the church to non-Christian religions, the council declared: "The Catholic Church rejects nothing which is true in these religions."[27] John Paul II comments that instead of being concerned about the existence of so many religions, we should rather marvel at the many elements that all of them have in common. He says that all the religions have the *semina Verbi* (seeds of the Logos) which the Holy Spirit uses to do his work outside the church.[28]

At the same time the pope affirms that the Catholic Church is necessary for salvation, because the Vatican Council II has declared that the church, "constituted and organized in the world as a society, subsists in the Catholic Church," and because "it is through Christ's Catholic Church alone, which is the all embracing means of salvation, that the fullness of the means of salvation can be obtained."[29] There is salvation outside the Catholic Church, but it is an incomplete salvation. In the final analysis, the ecumenical dream of Catholicism is that all human beings, even the animist and the atheist, will be integrated to the one church that *subsists* in the Roman Catholic Church—"the sacrament of salvation for the whole world."

It is true that in some respects the Catholic Church is the same; but although (superficially at least) her distinctive and fundamental dogmas remain unchanged, she has experienced several changes in response to internal and external pressures; and she has to go through more changes in the years to come. We pray that the Catholic Church may change in complete submission to God's written revelation, under the ministry of the Holy Spirit.

NOTES

1.   Juan Luis Segundo, *Teología de la Liberación. Respuesta al Cardenal Ratzinger* (Madrid: Ediciones Cristiandad, 1985), pp. 125-138.

2.   Juan José Tamayo-Acosta, *Para Comprender la Teología de la Liberación* (Navarra, España: Editorial Verbo Divino, 1990), pp. 83-84.

3.   Enrique Dussel, "Teología de la Liberación y Marxismo," in *Mysterium Salutis* (San Salvador, El Salvador: UCA Editores, 1991), pp. 122-124.

4.   Ibid., p. 125.

5.   Ibid., p. 126.

6.   Tamayo-Acosta, p. 79.

7.   Leonardo and Clodovis Boff, *Cómo Hacer Teología de la Liberación* (Bogotá, Colombia: Ediciones Paulinas, 1986), pp. 38-39.

8.   Pierre Bigó, "Análisis marxista y Materialismo Dialéctico," in *Otra Iglesia en la Base.* A publication of the Latin American Council of Latin American Bishops, Bogotá, Colombia, 1985, p. 301.

9.   Gustavo Gutiérrez M., *A Theology of Liberation.* With a new Introduction by the author (Maryknoll, NY: Orbis Books, 1988), pp. 19-20.

10.   Ibid., pp. 65-66.

11.   Ibid.

12.   Ibid, p. xxiv.

13.   Ibid., p. 156.

14.   Pierre Bigó, Debate en la Iglesia, Teología de la Liberación (Bogotá, Colombia: Ediciones Paulinas, 1992), p. 82.

15.   "Boff renuncia a la Teología de la Liberación, dice diario," *Prensa Libre,* Guatemala, September 30, 1991.

16. Flavio Tavares, "La Iglesia está bajo una dictadura," *Crítica,* Guatemala, January 31, 1993.

17. Jon Sobrino, *Jesucristo el Liberador* (San Salvador, El Salvador, 1991), p. 26.

18. "A New 'Liberation Theology" for the World: Faith and the Free Market," *Imprimis,* Hillsdale College, Hillsdale, Michigan, March 1991.

19. Gustavo Gutiérrez M., "La Evangelización de América Latina ante el año 2000," *Ciencia Tomista,* Facultad de Teología de San Esteban, Salamanca, España, Vol. CXVI, May-August, 1989.

20. "Mensaje de la IV Conferencia a los Pueblos de América Latina y el Caribe," *Santo Domingo. Conclusiones* (Guatemala: Conferencia Episcopal de Guatemala, 1992), par. 17.

21. Pope John Paul II, *Centesimus Annus* (Guatemala: Conferencia Episcopal, 1991), par. 26, p. 52.

22. John Paul II, "Discurso Inaugural," *Santo Domingo. Conclusiones,* par. 16, p. 10.

23. *Puebla. III General Conference of the Latin American Catholic Bishops* (Bogotá, Colombia: CELAM, 1979), pars. 372-374, p. 118.

24. *Santo Domingo. Conclusiones,* pars. 23-30, pp. 34-36.

25. Idem.

26. John Paul II, *Crossing the Threshold of Hope* (Barcelona, España: Plaza & James, 1994), pp. 207-209.

27. "Declaration on the Relationship of the Church to Non-Christian Religions," *The Documents of Vatican II* (New York: Guild Press, 1966), par. 2, p. 662.

28. John Paul II, *Crossing the Threshold of Hope,* pp. 96-97.

29. Ibid., p. 147.

16

Mission, Missions and Missionaries in Latin America

William Taylor

So many of my thoughts on Latin America crystallized during that long predawn ride from Maracay to the Caracas airport. I had spent a packed week of ministry in the country, with the honor of staying with some dear national friends; and now I was returning to my family. The ride with Jorge and Roberto became a transforming moment as we came to grips with issues raised in this book: the history and reality of Latin America, both strengths and weaknesses; the Latin idiosyncracies; religious currents surging through the continent; the role of a minority evangelical church in an increasingly hostile secular and Catholic world; the mission of the churches of Christ in the Latin American context; the nature of evangelical contextualization and ministerial preparation; cross-cultural missions; and finally, the crucial role of the foreign missions and missionaries.

Jorge (the analytical teacher) and his colleague Roberto (the pastor), together with their wives, represented the essence and promise of evangelicals in Latin America. Both could have taken a secular vocation and made more money, but both were intensely committed to Christ, to his churches, to leadership training, to Christian literature, to theological reflection based on the Word and from Latin America. They symbolized hope; and I was proud to know them, to share with them, to learn from them, to interact seriously with them, to be their friend, and to laugh, cry and pray together. It was a great ride to the airport, and as the dawn light conquered the night, I intuitively sensed that Jorge and Roberto also represented Christ's light overcoming Latin America's spiritual darkness.

A REVIEW OF THE TERRITORY WE HAVE COVERED

As I look back over the previous chapters, I congratulate readers for coming this far. We have traveled much and perhaps you are weary of details and statistics, of the overwhelming number of topics apparently important to Latin America. You now need to sift through the material, to evaluate and reason, seeking discernment of the Lord, looking toward some kinds of decisions you might need to make. But let us review the territory once more.

Our first major section of the book dealt with a number of themes. We attempted to survey the Latin American scenario; we delved into the history in search of understanding; we were hit in the face with the acute human crises of Latin America's population; we viewed the spiritual dimensions, marking the Latin openness to messages of hope and power; we risked a personal evaluation of the Latin American personality.

Then we moved to other issues, examples of evangelical contextualization from Latin America. We examined the different Christs of the continent; we spent a serious amount of time working through an understanding of Roman Catholicism in Latin America; we were exposed to the challenge of doing theology based on the Word and from the Latin context; and finally we evaluated the call for evangelical social responsibility and concluded with a study of the nature of the church's mission.

And now what? What is my responsibility as well as yours as we wrap up this book? Clearly we as authors want you the reader to conclude our time together with a solid understanding of what Latin america really is today, as a result of evaluating her history and culture. We want you to increase your sensitivity to the unique factors that make up this kaleidoscopic mosaic, this rich tapestry of Latin America. We want to promote in you a genuine love for the continent's culture and its people, a love that ultimately must come as part of the love of Christ.

But there is yet more. And I suggest that we conclude with some brief final observations on two critical topics: the nature of the church's mission in Latin America, and then the role of the foreign mission and its missionaries.

THE MISSION OF THE CHURCH WITHIN
THE CONTEXT OF LATIN AMERICA

I trust you were careful to sense the heartbeat of my friend and co-author as he developed his topics, particularly the mission of the church in Latin America. This concern probes directly into the heart of many issues that have provoked serious polemic for evangelicals in today's world.

The Issues

We are here speaking of the nature of the gospel and of the church and its biblical and contemporary mission. We cannot afford to ignore the cry of the people living on the underside of history. Nor can we capitulate to the demands of a purely political gospel of societal transformation. As I interact with and read the writings of key Latin American evangelicals, I see that they call for a biblical balance that takes into account the human socio-spiritual problems of people who do not live in a context of Anglo-Saxon prosperity. These committed men—Padilla, Escobar, Arana, Núñez, and others—are challenging us to reread Scripture with the insight and discernment that the Holy Spirit can give when there is also sensitivity to different histories and cultures.

The plea is to consider a complete and integrated gospel that deals with the fundamental spiritual alienation of humanity from God, an alienation that splinters all the relationships that humans sustain: those to God, to oneself, and to others. No serious Latin evangelical wants to dump the gospel and adopt mere humanistic reformation. But they do say that the social implications of the gospel are clear in Scripture and must be made clear today in the demands of the biblical gospel. Social responsibility must never become a substitute for the gospel, for there is no true gospel without the person and work of Jesus Christ. But at the same time, the gospel and social responsibility are intimately related. In some cases the social responsibility prepares the way for the gospel as Christian compassion is incarnated; in other cases it accompanies the gospel proclamation as a full partner; and in still other instances it is a product of the gospel.

We also are dealing with the issue of contextualization, that prickly and misunderstood task of churches around the world. If the Scripture is to have contemporary impact equal to that experienced by its first readers and hearers, then we must dedicate ourselves to the task of examining how this can take place within Latin American realities. As Latin evangelicals commit themselves to contextualization, their task will call for godly humility and trust. Humility is imperative for all because nationalistic pride can destroy the best Christian minds. Trust is imperative because the Holy Spirit must be their guide. In particular, Anglo-Saxons must trust the Spirit to lead their Latin colleagues. The postulates, process, and products may threaten some, but ultimately the matter calls for trust and prayer.

In the providence of the Lord, he may call Latin churches and leaders to take routes uncommon to the countries of the northern hemisphere. Latin American evangelicals need to develop more bonds with their brothers and sisters in Africa and Asia who have experienced similar histories of colonization and underdevelopment. And we can praise God for the vast number of gifted Christian men and women in the Two-Thirds World who are very capable of sharing the work of contextualization. There will be different emphases than in the North. These will be based on gifts, vocations, objectives, and the particular historical context being lived out. Latin American church history must increasingly be written and proclaimed by Latins themselves. They are capable and willing, and members of the Body of Christ worldwide will be enriched as we listen to one another.

A Full-Orbed Thrust

The power of the gospel in its fullness must be proclaimed in Latin America. This means the utilization of all the vast resources of God's people on the continent. It means a clear understanding of the unadulterated essence of the life-saving gospel that brings eternal salvation. We may have to re-examine and probably restructure some of the made-to-order-market-tested-gospel-formulas. But the centrality of the life and ministry of Christ, his death and resurrection, must be the core of the proclamation and persuasion.

We must preach the powerful gospel, power that transforms lives, families, vocations, communities, and even nations when fully unleashed. We will be called upon to understand and practice spiritual warfare, to understand powerful encounters with demonic forces that operate openly in the occult and spiritist worlds as well as in socio-political arenas. We must call Latin Americans to repentance before the Lamb, and we must call them to an understanding of the implications of a commitment to Christ that goes beyond easy-believism and a shallow Christian life. Believers must be confronted with their responsibilities before the Lord not only to evangelize but also to live out the gospel and its full implications in the social dimension.

The church in Latin America has generally been self-propagating, self-governing, and self-financing. Now the fourth "self" must come, self-theologizing. This includes doing theology in Latin America, preparing people for ministry through all forms of theological education (formal, nonformal, and even informal), modeling, mentoring, and writing. This task is not easy. Perhaps it will call for greater development of international and intercultural theological communities and fellowships where the richness of varied heritages and experiences are focused on self-theologizing. We must pray in particular for the individuals and groups dedicated to theological reflection based on the Word but who operate within the Latin world.

A WORD TO FOREIGN MISSION AGENCIES WORKING IN LATIN AMERICA

A very significant ceremony took place at COMIBAM in November 1987. The beginning of that historic congress was marked by a poignant ceremony of celebration—a time of thanksgiving for the foreign missionaries who left Europe and North America to bring the gospel and establish churches and institutions in Latin America. Latin Americans spoke in magnificent Spanish and Portuguese, thanking God for the legacy. Then a veteran North American former missionary to Latin America responded. God was praised, the thousands clapped with enthusiasm, and prayer was raised in thanksgiving, coupled with the realization of the enormous responsibility that lay upon Latin evangelicals. Speakers also frankly underscored the shortcomings of the foreign missionary during COMIBAM. I was one of those.

As I talk with Latin Christians, the vast majority are openly thankful to the expatriate missionaries and agencies that work in Latin America. In spite of the plethora of limitations and mistakes, there is appreciation. I frankly asked my Venezuelan friends Robert and Jorge: "What is the place of the foreign mission and missionary in Latin America today? Do you still want us?" There was quietness in the car as we sped toward the airport. Both of them pondered the question, an honest query that called for an honest answer. Then Jorge spoke: "Yes, there is a place today, but—" The "but" is crucial, for as we interacted with the topic both men spoke with heat and conviction of the benefits and then the unfortunate errors of Anglo-Saxon agencies and missionaries.

Let me focus on the missionary agencies for now. Patrick Johnstone reports that there are about 11,544 foreign missionaries in Latin America today.[1] How many agencies only God knows, but the thirteenth edition of the *Mission Handbook: North American Protestant Ministries Overseas* lists the major ones.[2] My concern right now is not for the number of agencies or for increasing their number and size. I am more concerned about the leadership of the foreign agencies working in Latin America. I assume that these leaders operate with high Christian motives and that they are ultimately led by the love of Christ, albeit in some cases they are misguided. What can be done to stimulate more culturally sensitive foreign mission agencies? Here are a few lines of thought.

How many of these organizations have Latin representation on their boards? Precious few, if my sources are correct. There are all kinds of reasons given, but they do not hold water today. Too many agencies are built upon the North American transnational corporation model. Anglo boards make decisions based on executive leadership input. Discussions are obviously in English, a fact that probably cannot be obviated for now. But too many times decisions affecting the Latin American churches are made without an iota of Latin input. Is this the right way to do God's business? And the same is true for those missions that work in Africa, Asia, the South Pacific, and Europe. There must be national representation. To excuse this lack with "Well, there just are not any qualified Latins" or "It just costs too much money to have them travel to our meetings" is simply not right.

Secondly, agencies are challenged to take decision-making processes to their fields of service, where there is greater direct access to godly Latin American leaders. Perhaps we need to rethink our entire authority structure in light of the demands of international partnership in order for the agenda to be guided and informed by national thinking. Surely national input is needed for decisions that affect institutional budgets and construction, the placing of missionaries and their orientation, and the setting of goals and priorities. It requires a painful transition. Mistakes will be made once again during the transitional process, but the results will ultimately outweigh the problems.

Thirdly, foreign agencies with formal institutions must make sure that local national boards are developed to assume full responsibility for those ministries. There will in all probability be an ongoing financial and staff partnership with the agency, but ultimate authority must reside in the local board. Tragic mistakes have been made in the past in the entire nationalization process; and the evangelical camp has lost more than one institution in Latin America. But this should not deter the process of serious nationalization, including the ultimate ownership of the properties.

Fourth, a word to the newer ministries coming to Latin America in recent years, whether youth organizations, specialized groups, or the international television experts invading Latin America with a high-tech gospel, capitalism, and expensive methodology. Beware of what is being done with the vast amounts of personnel, time, funds, and equipment. Be sensitive to the local churches and leadership, which will generally withhold their evaluation and opinions until asked. Some groups should stay "home."

Completely stop buying off with money and the promise of prestige those gifted church leaders who are dedicated to local congregational ministries. Obviously the Lord can lead them to change their ministries, but this decision should be made without financial temptation. Some years ago while I taught at Trinity Evangelical Divinity School in Illinois, an international recruiter of a large North American agency spoke with me. He knew of my experience in Latin America and asked me for the names of Latins who could fill seven key positions in their work. I frankly told him that I did know of people, but that I was reluctant to give the names, for the above-stated reasons. This prompted a most interesting discussion on the place of money and ministry in Two-Thirds World recruitment.

Fifth, all foreign-based ministries must re-examine the challenges of partnership in mission in Latin America. Some agencies still sadly continue subsidizing pastor's salaries, thereby further promoting the dependence and paternalism. This practice should be terminated at the local-church level. Ministry and economic partnerships are still needed at the institutional and capital-investment end, guided by constant dialogue. Scholarship programs that will provide further training in Latin America, Africa, Asia, Europe, or North America are greatly needed for gifted leaders. Theological institutions, literature ministries, development projects, and other strategic outreaches need foreign partners—personnel and finances.

The vast under-reached cities of Latin America require enormous creativity and investment in terms of evangelism and church planting. Here is fertile ground for experimenting with new partnership models. And as new agencies come to Latin America, there is also a challenge for these agencies themselves to work in cooperation with each other or with established national churches. Why duplicate efforts or multiply more church bodies than already exist? Here is an area calling for evangelical unity and sharing of both tasks and glory.

Finally, now is the time for missions agencies to initiate and hasten the serious process of organizational contextualization in Latin America.

Let us do it before tensions rise to the explosion stage. It can be done wisely, thus avoiding the charges of paternalism and neo-colonialism.

A WORD TO THE EXPATRIATE MISSIONARIES IN LATIN AMERICA

Some Initial Thoughts

Are you wanted in Latin America today? Yes, you are, but—and the "but" is of crucial importance, presenting a great challenge to the missionary. If you accept the challenge, the "but" will open doors of loving relationships and effective communication. In recent years and in preparation for this book I have asked scores of Latin American friends what they think about foreign missionaries—most of whom come from North America or Europe. I have asked my friends if they still need missionaries and, if so, what kind of missionary they want.

Significantly, the answers fall into clear patterns. They do want them to come, but they want them to live with the people, to learn from the people, to love the people, to serve the people, to understand their history, to appreciate their culture, to work alongside and perhaps under them as time develops. They do not speak—as expatriate missionaries tend to do—of "Working yourself out of a job." It is more, "Stay with us and work until the task is completed. Then move horizontally to another job."

My friends Roberto and Jorge affirmed that Venezuela did need missionaries, "but" they must be sensitive to culture, live outside the Anglo ghettos, curb their American lifestyle, renounce their paternalism, work as servants in dialogue with national colleagues, strive to contextualize their ministries, and be willing to relocate to areas of major need, such as under-reached Caracas.

The Fruit of Brainstorming Sessions

On different occasions I have asked Latin Americans to think through the advice they would give new missionaries to their countries. Here is their counsel, as well as the creativity of a number of former students of mine at the Central American Theological Seminary in Guatemala. I give them to you as they came, requiring you to evaluate each one on its relative importance and merit.

Suggestions for New Missionaries
and Their Adaptation to Latin America

1. Remove from your head your great American ideas of how things should be done here.

2. Do not think you have come to work with uncivilized people.

3. Do not teach so much theory, but practice your teaching in your life. Show us how it works in real life as you model the truth.

4. Read about Latin America and my country. Find out who our best authors are.

5. Have more contact with the people, not only in the churches but in your social life.

6. Live at an adequate level, neither too high above us nor too low below us. Adapt your lifestyle to the people with whom you work.

7. Do not talk in English when there are people present who do not understand it. This is rude on your part, and we tend to suspect that you are talking about us.

8. Do not impose your American customs on us or belittle ours. Do not try to make us into little North Americans.

9. Do something to meet the social needs of our people, whether it be literacy, relief, or development projects.

10. Do not feel that you are superior to us. We can sense pride even in small amounts. You came to serve in humility, and it is best that you not compare cultures, trying to prove yours is better.

11. Show love to people as you do in your country, and then learn how we do it here.

12. Learn our language well: our sayings and proverbs, our youth slang if appropriate, our subjunctive, our regional and national accents.

13. Try to learn our language so well that you speak without a foreign accent.

14. Read about our continental and national heroes: Bolívar, Miranda, Juárez, San Martín, and others.

15. Be willing to accept our suggestions. That may hurt, but we want to help. You have to accept them with humility. Learn the meaning of Proverbs 27:6 and 17.

16. Watch the way you speak to us. We are very sensitive to the tone of voice and the choice of words. We are touchy people.

17. Be more diplomatic in your relationships with us. Do not greet us as you *gringos* greet each other. You seem too cold and distant. Ask about our families and our personal lives.

18. Learn to touch us appropriately. You people seem very cold in human relations. There is nothing like a great *abrazo*.

19. See yourself as a co-equal with us, neither higher nor lower.

20. Develop serious and deep friends from among us, people with whom you can be transparent and vulnerable. This will take time and is costly. But you can ask them about the intimate things, about ideas and other topics. This step is risky, for the closer you get to us the more unhappy you might make your missionary colleagues.

21. Love without talking about it. Just show it.

22. Show that you lovingly expect much from us without coming across as a paternalistic chief.

23. Make disciples among us, leaving a human and reproducible legacy when you leave.

24. Eat and like our food, not just Pizza Hut and McDonald's. We also like to know what you eat at home as a family.

25. Learn to dress like Latins, using our styles and fabrics.

26. Be more flexible in terms of time. Slow down! Why are you always in a hurry, looking at your watch? There is more to life than time.

27. Learn and appreciate our music and instruments, both folk and classical.

28. Drop the terms *pounds* and *miles,* and then learn to give weights and distances in kilos and kilometers.

29. Struggle honestly with our struggles: social, historical, cultural, church, and Christian life. Do not just give us capitalistic answers, and do not reduce societal problems to simplistic spiritual solutions.

30. Learn to read the Bible from our perspective and culture. You will have to work at this, but it is worth it. Note how much of the Bible was written to people who lived in violence, injustice, and political uncertainty.

31. Remember that we think differently from the way you do, and our problem-solving is different from yours. Learn how we do it.

32. Come and stay with us for a long time. Short terms are shortcuts many times.

33. At the same time, be bold enough to examine whether or not you should stay in Latin America as a missionary. Perhaps some of you should return home, particularly if you cannot adjust here, or do not know why you came, or are having serious family problems, or cannot work with us.

Two Farewells of Missionaries

I shall never forget two contrasting farewells given to two different North American missionary families in Latin America. In one of the cases I was driving through a certain Central American country and dropped in to visit a pastor friend. The church rang with chatter and laughter. "What's going on?" I asked. The pastor replied frankly, "Well, we are giving a farewell party to a missionary family that is returning to their country. But to be honest, most of us don't know when they came, what they did, and why they are leaving. But we are giving a party." What stunningly sober words. A ministry of nothingness, leaving behind nothing. Surely other facets could explain the case, and probably the missionary couple was about to return home in profound frustration and defeat. But unfortunately, cases such as this true one represent a current reality in Latin America.

The other case was radically different. At the farewell service one veteran Latin Christian took the microphone and spoke warmly. "This missionary family leaves us, for a time. But from them we have learned many things: how to love the Lord and His church; how to love our spouses and children, and I in particular have learned this from them, even how to love our own culture, for their home is decorated with our art and artifacts. We will miss them, but they have left a legacy of transformed lives. They leave, but live with us still."

Leave a Legacy

I learned this lesson from my own parents and their ministry in Latin America: Leave a legacy. When my wife and I first drove to Costa Rica for language study in 1968, I found my father's footprints all over the country. He had indelibly marked lives, from humble *campesinos* to future presidential candidates. On one occasion I spoke with a Costa Rican pastor, and as we shared experiences I asked him how he had come to the Lord. It had been through my father, and now he was pastoring the church where as a lad I had accepted Christ through my father's ministry! As I traveled throughout Central America the same story came out time after time—men and women in the ministry because a young missionary had led them to Christ or had encouraged them to serve the Lord and his church. On one occasion I spoke at the chapel service at John Brown University. To my amazement I met a young student from Costa Rica whose grandparents had come to Christ through my parents' ministry. The reverberations continue.

I grew up with a living model of a modern Barnabas, a man who in biblical days quietly worked to bring people to Christ. He apparently did not have the powerful personality of Paul, or his eloquence. But humanly speaking, without Barnabas the church would be poor. This unassuming man left behind a phenomenal legacy: the church at Antioch, the very apostle Paul himself, and the gospel writer John Mark.

Barnabas becomes a model for today's missionary to Latin America, and by extension this can be applied to mission agencies. Expatriate missionaries as well as Latin leaders could well learn from Barnabas. What is the legacy you wish to leave behind? Make sure you do your work in the power of the Spirit; with a spirit of true humility; with a gradual identification with and bonding to Latin America, recognizing that this takes time; with a genuine love for people. Invest in the process of reproducing disciples who at the same time are given the liberty to develop according to their own personalities.

I am impressed that Barnabas did not demonstrate paternalism. Nor did he cling to his position of power in Antioch or on the first missionary journey. He became a beautiful model for the foreign missionary by the way he passed the leadership to his assistant, Paul. In Acts 13 we see how from the references to "Barnabas and Saul" we shift to "Paul and Barnabas." What happened here? A friend has called this "The Great Renunciation"—that is, Barnabas renounced his position of leader and transferred the torch into the hands of his brilliant and gifted assistant, Paul. Barnabas thus becomes a paradigm for today's missionary: go out and work with a ministry, or start one; then develop other leaders to work with you and learn from you; keep the future in focus, and then begin the process of the total transfer of responsibility and authority; if necessary, move on to another ministry in God's kingdom.

Where Are Missionaries Needed Today in Latin America?

The question of where missions are needed today in Latin America is crucial to the role any expatriate missionary would play in that continent. At the conclusion to chapter 4, I mentioned a variety of areas where the Latin American churches need partners. Let me look at these areas again.

First, missionaries are needed to reach the unreached peoples of Latin America. These include those Indian populations with little or no gospel witness, some needing a Bible translation. Wycliffe Bible Translators report in the tenth edition of their *Ethnologue* that Latin American countries have 191 languages with definite and potential needs for Bible translation.[3] But let us also include among the unreached groups the economic and social elites; military offiers; Indian, labor, and peasant officials; media leaders; university professors; and national intellectuals. And surely there are others.

A second group to consider is that of the under-reached populations. Include here the megacities, with Caracas and Mexico City showing that evangelicals have not taken seriously the challenge to establish vital churches in all the neighborhoods of these cities. While some ministries labor among university students (with the IFES-related groups the strongest), the vast majority of strategic students are not being touched by a powerful witness to Jesus Christ. Such a witness requires an understanding of apologetics from the Latin-American and not the Anglo-Saxon perspective. This means coming to grips with the claims of socialism and Marxism, critiquing capitalism for its basic greed motive, and pointing people to the One who alone brings purpose in life and life everlasting.

Yet another group, unreached or under-reached, are those living on the absolute underside of history. They are the street kids, the prostitutes and pimps, the dump dwellers. They are the most obviously hopeless; and ministry to them cannot be at a distance. It requires unusual incarnational commitment that, frankly, few Christians possess.

A fourth area of ministry is that which clusters together relief and developmental projects. The priority must be on tasks that provide long-term incentives and personal participation. These can be specifically focused, such as basic sanitation or portable water projects, housing and re-settlement programs. They can be geared to helping the little entrepreneur or small-project businessperson, such as Opportunity International (formerly IIDI), does. World Vision and World Relief have refocused their programs less on relief and more on preventive and developmental projects, and this is a good sign. Such ministries must be seen as just that, ministries. They may require graduate degrees in international development as well as profound cultural sensitivity.

Yet another need calls for partners in ministerial preparation, from the most popular level Bible institute or correspondence course all the way up to higher degrees in theological and missiological studies. As of today, no evangelical seminary in Latin America offers a doctorate in theology, but the plethora of programs operating are enough to daunt the researcher in this area. The continent requires a major commitment to the full utilization of all models of theological education, from extension (born in Guatemala in 1963) to residence programs (one of the largest and strongest is also in Guatemala), to anything else that works. Theological institutions must bravely accept Latin America's challenges from both the secular and spiritual courts. There is a desperate need for renewal and sharing of experiences and resources.

In the sixth place let me mention the specialized ministries that focus on leadership development, evangelism training and crusades, family and counseling programs, or other particular needs of the churches. Many times these missionaries serve as catalytic agents to bring about change, demonstrating new ministry models, publishing key literature, and stimulating the local churches to set new goals. One weakness of some of these ministries is that they run the risk of operating independently of the national church. They have international and creative leadership that purports to serve the churches, but not always is this the case. Some of them also have been accused of skimming off the cream of evangelical leadership for their own ministries. I see here a real need for initial and ongoing dialogue for such ministries. At the same time we thank God for these service teams, which have a strategic role to play.

A significantly growing target for creative ministry is that composed of immigrants from Asia. This includes the thousands of Chinese, Koreans, and Japanese, most of whom profess one of the traditional Oriental religions. Just in Central America there are some one hundred thousand Chinese, and in Peru about sixty thousad. Recent years have seen a large number of Middle East Arabs moving to Latin America, most of them Muslims. It will take new approaches to reach these peoples and establish vital churches that will minister to them adequately.

A final area I mention is the training of the new generation of Latin American cross-cultural missionaries. This requires a great deal of initial research and planning, avoiding the slavish copying of models that work in North America. The tendency will be to think that all we need to do is to add new courses or programs to existing theological institutions. This is inadequate. What is needed today is to study programs operating in Africa and Asia and then come up with new models for the Latin American realities. Veteran missionaries have much to share, particularly if they are sensitive and trained in linguistics, cultural studies, contextualization, and other missiological studies. Writers are urgently needed to create contextualized missions material.

Every expatriate missionary should keep in mind the legacy he or she wishes to leave in Latin America after the years invested in ministry. Ponder anew the life, ministry, and legacy of Barnabas.

What Kind of Preparation Does a New Missionary Need?

Clearly the kind of preparation a new missionary needs depends on the individual, personality and gifts,ministry goals, and the needs on the various fields of service. Many others have written on the preparation of missionaries, so I want to address a few items briefly. Missionaries tend to come with a checkered academic background. Today's Latin America needs people with as much formal training as possible. Whether it is a Bible college, a Christian liberal-arts school, a secular college, or a university, all candidates need further training in a number of areas. I am fully committed to the best pre-field preparation, particularly on the seminary level—if possible, one that will also offer cross-cultural studies and other missions courses.

Another area of study is specific to the Two-Thirds World, and in particular courses on international studies or on Latin American history, literature, culture, and contemporary issues. Perhaps the best place for such courses would be a university setting where one is challenged to see the world through secular eyes. I have never regretted for a moment all my university courses on Spanish-American literature. They became a treasure to draw upon as I learned, spoke, and taught in the context of Latin America. Illustrations emerged from that body of literature that affected Latin American listeners much more than those that came from the Anglo-Saxon worlds. Obviously, formal study of Spanish or Portuguese will be most helpful.

The Latin American church needs more and more expatriate servants with practical experience both in sheer living that brings personal maturity as well as in ministry. The former rush to "get to the field right away" now must be tempered by experience in the Lord's work. Commit more of your initial ministry mistakes in your home country.

Finally, as you move toward actual service in this continent in crisis, make sure you select your mission team wisely. This is much more important than the geographic area in which you will work. In the course of your service to the Lord you may change locations, but you may continue with the same organization, your team. Be sure the mission is biblically solid and culturally sensitive to Latin America. Assure yourself that the mission strategy is wise and that it is focused on the local church and its broad ministries. It is important that contemporary mission agencies have a broad continuum of ministries: from evangelism to discipleship to church planting to leadership training.

A FINAL WORD TO OUR READERS

May God bless you as you ponder Latin America today, learning her history, appreciating her cultural heritage, and loving her peoples. Some of you have already invested part or all of a career in Latin America. You in particular can understand more of this book than the rest. Others of your kind will follow. Still others of you will not invest a career in Latin America, but you are keenly interested in understanding this continent in crisis. Perhaps you have friends or family in Latin America, and you desire to be a more informed friend supporter. To all of you, we wish God's blessing on you.

Yes, the old Quiche words for *crisis* come back; *xak quieb cubij päkawi* ("Something I'm in and either way I go it's trouble, but that's just where we are"). What is the future of Latin America? Only God knows fully. Political, economic, and military systems attempt to bring peace, justice, liberty, and some kind of development and prosperity to a continent rich in natural and human resources. But these systems have a bankrupt core. The Christian yearns for the City of God, yet struggles to proclaim the gospel in all its fullness and power on earth, desiring to be obedient to the biblical demands of citizenship. What are we left to do? Praise and worship the Lamb, Lord of the universe and Savior of the world. May the name of the true Christ come to be exalted and served in Latin America.

NOTES

1. Patrick Johnstone, *Operation World* (Bromley, Kent, England: STL Books, 1986), pp. 62-67.

2. Samuel Wilson and John Siewert, eds., *Mission Handbook: North American Protestant Ministries Overseas*, 13th ed. (Monrovia, CA: MARC, 1986).

3. Barbara Grimes, ed., *Ethnologue: Languages of the World*, 10th ed. (Dallas: Wycliffe Bible Translators, 1984), pp. xi-xiv.

Annotated Bibliography

A recent computer list of books on Latin America offered 3,296 titles for sale just in the English-language! We suggest the following as a solid library for the beginning or advanced Christian student of Latin American. Obviously we are selective, and probably reflect our presuppositions and preferences, but we trust all will profit from this brief recommendation.

History and Culture of Latin America

Arciniegas, Germán. *Latin America: A Cultural History*. Translated by Joan MacLean. New York: Alfred A. Knopf, 1972.
> A magnificent and insightful survey by a great Colombian. Unfortunately out of print, but can be acquired in libraries.

Armesto, Felipe Fernández. *Columbus*. Oxford University Press, 1991.
> This superb Spanish author and Columbus scholar carefully uses primary and corroborated sources, placing the explorer in the context of his own world. Good chronology and maps.

Chang-Rodríguez, Eugenio. *Latinoamérica: su civilización y su cultura.* HarperCollinsPublishers, 1991.
> Well-written portrayal of Latin America, with strong regional perspective, emphasizing the cultural perspective. Good section on Brazilian distinctives. This is a text to accompany Benjamin Keen's *A History of Latin America.*

Collier, Simon, Thomas E. Skidmore, Harold Blakemore, gen. eds. *The Cambridge Encyclopedia of Latin America and the Caribbean.* Cambridge University Press, 1992.
> A comprehensive well-illustrated report of the entire continent plus the Caribbean. A brief four-page section on the Catholic Church in Latin America with scant reference to evangelicals.

Economist Country Profiles. The Economist Intelligence Unit (15 Regent Street, London, SW1Y, 4LR, United Kingdom) on a quarterly basis publishes its global research.
> All 19 nations included in *Crisis and Hope in Latin America* are carefully covered in these profiles.

Galeano, Eduardo. *Open Veins of Latin America: Five Centuries of the Pillage of a Continent.* Translated by Cedric Belfrage. New York: Monthly Review Press, 1973.
> Though dated, it is a well-written Marxist perspective of the continent, with heavy commitment to questioned dependency theories. Still in print.

Keen, Benjamin. *A History of Latin America.* 4th ed. Houghton Mifflin Company, 1992
> An excellent university text that in 630 pages covers all you might want to know about Latin America. Perhaps the most updated history. Strong regional and national sections. To be read in tandem with *Latinoamérica: su civilización y su cultura* by Eugenio Chang-Rodgríguez.

Morison, Samuel Eliot. *Admiral of the Ocean Sea—A Life of Christopher Columbus.* Little, Brown and Company, 1942.

> The classic scholarly work which brought the author the Pulitzer prize, one of many books emphasized during the multiple 1992 commemorations.

Stuart, Gene S. and George E. Stuart. *Lost Kingdoms of the Maya.* National Geographic Society, 1993.

> A splendid analysis and pictorial exposition of some of the most recent discoveries and interpretations of the complex, sophisticated and spiritually-oriented Maya.

Spiritual Dimensions of Latin America

Berg, Mike and Paul Pretiz. *The Gospel People.* MARC/LAM, 1992.

> A very readable place to start for the lay reader wanting insights on the growth and faces of Latin American evangelicalism. Of particular interest is their five-wave sequence of evangelicalism in Latin America.

Christian History. "What Happened When Columbus and Christianity Collided in the Americas?" *Issue 35 Vol. XI, No. 3).*

> Excellent articles related to the major theme, but ranging beyond the specific topics of Columbus and dealing with Christianity today in Latin America.

Cleary, Edward L. and Hannah Stewart-Gambino, eds. *Conflict and Competition: The Latin American Church in a Changing Environment.* Lynne Rienner Publishers, 1992.

> Careful analysis of contemporary crossroads experience of the institutional Catholic Church. Just Cleary's chapter, "Evangelicals and Competition in Guatemala," is worth the book, reflecting growing balance of some Catholic and academic scholars in their treatment of the Latin American religious arena.

Cook, Guillermo, ed. *New Face of the Church in Latin America: Between Tradition and Change.* Maryknoll: Orbis, 1994.

> A very profitable series of 21 essays moving across the eccelsiastical and thematic spectrum of the continent. The primary grid is that of Protestantism, the truly new face of the church in Latin America. Probably the most complete bibliography on the subject.

Deiros, Pablo Alberto, ed. *Historia del Cristianismo en América Latina.* Buenos Aires: Fraternidad Teológica Latinoamerica, 1992.

> For Spanish readers, a ground-breaking 847-page history of Latin Christianity written by one of Latin evangelicalism's most respected historians.

Dussell, Enrique. *A History of the Church in Latin America: Colonialism to Liberation.* Grand Rapids: Eerdmans, 1981.

> A Catholic, liberationist perspective of the Roman Catholic Church and its historical impact in Latin America. Systematic research, scholarly, penetrating.

Dussell, Enrique, ed. *The Church in Latin America, 1492-1992.* Maryknoll: Orbis, 1992.

> A wide-ranging series of essays with predominant focus on the Catholic Church. The first of three volumes focusing on the church in the Third World, giving a chronological and regional survey, followed by selected thematic presentations. Primarily a Catholic perspective. One challenging though minimalist chpater on Protestantism on the continent built primarily on a sociological model.

Escobar, Samuel. *Fe Evangélica y las Teologías de la Liberación.* El Paso: Casa Bautista de Publicaiones, 1987.

> An excellent study, still relevant, by one of Latin America's leading evangelicals. Helpful appendices and Spanish bibliography

Goodpasture, H. McKennie. *Cross and Sword*. Maryknoll: Orbis, 1989.

> A fascinating tour through 500 years of Latin religious history through the perspective of eye-witnesses of the church in Latin America, with anthologies of letters and other documentation from 1492 to the present. The author starts with Catholic sources and then interweaves Protestant ones as the centuries roll along.

Gutiérrez, Gustavo. *A Theology of Liberation: History, Politics and Salvation*. rev. ed. Translated and edited by Sister Caridad Inda and John Eagleson. Maryknoll: Orbis, 1988.

> The classic work on liberation theology, now in current edition with a new important introduction. Study of this seminal book should be followed by reading his more recent pastoral writings.

Johnstone, Patrick. *Operation World*. Zondervan, 1993.

> Excellent continental essay with extensive statistical data, as well as information on every Latin nation: general and religious status, with emphasis on task remaining for evangelicals.

MacKay, John A. *The Other Spanish Christ*. New York: MacMillan, 1932.

> The unparalleled classic on some of the spiritual dimensions of Latin America. Long out of print, but can be located in some libraries.

Martin, David. *Tongues of Fire: The Explosion of Protestantism in Latin America*. Blackwell, 1991.

> A most significant work by a British sociologist sympathetically documenting what secular and even Catholic scholars had wished to ignore. Now in a 1993, reasonably priced, paperback edition.

Núñez, Emilio Antonio. *Liberation Theology.* Translated by Paul E. Sywulka. Moody Press, 1985.
An outstanding work by a true scholar, unfortunately out of print, but still available in libraries. Written prior to the collapse of European/Russian ideological/political Marxism.

Stoll, David. *Is Latin America Turning Protestant? The Politics of Evangelical Growth.* University of California Press, 1990.
From an anthropological perspective Stoll analyzes evangelical growth in Latin America, correcting his own presuppositions by the data. Stoll and David Martin have impacted the academic and non-evangelical world with their books. Now in a 1991, reasonably priced, paperback edition.

Stoll, David and Virginia Barrard-Burnett, eds. *Rethinking Protestantism in Latin America.* Temple University Press, 1993.
The most recent example of growing balance in the reporting of Latin spiritual dimensions.

Compiled by William David Taylor
with the assistance of John Maust
January, 1996

Index of Persons

Index of Subjects

Minifundio, 60

Requerimento, 58

Regidores, 60

Reinoes, 60

COMIBAM, 41, 163, 173, 182, 459-460, 467-468, 495

CONELA, 172-173, 428, 466, 472

Conference of Latin American Bishops, Santo Domingo (1992), 485-488

Conference on the Nature and Mission of the Church, Wheaton (1983), 425-428, 430

Conquistadores, 49, 55, 326

Conscientising, 254-255

Constitutions of Latin America, 89

Contras of Nicaragua, 92-93

Contextualization, 7, 41, 171, 179-180, 258, 331-371, 465, 472, 493-494

Corn, 53, 65

Cosmic race, 31

Costa Rica, 155, 165, 303, 463

Council of Trent, 137

Criollos, 61, 67, 68, 81, 193, 384

Crossing the Threshold of Hope, 487

Cuba, 30, 36, 77, 90-91, 127, 441, 455-456

Culture in Latin America, 42-43

Death, cult of, 217-218

Declaration of Human Rights, 239

Declaration of the American Catholic Bishops, 309

Delegados de la Palabra, 280

Democracy, democratic capitalism, 93, 94, 104-106, 122-125, 354, 431-433

Dependency, 103-105, 123, 262-263

Development, developmentalism, 104-106, 262-263, 425

Document of Puebla, 486

Dominican Republic, 424, 469, 485

Dominican order, 63

Drug industry, 38, 441, 451-452

Dutch (Holland), 61, 151, 332

Ecuador, 27, 278, 366, 441

Ecumenical Institute, WCCC, 335

Education in Latin America, 64, 110-112, 140, 159, 195, 253, 256, 259, 364-369

El Dorado, 57

El Salvador, 1-2, 278, 283, 439-441, 483

England, Britain, 17, 61, 67, 71, 153, 232, 332, 377

Europe, 66

Enlightenment, encyclopaedists, 68, 193, 194

Evangelical Foreign Missions Association (EFMA), 409

"Evangelicals and Catholics Together," 470

Evangelii Nuntiandi, 245, 486, 488

France, 61, 66, 67, 68, 232

Family in Latin America, 64-65, 114-115, 206-210

"Fifth Wave" churches, 463, 472

First Charismatic Congress (1967), 302

Fraternidad Teológica Lat-